Douglas F. Greer
California State University, San José

INDUSTRIAL ORGANIZATION AND PUBLIC POLICY

Macmillan Publishing Co., Inc.
New York
Collier Macmillan Publishers
London

Macmillan Publishing Co., Inc.
866 Third Avenue, New York, New York 10022

Collier Macmillan Canada, Ltd.

Library of Congress Cataloging in Publication Data

Greer, Douglas F.
  Industrial organization and public policy.

  Includes index.
  1. Industrial organization (Economic theory)
2. Industry and state. I. Title.
HD2326.G73   658.1   78-31488
ISBN 0-02-347020-8

Printing: 2345678   Year:0123456

ACKNOWLEDGMENTS

Excerpts from *Pills, Profits, and Politics* by Milton Silverman and Philip R. Lee copyright 1974 by The Regents of the University of California. Reprinted by permission of the University of California Press.

Excerpts from *Industrial Market Structure and Economic Performance* by F. M. Scherer copyright 1970 by Rand McNally College Publishing Company. Reprinted by permission of the publisher.

Excerpts from *Antitrust Economics: Selected Legal Cases and Economic Models* by Eugene M. Singer copyright 1968 by Prentice-Hall, Inc., Englewood Cliffs, N. J. Reprinted by permission of the publisher.

Excerpts from *Regulation: A Case Approach* by Leonard W. Weiss and Allyn D. Strickland copyright 1976 by McGraw-Hill Book Company. Reprinted by permission of the publisher.

Excerpts from *The Wall Street Journal*, "The Sweet Success of Smell" by Jonathan Kwitny, and "Supermarket Scrap" by Joseph Winski, reprinted by permission of *The Wall Street Journal*, copyright by Dow Jones & Company, Inc, 1975 and 1976. All rights reserved.

INDUSTRIAL ORGANIZATION AND PUBLIC POLICY

For my parents, Fred and Sally

Preface

An author's relentless pursuit of his next sentence is what gets his book written. Relentless pursuit of all relevant material is what makes his book worthwhile. I have tried to pursue both ends diligently enough to lighten the reader's burden without skimping on content.

The book is intended for junior and senior level college students of industrial organization and public policy. In its sophistication, the book assumes that the reader brings to bear no more than some background in economic principles and a recollection of high school algebra. On either side of this mean, however, there is substantial variance. On the simple side are brief reviews of some essential principles, such as elasticity, for benefit of those who forget easily. On the tough side are explanations of Pareto optimality and monetarist theories of inflation. The book is unconventional in organization. Rather than lump theory and empiricism in the first half and policy in the second, as is so often done in books of this type, I have tried to integrate theory, empiricism, and policy. The integration is less than complete, however, because some potential users of the book may prefer the traditional, dichotomous sequence. Thus two chapters are offered on each major subject. The first chapter covers theory and empirical evidence, the second policy. Those who wish to ignore policy can simply exclude the policy chapters. Conversely, those most interested in policy can exercise an appropriately opposite selectivity.

Of the many reasons motivating the design, two deserve mention. First, for those who do have time enough to cover economics and policies together, the integration should prove illuminating. I think most students look upon theory and cross-section statistical evidence, which comprise the guts of the first chapter in each pairing, as rather abstract and therefore often nebulous. In contrast, most students look upon policies and the case studies they produce, both of which are found in the second chapter of each pairing, as down-to-earth and concrete. Assuming that any subject is most readily and thoroughly learned by exposure to both its abstract and practical aspects, I have tried to blend these complementary elements more conscientiously than is customary.

My second main reason for adopting this organization is to allow for an orderly introduction of much policy material that is unjustifiably slighted in conventional books. The last two decades have witnessed an explosion of new policies and major modifications to old policies that do not fit neatly into a dichotomous scheme, but which, nevertheless, ought to be reviewed by students of industrial organization. These policies include product standardization, disclosure labeling, grade rating, regulation of product safety and quality, wage-price controls, and corrective advertising. To be sure, antitrust and public utility regulation remain important, but they must move over to make room for these extensions of government activity. The focus of these new policies varies widely, touching the structure, conduct, and performance of industries. It is this variety of focus and impact that discourages use of the traditional order and encourages adoption of the present one. Indeed, the coverage of industrial policy is so broad that the book could find use in government and business courses.

My fascination for economics caught me unawares, altering my life's direction while I was still a college student. Thus I owe a special debt of gratitude to my former industrial organization professors—Robert E. Smith, who first kindled the fires of interest; Corwin D. Edwards, who impressed upon me the importance of asking the right questions; and Alfred E. Kahn, who taught me to hunt down the truth even when it hides in uncomfortable places. The inspiration and influence of these good fellows run deep; consciously or unconsciously they often guided my pencil.

Portions of the manuscript were critically reviewed by Steve Rhoades, Trudi Edwards, Corwin Edwards, Art Fraas, Steve Cox, Geoffrey Nunn, Norm Keiser, and John Landon. Their weeding improved the garden considerably. But none of these readers was given access to the entire plot, so none can be blamed in the least for remaining errors. Among my critical reviewers I owe more to a non-economist—Tony English, my editor at Macmillan—than to anyone else. His sacrifice of spring and summer delights to read my manuscript must have been maddening. Nevertheless, he kept his wits well enough intact to unsnarl sentences that even an illiterate contortion artist could not deliberately compose. In many ways his effort was surely more relentless than mine.

Finally, I have my family to thank. Encouragement, solace, patience, understanding, and unwarranted praise are offered to most authors by their families. I received full measure of the usual tributes. My debts pile higher, however. My wife Wendy typed and edited the entire manuscript, while my daughters Darby and Leah helped exorcise my atrocious spelling. Regrettably, I too often showed my gratitude by thinking of my next sentence rather than of them.

D. F..G.

Contents

four

PERFORMANCE   443

one

INTRODUCTION

1

Introduction and Overview

Because we live in a market-run society, we are apt to take for granted the puzzling—indeed almost paradoxical—nature of the market solution to the economic problem.

ROBERT HEILBRONER and LESTER THUROW[1]

Markets comprise the central nervous system of our trillion dollar economy. We rely on them for most of what life is all about—food, entertainment, fuel, transport, shelter, and so forth. Still, despite their overwhelming importance to us and our daily contact with them, markets are neither widely understood nor greatly appreciated. Most people seem to think of markets as merely places where fish, produce, or shares of equity stock are bought and sold. They fail to recognize the economist's broader use of the term, which encompasses an enormous variety of markets, major and minor, including those for aluminum, stereos, apparel, autos, steel, gasoline, soap, cosmetics, beer, motion pictures, insurance, and air travel. Moreover, people tend to ignore the large diversity of firms populating most markets, ranging from such pygmies as Harvey Aluminum, Star Gas, and Swift Airlines to such giants as ALCOA, ARCO, and TWA. On top of all this is a hodgepodge of several dozen different government regulations, many of which escape most people's notice, even when the intent of the regulation, as is true of our truth-in-lending and textile labeling laws, is to put people on notice.

Thus, the purpose of this book is to give the reader a broad understanding of markets and their regulation. In particular, we shall attempt (1) to bring some *order* to this almost chaotic diversity by developing a systematic way of looking at markets; (2) to *analyze* how markets function; (3) to *evaluate* how well

---

[1] Robert Heilbroner and Lester Thurow, *The Economic Problem*, 4th ed. (Englewood Cliffs, N.J.: Prentice-Hall, Inc.), p. 12.

various markets function in light of society's desires and expectations; and (4) to *explain* and *assess* many of the policies governing markets. Among the numerous issues that will be addressed along the way, the following are apt to be of greatest interest to the reader: Why are markets so important to the economy? What factors determine price and output? Why do just a few huge firms dominate some of our key markets, such as those for autos, computers, steel, and aluminum? What are the effects of such dominance on profits, wages, innovation, and efficiency? Why are soaps, cereals, and cosmetics heavily advertised, whereas sugar, cement, and coal go largely unpromoted by Madison Avenue? Does advertising foster market power? Has market power contributed to inflation or high unemployment? What do policy makers hope to accomplish with measures like truth-in-lending, grade rating, and product standardization? Should the government take action to break up big corporations or subsidize small ones? What has the government done about mergers, price fixing, false advertising, product safety, and inflation? Are there such things as "natural monopolies"? If there are, can they be regulated effectively? In a nutshell, under what conditions do our markets best serve the public interest?

Of course everything cannot be said all at once, so in this chapter we begin at the beginning. First, a few words need to be defined, including the word "market." Second, we shall briefly explore the place markets occupy in the scheme of things. Third, because evaluation is one of our objectives, a discussion of certain values held by our society is needed for later use in evaluating various types of markets and regulations. Fourth, to facilitate understanding and analysis, we need to devise a systematic way of looking at markets. Finally, we shall explain our particular methodology and indicate the organization of the remaining chapters.

Setting the Scene

Simply put, a **market** is an organized process by which buyers and sellers exchange goods and services for money, the medium of exchange. Notice that every market has two sides to it—a demand side (made up of buyers) and a supply side (made up of sellers). Notice also that markets can be local, regional, national, or international in scope. When the exchange alternatives of either buyers or sellers are geographically limited—as is true of barbering, grocery retailing, and cement manufacturing, for example—then exchange and competition are correspondingly limited in geographic scope. Strictly speaking, the word "industry" denotes a much broader concept than market because an industry can include numerous local or regional markets. When we speak of the construction industry or the banking industry, we usually refer to something more than local business. In practice, however, "market" and "industry" are often used synonymously, without careful distinction, a practice we too will follow when precision is not required. Indeed, economists commonly use the term "industrial organization" rather than "market organization" to describe the areas of study covered in this book.

The crucial importance of markets can be fully appreciated only after it is recognized that the "market" is the basic economic *institution* upholding our private free-enterprise capitalist system. An **institution** may be defined as selected elements of a scheme of values mobilized and coordinated to accomplish a particular purpose or function.[2] This definition implies that "markets" have two principal aspects—a *value* aspect and a *functional* aspect.

The Functional Aspect

With respect to function, we rely on markets to cope with the fundamental problem of scarcity, which is what economics is all about. Granted, some societies and some "wise men" have overcome their acquisitive desires by adopting the philosophy that human happiness and satisfaction may be attained only if people do not want things they cannot have; scarcity is no problem when wants are so severely curtailed. Granted, too, if everyone had an Aladdin's lamp, scarcity would be no problem even if material wants ran wild, for then our productive capabilities would know no bounds. But, alas, neither of these conditions holds for our society. We have neither limited wants nor unlimited resources. Quite the contrary, Americans are by far the most prosperous people who have ever lived; yet we still want more goods and services—more than our limited resources of land, capital, labor, energy, and time can produce. Proof of this statement is easy: markets, prices, wages, and all the other trappings of our economy would not exist save for scarcity (especially not textbooks about markets).

To be a little more specific about the *function* of markets, scarcity rudely forces us to make certain decisions. We simply cannot have our cake and eat it too. Somehow, the following decisions must be made:

1. *What goods and services shall we produce and in what amounts?* At first glance the answer may seem simple and obvious. We need such basics as food, clothing, and shelter. But even in this context our limitations impose trade-offs. Shall it be more "Twinkies" and less "Granola"; more apartments and fewer single-family dwellings; more sweaters and fewer jackets? Similarly, if we commit more of our resources to autos, trains, and planes, sacrifices will have to be made elsewhere. What combination of goods is most desirable?
2. *How are goods and services to be produced?* Many different methods of production are possible for most goods. Cigars, for instance, can be made by man as well as by machine. What mixture of the two will it be? Should autos be shipped from Detroit by truck or train? Should coal be mined

[2] Talcott Parsons and Neil Smelser, *Economy and Society* (New York: Free Press, 1965), p. 102.

by strip or underground methods? In short, what combination of resource commitments is most efficient?

3. *Who shall get and consume the goods and services we produce?* There
are two aspects to this question. One aspect relates to income distribution—what share of our total national income should each household
receive? At present, some enjoy riches and others suffer poverty, while
most of us hold down the middle. The other aspect relates to rationing
of specific goods. Not enough gasoline can be produced for everyone to
get as much as they would like. Hence some form of rationing is required.

4. *How shall we maintain flexibility for changes over time?* No condition
of scarcity is static, ironclad, or unchanging. Discoveries of new resource endowments, advances in technology, and better educational
attainments continually expand our productive capabilities. Consumer
tastes also alter. Thus we are confronted with questions of change. Shall
we convert to nuclear power, steam autos, digital watches, electronic
calculators, and nine-track tapes? Decisions of acceptance and rejection
must continually be made. Flexibility allows us to probe such new
opportunities as they arise.

Although every society that has ever existed has had to arrive at answers
to these four fundamental questions, only three basic institutional devices
(or answer machines) have so far evolved to handle them—tradition, command,
and the market. *Tradition* is typical of most primitive societies, wherein each
generation merely emulates its ancestor's pattern of life-support. *Command*
involves centralized decision making, usually by government authorities (as in
Communist China) but also by high priests, war lords, and the like. Elements of
tradition and command can of course be found in our own economy. But by
and large we entrust these decisions to the *market*, to millions of consumers,
workers, employers, land owners, investors, and proprietors, each pursuing self-
interest in the market place. *Thus, the function of markets is to coordinate and
control this decentralized decision-making process, which answers these four
crucial questions.* It should also be noted that private property and contract
assist markets in this task. *Private property* provides material incentives for
individual actions and enables (but not necessarily assures) decentralized
decision making. *Contract* allows individuals to determine their own terms of
exchange and permits stabilizing, long-run commitments.

The Value Aspect

As far as its values are concerned, our society generally believes that markets
tend to perform the function of coordination and control very nicely. That is to
say, the market system accords well with many of our society's values by (1)
typically providing fairly good answers to the four questions and (2) arriving at
these answers in a particularly appealing way. Exactly what these answers are
and exactly how the market system goes about arriving at them will be discussed

in subsequent chapters. Right now we need to explain which values we refer to and thereby specify what is meant here by "good" and "appealing."

In the present context, **values** are simply generalized concepts of the desirable. They are objectives, ends, or aims that guide our attitudes and actions. Among the most generalized concepts of the desirable are such notions as "welfare and happiness," "freedom," "justice," and "equality." These may be called **ultimate** values because they reign supreme in the minds of most western men and women. Indeed, they even justify occasional bloodshed (sometimes between men and women).

Although these are undeniably noble aims, they are also too vague and too ill-defined to provide a basis for specific institutional arrangements and policy decisions; so, for purposes of actual application, they can be translated into more specific concepts—like "full-employment" and "allocation efficiency"—which may be called **proximate** values. Table 1-1 presents a summary list of proximate values that are relevant here, together with the ultimate values from which they are derived. Allocation efficiency, full employment, clean environment, and health and safety, for example, are several proximate values that convey the

TABLE 1-1 Some Proximate Values and the Ultimate Values from Which They Derive

Ultimate Values	Proximate Values
Freedom	Free choice in consumption and occupation Free entry and investment Limited government intervention Free political parties National security
Equality	Diffusion of economic and political power Equal bargaining power for buyers/sellers Equal opportunity Limited income inequality
Justice and fairness	Prohibition of unfair practices Fair labor standards Honesty Full disclosure
Welfare and happiness	Allocation and technical efficiency Full employment Price stability Health and safety Clean environment
Progress	Rising real income Technological advancement

spirit of "welfare and happiness." The list is intended to be more illustrative than exhaustive, so only a brief discussion of it is warranted.

Freedom. Proximate values reflecting freedom include such notions as "free choice in consumption and occupation," and "free entry and investment." They imply active, unhampered participation in the economic decision-making process by all of us. The market furthers these objectives because, unlike tradition or command, the market affords free expression to individual choice in deciding answers to the key economic questions outlined earlier—what, how, who, and what's new? Unfettered individual choice is possible *only* under favorable circumstances, however. For if markets are burdened with barriers to entry, monopoly power, price fixing, allocations of customers, or similar restraints of trade—imposed *either* by government *or* by private groups—then this freedom is sharply curtailed. Although the government has often imposed these and other restraints (usually under the influence and for the benefit of special interest groups), most people in our society favor "limited government intervention" and "free political parties," both of which tend to inhibit centralized command and coercion. Thus, to the extent government intervention is properly called for, most would probably agree that it should be for purposes of *preventing* private restraints of trade rather than for *imposing* official restraints.

Equality. When one person's freedom encroaches upon another person's freedom, some criterion is needed to resolve the conflict; in our society the ideal criterion is "equality" or "equity."[3] This usually means that everybody's preferences and aspirations are weighted equally, as in the political cliché: one man, one vote. In economics, the notion that each individual's dollar counts the same as anyone else's dollar reflects a similar sentiment. Among the more important proximate values stemming from equality are "a wide diffusion of economic and political power," "equal bargaining power on both sides of an exchange transaction," "equal opportunity, regardless of race, religion, sex, or national origin," and "*limited inequality* in the distribution of income." Under favorable conditions, the market system can further these objectives as well as those associated with freedom.

Justice and Fairness. The market is often given high marks for justice and fairness because, under ideal circumstances, it generates answers to the key economic questions that are not arbitrary, imperious, despotic, or peremptory in nature. Adam Smith's metaphorical "invisible hand" eloquently illustrates this deduction. Unfortunately, real world circumstances often fall short of the ideal, so that free pursuit of profits in the market place may not always yield fair or just results. As Vernon Mund has written, "Profit can be made not only by producing more and better goods but also by using inferior materials, by artificially restricting supply to secure monopoly profits, by misleading and

---

[3] Robert A. Dahl and Charles E. Lindblom, *Politics, Economics, and Welfare* (New York: Harper & Row Publishers, 1963), p. 41.

deceiving consumers, and by exploiting labor."[4] Thus, to account for these sad possibilities and to introduce several forms of market regulation that will be discussed in later chapters, we have listed "full-disclosure," "honesty," and "prohibition of unfair practices" among the proximate values of Table 1-1.

Welfare, Happiness, and Progress. The foregoing discussion of freedom, equality, justice, and fairness helps to explain our earlier statement that the market system arrives at answers to the key economic questions in a *particularly appealing way*, but it remains to be demonstrated that the answers themselves are *fairly good answers*. In other words, as far as markets are concerned, the foregoing values relate more to the decision-making process than to the decisions made—to *means* rather than to *ends*. So, what about ends? Fortunately for us, the answers provided by the market system (again under favorable circumstances) comport fairly well with our society's concepts of welfare, happiness, and progress. As already indicated, a thorough exploration of these answers is deferred until later chapters, especially Chapter 2, when we can elaborate on the meaning of the phrases "favorable circumstances" and "ideal conditions" that have echoed interchangeably across these pages. Nevertheless, for a prelude, we can note briefly that the market system is generally efficient and flexible. Thus, markets answer the question "what will be produced" by allocating labor and material resources to the production of goods and services yielding the greatest social satisfaction. And, with respect to the question of how goods are produced, markets encourage the use of low-cost production techniques that consume the least amount of scarce resources possible for a given bundle of output. Finally, flexibility: the market is generally receptive to good new ideas and new resource capabilities so that, with each passing year, we can produce more and better goods with less and less time, effort, and waste; all of which implies progress. As regards "clean environment" and "health and safety," which are also mentioned as proximate values in Table 1-1, the market alone has not performed very well in the past, nor can it be expected to under most ordinary conditions. The reason for this failure will be discussed in Chapter 2.

Although these ultimate and proximate values are widely shared and vigorously advocated by most people in our society (why else would they pop up so conspicuously in most political speeches?), they are also sources of conflict, frustration, and disappointment simply because they are not always consistent with each other. Among the more obvious examples of inconsistency, consider the following:

1. "Health and safety" may be furthered by requiring seat belts and a collapsible steering wheel in every auto, but this requirement would inevitably interfere with "free choice in consumption."

[4] Vernon A. Mund, *Government and Business*, 4th ed. (New York: Harper & Row Publishers, 1965), p. 24.

2. Measures designed to procure a "clean environment," such as banning the use of sulfur laden coal (which is our most abundant energy resource), may seriously diminish what we can achieve in the way of "rising real income."

3. Enforcement of "honesty" and the "prohibition of unfair practices" in the marketing of products may conflict with many people's concepts of "limited government intervention."

4. Stockpiling a full year's requirements of crude petroleum in storage facilities may be horrendously costly in terms of "allocation and technical efficiency" but nevertheless may be judged vital to our "national security."

5. Patents may be deemed the best means of encouraging "technological progress," but each patent confers monopolistic privileges that run counter to both "free entry" and "diffusion of economic power."

Lest the picture painted by these examples look too bleak, we hasten to add that in many instances there may not be inconsistencies among values, and in other instances the inconsistencies may be so mild that they are readily amenable to resolution and compromise. Still, as just suggested, inconsistencies do exist and are often sharp, which helps to explain several important facts of political-economic life.

First, for various reasons (including material self-interest, educational background, emotional empathy, and social position) each individual gives differing *weights* and *definitions* to these values. It is the particular weight and definition that guides each person's judgment of conflicts among values, precluding the possibility of unanimous agreement on almost anything.

Second, several "economic philosophies" or "schools of thought" have evolved that differ primarily in terms of the weights they apply to these values and the definitions they give to them. Thus, for example, "conservatives" generally believe that "freedom" is superior to "equality" and "fairness." They prefer less government intervention—even at the expense of more private monopoly power, greater consumer deception, and aggravated income inequalities. In contrast, "reform liberals" often stress "equality" and "fairness" over "freedom," and their list of preferences is consequently quite different from that of "conservatives."

Third, people's definitions and weights are by no means static or immutable. They obviously change with time and events. (And whether you regard these changes as "good" or "bad" depends on your own value judgments.) Indeed, economic policy formulation has been described as "a trial and error process of self-correcting value judgments."[5] Nothing is absolute or final, especially in this field. *Knowledge* and *policy* have within them and between them certain irreconcilable inconsistencies. They are both undergoing continuous review and

[5] H. H. Liebhafsky's entire book *American Government and Business* (New York: Wiley and Sons, 1971) is devoted to this theme, but see especially Chapters 1, 2, 6, and 18.

revision, and opinions about both are strongly influenced by values. For these several reasons, we shall frequently return to this matter of value judgments.[6]

A System for Analysis

Having examined the place markets occupy in our economy, and having described the basic ideals that will be applied in our evaluation of markets, we are ready to develop a systematic way of looking at markets and categorizing their characteristics. Such a system is necessary if any headway is to be made in analyzing market operations or evaluating how well various markets perform their function. In essence, all that is required is (1) a workable categorization of the principal attributes of markets and (2) a theoretical scheme tying these attributes together. The process is analogous to analyzing the operation of an automobile or motorcycle—the categorization of attributes (or parts) would distinguish between the electrical system, fuel supply system, drive train, and so on, and the theoretical scheme would relate each of these attributes to the others to explain how the machine moved under its own power.[7] As we shall see, this "modeling" of the problem not only helps us organize our thoughts, it also helps us formulate testable hypotheses about how markets work. For example, one obvious and familiar hypothesis is that an unregulated monopoly sets higher prices than would prevail under competitive conditions.

The traditional model of markets, as originated by Edward Mason and expanded by Joe Bain, J. M. Clark, F. M. Scherer, and many other industrial organization economists, is outlined in Figure 1-1.[8] As indicated there, the principal components of market analysis are the basic conditions, structure, conduct, and performance. The **basic conditions** may be thought of as characteristics that are either unalterably inherent to the product (as is largely true of price elasticity of demand, purchase method, and product durability) or relatively impervious to easy manipulation by policy (as is largely true of growth rate, technology, and historical background). The elements of market **structure** also tend to be stable over time, but they can be affected by either private or government policy. Among the more important variables of structure are the number of sellers and their size distribution (both of which can be altered by antitrust divestiture and dissolution), product differentiation (determined chiefly by private advertising and promotion policy), and the condition of entry (which is

[6] For more extensive discussions of values and their importance see Liebhafsky, *ibid;* Donald Watson, *Economic Policy* (Boston: Houghton Mifflin, 1960), Chapters 2–6; and Duncan MacRae, Jr., *The Social Function of Social Science* (New Haven: Yale University Press, 1976).

[7] An interesting elaboration of this way of thinking may be found in Robert Pirsig's *Zen and the Art of Motorcycle Maintenance* (New York: Bantam Books, 1975).

[8] Basic sources include Edward Mason "Price and Production of Large-Scale Enterprise," *American Economic Review*, Supplement (March, 1939), pp. 61–74; Joe Bain, *Industrial Organization* (New York: Wiley & Sons, 1959); J. M. Clark, *Competition as a Dynamic Process* (Washington, D.C.: Brookings Institution, 1961); and F. M. Scherer, *Industrial Market Structure and Economic Performance* (Chicago: Rand McNally, 1970).

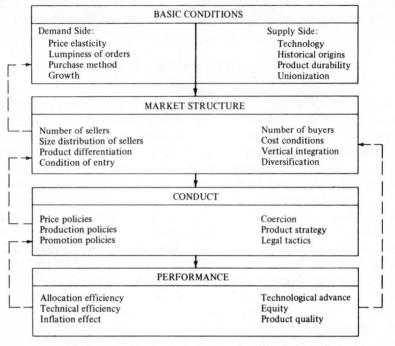

Figure 1-1. *A model of industrial organization analysis.*

affected by patents, licensing, and product differentiation, among other things). The word **conduct** denotes behavior, policy, and strategy on the part of firms in the market, so the several items listed under conduct in Figure 1-1 reflect action, not static condition. Finally, **performance** relates to achievements or end results as determined by such variables as efficiency, technological advances, and product quality. In short, structure and conduct relate to *how* the market functions within the limits of its basic conditions, whereas performance relates to *how well* the market functions.

The arrows of Figure 1-1 indicate possible relationships among these attributes. In particular, traditional theory assumes a causal flow running from the basic conditions and structure to conduct and performance. Technology and growth, for instance, could greatly influence the number and size distribution of firms in the market. In turn, the structural characteristics of number and size distribution might determine price and production policies (conduct) that cause good or bad allocation and technical efficiency (performance). The broken lines of Figure 1-1 represent causal flows running in the opposite direction from those of the traditional model. As recent research has increasingly turned its attention to these latter possibilities, they too will occasionally attract our attention.

12

Sticking with the traditional model for now, a more explicit portrayal of structure-conduct-performance relationships is contained in Table 1-2. Four traditional market types are summarized there—**perfect competition, monopolistic competition, oligopoly**, and **monopoly**. Among the more obvious theoretical relationships depicted is that between the number of firms and price policy. Notice first that under perfect competition the large number of firms prevents any one firm from being large enough to influence price; so these many firms have no price policy. They take prices as given by the market and independently determine their production with an eye to maximizing profits. Under oligopoly, however, with just a few sellers, each firm knows that its price and output actions are likely to affect its rivals' behavior; hence "recognized interdependence" is said to prevail in oligopoly. Only the monopolist enjoys full independence of *both* price and production policy because he is the sole supplier in his market.

Another simple example of causal flow concerns the relationship between product type and promotion policy. Intensive brand name advertising is likely to arise only for products that are differentiable; that is, products that people *believe* can have significant brand differences, whether or not the differences are real. Examples include drugs, cosmetics, soft drinks, and autos—each of which is vigorously advertised by brand. In contrast, standardized products—like milk, wheat, and potatoes—might be promoted on an industry-wide basis or by large segments of the industry (for example, Idaho peddles aristocratic potatoes), but the perfect substitutability of various suppliers' offerings of these products makes brand advertising and promotion by individual producers unprofitable. Table 1-2 also acknowledges the possibility of institutional or political advertising, which is generally practiced by firms self-conscious about their public image, as seems to be true of conspicuously large oligopolists and monopolists. Much recent environmental advertising would obviously come under this category.

The relationship between condition of entry and profits also deserves mention. According to the traditional theoretical model, industry profits (averaging all member firms) can be excessively high in the long run only if the entry of new firms into the industry is at least partially impeded. Otherwise, such high profits would attract newcomers seeking a piece of the profitable action. The new competition would in turn expand production, lower prices, and reduce profits. Thus, Table 1-2 specifies a positive, direct relationship between the height of barriers to entry (structure) and the likely level of industry profits (performance). On the whole, then, it may seem that perfect competition provides the "ideal circumstances" and "favorable conditions" alluded to earlier. To some extent it does, but, as we shall explain in the next chapter, this is only partly true.

Table 1-2 also serves to illustrate the two principal methodologies employed by industrial organization economists to analyze structure-conduct-performance relationships and test their significance—the "case study" approach and the "cross-section" approach. Under the former approach, the researcher

TABLE 1-2 Basic Market Types

Market Type	Structure			Conduct			Performance		
	Number of Firms	Entry Condition	Product Type	Price Policy	Production Policy	Promotion Policy*	Profits	Technical Efficiency	Progressiveness
Perfect Competition	Very large number	Easy	Standardized	None	Independent	b	Normal	Good	Poor perhaps
Monopolistic Competition	Large number	Easy	Differentiated	Unrecognized interdependence		a	Normal	Moderately good	Fair
Oligopoly	Few	Impeded	Standardized or differentiated	Recognized interdependence		a, b, c	Somewhat excessive	Poor perhaps	Good
Monopoly	One	Blocked	Perfectly differentiated	Independent		$a \equiv b$ c	Excessive	Poor perhaps	Poor perhaps

* Key: a = promotion of firm's brand product; b = industry or market wide advertising and promotion; c = institutional or political advertising.

14

narrows his focus to one industry or market for his "case study"; at the same time he usually considers almost all important aspects of the industry's structure, conduct, and performance. This approach is like viewing Table 1-2 *horizontally*, concentrating on only one row (for example, oligopoly), and moving from left to right across all the columns. In contrast, the cross-section approach is more inclusive of industries covered, but less comprehensive in its study of attributes or variables. With this approach one can usually focus on only a few items of structure, conduct, or performance (for example, the number of firms and profits). Thus the cross-section approach is like viewing Table 1-2 *vertically*, concentrating on relatively few columns, but including as many industries as the available data permit.

The two approaches have different advantages and disadvantages, so their contributions to our fund of knowledge are complementary. In particular, each industry is in some ways unique in its basic conditions, structure, or regulation. The case study approach can take these unique characteristics into account and assess their impact on conduct and performance. The main shortcoming of case studies, however, is that generalizations cannot reliably be drawn from them—that is, their conclusions may not be applicable to industries other than those under study. By contrast, the cross-section approach cannot include all the unique attributes of all the industries under its purview (because of data limitations and measurement problems), but with this approach the researcher can test the *general* validity of certain hypotheses by estimating statistically the relationships between the variables of structure, conduct and performance. For example, cross-section evidence indicates that industry profits are generally associated positively with the height of barriers to entry. However, certain unique features of a particular industry may have been left out of the cross-section analysis, thus precluding a direct and accurate application of this generalization to its specific case. Public pressure, flaccid demand, or some other factor that could only be accounted for by a thorough case study might cause low profits in a certain industry despite the presence of quite formidable barriers to entry. In sum, then, neither approach by itself is foolproof.

The case study and cross-section approaches differ not only in their substantive strengths and weaknesses. They also offer alternative ways to learn about the field of industrial organization, each of which has its pedagogical advantages and disadvantages. To most students' eyes, case studies appear concrete and lifelike, but the abstract overall view tends to be obscured by the wealth of detail they contain. On the other hand, cross-section evidence has opposite qualities—it provides an overall abstract view but lacks the concrete and often engrossing details one finds in case studies. Although this book is based primarily on the cross-section approach, both theoretically and empirically, it includes large doses of case study material. To blend approaches, we treat each major attribute of markets outlined in Figure 1-1 and Table 1-2 with a *pair* of chapters rather than just one chapter. As a glance at the table of contents will show, the first chapter of each pair presents "abstract" theories and cross-section evidence, whereas the second presents "concrete" case study illustrations and relevant policy provisions. Each pair of chapters is classified under the broad heading to which it corresponds, beginning with structure and ending with performance.

An Overview of Policies

Government policies concerning markets can also be classified within the structure-conduct-performance framework because, generally speaking, the immediate focus or proximate impact of such policies is limited to just one or a few of the market attributes outlined in Figure 1-1 and Table 1-2. Indeed, a chief reason for organizing this book into a sequence of structure, conduct, and performance discussions was the integrated treatment of policies and economics that could be achieved by such an organization. Most of the major policies that will be reviewed are outlined in Table 1-3, according to where they fit in this three-part scheme. Each policy has also been crossclassified in terms of how the policy relates to one important summary attribute of markets—*competition* Thus, the left hand side of Table 1-3 shows three designations concerning competition: (1) maintenance of competition, (2) setting the plane of competition, and (3) reliance on a "public utility" type of regulation instead of competition. It must be stressed that the resulting alignment of policies and market attributes is only a very loose representation of reality. Moreover, space limitations prevent the mention of numerous other policies, particularly those that constitute exemptions or special privileges. Nevertheless, the table serves as a solid and lofty perch from which to catch a panoramic view of the overall landscape that lies ahead.

Setting details aside until later, we may illustrate these points by highlighting some of the contents of Table 1-3. Mergers between firms in the same market, for example, are prohibited by the Clayton Act (as amended by the Celler-Kefauver Act of 1950) if their effect "may be substantially to lessen competition." The courts, when judging whether a given case produces this effect, examine the number of firms in the market, the trend in numbers over time, and the market shares of the merging firms, all of which obviously relate to two attributes of market structure, namely, the number and size distribution of firms. Thus, Table 1-3 lists "merger laws" under the column headed "Structure." And, since prosecutions of monopolization under the Sherman Act are grounded on similar types of evidence, particularly size of market share, monopoly law joins merger law under "Structure" in Table 1-3. Without further reference to judicial considerations, it should be fairly clear that the remaining policies listed under structure belong there, for they relate primarily to product differentiation.

Under the column headed "Conduct," our laws governing price fixing (collusion), price discrimination, exclusive dealing, tying, and false advertising proscribe certain kinds of business behavior. There can be no question that among these, price fixing and false advertising policies should be classified under conduct. Price fixing's *per se* illegality (regardless of the extent of market power behind it or its effect on performance) illustrates the reasons for this. On the other hand, as will be shown later, simply designating price discrimination, tying, and exclusive dealing policies under "Conduct" may be somewhat misleading, since standards of illegality in these cases require that structural circumstances be taken into account before violation can be determined.

"Performance" is the third classification. It will be recalled that allocation efficiency, technical efficiency, macroeconomic stability, and technological progress are attributes of major concern. As will be explained immediately following, performance measured by these attributes lies largely outside the purview or concern of policies designed to maintain competition. Hence, the first cell of the "Performance" column in Table 1-3 has been left blank. The remaining performance policies are divided into two categories: (1) those policies that apply to almost all industries, regardless of competitive structure (since structure may have no effect on these particular forms of performance), and (2) those policies that apply to specific industries regulated by government commissions rather than by competition.

The first category includes such policies as pollution control, occupational health, minimum safety requirements, and standards of purity for food and drugs (undeniably important matters of performance not hitherto mentioned because their connection to the traditional variables of structure and conduct is tenuous). The second category includes similar policies to some extent, but its main contents are profit regulation, service requirements, investment control, and supervision of innovation and technological change, for these policies typically come with the jurisdiction of numerous independent commissions that regulate these aspects of specific industries—for example the Interstate Commerce Commission, Civil Aeronautics Board, and the Federal Communications Commission. Instances of such direct performance regulation are usually rationalized on the ground that competitive structure cannot be attained or, if attainable, cannot be relied upon to provide desirable performance. For this reason the last structural policy cell of Table 1-3, corresponding to public utility type regulation, has been left blank, even though these industries are subject to certain forms of structural supervision.

Values, Attributes, and Policies Together

This chapter cannot be concluded without an explicit acknowledgement of the links between all three of its major components—value judgments, market attributes, and public policies. The ties connecting the latter two have just been dealt with, so all that remains is a brief exploration of whatever correspondence they may have to value judgments. To state the obvious: All public policies have

17

TABLE 1-3 Basic Government Policies Concerning Markets (Enforcement Agencies in Parentheses)

Policy Type	Structure	Conduct	Performance
Maintenance of competition	1. Monopoly law (DOJ) 2. Merger laws (DOJ, FTC)	1. Price fixing law (DOJ) 2. Price discrimination law (FTC) 3. Exclusive dealing law (DOJ, FTC) 4. Tying law (DOJ, FTC)	1. Health and safety disclosures (FTC, PSC, FDA) 2. Health and safety regulation in products, transportation, etc. (PSC, DOT) 3. Pollution limitations (EPA, S&LC)
Setting the plane of competition	1. Disclosure of information, truth-in-lending (FTC, FRB) 2. Grading and standardization agricultural products (USDA); general weights and measures (BOS) 3. Trade mark and copyright protection (DOC)	1. False advertising (FTC) 2. Deceptive practices (FTC)	

"Public utility" regulation

1. Price regulation in trucking, bus transit, railrods, airlines, telephone, electricity and gas, banking and insurance (ICC, CAB, FRB, FHLB, S&LC)	1. Profit regulation (S&LC, FPC, CAB, ICC)
2. Abandonment of service (ICC, CAB)	2. Service requirements (S&LC, ICC)
3. Credit availability (FRB)	3. Safety (DOT, S&LC, FAA, FPC, NRC)
	4. Innovation regulation (ICC)

Key:
DOJ = Department of Justice
FTC = Federal Trade Commission
FRB = Federal Reserve Board
USDA = U.S. Department of Agriculture
ICC = Interstate Commerce Commission
CAB = Civil Aeronautics Board

BOS = Bureau of Standards
PSC = Product Safety Commission
FDA = Food and Drug Administration
DOT = Department of Transportation
FHLB = Federal Home Loan Bank Board
DOC = Department of Commerce

EPA = Environmental Protection Agency
FPC = Federal Power Commission
FAA = Federal Aviation Agency
NRC = Nuclear Regulation Commission
S&LC = State and Local Commissions

some *purpose* or *objective*, usually (or hopefully) the furtherance of one or more social values. And, broadly speaking, the purpose of most policies governing markets is to further one or more of the ultimate and proximate values listed earlier in Table 1-1. This observation may be comforting (since it assures us that government officials act in the public interest, at least occasionally), but it is not really very illuminating. We need to know a few specifics. In particular which policies are designed to further which objectives? And which objectives are associated with which market attributes?

To best understand the answers to these questions, the reader must use his mind's eye to divide Table 1-1 into three main groups of ultimate values—(1) freedom and equality, (2) justice and fairness, and (3) welfare, happiness, and progress—retaining within each group the appropriate proximate values listed under each broad heading. Now (without straining your mind's eye too much) align the resulting three groups of values next to the three categories of market attributes outlined in Figure 1-1 that are, in principle, readily amenable to policy change—that is, (1) market structure, (2) conduct, and (3) performance. By this procedure it is possible to gain a loose appreciation for the fact that generally speaking, (1) policies dealing primarily with market structure have as their main purpose the furtherance of "freedom and equality," (2) policies dealing primarily with market conduct are typically designed to enhance "justice and fairness," and (3) policies dealing chiefly with performance usually have as their objective the enrichment of "welfare and happiness" or the encouragement of "progress." Finally, if tilted properly, the policy outline of Table 1-3 could join this rough conceptual alignment of values and market attributes to complete an overall pattern of correspondence among values, market attributes, and policies, as indicated in Table 1-4. This summary alignment is of course only a very crude representation of reality, for numerous overlaps and inconsistencies could easily be pointed out. Still, for introductory purposes, it has the benefit of brevity.

The interrelationships between values, policies, and market characteristics, together with some qualifications, may be illustrated with special reference to the antitrust laws, which have been labeled "Maintenance of competition" policies in Table 1-3, and which are probably the most important of all policies considered in this book because they constitute the "general rule" and therefore apply to most industries. Regarding values, antitrust policy could serve one or more of a wide variety of possible aims, nearly all of which may be grouped in the following three classes:[9]

1. *Maintenance of competition and limitation of business size*: This broad objective would draw its justification from the desirability of having (a) free entry and investment; (b) a large number of alternatives for exercising free choice in consumption and investment; (c) limited business

---

[9] For a more thorough treatment of antitrust objectives see Carl Kaysen and Donald Turner, *Antitrust Policy* (Cambridge: Harvard University Press, 1965), pp. 11–22.

TABLE 1-4   Overall   Correspondence   Among   Values,   Policies,   and Market Attributes

Values	Policies	Market Attributes
Freedom and equality	Maintenance of competitive opportunity	Structure and (to a lesser extent) conduct
Justice and fairness	Rules regarding pricing, promotion, tying, etc.	Conduct
Welfare, happiness, and progress	Direct regulation of performance	Performance

power, or a diffusion of economic power; and (d) equal bargaining power on both sides of the market. These aims embody certain desirable *economic* traits or conditions descriptive of *markets*, but antitrust could help to achieve certain *political* or *social* aims as well, for political and social power are often grounded on economic power, and economic power can stem either from prominance in a specific market or from participation in numerous markets (as is true of so-called conglomerates). Thus, this first class of objectives could include a dislike for huge business units as such and a disapproval of conduct that might injure small businesses. Many if not most of us believe that furtherance of these several aims tend to foster "freedom" and "equality" as defined earlier.

2. *Fair conduct*: The foregoing relates primarily to the *mere possession* of power, not to its *exercise*. In contrast, aims of "fair conduct" relate more to the way business power is used rather than its mere presence. Should large buyers be charged less than small buyers? Should a seller be allowed to tie the sale of two products together, like computers and punch cards, one of which is monopolistically controlled by patents or trade secrets? Should a manufacturer deny its wholesalers and retailers the right to sell another manufacturer's line of products? Also, what about group boycotts and aggregated rebates? Antitrust could attempt to lay down certain standards of fair business conduct that would curtail these kinds of practices without necessarily attacking the economic power that makes them onerous.

3. *Desirable economic performance*: Because market structure and conduct greatly affect market performance, antitrust policy could be concerned with structure and conduct *only* in so far as they might produce poor performance, while overlooking any concentrations of power or unfair practices that had no discernible effect on performance or promised potential improvements therein. Indeed, despite ample evidence to the contrary, a few economists believe that bigness brings about efficiency,

21

stability, and progress; that cartels are relatively harmless; and that "restrictive practices" are not really restrictive at all. Hence they emphatically favor having performance as the only goal, arguing that "the *process* of choice itself must not be a value,"[10] and that our policy objectives should be confined to "maximizing economic benefits, *whatever* the number of firms may turn out to be."[11]

Which of these three broad aims actually predominates? Notwithstanding the views of the performance minded minority, the general consensus among economists, legislators, and jurists seems to be that our antitrust policy should be aimed, primarily, at the maintenance of competition as an end in itself and, secondarily, at the enforcement of fair conduct. Bartlett's could publish an entire book of (unfamiliar) quotations supporting this assertion, but only a few will suffice here:

> The greatest common denominator in antitrust decisions is a commitment to smallness and decentralization as ways of discouraging the concentration of discretionary authority.—Donald Dewey[12]

> The grounds for the policy include not only dislike of restriction of output and of one-sided bargaining power but also desire to prevent excessive concentration of wealth and power, desire to keep open the channels of opportunity, and concern lest monopolistic controls of business lead to political oligarchy. — Corwin Edwards[13]

> Throughout the history of these [antitrust] statutes it has been constantly assumed that one of their purposes was to perpetuate and preserve, for its own sake and in spite of possible cost, an organization of industry in small units which can effectively compete with each other.—Judge Learned Hand[14]

As for the views of laymen, the reader need merely ask: Would most folks like to see each and every industry turned over to the control of two or three firms and the economy as a whole (including mining, manufacturing, transportation, finance, and wholesale and retail trade) subjected to the overwhelming dominance of only fifty corporations, assuming (for the sake of illustration) that economists believe this massive restructuring would eventually yield 5% greater efficiency, 3% less cyclical instability, and 4% faster growth in GNP? In all probability, your answer is no (or NO!). Moreover, the same answer would most likely greet a similar question regarding unfair or restrictive business

---

[10] C. E. Ferguson, *A Macroeconomic Theory of Workable Competition* (Durham: University of North Carolina Press, 1964), p. 56 (emphasis added).

[11] John McGee, *In Defense of Industrial Concentration* (New York: Praeger Publishers, 1971) p. 21 (emphasis added).

[12] Donald Dewey, "The New Learning: One Man's View," in *Industrial Concentration: The New Learning*, edited by H. J. Goldschmid, H. M. Mann, and J. F. Weston (Boston: Little, Brown and Co., 1974) p. 13.

[13] Corwin Edwards, *Maintaining Competition* (New York: McGraw Hill, 1949), p. 9.

[14] *United States v. Aluminum Company of America*, 148 F.2d 416 (1945).

practices. Thus our major antitrust policies have been assigned to the "Structure" and "Conduct" sections of Table 1-3, and it is not inappropriate to draw an association between these policies and certain broad classes of values addressed at the outset—freedom, equality, justice, and fairness. If, for one reason or another, the antitrust approach fails to satisfy these objectives in a specific industry, or if the approach is irrelevant to certain performance objectives (like clean air), or if the approach is considered *too* costly in terms of poor performance in an industry, then direct regulation of performance often ensues. But this step is usually taken only with great reluctance and often in response to crisis.

Summary

A few first steps towards an understanding of markets have now been taken. In a nutshell, the market system should be looked upon not only as the organized process by which buyers and sellers exchange goods and services but as an *institution*—the key institution upholding our private free-enterprise capitalistic economy. Because markets are institutional by nature, they embody certain social values, they perform an essential economic function, and they are the target of many governmental policies. In function, markets coordinate and control the largely decentralized decision-making process that provides answers to the four fundamental questions scarcity forces upon us: (1) What should be produced? (2) How should goods and services be produced? (3) Who shall get the benefits of our productive efforts? (4) How can we maintain flexibility for changes over time? Given their assigned task, markets may be analyzed and evaluated by both the specific *answers provided* and the *process by which the answers are obtained*. If the decision process seems "bad" but the answers themselves are considered "good," society might want to reject the system despite its considerable "goodness." Indeed, the way decisions are made may be important enough to people to make them willing to suffer an occasional bad answer in order to maintain a system or process to their liking. Ideally, of course, both the process of choice and the answers produced should conform to society's concepts of the desirable—that is, society's values.

Translating "process" and "answers" into a model of markets, we come up with a four-part categorization of market attributes—the basic conditions, structure, conduct, and performance. The last three command special attention because structure and conduct comprise the market's decision-making process, whereas performance consists of the achievements, outcomes, or answers provided by the process. In other words, structure refers to such factors as the number and size distribution of the decision makers (buyers and sellers), the condition of entry, and product differentiation. Conduct includes, among other things, price policy, production policy, promotion activity, and coercive tactics. Last, the principal attributes of performance are allocation and technical efficiency, progress, and aggregate economic stability.

Returning to goodness and badness, value judgments furnish standards for evaluating market structure, conduct, and performance. Moreover, value judgments guide policy formulation and enforcement. Antitrust policy provides an apt illustration of this junction of market attributes, value judgments, and public policies: (1) antitrust focuses most intently on structure and conduct, (2) its principal purpose is the maintenance of competition as an end in itself, and (3) maintenance of competition is, in essence, a shorthand way of saying freedom, equality, fairness, and justice, together with most of the relevant proximate values they represent.

2

Perfect Competition: A Specific Case and Possible Standard

Competition may be the spice of life, but in economics it has been more nearly the main dish.

GEORGE STIGLER

Chapter 1 described, in very general terms, the relationships among market structure, conduct, and performance. We now move from the general to the particular. This chapter provides a detailed theoretical treatment of structure, conduct, and performance as they relate to one particular type of market— perfect competition. This detailed treatment will accomplish two ends. First, it will illustrate theoretical **market analysis**; it will, in other words, demonstrate how buyers and sellers make market decisions under certain conditions. Second, analysis of the perfectly competitive market model will enable us to probe more thoroughly into the issue of **market evaluation**: What structure *ought* to prevail? What conduct decisions *ought* to be made? What performance *ought* to be realized? Before we can answer such questions, we must develop some theoretical **standard**, or **ideal conditions**, against which real world markets may be compared.

As the first word in the name of the model under review is "perfect," the reader already has the hint that economists for the most part, regard perfect competition the ideal situation, the standard against which all markets should be compared. Thus, in the first few sections that follow we shall attempt to demonstrate why, on economic grounds, perfect competition *might* be desirable. The word "might" needs stress because there are numerous reasons why we might *not* want perfect competition as our standard. These contrary reasons are discussed toward the end of the chapter. Finally, once we have covered both the pros and the cons of this "perfect" model, we shall conclude by specifying standards that are not exactly perfect, but which are nevertheless highly desirable.

Welfare Optimality

According to classical economic theory, the major microeconomic achievement of perfectly competitive markets is "welfare optimality" or "Pareto optimality," so named because Vilfredo Pareto, an Italian economist, first formulated the concept. To understand what is involved here, we begin by exploring the meaning of Pareto optimality and then determine how perfectly competitive markets can attain it.

The word "optimum" has a familiar ring. In simple English it means "most favorable." This meaning carries over to the word's use in economics, but in economics it is applied technically. It does not mean the same thing as "maximum." Maximum denotes the greatest value attainable in a given specific case. High performance dragsters illustrate a maximum. The objective of a dragster is merely the greatest speed while covering a quarter-mile distance from a standing start. Compare this goal (and the dragster's design) with the typical family car. The purpose of a family car is to serve diverse needs: Dad needs good gas mileage for commuting; mom needs room for groceries; junior (who is 18 years old) wants sporty lines with horsepower to match; and so on. It would be silly to speak of the maximum car in this case. In light of the diverse performances and the trade-offs implied—for example, greater horsepower and size reduce gas mileage efficiency—no single design or size or bundle of equipment may be considered absolutely the best.

It is likely that several models could qualify as "favorable" or "optimal" from the entire family's point of view. Selection of this optimal set might be based on some simple rule of elimination such as: reject a car whenever someone's favorite feature can be enhanced by selecting another car *without* detracting from the favorite feature of any other family member. Of course other rules are possible, especially rules favorable to certain individuals. One such rule might be that any car chosen *must* meet dad's minimum requirement of 25 miles per gallon, dad's wishes having priority in this case. Notice that (1) value judgments play a major role in determining which selection rule will be adopted, (2) conflicts may consequently arise, and (3) *scarcity* forces the family to make a choice and share (otherwise each member would own a car, or two maybe, precluding the need for a group decision rule).

The concept of Pareto optimality springs from very similar circumstances— namely, society's forced choice under the confines of scarcity as to *what* goods should be produced and *how* they should be produced. The formal definition of **Pareto optimality** is this: *a point in the processes of production and resource*

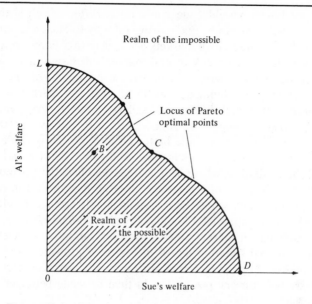

Figure 2-1. *Pareto optimal points for two-person society.*

allocation where it is impossible to make any person better off (as that person sees his own welfare) without at the same time making another person worse off (as that other person sees his own welfare). To state the same concept differently, we would *not* be at Pareto optimum if we could enhance the welfare of one or more members of society while we maintained without change the welfare of all others. So long as this possibility for clear-cut improvement exists, the result is said to be inefficient, nonoptimal, or unfavorable. Thus Pareto optimality is synonymous with allocation and technical efficiency.

Figure 2-1 depicts a Pareto optimal locus of points for a simple, two-person society (it being impossible to graph such curves for 200 million people). Movement to the right, parallel with the horizontal axis, indicates greater levels of welfare for Sue. Upward movement in the vertical direction would reflect betterment for Al. Points L and D on the graph indicate points of "maximum" for each individual. That is to say, if society completely ignored the welfare of Al and directed all of its resources and energy to the satisfaction of Sue's wants, scarcity would prevent us from making Sue any better off than is indicated by point D. Conversely, the single-minded pursuit of Al's welfare would be limited to point L. The curve LACD is thus a locus of Pareto optimal points because it delineates the realm of the possible for this society. From any point, such as B, inside the boundary, Sue can be made better off without spoiling Al's world by moving toward C. A move from B to A would represent a change that made *both* individuals better off simultaneously. In short, points like B are inefficient. Once society is on the LACD line, however, positive

27

movement is no longer possible. Sue can be made better off *only* at the expense of Al and, conversely, Al can be made better off only to Sue's discomfort.

How do perfectly competitive markets get society to a Pareto optimal solution of the scarcity problem? A formal answer will be given in subsequent sections after we define "perfectly competitive market." For the present, a tentative answer may be obtained if we recall that any market is simply an organized process by which buyers and sellers *exchange* goods and services. Whenever *free and voluntary* exchange occurs with no adverse third party effects, at least one person is made better off and no one is made worse off (as each party to the exchange sees his own well being). Notice that this is not the world of the Godfather, where people are given offers they "cannot refuse" (because the consequences of refusal are bloody). It is the world of free and voluntary exchange, and such exchange would simply not occur unless at least one person's lot were improved. Usually, of course, *both* parties to an exchange benefit. The exchange or market process therefore can move a society from an inefficient, suboptimal situation like *B* in Figure 2-1 toward an efficient, optimal situation like *A* or *C*. Once at *A* or *C*, mutually beneficial exchange is no longer possible because one person would then be made better off at the expense of another.

To be a bit more specific, Pareto optimal solutions require the simultaneous fulfillment of three necessary conditions. Their shorthand labels are consumption efficiency, production efficiency, and consumer sovereignty. Simply stated, they are almost self-evident requirements:

1. **Consumption efficiency:** Goods should go to the people who want them most—for example, tea should go to the tea drinkers, coffee to the coffee drinkers, and so on.
2. **Production efficiency:** As much of each desirable good should be produced as our resources and technical knowledge permit in light of the production of other desirable goods—for example, maintaining our production of corn, oats, and other crops, we should produce as much wheat as possible.
3. **Consumer sovereignty:** The goods people want most should be produced —for example, if Popeye, and only Popeye, likes spinach, we should concentrate our efforts on the production of goods other than spinach.

The role of free and voluntary exchange in achieving the first of these, consumption efficiency, may be appreciated in a simple example. Suppose that Al and Sue produce only two products—bread and jam. Suppose further that at the end of each season Al and Sue, working separately, have the following inventories of these commodities in their possession:

Al	*Sue*
375 loaves of bread	415 loaves of bread
250 jars of jam	436 jars of jam

Now each individual will have subjective preferences for these goods as determined by his or her taste and current inventories. Recalling that everyone "has a price," we express these relative preferences in substitution or trading ratios, such as the following:

Al	Sue
. . . would be willing to give up 1 loaf of bread to get 1 additional jar of jam (or vice-versa) . . .	. . . would be willing to give up 3 loaves of bread to get 1 additional jar of jam (or give up $\frac{1}{3}$ jar for 1 loaf) . . .
substitution ratio = 1 bread/1 jam	substitution ratio = 3 bread/1 jam

It is easy to see that, of the two individuals, Sue has the sweet tooth. Despite her comparatively abundant initial wealth of jam, she places a high value on jam in terms of the large amount of bread she is willing to give up in order to get still more jam. The important point, though, is that as long as these subjective substitution ratios differ, exchange between Al and Sue can benefit both of them. Sue would willingly offer Al $1\frac{1}{2}$ loaves of bread for an additional 1 jar of jam (indeed, she would willingly offer up to 3 loaves). Al would willingly accept this offer of $1\frac{1}{2}$ loaves, since this is a better deal than his subjective evaluation of 1 loaf for 1 jar. The ensuing exchange produces a flow of jam from Al's cupboard into Sue's, and a flow of bread from Sue's pantry into Al's.

Of course this cannot go on forever. Bread and jam go well together, and Sue and Al both know this. As Al's growing stock of bread rises relative to his diminishing stock of jam, his relative evaluation of jam will *rise*. And as Sue's growing stock of jam rises relative to her diminishing stock of bread, her relative evaluation of jam will *fall*. With Al's subjective preference ratio rising from 1/1 and Sue's falling from 3/1 they will eventually become equal. Suppose these folk end up as follows, in terms of stocks and ratios:

Al	Sue
447 loaves of bread	343 loaves of bread
191 jars of jam	495 jars of jam
substitution ratio = 2 bread/1 jam	substitution ratio = 2 bread/1 jam

Once their substitution ratios are equal at, say, 2/1, trade ceases and "consumption efficiency" is attained. No one can be made better off by trade without making someone else worse off. For later reference it is important to note that these subjective substitution ratios are actually *price* ratios. According to this last table, the "price" of a jar of jam is 2 loaves of bread, and the "price" of 1 loaf of bread is $\frac{1}{2}$ jar of jam:

Substitution Ratios	Price Ratio
$\text{Al's}\left(\dfrac{2 \text{ bread}}{1 \text{ jam}}\right) = \text{Sue's}\left(\dfrac{2 \text{ bread}}{1 \text{ jam}}\right)$	$=$ $\dfrac{\text{price of jam}}{\text{price of bread}}$

In monetary terms, jam would be worth $1.20 per jar if bread was $0.60 per loaf.

Efficiency in production, the second condition for Pareto optimum, may be illustrated by a diagram. Figure 2-2 depicts the production possibilities curve for bread and jam in this little two-person society. Devoting *all* of society's resources to the production of jam would yield 920 jars per year. Conversely, if no jam were produced and all effort centered on bread production, total output would be 1150 loaves of bread. The curved line spanning the distance between these two extreme points indicates all the possible combinations of bread and jam production—assuming *full employment, efficient use of resources, and application of the society's best production techniques.* In sum, this curve is quite similar to the welfare possibilities curve of Figure 2-1, but here we are looking at *production* possibilities, not *welfare* possibilities. As a consequence, each axis is scaled on the basis of quantity output per year (or some other time period).

Any point inside the curve (such as 600 loaves of bread and 300 jars of jam) falls short of "production efficiency" because more of one of these goods could be produced without reducing the output of the other, or the output of *both*

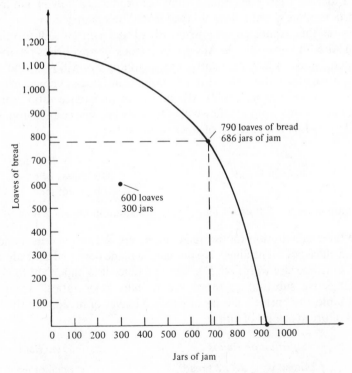

Figure 2-2. Bread and jam production possibilities curve.

goods could be increased simultaneously. Only those points *on* the possibilities curve are "efficient," for only on that curve can it be said that as much of each desirable good is being produced as is possible in light of the production of other desirable goods. The point representing 790 loaves of bread and 686 jars of jam is one such point, and we call special attention to that combination of goods because it designates the total output of Al and Sue in our preceding example of consumption efficiency. Total starting inventories in that example were $375 + 415 = 790$ loaves of bread, and $250 + 436 = 686$ jars of jam. Ending inventories were $447 + 343 = 790$ and $191 + 495 = 686$, respectively. Thus, by assumption, the example is continued here to show simultaneous compliance with both consumption and production efficiency.

Compliance with these two conditions is necessary but not sufficient for attainment of Pareto optimum, since the third condition—consumer sovereignty—must likewise be satisfied. To summarize: the first condition is an equality of everyone's substitution and price ratios. The second condition is met by being on the production possibilities curve. Finally, compliance with the third condition requires that the *slope* of the production possibilities curve be *equal* to the subjective substitution and price ratios. The slope of the production possibilities curve indicates the amount of bread that must be given up by society in order to produce an additional jar of jam and vice-versa (remember that scarcity forces this trade-off). Thus at the point for 790 loaves and 686 jars in Figure 2-2, the cost of 1 additional jar of jam is 3 foregone loaves of bread— if we are moving *down* the curve in the direction of more jam and less bread; whereas, the cost of an additional 3 loaves of bread is 1 foregone jar of jam—if we are moving *up* the curve in the direction of more bread and less jam. In formula notation we have

$$\text{slope of production possibilities curve} = \frac{3 \text{ loaves of bread}}{1 \text{ jar of jam}} = \frac{\text{cost of jam}}{\text{cost of bread}}$$

It follows, then, that consumers' sovereignty requires:

$$\frac{\text{cost of jam (at the margin)}}{\text{cost of bread (at the margin)}} = \frac{\text{price of jam}}{\text{price of bread}}$$

Or, stating the same relation in terms of nonmonetary quantities:

$$\underset{\substack{\text{Production} \\ \text{Possibilities}}}{\left(\frac{\text{loaves}}{\text{jars}}\right)} = \text{Al's}\left(\frac{\text{loaves}}{\text{jars}}\right) = \text{Sue's}\left(\frac{\text{loaves}}{\text{jars}}\right)$$

Slope   *Subjective Substitution Ratios of People*

If this condition is not met, then one person can be made better off without making the other worse off, that is, inefficiency exists. In particular, this condition is not met if the production possibilities slope is 3 loaves/1 jar while subjective preferences are 2 loaves/1 jar, which is the situation now prevailing in our example. Thus, at this point, we should be able to make one person better off or both better off even though we have already attended to consumption and production efficiency (the first two conditions).

Let's leave Sue alone, and deal solely with Al to demonstrate this. We could make Al just as well off as he is right now if we took 1 jar of his jam and gave him in return 2 loaves of bread. The current 3 loaves/1 jar production possibilities ratio indicates that physically we can do this—that is, society can give up 1 jar to get more bread. Indeed, it indicates that we can use Al's foregone 1 jar to produce 3 additional loaves of bread. If we did this and gave 2 of these loaves to Al to leave him just as well off as before, we would then have 1 loaf left over, 1 loaf that belonged to nobody. This added loaf could obviously be used to make Al better off, or, if we give half of it to each person, we could make both better off. Thus, the inequality between the production and consumption ratios was inefficient.

Under ideal circumstances, free and voluntary exchange would correct this inefficiency by expanding society's output of bread and reducing society's output of jam. The reduction of jam production would, in turn, reduce the production possibilities ratio of loaves-of-bread/jars-of-jam (because the slope of the production possibilities curve in Figure 2-2 is flatter toward the top, in the direction of more bread, than toward the bottom, in the direction of more jam), and raise the consumers' relative valuation of jam (that is, raise the loaves/jars ratio in consumption) as jam output falls and bread output rises. Finally, once all these ratios are equal, Pareto optimum will be achieved. No one can then be made better off without making someone else worse off. For future reference the key equality is

$$\frac{\text{cost of jam at the margin}}{\text{cost of bread at the margin}} = \frac{\text{price of jam}}{\text{price of bread}}$$

This can be written more simply as:

$$\frac{\text{price of jam}}{\text{price of bread}} = \frac{\text{cost of jam at the margin}}{\text{cost of bread at the margin}}$$

To translate the last of these relations into more explicit language, notice first that the *price* of bread indicates the value to society of using scarce resources *here*, in the production of bread. Notice next that the *cost* of bread reflects the value to society of using these scarce resources *elsewhere*, in the production of other goods such as jam. *Optimal allocation* of resources requires that

$$\text{value here} = \text{value elsewhere}$$

If value here (in bread) exceeds value elsewhere (in other goods), then price exceeds cost and resources should get out of elsewhere to move here. This inequality is called an **underallocation** of resources. On the other hand, if value here falls short of value elsewhere, then price is less than cost and resources should get out of here and go elsewhere to correct for an **overallocation** of resources to here. Under- and overallocations are both *mis*allocations.

Perfect Competition: Demand and Structure

We have defined Pareto optimum, explained the conditions required for its realization, and very vaguely suggested how perfectly competitive markets might achieve this optimum. We shall now define perfectly competitive markets in structural terms. Subsequent sections will take up perfectly competitive conduct and performance, showing more explicitly how perfect competition achieves the optimum. Structure relates primarily to demand as individual firms see it, conduct relates to supply, and performance relates to the combination or interaction of demand and supply. Thus, in essence, our plan is to explore demand, supply, and their interaction.[1]

Perfect competition is defined by four basic structural conditions. First, perfect competition requires a very large number of small buyers and sellers. Indeed, each buyer and each seller must be so small relative to the total market that none of them *individually* can affect product price by altering their volume of purchases, if they are buyers, or their level of output, if they are sellers. This is true even if one of these market participants takes the drastic step of leaving the market entirely. As a group they can affect price; individually, they cannot.

Second, the product of any one seller must be a perfect substitute for the product of any other seller. All that matters is price. Buyers do not care who supplies the product so long as price is the same for all sellers. In economists' jargon, the product is homogeneous or standardized.

Third, perfect competition requires that productive resources be freely mobile into and out of markets. Of course any such movement will take time, and in the short run some factors like land and capital are said to be "fixed" because of their short-run immobility once they are committed to production. However, in the long run, all factors are variable and perfectly mobile. This means an absence of barriers to new firm entry—that is, an absence of patents, economies of scale, large capital requirements, and the like.

Finally, perfect competition requires that all market participants have full knowledge of the economic and technical data relevant to their decision making.

---

[1] For a more complete discussion of perfect competition see E. Mansfield, *Microeconomics: Theory and Applications*, 2nd ed. (New York: W. W. Norton & Company, 1976), Chapter 7, or some other theory text.

Buyers must be aware of the price and product offerings of sellers. Sellers must know product prices, wage rates, materials costs, and interest rates. Moreover, it is assumed that all participants act rationally on this knowledge.

Under these several conditions the demand curve facing each individual firm will be perfectly elastic with respect to price. This is a supremely important statement, yet its specific content is meaningless without an understanding of two of its key terms "demand" and "elasticity." Although the reader is probably familiar with each concept, a brief review is perhaps warranted. In the very broad sense, **demand** refers to the quantity of product that would be purchased at various possible prices during some given period of time, holding all determinants of demand other than product price constant. Specifically, demand can refer (1) to the demand *of an individual buyer*, (2) to the demand *of all buyers* in the market taken together, or (3) to the demand *facing an individual seller* in the market. Generally speaking, structural conditions do not influence demand in the first two respects. That is to say, the purchases of a single buyer are only a function of product price, income, tastes, prices of substitute goods (for example, coffee for tea or vice-versa), prices of complements (for example, coffee and donuts), and expectations. Individual demand, as your own experience should tell you, is *not* a function of the number of sellers in the market or the condition of new firm entry. Similarly, since total market demand is simply the summation of all the demands of the individual buyers' in the market, total market demand is a function of the same variables that determine individual demand (price, incomes, tastes, prices of related goods, and expectations), plus one additional factor—the number of buyers in the market. Now the number of buyers was mentioned as a structural element. But the number is typically large, so in all but a few instances we are safe in saying that *market structure does not directly affect market-wide demand.* (A special exception concerning advertising will be taken up in later chapters.)

Figure 2-3 illustrates several **market-wide** demand curves. According to the conventional "law" of demand each demand curve must have a negative slope because price and quantity are inversely related. Thus, on curve $D_1 D_1$, an increase in the price of the product from P_1 to P_2 causes quantity demanded to drop from Q_1 to Q_2, resulting in a movement along the demand curve from point K to J. Such movements along the demand curve, under the impetus of price changes, should not be confused with *shifts* of demand, which are caused by changes in variables *other* than the product's price. An increase in income, for instance, is likely to shift demand outward from $D_1 D_1$ to $D_2 D_2$. Conversely, a reduction of income is likely to shift demand down from $D_1 D_1$ to $D_3 D_3$, resulting in fewer purchases than before at each possible price.

Later, it will be important to know just *how responsive* demand is to variations in price. To measure such responsiveness, economists rely on the **elasticity** of demand in relation to price, which is defined as follows:

$$\text{price elasticity of demand} = \frac{\text{percentage change in quantity demanded}}{\text{percentage change in price}}$$

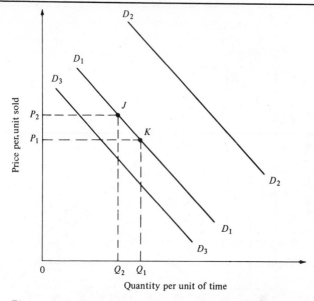

Figure 2-3. *Examples of market-wide product demand.*

Strictly speaking, the negative slope of demand always yields a negative elasticity, but the negative sign is usually suppressed for simplification. When the percentage change in quantity demanded exceeds the percentage change in price for some given price change, quantity demand is highly responsive to price and the elasticity ratio will be greater than 1. Conversely, if the percentage change in quantity demanded is less than the percentage change in price, demand is relatively *un*responsive to price variations and the elasticity will be less than 1. Finally, if both percentages are the same, the ratio will just equal 1. To summarize:

Elasticity Ratio	Demand is Said to Be
Greater than 1	Elastic
Less than 1	Inelastic
Equal 1	Unit elastic

All three of these situations may be illustrated on a single market-wide demand curve, Figure 2-4, since elasticity will vary along a linear demand curve. For purposes of illustration, the horizontal axis depicts quantity in billions of dozens of eggs, whereas the vertical axis is scaled in fractions of a dollar for the price per dozen. Notice, first, that a 10-cent drop in price from $1.00 to $0.90 or a 10-cent rise in price from $0.90 to $1.00 represents, on average, a percentage change of about 10.5% (0.10/0.95 = 0.1052). Associated with these prices are quantities of 1 billion and 2 billion dozen. Hence, on average up and down, the percentage change in quantity over this range of prices would be

35

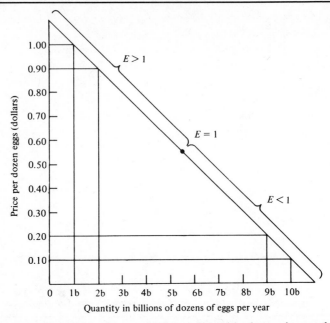

Figure 2-4. *Elasticities along a single market-wide demand curve for eggs.*

approximately 66.7% (1 billion/1.5 billion = 0.6666). Dividing the percentage change in quantity by the percentage change in price yields an elasticity of 66.7/10.5, or 6.35, which is obviously greater than 1.

Moving to the lower end of the demand curve, we notice next that a 10-cent change in price (up or down) relative to an original price of 10 or 20 cents is quite large, namely, 66.7% on average (0.10/0.15 = 0.6666). Associated with these prices are quantities of 9 and 10 billion dozen, which, when converted to percentage change, yield a relatively small number 10.5% (1 billion/9.5 billion = 0.1052). Thus, elasticity in this range of the demand curve is 10.5/66.7, or 0.157, which is clearly less than 1. Between the elastic and inelastic portions of the curve we naturally find unit elasticity.[2]

[2] The formula used to compute these elasticities is

$$\frac{\dfrac{Q_2 - Q_1}{(Q_1 + Q_2)/2}}{\dfrac{P_2 - P_1}{(P_1 + P_2)/2}}$$

This is called the "midpoint" formula because the midpoints, or averages, of the starting and ending values are used to compute the percentage change. The simple alternative is

$$\frac{(Q_2 - Q_1)/Q_1}{(P_2 - P_1)/P_1}$$

But use of this formula will yield differing elasticities depending upon whether the price change is assumed to be up or down.

Although the market-wide demand for eggs and other commodities tends to be inversely related to price and of varying elasticity, this cannot be the same view of demand held by the typical *individual firm* selling in the market, unless, of course, there is only one firm in the market (a monopolist). In the case of perfect competition the number of sellers is very large, and each seller is so small relative to the total market that it views its demand as in Figure 2-5—a horizontal line running parallel to the quantity axis and intersecting the vertical axis at the going market price. Market price can, of course, vary up and down over time, which would be shown here by up and down shifts of this demand line. However, Figure 2-5 says that neither the market price nor the firm's price can vary up or down *over the range of output* that this very small firm can produce. Notice that the quantity axis here is scaled in *thousands* of dozens of eggs per year instead of *billions* of dozens as in Figure 2-4, a modification necessitated by the small scale of the typical firm in this instance (think of Ma Kettle with a dozen hens).

Thus, market structure is a *crucial determinant* of demand as viewed by the typical firm in the market, even though structure generally does *not* influence the market-wide demand curve. In and of itself this finding may seem meaningless, but it is precisely through this influence on the firm's view of demand that structure subsequently influences firm conduct and, thereby, market conduct as well. How does the firm's view of demand influence firm conduct? By influencing the way firms in the market go about maximizing their profits—assuming that firms want to maximize profits. In summary,

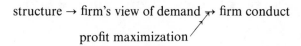

structure → firm's view of demand ↗ firm conduct

profit maximization ↗

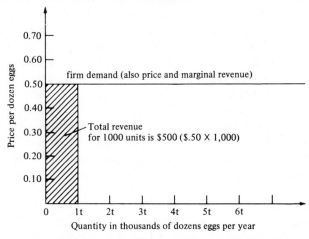

Figure 2-5. *Demand of a perfectly competitive seller.*

And the next step, before explicitly taking up conduct, is to extract the element of demand particularly relevant to the firm's profit maximizing calculation.

There are numerous profit maximizing rules of thumb (for example, "never give a sucker an even break"). The formal economic principle is, in essence, *equalize marginal revenue and marginal cost.* Because demand determines marginal revenue, we shall discuss the revenue portion of the formula first, postponing consideration of marginal cost until the next section. **Marginal revenue** *is the change in total revenue attributable to the sale of one more unit of output.* Indeed, "incremental revenue" might be a better name for it. As price and quantity are always the two basic components of demand and as total revenue is always price *times* quantity sold, there is a very intimate relationship between demand and marginal revenue. In the purely competitive case, the firm's total revenue will rise directly with quantity sold at a constant rate of increase because, according to the firm's demand curve, price is constant over the firm's range of product sales. In other words, the additional sale of one unit of output always adds to total revenue an amount that *just equals the price.* Hence, price and marginal revenue are equal when, as shown in Figure 2-5, the demand curve of the firm is a perfectly elastic. Using that figure's data, an additional sale of 1 dozen eggs adds 50 cents to the firm's total revenue regardless of whether it is the first dozen sold or the 3000th dozen sold. Hence, marginal revenue is 50 cents.

Perfect Competition: Supply and Conduct

Marginal cost, the second portion of the profit maximizing rule of thumb may be defined as *the addition to total costs due to the additional production of one unit of output.* What are "total costs"? In the short run, total costs are made up of two components—total fixed costs and total variable costs. The short run, as already mentioned, is a time period short enough for certain factors of production—such as land, buildings, and equipment—to be immobile. Those immobile factors generate **total fixed costs**—such as rent, debt repayments, and property taxes—that *in terms of total costs* do not vary with output. In terms of *cost per unit* of output or "average fixed cost," however, these costs actually decline with greater output because average fixed cost is the total fixed cost (a constant) divided by the number of units produced. Thus, as output rises these fixed costs are "spread" over a larger and larger number of units.

Total variable costs, on the other hand, are those costs associated with variable factors of production such as labor, raw materials, and purchased parts. In terms of *total* costs these costs *always* rise with greater amounts of output, but in terms of *per unit* or "average costs" these may fall, remain unchanged, or rise, depending on the prices and productivity of these variable factors as they are variously applied to the fixed factors. Average, or per-unit

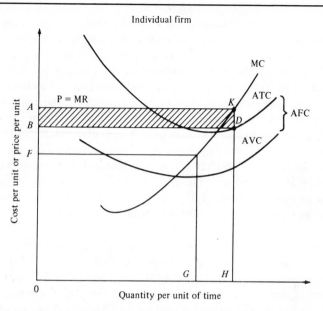

Figure 2-6. *Short-run cost curves of the firm together with perfectly competitive demand.*

variable cost is the total variable cost at some given level of output, divided by the number of units in that quantity of output. Thus, functionally speaking, if total variable cost rises less rapidly than quantity, per unit variable cost will fall; if total variable cost rises one-for-one with quantity at a constant rate, per unit variable cost will be constant; and, if the total rises more rapidly than the quantity, per unit variable cost will rise.

Figure 2-6 depicts this family of cost curves on a per-unit or average basis, according to conventional forms. ATC indicates short-run average total cost, and AVC indicates short-run average variable cost. Average fixed cost, AFC, constitutes the difference between ATC and AVC. When ATC is falling, marginal cost, MC, will be below ATC. Once ATC begins to rise, however, MC exceeds ATC. If the P = MR (price equals marginal revenue) line represents the individual firm's demand curve for a prevailing price of OA, profit maximization is achieved by producing OH units of output because, at that level of output, marginal cost just equals marginal revenue at point K. Bearing in mind that total profits are simply total revenue less total cost, the profit-maximizing firm will add to its output so long as the added revenue thereby obtained, MR, exceeds the added cost thereby incurred, MC. This is true of all output levels up to OH. However, once the added cost of added output, MC, exceeds the added revenue obtained, MR, total profits will begin to fall. Hence, the astute firm will not produce an output greater than OH. At output OH total economic profit is the shaded rectangle $BAKD$, which is the economic profit per unit, KD, times the number of units produced AK. This is called **economic profit** or **excess profit** because the average total costs *includes* a "normal" profit for the investors that is just sufficiently large, say 7% per year, to pay the cost of capital. Provision of this normal profit rate discourages the investors from withdrawing their capital in the long run and investing it elsewhere.

At price OF there would be neither excess profit nor normal profit; there would be a loss. Still, in the short run, the firm would continue to produce an amount OG, which would again equate marginal revenue (now OF) with marginal cost. The firm will thus minimize its losses. Only if price were to drop so low that the firm could not recover its variable cost AVC on each unit would it minimize loss by closing down. The firm should *never* lose in total dollars more than its total fixed cost. If it cannot even cover its variable cost on each unit, then its continued operation will result in losses exceeding total fixed cost.

Two major conclusions emerge from this analysis. First, since price equals marginal revenue for the perfectly competitive firm, the MR = MC profit rule of thumb causes price to equal marginal cost and fulfills the optimal welfare requirement stated earlier, at least for the firm. Second, the supply curve for the firm is identical to its marginal cost curve above the AVC curve. Over the range of possible prices, the quantity offered for sale by the firm may be read from the MC curve. It follows, then, that market-wide short-run supply is determined by simply adding up the short-run supplies of all individual firms in the market at each possible price, as is illustrated in Figure 2-7.

Abstracting from the thousands of firms required for perfect competition, we show only three in Figure 2-7, firms X, Y, and Z. Notice that at any given price, say P_1 or P_2, the marginal costs of all the firms are the same. This implies efficiency. Notice also that entry of new firms into the market would shift the market supply curve outward to the right. Conversely, exits would shift the aggregate supply curve inward toward the left. Of course contemplation of such shifts carries us into the long-run context because entry and exit can occur only in the long run. Before we discuss the long run in detail, however, we should ask what induces entry and what provokes exit? The answer is *profit*. If existing

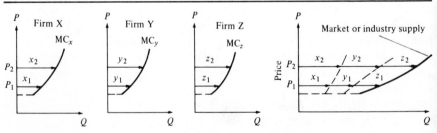

Figure 2-7. *Horizontal summation of firm supply curves for industry supply.*

40

firms are enjoying excess or economic profits, as illustrated by $AKDB$ in Figure 2-6, newcomers will enter for a shot at a piece of the action. Conversely, if existing firms are suffering losses, that is, earning less than normal (minimum) profits, exits will follow as investors seek to better their fortunes. Gold rushes provide striking examples of entry and exit—boom towns one year, ghost towns the next.

Demand, Supply, and Long-Run Performance

One robin doesn't make a spring. Neither does one "A" grade make a scholar. By much the same token, performance is a long-run matter for markets and industries. The long-run adjustment process of a perfectly competitive industry may be examined with the aid of Figure 2-8. Figure 2-8(a) shows the major short-run and long-run cost curves of a typical firm; Figure 2-8(b) depicts industry-wide supply and demand curves. The first thing to note is that price in the market is determined by the interaction of supply and demand. Thus, given demand D_1 and supply S_1, the market will generate a price of P_1. At any price above P_1, such as P_2, supply will exceed demand, causing sellers to cut price and trim output until the quantity demanded matches quantity supplied at equilibrium E. Conversely, at any price below P_1, quantity on D_1 exceeds quantity on S_1. In such circumstances, buyers will bid up the price until demand and supply converge upon equilibrium E. As viewed by the individual firm in Figure 2-8(a), price P_1 establishes the demand curve P_1d_1, which is perfectly elastic. Short-run profit maximization leads to an output of Q_1.

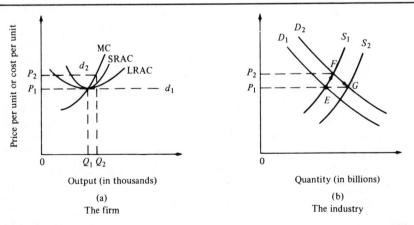

Figure 2-8. *Long-run adjustment and equilibrium for the firm and industry. MC = marginal cost; SRAC = short-run average cost; LRAC = long-run average cost.*

Of course changes in tastes, income, and other factors will cause demand to shift. If demand shifts from D_1 to D_2, point E will no longer represent equilibrium. In the short run, the enhanced demand will boost prices to P_2, inducing existing firms to move up along their short-run marginal cost curves (MC) to an output level Q_2. This translates into a movement *along* the short-run industry supply curve S_1 from E to F when viewed in the market-wide perspective of Figure 2-8(b). With price greater than short-run average total cost, SRAC, economic or excess profits mount up. New firms will enter the market and shift the supply curve to the right to S_2. Entry continues until price falls low enough to wipe out the prospect of excess profits for new entrants. In Figure 2-8 it is assumed that price returns to P_1, a movement that implies that, in the long run, industry supply has increased from E to G without any long-run change of price. S_1 and S_2 are, therefore, merely short-run supply curves, whereas the long-run supply curve would be perfectly horizontal, output being increased by increasing the number of firms with output OQ_1. The long-run supply curve could be horizontal in this way only if resource costs did not change with entry. More typical is the case in which resource costs rise with entry and expansion, giving the long-run supply curve some positive slope. In either case, the long-run supply curve is identical to the industry's long-run marginal costs. Finally, it should be noted that a downward shift of demand produces a reverse pattern of activity and effects.

The performance implications of this model may be evaluated according to how well it fulfills the three conditions underlying Pareto optimality:

1. **Consumption efficiency:** The freedom of buyers to enter and exit all markets, coupled with the fact that all buyers pay the same price for any given commodity, assures us that under perfect competition goods will go to the people who want them most. Price measures the marginal value of the product to each person who buys, and consumption efficiency requires the equalization of these marginal values among individuals.
2. **Production efficiency:** All firms in this "ideal" market are forced to use the production technique of lowest possible cost and to operate at a scale of output that places them at the low point on their short- and long-run average total cost curves (see Figure 2-8a). Moreover, marginal costs are equal across firms. Hence, as much of each desirable good is being produced as is possible in light of the production of all other desirable goods. (Another name for this is **technical efficiency**.)
3. **Consumer sovereignty:** Price is equal to long-run marginal cost, just as in the short run price is equal to short-run marginal cost. This means that allocation efficiency is achieved. Or, in less formal terms, the goods that people want most are being produced.

Outside this static Pareto framework, the perfectly competitive model also rates high marks for flexibility. As demands change, or as cost conditions alter, this market makes the adjustments needed to achieve a new welfare optimum solution.

Perfect Competition: The Imperfect Standard[3]

As we have just seen, the achievements of perfect competition are impressive. We might reasonably want to use this market model to evaluate real world industries—applauding those that live up to it, chastising and revamping those that do not. Unfortunately, things are not that easy. There are many reasons why we might *not* want perfect competition for our standard.

Unreality

Perhaps the most obvious shortcoming of the perfectly competitive model is its striking lack of reality. Thousands of sellers in every market? Perfectly standardized goods? Perfect mobility? Perfect knowledge? We were careful to stay within the bounds of economic possibility when we postulated positions for our economy in Figures 2-1 and 2-2. On similar grounds it could be argued that, because these conditions for perfection lie beyond the realm of known physical, social, and political possibility, they should not be adopted as our standard.

There may be appeal in this objection, but if this is all, it is not very compelling. In point of fact, there actually are a few industries that, at one time or another, have come fairly close to meeting the conditions for perfect competition. Agriculture, textile manufacturing (before the 1950s), and the stock market are often cited as examples. Moreover, all we are looking for here is a standard, an ideal, and most ideals are *by definition* unrealistic. To paraphrase an old saying: the stars are untouchable but they guide the mariner to his destination. Still, this realism argument against the perfectly competitive model can be made more compelling by tacking on some amendments. It has been shown that *partial* or *incomplete* progress toward the attainment of perfect competition everywhere may *not* constitute progress toward Pareto optimality. Indeed, steps that seemingly take us in the right direction, but not all the way, may actually take us in the wrong direction. In this light, the problem of unreality is quite serious.[4]

---

[3] This section draws heavily on Francis Bator, "The Anatomy of Market Failure," *Quarterly Journal of Economics*, (August, 1958); and Roland McKean, *Public Spending*, (New York: McGraw-Hill Book Co., 1968) Chapter 3.

[4] R. G. Lipsey and K. Lancaster, "The General Theory of Second Best," *Review of Economic Studies*, Vol. 24, No. 1 (1956), pp. 11–32.

Value Judgments

Another objection to the model of perfect competition, and Pareto optimum as well, is that each may easily be countered by appeal to inimical "value judgments." Note that wanting to attain Pareto optimality is itself merely one value judgment, one that might take second or third place (or even no-show) when compared to the many other value judgments people hold dear. Among the many values that we might rate more important than allocation and technical efficiency, four are worth special mention.

First, a grossly unequal distribution of income, such as that implied by point L in Figure 2-1, may be compatible with Pareto optimum but not compatible with society's sense of compassion, in which case we may willingly sacrifice allocation efficiency in order to attain a more just "equality." Though perhaps this point is valid, its force is weakened by the fact that perfect competition may actually be favorable to equality rather than unfavorable. Recall that price, in the long run, equalled average total cost for the representative firm, precluding supranormal profits. The absence of excess profits is generally conducive to an equitable income distribution.

Second, no society has honored the principle of consumer sovereignty completely and without reservation. True, our society is probably more liberal than most, accepting such nonsense items as towel warming racks, nothing boxes, pet rocks, and jeweled pill boxes. But many products and services are banned or restricted for reasons of morality ("pot," prostitution, and even liquor in some areas), or safety (inflammable fabrics, Red Dye No. 2, and certain toys), or environmental cleanliness (DDT, nonreturnable bottles in some states), or efficacy ("snake oil" medicines), or conservation (seashore zoning, fishing limits, whale oil products).

Third, there is no room in the perfectly competitive model for brand names, advertising, style variation, location advantages, and other forms of product variety because one of its conditions requires standardized products. Of course people like variety and relish style; hence, they seem willing to sacrifice efficiency in order to obtain them.

Finally, the perfectly competitive model is confined to pure *statics*. Like a bee fossilized in amber, it is perfect but cannot fly or move about or evolve. The model lacks *dynamics*; its conditions may inhibit rather than promote invention and innovation, the two key ingredients of technological change.

Market Failures

Of all the shortcomings of the perfectly competitive model, the most debilitating may be brought together and labeled "market failures." Assume, for the moment, that the foregoing qualifications could somehow be eliminated or "fixed." Assume also that during one massive spring cleaning of the economy we could in fact restructure all markets into the perfectly competitive mold. The theory of market failures states that, even if we could perform this Herculean feat, it is very *un*likely that we would thereafter attain Pareto optimum. We shall delve into several of these failures at greater length later, so at present we shall only touch lightly on them. In each instance the fundamental problem is one of *misallocation* because the basic equality, value here = value elsewhere, is practically unattainable. Put more technically, the result does not yield marginal social benefit = marginal social cost (MSB = MSC). Thus, we may begin by outlining these several failures according to the direction of the misallocation produced by the private competitive market:

Failure	*Inequality*	*Misallocation*
Economies of scale	MSB > MSC	Underallocation
External costs	MSB < MSC	Overallocation
External benefits	MSB > MSC	Underallocation
Public goods	MSB > MSC	Underallocation

Economies of scale cause the long-run average cost curve to decline as the size of the firm expands (see the negative portion of the *LRAC* curve in Figure 2-8a). In extreme cases, the size of a low cost producer may be so large as to fill the entire market's demand requirements, which means that a monopolist takes control and charges a price in excess of marginal cost. With price above marginal cost, MSB exceeds MSC.

External costs and external benefits are conceptually similar to each other, but of opposite effect. External costs are imposed on society and are *not* borne by producers or consumers in the course of production and consumption. Pollution provides the classic example of an external cost; pollution imposes costs of avoidance (air conditioning, moving out of town), of repair (painting, cleaning, medical treatment), and of raw damage (death, ugly air) that are not paid for out of the pockets of polluters, except in some form of emission taxation or through government intervention. Acting in their own best interests, market participants equate price with their own *private* marginal cost. But, when external costs are recognized and added to these private costs, the result is MSB < MSC. Correction of this overallocation requires a reallocation of resources away from pollution producing activities into other endeavors.

Conversely, external benefits lead to an underallocation of resources to products and services yielding social benefits that are above and beyond the private benefits people willingly pay the market price to obtain. In short, MSB > MSC. A government subsidy, as is true in education, might be an appropriate corrective in such cases.

Finally, there is the market failure concerning public goods. Public goods can be consumed by more than one individual at the same time at no additional expense. Indeed, it may cost something positive to exclude consumers from partaking of these goods. Because marginal cost is essentially zero for these goods, charging any positive price for their use (as would be required by a private profit-making enterprise) causes price to exceed marginal cost and MSB > MSC. Reliance on the private competitive market system to provide these goods would therefore lead to an underallocation—misallocation of resources. For this reason, government commonly provides these goods, as is true of national defense, general law enforcement (including antitrust enforcement), and many forms of pollution control.

Workable Competition: An Alternative Standard

Brick by brick we slowly built up the appealing edifice of perfect competition. Then, in the last section, we quickly tore it down. Where does this leave us? A devout agnostic would say it leaves us hanging in thin air, without so much as one star to guide us. Still, policy decisions must be made—good and bad decisions about what is good and bad. For the sake of policy and for other reasons, numerous economists, including J. M. Clark, Corwin Edwards, Walter Adams, and Alfred Kahn, have created the concept of **workable competition**, a set of *operational* norms or standards by which markets may be evaluated. In many ways, workable competition is a first cousin to perfect competition, if not a sibling. Factual *experience*, rather than theory, has shown that, even though the "perfection" of theory is not possible and probably undesirable, vigorous competition in the market place is generally better than no competition—better for political and social ends as well as for economic ends. Thus, borrowing heavily from F. M. Scherer, we conclude this chapter with an outline of some of the criteria of "workability" that have evolved in the literature:[5]

Structural Norms
1. The number of traders should be at least as large as scale economies permit.
2. There should be no artificial inhibitions on mobility and entry.
3. Where appropriate, there should be moderate and price-sensitive quality differentials in the products offered.
4. Buyers should be well informed about prices, quality, and other relevant data.

Conduct Criteria
5. Some uncertainty should exist in the minds of rivals as to whether price initiatives will be followed.
6. Firms should strive to achieve their goals independently, without collusion.

[5] F. M. Scherer, *Industrial Market Structure and Economic Performance* (Chicago: Rand McNally, 1970), p. 37. For other reviews of workable competition see S. Sosnick, "A Critique of Concepts of Workable Competition," *Quarterly Journal of Economics*, (August 1958) pp. 380–423; and H. H. Liebhafsky. *American Government and Business* (New York: John Wiley & Sons Inc., 1971), pp. 236–262.

7. There should be no unfair, exclusionary, predatory, or coercive tactics.
8. Inefficient suppliers and customers should not be shielded permanently.
9. Sales promotion should not be misleading.
10. Persistent, harmful price discrimination should be absent.

Performance Criteria
11. Firms' production operations should be efficient.
12. Promotional expenses should not be excessive.
13. Profits should be at levels just sufficient to reward investment, efficiency, and innovation.
14. Output levels and the range of qualities should be responsive to consumer demands.
15. Opportunities for introducing technically superior new products and processes should be exploited.
16. Prices should not intensify cyclical instability or inflation.
17. Success should accrue to sellers who best serve consumer wants.

It should be obvious that this approach is basically pragmatic, somewhat rough-and-ready, largely judgmental, certainly "unscientific," and rather imprecise. As H. H. Liebhafsky says, "Such an approach is not satisfactory to anyone who either believes that it is possible to achieve absolute certainty or who is driven into an attempt to achieve it as a matter of his personal emotional make-up."[6] Moreover, value judgments unavoidably enter any application of these criteria. Scherer correctly points out, for instance, that on many of the variables a line must be drawn separating "enough" from "not enough" or "too much". How much uncertainty should exist in the minds of rivals as to whether their price initiatives will be followed? How moderate should quality differentials be? What constitutes misleading sales promotion? How long must price discrimination persist before it becomes persistent? And so on.[7] Moreover, these various criteria need not be given equal weight. And, when some criteria are satisfied but not others, how is one to determine workability? If performance is fairly good but structure is irregular, what then? Some of the values that may influence our judgments on these issues were discussed earlier in Chapter 1. In subsequent chapters we shall discover what specific judgments have been made in the past. We shall also develop a body of information from which the reader may fashion his own informed judgments.

Summary

Pareto optimality is one rather widely accepted way of defining how well we are coping with the basic problem of scarcity. An optimum is achieved when

---

[6] Liebhafsky, *op. cit.*, p. 261.
[7] Scherer, *op. cit.*, p. 37.

no one can be made better off without making someone else worse off. The conditions necessary for this result are (1) efficiency in consumption, (2) efficiency in production, and (3) consumer sovereignty. Under ideal and rather unrealistic circumstances, perfect competition fulfills these conditions, thereby giving us reason to look favorably upon perfect competition as a possible standard for use in evaluating industries. Not only have we seen by it how well markets ought to function but we have also explored theoretically the more analytical issue of how markets do function. Broadly speaking, structure determines the firm's view of demand; conduct influences industry supply; and structure and conduct together crucially affect performance.

Nobody is perfect, and it turns out that perfect competition is an imperfect standard. It is among other things, (1) unrealistic, (2) unduly limited relative to the full spectrum of what is valued, and (3) inadequate to the task of getting us to an optimal solution in the face of market failures. Thus we are forced to rely on a less precise but more practical standard that avoids these weaknesses—workable competition. To the disappointment of perfectionists, workable competition isn't perfect either.

two

STRUCTURE

3

Introduction to Structure

Power tends to corrupt . . .

LORD ACTON

In the perfectly competitive market system of Chapter 2, decisions concerning what and how to produce were made by nobody in particular. They were made collectively by the balanced interaction of many faceless sellers and buyers. With decision making thus decentralized, power was also decentralized because "power" in this context is the ability to make and affect decisions. Once we depart from the world of perfect competition, all the key issues concerning market structure relate to power:

1. What is market power?
2. How can market power be measured?
3. What are the sources and causes of market power?
4. How can these sources and causes of power be measured?
5. What policies can be devised to control the distribution of power?

The purpose of this chapter is to provide introductory answers to the first three questions. It serves to preface the more detailed answers to all questions that follow in the next six chapters.

What is Market Power?

Market power *is the ability to influence market price perceptibly*. The key word here is "ability." A buyer or seller may have the ability to influence price but may not actually use that ability. Still, power would be present, just as a boxer's power

51

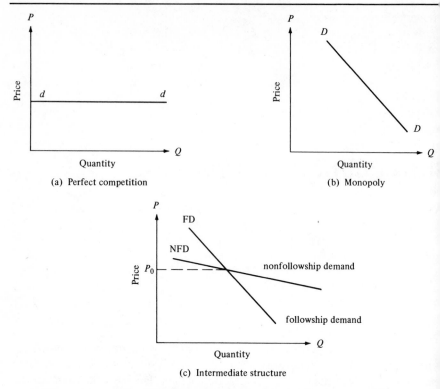

Figure 3-1. Firm demand conditions in alternative market structures

is always present, outside as well as inside the ring. Stress on ability is important because pricing behavior is not, in and of itself, a feature of market structure. Structure does, however, determine ability.

As already indicated in Chapter 2, variations in the features of market structure cause variations in the ways individual sellers view their demand and individual buyers view their supply. Assuming, as before, that a large number of buyers exists on the demand side, Figure 3-1 summarizes individual seller views of demand according to variations in market structure. Figure 3-1(a) depicts the horizontal demand curve of a perfectly competitive seller who has no power to influence price. At the other extreme, 3-1(b) shows a monopolist's demand curve, which is labeled *DD* because, by definition, this is the market-wide demand curve as well. The monopolist's power is reflected in the wide range of price-options offered by this demand curve.

Between these two extreme cases is an intermediate situation of "rivalry" among a limited number of sellers. Here the firm confronts two demand curves with downward slope, neither of which is the market-wide demand curve. The firm might perceive either one or both (or portions of both) of these demand curves, depending on what assumptions it makes concerning its rivals' behavior. If the firm assumes that its rivals will follow any price change it makes up or down from P_0, which is the going price, then it will consider the "following demand" curve the applicable demand curve. With rivals matching its every price move, the particular firm cannot gain or lose market share because it will neither take sales away from nor give sales to its rivals through any price change it makes. The downward slope derives entirely from sales variations at the market-wide level, with the individual firm always getting its constant share of market-wide sales. Thus this FD curve could also be called a "constant share" demand curve, and it is a close reflection of the market-wide demand curve.

In contrast, the "nonfollowship demand" curve of Figure 3-1(c) is based on the assumption that rivals in the market do *not* follow the price changes of the firm depicted but instead leave their prices unchanged at P_0. The elasticity of this NFD curve is much greater than the elasticity of the following curve because, without followship, the firm will win customers away from its rivals when it cuts price below P_0, or lose customers to its rivals when it raises price above P_0. With customers moving amongst firms as well as into and out of the market, the firm's market share will rise with a price cut and fall with a price hike. The NFD curve could therefore also be called a "changing market share curve." A firm confronting this set of demand curves has *some* power over price, but not as much as a monopolist.

How Can Market Power be Measured?

The **Rothschild index**, is a *theoretical* measure of market power based on a comparison of the slopes of the followship and nonfollowship demand curves.[1] Redrawing these curves in Figure 3-2 and labeling certain points for purposes of computation, we may summarize the Rothschild index as follows:

$$\text{Rothschild index} = \frac{\text{slope of NFD}}{\text{slope of FD}} = \frac{JK/JM}{JL/JM} = \frac{JK}{JL}$$

Under perfect competition the nonfollowship curve would be perfectly horizontal, yielding a ratio of JK/JL equal to zero. On the other hand, a monopolist would observe no difference between the followship and nonfollowship curves. Because the monopolist does not share the market with any rivals, there is no question whether they will or won't follow his price initiatives. When FD and NFD coalesce, the ratio JK/JL equals one. From these two extreme observations it should be clear that intermediate cases range between zero and one,

[1] K. W. Rothschild, "The Degree of Monopoly," *Economica* (February 1942), pp. 24–40.

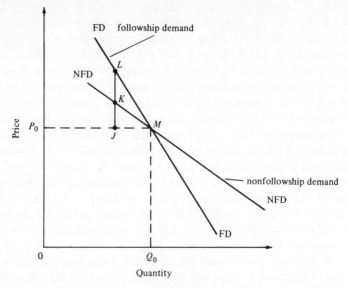

Figure 3-2. *The Rothschild index.*

varying directly with market power. In short, the Rothschild index provides one answer to the second question: "How can market power be measured?" Other, more practical, measures derive from the sources and causes of market power.

What are the Sources and Causes of Market Power?

The following chapters will focus on three structural characteristics that contribute to market power:

1. **Product differentiation:** The greater the degree of product differentiation, the steeper the nonfollowship demand curve and the greater the JK/JL ratio. With differentiation, many buyers prefer particular brands for *non*price reasons, such as style and advertising image. Product differentiation thus produces less price-induced brand switching and more stable market shares in the face of price differentials than would be observed with standardized products.

2. **Market share:** The larger the firm's market share, the closer NFD approaches FD and, consequently, the higher the JK/JL ratio. To see this relationship, consider a price cut by a firm with 1 % of the market and compare its effect to that of a price cut by a firm with 90 % of the

market. The small firm will have a highly elastic NFD curve because it can easily double or triple its sales and market share by cutting price. On the other hand, the monster with the 90% share already has so much of the market that, even if it takes the remaining 10% away from its rivals, it won't achieve much of a gain in sales or market share. When measuring the power of a *group* of firms, their market shares may be combined.

3. **Barriers to entry:** The effect of barriers is not directly observable in Figure 3-2 as it stands. Entry is a long-run matter, whereas these curves relate to the short run. However, let FD depict short-run demand, and NFD depict long-run demand (allowing sufficient time for entry to occur); then high barriers to entry will cause NFD to coincide more closely with FD above price P_0, and the JK/JL ratio will be greater the more formidable the barriers. In other words, we could look upon new entrants as nonfollowers who eventually come into the market charging price P_0, in the event the established firm boosts price above P_0. Accordingly, the long-run NFD curve will be more elastic under conditions of easy entry than it would be with difficult entry. (Price changes on the downside, below P_0, would relate to ease of rivals' exit rather than entry in this modified view of Figure 3-2.)

As already suggested in Chapter 1, there are numerous other elements of tructure that might influence market power—including growth, vertical ntegration, and diversification. Unfortunately, we have only enough space to ouch lightly on these other elements in various spots later. By concentrating on ifferentiation, market shares, and entry, we follow in the footsteps of Joe Bain, Richard Caves, and Willard Mueller.[2] It should also be stressed that the Rothschild index provides only one answer to the question, "How can market ower be measured?" And it is not necessarily the best answer.[3] Its greatest hortcoming is its purely theoretical nature. In practice, it is not possible to stimate the index accurately, so measures of differentiation, market share, and ntry barriers are used instead. That the index is based solely upon demand actors, to the exclusion of supply and cost conditions, is another weakness. As Edward Chamberlin has remarked, measuring market power is much like measuring one's health: "Some aspects of health can be measured and others annot. Among the former, we have body temperature, blood pressure, metabo-sm, weight, etc. But these do not lend themselves to the construction of a single

[2] Joe Bain, *Industrial Organization* (New York: John Wiley & Sons, 1959); R. Caves, *American dustry: Structure, Conduct and Performance* (Englewood Cliffs, N. J.: Prentice-Hall, 1964); *. F. Mueller, *A Primer on Monopoly and Competition* (New York: Random House, 1970).

[3] To list but a few other authors of such measures: A. G. Papandreou, "Market Structure and Monopoly Power," *American Economic Review* (September 1949), pp. 883–97; R. Triffin, *Mono-dlistic Competition and General Equilibrium Theory* (Cambridge, Mass.: Harvard University Press, 40); and Joe Bain, "The Profit Rate as a Measure of Monopoly Power," *Quarterly Journal of conomics* (February 1941), pp. 271–93.

index of health. Similarly, in economics it does not follow that because certai
indices are quantitative themselves they can be averaged or in some wa
reduced to a single index . . . ."[4]

The Lerner Measure

Another commonly cited theoretical index of market power—one tha
introduces costs and illustrates the misallocative effect of monopoly—is th
Lerner index:[5]

$$\text{Lerner index} = \frac{\text{price} - \text{marginal cost}}{\text{price}}$$

Under perfect competition there is no divergence between price and margin;
cost, in which case the Lerner index is equal to zero. With monopoly, howeve
the divergence can be substantial. Figure 3-3 depicts the profit maximizin
solution for a monopolist. As before, the rule of thumb for maximizing profit
marginal cost equals marginal revenue, which occurs at point E with outpu
OQ_1 and price OP_1. Although the MC = MR rule applies here as under perfec
competition, the result is markedly different in this case because the downwar
sloping demand of the monopolist generates a downward sloping margin;
revenue curve that lies below the demand curve. Recalling that marginal revenu
is the addition to total revenue due to the additional sale of one more unit (
output, we may illustrate the relationship between price, quantity, total revenu
and marginal revenue in the simplified schedule of Table 3-1.

Each extra unit sold *adds* to total revenue an amount equal to the price (
that unit, but from this the monopolist must *subtract* the price reductio:
necessary to sustain the sale of all preceding units. Thus in Table 3-1 the margin;
revenue of producing the third unit is $6 even though price at that point is $
because three units generate a total revenue of $24 ($8 × 3), whereas two uni
generate a total revenue of $18 ($9 × 2), and 24 − 18 = 6. Marginal revenu
is lower than price. And, as price declines, marginal revenue declines faste
Thus once again we have seen how structure, via its influence on the firm
view of demand, affects conduct.

Economic or excess profit per unit in Figure 3-3 is indicated by the distanc
DG. Total dollar excess profit is consequently the area $DGHP_1$. (Recall that AT
includes a normal profit.) The Lerner index would be DE/DQ_1, which is clear
greater than zero. In the extreme, with zero marginal cost, the index woul

[4] E. H. Chamberlain, "Measuring the Degree of Monopoly and Concentration," in *Monopo*
and Competition and their Regulation, edited by E. H. Chamberlin (New York: Macmillan, 195;

[5] A. P. Lerner, "The Concept of Monopoly and the Measurement of Monopoly Power
Review of Economic Studies (June 1934), pp. 157–75.

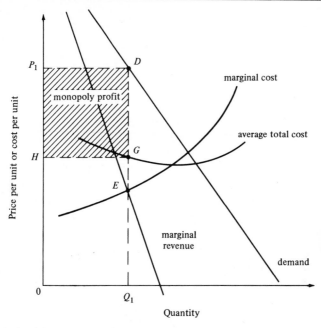

Figure 3-3. *Monopoly equilibrium solution and the Lerner index of power.*

qual one, indicating the ability of a seller to charge a price for a free good which obviously makes that seller a con artist). Despite the apparent impact of costs on this index, it actually measures the degree of monopoly solely in terms of the deviation of slope of the demand curve away from the perfectly competitive slope value of zero. Given MC = MR for profit maximization, the index converts to the inverse of the price elasticity of demand of the

TABLE 3-1   Marginal Revenue and Price

P ($)	Q (units)	TR(P × Q) ($)	Marginal Revenue ($)
11	0	0	
10	1	10	>10
9	2	18	>8
8	3	24	>6
7	4	28	>4
6	5	30	>2
5	6	30	>0
4	7	28	>-2

nonfollowship demand curve or, in the case of pure monopoly, the market-wide demand curve:[6]

$$\frac{P - MC}{P} = \frac{P - MR}{P} = \frac{1}{\text{price elasticity of demand NFD}}$$

In essence, then, the Lerner index does not differ very much from the Rothschild index. Both give emphasis to the demand side. Both are basically theoretical measures, incapable of being accurately or easily applied to the real world. Both vary between zero and one. And, both are "static," as opposed to "dynamic," in scope.

One distinction of relevance, however, is that the Lerner index is a measure of actual conduct—a measure of the *exercise* of power rather than its mere *existence*. Because we are presently more interested in the latter than in the former, we have given the Rothschild index primacy of place. We postpone further discussion of conduct and performance measures until after we have studied structure in finer detail.

Summary

Market power is the ability to influence price in the long or short run. Since price is always determined by prevailing supply and demand conditions, at least some control of supply or demand or both is required before such power can be said to exist. Even when the government wants to influence price it must resort to one of these controls, as is illustrated by the government's reliance on rationing tickets to "control" demand when it sets a legal price ceiling below the free-market equilibrium level. Where do the elements of market structure fit into the picture? They are the means, the elements, or the indices of demand and supply control. Product differentiation may be looked upon as a weak form of demand control. Similarly, a firm with a 70% market share may be said to control 70% of market supply. Also, high barriers to entry give existing firms some degree of control over long-run supply. Finally, in a different vein, these elements of structure will control the discussion of the next six chapters, although other elements receive mention as well.

[6] For a proof of this see J. V. Koch, *Industrial Organization and Prices* (Englewood Cliffs, N. J. Prentice-Hall, 1974), pp. 52–53.

4

Product Differentiation:
Theory and Cross-Section
Evidence

Go directly to your friendly local monster supermarket. Count the items on the shelves. There are 10,000 of them! And each package is calling out to the housewife . . . Hey, remember me? Remember my advertising, my promises? Remember my company?

STEPHEN FRANKFURT

Once upon a time, there was a colorless, odorless, and tasteless beverage that was produced by an essentially simple, easily imitated process. The producers of brand "S" couldn't make their brand any more colorless, odorless, or tasteless than other brands of this beverage. But, by advertising heavily and by pricing brand S above the others, they convinced many drinkers that S was the best. In particular, S's advertising stressed the gaiety and modernity of brand S because this theme would appeal to young, affluent adults to whom gaiety and modernity were important. As for pricing, the producers of S were so confident that consumers believed price was an index of quality that at one point they actually *raised* the price of S in response to a competitor's price *cut*. The sales of brand S soared.

This sounds like a fairy tale, but it's not. It's the true story of Smirnoff vodka.[1] Indeed, Smirnoff has been so successful with this marketing strategy that during the first half of the 1970s it became the number one brand of vodka and the number two brand among all hard liquors. Why do we tell the story here? Because it illustrates some of the causes and effects of "product differentiation." Our purpose in this chapter is to explore certain causes and effects of

[1] R. D. Buzzell, R. E. M. Nourse, J. B. Matthews, Jr., and T. Levitt, *Marketing: A Contemporary Analysis* (New York: McGraw-Hill, 1972), pp. 10–11.

product differentiation, beginning with its effects and ending with its causes. In our study of *effects*, we shall see that, when producers successfully differentiate their products, consumers may choose one brand over rival brands for nonprice reasons. Buyers believe that alternative brands of the same product are not perfect substitutes for each other, that they may have to pay more to get what they want. Under *causes*, it will be shown that these nonprice reasons for choice may be either real or imaginary, objective or subjective, depending on the various means by which differentiation is achieved. If nonprice differences between brands are real and objective, they are usually the result of manipulations of flavor, quality, warranty, service, store location, or something similar. If, on the other hand, they are merely imaginary, they are usually created by exhortative advertising, brand name connotation, or superficial variations in packaging.

These topics may sound intriguing enough, but this statement of purpose may leave the reader wondering: "Why are these topics treated as *structure* topics? They sound as if they might relate more closely to *conduct* rather than structure. Are we changing horses in midstream?" The answer is, of course, "No." Product differentiation will indeed be discussed later as a business policy or conduct variable, at which time we shall take up such issues as false advertising, competitive escalations of advertising, and the profitability of advertising. However, we cannot begin those discussions without this structural discussion. In particular, some products, like vodka, are highly *differentiable* whereas others are not. Moreover, certain classes of buyers are more *susceptible* to the influences of differentiation than other classes of buyers. Thus this chapter is primarily concerned with the differentiability of various products and the susceptibility of various buyers. There is no simple relationship between the causes and effects of product differentiation that applies uniformly across all products and purchasers. Exhortative advertising seems to work potently in some cases but not in others. The same holds true for styling, packaging, and other sources of differentiation. Thus, certain prior conditions may strengthen or weaken the cause-and-effect relationship, and these conditions are most appropriately discussed at this point.

Effects

Changes in Buyer Demand[2]

The key to understanding product differentiation lies in buyer behavior. If buyers act rationally, they will attempt to maximize their material well-being subject to the constraints of limited time and income. To put the matter simply,

---

[2] Much of this material may be found in E. H. Chamberlin, *The Theory of Monopolistic Competition* (Cambridge: Harvard University Press, 1933).

buyers try to get the most for their time and money. Pursuing this goal, consumers must make decisions at two levels: (1) Which products should be bought—for example, autos, lumber, or hamburgers? (2) Given a choice of product, which brand and model should be bought—for example, Datsun 280Z versus Porsche 924, McDonald's versus Burger King? If buyers think (and know for a fact) that all brands and models of a certain product are absolutely identical in their ability to satisfy certain needs, there would be *no* product differentiation. Buyers would maximize their welfare simply by purchasing the lowest priced brand or model. Sellers would be forced to compete solely on the basis of price (assuming they do compete). Competition by advertising or style change would not alter sales; it would only add to costs and subtract from profits. If, in contrast, the product can be successfully differentiated, then buyers can be persuaded by nonprice considerations that they get more for their money by choosing Brand Y over Brand X, or vice-versa. In essence, successful differentiation can either shift the individual seller's demand curve outward, enabling him to sell a larger quantity at a given price, or tilt his demand curve to a steeper slope, enabling him to raise his price without losing many customers. *In short, differentiation gives sellers some power over price.*

Figure 4-1 illustrates the first of these effects. A successful exhortative advertising campaign for Brand Y shifts the demand curve for Y from d_{y_1} to d_{y_2}, resulting in a greater volume of sales, Q_{y_2}, as compared with original sales, Q_{y_1}. At constant price P_y, total revenues (price times quantity) rise from $OP_yAQ_{y_1}$ to $OP_yBQ_{y_2}$, suggesting increased profits, provided the additional costs of producing and marketing Y are less than the added revenue. Alternatively, price could rise *while quantity is constant*. Assuming Brand X and Brand Y are to some degree substitutes, this favorable shift of tastes to Brand Y will shift the demand curve of Brand X to the left, lowering Brand X revenues.

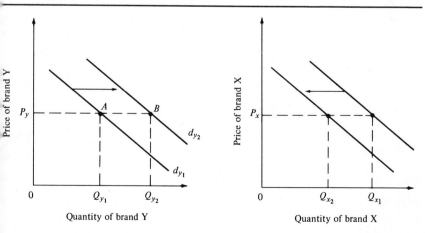

Figure 4-1. *A shift of sales to Brand Y by means of advertising or differentiation.*

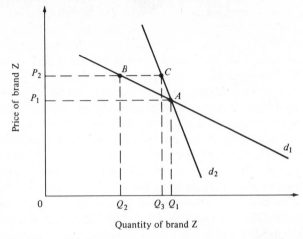

Figure 4-2. Reducing elasticity of demand by means of product differentiation.

Of course, sellers of Brand X might try to retaliate by changing their promotional pitch or boosting their advertising outlays, but, as already noted, we shall ignore such gamesmanship until later (Chapter 15).

Figure 4-2 illustrates the second possible effect of successful product differentiation. Let curve d_1 depict demand under conditions of little product differentiation. Then let d_2 depict demand after the introduction of a new advertising theme, which proclaims incessantly that "Brand Z folks would rather fight than switch." If the price of Brand Z had been raised prior to the new campaign from P_1 to P_2, sales would have fallen from Q_1 to Q_2, and total revenues would have dropped from area OP_1AQ_1 to area OP_2BQ_2. But, once most Brand Z buyers are convinced that they would rather fight than switch, the same increase in price would trim sales only slightly, from Q_1 to Q_3, and total sales receipts would actually rise to an amount represented by area OP_2CQ_3. In brief, product differentiation can reduce the price elasticity of demand as well as shift a brand's demand curve outward.

The Importance of Knowledge

The extent to which sellers can succeed in achieving these effects, and the means they must employ to do so, depends largely on buyer **knowledge**. Under the ideal circumstances of perfect competition, reviewed in Chapter 2, it was assumed that all buyers pursued their goal of welfare optimum with the aid of perfect knowledge. This implies that each buyer

1. Is an expert buyer, readily able to appraise product quality objectively.
2. Has a well-defined set of stable taste preferences or purchase requirements.

3. Is aware of all purchase alternatives and the terms offered by sellers.
4. Is able to calculate accurately the marginal gains and losses of choosing one combination of commodities over another to obtain the highest possible benefit for any given expenditure.[3]

If all buyers fitted this description, it would be very difficult for sellers to pull the wool over their eyes, to sell them goods they did not really want, to exaggerate the quality of one brand over another, or to charge outrageous prices for goods that were more cheaply available elsewhere.

It would in short, be impossible *artificially* to shift the demand curve or reduce its elasticity. Product differentiation could still occur under these ideal circumstances, but it would have to be based on genuine, objective, nonprice differences between brands (involving quality, durability, service, convenient location, or the like). Moreover, the intensity of effort put forth to differentiate brands and models, as measured by the amount of money spent on advertising, style changes, packaging, and such, would probably be quite low (or soft, as in "soft-sell") were buyer knowledge to approach perfection. By contrast, ignorance and gullibility improve the profitability of seller exhortation, "image building," functionless style variation, and related gimmicks that play on the subjective passions and preferences of buyers. With the variety and robustness of differentiation enriched by a lack of knowledge, it is not surprising that buyer ignorance and gullibility seem to be proportionately related to huge expenditures on bedazzling forms of product differentiation.

Having linked buyer knowledge to the shape and volume of differentiation activity, let us now take up the question of *what determines buyer knowledge* or the lack thereof. As already suggested, the answer comes in two parts—**buyer character** and **product type**. We can, for the moment, divide all buyers into two broad groups: (1) professional business buyers and (2) household consumers. We can also divide all products and services into two types: (1) search goods and (2) experience goods.

Among buyers, business and government buyers come about as close to being highly knowledgeable and fully informed as one could normally expect. Indeed, professional purchasing agents of large firms often specialize in buying such broad categories of goods and services as raw materials, construction, transportation, insurance, heavy machinery, and office supplies. Moreover, they often have the assistance of engineers, scientists, financial wizards, and other experts who conduct tests, arrange favorable credit terms, guide negotiations, and the like—all with an eye to maximizing profits. Perhaps the most important reason for this highly developed expertise is the ability of professional buyers to spread the costs of obtaining this expertise over a large volume of purchases. Thus, their absolute total dollar costs of purchasing may be huge, but on a *per unit* basis these costs will be small. (The aggregate savings gained from avoiding errors is also enormous.)

---

[3] Tibor Scitovsky, "Some Consequences of the Habit of Judging Quality by Price," *Review of Economic Studies*, Vol. 12, No. 2, pp. 477–85 (1944–1945).

On the other hand, we have the typical American householder, who, by comparison, is a 91 pound intellectual weakling. Although not a moron, he or she runs a very small scale operation. Of course, assistance from the spouse or helpmate may be offered, but it probably hinders as often as it helps in deciding which breakfast cereal is the most nutritious per dollar cost, which TV set is the most dependable, which laundry detergent gives the "whitest white," which bank offers the best loan terms, and so on.

Needless to say, many if not most of the thousands of decisions consumers make each year are terribly complex, precluding the cultivation of genuine low-cost per-unit expertise. Their ignorance forces them to rely on an array of homely little **cues**, many of which may not be accurate indicators of product value or quality at all. Studies have shown that consumers may judge the quality of identical hosiery on the basis of scent; the richness of ice cream flavor on color; the cleaning strength of detergent from suds level and aroma; the mildness of detergent on the basis of color; the thickness of syrup by darkness; the "pickup" of cars by the tension in the spring controlling the accelerator pedal; the quality of beer, floor wax, razor blades, lunch boxes, and carpeting, on price; the power of kitchen mixers on noise; and the quality of tape recorders on the basis of exaggerated advertising claims.[4] In short, household consumers are sensitive to all forms of product differentiation, subjective and objective alike. It is easy to see, then, why sellers of consumer goods account for the lion's share of all money spent on differentiation activities. In contrast, sellers of producers' goods are largely limited to rather objective (and genuine) forms of differentiation. They consequently tend to limit the intensity of their promotional efforts.

Lest we overstate the ignorance and gullibility of the typical household consumer, we hasten to add that product type will also determine the degree to which the purchase decision is made by hunch in the fog or by compass in the clear. Nearly all of the products just mentioned, and most of those that are prone to the greatest amount of subjective differentiation, are what may be called **experience goods**, that is, those whose utility can be fully assessed only *after* purchase. To evaluate brands of bottled beer accurately, for example, the consumer would obviously have to buy alternative brands in order to experience their taste. The same is true of canned foods, soaps, automobiles, appliances, and related products. It is largely the presence of hidden qualities in these goods that makes them liable to subjective as well as objective differentiation.

A second and contrasting category of commodities may be called **search goods**. In the case of search goods—like fresh fruits and vegetables, raw meat

---

[4] Donald F. Cox, "The Sorting Rule Model of the Consumer Product Evaluation Process," in *Risk and Information Handling in Consumer Behavior*, edited by D. F. Cox (Boston: Division of Research Graduate School of Business Administration Harvard University, 1967), pp. 324–68. A. G. Bedian, "Consumer Perception of Price as an Indicator of Product Quality," *MSU Business Topics* (Summer 1971), pp. 59–65; A. G. Woodside, "Relation of Price to Perception of Quality of New Products," *Journal of Applied Psychology* (February 1974), pp. 116–18; and R. W. Olshavsky and J. A. Miller, "Consumer Expectations, Product Performance and Perceived Product Quality," *Journal of Marketing Research* (February 1972), pp. 19–21.

TABLE 4-1   Differentiation by Broad Market Categories

		Type of Product	
		1. Search	2. Experience
Type of Buyer	1. Producer	Form: Objective Intensity: Low	Form: Mainly objective, some subjective Intensity: Moderate
	2. Consumer	Form: Mainly objective, some subjective Intensity: Moderate	Form: Both objective and subjective Intensity: High

apparel, shoes, jewelry, and maybe furniture as well—the consumer can judge on the basis of fairly simple inspection *prior* to actual purchase whether a given article is wholesome, handsomely styled, properly fitting, and reasonably priced for the level of quality it represents. At least in these instances, the consumer typically acts in a relatively well-informed manner, being much less sensitive to the blandishments of exhortative advertising, the attractiveness of package coloring, or the image conveyed by brand name.[5]

Goods and services bought by commercial enterprises or government agencies may also be divided into experience and search categories. The distinguishing characteristic of items in the latter classification is, again, the ability of the buyer to evaluate quality accurately before purchase, although on commercial and government planes the evaluation process is undoubtedly much more thoroughgoing than is the case in even the simplest of consumer goods. Thus, search goods bought by professional buyers include, among other things, raw materials, basic office supplies (such as pencils and paper), many semifinished articles, steel, and lumber. Although the high-powered capabilities of these buyers may seem to rule out the existence of producers' experience goods, it seems reasonable to place in this category such items as computers, aircraft, complex machinery, and financial services. To the limited extent that business or government buyers can be swayed by subjective forms of differentiation, these experience goods offer the best scope for such subjective differentiation.

Table 4-1 summarizes these several categorizations. Our division of buyers into two groups—producers and consumers, and our division of all products

[5] For elaborations on search and experience goods see R. H. Holton, "Consumer Behavior, Market Imperfections and Public Policy" in *Industrial Organization and Economic Development* edited by J. W. Markham and G. F. Papanek (Boston: Houghton-Mifflin, 1970), pp. 102–15; and Phillip Nelson, "Information and Consumer Behavior," *Journal of Political Economy* (March/April 1970), pp. 311–29.

into two groups—search and experience goods, define four broad market categories. The first division is made vertically, the second division horizontally, in Table 4-1, yielding a matrix of four cells. Brief notations within each cell summarize product differentiation in likely form and intensity.

In the case of producer search goods, differentiation centers on variations of size (for example, lumber), shape (for example, steel), composition (for example, metal alloys), terms of sale (for example, credit), and other objective or genuine features. The cost or intensity of differentiation in this case, as measured by differentiation expenditures relative to total sales revenues, is generally low, apparently ranging from 0 to 5% of sales. In brief, the goods of this cell closely approximate the standardized goods of the perfectly competitive model of Chapter 2.

At the opposite extreme are consumer experience goods. To be sure, these goods also vary objectively, but, more important, they are promoted on subjective appeals such as exhortative advertising (for example, cigarettes), packaging (for example, perfume), style (for example, autos), and brand image (you name it). Here total marketing costs may run as high as 50% of total sales revenue, although, on average, they appear to be in the neighborhood of 10–15% of total revenues. Accordingly, intensity of marketing effort is said to be "high" for these goods.

Between these two extremes we find producer experience goods and consumer search goods. Differentiation in these cases focuses primarily on objective product features, although subjective appeals undoubtedly influence buyers' decisions too. Marketing expenses for the intermediate goods appear to be more substantial than the skimpy outlays associated with producer search goods but less than those associated with consumer experience goods, which explains the "moderate" designation of Table 4-1.[6]

Some Problems and Qualifications

Although this four-part division of products helps in understanding differentiation, it has two possible shortcomings worthy of exploration—irrelevance and oversimplification. A skeptic might argue that these distinctions are meaningless or irrelevant to what really matters most—good industrial conduct and performance. Consider the distinction between search and experience goods as it applies to household consumers, for example. If one assumes that consumers act in a cold, calculating manner, with immutable preprogrammed taste preferences, one can demonstrate theoretically that they are no less efficient in their selection of experience goods than in their selection of search goods, despite the abundance of exhortative advertising accompanying experience goods sales. In brief, this theory asserts that consumers randomly

---

[6] Detailed cost data on all differentiation efforts are not publicly available. These rough estimates are derived primarily from E. L. Bailey, "Manufacturers' Marketing Costs," *The Conference Board Record* (October 1971), pp. 58–64; and D. Houghton, "Marketing Costs: What Ratio to Sales?" *Printers' Ink* (February 1, 1957), pp. 23–24, 54–55.

sample alternative brands of these products and learn from their past purchase experiences which ones they like and which ones they do not like. They then apply this acquired knowledge to more effectual purchasing over time because they accumulate a fund of knowledge comparable to search knowledge. It has even been argued that exhorative advertising *helps* consumers, that they need merely buy the most heavily advertised brand to get the best quality for their money.[7]

Although there may be some truth to this theory, contrary theories and contrary empirical tests abound.[8] There are obvious practical difficulties in keeping up with rapid technological change and in sample purchasing such items as automobiles, refrigerators, and color TVs. Moreover, there is the broader question of whether the "robot model" of consumer behavior is accurate— whether, that is, consumers really *learn to buy what they like* after random sampling. To summarize the opposing position, which supports the preceding division of products, it seems more accurate to say that consumers quite often *learn to like what they buy*, without any random sampling, especially in the case of experience goods. The literature supporting this latter viewpoint is too vast to review here, but one theory has been so thoroughly tested by marketing specialists and psychologists that it warrants special mention. It is the theory of **cognitive dissonance**.

This theory may be explained by tracing the thoughts and attitudes of someone buying a new color television set.[9] Prior to purchase the consumer is faced with the necessity of choosing between at least two alternatives—for example, Zenith and RCA—both of which have attractive features. Because both are attractive, some uncertainty is likely to develop *after* purchase as to the wisdom of the ultimate choice. These post purchase doubts may be called states of "cognitive dissonance," since the positive features of the rejected alternative and the negative features of the chosen alternative create a conflict in the consumer's mind. This dissonance cannot last, however. Humans generally strive toward contentment and shun frustration. The most obvious and easiest route to reduced restlessness in this context is a *change* of attitudes, a mental reranking of the alternatives to raise one's evaluation of the chosen set and lower one's assessment of the rejected ones. Thus, the consumer often learns to like what he chooses simply because he has made the choice, a behavior that does not jibe with the "robot model" of experience goods sampling. Although formal tests of this theory have occasionally failed to confirm it (which suggests that dissonance is not always a part of purchasing), the evidence in its favor is

---

[7] Phillip Nelson, "Advertising as Information," *Journal of Political Economy* (July/August 1974), pp. 729–54; and P. Nelson, "The Economic Consequences of Advertising," *Journal of Business* (April 1975), pp. 213–41.

[8] For surveys see R. J. Markin, Jr., *Consumer Behavior: A Cognitive Orientation*, (New York: Macmillan Publishing Co., 1974); and T. H. Meyers and W. H. Reynolds, *Consumer Behavior and Marketing Management* (Boston: Houghton Mifflin Co., 1967).

[9] S. H. Rewoldt, J. D. Scott, and M. R. Warshaw, *Introduction to Marketing Management*, Homewood, Ill.: Richard D. Irwin, Inc., 1973) p. 106.

impressive, covering a wide diversity of products—for example, autos, phonograph records, swim suits, candy, toothpaste, scouring pads, and spray disinfectants.[10]

What is the importance of these findings to us here? They lend credence to the search–experience goods dichotomy because they indicate a lack of full, objectively applied knowledge in the consumer's purchase of experience goods. In fact, one of the more interesting implications of this dichotomy concerns the relationship between price and product quality. Given the prepurchase evaluation possibilities of search goods, we ought to expect a strong positive correlation between their price level and brand or model quality. For a given product, low quality should sell only at a low price, whereas high quality should justifiably bring a high price. In contrast, the correlation between the price and brand quality of experience goods might be low, since, as we have seen, brands of these commodities are often selected on the basis of unreliable cues and the pull of prior purchase. Such correlations were computed for 35 products by Alfred Oxenfeldt, using Consumer's Union brand evaluation scores and price data. Results for the eight products with highest correlation (maximum possible is $+1.0$) and the eight products with lowest correlation (lowest possible is -1.0) are presented in Table 4-2. Notice that the eight products having highest correlation are all search goods, whereas seven of the eight products having lowest correlation could be considered experience goods (the single possible exception being men's hosiery).[11] Similar data are not available for producers' goods, but the reader can decide for himself whether producers' goods markets would have a better record than this.

Although these data further indicate that the four-part scheme of Table 4-1 is informative, the scheme does have one major shortcoming: it oversimplifies reality. Many, if not most, products have a blend of search and experience features, precluding any neat, clear-cut assignment to a search or experience good category. In addition, numerous product characteristics besides hidden versus observable qualities and buyer type influence differentiability. These

---

[10] G. D. Bell, "The Automobile Buyer After Purchase," *Journal of Marketing* (July 1967) pp 12–16; L. A. Losciuto and R. Perloff, "Influence of Product Preference on Dissonance Reduction *Journal of Marketing Research* (August 1967), pp. 286–90; R. Mittelstaedt, "A Dissonance Ap proach to Repeat Purchasing Behavior," *Journal of Marketing Research* (November 1969), pp 444–46; J. Jacoby and D. B. Kyner, "Brand Loyalty vs. Repeat Purchasing Behavior," *Journal of Marketing Research* (February 1973), pp. 1–9; J. B. Cohen and M. J. Houston, "Cognitive Consequences of Brand Loyalty," *Journal of Marketing Research* (February 1972), pp. 97–99 F. W. Winter, "The Effect of Purchase Characteristics on Post Decision Product Reevaluation," *Journal of Marketing Research* (May 1974), pp. 164–71; J. L. Ginter, "An Experimental Investi gation of Attitude Change and Choice of a New Brand," *Journal of Marketing Research* (February 1974), pp. 30–40.

[11] More recent computations of rank correlation may be found in R. T. Morris and C. S Bronson, "The Chaos of Competition Indicated by Consumer Reports," *Journal of Marketing* (July 1969), pp. 26–34. Unfortunately the Morris-Bronson sample of 48 products includes only experience goods. Their median coefficient was $+0.36$ and their mean was $+0.29$, a degree o association between price and quality that could be considered rather low. It is interesting to note that the products with negative correlations included lightweight vacuum cleaners (-0.66), nylon auto tires (-0.54), household detergents (-0.28), and color TV (-0.23).

TABLE 4-2   Coefficients of Rank Correlation Between Brand Quality Score and Brand Price

Product	Number of Brands Tested	Coefficient of Rank Correlation
Top eight products		
Boys' blouses (shirt type)	8	0.82
Men's hats	30	0.76
Women's slips (knitted)	28	0.75
Mechanical pencils	26	0.71
Women's slips (other than knit)	67	0.70
Men's shoes	52	0.70
Diapers, gauze	11	0.57
Children's shoes	8	0.55
Bottom eight products		
Yellow, white, and spice mixes	9	−0.11
Mayonnaise	25	−0.13
Men's hosiery (wool)	9	−0.20
Vacuum cleaners	17	−0.26
Biscuit mixes	10	−0.46
Hot roll mixes	3	−0.50
Waffle mixes	3	−0.50
Gingerbread mixes	6	−0.81

Source: Alfred R. Oxenfeldt, "Consumer Knowledge: Its Measurement and Extent," *Review of Economics and Statistics* (October 1950), p. 310.

other characteristics determine the potency of several specific causes of differentiation—advertising, styling, and packaging. Hence we turn next to these specific causes and these other characteristics.

Advertising as a Cause

Advertising and the Four-part Classification

The four-part classification of products and buyers predicted that advertising expenditures as a percentage of sales would be lowest for producer search goods and highest for consumer experience goods, with the remaining two classes falling in between. As a beginning to our discussion of advertising, let's look at some numbers that illustrate these relationships. Table 4-3 presents advertising/sales ratios for 24 broadly defined industries, each of which fits fairly

69

TABLE 4-3 Advertising Outlays as a Percentage of Sales by Broad Market Categories, 1972–73

Producer search goods

Farm products (unprocessed)	0.27%
Metals—mining	0.07
Nonmetallic minerals (except fuels)	0.27
Logging, lumber	0.18
Stone, clay, and glass products	0.59
Primary metals (e.g., iron and steel)	0.28
Average 0.28%	

Consumer search goods

Men's and boy's clothing	1.01%
Women's, children's, and infant's clothing	0.62
Household furniture	1.22
Footwear, except rubber	1.47
Leather products	1.85
Retail foodstores	0.97
Average 1.19%	

Producer experience goods

Farm machinery	1.01%
Office and computing machines	0.79
Metalworking machinery	0.85
Basic chemicals, plastics, synthetics	1.19
Service-industry machines	1.12
Business services, except advertising	1.41
Average 1.06%	

Consumer experience goods

Food and kindred products	2.27%
Soaps, cleansers, and toilet goods	8.78
Tires	1.50
Appliances	2.27
Clocks and watches	5.10
Hotels and other lodgings	2.12
Average 3.67%	

Source: U.S. Internal Revenue Service, *Source Book of Statistics of Income*, 1972–73 edition.

neatly into one of the four classes outlined in Table 4-1. Advertising intensity is indeed lowest for the producer search goods of Table 4-3, followed next by producer experience goods. The overall average for all listed producers' goods is 0.67% of sales revenue. In contrast, the overall average for all listed consumers' goods is nearly four times greater, at 2.43%. Most of this difference is attributable to the consumer experience goods category, which obviously contains the highest outlay ratios in the table.

Comparing all search goods with all experience goods, the averages are 0.74 and 2.37%, respectively. These data do not prove our earlier assertions concerning products and buyers. They are too sketchy to serve as proof. For example, one difference between producers and consumers that has not been mentioned but does affect these data, is the relatively few buyers of producer goods compared to the number of buyers of consumers' goods. "Personal selling" is therefore more efficient and advertising somewhat less efficient in the case of producers' goods as compared with consumers' goods. A *Printers' Ink* sample of producers' goods suppliers reveals that their advertising cost only 1.1% of sales; however, their "sales forces" in the field cost 6.3% of sales, yielding a total of 7.4% for all "selling expenses." Still, the same study estimated total selling expenses of consumer goods to be 9.5%, suggesting that the inclusion of nonadvertising selling expenses would not overturn the findings of Table 4-3.

Informative Versus Persuasive Advertising

Any reader devoting at least a quarter of his attention to what has been said will have noticed one slight irregularity in the previous paragraph. The adjective "exhortative," which heretofore has usually preceded the word "advertising," does not appear there. All advertising is lumped together without distinguishing exhortative advertising from any other kind. What other kind is there? The answer is easy. Much advertising is informative and may genuinely increase buyer knowledge rather than detract from it, warp it, or overwhelm it with exhortation.

The next question is much tougher to answer but unavoidable: How much advertising is beneficially informative and how much is merely persuasive? Defenders of advertising say *all* advertising is informative and none of it is persuasive. Hardboiled critics of advertising say all advertising is persuasive, or at least intended to be such, and none of it is informative. Some say the question cannot be answered because they cannot distinguish between information and persuasion. Finally, some take a middle ground by saying there is no clear-cut answer but much of it is informative, providing facts on prices, locations, and availabilities (for example, newspaper classified ads and mail order house catalogs), much of it is purely persuasive (for example, "Coke is the *real* thing"), and much of it is a blend of both (for example, the magazine car ad that gives you EPA miles per gallon, an itemization of standard equipment, and a pretty girl sitting in the passenger's seat).

71

We shall adopt this last view, if only because it seems to be the view held by most folks. In one of the most extensive opinion surveys ever taken, conducted by R. A. Bauer and S. A. Greyser, a large sample of people were asked, first, to press the,button on a counter "everytime you see or hear an ad," and, second, to fill out a card for each of these tallied ads that "you consider especially annoying, enjoyable, informative, or offensive." The results indicate that, of the hundreds of ads the average person is exposed to every day, he or she is conscious of only about 76 per day. Of these 76, only 6 of them, or 16%, are sufficiently moving to warrant the completion of a report card. Reactions to the rest were, "So what?" Of the 16% most noteworthy, 36% (or 5.8% of all tallied ads) were considered "informative" by the respondents.[12] (As for the rest of the notables, 23% were annoying, 36% were enjoyable, and 5% were offensive.) Of course the purpose of advertising is not to inform buyers—not in a purely cognitive, unbiased sense anyway. The idea is to sell goods by *influencing* buyers. It will therefore come as no surprise to learn that, when the same survey asked whether "advertising often persuades people to buy things they shouldn't buy," 73% of the respondents agreed. This response corresponds fairly well to earlier polls, taken in 1940 and 1950, that found 80% of those surveyed agreeing that "advertising leads people to buy things they don't need or can't afford."[13]

Although the information quotient for all major media was 36%, the ratings for individual media were quite diverse. The print media, as everyday experience indicates, seem to contain the highest proportions of informative ads, with 59% of especially noteworthy newspaper ads winning this designation in the survey. Magazines were a distant second with 48%, followed by radio with 40% and TV with 31%.[14] Thus, a fuller impression of information content can be gained by considering the distribution of all advertising outlays across the media. These data for 1974 are shown in Table 4-4. The total amount spent during that year came to well over $26 billion, or about 2% of the gross national product and 3% of all personal consumption expenditures in that year. Of this grand total, 39.2% went to newspapers, magazines, and farm and business publications, which entails more information than one who is used to watching TV might suppose. Much direct mail advertising is also fairly rich in information (despite its rude intrusiveness). F. M. Scherer may be on target when he says, "If a horseback generalization must be hazarded, it would be that half of all advertising expenditures cover messages of a primarily informative character, while the other half serve largely to persuade."[15]

---

[12] R. A. Bauer and Stephen A. Greyser, *Advertising in America: The Consumer View* (Boston: Division of Research Graduate School of Business Administration, Harvard University, 1968), pp. 175–83.

[13] *Ibid*, p. 71.

[14] Again, however, these are a very small minority of all counted ads. For an econometric test indicating very little, if any, information content in magazine ads, see L. L. Duetsch, "Some Evidence Concerning the Information Content of Advertising, *American Economist* (Spring 1974), pp. 48–53.

[15] F. M. Scherer, *Industrial Market Structure and Economic Performance* (Chicago: Rand McNally, 1970), p. 326.

TABLE 4-4   United States Advertising Expenditures in 1974 by Media

Medium	Millions of Dollars		Percent of Total	
Newspapers total	$ 8,001		29.9	
National		1,194		4.5
Local		6,807		25.4
Magazines	1,504		5.6	
Farm publications	72		0.3	
Television total	4,851		18.1	
Network		2,145		8.0
Spot		1,495		5.6
Local		1,211		4.5
Radio	1,837		6.9	
Direct mail	3,986		14.9	
Business publications	900		3.4	
Outdoor	345		1.3	
Miscellaneous	5,284		19.7	
Grand total	$26,780		100.0	

Source: Reprinted with permission from the December 29, 1975 issue of *Advertising Age*, p. 34. Copyright (1975) by Crain Communications, Inc.

Still another way of judging this issue is by product and buyer type. Anyone who has leafed through *Mining Magazine* or *Electrical Review* will conclude that advertising directed toward professional buyers is largely informative. "Because the audience for such advertising is expert," Corwin Edwards explains, "the characteristic advertisement in such publications is of a kind that might persuade an expert: it provides information, avoids garbled treatment of facts, and addresses itself to the reader's intelligence."[16] Alas, this obviously does not hold for most advertising aimed at consumers, but there does seem to be substantial variance across consumer products.

Drawing again from the Bauer–Greyser survey of consumer opinion, the variance may be seen in Table 4-5, which includes some data on producers' goods as well as consumers' goods because a number of the consumers surveyed were also producers (that is, businessmen). This table shows, for individual product groups, the distribution of especially noteworthy ads (as explained above) across the four categories of noteworthiness. It is easy to see that respondents were most often impressed by the informative nature of producer goods ads and, to a slightly lesser extent, consumer search goods ads. Moreover, in only a relatively few instances were these ads considered annoying or

[16] C. D. Edwards, "Advertising and Competition," *Business Horizons* (February 1968), p. 60.

TABLE 4-5   Per cent of Especially Noteworthy Advertisements Categorized as Being Informative, Enjoyable, Annoying, and Offensive

Industry Classification	Categorization			
	Informative	Enjoyable	Annoying	Offensive
Producer goods				
Agriculture and farming	84	11	5	0
Industrial materials	75	16	9	0
Freight, industrial development	82	18	0	0
Building materials and equipment	64	16	14	6
Consumer-search goods				
Apparel, footwear, accessories	52	25	17	6
Household furnishings	65	23	12	0
Retail and direct-by-mail	62	19	19	0
Horticulture	72	28	0	0
Consumer-experience goods				
Food and food products	31	54	14	1
Toilet goods and toiletries	31	35	31	3
Soaps, cleansers, polishes	28	24	45	3
Smoking materials	8	38	36	18
Confectionary and soft drinks	12	69	17	2
Beer, wine, liquor	5	50	22	23
Automobiles and accessories	48	31	20	1
Drugs and remedies	41	18	36	5

Source: R. A. Bauer and S. A. Greyser, *Advertising in America: The Consumer View* (Boston: Harvard University, 1968), pp. 296–97.

offensive. By stark contrast, ads promoting most consumer experience goods were apparently not very informative. They often gained noteworthy status on other counts, but these other counts seem more clearly associated with persuasive appeals—that is, enjoyable (attention grabbing) and annoying (repetitious). Indeed, the information content of these ads may be overstated by these data because respondents frequently labeled an ad "informative" on grounds that they "felt they were in the situation," they "wanted to buy the product," or they "used the product," all of which reasons fall outside the realm of what could justifiably be considered informative.[17]

[17] Bauer and Greyser, *op. cit.*, p. 203.

A plausible explanation for this large difference between search goods and experience goods advertising rests on the prepurchase evaluation that can be made of search goods. If the advertised properties of search goods stray too far from their actual properties, consumers are readily able to detect the discrepancies and penalize the promoters with refusals to buy. Advertisers of these products therefore feel constrained to use a more informative approach. They have relatively little use for exaggeration, "puffery," humor, sex, jingles, plays on insecurity, and cajolery, all of which may be found in the tool boxes of experience goods advertisers.[18] Recalling the advertising expenditures data of Table 4-3, we can postulate a rather interesting conclusion: advertising intensity and information content are *inversely* related. Generally speaking, the greater the dollar outlay relative to product sales, the lower is the information content of the advertising messages. Furthermore, in terms of adequate amounts and efficient applications of buyer knowledge, it seems that advertising is *least* informative where the need for information is greatest (consumer experience goods), whereas it is most informative where the need for information is least (producer search goods).[19] This paradox makes it clear that the purpose of advertising is *not* to inform buyers; it is to gain sales by influencing buyers.

Advertising and Persuasion

Economists have no theories of how consumers' tastes change or how persuasion works, but most academic social psychologists and many marketing experts earn their daily bread by conjuring up such theories and testing them empirically. Since this is an economics book, we can do little more than touch on these theories and research and refer readers who have an interest in pursuing the subject further to a few surveys of this vast, yet fascinating, literature.[20] Our purpose is to determine the degree to which various products may be differentiated, although we shall now confine our attention to products lying within the broad consumer experience category. As we have seen, subjective differentiation and exhortative advertising are most significant for that group of goods.

Before discussing specific subcategories of these products, however, we should clarify our use of the word "persuasion" by reviewing briefly several

[18] P. Nelson, "Advertising as Information," *op. cit.*, p. 730.

[19] See T. Scitovsky, *Welfare and Competition* (Homewood Ill.: Richard D. Irwin, Inc., 1951), Chapter XVIII, for an elaboration of this point.

[20] P. Zimbardo and E. B. Ebbesen, *Influencing Attitudes and Changing Behavior* (Reading, Mass.: Addison-Wesley, 1969); H. C. Triandis, *Attitude and Attitude Change* (New York: John Wiley & Sons, 1971); M. Fishbein and I. Aizen, *Belief, Attitude, Intention and Behavior: An Introduction to Theory and Research* (Reading, Mass.: Addison-Wesley, 1975); R. L. Applbaum and K. W. E. Anatol, *Strategies for Persuasive Communication* (Columbus, Ohio: Chas. E. Merrill Publishing Co., 1974); and G. R. Miller and M. Burgoon, *New Techniques of Persuasion* (New York: Harper & Row, 1973).

thoroughly tested, well-established exhortative advertising techniques that are now commonly used to promote most consumer goods:

- There will be more opinion change in the desired direction if the communicator has high credibility than if he has low credibility, where credibility is expertise and trustworthiness. Thus, regarding expertise, race drivers sell oil, singers sell Memorex tape, a washer repairman sells Maytag, and so on. With respect to trustworthiness, we see "the friendly corner druggist" giving a pitch for Crest toothpaste, "neighbors" recommending Johnson's wax, and "dad" urging us to buy a Kodak camera.
- Present one side of the argument when the audience is generally friendly, but present both sides or present comparisons when the audience starts out disagreeing with you. Thus, number one selling brands very rarely mention competing products, but Avis is No. 2 to Hertz, so it tries harder; B. F. Goodrich touts its lack of a blimp; and so on.
- A person's opinions and attitudes are strongly influenced by groups to which he belongs and wants to belong. Athletes and entertainers therefore give testimonials for everything under the sun. You drink Pepsi if you want to join the Pepsi generation, and so on.
- Repeating a communication tends to prolong its influence and slight variations of the repetition are advantageous. Thus, how many ways can you break a Benson and Hedges? Would you like a nickel for every time you've heard that "Coke is the *real* thing"?
- Audience participation helps to overcome resistance, and attitude change is more persistent over time if the receiver actively participates in, rather than passively receives, the communication. Accordingly, we are asked to find the answers to such questions as: What do Isuzus do? What's a Moscow Mule? (Smirnoff and 7-Up.) Why smoke Now?[21]

Of course persuasive techniques are not sure-fire. People are not led around by rings in their noses, at least not most of them nor most of the time.[22] And some consumer experience goods are more promotion prone than others.

[21] This list borrows heavily from Zimbardo and Ebbesen, *op. cit.*, pp. 20–23. See also J. E. Weber and R. W. Hansen, "The Majority Effect and Brand Choice," *Journal of Marketing Research* (August 1972), pp. 320–23; A. G. Sawyer, "The Effects of Repetition of Refutational and Supportive Advertising Appeals," *Journal of Marketing Research* (February 1973), pp. 23–33; J. L. McCullough and T. M. Ostrom "Repetition of Highly Similar Messages and Attitude Change," *Journal of Applied Psychology* (June 1974), pp. 395–97; and Leo Bogart, *Strategy in Advertising* (New York: Harcourt, Brace & World, Inc., 1967).

[22] For obvious reasons advertising apologists like to stress this point when addressing the general public or defending themselves against charges of false advertising; see e.g., A. A. Achenbaum, "Advertising Doesn't Manipulate Consumers," *Journal of Advertising Research* (April 1972), pp. 3–13; and the trial record *In the Matter of the Firestone Tire & Rubber Co.* Federal Trade Commission Docket No. 8818 (1971). They understandably sing a different tune, however, when trying to win the accounts of advertisers.

Among the various product characteristics that determine the effectiveness of exhortative advertising, the following seem particularly important:[23]

1. The degree of interest or "involvement" people have for the product.
2. The presence of powerful emotional buying motives like health, romance, and safety.
3. The perceived risk of getting stuck with a "lemon," especially one that's high-priced.
4. The frequency of purchase and growth of demand.

Interest and Involvement. How interested are you in salt? Do you get involved when reading an ad for weed killer? Probably not. On the other hand, what about stereos or cars? When one's interest in a product is high, one is obviously more likely to read magazine ads or pay attention to TV "spots" about the product than otherwise. Hence, because audience attention is a prequisite to exhortation, high-interest products seem more promotion prone than low-interest products.[24]

A survey designed to test interest and involvement across various products asked a representative sample of 1603 people several questions concerning (a) pleasantness (or unpleasantness) associated with product use; (b) interest in reading or hearing about new developments in the product; and (c) interest in talking about the product with friends. The tabulated answers to these questions were then converted into a single index of the proportion of people who expressed "high" overall interest as opposed to "low" overall interest for each product included in the survey. The products of greatest interest to men seem to be new cars and pain and tension relievers. In contrast, women seem to be most interested in packaged mixes, canned vegetables, coffee, make-up, and washers. (Women, wives especially, are also more interested in life insurance than are men.)

These differences by sex explain why advertisers try to aim their messages at appropriate segments of the population. When the responses of both sexes are added together, the top two ranked products turn out to be cars and pain and tension relievers.[25] Unfortunately, the products included in the questionnaire were limited to those that are commonly advertised in newspapers, so we do not have involvement scores for products that are heavily advertised in other media such as TV (for example, detergents and breakfast cereals), or that receive little advertising of any kind (for example, sugar and salt). Nevertheless, it does appear from these data that high interest is positively associated with voluminous advertising.

---

[23] One of the earliest such listings is that of Neil Borden, *The Economic Effects of Advertising* (Chicago: Richard D. Irwin Publishers, 1942), pp. 424–28.

[24] H. E. Krugman, "The Measurement of Advertising Involvement," *Public Opinion Quarterly* (Winter 1966–67), pp. 583–96.

[25] *A Study of the Opportunity for Exposure to National Newspaper Advertising,* Supervised by the Bureau of Advertising, ANPA, for the Newsprint Information Committee, 1965.

TABLE 4-6 Advertising Outlays of Selected Firms, 1974

Rank in Terms of Dollars Spent	Firm	Product Area	Millions of Dollars Spent	Advertising as a Per Cent of Sales
1	Proctor & Gamble	Soaps	325	7.3
2	General Motors	Autos	247	0.9
3	Sears, Roebuck	Retailing	220	1.7
4	General Foods	Foods	189	6.9
5	Warner–Lambert	Drugs and cosmetics	156	14.3
6	Bristol–Meyers	Drugs and cosmetics	150	9.4
7	American Home Products	Drugs and cosmetics	135	8.8
8	Ford Motor Company	Autos	132	0.6
9	Colgate–Palmolive	Soaps	118	10.7
11	R. J. Reynolds	Tobacco	102	2.3
13	Heublein	Liquor	97	6.4
16	Sterling Drug	Drugs and cosmetics	85	15.1
19	Richardson–Merrill	Drugs and cosmetics	84	14.5
21	General Electric	Appliances, TV, radio	80	0.6
27	Goodyear Tire & Rubber	Tires	73	1.4
33	Nabisco	Foods	68	5.7
37	Firestone Tire & Rubber	Tires	61	1.7
39	McDonalds	Foods	59	3.0
56	Revlon	Cosmetics	40	6.6
57	Alberto–Culver	Cosmetics	40	26.2

Source: Reprinted with permission from *Advertising Age*, August 18, 1975, p. 30. Copyright (1975) by Crain Communications, Inc.

Emotional Connotations. Some products naturally lend themselves to strong emotional appeals like health (drugs, vitamins, toothpaste, for example), sex and romance (perfumes, cosmetics, mouthwash), safety (smoke detectors, tires, shock absorbers), and security (travelers' checks, insurance). The implications of having the opportunity to exploit these appeals should be obvious to the reader, for they make the job of persuasion easier and more profitable. What is probably not so obvious is the subtlety and sophistication with which these opportunities can be exploited.[26] The persuasive power of sex, for instance, does not work equally well across all products. Nor is sex appeal simply a matter of getting a bikini-clad girl into the picture.[27] To adapt Hai Karate's ad line, advertisers must "be careful how they use it."

Perceived Risk Inherent in the Purchase. The purchase and consumption of most products involves certain risks—the risk of financial loss from product failure, the risk of embarrassment before the eyes of friends and, still more important, the risk of injury or property damage. Generally speaking, it appears that the persuasive influence of advertising is greatest when perceived risk is low.[28] Advertising tends to work best, therefore, for products that are low in price, low in obvious physical danger, and low in "importance" to the consumer. According to one study, for example, advertising induced twice as much brand switching among household food wraps as it did for ground coffee, and the housewives involved in the study thought that the proper choice of coffee was much more "important" than the proper choice of wrap.[29] As regards price, consumers apparently do not weigh price differences very carefully when prices are low, enabling promoters to induce purchase on nonprice grounds.

Purchase Frequency and Sales Growth. High purchase frequency (as with milk, margarine, and bread) implies greater consumer knowledge about the product than low purchase frequency (as with most durables). Moreover, other things being equal, frequently purchased items tend to gobble up large portions of one's budget, provoking greater price consciousness among consumers. For these several reasons, high frequency of purchase is likely to lessen the effectiveness of exhortative advertising and other nonprice promotional efforts.

Going from the extreme of frequently purchased, well-established products to the other of relatively new, never-before-purchased products provides an

---

[26] On the use of fear see B. Sternthal and C. S. Craig, "Fear Appeals: Revisited and Revised," *Journal of Consumer Research* (December 1974), pp. 22–34. On the use of sex see Myers and Reynolds, *op. cit.* pp. 91–93, and Zimbardo and Ebbesen, *op. cit.* pp. 34–38.

[27] R. N. Kanungo and S. Pang, "Effects of Human Models on Perceived Product Quality," *Journal of Applied Psychology* (April 1973), pp. 172–78.

[28] J. A. Barach, "Advertising Effectiveness and Risk in the Consumer Decision Process," *Journal of Marketing Research* (August 1969), pp. 314–20; T. Levitt, "Persuasibility of Purchasing Agents and Chemists: Effects of Source, Presentation, Risk, Audience Competence, and Time," in Cox (ed.), *Risk Taking and Information Handling in Consumer Behavior, op. cit.*, pp. 541–58; and L. G. Schiffman "Perceived Risk in New Product Trial by Elderly Consumers," *Journal of Marketing Research* (February 1972), pp. 106–08.

[29] Barach, *op. cit.*

interesting contrast. Rapidly growing product sales usually stem from a relatively quick accumulation of new users of the product or new uses for the product, or both. Thus, rapid growth provides a fertile field for advertising because advertising may effectively "spread the news," encouraging these conversions and new applications. Of course, intensive advertising may *cause* rapid growth as well as *be caused* by it. Much the same could be said of some of the other factors outlined previously. (Thus, a prime function of advertising is to stimulate interest in products and reduce perceived risk—which implies that high "product interest" and low perceived risk may be as much effects of intensive advertising as they are causes of it.) Still, the important point to be made here is that rapid growth generally improves the persuasive possibilities of advertising, just as do high product interest, strong emotional ties, low risk, low price, and relatively infrequent purchase patterns.

Advertising Data by Company

Taken together, the several factors discussed in the preceding section help to explain why some firms advertise more heavily than others. Table 4-6 shows total dollar outlay and advertising as a percentage of sales for some of the top advertisers in the United States. By both measures of intensity, the leaders are manufacturers of soaps and cleansers, drugs and cosmetics, tobacco, foods, and liquor. Auto firms rank high in total expenditures but low in costs relative to sales. Since the latter measure is economically the more meaningful, autos may be considered moderately advertised, perhaps because of their high-price, high-risk character. (On the other hand, outlay per individual prospective car buyer is substantial.) Although not mentioned in the table, sellers of gum, candy, soft drinks, and beer are also among the top.

Other Causes of Differentiation

Data about causes of differentiation other than advertising are not recorded accurately enough to support a detailed discussion of their use or impact. Nevertheless, a few words about these other influences are appropriate.

Style and Image

Products and brands are often purchased not only for their functional qualities but for the favorable impression they make (or presumably will make) on other people. Fashion and style serve "as an outward emblem of personal distinction or of membership in some group to which distinction is ascribed."[30]

---

[30] D. E. Robinson, "The Economics of Fashion Demand," *Quarterly Journal of Economics* (August 1961), p. 380.

Sociologists call this "reference-group" influence. And it has been observed that: "The conspicuousness of the product is perhaps the most general attribute bearing on its susceptibility to reference group influence: (1) The item must be one that can be seen and identified by others; (2) it must be conspicuous in the sense of standing out and being noticed—i.e., no matter how visible the product is, if everyone owns one, it is not conspicuous in the second sense."[31]

Among the most obvious products fitting the style and image category are clothes, cars, and furniture, all of which are subject to style variation. Less obvious are cigarettes, beer, liquor, and magazines. Advertisers of these products are advised to stress the kinds of people who buy the product or brand, "reinforcing and broadening, where possible, the existing stereotypes of users."[32] For less conspicuous products, like laundry soap, canned foods, and weed killer, where "neither product nor brand appear to be associated strongly with group influences, advertising should emphasize the product's attributes, intrinsic qualities, price, and advantages over competing products."

Packaging and Brand Name

Packaging affects appearance, convenience in storage or use, shelf-life, waste disposal, safety, brand image, and, consequently, sales. Four examples will suffice:

- The Color Research Institute asked housewives to test a single (identical) detergent packaged in three differently colored boxes—one blue, one brilliant yellow, one a mix of blue and yellow. After several weeks the housewives reported that one was too weak (blue), one too strong (yellow), and one was just right (the combination).[33]
- Kraft salad dressing formerly came in cylindrical bottles; however, Wishbone enjoyed great success with its wide-bottom flask bottle, partly because it gave Wishbone more "shelf facings" than Kraft's. Hence, Kraft had to copy.[34]
- In a survey test, consumers were shown two identical items—one packaged, the other not—and were asked to estimate their price. The packaged items were always judged to sell at a higher price than the unpackaged ones.[35]
- Blue and white work best for toothpaste. Yellow—never.[36]

[31] Rewoldt, Scott, and Warshaw, *op. cit.*, p. 123.
[32] *Ibid*, p. 125.
[33] V. Packard, *The Hidden Persuaders* (New York: David McKay Co., 1957), pp. 16–17.
[34] W. P. Margulies, *Packaging Power* (New York: World Publishing Co., 1970), p. 59
[35] P. G. Scotese, "The Retail Level," in *Creative Pricing* edited by E. Marting (American Marketing Association: 1968), pp. 110–11.
[36] R. C. Griffin and S. Sacharow, *Principles of Package Development* (Westport Conn.: AVI Publishing Co., 1972), p. 220.

Needless to say, brand names are also influential, especially for perfumes, cosmetics, drugs, autos, paper products, snack foods, pet foods, and other consumer experience goods. Indeed, name alone undoubtedly explains the mild success of Screaming Yellow Zonkers (and the Edsel might still be with us if it had been called the Eagle).

Location and Retailing[37]

In retailing we find differentiation in the clerk's friendly smile, the breadth of product selection, the services offered, the availability of credit, and the convenience of store location. Of these, location is often the most important, and its effect depends crucially on the kinds of goods being retailed. Thus one last distinction is needed: that between convenience goods and shopping goods. The distinction is based primarily on frequency of purchase and product price because **convenience goods** are relatively inexpensive items that people buy regularly, such as food, cigarettes, beverages, drugs, and gasoline. **Shopping goods**, on the other hand, are more costly and more intermittently purchased— appliances, stereos, autos, furniture, and apparel, for example. Locating close to consumers has obvious advantages for convenience goods retailers, since consumers value their time and transportation expenses. Convenience may be so important that some retailers (the back-road neighborhood gas station, and the "7–11" store around the corner) may *specialize* in convenience, extracting a price premium from those consumers who particularly favor ease of access.

Thus, food stores, gas stations, and drug stores dot the landscape here and there; however, shopping goods retailers tend to be clustered closer together in the heart of town, along major thoroughfares, or in large shopping centers. Such clustering enables people who are "in the market" for a new car, stereo, washing machine, or suit of clothes to shop around before they buy, comparing prices, terms, styles, service facilities, and so forth. Moreover, at least *in theory*, such comparison shopping could cause price elasticity of demand for each one of these retailers to exceed that confronting individual convenience goods retailers. In the course of shopping for a "big ticket" item, people could become sufficiently price conscious to suffer a little inconvenience willingly if it produced substantial price savings. In fact, this is not true of a substantial number of consumers. Survey evidence indicates that many consumers visit only one seller for shopping goods as well as for convenience goods. For such major items as new cars, television sets, refrigerators, washing machines, and so on, approximately half of all buyers surveyed said they went to only one store, the one where they made their purchase.[38] This statistic does not necessarily imply

---

[37] This section borrows from L. W. Weiss, *Economics and American Industry* (New York: John Wiley & Sons, 1961), pp. 392–94.

[38] Frederick E. May, "Buying Behavior: Some Research Findings," *Journal of Business* (October 1965), p. 391, and the references therein. See also J. W. Newman and R. Staelin, "Prepurchase Information Seeking for New Cars and Major Household Appliances," *Journal of Marketing Research* (August 1972), pp. 249–57.

that price elasticity at shopping goods retailers is low or that they do not compete in price offerings. All it takes to raise elasticity and encourage price rivalry among retailers is for them to face a measurable, though not necessarily dominant, contingent of price conscious buyers. Still, this statistic does suggest that even shopping goods retailers may have some leeway to use location as a means of differentiating their "product."

Finally, it is important to note that this distinction between convenience goods and shopping goods affects more than just store location. It also affects the retailer's *contribution* to the differentiation of the *specific brands* he sells. In the case of convenience goods, retailers typically offer little or no sales assistance, repair service, or other help. Moreover, the low price and frequent purchase of these goods make "in-store" information search by consumers rather costly relative to the potential benefits. Buyers therefore enter convenience stores "presold," and the retailer's contribution to specific brand differentiation is slight. This places the major burden of building brand image and preselling on the manufacturer.

The contrast in the case of shopping goods is notable. Retailers of these products do offer sales assistance, demonstrations, credit, repair service, delivery service, and so on—each of which greatly affects brand differentiation. Then too, the consumer in this case considers the purchase relatively important and expensive, an attitude that boosts the potential benefits of his or her in-store information search. All this adds up to the retailer of shopping goods having considerably more power over brand differentiation than the retailer of convenience goods has. And manufacturers cannot presell shopping goods as readily as they can convenience goods.

These distinctions have been emphasized by Michael Porter, who has also demonstrated their empirical importance.[39] We shall return to Porter's work later. For now, we merely need note that he found manufacturer's average advertising as a percentage sales to be 4.7 % for 19 convenience goods industries, and 2.1 % for 23 shopping goods industries. This comparison together with the factors discussed earlier, may help to explain why, in Table 4-6, the advertising/sales ratios of auto, appliance, and tire manufacturers tend to be relatively low.

Summary

A general class of product is differentiated if nonprice considerations influence the brand and model preferences of buyers. The major effects of successful differentiation give sellers some power over price. That is, differentiation can shift the demand curve outward and also reduce price elasticity of demand. This differentiation may be based on objective features such as quality, warranty,

---

[39] Michael E. Porter, "Consumer Behavior, Retailer Power and Market Performance in Consumer Goods Industries," *Review of Economics and Statistics* (November 1974), pp. 419–36.

service, location, dimension, and flavor. On the other hand, it may also be based on purely subjective buyer preferences, such as those cultivated by exhortative advertising, styling, brand name connotation, and superfluous packaging variation.

Form and strength of differentiation depend heavily on buyer knowledge, which, in turn, depends on buyer and product characteristics. Professional buyers are much more knowledgeable than consumers, so they are much less susceptible to differentiation, especially its subjective forms. Similarly, the subjective differentiability of search goods is limited by the fact that buyers can readily evaluate the quality of search goods prior to purchase. This is not true of experience goods, whose hidden qualities can be thoroughly evaluated only after purchase. Indeed, it appears that, among consumers, certain psychological effects, such as cognitive dissonance, preclude an objective, thoroughgoing evaluation of these goods even after purchase. As a consequence, consumer experience goods are most prone to subjective differentiation and least prone to efficient purchase.

Among the specific causes of differentiation, advertising predominates. Its intensity is subdued and its content most informative when buyer knowledge is well developed, as in the case of producer search goods. At the other extreme, however, we find billions of dollars being spent for the persuasive promotion of consumer experience goods. The effectiveness of such efforts seems to vary across products within the broad category of consumer experience goods, because such effectiveness is largely determined by numerous product characteristics. Among the most important are (1) consumers' "interest" in the product; (2) the emotional connotations associated with the product—for example, health, romance, safety, and security; (3) perceived risk and absolute price; and (4) frequency of purchase and rate of sales growth.

Finally, we discussed several probable causes of differentiation other than advertising. Detailed data concerning these other causes are not readily available. Nevertheless, it does appear that style variation, packaging, and location often contribute substantially to differentiation. The distinction between convenience goods and shopping goods largely determines the importance of location. The same distinction affects the potency of manufacturers' advertising.

5

Product Differentiation: Practice and Policy

Ironically, standards have not been completely standardized.

DAVID HEMENWAY

During a few weeks of the early 1960s, 42 Texas housewives shopped for bread in a most unusual way. Twelve special home deliveries were made to them. On each occasion the women were asked to select one of four loaves of bread marked "L," "M," "P," or "H." Except for these labels, the loaves were identical—same batch, same slicing, same wrap—but the women were not told this. The deliveries were arranged not by a baker but by a professor of marketing, W. T. Tucker. He wanted to see if the women would develop "brand loyalty" (product differentiation) based on nothing more than lettered labels. Defining "brand loyalty" to be three successive choices of the same brand, he found that by the last delivery half the women in the study had become "brand loyal." There were also clear indications that, if deliveries had continued, many more would have become loyal to one brand.[1]

To test the strength of this loyalty, Professor Tucker added a special twist. Once a housewife displayed loyalty, a new penny was attached to the brand she had chosen least often. If she remained faithful to her favored brand despite this enticement, one more penny was added to the neglected brand each delivery until she switched or the study ended. Before deliveries ended, six of the brand-loyal women did switch to the "premium" brand for enticements varying between 2 and 7 cents. Eight women remained unmoved. The premiums

---

[1] W. T. Tucker, "The Development of Brand Loyalty," *Journal of Marketing Research* (August 1964), pp. 32–35.

85

they refused varied from 1 to 7 cents, and averaged 3.5 cents. A hint of the thinking involved here was given by one woman who said, "No wonder you put the special on brand P. It's the worst of all." For these and other reasons, Tucker concluded that "loyalties are more than trivial, even though they are based on what may seem trivial distinctions."

Tucker's study provides an apt introduction to two detailed case studies concerning beer and computers that occupy the first third of this chapter. The purpose of these case studies is to pump life into the abstract theory and cross-section evidence of the preceding chapter. The main message they convey is simply this: *Trademarks may serve merely to identify the "origin" of goods, but consumers often go further by relying on trademarks to identify a given level of product quality. This reliance often grants sellers some power over price.*

In the last two thirds of this chapter we shall review certain policies that affect product differentiation. These policies are related to the case studies and our previous evidence by the following hypothesis: *If quality identifications could be made independent of trademarks, the market power generated by trademarks would weaken and in some instances even die.* To achieve this independent identification, policies would have to make consumers behave more like professional buyers, or make experience goods more like search goods. In short, buyers must be well informed, or readily informed. And, indeed, these are the broad objectives of such policies as the Textile Fiber Products Identification Act, the Fair Packaging and Labeling Act, the Truth in Lending Law, and the grade rating and labeling activities of the U. S. Department of Agriculture, all of which are discussed in this chapter.

There are many other policies relating to product differentiation or product quality besides those concerning information disclosure. We should, therefore, distinguish between the policies of immediate concern and two other broad groups of policies: (1) those that prohibit deceptive and useless sales promotion, and (2) those that directly regulate product quality, efficacy, and safety. Policies governing deceptive practices, which are discussed in Chapter 16 under "conduct," are generally *pro*scriptive and negative. They *prohibit* certain types of misleading conduct, such as false advertising and misrepresentation; however, they do not require sellers to make informative pronouncements. In contrast, the disclosure policies of the present chapter are generally *pre*scriptive and positive; they require disclosures.

Policies that directly regulate product quality, efficacy, and safety are covered in Chapter 26. Under them, businessmen seem to be confronted with as many "thou shalts" as "thou shalt nots." In these cases the government attempts to protect consumers from unsafe, impure, ineffective, and low quality products by *directly regulating* product features and production processes. Examples include bans against highly flammable fabrics and unsafe tires, control of automobile exhaust emissions, inspection of food processing plants, and surveillance of drug effectiveness. In contrast to the disclosure approach, the consumer is denied a free choice in these instances. Instead of attempting to secure good market structure in hopes that good performance will ensue, product performance is regulated directly. One argument for this direct regulation is that structure may not affect these kinds of performance. Although the boundary lines between the disclosure, deception, and performance policy groups are often vague, this classification organizes our approach to consumerism as it pertains to industrial organization.[2]

Case Studies

Beer

Legend has it that cockroaches are strongly attracted to beer. Indeed, they will even drown in it if given the chance. The author is a believer. He has built ramps to bowls of brew to give roaches the chance, and they took it. Legend also holds that cockroaches favor certain brands of beer, but the author's experiments do not confirm this. Many folks are like cockroaches in that they, too, are attracted to beer. But they, unlike cockroaches, reveal a substantial degree of brand loyalty, loyalty that is expressed even at the expense of burdening their already overburdened budgets.

One revealing study is that of A. G. Woodside, who wanted to test the hypothesis "that many products have meaning and significance for consumers far beyond the physical attributes of the products themselves and that these hidden values in products are a major influence on the consumer's purchase decision."[3] Because the hypothesis was psychological, Woodside chose a psychological testing technique known as indirect questioning. His subjects were 157 business students attending the University of South Carolina. The instructions to each student ran: (1) read a shopping list allegedly written by a student planning a "small informal party," (2) "project yourself into the situation," and (3) write a brief description of the party planner's "personality and character." Three shopping lists were used, although the students were not aware of this because they were segregated into three groups. The lists were identical except for the fifth of the seven items. Two cases of Pabst Blue Ribbon beer was the fifth item on one list; two cases of another brand known to us only as Brand X was the fifth item on the second list; and no beer was mentioned on the third. Woodside chose Pabst because "of its apparently distinctive image" and its ranking at the time among the top three national brands of beer. He does not disclose the identity of Brand X in his article because the test results were unfavorable to it. However, he does tell us that Brand X was ranked among the top ten, and that "Brand X's sales and market share are dropping, suggesting a weak or unfavorable image." Woodside included the no-beer list to serve as a control or

---

[2] For a discussion of this categorization scheme see R. H. Leftwich and A. M. Sharp, *Economics of Social Issues* (Dallas: Business Publications, Inc., 1976), Chapter 7.

[3] A. G. Woodside, "A Shopping List Experiment of Beer Brand Images," *Journal of Applied Psychology* (December 1972), pp. 512–13.

TABLE 5-1   Percentage of Students' Assessments Classified as Favorable, Unfavorable, and Neutral

Sample	Favorable (%)	Unfavorable (%)	Neutral (%)	Total (%)
Pabst	62	15	23	100
Brand X	29	40	31	100
No beer	38	40	22	100
Average	43	31	26	100

Source: A. G. Woodside, "A Shopping List Experiment of Beer Brand Images," *Journal of Applied Psychology* (December 1972), p. 513.

standard against which the results of the other two lists could be compared. Among the items included on all three lists were "5 lbs. hamburger," "3 packages Sunbeam hamburger buns," and "1 jar Del Monte dill pickles."

The student's assessments of the fictitious shopper's personality were processed in two ways. First, each assessment was judged to be generally favorable, unfavorable, or neutral. Woodside then summarized the scores for each shopping list in terms of the *proportion* of the assessments that were favorable, unfavorable, or neutral. These results are shown in Table 5-1. There it may be seen that a substantial majority of the students describing the Pabst party planner had favorable assessments. In contrast, only 29% of those viewing the Brand X list had favorable opinions, whereas 40% held negative views. Even the no-beer list did better than this.

The second approach looked at the specific personality traits that were attributed to the party planners. In this connection Woodside found that the Brand X buyer was described as "unintelligent" and "unimaginative" by more than one third of those viewing the Brand X list. On the other hand, only 9% of the Pabst students held similar impressions of their party planner.

These results are inherently interesting. What makes them more than merely interesting—perhaps even astounding—is the fact that beer drinkers cannot taste any difference between all but a few brands of American beer. This lack of any "genuine" difference among beers has been demonstrated by numerous researchers in a variety of ways, but all of them rely on one basic approach— the "blind" taste test. One of the most comprehensive of these studies was conducted by R. I. Allison and K. P. Uhl.[4] Their test went through two rounds using five well-known national or regional brands of beer on a sample of 326

[4] R. I. Allison and K. P. Uhl, "Influence of Beer Brand Identification on Taste Perception," *Journal of Marketing Research* (August 1964), pp. 36–39. Another example of this genre is S. H. Rewoldt, J. D. Scott, and M. R. Warshaw, *Introduction to Marketing Management* (Homewood, Ill.: Richard D. Irwin, Inc., 1973) Case 2-1, "Falstaff Brewing Corporation," pp. 177–90.

who drank beer at least three times a week. Round one was designed to answer these questions:

1. Could beer drinkers, in general, distinguish among various beers in a blind test?
2. Could beer drinkers identify "their" brands in a blind test?

For this purpose each participant tested and evaluated (at their leisure) a six-pack of various unlabeled bottled beers, identified only by lettered tags— AB, CD, EF, GH, and IJ. The regular labels were soaked off and the bottle caps were wire brushed clean.

Possible scoring ranged from zero, which would be "very poor," to 100, which would be "excellent." On average, *all* beers scored within one point of 64, and there was no significant difference between brands. Thus the first answer is clearly "No." Drinkers cannot, in general, distinguish between brands.

The answer to the second question is found in Table 5-2. There the drinkers are segregated into five groups, depending on which of the five brands they claimed was their usual brand, as shown by the left-hand column. The blind ratings of the beers are presented in the body of the table. Thus, for example, drinkers who claimed EF was "their" brand rated EF at 65.0, but gave CD a rating of 74.5. And those who favored a fully dressed GH gave the nude GH a lowly 60.0 rating, which compared quite unfavorably to their rating of the nude IJ. As indicated by the right-hand column of Table 5-2, the answer to question 2 was negative in every case.

Round two was designed to answer one further question:

3. If the labels were left on, how would they influence the evaluations of various brands?

For this purpose Allison and Uhl picked up the unlabeled empties and gave each drinker a six-pack of labeled beer to taste and rate in the same fashion as in round one. Table 5-3 reveals these results. The first thing to note is that, generally speaking, the labels seem to have improved the taste of all five beers to all drinkers because the numbers in Table 5-3 usually exceed their corresponding numbers in Table 5-2 by a substantial margin. Note next that this "improvement" is especially evident in the way the drinkers rated their "own" brands, as revealed by a comparison of the diagonal entries of Tables 5-2 and 5-3. Thus AB devotees boosted their rating of AB by 10.3 points once it was labeled, and the other increments were CD, 18.0 points; EF, 17.3; GH, 20.0; and IJ, 7.9. It is not unreasonable to conclude that drinkers generally rated "their" brand above the others when brand image could prompt their taste buds. Statistically significant divergences in this brand-name "improvement" direction are indicated in the right-hand column of Table 5-3. A similar effect was observed by J. D. McConnell, who in a separate test conducted during the late 1960s observed that beer drinkers claimed to taste quality differences among three

TABLE 5-2 Drinkers' Loyalty to "Their" Brand in Blind Test (Own Brand Rating on the Diagonal)

Brand Drunk Most Often	Taste Test Ratings by Brand Rated					Own Brand Rates Significantly Higher Than All Others?
	AB	CD	EF	GH	IJ	
AB	67.0	62.4*	57.7*	65.0	65.8	No
CD	64.9	65.6	65.4	63.2	63.9	No
EF	68.8	74.5*	65.0	62.5	61.4	No
GH	55.4	59.2	68.7	60.0	71.4*	No
IJ	68.4	60.5*	69.2	62.0	65.6	No

* Brand significantly different from user's own brand.
Source: R. I. Allison and K. P. Uhl, "Influence of Beer Brand Identification on Taste Perception," *Journal of Marketing Research* (August 1964), p. 38. Reprinted by permission of the American Marketing Association.

TABLE 5-3 Drinkers' Loyalty to "Their" Brand in Label Test (Own Brand Rating on the Diagonal)

Brand Drunk Most Often	Taste Test Ratings by Brand Rated					Own Brand Rates Significantly Higher?
	AB	CD	EF	GH	IJ	
AB	77.3	61.1	62.8	73.4	63.1	Yes
CD	66.3	83.6	67.4	78.3	63.1	Yes
EF	67.3	71.5	82.3	71.9	71.5	Yes
GH	73.1	72.5	77.5	80.0	67.5	Only over IJ
IJ	70.3	69.3	67.2	76.7	73.5	Only over EF

Source: Allison and Uhl, *op. cit.*, p. 39.

"brands" where in fact no quality difference existed. In this case the *same* beer was labeled "P," "L," and "M," which labels were said to be priced $0.99, $1.20, and $1.30 per six-pack, respectively. After 2 months of 24 home deliveries to each drinker, the "high-priced" brand outscored the other two on quality by a wide margin. One drinker said of one of the brands he thought was cheap: "I could never finish a bottle."[5]

This is not to say that *all* brands of beer are identical; or that cheap beer is

[5] J. D. McConnell, "The Price-Quality Relationship in an Experimental Setting," *Journal of Marketing Research* (August 1968), pp. 300–03.

always the best buy. (The author has done more with beer than catch cockroaches.) Still, the evidence indicates that brand image is of utmost importance.[6]

Computers

On a number of counts the computer industry is truly remarkable. Few other industries have contributed as much to science fiction. Few have grown as rapidly. And, few producer goods industries can match computers in strength of product differentiation. Although product differentiation for most consumer goods seems to be based on advertising, differentiation in the computer industry is based primarily on close customer-manufacturer contacts. As Gerald Brock has written, "The user is not purchasing just a machine but a relationship with a manufacturer":

> Manufacturers often promise an undefined amount of help in getting the installation running, which is difficult to value. Most manufacturers have application programs available, either directly through the manufacturer or through a user's group, and plan upgrades of either the hardware or software within the time the user plans to keep a machine installed. The user's expectations about the characteristics and compatibility of the manufacturer's follow-on line of machines have an important influence on selection . . . his beliefs about the reliability and stability of the manufacturer may be as important or even more important than the actual measured performance and price of the machine being considered.[7]

These observations are particularly apropos of the heart of computer installations—the central processing unit, or CPU. These units are complex, costly, delicate—and IBM's special claim to fame. Indeed, IBM's dominance of this aspect of the business led one industry expert to remark that "IBM doesn't have to sell equipment at the same price-performance ratio as its competitors .... Most customers won't take the risk of leaving IBM for less than 30% improvement."[8]

The peripheral equipment of computer systems—such as tape drives and disk memories—may be considered much less differentiable. The choice between IBM and competitive "plug compatible" peripheral equipment is relatively straightforward because rivals have successfully copied IBM's specifications and because no substitution of the complete computer system is involved. Still, even in this simplified situation, IBM enjoys an impressive amount of brand loyalty. To measure the intensity of this loyalty, IBM itself conducted a questionnaire survey of its disk customers, asking them how much lower competitive disk equipment would have to be priced in order for these customers to switch from IBM to a competitor. As may be seen in Table 5-4, IBM would apparently retain 92% of its customers despite competitive discounts of 10%.

[6] For a brief review of other taste tests (covering cola drinks and cigarettes as well as beer) the interested reader should consult J. H. Meyers and W. H. Reynolds, *Consumer Behavior and Marketing Management* (Boston: Houghton Mifflin Co., 1967), pp. 16–19.
[7] Gerald W. Brock, *The U.S. Computer Industry: A Study of Market Power* (Cambridge, Mass.: Ballinger Publishing Co., 1975), p. 46.
[8] "Itel's Powerful New Computer," *Business Week* (October 25, 1976), p. 74.

TABLE 5-4   IBM Disk Customer Loyalty in the Face of Competitor's Discounts

| Competitive Discount (%) | IBM Customers Remaining with IBM | | |
	Overall (%)	2319A Users (%)	3330 Users (%)
1–5%	97	99	94
6–10	92	95	88
11–15	70	58	64
16–20	46	37	36
Over 20	31	23	22

Source: G. Brock, *The U. S. Computer Industry: A Study of Market Power* (Cambridge Mass.: Ballinger Publishing Co., 1975) p. 48. Reprinted by permission.

Furthermore, almost half of IBM's customers were willing to pass up competitive equipment that was priced as much as 20% below IBM's equipment. It seems, then, that IBM's customers and Pabst's two-legged clientele share at least two things in common—they are human and they tend to be loyal to their chosen brand.

A Bit of Theory

It may seem to the reader that these two groups also have in common a good deal of irrationality, but this is not necessarily so. They may merely be uniformed or misinformed. If after being informed that Brand X and Brand Y are virtually identical, the buyer still chooses the more expensive brand, he might then be considered irrational. Of course the key phrase here is "being informed." Consumers are repeatedly "informed" by advertisements that "they may have to pay a little more but they get *so much* more from Brand X." For this reason many people do not believe (or are not persuaded by) truly objective and authoritative information to the contrary, such as that which might be provided by *Consumer Reports* or the government.[9]

---

[9] An intriguing study of this issue is provided by G. Scherhorn and K. Wieken (S & W) of West Germany. Despite the fact that all heavy duty laundry detergents are pretty much the same, S & W found that $\frac{7}{8}$ of a large sample of German housewives bought expensive detergents because of "preferences resulting from misinformation about quality." Only $\frac{1}{8}$ had "no preferences for certain brands . . . or brand name detergents in general." Having thus identified the true believers, S & W then sent them a large amount of authoratitive but readable "counterinformation," which explained why most detergents were alike and why they were wasting money on the expensive brands. Follow-up interviews disclosed that only 55% of the housewives were "generally convinced by the counter-information that all detergents tend to meet the same standards of quality," and only "$\frac{1}{3}$ of the buyers interviewed were ready to buy the detergent which was actually the cheapest." G. Scherhorn and K. Wieken, "On the Effect of Counter-Information on Consumers," in *Human Behavior in Economic Analysis*, edited by B. Strumpel, J. Morgan, and E. Zahn (San Francisco: Jossey-Bass Inc., 1972), pp. 421–31.

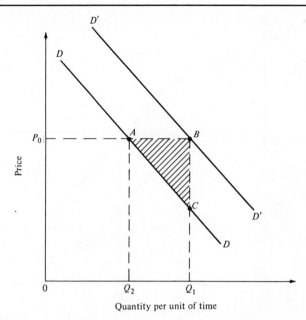

Figure 5-1. *The monetary loss from an error of commission.*

Setting this problem aside, we may conclude these case studies and preface our discussion of public policy with a brief explanation of the monetary benefits of correct information and rational action.[10] In essence, benefits arise from *error avoidance.* So much is obvious. Less obvious is the fact that there are two types of errors to be avoided—errors of commission and omission.

An **error of commission** occurs when the buyer makes a purchase on the basis of an excessively favorable prepurchase assessment of the acquired good. In other words, the buyer gets not what he thinks he is getting but something less. The monetary loss of making such an error (or the gain from avoiding same) is illustrated in Figure 5-1 as the shaded area *ABC.* The demand curve *DACD* refers to what demand would be like if the good were correctly evaluated, whereas *D'BD'* depicts an erroneously optimistic level of demand. The latter lies to the right of the former since the uninformed buyer wants to buy more at each possible price than he would if he were fully informed. Thus, given a fixed price equal to OP_0 (or constant marginal costs of supply indicated by

[10] This section draws heavily from S. Peltzman, "An Evaluation of Consumer Protection Legislation: The 1962 Drug Amendments," *Journal of Political Economy* (Sept./Oct. 1973) pp. 1049–91; T. McGuire, R. Nelson, and T. Spavins, "Comment on the Peltzman Paper," *Journal of Political Economy* (June 1975), pp. 655–61; M. R. Darby and E. Karni, "Free Competition and the Optimal Amount of Fraud," *Journal of Law and Economics* (April 1973), pp. 67–88; George Akerlof, "The Market for 'Lemons': Quality Uncertainty and the Market Mechanism," *Quarterly Journal of Economics* (August 1970), pp. 488–500; and R. H. Nelson, "The Economics of Honest Trade Practices," *Journal of Industrial Economics* (June 1976), pp. 281–93.

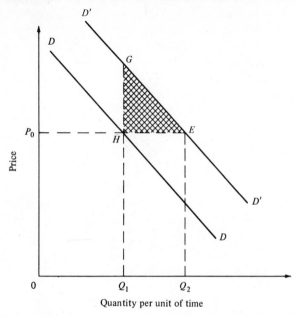

Figure 5-2. *The monetary loss from an error of omission.*

P_0AB), the consumer buys an excess equal to the difference between Q_1 and Q_2, that is, $Q_1 - Q_2$. The amount he pays for this excess is the area Q_2ABQ_1, price times the excess quantity. However, the *true value* of the extra units amounts only to Q_2ACQ_1, or the trapezoid below A and C. Thus, the difference between dollar outlay Q_2ABQ_1 and true value Q_2ACQ_1 is ABC, the net loss.

Errors of omission are the opposite. They occur when the buyer buys *less* than he would with full knowledge. The monetary loss from making such an error is illustrated in Figure 5-2 by the area GHE. In this case the demand curve $D'GED'$ depicts what the demand would be like if the commodity were correctly evaluated, whereas DHD represents the erroneously pessimistic demand of buyers who underestimate the value of the product. Given a constant price P_0, a corrective movement from the poorly chosen amount Q_1 to the proper amount Q_2 requires an additional cash outlay equal to area Q_1HEQ_2. But the move yields a greater addition to total benefit, indicated by Q_1GEQ_2. Subtracting the added cost from this added benefit yields a *net* benefit of HGE, which in technical jargon is the amount of "consumer's surplus" the consumer misses out on when he errs in the direction of omission. It may now be seen that errors of omission lead to *under*allocations of resources to the particular products or brands, whereas errors of commission lead to *over*allocations to the chosen products or brands. Needless to say, both forms of error are *mis*allocations, and they often represent opposite sides of the same coin. When someone over-values Pabst, for instance, he is probably also undervaluing Brand X.

The next question is: What policies can assist buyers in avoiding these errors? Incredible though it may seem in light of what has been said to this point, one such policy is the issuance and enforcement of *trademarks*. To see this most clearly, the reader might try imagining what the world would be like in the absence of trademarks. Without them how could *Consumer Reports* tell us (in December 1975) that a VW "Rabbit" was better than a Subaru? Or how could a friend advise us that Levi's trousers are a good buy? How could we be sure that, having been wholly satisfied with an Arrow shirt, we could ever get another one from the same manufacturer? How could we sue the Coca-Cola Company for damages if we found a dead mouse in one of its soda bottles? In other words, it can be argued that, to the extent consumers do learn from experience and to the extent they do learn to buy what they like (rather than like what they buy), trademarks can minimize *repeated* errors merely by identifying good, bad, and mediocre goods and services. Similarly, trademarks are necessary to spreading an individual's or a testing agency's specific knowledge to others. And, finally, in extreme cases of error, individual producers may be held legally as well as economically accountable for their share in any disaster. As Richard Caves and William Murphy have so aptly put it, "By offering the seller's good name as hostage, the trademark provides the buyer with cheap information and assurance about product quality."[11]

Despite these considerable social benefits, the trademark laws as they stand also involve specific *social costs*. Trademark policies are based on the assumption that trademarks serve primarily to identify the *origin* of goods, and that the purposes of such identification are twofold:[12]

1. Protection is furnished the seller from "unfair" competition through the infringement of his mark by an imitator or poacher.
2. Protection is furnished buyers who might be deceived into purchasing the goods of one seller in the belief that the goods are another's.

Unfortunately, this emphasis on origin adds substantially to the social costs of the trademark system without contributing to its social benefits. Benefits derive from the *identification of a given level of quality*, not from the identification of a given origin. Identification of origin on an exclusive, perpetual, and carefully protected basis, as is now practiced, may serve *indirectly* to identify a given level of quality. But it also often facilitates the creation of substantial market power,

---

[11] R. E. Caves and W. F. Murphy II, "Franchising: Firms, Markets, and Intangible Assets," *Southern Economic Journal* (April 1976), pp. 572–86. It may be worth noting that even the Russians use trademarks: "This makes it easy to establish the actual producer of the product in case it is necessary to call him to account for the poor quality of his goods. For this reason it is one of the most effective weapons in the battle for the quality of products . . ." M. I. Goldman, "Product differentiation and Advertising: Some Lessons From Soviet Experience," *Journal of Political Economy* (August 1960), pp. 346–57. Note too, however, that communists are not always "called to account" in the same manner as capitalists.

[12] E. W. Kintner and J. L. Lahr, *An Intellectual Property Law Primer* (New York: Macmillan Publishing Co., 1975) p. 250.

power that translates into social costs, power achieved by exhortative advertising and other means of questionable social worth. As we shall see even more thoroughly later, the available evidence indicates that, when quality guarantees or quality identifications are established independently of trademarks (by professional buyers themselves, by government grade rating and standardization, by consumers search shopping for easily analyzable goods, and so on), monopoly power cannot be based on trademark differentiation and advertising, and burdensome social costs are avoided. The effects of the trademark system are therefore negative when (1) trademarks (and the persuasive advertising promoting them) provide the sole or major source of quality identification for the product *and* (2) grants of exclusive trademark use protect the goodwill (or monopoly) profits that attach to trademarks under such circumstances. Corrective policies should therefore be focused on one or both of the following objectives:

1. Permit trademarks to identify or guarantee quality but remove the rights of exclusivity and perpetuity currently awarded them.
2. Establish quality identifications and guarantees that are *independent* of the trademark system.

With respect to the first, nonexclusive trademark use, Edward Chamberlin once suggested a policy that would permit brand imitation as long as quality was maintained.[13] Such a policy would, of course, focus the law on identifying quality instead of origin. But this policy is rather radical, and its adoption is unlikely. Still, in some ways it would be only a small step beyond the rapidly spreading practice of franchising, whereby many producers are licensed to use the same trademark. Indeed, franchising has grown to such a point in the United States that it is no longer accurate to say that trademarks always identify origin. Among the many trademarks that do not identify origin are McDonald's, Mister Donut, Abbey Rents, Avis, Fruit of the Loom, BVD, Serta, and Arnold Palmer Dry Cleaning Centers.[14] In such instances a given level of quality (not necessarily high quality) is assured, since under United States law the owner of a trademark may license others to use the mark only as long as the licensor controls the "nature and quality" of the goods or services offered by the licensee-franchisee. If the owner of the mark does not exercise "control," the mark may be freely imitated by competitors.

With respect to the second possible focus of policy, quality identifications and guarantees that are independent of the trademark system, regulations abound. They merit the entire section that follows.

---

[13] Edward H. Chamberlin, *The Theory of Monopolistic Competition*, 8th ed. (Harvard University Press, 1962), p. 273; see also M. L. Greenhut, "Free Entry and the Trade Mark-Trade Name Product," *Southern Economic Journal* (October 1957), pp. 170–81.

[14] Standards of scholarship require that I identify the origin of these examples: Donald N. Thompson, *Franchise Operations and Antitrust* (Lexington, Mass.: Heath Lexington Books, 1971) pp. 5–27.

Standardization and Disclosure

As suggested by the heading "Standardization and Disclosure," information or identification policies other than trademarks may be divided into two categories.[15] And, as suggested by the items listed for each category, the ultimate purpose of these policies is to assist buyers—particularly consumers—in avoiding errors:

A. Standardization for easier price comparisons
   1. Simplified quantity labeling
   2. Uniform sizes
   3. Price standardization, e.g., "unit" pricing
B. Quality disclosures
   1. Ingredient disclosure
   2. Open dating of perishables
   3. Specific performance disclosures
   4. Grade rating

Standardization policies typically promote simplification or uniformity or both. The distinction between simplification and uniformity may be seen by an easy example. Suppose ten brick manufacturers were each making the same 50 kinds of brick. Since each producer offered a full range of 50 kinds, each firm's bricks would match those of the others and there would be perfect **uniformity** among sellers. With 50 varieties, however, the situation would not be simple. **Simplification** could be achieved if these firms agreed to cut down the number of their offerings to, say, 12 common types. This would yield a combination of simplification and uniformity—ten firms, each producing the same 12 kinds of brick. Alternatively, simplification could be achieved at the expense of uniformity. If each of the ten brick makers cut back their offerings to four *unique* items, with no one producing the same item, uniformity would disappear. The total, industry-wide variety, however, would have been simplified from 50 down to 40. As far as buyer errors are concerned, uniformity facilitates the comparison of different seller's offerings, whereas simplification may help to keep buyers' minds from boggling.

Quality disclosures are quite different. They sharpen the buyer's awareness of "better" or "worse." For example, all mattress manufacturers may uniformly adhere to a few simple sizes—twin, double, queen, and king. But this says nothing about the range of quality (and some mattresses may feel as if they were made from 50 kinds of brick). Disclosure of ingredients might be helpful

---

[15] This division and much else in this section owe their origin to David Hemenway, *Industrywide Voluntary Product Standards* (Cambridge, Mass.: Ballinger Publishing Co., 1975).

in this case, and grade rating would be even more helpful. Policies revealing ingredients and grades may thus be considered quality disclosures.

Before we take a detailed look at specific policies, one more preliminary point needs attention: Why must we rely on the *government* to elevate consumer knowledge and information? What is wrong with relying on free *private* enterprise? If information is a desirable "good," ought not profit opportunities abound for anyone who wants to supply information? The answer to all these questions is, in a word, *imperfections.* The nature of the commodity in question—information—is such that imperfections stand in the way of its optimal provision by private enterprise.

Among the many problems that discourage optimal private provision, two seem paramount. First, sellers of information may face the same problem as the little boy who climbs and shakes the apple tree but gets few of the fallen apples because his buddies on the ground run off with the loot before he can get down. This is "inappropriability," and it often applies to information because information may be spread by means outside the control of the information's original producer—for example, piracy by word of mouth. When a private producer of information is not rewarded in just proportion to the social value of his effort, he extends less effort than is socially optimal. A second and more striking problem arises because buyers of information cannot be truly *well informed* about the information they want to buy. If they were, they would not then need to buy the information.[16] In other words, the seller of information cannot let potential buyers meticulously examine his product prior to sale lest he thereby give it away free. Buyers of information therefore do not know the value of the product they seek (information) until after they buy it. They are consequently vulnerable to errors of commission and omission. Only with objective, outside, nonmarket assistance can they overcome this handicap.

Standardization for Easy Price Comparisons

Simplified Quantity Labeling. Try this little test on yourself. Which box of detergent is the best buy—25 "jumbo" ounces for 53¢; $1\frac{1}{2}$ pounds for 49¢; or $27\frac{1}{2}$ "full" ounces for 55¢? Prior to the Fair Packaging and Labeling Act of 1966 (FPLA), grocery shoppers took, and failed, real-life tests like this more often than they probably care to remember. In 1965, for instance, a selected sample of 33 married women who were students or the wives of students at Eastern Michigan University were asked to pick the most economical package for each of 20 supermarket products. Despite their above average intelligence and their stimulated attention, these women typically spent 9.14 % more on these groceries than they should have.[17] Small wonder they erred, what with the commingling

[16] Kenneth Arrow, "Economic Welfare and the Allocation of Resources for Invention," in *The Rate and Direction of Inventive Activity: Economic and Social Factors* (New York: National Bureau of Economic Research, 1962).

[17] M. P. Friedman, "Consumer Confusion in the Selection of Supermarket Products," *Journal of Applied Psychology* (December 1966), pp. 529–34.

of weight and fluid volumes for the same products; the use of meaningless adjectives, such as "jumbo" and "full"; the frequent appearance of fractional quantity units; and the designation of servings as "small," "medium," and "large," without any common standard of reference.

The Fair Packaging and Labeling Act tidied things up a bit by providing

1. The net quantity be stated in a uniform and prominent location on the package.
2. The net quantity be clearly expressed in a unit of measure appropriate to the product.
3. The net quantity of a "serving" must be stated if servings are mentioned.

This may not seem like much, but early and final versions of FPLA were vigorously opposed by business interests. It took 5 years of Congressional hearings and a persistent effort on the part of the late Senator Hart of Michigan to get FPLA passed. Some opponents claimed that it was "a power grab based on the fallacious concepts that the consumer is Casper Milquetoast, business is Al Capone, and government is Superman."[18] Their opposition was based on what they apparently thought was a more accurate concept—the housewife as Superwoman. "We suggest," argued the editor of *Food Field Reporter*, "that the housewife...should be expected to take the time to divide fractionalized weights into fractionalized prices in order to determine the 'best buy'."[19] Still others worried about what would happen to the Barbie doll: "Will the package have to say, in compliance with the act's rules, 'One doll, net,' on quantity, and then, on size, '34-21-34'?"[20] Despite such criticism, the FPLA seems to have worked fairly well. The Federal Trade Commission and Food and Drug Administration have encountered problems while enforcing the Act, but nothing insuperable. The problem of what to do with Barbie, for instance, was solved when the Federal Trade Commission declared that she was among the many commodities that were not covered by the Act—toys, chinaware, books, souvenirs, and mouse traps, to name only a few. If anything, the main problem may be that the Act did not go far enough.

Uniform Package Sizes. As already suggested, it would be easier for consumers to compare the price per unit of various brands and volumes if sellers adhered to a few common sizes of packaging. Senator Hart tried to have some compulsory rules for packaging uniformity or "standardization" written into FPLA, but they were defeated by the opposition. Several *nonmandatory* standards have emerged from under the voluntary sections of the Act. Dry cereals, for example, are supposed to be packaged in whole ounces only. Jellies and preserves are

---

[18] Michigan Chamber of Commerce, as quoted by R. L. Birmingham, "The Consumer as King: The Economics of Precarious Sovereignity," in *Consumerism*, edited by D. A. Aaker and G. S. Day (New York: Free Press, 1974), p. 186.

[19] A. Q. Mowbray. *The Thumb on the Scale* (New York: J. B. Lippincott Co., 1967), p. 72.

[20] *New York Times*, June 8, 1969.

TABLE 5-5   Selected Canadian Standardization Regulations

Product	Prescribed Weight or Volume
Jellies and jams	$2\frac{1}{2}$, 6, 9, 12, 24, or 48 ounces
Eggs	Multiples of 12
Frozen peas, corn, liver beans, and spinach	12 ounces or 2 pounds
Fruit and vegetable juices	$5\frac{1}{2}$, 6, 10, 14, 19, 28, 48, or 100 fluid ounces
Single-ply paper napkins	Multiples of 30 napkins
Liquid/ lotion shampoos	Multiples of 25 milliliters between 25 and 250 milliliters; Multiples of 50 milliliters over 250 milliliters

Source: *Package Standardization, Unit Pricing, Deceptive Packaging* (Paris: Organization for Economic Co-operation and Development, 1975), pp. 31–35.

now supposed to come in sizes of 10, 12, 16, 18, 20, 24, 28, 32, 48, or 64 ounces. However, these voluntary standards do not seem to be very helpful. For more stringent action we must look to state and foreign laws. In the United States, several states have standardized the packaging of bread, butter, margarine, flour, corn meal, and milk. Among foreign countries, Germany, France, England, and Canada have rather extensive mandatory standardization.[21] A few examples of Canadian policy are shown in Table 5-5.

Price Standardization. Price standardization is an approach still more helpful to consumers than package uniformity and simplification. It may be found in two major forms—unit pricing and truth-in-lending. **Unit pricing** translates all package prices into a price per standard weight or measure, such as 25.3 cents per pound, or 71.4 cents per hundred count. Representing price in this way helps consumers compare prices without superhuman computations. Numerous studies have shown that unit pricing greatly reduces price comparison errors. One such study found that with unit pricing people could pick the least cost item 25% more often than without, and at the same time cut down their shopping time considerably.[22] Extensive national regulation policies of this type exist only in Germany and Switzerland. In the United States, 11 states have adopted unit-pricing regulations, led by Massachusetts in 1971.[23] Although United States laws thus have restricted application, many grocery stores have

[21] Committee on Consumer Policy, *Package Standardization, Unit Pricing, Deceptive Packaging* (Paris: Organization for Economic Co-operation and Development, 1975).

[22] For a summary of this and other studies see General Accounting Office, *Report to the Congress on Food Labeling: Goals, Shortcomings, and Proposed Changes* (#MWD-75-19) January 1975. This is the main source for this section.

[23] *State Consumer Action: Summary '74*, Office of Consumer Affairs, Department of Health, Education, and Welfare [Pub. No. (OS) 75-116], pp. ix–x.

voluntarily adopted unit pricing. As a result, it appears that roughly half of all chain-operated supermarkets in the United States and one fourth of all independent supermarkets use unit pricing of some kind.

Of course, retailer adoption and actual consumer use of unit pricing are two different things. Surveys of consumers' use of unit pricing, where it is available, have shown a wide variation of shoppers claiming usage—from 9 to 68%—with an average of only 34%. In accord with the view that the typical shopper is not Superperson, it appears that one reason for this limited reliance on unit pricing is a complete lack of awareness. One study showed that 28% of those not using unit pricing simply didn't know about it. Obviously, limited use also limits the benefits that can be attributed to unit pricing. Thus, one survey estimated that only about 8.8% of observed purchases probably involved the use of unit pricing, and another study concluded that active use saves consumers only about 3% on their grocery bill. Multiplying these two estimates yields an estimated saving of no more than 0.264% on the cost of all purchases. Although this estimate is indeed small, it nevertheless appears to be greater than the costs borne by those retailers who have adopted unit pricing. Many consumer advocates therefore urge that federal legislation require nationwide unit pricing. They also argue that consumers be more thoroughly educated about its use.

Truth-in-lending (TIL) is one form of price standardization that since 1969 has been provided by United States government regulations.[24] However, the scope of these regulations is limited to consumer credit. Before adoption of TIL, numerous studies indicated that only a few people knew how much they actually paid for credit. Two such studies in the 1950s, for instance, indicated that 66–70% of consumers did not have even a vague idea of the annual *percentage rate*, let alone the dollar value, of interest they were paying on their *recent* installment purchases. They almost certainly did not know the interest rates charged by other credit suppliers, information that is, of course, necessary to comparative shopping. Why this vast ignorance? To make a long story short, there was no price standardization in the credit industry. One lender would use the "add-on" method; others would use a "discount rate," or an "annual percentage rate," or "monthly rate," or some combination of all three. Depending on the method, the price for the same amount of credit might be quoted as being 1%, 7%, 12.83%, or 16%. Indeed, some lenders would not quote *any* rate of charge. They would merely state the number and amount of the monthly payments required.

The purpose of the Truth in Lending Law is to let consumers know exactly what the price of credit is and to let them compare the prices of various lenders. Moreover, as argued by the late Senator Paul Douglas (an early sponsor of the legislation and also a prominent economist): "The benefits of effective

---

[24] Material for this topic may be found in *Consumer Credit in the United States*, Report of the National Commission on Consumer Finance (Washington D.C.: U.S. Government Printing Office, 1972) Chapter 10; and *Technical Studies, Vol I*, of the same Commission, which includes papers by R. P. Shay, M. W. Schober, G. S. Day, and W. K. Brandt.

competition cannot be realized if the buyers (borrowers) do not have adequate knowledge of the alternatives which are available to them." To achieve these ends the law requires disclosure of two fundamental aspects of credit prices:

1. The *finance charge*, which is the amount of money paid to obtain the credit.
2. The *annual percentage rate*, or APR, which provides a simple way of comparing credit prices regardless of the dollar amount charged or the length of time over which payments are made.

This summary makes enforcement of the law by the Federal Reserve Board of Governors and the Federal Trade Commission sound easy, but it's not. The former's Regulation "Z" runs to nearly 100 fine-printed pages. Still, this summary is not misleading, and from the consumer's viewpoint things are indeed simpler. Several studies of credit-cost awareness subsequent to TIL have discovered significant improvement in debtor knowledge. This is especially true of their credit card accounts, which now include an APR disclosure with each monthly bill.

Quality Disclosures

Critics of the policies ticked off heretofore correctly point out that they simply make price comparisons easier; they do not take into account differences in the *quality* of competing brands or products. Furthermore, some critics assert that these policies cause consumers to *overemphasize* price per unit and *overlook* quality per dollar spent. The latter argument is probably questionable. In any event, the general purpose of the following policies is to help buyers identify quality.

Simple Disclosure of Ingredients. The Wool Products Labeling Act of 1939, the Fur Products Labeling Act of 1951, and the Textile Fiber Products Identification Act of 1958 call for the disclosure of ingredients in fur and fiber products. All are enforced by the Federal Trade Commision. Under the first of these, almost all wool products must bear labels showing the percentage of the total fiber weight of "virgin" wool, reprocessed wool, and reused wool. Inclusion of any other fiber must also be identified by generic name (as opposed to trade name) if it exceeds 5% of the total. Similarly, the Fur Act requires fur product labels that disclose the true English name of the animal that grew the fur; the animal's home country if the fur is imported; whether the fur is bleached, dyed, or otherwise artificially colored; and whether it is composed of paws, bellies, scraps, or waste fur. Thus, rabbit cannot be passed off as "Baltic Lion," and sheared muskrat cannot be called "Hudson Seal"—not as long as the FTC's agents stay awake on the job.

Finally, the main purpose of the Textile Act is to reduce confusion that might be caused by the proliferation of manmade chemical fibers and their many trade names. The law requires labels revealing the *generic* names and percentages of all fibers that go into a fabric, except those that constitute less than 5% of the fabric. Thus Dacron, which is a trade name, must be identified as "polyester," its generic name. Over 700 other trade names must be identified as belonging to one of seventeen generic families specified by the FTC. These include—besides polyester—nylon, rayon, acetate, rubber, saran, acrylic, and spandex. To the extent consumers know the properties of these generic fibers in terms of washing, pressing, dying, and wearing them, the law helps. To the extent consumers do not know, it does not help.

Ingredient labeling regulations for food products has a shorter but more complicated history.[25] Since about 1972 the Food and Drug Administration (FDA) has vigorously expanded its activity in labeling so that detailed disclosures of composition are now required on the labels of most food products. The disclosures include:

1. Nutrition information, such as vitamins, minerals, caloric content, carbohydrate content, and protein.
2. Information on cholesterol, fat, and fatty acid composition.
3. Special information on foods intended for infants, nursing mothers, diabetics, the allergic, and the obese.
4. Defining natural and artificial flavors, spices, and colorings.

An example of the FDA's efforts pertinent to our earlier discussion is its attempt to get ingredient listings on all alcoholic beverages. Whether the FDA succeeds is at this writing uncertain. Many wineries oppose the measure on grounds that the fermentation process changes their ingredients over time. The FDA ruled therefore that if the regulation ever went into effect only the "starting" ingredients need to be revealed. Many brewers oppose it because they would then have to disclose the fact that their beer included more than just water, barley, malt, corn, and hops. They would also have to mention kelcoloid, which many though not all brewers use to fluff-up their foamy heads.[26]

Open Dating. Freshness is obviously an important aspect of the quality of perishable food products. For many years food manufacturers dated their products for inventory control and retailer rotation. Until recently, however, these dates were disguised by codes not known to the public. Open dating is simply uncoded dating. As of 1975, federal law did not require open dating, but 12 states had some form of dating regulation, and many grocery chains had voluntarily adopted it. One problem that remains to be resolved is uniformity. A confusing variety of dating methods have so far been used—"pull date," "packing date," "expiration date," and so on.

---

[25] L. E. Hicks, *Product Labeling and the Law* (New York, AMACOM Division of American Management Associations, 1974).

[26] "Protests foam up over labeling rules," *Business Week* (December 8, 1975), pp. 23–24.

Another form of open dating relates to autos. As of 1975, 37 states had entered the snake pit of used car sales by prohibiting odometer tampering. Thereafter, the federal government also stepped in with passage of the Motor Vehicle Information and Cost Savings Act. This law requires a written, true-mileage disclosure statement at the time of sale for all self-propelled vehicles except those that are over 24 years old or exceed 16,000 pounds. Moreover, the law prohibits disconnecting or resetting the odometer with intent to change the mileage reading or knowingly falsifying the written odometer statement.

Specific Performance Disclosures. Beginning with the 1977 models, all new cars sold in the United States have had labels disclosing the estimated number of miles they get per gallon of gas and an estimate of what yearly fuel cost would be if 15,000 miles were traveled per year. Thus, for example, the 1977 Volkswagen Rabbit Diesel, with a 90-cubic-inch engine, reportedly travels 44 miles per gallon and costs $188 in annual fuel expense. By contrast, the 1977 Dodge Royal Monaco with a 440-cubic-inch engine brandished a sticker saying that a standard year's travel in one of them would cost $886, since it averaged only 11 miles per gallon. The Federal Energy Act of 1975 requires these disclosures on the theory that they assist efficiency comparisons and in the hope that car buyers will react to these revelations by shying away from gas guzzlers. The Act also requires that efficiency ratings appear on major home appliances.

Another illustration of specific performance disclosure is gasoline octane posting, which has been with us in one form or another since 1973, but only haphazardly enforced. The Federal Trade Commission, which has been the most vigorous advocate of octane-posting; has argued that in the absence of octane-posting, motorists would waste more then $300 million a year by purchasing gasoline with higher octane than they really need. Most people seem to think that higher octane produces greater power. But this is not true. Octane indicates only the antiknock properties of gasoline. The major brand petroleum companies have persistently opposed octane-posting for fear that it would lead people to recognize that all brands of gasoline of a given octane rating were pretty much alike (which they are).[27]

Grade Rating. Disclosures of ingredients, freshness, dimensions, specific performance and the like may guide buyers toward ideal purchasing patterns. But how close to the ideal can these raw data take them? Several recent studies have demonstrated formally what most students already know from informal experience—namely, the information processing capabilities of the human mind are quite limited. Indeed, some evidence even suggests that beyond a

---

[27] See *Business Week* (May 31, 1976), p. 21 and F. C. Allvine and J. M. Patterson, *Competition Limited: The Marketing of Gasoline* (Bloomington, Ind.: Indiana University Press, 1972) pp. 24–25. It may be worth noting that the petroleum industry itself imposes extensive standards on its suppliers. According to the American Petroleum Institute: "All of our standards are written from the point of view of a consuming industry . . . . Our motive simply is to provide uniform performance requirements to the widest possible range of suppliers." Hemenway, *op. cit.*, p. 66.

certain point additional information merely confuses and frustrates consumers. Thereafter they no longer move toward their ideal decision, but rather *away* from it.[28] Thus grade rating is often recommended as a means of simplifying complex quality information into an ABC format.[29]

The most active federal agency in this respect is the U. S. Department of Agriculture, whose agents grade meat, eggs, butter, poultry, grain, fruits, and vegetables. Beef, for example, is graded "prime," "choice," "good," "standard," and so on. This grading is not compulsory. Hence, large brand-name meat packers like Armour, Swift, Morrell, and Wilson are given some elbow room to resist it. They prefer to promote the sale of beef under their own brand names whenever and wherever possible. Among the statistics that reflect resistance to grading, we find that during the 1950s only 27% of national packer beef was USDA graded, and all but one of the national brand-name packers advocated an end to federal grading. In contrast, the main supporters of the system are independent packers, retail food chains, independent retailers, and consumers. During 1955, for instance, 94% of all beef sold by retail food chains was USDA graded, and 85% of all chains surveyed said they favored compulsory grading or continuation of the present system. These and related data led W. F. Williams, E. K. Bowen, and F. C. Genovese to conclude that:

1. Grade standards have tended to intensify competition.
2. Unbranded packers and wholesalers increased in numbers and volume of meat processed, whereas branded packers declined greatly in number.
3. The system has tended to increase the accuracy, ease, and effectiveness of prices in reflecting value differences at each stage in the marketing system for beef by assisting consumers in the expression of their preferences.[30]

Perhaps the clearest demonstration of how grading can reduce a buyer's erroneous reliance on brand names is provided by Louis Bucklin in his study of auto tire grading.[31] He first asked a group of 40 consumers to study typical advertisements of four different tires—Firestone, Falcon, Goodyear, and

---

[28] J. Jacoby, D. E. Speller, and Carol A. Kohn, "Brand Choice Behavior as a Function of Information Load," *Journal of Marketing Research* (February 1974), pp. 63–69; and J. Jacoby, D. E. Speller, and C. K. Berning, "Brand Choice Behavior as a Function of Information Load: Replication and Extention," *Journal of Consumer Research* (June 1974), pp. 33–42.

[29] J. R. Bettman, "Issues in Designing Consumer Information Environments," *Journal of Consumer Research* (December 1975), pp. 169–77.

[30] Willard F. Williams, E. K. Bowen, and F. C. Genovese, *Economic Effects of U.S. Grades for Beef*, U.S. Department of Agriculture Marketing Research Report No. 298 (Washington D.C., 1959) pp. vii, 158–80.

[31] Louis P. Bucklin, "The Uniform Grading System for Tires: Its Effect upon Consumers and Industry Competition," *Antitrust Bulletin* (Winter 1974), pp. 783–801. For an argument and evidence that grading ought to be adopted for detergents, see Steven R. Cox, "Consumer Information and Competition in the Synthetic Detergent Industry," *Nebraska Journal of Economics and Business* (Summer 1976), pp. 41–58.

TABLE 5-6 Summary of United States Standardization and Disclosure Policies

Policy	Enforcement Agencies*	Products Covered
A. Standardization		
1. Fair Packaging and Labeling Act (1966)	FTC, FDA	Grocery store items, e.g., foods and detergents
2. Size uniformity and simplification	Various state authorities	Bread, margarine, flour, dairy products
3. Unit pricing	Various state authorities	Grocery store items
4. Truth in Lending Act (1969)	FTC, FRB	Consumer credit
B. Quality Disclosures		
1. Ingredient labeling:		
Wool Products Labeling Act (1939)	FTC	Wool products
Fur Product Labeling Act (1951)	FTC	Furs
Textile Fiber Identification Act (1958)	FTC	Textiles, apparel, etc.
Food, Drug and Cosmetic Act	FDA	Food products
2. Open dating of perishables	Various state authorities	Grocery perishables
3. Antitampering Odometer Law (1972)	NHTSA	Cars and trucks
4. Performance disclosures:		
Fuel efficiency	FEA	Autos, appliances
Octane rating	FTC, FEA	Gasoline
Tar and nicotine	FTC	Cigarettes
On time performance	ICC	Moving van services
5. Grade rating	USDA	Meat, eggs, butter, etc.
	NHTSA	Tires

* Key: FTC—Federal Trade Commission; FDA—Food and Drug Administration; FRB—Federal Reserve Board of Governors; NHTSA—National Highway Traffic Safety Administration; FEA—Federal Energy Administration; ICC—Interstate Commerce Commission; USDA—U.S. Department of Agriculture.

Cambridge. Next, after telling them that the depicted Firestone tire was priced at $25, he asked them how much they would be willing to pay for the other three tires. Since the advertisements made the tires seem quite similar in terms of fiberglass belting, number of plies, and so forth, these consumers gave dollar values that were, on average, close to $25—that is, Goodyear $26.60, Falcon $24.60, and Cambridge $22.40. Note, however, that these last two, less-heavily advertised, local brands were discounted to prices below $25.

To test the effect of grading, Bucklin then went through the same steps with another group of 40 consumers, but he added to each advertisement a three-part grade designation for treadwear durability, traction, and high-speed performance. An explanation of the grading system was also provided. This time the amounts the consumers said they would be willing to pay were dramatically different—Goodyear $39.60, Falcon $35.40, and Cambridge $54.00. This enormous shift of the little-known Cambridge brand from the lowest valued tire to the highest valued led Bucklin to observe: "Distributor and local brands have traditionally sold at prices below those of the major brands. It is possible that quality differentials have caused some of this, but much may be attributed to the promotional position of these major products." In the future this promotional edge may carry less weight because the National Highway Traffic Safety Administration has developed a grading system that should be operating by the time this book is printed.

Summary

Most folks cannot taste any difference between different brands of beer, and computers are bought by expert buyers. Nevertheless, our case studies disclose substantial product differentiation in both industries. This does not necessarily mean that in these instances (and others like them) buyers are irrational. They may merely be uniformed or misinformed. And they may rely heavily on trademarks to guide their purchasing decisions, since in a roundabout way trademarks may often help buyers avoid errors of commission or omission. On the other hand, too heavy a reliance on trademarks and the advertising promoting them may *cause* errors of commission or omission, in which case the owners of prominent trademarks gain at the expense of buyers.

Corrective policies have to focus on one or both of the following objectives: (1) Permit trademarks to identify quality, but remove the rights of ownership exclusivity and perpetuity that presently prevail. (2) Establish quality identifications independent of the trademark system. The first objective apparently lies outside the realm of political possibility. The second has been furthered by two broad classes of policies—standardization (which includes simplified quantity labeling, uniform sizes, and unit pricing) and quality disclosures (which include ingredient labeling, open dating, performance disclosure, and grade rating). These are outlined in Table 5-6.

Evidence that these measures lessen consumer reliance on trademarks for cues to quality, invigorate price competition, and build closer correspondence between price and quality is provided by the meat packing industry, where grade rating has been applied for decades.

Finally, it may be worth noting that sellers in some markets have *voluntarily* adopted quality-rating practices such as these. In almost every instance of voluntary seller adoption, however, the buyers involved were not household consumers. They were business or government buyers powerful enough to "persuade" their suppliers that these practices were desirable (even necessary).

6

Concentration and Number of Firms: Theory and Cross-Section Evidence

Seller concentration has for a long time received more attention from economists and those concerned with public policy towards industry than any other single characteristic of industrial structure.

DOUGLAS NEEDHAM

Two questions haunt the minds of humans, especially when reading report cards or opening presents:

1. Do I get what I deserve?
2. Do I deserve what I get?

The answers are limited to five possible combinations, each of which is sketched in Figure 6-1. If the answer to both questions is "no," then getting and deserving do not coincide at all, as indicated by the two separate circles at the top of Figure 6-1. Moving to the middle tier, we see that if it is a "yes-no" combination for questions 1 and 2, respectively, we tend to get more than we deserve. Conversely, a "no-yes" combination implies that we deserve more than we get. In an ideal world we would always get what we deserve and deserve what we get, yielding "yes" answers to both questions. Finally, and more realistically, the most accurate answers for most of us are probably "sometimes" and "sometimes," as depicted by the partially overlapping circles in the southeast corner of Figure 6-1.

Of course these questions apply to more than just grades and gifts. On a personal level they may apply to any number of important things—social

109

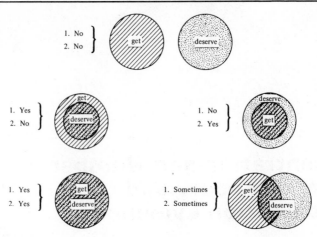

Figure 6-1. Possible answers to the questions: 1. Do I get what I deserve? 2. Do I deserve what I get?

status, vacation time, love, whatever. In the present context, we shall be exploring a series of similar questions important to industrial organization. To measure the presence of market power for any particular market, we can get an estimate of the number of firms, the Gini coefficient, or the concentration ratio. But, which one of these statistics best depicts the population and size distribution of firms in relation to sellers' power over price? Given an answer to this question, how do we define the relevant market to include all the firms that deserve to be included and to exclude all the firms that deserve to be excluded from our statistical calculations? Are Coca-Cola and Pabst in the same market, for instance?

Turning to the issue of what *causes* a given number and size distribution of firms, we ask whether firms get the market shares they deserve. Do General Motors, Ford, and Chrysler, for example, deserve, by their efficiency and quality of product, to account for 83% of all cars sold in the U.S.? Or, did they attain their dominant position merely by acquiring former competitors and hiding behind tariff barriers that inhibited imports? Finally, the federal government has by *policy* broken up large companies, such as Standard Oil of New Jersey (now Exxon) and prohibited numerous attempts at merger, such as Brown Shoe with Kinney, and Clorox with Procter & Gamble. Did these firms deserve what they got? Did they get what they deserved?

These questions highlight the issues taken up in this and the next three chapters. In this chapter, we first discuss various statistical measures of the number and size distribution of firms. Next we review the historic and present conditions of market concentration in the United States and abroad. We then consider the causes of those conditions. Finally, we shall move from individual markets to the economy as a whole and consider aggregate concentration.

11

Statistical Measures

Several statistical measures of structural power have been devised. Which of these is used in any given instance depends on data availabilities and the immediate purpose. A good measure is one that is easy to calculate, sensitive to major structural changes over time, and indicative of differences in structural power across diverse markets and firms. Above all, *an effective measure must provide fairly accurate predictions of market conduct and performance*; otherwise, it is useless. For this reason, considerations of conduct and performance necessarily intrude in our current discussion. References to a measure's potential weaknesses are most often couched in terms of that measure's lack of predictive force. Still, we shall not lose sight of our present focus, which is primarily structural.

The Number of Firms

The most obvious structural measure of market power is the number of sellers. As outlined earlier (in Chapter 1), pure competition and monopolistic competition each require a large number of sellers. Monopoly entails just one seller. In between, oligopoly is characterized by the presence of only a "few" sellers.

In terms of ease of computation and sensitivity to changes over time, this measure has certain advantages. Moreover, the number of sellers is likely to influence behavior because numbers may influence each firm's *expectations regarding the behavior of its rivals*. This influence is most clearly seen in extreme cases. By definition, a firm blessed with monopoly has no rivals, so it may operate in an isolated, independent fashion. At the other extreme, a purely competitive firm has so many rivals that it also acts independently. It can safely assume that its action will not affect the price or production policies of its multitudinous competitors.

Between these extremes, where "few" could mean anything from 2 to 52, numbers retain their relevance; however, their predictive capabilities are reduced. As Douglas Needham explains: "The extent to which the behavior of one firm will influence other firms noticeably may well be related to the number of firms in the market. The smaller the number of sellers, for example, the larger, on average, will be the fractions of a particular market supplied by individual sellers, and any given percentage gain in sales by one seller at the expense of the others results in a more noticeable loss to each of the others and is more likely to invite retaliation. There is, however, no single number of sellers which will in all circumstances distinguish oligopoly market situations from market situations characterized by behavior which is heedless of rival's reactions."[1]

[1] Douglas Needham, *Economic Analysis and Industrial Structure* (New York: Holt, Rinehart and Winston, Inc., 1969), p. 84.

111

TABLE 6-1   Cumulated Percentages for Sample Lorenz Curve

Firm	Sales (%)	Sales Cumulated From Smallest Firm (%)	Number of Firms Cumulated (%)
A	5	5	25
B	10	15	50
C	15	30	75
D	70	100	100

In short, the number of firms is positively correlated with "the fractions of a particular market supplied by individual sellers." But since these fractions, or divisions, probably influence behavior more directly than mere numbers, it may be better to rely on a measure that actually involves these fractions. Indeed, markets are often comprised of a "central core" of a few very large firms and a behaviorally inconsequential "fringe" of many small firms. In these instances a raw tally of total numbers may give a false impression of competitive dispersion. A case in point is the computer industry, which has been called "Snow White and the Seven Dwarfs" because IBM's 70% share dwarfs its seven rivals.

The Lorenz Curve and Gini Coefficient

Two measures of fractions are the Lorenz curve and its companion statistic, the Gini coefficient. The absolute number of firms is almost completely suppressed by these measures because they reflect *inequality*, or *relative concentration*, more than anything else.

This may be illustrated with a good example developed by Eugene Singer. Imagine, if you will, four firms in a market with the following percentage shares of market sales (or some other indicator of size, such as assets or employees): firm A, 5%; firm B, 10%; firm C, 15%; and firm D, 70%. The key computations that generate the **Lorenz curve** are (1) the per cent of market sales cumulated from the smallest sized firm, and (2) the per cent of the number of firms, cumulated again from the smallest sized firm to the largest. These computations are shown in Table 6-1. Thus, beginning with A, which is the smallest, 25% of all the firms account for 5% of market sales; 50% of the firms (A plus B) account for 15% of the sales; and so forth. The resulting Lorenz curve is shown in Figure 6-2 as $RWVUS$. With the per cent of total market sales on the vertical axis, and the per cent of the number of firms on the horizontal axis, both axes are limited to maximum values of 100%. Hence Figure 6-2 forms a square. Inside the square, curve $RWVUS$ traces the paired values of the third and fourth columns of Table 6-1, beginning with the smallest firm, closest to the origin.

[2] Eugene M. Singer, *Antitrust Economics* (Englewood Cliffs, N. J.: Prentice Hall, 1968), p. 14

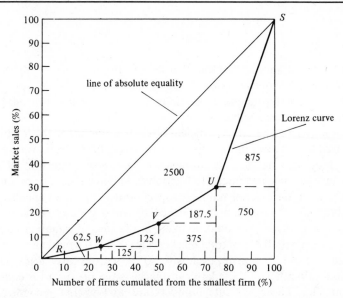

Figure 6-2. *The Lorenz curve and the Gini coefficient of inequality.*

This Lorenz curve may be compared to the straight diagonal line, *RS*, which bisects the square. If each of the four firms had 25% of market sales, the Lorenz curve would match this diagonal line; then 25% of the firms would have 25% of the sales; 50% would have 50%, and so on. Thus, the diagonal indicates an **equal size distribution**. And the more *un*equal the distribution of sales, the greater the divergence between the Lorenz curve and the diagonal. With extreme inequality of shares, the Lorenz curve would look more like a half-open jacknife than the quarter-moon shaped curve of Figure 6-2.

The area between the diagonal and the Lorenz curve, which in the present example equals 2500 percentage points, is often called the **area of concentration**. The **Gini coefficient** summarizes the degree of inequality, since this statistic is the ratio of the area of concentration to the total area under the diagonal. The total area under the diagonal is always 5000, because $\frac{1}{2} \times (100 \times 100) = 5000$. As for the area of concentration, one must add up the areas of the dashed lined triangles and rectangles lying beneath the Lorenz curve, and then subtract the result from 5000. Thus, in our present example:

1. Sum of areas under the Lorenz curve:

$$62.5 + 125 + 125 + 375 + 187.5 + 750 + 875 = 2500$$

2. Area of concentration:

$$5000 - 2500 = 2500$$

113

3. Gini coefficient:

$$2500/5000 = 0.50$$

More generally, it should be clear that, as the Lorenz curve approaches the diagonal, the area of concentration shrinks and the Gini coefficient approaches 0 Conversely, as greater inequality expands the area of concentration, the Gini coefficient approaches a value of 1.

The Lorenz curve and Gini coefficient obviously emphasize the fractions that were ignored by the raw number-of-firms measure. Therefore, they have appeal however, they also have many drawbacks. The most important of these is that they give *too much* emphasis to fractions and percentages, so much, in fact that they neglect the absolute numbers aspect of structure to an uncalled for and undesirable degree.[3] For example, a Gini coefficient of 0 may give the impression of intense competition, as would be likely in the case of a market comprising 1000 firms, each with 0.1 % of total market sales. Yet, a 0 would also derive from the presence of only two firms, each with 50 %; or from three firms, each with $33\frac{1}{3}$ %. And, in neither of these latter instances is the prospect for competition very promising. These absolute numbers are so low that recognized inter dependence could very well lead to behavior approaching that of monopoly Similarly, a decline in the number of sellers in a market could be associated with a *decline* in the Gini coefficient, since it would leave the remaining firms more equal in size if the departing firms were all quite small.[4] The opposite could hold for increases in firm numbers. As a result, changes in structure over time would not be depicted properly. Finally, another drawback of these measures is the large amount of data required for computation. Information on the market share of every firm in the market must be gathered before these statistics can be constructed, something which is often impossible or costly.

The Concentration Ratio

The **concentration ratio** combines absolute numbers *and* fractions. It is the per cent of market sales (or some other measure of size, such as assets, employ ment, or value added) accounted for by an absolute number of the largest firms in the market—for example, the 4 or 8 or 20 largest firms. Because the concentra tion ratio involves both an absolute number of firms and their size distribution and because it is also fairly easily constructed, it has become the most readily available and most widely used of all measures of structural power.

Figure 6-3 illustrates two concentration curves and the concentration ratios they generate. The vertical axis is exactly the same as that for the Lorenz curve of Figure 6-2—that is, per cent of total market sales. Its horizontal axis, however

[3] M. A. Adelman, "The Measurement of Industrial Concentration," *Review of Economics and Statistics* (November 1951), pp. 269–96.

[4] J. M. Blair, "Statistical Measures of Concentration in Business: Problems of Compiling an Interpretation," *Bulletin of the Oxford University Institute of Statistics* (November 1956), p. 356.

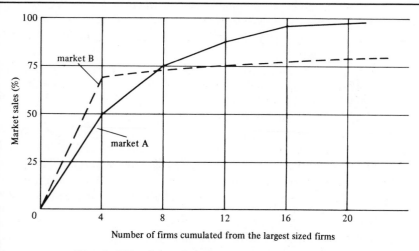

Figure 6-3. *Concentration curves for two markets.*

s scaled in terms of the absolute number of firms instead of the per cent of number of firms. Another difference here is that the firms of Figure 6-3 are not cumulated from the smallest first. Instead, cumulation begins with the largest firm at the origin. Thus, the *height* of the curve above a given number of firms is the concentration ratio associated with that number. It is the percentage of total market sales accounted for by a given number of leading firms. Thus the four-firm concentration ratio for market A is 50. And the eight-firm concentration ratio for market A is 75.

Among the many virtues of the concentration ratio, two deserve special mention. First, it is the combination of firm numbers *and* size distribution rather than one or the other alone that is most closely connected with behavior. To quote Gideon Rosenbluth, "Economic theory suggests that concentration as defined here is an important determinant of market behavior and market results."[5] Second, concentration ratios are fairly precise and easily understood indexes of market power. As we shall see in the next chapter, they appear in the courtrooms of statistically untrained judges almost as often as they appear in the writings of sophisticated scholars.

This is not to say that the concentration ratio is perfect. Nothing is. Of its many faults, the following three must be counted important:

1. Unlike the Lorenz curve, the concentration ratio describes only one slice of the market's size distribution of firms. It does not summarize conditions for all firms, only those for the top four or top eight or such.

[5] Gideon Rosenbluth, "Measures of Concentration," in *Business Concentration and Price Policy*, edited by G. J. Stigler (Princeton, N. J.: Princeton University Press, 1955), p. 57.

The resulting potential ambiguity is illustrated in Figure 6-3, where market B is more concentrated than market A at the four-firm level, whereas, conversely, market A is more concentrated than market B at the 12-firm level.

2. Even if we settle on one given number of firms as being the best of all possible slices, the concentration ratio provides no information about the size distribution of firms within that slice. Thus in Figure 6-3 we are ignorant of the size distribution of firms 1, 2, 3, and 4.

3. The concentration ratio does not reflect upon other aspects of structure that might be important to behavior, other aspects such as *turnover* (changes in the ranking of given firms) and the condition of entry. Other measures have this failing, too, and turnover and concentration are correlated, but this fact does not wholly alleviate the problem.

Many scholars have tried to invent a summary index that would rectify thes problems.[6] Unfortunately, they have had about the same success they woul have had looking for an honest politician. Some progress has been made, b no index has turned up whose combined purity and convenience exceeds tha of the concentration ratio. In the interests of science, we shall briefly review on of the more promising and interesting of these substitute indexes before re turning to a more detailed discussion of concentration ratios.

The Herfindahl Index. This summary index is the sum of the squares of th sizes of firms in a market, in which sizes are expressed as a proportion of tot market sales (or assets, or employment).[7] In mathematical notation:

$$\text{Herfindahl index} = \sum \left(\frac{X_i}{T} \right)^2 \qquad (i = 1, 2, 3, \ldots, n)$$

where T represents total market sales, X_i represents the sales of individual fir i, and n is the number of firms in the market. In terms of our earlier example four firms with 5, 10, 15, and 70 % of total market sales:

$$\text{Herfindahl index} = (0.05)^2 + (0.10)^2 + (0.15)^2 + (0.70)^2 = 0.525$$

[6] For clever examples see Janos Horvath, "Suggestion for a Comprehensive Measure of Co centration," *Southern Economic Journal* (April 1970), pp. 446–52; Ann Horowitz and Ira Horowi "Entropy, Markov Processes and Competition in the Brewing Industry," *Journal of Industr Economics* (July 1968), pp. 196–211; Irwin Bernhardt and Kenneth D. Mackenzie, "Measuri Seller Unconcentration, Segmentation, and Product Differentiation," *Western Economic Journ* (December 1968), pp. 395–403; J. L. Hexter and John W. Snow, "Mergers, Asymmetry and An trust," *Antitrust Bulletin* (Summer 1974), pp. 401–19.

[7] O. C. Herfindahl, *Concentration in The Steel Industry*, Ph.D. dissertation (New York: C umbia University, 1950).

Under pure competition the index would equal 0. Under monopoly it would equal 1. These extremes are perhaps most readily seen by the fact that, if all firms in the market were of equal size, the Herfindahl index would equal $1/n$, which is the inverse of the total number of firms. With n equal to 1, this ratio also equals 1. As the value of n increases, this ratio collapses toward 0.

Because the Herfindahl index appropriately registers the impact of absolute numbers as well as size inequality, and because the index takes account of all firms in the market simultaneously, it is held in high regard. Even so, it is not widely used because it has one major drawback—its computation requires comprehensive market share data which, as we already pointed out, are terribly scarce.

The Importance of Proper Market Definition

To this point we have tossed the word "market" around offhandedly. But "market" deserves the same careful handling we would give a stink bomb. This warning applies regardless of whether one is using raw numbers, the Gini coefficient, the concentration ratio, or the Herfindahl index because market definition determines the total scope of activity against which shares and numbers are computed. Indeed, the predictive accuracy of one's structural measure may depend more heavily on the proper choice of market definitions than on the proper choice of statistical index. All the indexes considered previously correlate well with each other. The rank correlation coefficient between the three-firm sales concentration ratio and the Herfindahl index, for example, was found by Gideon Rosenbluth to be $+0.98$ for 96 Canadian manufacturing markets.[8] Similar results have turned up in other studies of alternative statistical forms.[9] Thus, if a market has a high four-firm concentration ratio, it will probably also have a high Herfindahl index, a high Gini coefficient, a high eight-firm concentration ratio, a high 20-firm concentration ratio, and a small number of firms. The same could be said of the choice between sales, assets, employment, value added, and most other units of quantity used for measuring size. Concentration ratios based on these various units of measure are all highly correlated.[10] For this reason we shall ignore the debate over alternative units of measure. Broadly speaking, the most commonly used size variable is sales (also referred to as value of shipments).

[8] Rosenbluth, *op. cit.*, p. 69.

[9] R. W. Kilpatrick, "The Choice Among Alternative Measures of Industrial Concentration," *Review of Economics and Statistics* (May 1967), pp. 258–60; Christian Marfels, "A Bird's Eye View Measures of Concentration," *Antitrust Bulletin* (Fall 1975), pp. 485–501.

[10] Rosenbluth, *op. cit.*, pp. 89–92; and John Blair, testimony, *Economic Concentration*, Part 5, Hearings before the Subcommittee on Antitrust and Monopoly of the Committee on the Judiciary, U.S. Senate (1966), pp. 1894–902.

The problem of market definition centers on the following questions:

1. Does the "market" include those firms that deserve to be in it? That is, *does it include all firms that compete with each other?*
2. Does the "market" exclude those firms that deserve to be out of it? That is, *does it exclude noncompeting firms?*

If a definition fails to include deserving firms, the definition is said to be **too narrow**, and the concentration ratio will usually be biased upward. If on the other hand, it fails to exclude *non*deserving firms, then it is said to be **too broad**, and the concentration ratio will tend to be biased downward. In the case of either error, the concentration ratio will not predict behavior or performance very well.

This problem of defining the market so as to include competitors while excluding noncompetitors may be further broken into two parts: product delineation and geographic scope.

Product delineation may be illustrated by taking a look at the procedures by which the U. S. Bureau of the Census computes concentration ratios in manufacturing industries. These computations are based on definitions in the federal government's Standard Industrial Classification Code, abbreviated SIC. The SIC refers to markets as industries, and it delineates market breadth with a system of numerical codes. At the broadest level are twenty separate two-digit *major industry groups,* such as "Food and kindred products" (20), "Textile mill products" (22), "Primary metal products" (34), and "Transportation equipment" (37). In turn, each of these two-digit definitions is broken down into narrower three-digit *industry groups,* which are themselves subdivided into still narrower four-digit *industries,* and so on down to the very narrow seven-digit *product.* This progressive subdivision is illustrated in Table 6-2, which displays parts of SIC major industry 20. The sales activities of each firm must be assigned to the different major industry groups, industries, products, and so on. Few firms confine their operations to just one product, or even one industry. Once sales activities are assigned, total sales are computed for each digited market. Firm shares follow. Concentration ratios are then computed, but only a

TABLE 6-2 Examples Taken from the SIC System

SIC Code	Number of Digits	Designation	Name
20	2	Major industry group	Food and kindred products
203	3	Industry group	Canning, preserving
2037	4	Product group or industry	Frozen fruits and vegetables
20371	5	Product class	Frozen fruits, juices, and aid
2037135	7	Product	Frozen strawberries

TABLE 6-3   1972 Concentration Ratios for Selected Industries

SIC Code	Name	Four-Firm Ratio	Eight-Firm Ratio
37111	Passenger cars (five-digit)	99+	100
2043	Cereal breakfast foods	90	98
3633	Household laundry equipment	83	98
3334	Primary aluminum	79	92
3724	Aircraft engines	74	83
3411	Metal cans	66	79
2841	Soap and other detergents	62	74
2062	Cane sugar refining	59	85
3221	Glass containers	55	76
3613	Motors and generators	47	59
3312	Blast furnaces and steel mills	45	65
2522	Metal office furniture	42	54
3143	Men's footwear, except athletic	34	51
2211	Weaving mills, cotton	31	48
2631	Paperboard mills	29	44
3533	Oilfield machinery	28	42
2834	Pharmaceutical preparations	26	44
2272	Tufted carpets and rugs	20	33
2421	Sawmills and planing mills	18	23
3544	Special dies, tools, jigs	7	10

Source: U. S. Bureau of the Census, *Census of Manufactures, 1972, Concentration Ratios in Manufacturing,* MC72 (SR)-2, Washington, D.C., 1975.

the four- and five-digit level. Since there are approximately 430 four-digit industries and 1000 five-digit product classes, we can present no more than a small sample of 1972 Census concentration ratios in Table 6-3.

Most research has used ratios for SIC four-digit industries, since they generally represent definitions of about the right amount of detail. Still, the SIC system was not designed primarily for the computation of concentration ratios. The SIC definitions give heavy weight to similarity of production processes (or producer's substitutability) as well as to similarity of product uses (or consumer's substitutability). Although the ideal definition of a market ought to take account of substitution possibilities in *both* production and consumption, the SIC's heavy emphasis on the former yields many four-digit industries that may be considered too broad or too narrow.

Cane sugar refining, 2062, for example, is too narrow because it excludes beet sugar refining (see Table 6-3). Conversely, pharmaceutical preparations, 2834, is too broad because it includes a wide variety of drugs that are not close

TABLE 6-4   National Versus Regional and Local Markets

SIC Code	Name	National Four-Firm Ratio	Average Regional or Local Four-Firm Ratio
	Regional Market Products		
2095	Roasted coffee	52	71
2791	Typesetting	6	19
2911	Petroleum refining	34	52
3241	Cement, hydraulic	29	55
3446	Architectural metal work	13	37
	Local Market Products		
2024	Ice cream	37	70
2026	Fluid milk	23	57
2051	Bread and related items	23	47
2711	Newspapers	15	73
3251	Brick and structural tile	12	87
3273	Concrete	4	52

Source: David Schwartzman and Joan Bodoff, "Concentration in Regional and Local Industries," *Southern Economic Journal* (January 1971), pp. 343–48.

substitutes from the patient's point of view. In Table 6-3 this industry has a four-firm concentration ratio of 26%, but in narrower therapeutic groups we find four-firm ratios such as: anesthetics, 69; antiarthritics, 95; antispasmodics 59; cardiovascular hypotensives, 79; diabetic therapy, 93; diuretics, 64; and sulfonamides, 79.[11] This discrepancy between broad and narrow definitions in drugs arises because a few firms tend to dominate each therapeutic group but the same firms do not dominate *all* therapeutic groups. When all therapeutic groups are lumped together, the fraction of the "total" business accounted for by any one firm then shrinks.

Another source of error is the exclusion of all imports and exports from Census computations.[12] In particular, significant imports will leave the Census ratio biased upward. The four-firm ratio for passenger cars, for instance, is said to be 99+ in Table 6-3 because there are essentially only four United States producers—General Motors, Ford, Chrysler, and AMC. But in 1976 imports accounted for 17% of all cars sold in the United States. Hence, a more accurate four-firm ratio for that year would be 83%.

[11] John Vernon, "Concentration, Promotion and Market Share Stability in the Pharmaceutical Industry," *Journal of Industrial Economics* (July 1971), pp. 246–66.
[12] Werner Sichel, "The Foreign Competition Omission in Census Concentration Ratios: A Empirical Evaluation," *Antitrust Bulletin* (Spring 1975), pp. 89–105.

To illustrate the problem of **geographic scope**, we may mention the high transportation costs that prevent petroleum refiners on the east coast from competing with those on the west coast. Refiners do not always operate in more than one region, or all regions. Standard Oil of California, for example, accounts for 16.3% of gasoline sales in Pacific coast states, but 0% in New England and South Atlantic states. The four-firm *national* concentration ratio of 34 in 1973 thus falls below most of the more relevant four-firm *regional* ratios. Sampling a few of these, we see: New England, 41.4; Mid-Atlantic, 41.6; South Atlantic, 37.9; West North Central, 34.2; and Pacific, 51.5.[13] Other products experiencing high transportation costs or easy perishability are listed in Table 6-4. In every case the nationwide concentration ratio understates concentration as it is viewed at the more relevant regional or local level. We shall return to this matter of market definition in the next chapter when discussing merger policy.

Market Concentration Patterns and Trends

Lest this chapter degenerate into a drab parade of procedural issues, we ought now to get down to brass tacks. Just how much concentration is there anyway? And what, if anything, has been the trend over time? A generalized answer to these questions includes the following observations.

Manufacturing

In manufacturing, it appears that oligopoly and, to a lesser extent, monopolistic competition predominate. After subjectively adjusting raw 1966 Census four-firm concentration ratios for the various biases surveyed previously (both positive and negative), William Shepherd found that the weighted average concentration ratio for relevant manufacturing markets was 60.3% (see Figure 6-4). He also concluded that three fifths of all manufacturing activity takes place in markets where four-firm concentration exceeds 50%. Moreover, although extreme cases of high concentration in the 90–100% range were relatively rare, occurring only 17% of the time, extremely low concentration in the 0–10% range was even rarer.[14] Compared with raw, unadjusted Census data, which yield a weighted average ratio of just 39% in 1966 (see Figure 6-4 again), these adjusted data obviously depict a predominance of oligopoly for manufacturing.

---

[13] Thomas D. Duchesneau, *Competition in the U. S. Energy Industry* (Cambridge Mass.: Ballinger Publishing Co., 1975), pp. 46–47.

[14] William G. Shepherd, *Market Power and Economic Welfare* (New York: Random House, 1970), pp. 106–07. See also Carl Kaysen and Donald F. Turner, *Antitrust Policy* (Cambridge, Mass.: Harvard University Press, 1965), pp. 26–33, for similar but earlier data and conclusions.

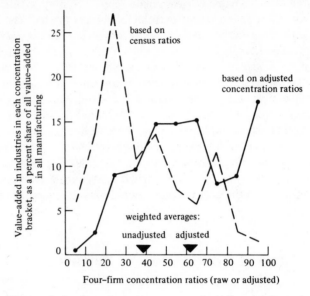

Figure 6-4. *Concentration patterns in U.S. manufacturing.*

As regards the *trend* in manufacturing markets, there seems to be relativel[y] little change in weighted average concentration over the last three decade[s] Although estimates of trend are hampered by intermittent changes in the SI[C] system (changes that abolish some industry codes, merge others, and create ne[w] ones), weighted average concentration ratios have been computed for 16[6] comparable industries over the 1947–1970 period, and for 292 comparabl[e] Census industries over the 1958–1970 period. Among the 166 most enduringl[y] defined industries, average four-firm concentration (unadjusted for breadth o[f] definition) rose slightly from 40.5% in 1947 to 42.6% in 1970. Similarly, amon[g] the 292 industries available for the shorter period, average four-firm concentra[-] tion sneaked up to 41.5% in 1970 from 40.9% in 1958.[15]

Over the still longer haul, starting way, way back in the late 1800s, the problem[s] of estimation are even more serious. Ancient data are both sketchy and un[-] reliable. It appears, however, that enormous increases in market concentratio[n] occurred between 1895 and 1902 as a result of a massive wave of mergers ([a] wave that will be discussed in detail later). Then between 1909 and onset of th[e] current age of relative stability in 1947, the pattern is obscured. Some scholar[s] believe, on the one hand, that market concentration declined or stayed th[e]

---

[15] Willard F. Mueller and Larry G. Hamm, "Trends in Industrial Market Concentratio[n] 1947 to 1970," *Review of Economics and Statistics* (November 1974), p. 512. See also J. Fred Westo[n] and Stanley I. Ornstein, *The Impact of Large Firms on the U.S. Economy* (Lexington, Mass.: D. [C.] Heath & Co., 1973), p. 12. Without restricting their sample to industries of constant SIC definitio[n] they find average concentration in manufacturing to have been 33.8 in 1947 and 34.2 in 1967.

same over the first half of this century.[16] On the other hand, in the most recent study of long-term trends in manufacturing, Alfred Chandler, Jr., determined that "The percentage of total product value produced by the oligopolists rose from 16% in 1909 to 21% in 1929, and then jumped to 28% at the end of the depression in 1939. Since World War II the figure has remained stable, being 26% in 1947, 25% in 1958, and then up to 27% in 1963."[17] "Oligopoly" in this case is defined as an industry "in which six or fewer firms contributed 50%, or twelve or fewer contributed 75% of the total product value."

Note that differences of opinion can crop up from any number of causes—for example, differing sources of concentration change, such as oligopoly industries getting bigger or big industries getting more oligopolistic. In any event, whatever changes did, in fact, occur over the 1909–1947 period, they were apparently not earthshaking enough to knock you off your chair. In sum, manufacturing market concentration is currently rather high, and it has been that way for some time. Other sectors of the economy have been measured and studied less intensively than manufacturing, primarily because the Census Bureau does not publish concentration ratios for nonmanufacturing industries. Nevertheless, nonmanufacturing industries are of interest. They account for approximately 70% of our gross national product, so they are obviously crucial to the economy.

Atomistic Industries

Speaking broadly, and beginning at the competitive end of the spectrum, we may note first that, in the United States, market structures are *unconcentrated* and even atomistic in *agriculture, forestry, fisheries, contract construction*, and *services* (all of which together account for about 20% of national income). In the services sector, for instance, it has been very roughly estimated that, on average, local market four-firm concentration for hotel services is 8%; laundries, 13%; eating and drinking establishments, 8%; and automobile repair service establishments, 12%.[18] Of course, these are just generalizations, and they mask pockets of moderately high concentration in certain localities and in certain unusual lines of product or service (such as farming chinese vegetables, repairing lawn mowers, or servicing cryogenic caskets). Moreover, these generalizations are somewhat misleading in their implication of vigorous rivalry. In many of these fields there is strong product differentiation (as in medical services), official government intervention inhibiting competition (as in agriculture), government ownership of substantial shares of the business or resource (as in forestry), and institutional constraints on competition of various kinds (like union organization of barbers and codes of "ethics" for dentists).

---

[16] G. Warren Nutter, *The Extent of Enterprise Monopoly in the United States: 1899–1939* (Chicago: University of Chicago Press, 1951), and M. A. Adelman, *op. cit.*

[17] Alfred D. Chandler, Jr., "The Structure of American Industry in the Twentieth Century: A Historical Overview," *Business History Review* (Autumn 1969), p. 257.

[18] Kenneth D. Boyer, "Informative and Goodwill Advertising," *Review of Economics and Statistics* (November 1974), p. 547. The estimates are for 1963.

TABLE 6-5   Selected Estimates of Local Market Concentration in United States Retailing—Early 1960's

Retail Group	Four-Firm Concentration Ratio (%)
Grocery stores (SMSA average)	50.1
Atlanta, Georgia	60.5
Cincinnati, Ohio	49.0
Houston, Texas	35.1
Madison, Wisconsin	40.6
Portland, Oregon	35.3
San Diego, California	52.5
Washington, D. C.	67.3
Department stores	34.0
Variety stores	55.0
Hardware stores	25.0
Furniture stores	25.0
Drug stores	39.0
Apparel and accessory stores	10.0

Sources: Grocery retailing: Federal Trade Commission, *Economic Report on the Structure and Competitive Behavior of Food Retailing* (Washington, D.C., 1966), pp. 366–72. Other observations: Kenneth D. Boyer, "Informative and Goodwill Advertising," *Review of Economics and Statistics* (November 1974), p. 547.

The Retail Trade

Retail trade also displays many atomistic features, but its oligopolistic tendencies are much more evident than in the sectors just mentioned. In a nationwide definition of the market, four large retail grocery chains (including A & P and Safeway) account for about 19% of total grocery sales, whereas four huge general merchandising chains (including Sears and Penneys) have a 17% merchandising-market share.[19] Both statistics are fairly low but deceptive. A switch to more relevant local market definitions reveals generally higher concentration ratios and a degree of local diversity that is sufficient to include many instances of tight-knit local oligopoly. In 1963, for instance, grocery retailing concentration at the local level ranged from 23.5% for four firms in Fresno, California, to 75.6% in Great Falls, Montana. Of the 216 cities with ratios between these bounds, a few are mentioned in Table 6-5.

Table 6-5 also contains selected estimates of local four-firm concentration—that is, multicity *averages* thereof—for grocery stores, department stores, and

[19] Leonard W. Weiss, *Case Studies in American Industry* (New York, John Wiley & Sons, 1971) p. 220.

TABLE 6-6   National United States Four-Firm Concentration Ratios for Major Fuels and Combined Energy Mining, 1955 and 1970

Industry	Top Four Firms 1955	Top Four Firms 1970	Top Eight Firms 1955	Top Eight Firms 1970
Crude oil	21.2	31.0	35.9	49.1
Natural Gas	18.6	24.4	30.4	39.1
Coal	17.8	30.7	25.4	41.2
Uranium	77.9	55.3	99.1	80.0
Energy ($)	16.1	23.4	27.2	37.8

Note: Natural gas production includes United States and Canada. Uranium concentration is measured at the milling stage.

Source: Joseph Mulholland and Douglas Webbink, *Economic Report on Concentration Levels and Trends in the Energy Sector of the U. S. Economy* (Washington, D. C.: Federal Trade Commission, 1974), p. 148.

several other kinds of retailing. Hence, average local concentration among grocery stores was 50.1% in 1963. The other averages in the table indicate a lower level of concentration in every other branch of retail trade except variety stores, which averaged 55% in 1963. One's overall impression of retailing thus hovers between monopolistic competition and loose-knit oligopoly. On top of this, there are signs that concentration in this sector is on the rise.

Mining

Mining brings us another mixed bag. In the life-and-death area of energy mining—which deserves a table all its own and gets it, Table 6-6—we find only moderate levels of concentration on a national market basis. The four-firm ratios for crude oil production, natural gas extraction, and coal mining were 31.0, 24.4, and 30.7% respectively, in 1970. The uranium ratios are twice as high. If one assumes that all these fuels are close substitutes for each other (which is doubtful[20]) then the broader product definition "energy" yields rather low ratios.

[20] David Schwartzman, "The Cross-Elasticity of Demand and Industry Boundaries: Coal, Oil, Gas, and Uranium," *Antitrust Bulletin* (Fall 1973), pp. 483–507.

Lest these numbers lead the reader to conclude that competition runs rampant in this sector, we should also mention that (1) government intervention produces much ossification, (2) the current trend in concentration is clearly skyward (see Table 6-6), and (3) by narrower, but perhaps more defensible geographic definitions of fuel markets, oligopolistic firms seem to be in control.[21] Furthermore, the energy sector can claim the greatest cartel in all history—the Organization of Petroleum Exporting Countries, or OPEC.

Broad generalizations for other areas of mining are equally difficult. On the one hand we find substantial four-firm control in the United States for gold (79.9), copper (74.8), sulfur (72.0), iron ore (63.9), and lead and zinc (47.0).[22] On the other hand, there are several areas of mining that are fairly atomistic—limestone, common sand and gravel, and phosphate, for example.

Finance

Banking, insurance, and other forms of finance are primarily local operations, although some large corporate buyers of these services have the option of easily shifting their accounts and lines of credit across state boundaries, thereby adding an element of nationwide scope. Local concentration in commercial banking tends to be moderate or high. The following 1970 sample of *three-firm* concentration ratios is based on deposits: Atlanta 65.6; Baltimore, 64.2; Chicago, 43.1; Columbus, Ohio, 93.4; Des Moines, 70.6; Indianapolis, 79.9; New York, 48.0; Phoenix, 92.8; Pittsburg, 80.0; and San Francisco, 77.7.[23] Since by law banks cannot freely operate across state lines, national market three-firm concentration based on deposits is only 9.6%. Moreover, one must sum up all the deposits of the nation's 50 largest banks to account for 60% of total United States deposits.

Local market concentration in life insurance, which illustrates another area of finance, is not quite as high as in banking. New Jersey is the most concentrated of all state markets, with a four-firm ratio of 56.2% in 1968.[24] Detracting somewhat from the significance of all ratios for finance is the fact that financial institutions are to various degrees exempted from the antitrust laws and subjected rather, to state and federal government regulation.

---

[21] See, e.g., John W. Wilson, testimony in *The National Gas Industry*, Hearings before the Subcommittee on Antitrust and Monopoly, Part I, U.S. Senate (1973), pp. 456–504.

[22] J. P. Mulholland and D. W. Webbink, *Concentration Levels and Trends in the Energy Sector of the U.S. Economy* (Washington, D.C.: Federal Trade Commission, 1974), p. 139.

[23] Federal Deposit Insurance Corporation, *Summary of Accounts and Deposits in All Commercial Banks, June 30, 1970* (Washington, D.C.), pp. 18–20.

[24] J. D. Cummins, H. S. Denenberg, and W. C. Scheel, "Concentration in the U.S. Life Insurance Industry," *Journal of Risk and Insurance* (June 1972), pp. 177–99. For statewide concentration ratios in consumer finance, see Milton W. Schober and Robert P. Shay, *State and Regional Estimates of the Price and Volume of the Major Types of Consumer Installment Credit in Mid-1971*, Technical Study, Vol. III, National Commission on Consumer Finance (Washington, D.C., 1973), pp. 145–6.

The Regulated Sectors

Last but considerably more than least are several sectors in which regulation is even more stringent and monopoly power even more in evidence. Indeed, these may be called the regulated sectors. Here, air transport, pipeline transport, railroading, and intercity bus services exemplify tight-knit oligopoly. Communications provides further examples of oligopoly—radio and television broadcasting, in particular. It also includes telephone communications, which, as everyone over age 5 knows, constitutes a massive monopoly incarnate. Electricity, gas, and water are also supplied by local and regional monopolies, many of which are owned by government agencies.

Conclusion

Where does this cascade of statistics leave us? Is any grand summary possible? Many observers seem to think so, but opinions differ:

> The extent of shared monopoly can modestly be called staggering.
>
> Mark Green[25]

> While there are *some* markets in which the number of competitors is limited, there is not an important national market today (with the possible exception of telephone service) which lacks active competition.
>
> Lee Loevinger[26]

Of course anyone can play this game. If the reader would like to try his hand at it, fine. A good approach might be to throw darts at a random listing of all markets. My guess is that two market categories—oligopoly and monopolistic competition—would account for roughly 80% of all your hits.

The Causes of Concentration

The next question is what produces concentration? Unfortunately, the answer is complex, so much so that we cannot possibly provide a thorough reply in the remainder of this chapter. All we can do here is outline the various main parts of the answer, refer to subsequent chapters for each item in the outline that is discussed in detail later, and discuss the outline briefly, paying particular

[25] *The Closed Enterprise System* (New York: Grossman Publishers, 1972), pp. 7–8. (A Nader Study Group Report.)
[26] "The Closed Mind Inquiry—Antitrust Report is Raiders' Nadir," *Antitrust Bulletin* (Fall 1972), p. 758 (emphasis added).

attention to those points that are not discussed extensively later on. First the outline:

A. Chance or luck.
B. Technical causes or prior conditions.
  1. Size of the market (Chapter 8, Barriers to Entry)
  2. Economies of scale (Chapter 8, Barriers to Entry)
  3. Scarce resources (Chapter 8, Barriers to Entry)
  4. Market growth rate (Chapter 8, Barriers to Entry)
C. Government policy.
  1. Antitrust (Chapter 7, Mergers; Chapter 9, Monopoly; Chapter 14, Restrictive Practices)
  2. Patents, licenses, tariffs, quotas (Chapter 9, Monopoly; Chapter 24, Patent Policy)
  3. Procurement policy
  4. Miscellaneous regulations (Chapter 20, Public Utility Regulation)
D. Business policies (within the context of the foregoing).
  1. Mergers (Chapter 7, Mergers)
  2. Restrictive practices (Chapter 9, Monopoly; Chapters 12, 13, Conduct)
  3. Product differentiation (Chapters 15, 16, Conduct)

Perusal of the outline should reveal why a detailed discussion of all items is inappropriate here. The list is not only long, it contains many items, such as antitrust policy and restrictive practices, that simply do not fit in the present context. Furthermore, many factors, such as economies of scale and scarce resources, transcend in structural importance their contribution to concentration. That is to say, they influence market power in their own right, independent of their contribution to concentration.

Chance or Luck

What do you suppose would happen if you and ten of your friends got together for an all night gambling session? Assume that each of you brought $50 to fritter away, and that every game played was one of *pure* chance—bingo perhaps—with all of you having *identical* chances of winning. Although conditions are such that getting and deserving are completely disconnected, what do you suppose would be the distribution of money by the break of dawn? Would everyone leave with $50? The laws of probability say "no" (and your own experience may lead you to agree). A few of you would put together a string of lucky games. A few would lose regularly. The rest would be distributed in between. The result is such a concentration of winnings (and losings) that two of you would end up with, say, six elevenths or 54.5 % of the total $550 in original funds.

TABLE 6-7   Four-Firm Concentration Ratios Resulting from Simulation Runs of a Stochastic Growth Process

	Four-Firm Concentration Ratio at Year:					
	1	20	40	60	80	100
Run 1	8.0	19.5	29.3	36.3	40.7	44.9
Run 2	8.0	20.3	21.4	28.1	37.5	41.6
Run 3	8.0	18.8	28.9	44.6	43.1	47.1
Run 4	8.0	20.9	26.7	31.8	41.9	41.0
Run 5	8.0	23.5	33.2	43.8	60.4	60.5
Run 6	8.0	21.3	26.6	29.7	35.8	51.2
Average for 16 runs	8.0	20.4	27.0	33.8	42.1	46.7

Source: Frederick M. Scherer, *Industrial Market Structure and Economic Performance* (Chicago: Rand McNally & Co., 1970), p. 126. Reprinted by permission.

Several economists have argued that similar principles apply to firms in markets, that chance explains much concentration.[27] This is best seen by way of a computer simulation experiment conducted by F. M. Scherer. He simulated 16 separate histories of a single market under the following set of assumptions:

1. The market starts the first year with 50 firms, each with $100,000 in sales and a 2% market share. (The four-firm concentration ratio starts then at 8%.)
2. Each firm has *identical chances* for growth, these chances being specified in terms of each firm annually drawing a year's growth from an identical probability distribution.
3. The probability distribution from which these annual growth rates are drawn provides for an *average* annual growth rate of 6%, but a *variance* of growth rates around this average such that the distribution is normal with standard deviation of 16%. Thus, each year about half the firms will grow faster than 6%, the other half slower. On average, though, they all grow at about 6%.

Table 6-7 shows the results of the first six of Scherer's 16 computer runs, together with averages for all 16 simulations on the bottom line. The numbers are four-firm concentration ratios taken at 20 year intervals up to 100 years. Since Lady Luck is at work, the results are not the same for any pair of runs, but the message is clear. Concentration rises rapidly at first, more than doubling in the first 20 years. It rises more slowly thereafter.

[27] P. E. Hart and S. J. Prais, "The Analysis of Business Concentration," *Journal of the Royal Statistic Society*, Series A (Part I, 1956), pp. 150–81; Herbert A. Simon and C. P. Bonini, "The Size Distribution of Business Firms," *American Economic Review* (September 1958), pp. 607–17.

The key to understanding how pure chance could produce these results lies in understanding the following sequence of events: Half of the firms will enjoy better than average growth the first year. Half of that half, or one quarter, will enjoy better than average growth a second year because the same probability distribution applies anew annually to *each segment* of firms and *each firm* regardless of the prior year's experience. Half of that quarter, or one eighth, will enjoy better than average growth in the third year, which means they enjoy three consecutive boom years. Half of that eighth, or one sixteenth, will have better than average growth in the fourth year . . . and so on. In short, the leaders have enjoyed a run of good luck, whether or not they deserved it.

The assumptions of this experiment conform to what is called **Gibrat's Law** of proportionate growth. Although real world markets do not conform exactly to these assumptions, there are various forms of evidence that suggest Gibrat's law or something like it is at work.[28] One of the more prominent findings is that, *on average*, the percentage growth of small firms is about the same as that of large firms.[29] This independence of size and growth was implicitly assumed for Scherer's experiment.

Still, happenstance cannot be the whole story. It helps to explain why there is always *some* concentration in just about every market, and why the "bad guys" sometimes outstrip the "good." But there is a great deal of *systematic* variation in concentration across markets, something incompatible with pure happenstance. What do we mean by systematic variation? For one thing, similar markets in diverse nations show consistent patterns in degree of concentration. If autos and cigarettes are highly concentrated in the United States, they are likely to be highly concentrated in Britain, France, and Sweden as well. Table 6-8 shows the composite ranking of 17 two-digit industries for 12 European and North American countries, as computed by Frederic Pryor, a leading authority on this subject. Averaged over these nations, tobacco and transportation equipment were the most highly concentrated of all manufacturing industries, whereas lumber and furniture were the least concentrated. The concordance coefficient, which indicates the *similarity* of rank orderings across all these 12 nations, was $+0.51$ and highly significant.[30]

Additionally, when any two nations' rank orders are compared, the correlation coefficient thereby produced is always highly positive.[31] This does *not* mean that the *average level* of market concentration for all industries taken together is the

[28] See, for example, S. J. Prais, "A New Look at the Growth of Industrial Concentration," *Oxford Economic Papers* (July 1974), pp. 273–88.

[29] Stephen Hymer and Peter Pashigian, "Firm Size and Rate of Growth," *Journal of Political Economy* (December 1962), pp. 556–69; M. Marcus, "A Note of the Determinants of the Growth of Firms and Gibrat's Law," *Canadian Journal of Economics* (November 1969), pp. 587–89.

[30] F. L. Pryor, "An International Comparison of Concentration Ratios," *Review of Economics and Statistics* (May 1972), p. 51.

[31] Besides Pryor see K. D. George and T. S. Ward, *The Structure of Industry in the EEC* (Cambridge, U.K.: Cambridge University Press, 1975), p. 16; Gideon Rosenbluth, *Concentration in Canadian Manufacturing Industries* (Princeton: Princeton University Press, 1957); R. E. Caves and M. Uekusa, *Industrial Organization in Japan* (Washington, D.C.: Brookings Institution, 1976), pp. 19–25.

TABLE 6-8 **High to Low Concentration Rankings for Two-Digit Industries—United States and Abroad**

SIC Code	Industry	12-Country Composite Rank	United States As of 1963	United States As of 1929
21	Tobacco products	1	1	1
37	Transportation equipment	2	3	6
35	Machinery (except electric)	3	11	9
29	Petroleum and coal products	4	2	3
28	Chemicals	5	6	7
30	Rubber products	6	8	2
36	Electrical equipment	7	5	8
32	Stone, clay and glass	8	7	14
34	Fabricated metal products	9	13	12
33	Primary metals	10	4	4
20	Food and kindred products	11	10	5
26	Paper products	12	12	11
22	Textiles	13	9	10
31	Leather products	14	15	15
23	Apparel	15	14	13
24	Lumber and wood	16	16	16
25	Furniture and fixtures	17	17	17

Sources: Twelve countries: Frederic L. Pryor, "An International Comparison of Concentration Ratios," *Review of Economics and Statistics* (May 1972), p. 135. United States figures: Derived from Alfred D. Chandler, Jr., "The Structure of American Industry in the Twentieth Century: A Historical Overview," *Business History Review* (Autumn 1969), pp. 258–59.

same among nations. That is a separate issue. The average height of Pygmies is less than ours, even though their age-height rank ordering correlates with ours. For average market concentration in manufacturing, Pryor finds that, "France, West Germany, and Italy, have weighted concentration ratios somewhat lower than the United States, while ... Japan, the Netherlands, and the United Kingdom, have weighted concentration ratios only slightly higher than the United States. In only five nations are concentration ratios clearly higher [by about 50%], namely, Belgium, Canada, Sweden, Switzerland, and Yugoslavia."[32]

Table 6-8 also reports the rank order of two-digit industries in the United States as of 1963. These rankings may be compared with the 12-country composite rankings to support our assertion that patterns in degree of concentration

[32] F. L. Pryor, *op. cit.*, p. 134. For corroboration concerning the United Kingdom, France, Germany, and Italy, see George and Ward, *op. cit.*, p. 17

are consistent across nations. More important, they may be compared with the rankings of the last column, which are for the United States in 1929. This latter comparison reveals a second type of systematic pattern. That is, interindustry differences tend to be quite stable over long periods of time. Tobacco and transport equipment have perched high atop the list for over a quarter of a century, whereas leather, apparel, lumber, and furniture have invariably roosted on the bottom. We thus have a pattern of persistence at odds with a pattern of pure chance.

Technical Causes

A third form of systematic pattern could be claimed if intermarket differences in concentration were closely associated with variations in technological conditions or prior circumstances that could reasonably be expected to affect concentration. In general, such an association does seem to be borne out by research.

Consider first the relationship between market size and concentration. We have already seen how a stringently narrow definition of the market tends to increase measured concentration, whereas an excessively broad definition has the effect of decreasing apparent concentration. Going beyond mere definition to a more substantive association, the same inverse relationship holds between economic market size and concentration, everything else being equal.[33] Large markets, measured by volume of business or buyer population or whatever, seem to have more "room" for a larger number of sellers than small markets. Consequently, large markets have lower concentration ratios than small markets. To take just one example, Table 6-9 reproduces average *two-firm* concentration ratios for commercial banks, categorizing them in terms of four different city sizes and three different types of branching regulation. Note in particular that, for each type of branching policy taken individually, concentration is greatest in areas of smallest population; whereas it is lowest in areas of largest population. In states that permit statewide branching, for instance, the ratio falls from 69.5 to 55.0. An even healthier drop from 68.5 to 42.7% occurs in unit banking states, where each banking firm is limited to only one office. Since branching is banned in these states, additional banking *firms* are almost a necessity for serving the additional demand that goes with additional population.

Economies of scale are another causal factor. They will be discussed at appropriate length in Chapter 8. Suffice it to say here that size of market alone is not enough. The size of *firm* required to achieve all efficiencies (and thereby

---

[33] George and Ward, *op. cit.*, pp. 22–23; Caves and Uekusa, *op. cit.*, pp. 22–25; F. M. Scherer, A. Beckenstein, E. Kaufer, and R. D. Murphy, *The Economics of Multi-Plant Operation an International Comparisons Study* (Cambridge, Mass.: Harvard University Press, 1975), pp. 221–23; M. D. Intriligator, S. I. Ornstein, R. E. Shrieves, and J. F. Weston, "Determinants of Market Structure," *Southern Economic Journal* (April 1973), pp. 612–25; Peter Pashigian, "The Effect of Market Size on Concentration," *International Economics Review* (October 1969), pp. 291–314.

TABLE 6-9   Percentage of Total Deposits Held by Largest Two Banking Organizations in Metropolitan Areas 1968

Population of Standard Metropolitan Statistical Area (SMSA)	Statewide Branching States (%)	Limited Branching States (%)	Unit Branching States (%)
50–100,00	69.5	65.4	68.5
100,000–500,000	68.5	64.4	53.5
500,000–1,000,000	69.1	57.7	47.8
1,000,000 and over	55.0	51.5	42.7

Source: "Recent Changes in the Structure of Commercial Banking," *Federal Reserve Bulletin* (March 1970), p. 207.

attain lowest possible cost per unit of output) is also important. If, for example, low-cost auto production required an output of *at least* 1 million cars per year, then an auto market of 10 million sales per year could be served by ten auto makers of efficient scale. If, on the other hand, efficient scale coincided with 5 million units, then there would be "room" for only two low-cost producers, a condition that would obviously aggravate concentration considerably. Stated differently, minimum efficient size and concentration should be positively correlated across markets. Without going into the details now, this association has been found.[34]

A scarcity of resource inputs, such as a scarcity of mineral deposits or uniquely skilled labor, may have a positive effect on concentration similar to the effect of economies of scale. Unfortunately, the data necessary for a cross-section test of this possibility are not available; however, some sketchy case history evidence will be reviewed later. By contrast, one of the more thoroughly researched hypotheses is that rapid growth in market demand tends to reduce concentration. It would of course be preposterous to suppose that the few leading firms of any market would consciously stand pat while the market grew up rapidly around them, permitting disproportionate expansions of their lesser rivals and a flood of entering newcomers. Still, a hypothesis that rapid growth diminishes concentration must infer some degree of such differential behavior. Accordingly, it has been theorized that leading firms tend to (1) be timid for fear of antitrust prosecution, (2) look more toward diversifying outside the market than merely keeping up within the market, or (3) suffer from the sluggishness that often

[34] R. E. Caves, J. Khalilzadeh-Shirazi, and M. E. Porter, "Scale Economies in Statistical Analyses of Market Power," *Review of Economics and Statistics* (May 1975), pp. 133–40; Caves and Uekusa, *op. cit.*, pp. 22–25; D. F. Greer, "Advertising and Market Concentration," *Southern Economic Journal* (July 1971), pp. 19–32; and L. W. Weiss, "Optimal Plant Size and the Extent of Suboptimal Capacity," in *Essays on Industrial Organization in Honor of Joe S. Bain*, edited by R. T. Masson and P. D. Qualls (Cambridge, Mass.: Ballinger Publishing Co., 1976), p. 135.

accompanies large size. However true these possibilities may or may not be, there is a substantial body of evidence indicating that *changes* in concentration *are* inversely associated with market rate of growth.[35] The association is, however, often weak statistically and of low magnitude. In particular, it has been estimated that a 100-percentage-point increase in market size would usually be necessary to trim four-firm concentration by 2 or 3 percentage points. Slim pickings, indeed.

Government Policies

Unlike the foregoing factors, which are largely attributable to Lady Luck or Mother Nature, government policies and business policies are obviously the work of lesser breeds, namely, government officials and businessmen. Among government officials, we find an amazing amount of ambivalence; some would even say schizophrenia. Fritz Machlup neatly summarized the situation when he wrote that "Governments, apparently, have never been able to make up their minds as to which they dislike more, competition or monopoly."[36] On the anti-monopoly side, government has created and mobilized various antitrust laws to dissolve excessive concentrations of market power or to prevent such concentrations from occurring in the first place. On the other side are a host of anticompetitive government policies.[37] These include **tariffs** and **quotas**, restricting the free flow of imports; **licenses**, inhibiting the entry of finance companies, taxi cabs, liquor stores, barbers, beauticians, landscape architects, and various other professionals; **franchises**, granting rights of monopoly to bus lines, athletic stadium concessionaires, water companies, electric and gas companies, and other businesses; and **patents**, awarding 17-year monopolies over the use of new inventions and innovations. The effects of these policies on concentration should be obvious.

The effects of slightly more subtle policies governing commercial bank branching may be seen by referring again to Table 6-9. Local two-bank concentration ratios are more than 10 percentage points higher in statewide branching states than in unit banking states for each size class of city, except the very smallest. Cities in the 50,000–1000,000 population range are usually served by just a few bank offices regardless of branching regulations; hence, the effect in their cases is negligible.

---

[35] Ralph L. Nelson, *Concentration in the Manufacturing Industries of the United States* (New Haven, Conn.: Yale University Press, 1963), pp. 50–56; W. G. Shepherd, "Trends of Concentration in American Manufacturing Industries, 1947–1958," *Review of Economics and Statistics* (May 1964), pp. 200–12; D. R. Kamerschen, "Market Growth and Industry Concentration," *Journal of the American Statistical Association* (March 1968), pp. 228–41; J. A. Dalton and S. A. Rhoades, "Growth and Product Differentiability as Factors Influencing Changes in Concentration," *Journal of Industrial Economics* (March 1974), pp. 235–40.

[36] Fritz Machlup, *Political Economy of Monopoly* (Baltimore: The Johns Hopkins University Press, 1952), p. 182.

[37] Walter Adams and Horace M. Gray, *Monopoly in America: The Government as Promoter* (New York: Macmillan Publishing Co., 1955).

TABLE 6-10   Selected Major Mergers Causing High Concentration 1895–1904

Company (or Combine)	Number of Firms Disappearing	Rough Estimate of Market Controlled (%)
U. S. Steel	170	65
U. S. Gypsum	29	80
American Tobacco	162	90
American Smelting & Refining	12	85
DuPont de Nemours	65	85
Diamond Match	38	85
American Can	64	65–75
International Harvester	4	70
National Biscuit (Nabisco)	27	70
Otis Elevator	6	65

Source: Ralph L. Nelson, *Merger Movements in American Industry 1895–1956* (Princeton, N. J.: Princeton University Press, 1959), pp. 161–62.

Government procurement policy also has an effect. Briefly stated, the federal government's multibillion dollar purchases of tanks, planes, ships, electronic equipment, and most other durable goods are concentrated among a relatively few supplying firms. In light of the ample concentration caused by factors *unrelated* to government procurement, it is not surprising that these purchases should also be concentrated. The government, moreover, obviously has special needs—particularly in the case of complex weapon systems—needs that often force it to show some favoritism toward Gargantuan suppliers. It has nonetheless been argued rather persuasively that the government's expenditures are *more* highly concentrated than these two rationalizations justify.[38] The government's ambivalence thus takes many forms, bringing to mind once again two important observations of Chapter 1: Society's value judgments are numerous, and they are not necessarily consistent either in principle or in imperfect practice.

Business Policies

Table 6-10 offers evidence of the potential and actual effects of business mergers. It not only summarizes the merger history of the ten companies listed

[38] *Ibid.*, Chapter V; U. S. General Accounting Office, *More Competition in Emergency Defense Procurements Found Possible*, B-171561 (Washington, D.C., March 25, 1971) and *Opportunities for Savings by Increasing Competition in Procurement of Commercial Equipment*, B-164018 (Washington D.C., February 26, 1971).

but also reflects the history of dozens of other modern-day mammoths that likewise rose to power through combination around the turn of the century. The ten firms of Table 6-10 accounted for the disappearance of 577 formerly independent rivals during this period. The consequences are obvious in the last column of the table, which provides rough estimates of the market shares these combinations acquired. United States antitrust policy currently stands in the way of further merger-built oligopoly. This is not the case in England and West Germany, however, where recent merger activity has contributed substantially to concentration in many major industries.[39]

Less measurable but no less deserving of mention are various business policies that have come to be called "restrictive practices." These include group boycotts, collective rebates, predatory price discrimination, barrier pricing, and exclusive dealing. They generally have no immediate effect on concentration, but over the long haul they can cement existing market power or extend it, as will be shown later when we take up conduct in earnest.

Finally, it appears that under certain circumstances product differentiation may foster concentration. Using a measure of product differentiation based on advertising as a percent of sales, Willard Mueller and Larry Hamm found that 16 consumer goods industries with "high" product differentiation experienced a big jump in four-firm concentration from 49.6 in 1947 to 62.3 in 1970. Over the same period, concentration in undifferentiated consumer-goods industries and producer-goods industries generally was unchanged or fell.[40] (These data may seem to conflict with our earlier observation that average concentration in manufacturing has not changed much since 1947, but a constant average is obviously consistent with substantial ups and downs among the average's component numbers.) Exactly how the *level* of advertising could effect *changes* in concentration is not exactly clear, but something seems to be going on. Later we shall explore this area further, paying particular attention to levels of *both* advertising and concentration or to changes in both (see Chapter 15).

Aggregate Concentration

Let us now broaden our view a bit. Let us leave the low lands of market concentration, and climb into the mountains for a brief look at what is called **aggregate concentration** or **economy-wide concentration**. As these latter names imply, our new viewpoint involves a look at the share of *total* economic activity

---

[39] M. A. Utton, "The Effect of Mergers on Concentration: U. K. Manufacturing Industry, 1954–65," *Journal of Industrial Economics* (November 1971), pp. 42–58; Jürgen Müller, "The Impact of Mergers on Concentration: A Study of Eleven West German Industries," same *Journal* (December 1976), pp. 113–32.

[40] Willard F. Mueller and Larry G. Hamm, "Trends in Industrial Market Concentration, 1947 to 1970," *Review of Economics and Statistics* (November 1974), p. 513.

accounted for by some relatively small group of enterprises, regardless of their specific markets. Although market and aggregate concentration are in fact related, they are quite different in principle. The many individual markets in the economy could all be highly concentrated. Yet, if the firms in each market were also highly specialized, limiting their activities to just one market, they could then be relatively small and numerous when compared to the economy as a whole. The result: relatively low aggregate concentration despite considerable market concentration. On the other hand, it is possible to have high aggregate concentration together with low market concentration. This would occur if a group of very large firms controlled a dominant portion of total economic activity, but with each firm's individual operations so diversified across a large number of markets that no single operation accounted for a major share of any one market.

Despite these theoretical possibilities, market and aggregate concentration are closely connected in several ways. First, firms that control large shares of the entire economy also hold dominant positions in major industries. Exxon and Texaco both rank among the ten largest United States corporations while they hold the lead positions in petroleum production. The same could be said of GM and Ford in automobiles, and IBM in computers. Indeed, every one of the 100 largest manufacturing firms in the economy was among the top four firms in at least one industry in 1963.[41]

Second, many of the overall leaders are highly diversified. LTV is into steel, aerospace, meat packing, sporting goods, pharmaceuticals, and electronics. ITT, FMC, and Litton are into so many different things that an abridged list for each would mislead you and a complete list would bore you. Thus, many, if not most, of the top 100 are referred to as **conglomerates**. They are not "in" an industry; they stand astride many.

Finally aggregate dominance and diversification may augment a firm's power within specific markets. This is especially true of diversification in the form of **vertical integration**, that is, single firm operation at several stages in the production and distribution of a given product. Major petroleum companies, for example, combine crude oil extraction, pipeline transportation, refining, and retail marketing. The linkage between market concentration and aggregate concentration may thus be more than just a statistical phenomenon.

Table 6-11 summarizes the current situation and recent trend in six broad sectors of the United States economy. By the end of 1974, the top 200 manufacturers (or about 0.1% of all manufacturing companies) accounted for 60.7% of all manufacturing employment. Their share of assets, sales, and other manufacturing aggregates is quite similar. The 1974 share of the top 50 firms in each of the other sectors except merchandising is also hefty—banks, 36.0; life insurance, 80.1; and so on. Taking all these sectors together, 750 leading firms are represented. These 750 accounted for 55.3% of the total employment in these sectors

---

[41] *Concentration Ratios in Manufacturing Industry, 1963*, Part II, Subcommittee on Antitrust and Monopoly, U. S. Senate, 90th Congress (1967), p. 284.

TABLE 6-11   Concentration of Employment Among 750 of the Largest United States Companies in Six Broad Business Divisions, 1955, 1965, and 1974

Largest Firms by Business Division	Percentage of Business Division Indicated by Row Heading at Left		
	1955	1965	1974
Top 50 manufacturers	23.7	29.9	31.4
Top 200 manufacturers	39.5	53.0	60.7
Top 500 manufacturers	50.1	67.8	79.9
Top 50 commercial banks	27.8	31.2	36.0
Top 50 life insurance firms	70.0	80.2	80.1
Top 50 transport companies	39.3	37.0	33.6
Top 50 public utilities	87.4	86.9	87.8
Top 50 merchandisers	14.0	18.3	20.3
Total of all top 750 firms	39.7	50.5	55.3

Source: William N. Leonard, "Mergers, Industrial Concentration, and Antitrust Policy," *Journal of Economic Issues* (June 1976), p. 358.

in 1974. Furthermore, aggregate concentration has been rising since 1955 in all but transportation and public utilities. The rise for manufacturing is especially steep, amounting to over 20 percentage points and 50%. If we recall that *average market* concentration in manufacturing has not risen over this period, we must attribute this upward trend to growing diversification and an especially rapid growth of industries controlled by relatively large firms. Similar upward trends have been observed in other developed countries.[42]

These numbers may chill your spine or warm your heart. Your reaction probably depends on your political persuasion, your father's occupation, your susceptibility to corporate "image" advertising, or your viewing of the movie *Network*. It probably does not depend on your knowledge of economics. If it does not, then you should not feel alone. You should feel a greater appreciation for the comments in Chapter 1 concerning noneconomic value judgments.

The recent upward trend in aggregate concentration is merely a continuation of an ascent that stretches back to the first decades of our century. The numbers demonstrating this are many and varied, but Figure 6-5 depicts a summary primarily concerned with manufacturing. Different measures of size, different definitions of scope, and different notions of how many firms constitutes a

---

[42] K. D. George and T. S. Ward, *op. cit.*, pp. 49–50. For example, Britain's top 100 industrial companies accounted for 46.5% of United Kingdom industrial assets in 1948 and 63.7% in 1968.

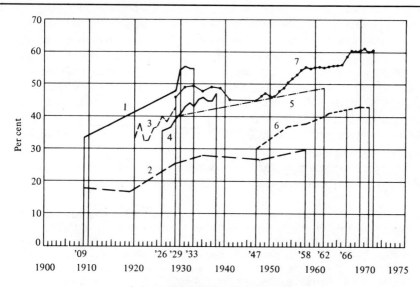

1 Assets, 200 largest nonfinancial corps.
2 Assets, 100 largest mfg., min. & dist. corps.
3 Net income, 200 largest nonfinancial corps.
4 Net working capital, 316 large mfg. corps.
5 Assets, 100 largest mfg. corps.
6 Value added by mfr., 200 largest mfg. cos.
7 Assets, 200 largest mfg. corps.

Figure 6-5. The long-term trend of aggregate concentration: Seven individual series. Source: John M. Blair, Economic Concentration (New York: Harcourt Brace Jovanovich, 1972), p. 63.

"few" obviously affect the picture.[43] But, generally speaking, aggregate concentration has risen. Note also that the period of the 1950s and 1960s witnessed a particularly rapid spurt, as did the period of the late 1920s and early 1930s. Long run trends outside the United States are an unsolved mystery.

Some commentators have tried to argue that there is no cause for alarm in this trend. They claim that although the *share* of the top 100 or so may be rising, the *identity* of the top 100 is constantly changing, implying turnover and competition. There is a grain of truth to this. Our high-altitude vantage point is not Mt. Olympus, so those we see up here do not enjoy eternal life. By raw count, 51

---

[43] This area of study has been described as a statistical Disneyland. I rather think of it as a monstrous maze. In either case we have no time for a tour. Those interested should consult the references of this chapter plus John Blair, *Economic Concentration* (New York: Harcourt Brace Jovanovich Inc., 1972), Chapter 4 (the secondary source for Figure 6-5); and D. W. Penn, "Aggregate Concentration: A Statistical Note," *Antitrust Bulletin* (Spring 1976), pp. 91–98. To give but two examples of complications, the Census value added series of Figure 6-5 is biased downward because of a classification system that excludes the large petroleum companies. Conversely, the FTC asset series is biased upward because it includes foreign as well as domestic assets.

firms listed among the top 100 industrials in 1919 were still among the top 100 half a century later in 1969. Whether this is a large or small number depends on your value judgments. Before passing sentence, however, you should learn what happened to the 49 nonsurvivors. Only 10 could be considered true failures, exiting by liquidation or suffering a decline in sales. Nine continued to grow and are still more-or-less close to the top, but faster growers displaced them. Finally, 30 of the 49 dropouts merged with other large firms, thus hardly making competitive exits.[44] Truly "competitive" exits have not only been rather rare but their frequency has diminished with time.[45] The top manufacturers are apparently becoming more and more entrenched.

In regard to areas *other* than manufacturing, the best work to date is that of Richard Edwards. He summarizes his findings this way:[46]

> Leaders which had emerged by 1919 continued in 1969 to dominate these other areas. The thirty-six telephone, gas, and electric companies listed as "large" in 1919 include eight of the top ten utility companies in 1969 . . . Of the top fifteen life insurance companies in 1917, fourteen continue among the top fifteen half a century later. The eight merchandising firms with 1919 assets greater than $20 million include six of the largest ten merchandising firms by assets in 1969. Nine of the largest fifteen banks in 1922 continued among the top fifteen in 1967; five of the remaining six were acquired by banks now among the top fifteen.

He concludes by saying that "The list could go on, but what is important is the extent to which the industrial structure established by the end of the First World War has continued to the present."

Summary

Measuring market concentration involves several steps and various options. First, one or more statistical indexes ought to be selected. A good index should provide good predictions of conduct and performance. It should also be fairly easy to compute. Our survey of possibilities indicates that (1) the absolute number of firms neglected fractional shares, (2) the Gini coefficient neglected absolute numbers, (3) the Herfindahl index registered both numbers and shares in overall summary fashion but was difficult to compile, and (4) the concentration ratio combines numbers and shares while being fairly inexpensive to

---

[44] Richard C. Edwards, "Stages in Corporate Stability and the Risks of Corporate Failure," *Journal of Economic History* (June 1975), pp. 428–57. It should be noted that turnover was greater per year during the two decades prior to 1919, so an earlier base year would suggest greater long-run turnover. We use 1919 in the text to attain comparability with our later data for nonmanufacturing.

[45] N. Collins and L. Preston, "The Size Structure of the Largest Industrial Firms, 1909–1958," *American Economic Review* (December 1961), pp. 986–1011; S. E. Boyle and J. P. McKenna, "Size Mobility of the 100 and 200 Largest U. S. Manufacturing Corporations: 1911–1964," *Antitrust Bulletin* (Fall 1970), pp. 505–19.

[46] Richard Edwards, *op. cit.*, p. 442.

compile. For the sake of consistency, it is fortunate that all the main indexes yield numbers that correlate well with each other.

Second, a choice must be made of size measure—sales, employment, assets, or something else. We have glossed over this problem. But for our purposes the differences between measures are not crucial.

Third, the market must be defined. Proper definition requires the inclusion of closely competitive offerings and the exclusion of noncompetitive offerings. A definition that is too narrow excludes competitive offerings. One that is too broad includes noncompetitive offerings. These criteria apply to both product breadth and geographic scope.

The data generated from taking these steps indicate a variety of conditions across the economy's many markets and several sectors. In general, four-firm concentration ratios either below 10 or above 90 are relatively rare. Observations in the 30 to 70 range are much more common. In addition, sector averages are either moving up or holding steady. Broadly based downward trends are absent. As for the causes of concentration, a summary outline has already been provided.

Aggregate or economy-wide concentration is also of interest. The top 200 United States manufacturing firms currently account for roughly 60% of all manufacturing activity. If the future follows precedent, manufacturing concentration will be even greater in 1985. If we add commercial banking, life insurance, transport, public utilities, and merchandizing to manufacturing for one grand aggregate, 750 firms employ over 55% of the workers. This share, too, has been on the move upward.

7

Concentration and Oligopoly: Merger Practice and Policy

The game of picking up companies is open to everybody. All you have to do is have indefatigable drive, a desire to perpetuate yourself or your family in control of an industry, or an unabsorbed appetite for corporate power.

MESHULAM RIKLIS (who parlayed
$25,000 into a $755 million empire
fittingly called Rapid-American, Inc.)

A long standing record was broken in 1967. Mergers in manufacturing and mining numbered 1496, thereby exceeding the previous high of 1245 in 1929. As if this were not enough, that previous high was nearly doubled the very next year, 1968, when 2407 mergers were recorded. Then, in 1969, 2307 more were tallied. Business partisans reacted as if capitalism had achieved its millenium; critics proclaimed the end of the world.

The purpose of this chapter is to explore this proliferation of mergers and related matters. Mergers are a major cause of concentration and, consequently, a major headache for the antitrust enforcement agencies. We begin with a brief description of various types of mergers and proceed with a historical review of mergers, an outline of their causes, and a run-down of policy developments.

Merger Types

The union of two or more direct competitors is called a **horizontal** merger. The combining companies operate in the same market, as is illustrated in

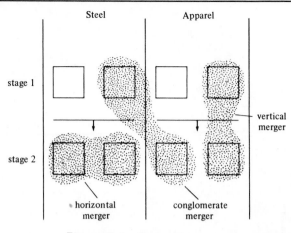

Figure 7-1. *Types of mergers.*

Figure 7-1. Bethlehem Steel's acquisition of the Youngstown Sheet and Tube Company in 1957 is an example. A **vertical** merger links companies that operate at different stages of the production-distribution process. This too is illustrated in Figure 7-1, and Bethlehem would provide an example of this type were it to acquire the Chrysler Corporation, a big buyer of steel. Broadly speaking, **conglomerate** mergers are all those that are neither horizontal nor vertical. This conglomerate definition covers a lot of ground, however, so the category may be subdivided into three classes: (1) **product extension**, involving producers of two different but related products, such as bleach and detergent; (2) **market extension**, involving firms producing the same product but occupying different geographic markets, for example, dairies in two distant towns; and (3) **pure conglomerate**, involving firms with nothing at all in common, as would be true of a retail grocer and a furniture manufacturer.

Some History

A glance at Figure 7-2 reveals why it is customary to speak of three major merger movements in American history. The first movement occurred around the turn of the century. Over the 7-year period 1897–1903, 2864 mergers were recorded in mining and manufacturing. Measured against our current and more recently set records, this record may not seem like much; however, measured against the economy of 1900 and the resulting market concentration, this first great wave was truly awesome. Horizontal mergers dominated the scene. Moreover, simultaneous *multiple* mergers, which are now very rare, were an everyday affair. Ralph Nelson found that mergers involving at least

143

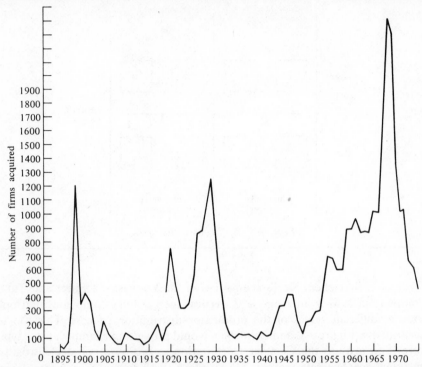

Figure 7-2. Number of manufacturing and mining firms acquired, 1895–1975
Source: Ralph L. Nelson, Merger Movements in American Industry, 1895–1956
(1959), p. 37; Temporary National Economic Committee, The Structure of American
Industry, Monograph 27 (1941), p. 233; Federal Trade Commission, Bureau of
Economics.

five firms accounted for 75% of firm disappearances during this period.[1] As
we saw in Table 6-10 in the last chapter, the turn-of-the-century merger boom
produced such giant companies as U. S. Steel, U. S. Gypsum, International
Harvester, DuPont, American Tobacco, International Paper, American Sugar
Refining, American Can, U. S. Rubber, Pittsburg Plate Glass, and National
Biscuit. The King Kong of these combinations was U. S. Steel. U. S. Steel was
our country's first billion dollar corporation, and its assets almost equaled
one fourth of the economy's gross national product in 1901.[2] A comparable
amount today would be $300 billion. Jesse Markham summarized the overall
movement neatly when he wrote, "The conversion of approximately 71 important oligopolistic or near-competitive industries into near monopolies by

[1] Ralph L. Nelson, *Merger Movements in American Industry*, 1895–1956 (Princeton, N. J.:
Princeton University Press, 1959) p. 29.
[2] D. O. Parsons and E. J. Ray, "The United States Steel Consolidation: The Creation of Market
Control," *Journal of Law and Economics* (April 1975), p. 183.

merger between 1890 and 1904 left an imprint on the structure of the American economy that fifty years have not yet erased."[3]

The second major merger wave arose during the Roaring Twenties. From 1925 through 1930, 5382 mergers were recorded for manufacturing and mining. During the peak year of 1929, ownership shares moved at the feverish pace of more than four mergers per business day. This second movement exceeded the first not only in numbers tallied but also in variety of merger types. Horizontal mergers were again very popular, but vertical, market-extension, and product-extension mergers were also in vogue. It was during this second period that General Foods Corporation put together a string of product-extension acquisitions to become the first truly big food conglomerate. Its acquisitions included Maxwell House Coffee, Jello, Baker's Chocolate, Sanka, Birds Eye, and Swans Down Cake Flour. National Dairy Products and Borden, whose acquisitions of local dairies topped out at more than 400, provided examples of market-extension mergers. Unlike the first merger movement, these years also witnessed countless mergers in sectors other than manufacturing and mining. According to Markham, at least 2750 utilities, 1060 banks, and 10,520 retail stores were swallowed up by acquisition during the twenties.[4]

After two decades of nothing more than a rather meager ripple in the late 1940s, momentum began to build once again in the mid-1950s. Thereafter, the movement swelled incredibly. It was almost as if one of every two American business leaders was suddenly struck with the zeal of a crusader, the determination of a bulldog, and the endurance of a long-distance runner—all for the sole purpose of quickly restructuring the ownership pattern of United States industry. From 1960 through 1970 the Federal Trade Commission recorded 25,598 mergers. Slightly more than half of these were in manufacturing and mining. The total value of manufacturing and mining assets acquired over this period exceeded $65 billion. This sector's peak year was 1968, when 2407 firms amounting to more than $13.3 billion were acquired. Putting the matter in relative terms and using an averaging process, we can deduce that, over the period 1953–1968, approximately 21% of all manufacturing and mining assets were acquired.[5]

This combining activity was not confined to small firms. In mining and manufacturing, 1280 firms with assets of $10 million or more disappeared by merger over the period 1948–1968. If *no* mergers had occurred during these years, the number of "large" firms ($10 million plus) would have been approximately 25–50% greater than it actually was in 1968.[6] Looking at it from the viewpoint of *acquiring* firms rather than the acquired, this nation's 100

---

[3] Jesse W. Markham, "Survey of the Evidence and Findings on Mergers," in *Business Concentration and Price Policy* (Princeton, N. J.: Princeton University Press, 1955), p. 180.

[4] *Ibid.*, pp. 168–69.

[5] Federal Trade Commission, *Economic Report on Corporate Mergers* (Washington, D.C., 1969), p. 666.

[6] *Ibid.*, p. 670; Michael Gort and T. F. Hogarty, "New Evidence on Mergers," *Journal of Law and Economics* (April 1970), p. 168.

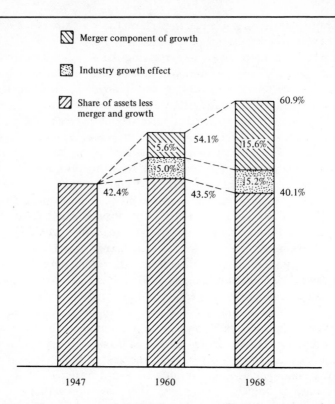

Figure 7-3. Share of assets of 200 largest manufacturing corporations of 1968 and accumulative components of growth; 1947, 1960, and 1968. Source: Federal Trade Commission, Economic Report on Corporate Mergers (1969), p. 192.

largest and 200 largest manufacturers (as of 1968) accounted, respectively, for 44% and 66% of all manufacturing and mining assets acquired over the 1948–1968 period. The list of big and busy buyers includes Gulf & Western Industries (67 companies worth $2.9 billion), LTV (23 companies worth $1.9 billion), ITT (47 companies worth $1.5 billion), Teledyne (125 companies worth $1.0 billion), and Litton Industries (79 companies worth $0.6 billion).[7]

Under the circumstances, concentration swelled—as should astonish no one. For the impact on *aggregate* concentration, Figure 7-3 shows the share of corporate manufacturing assets held by the 200 largest corporations of 1968 in 1947, 1960, and 1968. Over the 1947–1960 period, these corporations increased their share of assets by 11.7 percentage points, of which 5.6 points were due to mergers. Another 10 percentage points were added by mergers over

[7] Federal Trade Commission, *op. cit.*, pp. 260–61.

1960–1968, yielding a total of 15.6 percentage points from merger.[8] After the late sixties peak, mergers contributed very little to further increments in aggregate concentration.

With respect to *market* concentration, the effects have not been nearly so dramatic (except in a few product lines like textiles). Horizontal mergers affecting single markets have become much less numerous than conglomerate mergers. Between 1926 and 1930, horizontal mergers accounted for 67.6% of all mergers, whereas conglomerates accounted for 27.6%. The ratio was reversed during the record breaking sixties; in *numbers* of mergers it was 7.7% horizontal and 81.6% conglomerate for the period 1966–1968.[9] Figure 7-4 shows the trend of the last three decades in percentage of *assets* acquired by merger type. As we shall see shortly, much of this trend away from horizontal couplings and toward conglomerate couplings, especially toward pure conglomerates, was partly due to public policy. The enforcement agencies cracked down rather hard on horizontal mergers whereas they generally ignored conglomerates.

Perhaps the most notable structural effect of these events is to be found in single firm diversification. When diversification is measured simply by the *number* of industries in which a given firm operates, the recent spread of diversification, most of it by merger, appears to be nothing short of stupendous. During the ascending sixties, up through 1968, our 290 largest manufacturing companies added to the *average number* of industries in which they operated by 50%.[10] The specific jumps in averages were from 13 to 20 for four-digit industries, 9 to 14 for three-digit minor industry groups, and from 4 to 6 for two-digit major groups.

However, simply counting the tentacles of these enterprising octopi may be misleading. They may merely dabble lightly here and there while concentrating the vast bulk of their resources and efforts in just one or a few four-digit industries. Thus an alternative index of diversification is the firm's *primary* product sales relative to its *total sales* of all products. This might be considered a "weighted" index. And when measured in this way, the *rate of spread* of diversification appears not to have been nearly as rapid as suggested by the

---

[8] See also Lee E. Preston, "Giant Firms, Large Mergers and Concentration: Patterns and Policy Alternatives 1954–68," *Industrial Organization Review*, Vol. I, No. 1 (1973), pp. 35–46. Some people try to minimize the contribution of mergers by arguing that the history of the *present* top 200 (or 100) is largely irrelevant. They argue that we should instead take the top 200 of, say, 1947 as our yardstick. This latter group of firms will not have grown as much by merger because of some displacement by more aggressive acquirers. Their *current* share of all assets will also be much less than the top 200 of 1968 or 1978. However, the problem with this approach is obvious: Things would not be hunky-dory even if the top 200 of 1947 had by now shrunk to a negligible 3% of all assets, if at the same time the present top 200 controlled 90%.

[9] These are FTC estimates. Some have criticized the FTC for underestimating the recent incidence of horizontal mergers, but the downward trend still holds. Harvey Paul, "The Composition of Mergers in the United States During the 1963–1968 Period," *Industrial Organization Review*, Vol. I, No. 2 (1973), pp. 123–31.

[10] Federal Trade Commission, *op. cit.*, p. 221.

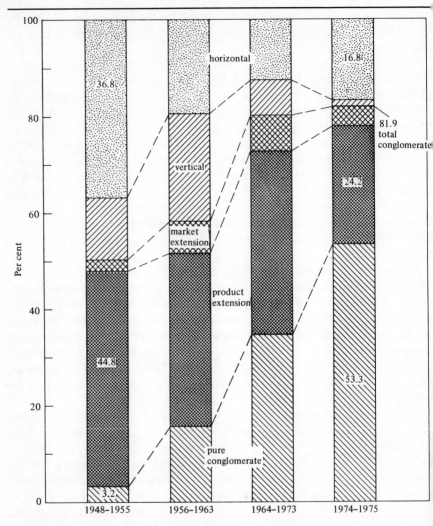

Figure 7-4. *Distribution of total acquired assets in large manufacturing and minin mergers, by type, 1948–1975. Source: Federal Trade Commission, Bureau Economics.*

raw numbers index. Charles Berry made some alternative estimates like thes but they are not comparable to the 50% raw numbers rate just mentione They refer to more firms over fewer years during the sixties.[11] Even so, roug extrapolation suggests a comparable growth rate of about 15–20% using "weighted" index of diversification.

[11] Charles H. Berry, *Corporate Growth and Diversification* (Princeton, N. J.: Princeton Ur versity Press, 1975), pp. 60–64.

Reasons for Merger

When counting the *reasons* for merger, one can get by with only the fingers on one hand, but just barely. In simplest terms, corporate marriage is merely a matter of finding a price that buyers are willing to pay and sellers are willing to accept. Going beyond this truism, however, we encounter complexities. Some motives are constant in the sense that they explain a fairly steady stream of mergers year in and year out. Other motives are more cyclical, a characteristic that helps explain why merger activity heats up and cools down over time. In other words, there are two interrelated issues—underlying cause and timing.

Timing of Mergers

Let us consider timing first. Several researchers have found a high positive correlation between the number of mergers per year and the general business cycle.[12] Merger frequency tends to rise and fall as the average level of stock market prices rises and falls. Ralph Nelson found a positive correlation of 0.47 between stock market price increases and all mergers in manufacturing over the period 1895–1954. Similarly, Willard Mueller found that, over the period 1919–1962, about 80% of the year-to-year variation in dairy company merger activity was positively associated with variations in average industrial stock prices.

Exactly why this correlation exists is not entirely clear. Experts speculate that owners of firms expecting eventually to sell out may feel they can get the best deal when stock prices are generally high. Conversely, from the buyers point of view, the basic problem is raising enough cash and securities to make an attractive offer. Hence, acquiring firms may find funds for acquisitions easier and cheaper to come by when stock prices are high. Notice in Figure 7-2 that merger activity wound down during the recessions of the early 1970s. As this is written (in 1977) a recovery brings some signs that a new wave may be getting underway. One such sign: in December 1976 the General Electric Company completed the largest corporate merger to date in terms of absolute (and now inflated) dollars, paying $2.17 billion in stock for Utah International Inc., a mammoth mining and natural-resources enterprise.[13]

Underlying Causes of Mergers

Underlying causes involve as much intuitive understanding as timing does. They are, however, less mysterious. Sellers and buyers may see things

---

[12] Nelson, *op. cit.*, pp. 106–26; Markham, *op. cit.*, pp. 146–54; and Willard Mueller, testimony n *Economic Concentration*, Hearings before the Senate Subcommittee on Antitrust and Monopoly, *art 2 (1965), p. 506.

[13] *Wall Street Journal*, February 18, 1977.

differently while benefiting mutually.[14] Sellers appear to have two major reasons for wanting to seek out a buyer. First, and most obvious, is the "failing firm" problem. As every used car owner knows, poor performance may prompt a sale. In the case of business enterprises, failure is measured not so much in terms of physical deterioration as it is in terms of declining revenues, disappointing profits, recurring losses, and even bankruptcy. Although any such aspect of failure may be an important motive for the sale of a small firm, it could be no more than a very minor motive for most sales of large firms. It has been estimated, for example, that only about 4.8 % of all "large" firms bought between 1948 and 1968 were suffering losses before their acquisition, where "large" was defined as having at least $10 million in assets.[15] In addition, estimated median profit rates for large acquired firms were 8.8, 9.2, and 10.2 % for horizontal, vertical, and conglomerate categories, respectfully. Thus, few of them stood (or lay) at death's door. Note too that, if failure was a major factor, merger frequency would not rise during business booms and fall during busts. It would be the other way around.

A second class of seller's motives relates to individually or family owned firms that are typically small. Merger may be the easiest means for an aging owner-manager to "cash-in" on his life-time effort and perpetuate the business after his retirement. Some income and estate tax considerations also favor the sale of such firms. Merger may likewise provide easier access to capital markets. Again, however, these seem to be minor factors, mere droplets in the tidal waves of time past. To the extent *large* sellers *actively* seek out buyers rather than wait to be wooed, their motives are usually more subtle (for example, running away from a despised suitor).

Of greater importance and keener interest are the buyers' motives. After all, the prices buyers pay to former owners typically exceed the book value of the purchased firms' assets and the market value of the former owners' stock holdings. This excess, or "premium," usually varies between 10 and 30 %, but may go as high as 50 % or more.[16] In early 1977, for example, prospective acquirers of Milgo Electronics were offering to pay $36 a share, whereas the former selling price was only $20 a share. Indeed, buyers may be so aggressive that they occasionally pull a "raid" or "take-over," in which case they succeed in buying a firm whose management opposes the acquisition. Stock owners who sell out against the management's wishes in these instances may no dislike their reluctant managers (although they frequently do); they may merely feel they have received an "offer they cannot refuse." Lest this give the impres-

[14] For an excellent discussion of causes see Peter O. Steiner, *Mergers: Motives, Effects, Policies* (Ann Arbor, Mich.: University of Michigan Press, 1975), especially Chapter 2.

[15] Stanley E. Boyle, "Pre-Merger Growth and Profit Characteristics of Large Conglomerate Mergers in the United States: 1948–1968," *St. Johns Law Review* (Spring 1970, Special Edition) pp. 160–61. See also Robert L. Conn, "The Failing Firm/Industry Doctrines in Conglomerate Mergers," *Journal of Industrial Economics* (March 1976), pp. 181–87.

[16] Steiner, *op. cit.*, p. 179; Gort and Hogarty, *op. cit.*; J. Fred Weston, "Determination of Share Exchange Ratios in Mergers," in *The Corporate Merger*, edited by W. Alberts and J. Segall (Chicago: University of Chicago Press, 1974), pp. 131–38.

150

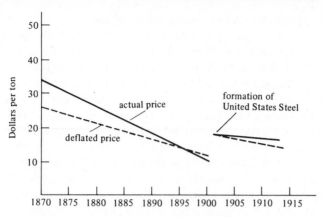

Figure 7-5. Pig iron price trend, before and after U.S. Steel. Source: Parsons and Ray, "The United States Steel Consolidation: The Creation of Market Control." Journal of Law and Economics (April 1975), p. 186.

sion that all merger motives are one sided, we hasten to add that the following list of buyer's motives includes items that could very well be considered "mutual" motives. Buyers and sellers may both benefit if the whole is worth more than the sum of its parts.

Monopoly Power. U. S. Steel was apparently worth more than the sum of its 170 parts. Prior to merger in 1901, the total value of the tangible property of the separate firms stood at roughly $700 million. After merger, U. S. Steel estimated its value at close to $1400 million. Why the enormous difference? A complete answer must await our discussion of conduct and performance. But this example is too good to pass up simply for the sake of textbook organization. Thus the answer is "market power." After merger, U. S. Steel produced two thirds of all United States semifinished steel and similar percentages of all rails, tin plate, rods, and other products. The consequences for the price of pig iron are pictured in Figure 7-5, which shows two price trend lines, one deflated by the wholesale price index, the other not. The discontinuous price jump of about 50% in 1901 coincides with the formation of U. S. Steel.

This may lead the astute reader to suspect a substantial rise in annual profit rates also, and he would be correct. Unfortunately, the profit side of the story cannot be shown so easily because of the change in ownership structure. If compared with the premerger value of $700 million, resulting profits would be handsome indeed; however, estimates actually reveal that, after merger, U. S. Steel common stockholders earned only about 9% return in dividends and higher stock prices during the first decade of incorporation. This is respectable but not excessive.

Where, then, did the profits go? They went to the former owners of the constituent companies and to the organizers of the merger, as is indicated by the $1400 million postmerger evaluation, or price paid in the transaction. Thus, a par value of $50 million in U. S. Steel stock was exchanged for $2 million worth of Federal Steel stock; a par value of $40 million in U. S. Steel stock was exchanged for $13 million worth of National Steel stock; and so on. As for the organizers or "promoters," J. P. Morgan's banking syndicate took $62.5 million. These added millions in capitalization represent the discounted future value of the *expected* excess profits that would accrue to the company after the merger. If the Steel Corporation had not been able to raise prices, profits to its stock holders relative to the new capitalization would have been very low, and the market value of the Corporation's stock would have therefore plummeted. To the very good fortune of those who got in on the ground floor, however, this did not happen. They could "cash-in" on their excess profit simply by selling their U. S. Steel stock. And those who bought it could make a "normal" return of 9% on their investment.[17] As F. M. Scherer explains, "the value of a company's common stock depends upon investor expectations regarding its future profits. If competition can be eliminated through merger, profits will presumably rise, and so the new consolidated firm's shares are worth more than the sum of the original companies' shares."[18]

U. S. Steel provides just one example. As we have already seen, there were many other huge horizontal mergers at the turn of the century that were probably motivated by the rewards of monopoly. The 70–90% market shares of those days speak fairly plainly for themselves. But a more explicit statement was made by Thomas Edison when he explained the formation of the General Electric Company in this way: "The consolidation of the companies . . . will do away with a competition which has become so sharp that the product of the factories has been worth little more than ordinary hardware."[19] Such bold talk and such merger-acquired market shares are largely a thing of the past. Present policy may be permissive in some ways, but it is not that permissive.

Whether market power could motivate vertical and conglomerate mergers as well as horizontal mergers is a much debated question. These other forms of merger produce no immediate or obvious increases in market share for the consolidated firm, nor do they promise added *market* concentration. Hence theories and empirical tests of possible adverse competitive effects of these mergers must attack the question indirectly. Since these indirect approaches entail rather circuitous routes through the territory of entry barriers and conduct, these topics will be dealt with in detail later. However, to anticipate briefly the case of vertical mergers, we can state that they may open up or

---

[17] Most of the data may be found in Parsons and Ray, *op. cit.* (see footnote 2).

[18] F. M. Scherer, *Industrial Market Structure and Economic Performance* (Chicago: Rand McNally, 1970), p. 113.

[19] H. C. Passer, *The Electrical Manufacturers: 1875–1900* (Cambridge, Mass.: Harvard University Press, 1953), p. 326.

ortunities for *price discrimination* and strengthen *barriers to entry*.[20] U. S. Steel provides an example of the barriers effect because the main source of its market power was its aggressive vertical acquisition of most iron ore supplies n North America. Charles Schwab, a prominent steel executive of the day, explained the consequences of U. S. Steel's 75% ore control while testifying n 1911:

> *Mr. Schwab.* I do not believe there will be any great development in iron and steel by new companies, but rather development by the companies now in business.
> *Mr. Chairman.* Now, explain that to us.
> *Mr. Schwab.* For the reason that the possibility of a new company getting at a sufficiently large supply of raw materials would make it exceedingly difficult if not impossible.[21]

To anticipate the case of conglomerate mergers, we can note that the greater ize and diversity they gain improves the possibility of *reciprocity*. This is a olicy of "I buy from you if you buy from me," and it may tend to foreclose ivals from affected markets. Conglomerate mergers may also eliminate *potential* competitors. In either event, profits might follow from the added power mplied. Substantiation or refutation of these and other possible effects is lifficult in particular cases and in general. However, several researchers have ound that the market shares of firms acquired by conglomerates do not usually grow inordinately after acquisition. They say this shows an absence of dverse competitive effect,[22] implying that most conglomerate mergers could not be motivated by quests for market power.

Risk Spreading Through Diversification. Suppose you want to get 2 dozen ggs delivered to your grandmother. Suppose further that she lives in the woods, nd the only available delivery service relies on brave but clumsy six year old girls attired in red. Experience shows that stumbles over roots and stones make uccessful egg delivery by any one girl a 50:50 proposition (even apart from he danger of wolves). Your problem then is this: If you want at least *some* of our 2 dozen eggs to get through, what delivery arrangements should you make? Placing the entire shipment in the hands of one girl means a 0.5 probability hat *none* will arrive. However, if you give 1 dozen to one girl and 1 dozen to nother, there is only one chance in four that no eggs will be delivered because hat is the probability of both girls falling down. Similarly, the split shipment ffers one chance in four that all eggs will arrive safely. Two times in every

---

[20] Willard F. Mueller, "Public Policy Toward Vertical Mergers," in *Public Policy Toward Mergers*, edited by F. Weston and S. Peltzman (Pacific Palisades, Calif.: Goodyear, 1969), pp. 50–66.

[21] Parsons and Ray, *op. cit.*, p. 198.

[22] L. G. Goldberg, "Conglomerate Mergers and Concentration Ratios," *Review of Economics nd Statistics* (August 1974), pp. 303–09; S. E. Boyle and P. W. Jaynes, *Economic Report on Conomerate Merger Performance* (Washington, D.C.: Federal Trade Commission, 1972), pp. 82–83.

four, 1 dozen will be broken and 1 dozen will get through. This example was developed by Roger Sherman to demonstrate the power of diversification in reducing risks.[23] He also demonstrates that still further diversification yields further risk reduction: "The best thing to do is to send 24 girls, each with one egg. The chance that no egg will arrive is then infinitesimally small, and it becomes very probable that about 12 eggs will arrive safely." The obvious moral (don't put all your eggs in one basket) may motivate many vertical and conglomerate mergers.

Diversification, however, is not always favorable; nor is merger the only means of achieving diversification. The conditions required for a positive effect for an acquiring firm are more limited than this simple example suggests.[24] In particular, the variances of the components of a combination must be essentially independent of each other. (The independence of several delivery girls would be severely compromised if they all held hands and thereby tripped over each other.) Failure to meet the conditions necessary for risk reduction may explain why researchers have been unable to find any risk reduction among conglomerate mergers generally.[25] Indeed, the gyrations of some conglomerates, such as LTV and Litton, offer evidence that mergers often augment risk rather than reduce it.

Economies of Scale. The larger size that mergers bring to combinations may yield lower costs of various kinds. These efficiencies may be divided into two broad groups—pecuniary economies and technical economies. **Pecuniary economies** are monetary savings derived from buying inputs more cheaply. Pecuniary gains thus include such things as larger "volume discounts" for the bulk purchase of raw materials or advertising space, lower interest rates on borrowed capital, and greater negotiating strength vis-a-vis labor, tax assessors, and others. In contrast, **technical economies** of scale are "genuine" cost savings. They imply fewer real inputs for a given level of output. Their primary sources are (1) greater specialization of equipment and operators, (2) high speed automation, (3) scaled-up equipment, and (4), in the case of vertical mergers, a refined coordination of effort between several stages of the production process.

We shall explore these efficiencies in a broader context in the next chapter. The question of immediate interest is whether mergers really produce such economies. Briefly, the answer is "yes" and "no." It is "yes" if we look only at the justifications businessmen most frequently offer the public for their mergers. It is "no" if we look at the evidence assembled and assessed by economists.

---

[23] Roger Sherman, *The Economics of Industry* (Boston: Little, Brown and Co., 1974), p. 105.

[24] H. Bierman, Jr. and J. L. Thomas, "A Note on Mergers and Risk," *Antitrust Bulletin* (Fa 1974), pp. 523–29.

[25] B. Lev and G. Mandelker, "The Microeconomic Consequences of Corporate Mergers," *Journal of Business* (January 1972), pp. 85–104; Samuel R. Reid, *The New Industrial Order* (New York: McGraw-Hill, 1976), pp. 94–98; R. W. Melicher and D. F. Rush, "The Performance of Conglomerate Firms: Recent Risk and Return Experience," *Journal of Finance* (May 1973), pp. 381–88.

Although *some* mergers may yield economies, they usually do not. Seeking *direct* evidence of cost savings, M. A. Utton studied British mergers important enough to be reported to the U. K. Monopolies Commission and found that "the evidence in merger reports has so far been unconvincing and the estimated savings very small."[26]

Indirect evidence afforded by studies of the profitability of mergers suggests that, at least in recent times, mergers have not, on the whole, been especially profitable. Compared to *non*acquiring firms (or relatively infrequent acquirers), aggressive acquirers experience no greater profits.[27] A few studies have even gone so far as to argue that, since World War II, firm merger activity and profitability are inversely related. When profits are sacrificed for the sake of rapid growth by merger, we may infer that growth, or speculative factors associated with growth, may be major motives.

Speculative and Financial Motives. Several influences may raise the price of an acquiring company's stock after a merger or series of mergers, even *without* any increment in market power, or economies of scale, or reduced risk, or enhanced real profit flows, or changes of the real assets under the combined control of the merging companies. Such stock price increases stem from speculation and often feed further speculation. They may stem from the mere *expectation* of real changes, as would be the case if investors expected a merger to capture as much market power as U. S. Steel acquired. Indeed, around the turn of the century many merger "promoters" exploited the expectations of investors by arranging mergers that had little chance of achieving real monopoly power while exaggerating monopoly power's prospects, planting rumors, and pointing to U. S. Steel's success. Once expectations were running wild and the deal was closed, promoters would hasten to sell the stock they obtained as a promotion fee to unsuspecting investor-speculators. These unfortunate folks often "took a bath." Shaw Livermore estimated that 141 of a sample of 328 mergers consumated between 1888 and 1905 were financial failures.[28]

Disclosure regulations have long since discouraged this unscrupulous practice. More recently (and more significantly for our own pocket books) we have the use of what Wall Streeters call "Confederate money." Assume the GO-GO Corporation has 1 million shares outstanding, and has annual profits of $1 million, or $1 per share. Its growth prospects are good, so its shares sell

---

[26] M. A. Utton, "British Merger Policy," in *Competition Policy in the UK and EEC*, edited by K. D. George and C. Joll (Cambridge, U. K.: Cambridge University Press, 1975), p. 108. See also Scherer's review of other British evidence, *op. cit.*, pp. 116–17 and G. Meeks, *Disappointing Marriage: A Study of the Gains from Merger* (Cambridge, U. K.: Cambridge University Press, 1977).

[27] For reviews of this evidence see Reid, *op. cit.*, pp. 103–09; Steiner, *op. cit.*, 190–95; T. F. Hogarty, "Profits from Merger: The Evidence of Fifty Years," *St. Johns Law Review* (Spring 1970, Special Edition), pp. 378–83. See also R. H. Mason and M. B. Goudzwaard, "Performance of Conglomerate Firms: A Portfolio Approach," *Journal of Finance* (March 1976), pp. 39–48.

[28] Shaw Livermore, "The Success of Industrial Mergers," *Quarterly Journal of Economics* (November 1935), pp. 68–96.

at $30 per share, resulting in a price earnings ratio of 30 : 1. Assume next that a second corporation called SLOW also has 1 million shares outstanding earning $1 each, but they are selling for $10 apiece because SLOW's internal growth is nil. If GO-GO's managers propose to buy SLOW, offering one-half of a new share of GO-GO in exchange for every one share of SLOW, the offer would be attractive to SLOW's stockholders. The half share of GO-GO is valued at $15 on the open market, whereas each share of SLOW is worth only $10.

Why in the world would GO-GO make such a generous offer? Its issue of 500,000 new GO-GO shares to buy SLOW would boost its capitalization to 1,500,000 shares outstanding. However, the addition of SLOW's $1,000,000 in earnings to GO-GO's $1,000,000 in earnings yields total earnings of $2,000,000. The new total earnings work out not to $1 a share, as before merger but to $1.33 a share. Thus, although nothing "genuine" has changed in the companies, their combined earnings per share are one third more lucrative after merger. Furthermore, GO-GO can continue to increase its earnings per share as long as it acquires companies with lower price-earnings ratios. How you may ask, can GO-GO maintain a high price-earnings ratio to make such acquisitions? It can as long as it continues to boost its earnings per share by buying companies.

Notice the circularity, however. GO-GO is building a house on sand. It earnings per share rise as a result of the acquisition of relatively slow and stodgy companies with relatively low price-earnings ratios rather than in response to real internal growth. Once acquisitions stop, the slow and stodgy real earnings cannot support the fantastically inflated price of GO-GO's stock. The ensuing result is well illustrated by true-life examples. Between year-end 1968 and year end 1974, when merger activity had died down, the total market value of LTV's stock fell 83%, Litton's plummeted 94%, Textron's dropped 66%, FMC's slumped 70%, and ITT's sank 63%. In contrast, the Dow Jones industrial average fell no more than 25% over the same period.[29] Other evidence also indicates that price-earnings manipulation played a major role in the merger movement of the sixties.[30] Exactly how major is a matter of opinion. Some experts estimate that its role was the principal reason behind at least 20% of all mergers occurring in 1967.[31]

Growth and Personal Aggrandizement. This survey would not be complete without mention of sheer growth and personal aggrandizement as motives. Just how important they are it is impossible to say. The Napoleonic aspiration of acquisitive business leaders cannot be captured by statistics, except insofar as statistics may disprove the importance of other, more publicly professed and more socially acceptable motives, such as economies of scale. You, the reader, are free to judge for yourself. You may draw upon your knowledge

---

[29] Reid, *op. cit.*, p. 97.

[30] Steiner, *op. cit.*, pp. 203–04; Walter J. Mead, "Instantaneous Merger Profit as a Conglomerate Merger Motive," *Western Economic Journal* (December 1969), pp. 295–306.

[31] *Business Week*, March 2, 1968, p. 42.

of human nature and your reading of whatever biographical material you may wish to look into. Two typical examples you will find are

- Harold Geneen led ITT in the acquisition of more than 250 companies. A close colleague of his once said, "Three things should be written on Hall Geneen's tombstone—earnings per share, 15% growth per year, and size."[32]
- Charles G. Bluhdorn, who guided Gulf & Western Industries through more than 80 acquisitions in 11 years, had this to say about his company and himself: "No mountain is high enough for us, nothing is impossible. The sky is the limit. . . . I came to this country without a penny, and built a company with 100,000 employees. This is what America is all about . . . to be able to do what I've done is a matter of pride to me and to the country."[33]

To summarize, the motives for merger are many and varied. No one explanation clearly surpasses all others. At any one time, there is a diversity of inducements; over time, trends of intention shift.

Merger Policy

There are two keys to understanding United States government policy toward mergers. First, the private interests and motives of business managers and stockholders are *not* accorded any weight in such policy. Why? As far as a merger may be socially beneficial, the benefits are almost always attainable by means *other* than merger. Economies of scale and diversification, for example, can be achieved by internal expansion as successfully as by merger. In the case of the failing firm or the aging owner-manager in search of a friendly savior, a strict rule denying anticompetitive mergers would probably exclude no more than a few prospective buyers, leaving open the possibility of sale to any number of other possible—and more suitable—acquirers. Conversely, for motives that are grounded on purely private gains or socially detrimental pursuits, a strict policy will either be neutral or favorable to the public interest.[34]

The second key was introduced in Chapter 1. Maintenance of competition by structural dispersal of power is a policy objective in and of itself. Many if not most congressmen and judges believe that the growth of large economic groups could lead only to increasing government control; freedom would corrode and the nation would drift into some form of totalitarianism."[35]

For these several reasons, the law governing most mergers has a structural focus and is designed to curb market power in the early stages (to "nip it in the

[32] Spoken by Richard H. Griebel, a former ITT executive and president of Lehigh Valley Industries, *Business Week*, May 9, 1970, p. 61. For more on Geneen see Anthony Sampson, *The Sovereign State of ITT* (Fawcett Crest Paperback, 1974).

[33] *Business Week*, July 5, 1969, p. 34.

[34] Derek C. Bok, "Section 7 of the Clayton Act and the Merging of Law and Economics," *Harvard Law Review* (1960), p. 308.

[35] *Ibid.*, p. 235.

bud" before it fully blossoms). Section 7 of the Clayton Act of 1914 prohibited potentially anticompetitive mergers—but it had enormous loopholes. These were not plugged until 1950, with passage of the Celler–Kefauver Amendment (which has some loopholes of its own). The amended statute outlaws mergers

> where in any line of commerce in any section of the country, the effect of such acquisition may be substantially to lessen competition, or tend to create a monopoly.

The Act is enforced by the Justice Department, which argues its cases in the federal courts; and by the Federal Trade Commission, whose judgments may or may not be appealed to high federal courts by dissatisfied defendants. Hundreds of cases have been decided under the Act, but we shall review only a few of the more important ones. Before we do, a brief outline of what to look for may be helpful:

1. The phrase "in any line of commerce" refers to product markets. Major factors affecting the courts' definition of relevant product markets include (a) the product's physical characteristics and uses, (b) unique production facilities, (c) distinct customers, (d) cross–elasticity of demand with substitutes, and (e) the absolute price level of possible substitutes.
2. The phrase "in any section of the country" refers to particular geographic markets. Major factors affecting the courts' definition of relevant geographic markets include (a) the costs of transportation, (b) legal restrictions on geographic scope, (c) the extent to which local demand is met by outside supply—for example, little in from outside, and (d) the extent to which local production is shipped to other areas—for example, little out from inside.[36]
3. The phrase "may be ... to lessen competition" reflects the importance of *probable* adverse effect. In this regard the major factors considered by the courts include (a) the market shares and ranks of the merging firms, (b) concentration in the market, (c) *trends* in market shares and concentration, (d) merger history in the market, (e) declines in the absolute number of firms, and (f) the elimination of a strong, competitively vigorous independent firm.

Horizontal Mergers

The Bethlehem-Youngstown Case (1958)[37]

Bethlehem Steel's acquisition of Youngstown Sheet & Tube in 1957 was the first large merger challenged under the Cellar–Kefauver Act. The firms ranked

---

[36] K. G. Elzinga and T. F. Hogarty, "The Problem of Geographic Market Delineation in Antimerger Suits," *Antitrust Bulletin* (Spring 1973), pp. 45–81.
[37] *United States v. Bethlehem Steel Corp.*, 168 F. Supp. 576 (1958).

second and sixth nationally among steel producers. Their combined ingot capacity amounted to 21% of total industry capacity. The number one firm, U. S. Steel, had a 30% share at the time, so this merger would have boosted the share of U. S. Steel and Bethlehem taken together from 45 to 50%. In the court's opinion, "This would add substantially to concentration in an already highly concentrated industry and reduce unduly the already limited number of integrated steel companies." The court was also impressed by the fact that, historically, mergers accounted "for the existing high degree of concentration in the industry." Aside from U. S. Steel's origins, "Bethlehem's growth in substantial measure is the result of mergers."

Bethlehem's defense argument for acquisition of Youngstown Sheet & Tube was that the national market was not the relevant geographic market for steel products. It's attorneys urged acceptance of three separate markets within the United States—eastern, midcontinental, and western. Since all of Youngstown's plants were located in the midcontinent area whereas all of Bethlehem's plants were either eastern or western, the defense went on to argue that the high costs of steel transportation prevented head-on competition between the merging firms. Moreover, they claimed that the acquisition would bring Bethlehem into the Chicago area, where it could then compete more effectively with U.S. Steel, the dominant force in that area.

The court rejected these arguments. It said that, even though Bethlehem did not have ingot capacity in the midcontinent area, Bethlehem's annual shipments of more than 2 million tons into the area indicated direct competition with Youngstown. Direct rivalry prevailed in other sections of the country as well. Furthermore, the court recognized that market delineation "must be made on the basis of where *potentially* they could make sales." In other words, Bethlehem was surely capable of entering the Chicago market by internal expansion instead of by acquisition. As for the argument that the combined companies could better compete with U. S. Steel, the same faulty logic could justify successive merger until just two or three firms were left in the industry, a situation that could hardly be considered competitive. Thus the merger was enjoined. The benefits of the court's denial were realized for all to see when a few years later Bethlehem *did* build a massive steel plant 30 miles east of Chicago.

The Continental Can Case (1964)[38]

In this case the Supreme Court held illegal a merger between Continental Can, the nation's second largest manufacturer of metal containers, and Hazel–Atlas Glass Company, the nation's third largest producer of glass containers. It was generally agreed that the entire country constituted the geographic market. Thus product market delineation became the critical issue. Table 7-1 shows the shares of these companies under alternative product market definitions. Continental produced no glass containers, and Hazel–Atlas produced no metal

[38] *United States v. Continental Can Co.*, 378 U. S. 441 (1964).

TABLE 7-1 Percentage of Metal and Glass Container Shipments Accounted for by Continental Can and Hazel-Atlas, 1955

Product Market	Continental Can	Hazel-Atlas	Continental and Hazel-Atlas Combined
Metal containers	33.0	None	33.0
Glass containers	None	9.6	9.6
Metal and glass containers	21.9	3.1	25.0

Source: *U.S.* v. *Continental Can Co.* 378 U.S. 441 (1964).

cans. A narrow definition that kept the two products separate would therefore mean no change in market shares as a result of the merger. Conversely, a broad definition combining metal and glass would imply direct competition between the companies and a jump in market share for Continental from 21.9 to 25%. Note that a still broader definition, one including paper and plastic as well as metal and glass, would also place these firms in the same market, but it would give them much lower market shares.

A majority of the Court thought that metal and glass containers combined could be considered a proper "line of commerce" for purposes of Section 7:

> Metal has replaced glass and glass has replaced metal as the leading container for some important uses; both are used for other purposes; each is trying to expand its share of the market at the expense of the other; and each is attempting to preempt for itself every use for which its product is physically suitable, even though some such uses have traditionally been regarded as the exclusive domain of the competing industry.

Up to that time this interproduct competition had been especially sharp for packaging beer, soft drinks, and baby food. To a lesser degree it extended to household chemicals and other areas. From recognition of these aspects of competition, it was a small step to a conclusion of merger illegality. The firms were large and highly ranked. Moreover, "the product market embracing the combined metal and glass container industries was dominated by six firms having a total of 70.1% of the business." The Court felt that where "concentration is already great, the importance of preventing even slight increases in concentration ... is correspondingly great."

The Von's Case (1966)[39]

This case is to horizontal mergers what the sixth commandment is to homicide. The acquisition was denied, although neither firm involved was really

[39] *United States v. Von's Grocery Co.*, 384 U. S. 270 (1966).

very big and, by usual standards, the market was not highly concentrated. Von's ranked third among retail grocery store chains in the Los Angeles area when in 1960 it acquired Shopping Bag Food Stores, which ranked sixth. Their market shares were, respectively, 4.3 and 3.2%. Hence, their combined sales amounted to 7.5%. This would have boosted the four-firm concentration ratio in the Los Angeles market from 24.4% before merger to 28.8% after. Moreover, 8-firm and 12-firm concentration had been on the rise prior to merger.

These facts might have been moderately damning. But Justice Black chose to neglect them when writing the Supreme Court's majority opinion. He stressed other factors:

> the number of owners operating a single store in the Los Angeles retail grocery market decreased from 5,365 in 1950 to 3,818 in 1961. By 1963, three years after merger, the number of single store owners had dropped still further to 3,590. During roughly the same period from 1953 to 1962 the number of chains with two or more grocery stores increased from 96 to 150. While the grocery business was being concentrated into the hands of fewer and fewer owners, the small companies were continually being absorbed by the larger firms through mergers.

Indeed, Black defines concentration in terms of the *number* of independent firms. He goes on to state that "the basic purpose of the 1950 Celler–Kefauver Bill was to prevent economic concentration in the American economy by keeping a large number of small competitors in business." By this reasoning, a divestiture order was unavoidable.

However laudable these sentiments might be, we may question as a matter of economics whether the massive demise of mom-and-pop grocery stores in Los Angeles was due to mergers like the one denied. Divestiture of Shopping Bag did not resurrect them. They fell by the wayside for reasons of economies of scale, cheap automobile transportation to shopping centers, easy parking in the shopping centers, and the like. In any event, divestiture could have been justified on more conventional grounds. Thus the Court seems to have set a stringent legal standard while deferring to a moderate standard of economic proficiency.

The Pabst Case (1966)[40]

Both standards carried over into the Pabst case, another denial decided just after the Von's case. In 1958 Pabst was the nation's tenth largest brewer. It acquired Blatz, the eighteenth largest. This merger made Pabst the nation's fifth largest brewer with 4.49% of nationwide sales volume. Thus, in terms of a broad national definition of the market, the ranks and shares involved here were rather low, even lower than those in Von's. Government prosecutors therefore argued acceptance of Wisconsin and a three-state area made up of Wisconsin, Illinois, and Michigan as relevant geographic markets. In Wisconsin,

---

[40] *United States v. Pabst Brewing Co.*, 384 U. S. 540 (1966).

for instance, Blatz had been the largest seller and Pabst had been fourth; after the merger Pabst was first with 23.95% of state sales. The Supreme Court bought the idea of limited state markets without any economic justification:

> The language of [the Act] requires merely that the Government prove the merger has a substantial anticompetitive effect somewhere in the United States—"in *any* section" of the United States. This phrase does not call for the delineation of a "section of the country" by metes and bounds as a surveyor would lay off a plot of ground.

Although the resulting thumbs-down decision may have been correct, the Court's cavalier treatment of the market definition problem has been strongly criticized. Unfortunately, few critics have suggested constructive analytical procedures for use in future cases.[41]

Several years after *Von's* and *Pabst*, the Justice Department promulgated a set of "Merger Guidelines." The Guidelines indicate which horizontal, vertical, and conglomerate mergers are likely to be challenged by the government in light of prevailing case law. The principles give explicit guidance to enterprises contemplating mergers and give some consistency to official policy. For horizontal mergers, the Guidelines are primarily structural, as shown in Table 7-2. Notice in particular that the percentages are so arranged that, as the market share of the acquiring firm becomes larger, the threshold size of the acquisitions that will be challenged becomes smaller. These Guidelines and the stern stand of the Supreme Court have led commentators to conclude that large horizontal mergers are now almost *per se* illegal in the United States.[42]

Vertical Mergers

Short of monopoly, the critical issue in nearly all vertical merger cases is "foreclosure." Before merger, numerous suppliers can compete for each independent user's purchases. After merger, supplier and user are linked by common ownership. Products then typically flow between the merged firms as far as is practicable, and the sales opportunities of other suppliers diminish. If the vertical linkage is trivial, as would be true of a farmer owning a roadside vegetable stand, competition is not affected. If, on the other hand, the foreclosure covers a wide portion of the total market, there may be anticompetitive consequences.

The Brown Shoe Case (1962)[43]

In 1955, the date of this merger, Brown was the fourth largest manufacturer of shoes in the United States, accounting for about 4% of total shoe production.

---

[41] A major exception: Elzinga and Hogarty, *op. cit.* (see footnote 36).

[42] I say "almost" because some big ones have gotten away, such as Warner-Lamber with Park, Davis in drugs, and National Steel with Granite City Steel.

[43] *Brown Shoe Company v. United States*, 370 U. S. 294 (1962).

TABLE 7-2 Summary of Justice Department Horizontal "Merger Guidelines"

The process of market definition may result in identification of *several* appropriate markets in which to test the probable competitive effects of a particular merger. The standards most often applied in determining a challenge may be stated in terms of the sizes of the merging firms' market shares.

1. Where the four-firm concentration ratio is 75% or more, the following will ordinarily be challenged:

Acquiring Firm		Acquired firm
4% or more	and	4% or more
10% or more	and	2% or more
15% or more	and	1% or more

2. Where the four-firm concentration ratio is less than 75%, the following will ordinarily be challenged:

Acquiring firm		Acquired firm
5% or more	and	5% or more
10% or more	and	4% or more
15% or more	and	3% or more
20% or more	and	2% or more
25% or more	and	1% or more

3. If market concentration has been increasing substantially, all mergers over 2% will ordinarily be challenged.
4. Any acquisition of a competitor that is a particularly "disturbing," "disruptive," or otherwise unusually competitive factor in the market.
5. Failing firms are exempt if they face a "clear probability" of failure and have tried unsuccessfully to meet these guidelines.
6. Claims of scalar economies will *not* exempt a merger.

Source: Department of Justice, "Merger Guidelines" (May 30, 1968), reprinted in *The Journal of Reprints for Antitrust Law and Economics* (Summer 1969), pp. 181–98.

It acquired the Kinney Company, which at the time was the nation's largest independent retail shoe chain, with over 400 stores in more than 270 cities and about 1.2% of all retail shoe sales by dollar volume. The case had horizontal as well as vertical aspects because Brown already owned, or controlled contractually, over 1230 retail shops. But most of these were, like Kinney, *acquired* by Brown. Hence, we shall focus solely on the vertical aspects.

On these vertical aspects the Supreme Court stressed several points. First, since Kinney was the largest independent retail chain, the Court felt that, in this industry, "no merger between a manufacturer and an independent retailer could involve a larger potential market foreclosure." Second, the evidence showed that Brown would use the acquisition "to force Brown shoes into

Kinney stores." Third, there was a *trend* toward vertical integration in the industry, a trend in which the acquiring manufacturers had "become increasingly important sources of supply for their acquired outlets," and the "necessary corollary of these trends is the foreclosure of independent manufacturers from markets otherwise open to them." Although Brown's attorneys argued that the shoe industry was composed of a large number of manufacturers and retailers, the Court rejected their arguments on grounds that "remaining vigor cannot immunize a merger if the trend in that industry is toward oligopoly." The Court thus ordered divestiture.

The Cement Cases (1961–1967)

Approximately three fourths of all cement is used to produce ready-mixed concrete (cement premixed with sand or other aggregate). Prior to 1960 there was virtually no integration between the cement and ready-mixed concrete industries. By 1966, however, after an outbreak of merger activity, at least 40 ready-mix concrete companies had been acquired by leading cement companies, and several large producers of ready-mixed concrete had begun to make cement. The Federal Trade Commission issued a series of complaints, directed its staff to make an industry-wide investigation, and in January 1967 issued a policy statement challenging vertical mergers in the industry, all of which seems to have reduced acquisition activity appreciably.[44]

In the eyes of the FTC, the relevant geographic markets were regional because 90% of all cement is shipped no more than 160 miles. Within the regional markets four-firm concentration typically exceeded 50%, in part because of economies of scale. Thus it was felt that the vertical merger movement threatened foreclosure in at least some regional markets. Areas particularly affected were Kansas City, Richmond, and Memphis, where more than 30% of all cement produced was consumed by "captive" ready-mix concrete companies. According to the Commission:

> When one or more major ready-mixed concrete firms are tied through ownership to particular cement suppliers, the resulting foreclosure not only may be significant in the short run, but may impose heavy long-run burdens on the disadvantaged cement suppliers who continue selling in markets affected by integration. Acquisitions of leading cement consumers in markets containing comparatively few volume buyers may have the effect of substantially disrupting the competitive situation at the cement level . . . .

The FTC's crackdown on cement acquisitions and the decision in the *Brown Shoe* case inspired the vertical merger portion of the Justice Department's "Merger Guidelines." The Guidelines state that vertical acquisitions will

---

[44] Federal Trade Commission, *Economic Report on Mergers and Vertical Integration in the Cement Industry* (Washington, D.C., 1966); Enforcement Policy with Respect to Vertical Mergers in the Cement Industry, January 1967, in Commerce Clearing House, 1971 *Trade Regulation Reports*, #4520.

ordinarily be challenged if the supplying firm makes 10% or more of the sales in its market and merges with any purchaser that accounts for 6% or more of total purchases. Furthermore, even lower market shares may be challenged if "there has been or is developing, a significant trend toward vertical integration by merger."

Conglomerate Mergers

The record-breaking merger statistics of the sixties show that the law has been almost inconsequential when it comes to conglomerate acquisitions. If a big conglomerate merger can be twisted into a horizontal or vertical configuration (as happened in the *Continental Can/Hazel–Atlas Glass* case), its chances of legal survival shrink considerably. If, however, it can withstand twisting, its chances of challenge must be somewhere below one in a thousand. In other words, officials are reluctant to apply curbs except where mergers clearly affect *particular markets*. Even so, the few cases that have been successfully brought in this area, as well as the Justice Department's Guidelines, seem to indicate some degree of vulnerability if the conglomerate merger involves two truly dominant firms (IBM and GM, say), or two very large firms (for example, Texaco and Ford Motors), or potential entrants (like U. S. Steel and ALCOA Aluminum), or some blatantly bad behavior subsequent to merger (for example, reciprocity or predatory pricing).

The Procter & Gamble Case (1967)[45]

Procter & Gamble's 1958 acquisition of Clorox Chemical Co. could be considered a product extension merger. Among other things, Procter was the dominant producer of soaps and detergents, accounting for 54.4% of all packaged detergent sales. Clorox, on the other hand, was the nation's leading manufacturer of household liquid bleach, with approximately 48.8% of total sales at the time. As these statistics suggest, the markets for detergents and bleach were both highly concentrated. The Supreme Court decided that the merger was illegal, but not wholly or even mainly because of these market shares.

Anticompetitive effects were found in several respects. First, and most obviously, Procter was a prime prospective entrant into the bleach industry. Thus, 'the merger would seriously diminish potential competition by eliminating Procter as a potential entrant." Indeed, prior to the acquisition, "Procter was in the course of diversifying into product lines related to its basic detergent-soap-cleanser business," and liquid bleach was a distinct possibility because t is used with detergent.

Second, the Court expressed concern that the merger would confer anticompetitive advantages in the realm or marketing. Although all liquid bleach

---

[45] *Federal Trade Commission v. Procter & Gamble Co.*, 386 U. S. 568 (1967).

is chemically identical (5.25% sodium hypochlorite and 94.75% water), it is nevertheless highly differentiated. Clorox spent more than 12% of its sales revenues on advertising, and priced its bleach at a premium relative to unadvertised brands. For its part, Procter was the nation's leading advertiser (and still is).

The Court therefore felt that Procter would unduly strengthen Clorox against other firms in the bleach market by extending to Clorox the same volume discounts on advertising that it received from the advertising media. Moreover, "retailers might be induced to give Clorox preferred shelf space since it would be manufactured by Procter, which also produced a number of other products marketed by retailers." In sum, "the substitution of the powerful acquiring firm for the smaller, but already dominant, firm may substantially reduce the competitive structure of the industry by raising entry barriers and dissuading the smaller firms from aggressively competing."

The ITT-Grinnell Case (1970)[46]

This case is of interest because the Justice Department tried to argue that a finding of specific anticompetitive effect in specific product and geographic markets was *not* required for illegality. It argued instead that, in the wake of a "trend among large diversified industrial firms to acquire other large corporations," it could be concluded that "anticompetitive consequences will appear in numerous though *undesignated* individual 'lines of commerce'."

The merger at issue was ITT's acquisition of Grinnell, a very large manufacturer of automatic sprinkler devices and related products. Since ITT had been a major participant in the conglomerate merger mania, and since Grinnell was big, this was as good a case as any to test the theory that adding to *aggregate concentration* alone was offensive under the law. But the District Court did not agree, and the Justice Department lost:

> The Court's short answer to this claim . . . is that the legislative history, the statute itself and the controlling decisional law all make it clear beyond a peradventure of a doubt that in a Section 7 case the alleged anticompetitive effects of a merger must be examined in the context of *specific product and geographic markets*; and the determination of such markets is a necessary predicate to a determination of whether there has been a substantial lessening of competition within an area of effective competition. To ask the Court to rule with respect to alleged anticompetitive consequences in *undesignated lines of commerce* is tantamount to asking the Court to engage in judicial legislation. This the Court most emphatically refuses to do.

The District Court opinion was not reviewed by the Supreme Court because the case was settled by consent decree prior to appeal.[47] Thus, the law is still

---

[46] *United States v. International Telephone and Telegraph Corp.*, 324 F. Supp. 19 (D. Conn. 1970).

[47] For a similar district court opinion see *United States v. Northwest Industries*, 301 F. Supp. 1066 (N. D. Ill. 1969) at 1096.

in flux. For the present, though, we have finally bumped into the outer limit of the law. As this limit is limited, conglomerate mergers proceed apace.

In a concluding note, we ought to acknowledge that judicial statements of legality tell only part of the story. *Remedies* are equally important. For if illegal mergers are allowed to stand, they might just as well be declared legal. In an extensive study of remedies in horizontal, vertical, and conglomerate cases won by the government, Kenneth Elzinga found few instances of truly effective relief.[48] Firms illegally acquired were only rarely returned to full-fledged independent status. Most often there was no relief whatsoever—or only a ban on future acquisitions, or partial divestiture, or divestiture of a nonviable firm, or divestiture to a strong horizontal competitor. The last form of phoney relief is illustrated by the Continental Can case discussed earlier. Continental had to sell the Hazel–Atlas Glass company. But it sold Hazel to the Brockway Glass Company, which was the fourth largest producer of *glass* products in the country. Had Brockway bought Hazel–Atlas in the first place, it would most likely have perpetrated an illegal horizontal merger.

Summary

History reveals an annual stream of mergers that occasionally swells to a flood. Around the turn of the century thousands of multifirm horizontal mergers transformed many manufacturing and mining industries into tight-knit oligopolies and near monopolies. A second major movement during the late 1920s brought further horizontal couplings and introduced extensive vertical and conglomerate activity as well. Most recently, the 1950s and 1960s witnessed the largest merger movement of all. During the 1960s 25,598 mergers were recorded, involving scores of billions of dollars in assets. Most acquisitions were conglomerate in nature, and the most active acquirers were conglomerates.

Generally speaking, merger frequency tends to rise and fall as the average level of stock market prices rises and falls. Thus, the timing of mergers is influenced by financial considerations. In addition, there are several basic underlying stimulants to merger, all of which have played some role in the past, none of which has clearly dominated the scene: (1) The pursuit of market power is most clearly associated with horizontal mergers. The first merger movement provides the best examples of this—including the U. S. Steel merger of 1901. (2) A desire to diversify, and thereby reduce risk, motivates many conglomerate mergers. Although some mergers may further this goal, most apparently do not. (3) Businessmen like to justify their mergers with claims of efficiency or economies of scale. Such claims may occasionally be valid, but the available

---

[48] Kenneth G. Elzinga, "The Antimerger Law: Pyrrhic Victories?" *Journal of Law and Economics* (April 1969), pp. 43–78.

evidence indicates that these claims are overly optimistic (if that is the right word). (4) Speculation contributed substantially to the merger movement of the sixties. (5) We cannot rule out growth and personal aggrandizement, although these factors are difficult to quantify.

As for policy, most law makers seem to favor stringent structural standards that ignore motives. To the extent that a merger may be socially beneficial, the benefits are usually attainable by other means, such as internal expansion or mutual fund organizations for investments. Errors of denial can thus be fairly easily rectified. However, structural stringency has been achieved only in the case of horizontal mergers and, to a lesser extent, vertical mergers. Conglomerate mergers are largely untouchable under current law, unless they can be pushed or pulled into vertical or horizontal shape by manipulations of "the market's" definition.

8

Barriers to Entry: Theory and Cross-Section Evidence

An oligopolistic industry may not be oligopolistic for long if every Tom, Dick, and Harry can enter.

EDWIN MANSFIELD

Imitation, plagiarism, and copy-cat behavior are generally frowned upon. There are permissible exceptions, though. A trial lawyer loves to have judges plagiarize from his "briefs" when they write their opinions because the opinions will then be favorable to the lawyer's clients. An economist likes to see imitation in the form of market entry because significant entry often brings lower prices, greater product diversity, better quality, and the like. In other words, **entry** is merely a shorthand way of saying that a firm *new to the market* has begun to offer a product or service that is a close *substitute* for the products or services of firms already established in the market. The newcomer may be established in another market and may merely ape the sellers already in the market entered. On the other hand, the newcomer could be a spanking-new firm and might do more than merely ape existing sellers. It might offer buyers something special, such as lower prices or faster service. If one of the new offerings is particularly successful in taking business away from established firms, those firms may end up imitating the entrant. All this adds up to intensified competition.

Of course entry does not occur at the drop of a hat. Attempted entry costs money, and there is no assurance that an attempt will prosper—that the newcomer will become in time a profitable old-timer. Entry hinges on two conditions—motivation and ability. For **motivation**, the prospects of eventually earning a substantial profit must be good. In **ability**, the potential entrant must

169

be legally and financially capable of making the attempt. Any factor that reduces the motivation or ability of potential entrants despite established firms' excessively high profits may be called a **barrier to entry**. It is the purpose of this chapter to identify, explain, and measure various barriers to entry. As stated earlier, in Chapter 3, we are interested in barriers to entry for the same reason we were interested in product differentiation and concentration: they are a major source of market power. If barriers to entry are formidable, established firms have yet another source of power over price. The concept of barriers is thus useful in explaining conduct and performance. It also helps to explain variances in observed concentration, because high barriers tend to be associated with high concentration. The concept is useful, moreover, in assessing public policy, for not all barriers are "naturally" or "technologically" determined; some are artificial and due to human manipulation.

We begin by briefly indentifying and classifying various possible structural barriers. We then review some evidence concerning their prevalence. Finally, we take a penetrating look at each main barrier.

An Overview of Barriers to Entry

Joe Bain, an early pioneer in research on barriers to entry, defined a barrier as anything conferring advantages on "established sellers in an industry over potential entrant sellers, these advantages being reflected in the extent to which established sellers can persistently raise their prices above a competitive level without attracting new firms to enter the industry."[1] When entry is easy, the advantages of established sellers are slight. When entry is difficult, the advantages of established sellers are great, and barriers may balloon to gargantuan proportions. Following Bain, barriers may be classified into four broad groups: (1) absolute unit cost differences, (2) economies of scale, (3) capital cost requirements, and (4) product differentiation.[2]

Absolute Cost-Advantage Barriers

The first category of barriers comprises absolute cost advantages of established firms. If for any given level of output the established firms can produce and market their wares at a lower cost per unit than newcomers, then any newcomer takes on the established firms with both hands tied behind its back. Take a look at Figure 8-1. Assuming unit costs go neither up nor down as a function of output, total unit costs (TUC) for the entrant are indicated by the uppermost horizontal line of Figure 8-1. The lower TUC line of a typical established firm shows cost advantages at every level of output. If the potential

[1] Joe S. Bain, *Barriers to New Competition* (Cambridge, Mass.: Harvard University Press, 1956) p. 3.
[2] *Ibid*, pp. 15–16.

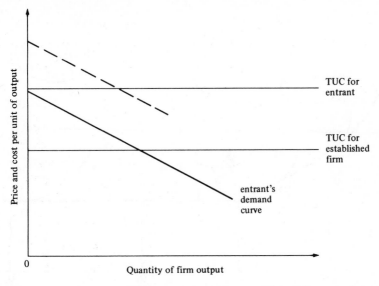

Figure 8-1. *Absolute cost differences between established firms and potential entrants.*

entrant expects his demand curve to be as depicted by the solid, negatively sloped line, then there is *no* level of output where he can cover his costs with revenues. The prospect's TUC lies above his expected demand at every point. If, on the other hand, the entrant's expected demand curve were more generously located, as suggested by the loftier, dashed demand line, or if the entrant's unit costs were lower, then entry would appear profitable—even if on a rather small scale. What is likely to raise the potential entrant's unit costs above those of established firms? The entrant may have to pay more for scarce raw materials, ship them greater distances, use inferior production technologies, or pay higher interest rates on borrowed capital.

Barriers Owing to Economies of Scale

Scalar economies constitute the second general class of barriers. In these instances the unit cost curves confronting potential entrants and established firms are quite similar in elevation and shape. But the *shape* of the curve itself is such as to give established firms an advantage. Figure 8-2 shows the derivation of a long-run unit cost curve for a single plant (or a single-plant firm) that reflects economies of scale. The long-run unit cost curve is best thought of as a *hypothetical* construct that carries real consequences. The potential entrant's engineers could design various possible plants of *identical* output capacity that used *different* production technologies. The resulting short-run unit cost curves might be depicted in Figure 8-2 as *A*, *B*, and *C* for output Q_1.

171

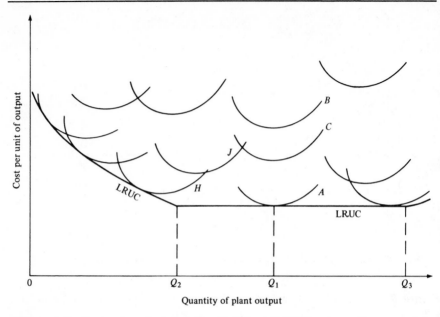

Figure 8-2. Derivation of a Long-Run Unit Cost (LRUC) curve with economies of scale.

Of course it is also possible to hypothesize plants of *differing* output capacity but *identical* technological style. The resulting short-run cost curves in this case could be those labelled *H*, *J*, and *C* in Figure 8-2. The short-run cost curves of other plants may look like clusters of fish scales, but they illustrate the diversity of conceivable designs and capacities. Although the possibilities thus seem rich, only the *lowest* cost possibility would be chosen by rational businessmen for any given level of projected output. For output Q_1 the choice is *A*, for example. Hence, the lower boundary, or "envelope" curve, depicts the long-run average cost curve confronting potential entrants. The curve declines up to output Q_2 because added size brings added efficiency. Beyond Q_2, size confers no additional advantages. Hence Q_2 is often called the **minimum efficient scale (MES)**. Beyond Q_3 it is assumed that added size yields *dis*economies, as indicated by a rise in LRUC.

How do scalar economies inhibit entry? The answer is not self-evident. We have already said that given enough money anyone—entrants and established firms alike—could build an MES plant easy as pie. The problem is that existing firms will have *already* built efficient plants. And the added output of an entrant's efficient plant may be so large relative to industry demand that, after entry, product price will fall below the entrant's (and established firms') cost per unit. In other words, there may not be room in the industry for an additional seller when efficient output is large relative to existing output and demand.

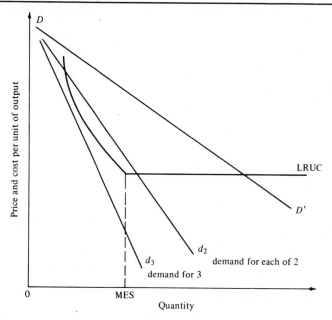

Figure 8-3. Economies of scale acting as a barrier to the entry of a third firm.

For example, assume that DD' is industry demand in Figure 8-3. Assume further that LRUC is the long-run unit cost curve confronting any firm. With two existing firms sharing total industry demand equally, each firm would view its demand as d_2, which is one half of DD' at each possible price. Since d_2 lies above LRUC over a considerable range, each of the two firms could produce and sell at a profit. However, a potential entrant would not have such a favorable view of the situation. If it is assumed that demand would be split evenly three ways in the event of a third firm's entry (a very optimistic assumption for a new entrant to make), each firm's demand would then become d_3, which is one third of DD' at each possible price. But given d_3, there is *no* plant scale that yields a profit to the entrant. There is no point at which LRUC falls below d_3. The result: no third firm entry.

A shift left of LRUC, and a consequentially lower level of MES output, would permit entry. Likewise, a LRUC curve that rose less sharply to the left of MES would also allow entry. But, as it stands, Figure 8-3 looks more like a bear pit than a welcome mat to third party prospects. Note, too, that a substantial shift outward to the right of the DD' line would make room for new entrants. Hence it is cost *relative* to demand that really counts. And rapidly growing demand may foster entry.

As stated in the preceding chapter, economies of scale may be of two types— pecuniary economies and technical economies. The former are merely monetary

173

savings on the purchase of inputs derived from the greater bargaining power that often goes with greater size. Quantity and volume discounts are of this type. On the other hand, technical economies constitute "real" savings in the sense that fewer of society's scarce resources are used up in the production-distribution process. Each type of saving will be explored fully in the next few pages. (It should also be noted that economies of scale may derive from multi-plant operations as well as large single-plant operations.)

Capital Cost Barriers

Third, we are now in a position to appreciate capital cost barriers to entry. Minimum efficient scale, MES as defined above, will in part determine the total capital outlay required for efficient entry. Generally speaking, a large MES necessitates a large capital cost outlay. However, since the prices of equipment and construction materials also enter the picture, MES does not always determine the cost. In any event, if the capital costs of efficient entry are appreciably more than what you and your friends can scrape together from your savings, say $1 billion, then capital costs pose a barrier to entry—even when MES plant is small relative to industry demand.

This barrier might be classified with the other absolute cost barriers mentioned earlier, since its effect often shows up in higher costs of borrowing, namely, higher interest rates. On the other hand, there are several features of this barrier that distinguish it. For one thing, it is closely connected to scalar elements, whereas other absolute unit cost differences are not. Second, the deterrence of this barrier depends on the nature of the potential entrant as well as the nature of the industry. If the prime potential entrant is already large—a General Motors, say, or an Exxon—then even enormous capital costs pose no great problems.

Barriers Caused by Product Differentiation

Fourth and finally, product differentiation may present a barrier to entry. A newcomer to some industry may face no absolute cost disadvantages in production, no difficulties in building a plant of efficient scale, and no trouble raising capital for that plant. The newcomer may nevertheless find the going tough if that industry deals in a highly differentiated product because successful entry would then depend on more than passing these tests in production. It would also require mastery of *marketing* problems, for the newcomer would then have to woo customers away from established firms with more than satisfactory prices. Marketing a differentiated product entails substantial costs, just as production entails costs—that is, the costs of advertising, packaging, style, and so on. And these marketing costs may pose problems for an entrant if they display characteristics similar to those displayed by production cost. That is to say, there may be absolute unit cost disadvantages, economies of scale, or high initial capital costs associated with a newcomer's differential ion effort. Indeed, in theory, "product differentiation" cannot be sharply differentiated as a separate class of barrier. For reasons that will become clear shortly, however, it deserves special treatment.

Other Barriers to Entry

Each of the four barriers presented can be considered a structural barrier to entry. Various behavioral or conduct barriers should also be acknowledged. Established firms, for example, may vigorously escalate their advertising outlays when an entrant appears on the horizon. Used thus, advertising poses a problem for the entrant above and beyond any advertising economies of scale or other effects mentioned previously. Other behavioral possibilities include collective boycotts, collective aggregated rebates, and predatory pricing. However, behavioral barriers will be taken up in detail later in Chapter 9 (concerning monopoly policy) and Part III (concerning conduct).

In addition, there are various legal barriers to entry. In the extreme, these take the form of licensing, chartering, and franchising regulations administered by local, state, or federal government authorities. Patents also constitute a legal barrier. Discussion of these legal barriers is also postponed, for they fit best in a broad review of regulation and patent policy.[3]

Evidence on the Relative Importance of Barriers in Manufacturing

Before we zero in on some of these barriers and their measurements, it may be helpful to review what little research has been done on the question of which barriers prove the most formidable and most frequently observed. The real trail blazer on this issue was again Bain, who by means of questionnaire surveys and other techniques assessed the prevalence of the four broad types of barriers outlined among 20 major United States manufacturing industries during the late 1940s and early 1950s. Bain concluded from his survey that product differentiation was most important, gaining a "very high" barrier rating in five of his sampled industries and a "substantial" rating in eight. Coming a close second was the capital-cost-requirements barrier, which he rated as "very high" in five industries and "substantial" in five more. Economies of scale were judged to be "very high" barriers in three industries and "substantial" in seven. Finally, absolute cost barriers seemed to be rather inconsequential except in three industries with close connections to mining—steel, copper, and gypsum.[4]

---

[3] See Chapters 20, 24, and 25.

[4] Bain, *op. cit.*, Chapter 6.

TABLE 8-1   Summary of Japanese Survey Concerning Barriers to Entry

Difficulty Cited	Number of Respondents	Percent of Respondents
Control of distributive outlets	96	53
Brand image	92	51
Lack of specialized skills (technical or marketing)	80	44
Capital requirements	58	32
Patents and speciality technology	45	25
Low profitability or slow growth of demand	42	23
Scarcity of land or water	29	16

Source: Richard E. Caves and Masu Uekusa, *Industrial Organization in Japan* (Washington, D. C.: The Brookings Institution, 1976), p. 35.

One of the more interesting aspects of Bain's research is that its conclusions are very similar to the results of a survey taken in Japan more than 20 years later. A total of 182 Japanese businessmen were asked to indicate the major "difficulties faced by large public corporations in entering new industries." A summary of their replies is shown in Table 8-1 by the number and percentage of respondents citing each item. (Note that they often cited more than one.) Most often mentioned were two items relating to product differentiation—control of distributive outlets and brand image. At the other extreme is an item that would raise absolute production costs—scarcity of land or water. In between, we find capital requirements. Unfortunately, economies of scale were apparently not included in the survey (although "slow growth of demand" would tend to incorporate scalar effects).

The most comprehensive cross-section statistical study to date is by Dale Orr.[5] Testing the impact of nine different factors on the entry experience of 71 Canadian industries during the mid-1960s, he found that capital requirements, advertising as a per cent of sales, concentration, and size of the industry measured in total sales were all very significant determinants of entry in the expected directions. It is appropriate that intense advertising (which reflects product differentiation) was a significant deterrent to newcomers only in *consumer goods* industries, not in producer goods industries. Although statistical problems prevented a direct test of economies of scale, entry experience was inversely related to capital requirements and concentration—both of which correlate closely with minimum efficient plant size. These results seem to

[5] Dale Orr, "The Determinants of Entry: A Study of the Canadian Manufacturing Industries," *Review of Economics and Statistics* (February 1974), pp. 58–66.

176

support the hypothesis that substantial economies of scale adversely affect entry. As for the remaining variables tested, Orr found that "research and development intensity and risk are modest barriers to entry, while past profit rates and past industry growth rate had a positive but weak impact on entry."[6]

For our own detailed study of barriers we shall adopt Bain's four broad classifications—absolute costs, economies of scale, capital costs, and product differentiation. Each is treated in turn.

Absolute Cost Differences

Of all the major barriers, absolute cost differences seem to be the easiest to conceptualize but the hardest to measure systematically across industries. The sources of such differences are diverse and often subtle. The best evidence available tends to be anecdotal and limited to particular industries. Here are a few examples:

1. *Lumber milling*: Established firms owning vast timber lands have an advantage in timber costs over potential entrants. "The original cost of timber to the Weyerhaeuser Company in 1900 was estimated at 10 cents per thousand board feet, whereas the 1959–1962 average out-of-pocket cost of timber purchased from the national forests of the Douglas fir region was about 24 dollars per thousand board feet." Moreover, new entrants often cannot locate as close to logging activity as entrenched firms. In the Oakridge area of Oregon, this means that entrants end up "paying an estimated 3 to 5 dollars more per thousand board feet for transportation, which increases the average stumpage cost of Oakridge timber by 15 to 25 percent."[7]
2. *Aluminum*: "The entry barriers which are most relevant to the aluminum industry are high capital requirements, availability of high quality, easily accessible bauxite ore, and access to inexpensive sources of electric power."[8]
3. *Petroleum refining in California*: The major refiners own a network of pipelines that crisscross the Los Angeles Basin. Lacking access to those pipelines newly entering refiners must pay the added cost of trucking crude oil to their refineries.[9]

---

[6] *Ibid.*, p. 65. For a similar but less comprehensive study see E. Mansfield, "Entry, Gibrat's Law, Innovation, and the Growth of Firms," *American Economic Review* (December 1962), pp. 1021–51.

[7] Walter J. Mead, *Competition and Oligopsony in the Douglas Fir Lumber Industry* (Berkeley, Calif.: University of California Press, 1966), pp. 113, 222–23.

[8] Council on Wage and Price Stability, *Aluminum Prices 1974–75* (Washington, D.C., 1976) p. 27.

[9] Federal Trade Commission, *Staff Report on the Structure, Conduct and Performance of the Western States Petroleum Industry* (Washington, D.C., 1975), p. 46.

Economies of Scale

In striking contrast to absolute cost differences, plant economies of scal have been relatively thoroughly studied and systematically measured. As result there is no question that economies of scale do exist. Among the cause that lower unit production costs as scale increases are the following.[10]

Specialization of labor: As the number of workers multiplies with plant size, individual workers specialize their activities, thereby becoming more proficient and productive. As a group, then, they can produce more with less labor time and labor cost.

Specialization of machinery: Small scale operations often must rely on multipurpose machinery and equipment that do many different jobs but no job really well. Large-volume operations permit specialization of equipment, as in the case of iron blast furnaces and cement kilns.

Economies of increased dimensions: Capital equipment in the form of tanks, vessels, and pipelines generate economies because a doubling of their surface area more than doubles their volume capacity. This is often summarized by the 0.6 rule, which states that, if capacity is multiplied by a factor of x, then capital cost is multiplied by $x^{0.6}$. This rule goes a long way toward explaining the evolution of super crude-oil tankers the size of the Empire State building. On long voyages, delivering a barrel of oil in a tanker of more than 100,000 dead weight tons (dwt) capacity costs only one fourth as much as delivery in a 25,000-ton tanker. Above 100,000 dwt, the cost savings taper off; a 250,000 dwt ship is only about 5 % more efficient than a 100,000 tonner.

Indivisibilities: There are many costs independent of scale, or fixed, over certain levels of output. When translated into per unit costs (dollars fixed/quantity), these fall with added output. Ball bearing production affords an example: "Setting up an automatic screw machine to cut bearing races takes about eight hours. Once ready, the machine produces from 80 to 140 parts per hour. An increase in the total number of parts produced in a batch from, say, 5,000 to 10,000, reduces unit costs by more than 10 percent due to the broader spreading of setup time and skilled labor costs."[11]

Massed reserves: Breakdowns, interruptions, and other contingencies are inevitable. The unit cost of being prepared is probably lower with larger

[10] E. A. G. Robinson, *The Structure of Competitive Industry* (Chicago: University of Chicag Press, 1958).

[11] F. M. Scherer, "Economics of Scale and Industrial Concentration," *Industrial Concentratio The New Learning*, edited by H. Goldschmid, H. M. Mann, and J. F. Weston (Boston: Little, Brow 1974) p. 33.

scales. For instance, a plant with 20 identical machines will stock less than 20 times the spare parts that a plant with only one machine would. The firm with 20 machines can safely assume that all its machines are not going to break down simultaneously.

*Dis*economies of scale are obviously another possibility. In their case increased size tends to drive unit costs up rather than down. But theory and empirical evidence related to diseconomies at the plant level are not nearly as refined or as pervasive as those concerning economies. At the multiplant firm level there is some positive probability of stretching management too thin or of encountering some other size-related inefficiency. At the individual plant level, however, the chances are slimmer. Significant diseconomies have been observed where the main raw material input is not standardized in quality or dimension, as is true of lumber milling,[12] but these conditions are uncommon.

Perhaps the only general source of plant diseconomies is outbound transportation. Plant expansion typically implies higher unit transportation costs because a large plant's output must be shipped farther afield than a small plant's output, everything else being equal. Where transportation costs bulk large relative to product value—as is the case for cement, petroleum, and steel—there is a limit to the geographic area that one plant can serve efficiently. This axiom could obviously be translated into a size limit for plants, but for present purposes, this will not be done.

If such transportation costs were included in the economies-diseconomies calculation, the optimum size of plant and the onset of diseconomies would vary greatly, even within a given industry, depending on the population density of the market assumed to be served by the plant. The estimated MES (Q_2 in Figure 8-2) and the estimated maximum efficient scale (Q_3 in Figure 8-2) would then be large for a plant located in the Boston–New York–Newark megalopolis, but small for a plant located in Cheyenne, Wyoming. Very few interindustry generalizations could be made about MES in the face of such fluctuating cost functions. Hence, it is best to ignore transportation costs when calculating MES. They can be better taken into account when computing the geographic market against which the MES plant is to be compared. This geographic comparison partly indicates warranted or justifiable concentration, as will be shown shortly.

Of course, the effects of various sources of economies, or the lack thereof, differ from industry to industry. They may lead to a relatively small MES, as indicated by MES_1 in Figure 8-4, or a larger one, as indicated by MES_2. They also influence the behavior of costs below MES. Thus in Figure 8-4, $ADGH$ and $BDGH$ are two cost curves sharing the same MES. But unit costs of the former rise only slightly at scales less than MES_1, whereas those of the latter rise sharply toward point B.

---

[12] W. J. Mead, *op. cit.*, pp. 11–31.

179

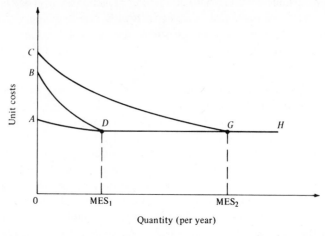

Figure 8-4. Alternative configurations of the long-run unit cost curve.

According to Louis Bucklin, these three curves crudely illustrate the cos[t] conditions observed in three broad categories of merchant wholesaling.[13] I[n] the case of meat and meat products wholesaling, processing and packing cost[s] are very important. They are also sensitive to volume increases because "han[-] dling activities may be automated." Hence *CGH* reflects the long-run uni[t] costs of these enterprises. In contrast, electrical appliance wholesalers do ver[y] little processing or packing, but they must carry inventories for a wide variet[y] of goods. "When broad lines are carried," Bucklin explains, "the demand fo[r] many items will be relatively light." Unless the business operates at hig[h] volume, and thereby reduces cost per unit, its turnover will be low and it[s] inventory costs per unit high. In fact, appliance wholesalers' costs look muc[h] like *BDGH*. In contrast, *ADGH* reflects observed costs in beer wholesaling[.] Beer wholesalers have neither processing duties nor wide-line inventories[.] They merely supply numerous taverns, liquor stores, restaurants, and othe[r] retail outlets. "Deliveries to small buyers are particularly burdensome, re[-] quiring much personal attention and offering scant opportunity for auto[-] mation." In the case of beer Bucklin found that small wholesale establishment[s] have costs quite comparable to larger ones. Economies are virtually non[-] existent. In terms of barrier effect, *CGH* would clearly pose the most ominou[s] hurdle, *ADGH* the least, and *BDGH* would be in between.

Bucklin's estimates for wholesale trade were based on what is called "statis[-] tical estimation." Two other widely used techniques are the "survivor" and th[e] "engineering" techniques. Each estimation technique has its advantages an[d]

---

[13] Louis P. Bucklin, *Competition and Evolution in the Distributive Trades* (Englewood Cliff[s] N. J.: Prentice-Hall, 1972) pp. 253–55.

disadvantages.[14] However, the engineering approach seems to be regarded by most economists as the most reliable, especially for comprehensive multi-industry comparative studies. By this approach industrial engineers, planning experts, and other industry "insiders" actually responsible for making plant-size decisions are canvassed and questioned about how costs vary with scale and what factors generate economies or diseconomies. The work involved in any large study of this kind is almost preposterous, and for many years Joe Bain was the only researcher with sufficient drive, patience, and skill to undertake the task. Now his efforts have been supplemented and superseded by the work of three scholars—F. M. Scherer, C. F. Pratton, and L. W. Weiss. The first two each headed a team of researchers; the last worked alone.

Taken together, their studies contain estimates of plant economies of scale for 33 industries as of the late 1960s and early 1970s. The results for 23 of these industries are summarized in columns (1) and (2) of Table 8-2. Some industries were studied by more than one of these researchers: in such cases the numbers reported in Table 8-2 are average or consensus figures. Where overlaps occurred, the estimates substantially agreed so that this summary procedure does no violence to their findings.

To simplify interindustry comparison, the estimated MES of each industry in column (1) is expressed as a percentage of total United States output in 1967. In addition, the industries are arrayed from highest MES to lowest. At one extreme, efficient turbogenerator production required a plant size that would account for 23% of total United States output. At the other extreme, efficient shoe production could be achieved with a plant that was so small relative to total industry output as to account for only 0.2% of production.

Column (2) shows how sharply the unit cost curve rises at scales less than MES. It shows the percentage increase in unit costs that would occur by moving from a full MES plant to one just half the size (in a few cases it is one third MES, which was Scherer's standard). It is rather interesting to note that high levels of MES, such as those observed for manmade fibers and cigarettes, are not always—or even usually—associated with high rates of cost increase at suboptimal scales. In other words, the figures of columns (1) and (2) do not correlate closely.

When the figures of column (1) are multiplied by a factor of 4, the result is column (3). This result is a rough indication of what the national four-firm concentration ratio would be like in each industry if each firm among the top four had a level of output matching MES. In other words, column (3) could be considered the degree of concentration "warranted" by economies of scale at the plant level. These figures may be compared with those of column (4), which are the actual four-firm concentration ratios of these industries in 1967. It is easy to see that columns (3) and (4) are correlated; with high values typically

[14] A. A. Walters, "Production and Cost Functions: An Econometric Survey," *Econometrica* (January-April 1963), pp. 39–52; William G. Sheperd, "What Does the Survivor Technique Show about Economies of Scale?" *Southern Economic Journal* (July 1967), pp. 113–22.

TABLE 8-2 Minimum Efficient Scale Plants, Costs of Suboptimal Plants, and Concentration Ratios in United States Manufacturing, Circa 1967

Industry	(1) MES as a Percentage of U.S. 1967 Output	(2) Increase in Unit Cost at 1/2 MES (%)	(3) "Warranted" Concentration Ratio	(4) Actual Concentration Ratio 1967
Turbogenerators	23.0	not available	92	100
Refrigerators	13.0	7	52	73
Home laundry equipment	11.2	8	45	78
Manmade fiber	11.1	5	44	86
Aircraft (commercial)	10.0	20	40	69
Synthetic rubber	7.2	15	29	61
Cigarettes	6.6	2.2	26	81
Transformers	4.9	7.9	19	65
Paperboard	4.4	8	18	27

...naces and steel	2.7	10	11	48
Detergents	2.4	2.5	10	88
Storage batteries	1.9	4.6	8	61
Petroleum refining	1.8	4.0	7	33
Cement	1.7	13	7	29
Glass containers	1.5	11	6	60
Ball and roller bearings	1.4	8	6	54
Paints, varnishes	1.4	4.4	6	22
Beer	1.1	10	4	40
Flour mills	0.7	3	3	30
Machine tools	0.3	5	1	21
Cotton textiles	0.2	5	1	36
Shoes	0.2	1.5	1	26

Sources: F. M. Scherer, A. Beckenstein, E. Kaufer, and R. D. Murphy, *The Economics of Multi-Plant Operation* (Cambridge, Mass.: Harvard University Press, 1975), Chapter 3; C. F. Pratton, *Economies of Scale in Manufacturing Industries* (New York: Cambridge University Press, 1971); L. W. Weiss, "Optimal Plant Size and the Extent of Suboptimal Capacity," in *Essays on Industrial Organization in Honor of Joe S. Bain,* edited by R. T. Masson and P. D. Qualls (Cambridge, Mass.: Ballinger Publishing Co., 1976), pp. 123–41.

at the top and low values at the bottom. In a few instances actual and warranted concentration nearly coincide. Aside from these few instances, however, actual concentration is much higher than it would be if each leading firm operated one MES plant. As Scherer concludes, "nationwide oligopoly and high seller concentration cannot be viewed primarily as the inevitable consequence of production scale economies at the plant level."[15]

Now Scherer's is an *extremely* important conclusion. It indicates that policies aimed at the attainment and maintenance of competitive market structures are *not* hopelessly at odds with the cost conditions underlying most industries,[16] that most industries need *not* be dominated by only a few giants in order to be efficient. (It carries political and social implications as well.) Still the conclusion must be qualified in two respects.

First, the minimum efficient market share estimates of Table 8-2 are based on the assumption that the relevant market for every industry is nationwide. In our previous chapters, this assumption has been shown often inappropriate. Indeed, thirteen of the industries listed in Table 8-2 could be considered at least partly regional on the basis of their transportation costs. Notable among them are cement, petroleum, glass containers, and steel, all of which have transportation costs exceeding 5% of product value on a typical haul. Weiss estimates, for example, that there are approximately 24 separate regional cement markets in the United States.[17] Cement's MES, compared to the average regional market, produces a market share of 40% for one plant instead of 1.7% as suggested by Table 8-2.

This is an extreme case, but it hits the nail on the head. When the other regional industries of Table 8-2 are adjusted in like manner, their "warranted" four-firm concentration ratios rise substantially. The average concentration ratio of column (3) as it stands is 19.6%. After adjustment for regional markets the average jumps to 35.7%. Instead of having four industries with warranted concentration greater than 40, adjustment yields a total of eight. A "relevant market" qualification is thus justified. Having said as much, we should also note that these particular data overstate the qualification that would be necessary if this sample of industries were truly representative. The sample is biased in the direction of more regional market fragmentation than would be found for all manufacturing industries. Whereas 57% of the industries listed in Table 8-2 are regional, only about 33% of all United States four-digit industries could be so classified.

Our second qualification also pushes in the direction of greater warranted four-firm concentration than Table 8-2 suggests. This qualification, however, has nothing to do with breadth of relevant market definition. It has to do instead with the implicit assumption that just one plant is sufficient for a firm

[15] F. M. Scherer, *op. cit.*, p. 28.
[16] C. Kaysen and D. Turner, *Antitrust Policy* (Cambridge, Mass.: Harvard University Press, 1965), p. 6.
[17] L. W. Weiss, "The Geographic Scope of Markets in Manufacturing," *Review of Economics and Statistics* (August 1972), pp. 245–66.

1

o gain all possible economies. In cases where substantial additional economies could be achieved from *multiplant* operations, the warranted national concentration ratios of column (3) could be increased (without affecting regional ratios). One problem with the continued use of the word "warranted" in this connection is that many multiplant economies tend to be purely pecuniary as opposed to real. The word "warranted" was not warped when applied to single plants because most economies in the case of single plants constitute genuine social savings. But pecuniary economies cannot claim social benefits. In any event, this area of multiplant economies has been more thoroughly and expertly explored by Scherer's team than by anyone else, so we shall press his findings into service here.

Scherer's results cover 12 industries, as shown in Table 8-3. Column (1) summarizes the main sources of multiplant economies. Column (2) gives Scherer's estimate of MES plant size. Column (3) shows the estimated number of MES plants that a firm needs to exploit all major multiplant economies of scale. When the plant shares of column (2) are multiplied by the number of plants in column (3), the result is the estimated national market share of an efficient *firm* in column (4). These estimates range from a high of 20% for refrigerators to a low of 1% for fabric weaving. They do indeed indicate a greater level of warranted concentration than was suggested by our consideration of single plant economies alone (ignoring for the moment the fact that pecuniary economies may not be "warranted"). The minimum market share for an efficient shoe producer would be 1% instead of 0.2%; for an efficient bottle producer, 4–6% instead of 1.5%; and so on.

Still, despite this accounting for multiplant economies, warranted concentration remains low in most industries. Compared with the average national market shares of big-three member firms reported in column (5) of Table 8-3, the efficient market shares of column (4) are quite small. The only exceptions are beer, refrigerators, and, perhaps, petroleum refining. To the extent that these estimates are valid, "national market seller concentration appears in most industries to be much higher than it needs to be for leading firms to take advantage of all but slight residual multiplant scale economies."[18]

In sum, neither of these two major qualifications—regional market definition and multiplant economies—severely damages our earlier conclusion. Each has been significant in the experience of several industries, implying in these instances the presence of formidable barriers and the inevitability of substantial market concentration. Yet economies of scale appear to pose no more than a moderate barrier to entry for the majority of United States manufacturing industries, and they "warrant" no more than moderate concentration. This optimistic conclusion cannot be equally applicable to countries having sparser populations and lower levels of income than the United States. Minimum efficient scales would gobble up larger percentage chunks of their smaller

---

[18] F. M. Scherer, A. Beckenstein, E. Kaufer, and R. D. Murphy, *The Economics of Multiplant Operation* (Cambridge, Mass.: Harvard Univ. Press, 1975), p. 339.

TABLE 8-3 Summary of Main Sources of Multi-Plant Economies and Firm Size Required to Experience Not More Than Slight Price/Cost Handicaps (12 Industries)

Industry	(1) Major Sources of Possible Multiplant Economies	(2) Estimated MES Plant Market Share (%)	(3) Number of MES Plants Needed to Have Not More Than Slight Disadvantage	(4) Share of U.S. Market Required in 1967 (%)	(5) Average Market Share per U.S. Big Three Member Firm (%)
Beer	Advertising, massed reserves	3.4	3–4	10–14	13
Cigarettes	Advertising, massed reserves	6.6	1–2	6–12	23
Fabric weaving	Market access, capital	0.2	3–6	1	10
Paints	Vertical ties, research	1.4	1	1.4	9
Petrol refining	Advertising, vertical ties, capital	1.9	2–3	4–6	8
Shoes	Advertising, massed reserves	0.2	3–6	1	6
Glass bottles	Capital, research	1.5	3–4	4–6	22
Cement	Capital	1.7	1	2	7
Steel	Capital	2.6	1	3	14
Bearings	Market access, research	1.4	3–5	4–7	14
Refrigerators	Market access	14.1	4–8 (multiproduct)	14–20	21
Storage batteries	Market access, massed reserves	1.9	1	2	18

Source: F. M. Scherer, A. Beckenstein, E. Kaufer, and R. D. Murphy, *The Economics of Multi-Plant Operation: An International Comparison* (Cambridge, Mass.: Harvard University Press, 1975), pp. 94, 334-36.

economic markets. Even abroad, however, economies of scale probably generate less concentration than many people seem to think.[19]

Capital Costs

The significance of capital costs may be inferred from column (1) of Table 8-3. Evidence abounds that small firms pay a higher price for their capital funds than larger firms do. The questions remaining are the following: What are the sources of this cost differential? Does it reflect real economies or just pecuniary advantages? As luck would have it, the answers are mixed because the differential is a product of at least three factors—transaction costs, risk, and loan market imperfections.

Transaction Costs

The effect of transactions costs may be appreciated in a personal analogy. When you borrow money from a bank to buy a car, there are certain fixed costs associated with the transaction. These include the bank's costs of reviewing your application, checking-out your credit record, posting your loan on the books, and processing your payments. For the most part, the absolute dollar value of these costs does not vary with the size of your loan. In cost *per dollar borrowed*, therefore, these costs fall as loan size increases, permitting lower interest rates on larger loans.

Multiply this example by the sum you would like to win in a lottery and you have some idea of the situation confronting small businesses requiring small loans. Indeed, the principle applies to equity stock issues as well as loans. This probably explains, at least in part, why average common stock flotation costs "for a cross section of manufacturing corporation issues during the early 1950s ranged from 20 percent of the funds raised for issues totaling less than $500,000 through 10 percent for issues in the $2–5 million bracket to 5.5 percent for issues between $20 million and $50 million."[20] Savings of transactions costs obviously qualify as "real" social savings.

---

[19] The view that observed concentration cannot, in general, be justified by real economies is not held by all economists. John McGee claims that "the *existing* structure of industry is the *efficient* structure." ("Efficiency and Economies of Size," in *Industrial Concentration: the New Learning, op. cit.*, p. 93; and John McGee, *In Defense of Industrial Concentration*, New York: Praeger, 1971). There are two problems with this extreme position, however. First, it is based on the premise that firms get big *only* by virtue of their efficiency, which is not true. As we have seen, efficiency may often produce bigness, but bigness is also the result of other factors, such as luck and mergers (O. E. Williamson, "Dominant Firms . . . Considerations," *Harvard Law Review*, June 1972, pp. 1512–22). Second, McGee's argument verges on tautology. He asserts that markets are "biased toward efficiency . . ." and "market results *are* evidence of efficiency." In other words, he claims that we know big firms are better simply because they are big! On this shortcoming see Joseph Brodley, "Massive Size, Classical Economics, and the Search for Humanistic Value," *Stanford Law Review* (June 1972), pp. 1155–78.

[20] Scherer, Beckenstein, Kaufer, and Murphy, *op. cit.*, pp. 284–85. See also S. H. Archer and L. G. Faerber, "Firm Size and the Cost of Externally Secured Equity Capital," *Journal of Finance* (March 1966), pp. 69–83.

Risk

As regards risk, small companies seem to suffer greater fluctuations in their sales and profits than big companies. The higher risks of default that small firms present lenders and investors must be compensated by higher interest rates on loans and bonds or by a price premium on equity stock issues. In the case of bonds, for example, W. B. Hickman found that relatively small firms did default more often than large corporations. Consequently, interest rates paid were inversely related to firm size. However, Hickman also found a large "fudge" factor that worked to the disadvantage of small firms. He found that even after adjustment for default losses, the relation of interest rates to size was inverted. In other words, small companies apparently pay a risk premium that exceeds the actual risk of default.[21] Whether reduction of this superfluous surcharge could be counted as a real economy for a large firm is questionable.

Loan Market Imperfections

Perhaps the clearest cases of pecuniary economies in this context are those associated with market "imperfections." Suppose that competition among banks for the extension of business loans is imperfect in the following way. Locally and regionally bank concentration is high, but nationally bank concentration is low because banks cannot engage in interstate branching. Suppose also that small borrowers are pretty much confined to dealing with the banks in their own local area, whereas huge borrowers such as GM, GE, and GT & are sufficiently well known, sufficiently diverse in their operations, and sufficiently big to take their business of borrowing anywhere they fancy. Under these suppositions, you would expect banks to exploit their local market power over small firms by charging them high rates of interest. But, in the big-league nationwide market, you would expect competition to keep interest charges a minimum.

Abundant evidence confirms these suppositions. Numerous cross-section studies have shown that business loan interest rates rise with local bank concentration, but only on loans to small businesses, not on those to big businesses.[22] One study concluded that "The level of market concentration has statistically significant impact on rates paid by firms with assets up to at least $5 million."[23]

On top of all this, a small firm may have difficulty raising capital at any price even if the firm has proved itself successful. Such is the story behind Atari Inc.

---

[21] W. B. Hickman, *Corporate Bond Quality and Investor Experience* (Princeton, N. J.: Princeton University Press, 1958).

[22] Fine examples include F. R. Edwards, "Concentration in Banking and Its Effect on Business Loan Rates," *Review of Economics and Statistics* (August 1964), pp. 294–300; Paul A. Meyer, "Price Discrimination, Regional Loan Rates, and the Structure of the Banking Industry," *Journal of Finance* (March 1967), pp. 37–48.

[23] Donald Jacobs, *Business Loan Costs and Bank Market Structure* (New York: Columbia University Press, 1971), p. 57.

hich was founded by Nolan Bushnell not long after he graduated from the niversity of Utah in 1968. Atari introduced the world to "Pong," "Gran rak 10," and other now famous video games. Bushnell first put $250 of his wn savings into his company. Then he guided it through an enormous spurt growth, but he could not raise enough capital to keep up with his market. Unable to meet the demand stimulated by Pong's success, Atari watched censees and competitors walk off with most of the spoils. 'We sold fewer imes of the Pong type than anybody else,' Bushnell says, 'because we didn't ave the cash to produce what the market demanded.'"[24] He finally sold out r $15 million to Warner Communications, Inc., a giant conglomerate rich in ash. *Business Week* summarized the situation: "When a small company in-ndes a big market, success can be almost as hard to cope with financially as ilure."[24]

Product Differentiation (Again)

A blend of barrier concepts is involved in product differentiation. We first onsider advertising and then turn to other forms of differentiation.

dvertising

According to William Comanor and Thomas Wilson, advertising often ymies new entrants with a triple whammy: (1) it raises the absolute costs of ing business due to "carry-overs"; (2) it entails economies of scale; and (3) adds substantially to the capital costs of entry.[25] Comanor and Wilson do it argue that advertising always or inevitably has these effects. Rather, they gue that it *can* have these effects under certain circumstances. Our job now to delineate these circumstances.

The Carry-Over Effect. One of the main characteristics of advertising that ay give established firms an advantage over entrants is its "lagged" or "carry-er" effect. January's advertising brings in September sales, and the lag may en last for years. There are several reasons for this extension of advertising ect:[26]

• Continued brand loyalty, though probably maintained by customer satisfaction, may have its origin in the persuasiveness of a single, long-forgotten ad.

---

[24] *Business Week*, November 15, 1976, p. 120.
[25] William S. Comanor and Thomas A. Wilson, "Advertising Market Structure and Perfor-nce," *Review of Economics and Statistics* (November 1967), pp. 425–26; William S. Comanor d Thomas A. Wilson, *Advertising and Market Power* (Cambridge, Mass.: Harvard University ss, 1974), Chapter 4.
[26] K. S. Palda, *The Measurement of Cumulative Advertising Effects* (Englewood Cliffs N. J.: ntice-Hall, 1964), p. 9.

- It may take a series of ads to break through the sales resistance of buyers. The last ad triggering the purchase cannot get all the credit.
- The potential customer, persuaded though he may be, may not be "in the market" for the product until later. This is particularly true of durables, such as tires and appliances.

Thus if the annual advertising outlay of each established firm in a market is $10 million, and if all the firms enjoy an equal volume of sales, it is not enough for a new entrant to spend his $10 million on advertising. He will *not* gain sales equal to the established firms during his first year in business, even if his product offering is identical to that of established firms in every other particular – price, quality, availability, and so forth. He is confronted by the aggregation of entrenchment. Only *some* of the sales of the established firms during the new firm's entry year are generated by their $10 million outlay of that year. The additional sales of each are attributable to advertising outlays of *previous* years.

If the advertising outlays of established firms have a carry-over effect of 0.4 (that is, an annual decay rate of 0.6), each established firm enjoys sales from its $10 million spent in the year *prior* to entry worth the equivalent of $4 million in advertising outlays the year *after* entry (0.4 × $10 million). From advertising *two* years previously each gains sales worth $1.6 million in terms of what it would cost them in current advertising dollars (0.4 × 0.4 × $10 million). Adding other prior years, this may be summarized in an equation:

$$\text{established firm's advertising value per year} = \underbrace{\$10m}_{\text{current}} + \underbrace{\$4m + \$1.6m + \$0.64m + \$0.256m + \cdots}_{\text{carry-over}}$$

In other words, the entrant would have to spend approximately $16.67 million during its first year in the market in order to match the advertising potency of each established firm—$10 million to match their current year's outlay plus $6.67 million to make up for lost time and counter established firm carry-over. Another way of looking at this phenomenon is to consider that, even if the established firms happened to spend nothing whatever on advertising during the entrant's first year, the entrant would have to spend $6.67 million on advertising just to pull even with them in the battle for customers. Thus the entrant's advertising costs per unit of sale will, in at least the first year, exceed those of established firms at every level of possible output.

Of course this is a simplified example. The 0.4 carry-over is only illustrative. Actual estimates of carry-over vary, depending on the commodity and the firm in question, and the lag structure assumed is only one of a number possible. Still, the main point is adequately represented, and significant carry-over effect have been found for a wide variety of products.[27] Perhaps the main short-coming of the carry-over argument is that, *under ideal circumstances*, the disadvantage of the entrant eventually fades away as the entrant himself builds up goodwill carry-over.[28] However, lest the reader take this positive note too much to heart—and take on Coke and Pepsi with his own brand of cola drink— we hasten to add that this note of optimism does not remove the barrier. The initial disadvantage must still be covered by capital expenditures. The problem converts into one of capital requirements. Moreover, circumstances are rarely, if ever, ideal for entrants. The carry-over of the entrant's advertising is likely to be much less than that of the established firm's advertising, something which poses a further disadvantage.[29] On top of all this, buyers may have strong loyalties to established sellers for reasons other than advertising. Recall Tucker's experiment with bread brand loyalty, reviewed in Chapter 5. Indeed, Comanor and Wilson go so far as to argue that advertising need not have a carry-over effect in order to create absolute cost disadvantages for entrants.[30]

Economies of Scale. As for economies of scale in advertising, it would be a pretty good bet that they are present whenever we observe an inverse relation-ship between market share and firm advertising outlays relative to sales, while leading firms are gaining market share or holding steady. To illustrate, these were the advertising outlays *per car sold* for United States auto manufacturers over the period 1954–1957: GM, $26.56; Ford, $27.22; Chrysler, $47.76; Studebaker–Packard, $64.04; and American Motors, $57.89.[31] Despite the relatively low outlays per car, leading firms GM and Ford thrived. Contrary-wise, the relatively enormous outlays of Studebaker–Packard failed to keep it alive. Another example comes from breakfast cereals. In 1964 selling and ad-vertising expenses of the largest four firms were 14.9% of sales, for the next four 17.7%, and for all others 19.8%.[32] Despite the relatively low expenditures of the top four, their combined market share was on the rise at the time. Or take liquor (just one shot): Case sales of the leading brand in the early 1960s exceeded case sales of the next leading brand by more than 300%, while its

---

[27] See Jean Jacques Lambin, *Advertising, Competition and Market Conduct in Oligopoly over Time* (Amsterdam: North-Holland Publishing Company, 1976), pp. 94–96; and Darral G. Clarke, "Econometric Measurement of the Duration of Advertising Effect on Sales," *Journal of Marketing Research* (November 1976), pp. 345–57.

[28] For a theoretical demonstration of no barrier under idealized conditions see R. Schmalensee, "Brand Loyalty and Barriers to Entry," *Southern Economic Journal* (April 1974), pp. 579–88. For contrary theorizing see John M. Vernon, *Market Structure and Industrial Performance: A Review of Statistical Findings* (Boston: Allyn and Bacon, Inc., 1972), p. 219.

[29] An empirical example is provided by N. E. Beckwith, "Multivariate Analysis of Sales Re-spones of Competing Brands to Advertising," *Journal of Marketing Research* (May 1972), pp. 68–76.

[30] Comanor and Wilson, *op. cit.* (1974), pp. 48–49.

[31] L. W. Weiss, *Economics and American Industry* (New York: John Wiley & Sons, 1961), p. 342. For more detailed data see Charles E. Edwards, *Dynamics of the United States Automobile Industry* (Columbia, S.C.: University of South Carolina Press, 1965), p. 219.

[32] National Commission on Food Marketing, *Studies of Organization and Competition in Grocery Manufacturing*, Study No. 6 (Washington, D.C.: U.S.G.P.O., 1966), p. 206.

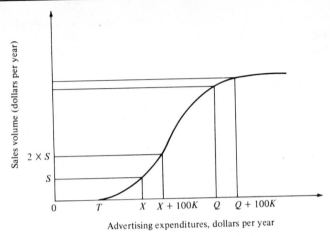

Figure 8-5. Sales volume as a function of advertising outlay, holding other factors constant.

advertising expenditure per case was only half as great.[33] Economies of scale here are obvious; however, they are *not* obvious for all products at all times.[34] In many instances they are either completely absent or not strong enough to make much difference.

Whether such economies arise depends on how sales respond to various levels of advertising outlay. Consider Figure 8-5, which depicts sales volume (on the vertical axis) as a function of the firm's advertising expenditures (on the horizontal axis), holding other elements such as price and rival firm advertising constant. At very low levels of advertising outlay, below threshold T, advertising has little or no effect on sales. Because we are presently interested in the experience of entering firms, the OT range assumes no positive sales at all. (For an established firm the entire function would have to be shifted upward to reflect the fact that even with zero current outlays there would be some positive level of sales attributable to carry-over.) Explanations as to why such a threshold may be present are many and varied, depending on the product and market:[35]

[33] James M. Ferguson, "Advertising and Liquor," *Journal of Business* (October 1967), pp. 414–34.

[34] R. Schmalensee, *On the Economics of Advertising* (Amsterdam: North-Holland Press, 1972); J. L. Simon and G. H. Crain, "The Advertising Ratio and Economies of Scale," *Journal of Advertising Research* (September 1966), pp. 37–43; J. M. Ferguson, *Advertising and Competition: Theory, Measurement, Fact* (Cambridge, Mass.: Ballinger, 1974) Chapter 4; D. Greer, "Product Differentiation and Concentration in the Brewing Industry," *Journal of Industrial Economics* (July 1971), pp. 19–32.

[35] R. D. Buzzell, R. E. M. Nourse, J. B. Matthews, Jr., and T. Levitt, *Marketing: A Contemporary Analysis* (New York: McGraw-Hill, 1972) pp. 533–34.

- It may be impossible to buy key forms of advertising below certain minimum quantities. For instance, the smallest amount of national television advertising possible could not be bought with pocket change. The time and production costs of putting even a 10-second "spot" on the air are substantial.
- There may be a "psychological threshold" in the minds of potential buyers that may be broken only by some minimum volume of promotion.
- There may be a minimum volume of promotion needed to induce retailers and wholesalers to carry the manufacturer's product line.

Beyond threshold T, the sales response function enters a range of increasing returns. Here, increasing amounts of promotion yield *more* that proportionate increases in sales revenues. An addition of $100,000 in expenditure to outlay X does not double total outlay but it does double sales volume from S to $2 \times S$ on the vertical axis. The reasons sales may climb at an increasing rate are similar to those underlying the threshold effect. A firm can gain efficiency in this range by hiring marketing specialists (instead of having their shipping clerks dabble in ad design), by allocating its money among the various media more and more efficiently, by exploiting a "band wagon" promotional pitch, by gaining discounts in its purchase of advertising messages; and by other means.[36]

It is the combination of threshold and increasing returns effects that is relevant to economies of scale. Over this range (roughly 0 to $X + 100K$ in Figure 8-5) advertising costs *as a percentage of sales* start out very high and then fall as absolute (total dollar) advertising outlay increases. This is not the end of the story, however. The presence of a threshold and increasing returns is quite commonly observed.[37] But, if these effects do not extend into very large levels of absolute outlay, then all economies could easily be exploited by rather small firms and new entrants. And beyond this small-firm range of economies, diminishing returns set in. Additional advertising outlays will eventually stimulate *less* than proportionate increases in sales revenues, as shown by Q and $Q + 100K$ in Figure 8-5. The reason for this diminishing stimulation is fairly obvious:

> Once salesmen have called on all the prospective customers with high purchase potential, they must turn to less and less promising prospects. Once advertising messages have reached the primary audiences with sufficient frequency, additional messages must be directed to audiences with lower and lower levels of response.[38]

[36] An example of discounts is provided by the Hearst Corporation (owner of Cosmopolitan, Good Housekeeping, and other magazines). In 1976 it offered discounts to advertisers who bought space in any three of its magazines according to the following schedule: 12 pages, 5% off; 15 pages, 6%; 18 pages, 7%; 21 pages, 8%; 24 pages, 9%. (*Wall Street Journal*, November 14, 1975, p. 3). However, discounts are not available in certain other media.

[37] Buzzell, *et. al., op. cit.*, pp. 533–34; A. G. Rao and P. B. Miller, "Advertising/Sales Response Functions," *Journal of Advertising Research* (April 1975), pp. 7–15; J. J. Lambin, *op. cit.*, pp. 27–30. For exceptions see Julian Simon, *Issues in the Economics of Advertising* (Urbana, Ill.: University of Illinois Press, 1970).

[38] Buzzell, *et. al., op. cit.*, p. 534.

Indeed, beyond $Q + 100K$," advertising may reach a point of complete satura tion, where further promotion adds nothing at all to sales.

In sum, economies of scale are substantial only where the threshold effect and increasing returns operate over a large range. This is reflected in the following *Business Week* quote concerning entry into the cosmetics industry:

> "The real challenge is simply gaining distribution," says market researcher Solomon Dutka . . . "to have sales volume and to be a factor in this business, you must have distribution. Yet to gain distribution, you must have sales volume or the big store groups won't bother with you. So when somebody tries to get into this business . . . they have to create volume artificially"—meaning the use of heavy and costly adver tising and promotion.[39]

Unfortunately, no one can accurately estimate the range of threshold effec and increasing returns for particular industries. Moreover, experts do no agree on what causes short or long ranges. Comanor and Wilson give some evidence that economies of scale are most prevalent in industries with high advertising/sales ratios, but their findings are not wholly supported by other evidence.[40] This author's pet theory is that economies loom largest in con sumer goods industries experiencing frequent style changes (autos and cos metics), or new titles and editions (books and records), or rapid brand multi plication (breakfast cereals and cigarettes).[41] The turbulent and continua changes endemic to these industries force successful firms to cross the threshold level of advertising outlay recurrently, not just once-and-for-all. The expense of each crossing may be thought of as a "fixed" expense of doing busines (unrelated to the level of output) because sales are not a function of advertising until after the threshold is crossed. Given high "fixed" promotional expenses in these industries, the largest firms will have the lowest advertising costs *per unit of sales* because they will be able to spread these costs over a larger volume of sales than smaller firms.

Advertising Increases Capital Cost of Entry. Finally, if economies of scale o goodwill carry-overs exist in advertising, the need to obtain substantial funds for advertising will increase the capital requirements for new entry well beyond those needed for physical plant and equipment. As Comanor and Wilson poin out, "this investment in market penetration will involve a particularly risky use of funds since it does not generally create tangible assets which can be resold in the event of failure."[42]

To end on a more positive note, we should mention that advertising can *assist* entry as well as curtail it. How better could a newcomer call attention

---

[39] *Business Week*, November 29, 1976, p. 44.

[40] Comanor and Wilson, *op. cit.* (1974), p. 214. Compare Simon and Crain, *op. cit.*, p. 41. A major weakness of the Simon-Crain study, however, is its failure to separate consumer and produce goods.

[41] D. Greer, "Some Case History Evidence on the Advertising-Concentration Relationship," *The Antitrust Bulletin* (Summer 1972), pp. 320–24.

[42] Comanor and Wilson, *op. cit.* (1967), p. 426.

to his new offering than by advertising vigorously? This procompetitive possibility is fully explored in Chapter 15. For now, no more need be said except that the procompetitive effect can easily be outweighed by the anticompetitive, barrier effects outlined previously. Empirical verification of a net procompetitive effect is limited to consumer search goods and consumer search services, such as retailing. Where retailer advertising as a percentage of sales is high, profits tend to be low, indicating intense competition.[43] Conversely, experience goods industries demonstrate just the opposite: high advertising is associated with high profits, as one would expect if advertising constituted a barrier to entry.[44] In short, it appears that advertising builds the highest barriers in consumer experience goods industries. In other industries (consumer search goods and perhaps producer goods), it may on balance be neutral or even beneficial to entry and competition.

Other Product Differentiation Barriers

The first thing to acknowledge with respect to other forms of differentiation is that they too may harbor economies of scale. R. D. Peterson and C. R. MacPhee find that, in the medical equipment and supplies industry, where salesmen's salaries and expenses account for most promotional expenses, small firms incur selling costs per sales dollar twice as high as those of large firms.[45] Style change in the auto industry provides another example. John Menge and Lawrence White have shown that the costs of special tools and dies may decline with increasing firm size.[46]

Aside from scaler effects, however, there are a number of factors in this area that may favor established firms still further. If the product is one for which consumers switch brands frequently or commonly buy more than one brand, then brand proliferation by existing firms may reduce a newcomer's expected sales.[47] Assume for the sake of illustration that the newcomer's brand would be the fourth in an industry in which three existing firms supply one brand apiece. The newcomer would get 25% of all the random brand switchers his first year. Now let's switch assumptions. Assume that each of the three existing firms has five brands, yielding a total of 15 existing brands. Then the newcomer

[43] Kenneth D. Boyer, "Information and Goodwill Advertising," *Review of Economics and Statistics* (November 1974), pp. 541–48.

[44] We shall explore these studies in detail in Chapter 15. Two key ones, however, are M. E. Porter, "Consumer Behavior, Retailer Power and Market Performance in Consumer Goods Industries," *Review of Economics and Statistics* (November 1974), pp. 419–36; Phillip Nelson, "The Economic Consequences of Advertising," *Journal of Business* (April 1975), p. 237.

[45] R. D. Peterson and C. R. MacPhee, *Economic Organization in Medical Equipment and Supply* (Lexington, Mass.: Lexington Books, 1973), pp. 58–59.

[46] J. A. Menge, "Style Change Costs as a Market Weapon," *Quarterly Journal of Economics* (November 1962), pp. 632–47; Lawrence White, *The Automobile Industry Since 1945* (Cambridge, Mass.: Harvard University Press, 1971), pp. 39–41.

[47] R. G. Lipsey, G. R. Sparks, P. O. Steiner, *Economics*, 2nd ed. (New York: Harper & Row, 1976), p. 300; Steven R. Cox, "Consumer Information and Competition in the Synthetic Detergent Industry," *Nebraska Journal of Economics and Business* (Summer 1976), pp. 41–58.

entering with one brand would get only one sixteenth, or 6.25%, of the random switchers.[48] Still another type of barrier arose among grocery retailers in connection with trading stamps. During the 1960s, when trading stamps were in vogue, the largest retail food chains enjoyed, in the use of trading stamps exclusive advantages that could not be topped by smaller retailers.[49]

Summary

We can execute a neat exit from this chapter on entry by reiterating just a few key points:

1. Anything giving established firms substantial advantages over potential entrant firms constitutes a barrier to entry.
2. Because barriers are a source of market power, they will be useful in explaining conduct and performance.
3. Virtually all structural barriers to entry can be classified into four factor groups: absolute unit cost differences, economies of scale, capital costs, and product differentiation. Product differentiation is a blend of the first three factors.
4. Absolute cost differences raise the entrant's costs of doing business (at every level of output) compared to the costs for established firms.
5. Economies of scale cause unit costs to fall with added size of plant or firm. If minimum efficient scale is large relative to total industry output, there will be little "room" in the industry for a large number of plants and firms, thus occasioning substantial barriers and fostering high concentration.
6. The capital costs of entry may be great, in which case new entrants will have difficulty raising funds at costs comparable to those of large established firms. To some degree this cost differential reflects real economies, for example, transaction costs. The differential is also caused by capital market imperfections, in which case it largely reflects pecuniary economies.
7. Empirical studies of entry barriers disclose a particularly potent effect for product differentiation in consumer experience goods industries. This is not so true of producer and consumer search goods, at least as regards advertising. Still, the influence of other forms of differentiation may often be significant even in these instances.
8. (Behavioral and legal barriers have been saved for later treatment.)

[48] Of course, the firm could enter with five brands instead of one, in which case it would boost its chances with any switcher back up to 25%. However, this would require the crossing of five Figure 8-4 type thresholds instead of one, leaving it at a disadvantage.

[49] Federal Trade Commission, *Economic Report on the Structure and Competitive Behavior of Food Retailing* (Washington, D.C.: U.S.G.P.O., 1966), pp. 242–44.

9

Barriers to Entry, Concentration and Monopoly: Practice and Policy

In this society of ours, we depend on diffusion of power as the best means of achieving political democracy . . . . If we fail the danger is clear to anyone who has studied history— particularly that of the Axis powers prior to World War II.

SENATOR PHILIP A. HART

As this chapter is being written, the U. S. Department of Justice is prosecuting IBM on charges of monopolizing the computer industry in violation of the Sherman Act. Should IBM lose the district court trial, it can appeal. If it loses its appeals, it could find itself broken up into several separate companies. Such was the fate of the Standard Oil Company of New Jersey (now Exxon) the American Tobacco Company (Winstons, Salems), and a number of other business behemoths. The objective of this chapter is to trace developments from passage of the Sherman Act in 1890 to IBM's present predicament, and simultaneously, to apply and extend our previous discussions of concentration and barriers to entry. We begin by exploring the wording of the Sherman Act and its interpretation by federal courts. Next we spotlight four relatively recent cases—Alcoa, United Shoe Machinery, United Fruit, and IBM. We conclude by reviewing some proposals to "toughen" the law.

The Sherman Act

The Sherman Act was passed in 1890 in response to public outcries that something ought to be done about the large "trusts" that were beginning to

197

flourish at that time. The first big trust was Standard Oil, formed in 1882. It was followed quickly by the Whiskey Trust, the Sugar Trust, the Lead Trust and the Cotton Oil Trust. Senator Sherman exclaimed that without federal action the country would soon have "a trust for every production and a master to fix the price for every necessity of life." Hence, his Sherman Act.

Broadly speaking, the Act contains two main sections outlawing (1) collusive restraints of trade and (2) monopolization. The first refers to collective conduct such as price fixing. We postpone treatment of restraints of trade until Chapter 12, where we take up such conduct in earnest. As for monopolization, Section 2 of the Sherman Act states that:

> Every person who shall monopolize, or attempt to monopolize, or combine or conspire with any other person or persons, to monopolize any part of the trade or commerce among the several States, or with foreign nations, shall be deemed guilty of a misdemeanor . . .

Although Section 2 covers those who "combine or conspire" to monopolize, it is primarily concerned with single firm activities and structural conditions. Having said that, we have not—unlike Budweiser—said it all. Why the word "monopolize"? Why not "monopoly"? What is the test of monopolization? How large a market share is required? What is meant by a "part of trade or commerce"? Is it the same thing as the "relevant market"?

Answers to these questions cannot be found in the Act's language; the words are merely landmines, set to explode when tripped by specific cases. The riddles are solved in the courts' interpretations of the language and the kinds of things they have deemed illegal. This may seem like a simple task. The Sherman Act is, after all, approaching its hundredth anniversary, and several hundred cases have been brought by the Justice Department under Section 2. Most issues, it would seem, should be settled now. Unfortunately, they are not. Judicial personnel, economic knowledge, political philosophies, and business practices change over time, much as fashion changes. Even more significant, the wording of the statute was left vague enough to invoke extensive judgment, opinion, estimation, insight, and even hunch.

A Sherman Act Section 2 violation is not as clear cut as shop lifting or murder. Price fixing is similar to these crimes in that, under Section 1, it is a *per se* offense. Just as one can be caught in the act of shoplifting, so a group of competitors can be caught in a smoke filled room conspiring to raise their price. *Per se* rules may be mechanically applied, but monopolizers cannot be caught in the act. They are never really caught at all. They are accused and judged by what has come to be called a "rule of reason." Merger trials, as already suggested, although not explicitly acknowledged, are also governed largely by rule of reason. In monopoly cases, however, the courts' discretionary reasoning is much more evident. The result is drawn out deliberations. Trials of three years are not unheard of, and in one case more than 1200 witnesses testified.

The crime of monopolization is not established without proof of two factors: (1) substantial market power, and (2) intent. As Justice William Douglas wrote in the *Grinnell* case, the offense of monopoly "has two elements: (1) the possession of monopoly power in the relevant market and (2) willful acquisition or maintenance of that power . . ."[1] Reason is exercised to establish both elements. In appraising monopoly power, the courts have considered barriers to entry of various kinds—including patents, pecuniary and real economies of scale, product differentiation, absolute capital costs, and several conduct-related barriers. Profits, too, have come under review. The one index of monopoly power consistently receiving greatest attention, however, is the market share of the accused. Indeed, although the Supreme Court has defined monopoly power as "the power to control prices or exclude competition," it has acted as if the "existence of such power ordinarily may be inferred from the predominant share of the market." (*Grinnell* again.) In this interpretation, reason must be called upon to answer two key questions: What is the relevant market? What market share is sufficient to establish unlawful power?

Market Definition

The factors entering decisions on the issue of relevant market are pretty much the same as those encountered in merger cases:

1. The physical characteristics of the products.
2. The end uses of the products.
3. The cross-elasticity of demand between products.
4. The absolute level of various sellers' costs.
5. The absolute level of product prices, apart from consideration of cross-elasticities.
6. The geographic extent of the market.

The diversity of judgments the relevant market has provoked may be illustrated with two contrasting cases.

In *duPont* (1956) a majority of the Supreme Court defined the market broadly to include *all* flexible packaging materials (cellophane, saran, foil, pliofilm, polyethylene, and so on) instead of merely cellophane, which duPont dominated.[2] The decisive argument for the Court's majority was cross-elasticity of demand, as may be seen from the opinion:

> If a slight decrease in the price of cellophane causes a considerable number of customers of other flexible wrappings to switch to cellophane, it would be an indication that a high cross-elasticity of demand exists between them; that the products compete in the same market. The court below held that the "great sensitivity of customers in the flexible packaging markets to price or quality changes" prevented duPont from possessing monopoly control over price . . . . We conclude that cellophane's interchangeability with other materials mentioned suffices to make it a part of this flexible packaging material market.

[1] *U. S. v. Grinnell Corporation*, 384 U. S. 563 (1966).
[2] *U. S. v. E. I. duPont de Nemours Company*, 351 U. S. 377 (1956).

Although duPont produced 75% of all cellophane sold in the United States, this amounted to only 14% of all "flexible packaging." Hence the broad definition made a big difference, and duPont won acquittal.

Three dissenting justices had doubts. They felt that cellophane was virtually unique. Cellophane's price, in particular, had been two to seven times higher than that of many comparable materials between 1924 and 1950. Yet during this period "cellophane enjoyed phenomenal growth," *more* growth than could be expected "if close substitutes were available at from one seventh to one half cellophane's price." Furthermore, they thought cross elasticity was low, not high. The price of cellophane fell substantially while other prices remained unchanged. Indeed, "during the period 1933–1946 the prices for glassine and waxed paper actually increased in the face of a 21% decline in the price of cellophane." If substantial "shifts of business" due to "price sensitivity" had in fact occurred, producers of these rival materials would have had to follow cellophane's price down lest they lose sales.[3]

Ten years later, in the *Grinnell* case (1966) a majority of the Court spoke as the minority did in *duPont*. They defined the market narrowly to include only "accredited central station protective services" (whereby a client's property is wired for burglaries and fires, signals of which are then sent electronically to a continuously manned central station accredited by insurance underwriters). Other means of property protection were excluded from the relevant market for various reasons:[4]

> Watchmen service is far more costly and less reliable. Systems that set off an audible alarm at the site of a fire or burglary are cheaper but often less reliable. They may be inoperable without anyone's knowing it . . . Proprietary systems that a customer purchases and operates are available, but they can be used only by a very large business or by government . . . . And, as noted, insurance companies generally allow a greater reduction in premiums for accredited central station service than for other types of protection.

Because Grinnell had 87% of the market as defined, the Court could not let it off the hook like an undersized trout. Grinnell suffered some dismemberment.

Market Share

The cases cited indicate that a market share of 14% does not amount to illegal monopoly but 87% does. What about the area in between? What market share does make an illegal "monopoly"? In two major cases the Supreme Court

[3] For an economic critique see, G. W. Stocking and W. F. Mueller, "The Cellophane Case and the New Competition," *American Economic Review* (March 1955), pp. 29–63.

[4] *U.S. v. Grinnell Corporation et al.*, 384 U. S. 563 (1966).

ruled that 64% of the farm machinery industry and 50% of the steel industry did not amount to monopoly. An influential appeals court judge, Learned Hand, once expressed the opinion that, while any percentage over 90 "is enough to constitute a monopoly; it is doubtful whether sixty or sixty-four percent would be enough; and certainly thirty-three percent is not."[5] For these several reasons the consensus seems to hold that market shares below 60% lie snugly beneath the Court's reach. And even 70 or 75% may manage to escape its grasp. The lack of exact definition makes the present IBM case a cliff-hanger. IBM's market share lies in the 65–75% range.

Actually, there is even more uncertainty than these figures suggest. In the early days of Sherman Act enforcement, the Court convicted "abusive" combinations with as little as 20% of the market (in coal railroading) and acquitted "well behaved" monopolists with as much as 90% (shoe making machinery). Moreover, some very large market shares have escaped prosecution altogether, while also avoiding the alternative treatments of government regulation and public ownership (which are common among "natural monopolies," such as telephone service and electricity supply). The freedom of judgment allowed by the rule of reason explains much of this variability but not all.[6]

The issue of *intent* is also important. Generally speaking, there is a trade-off between the market share and the degree of intent the prosecuting attorneys must prove to win a guilty verdict. A clear-cut case of 95% market share would now probably run afoul of the law, despite very little proof of intent. Conversely, intent would gain importance when a market share of less than 60% was involved. Indeed, it will be recalled that Section 2 of the Sherman Act forbids mere *attempts* to monopolize as well as monopolization itself. The requirements for proving a charge of "attempt" are now much more rigorous with respect to intent than they are in cases of pure monopolization. On the other hand, the requirements of proof in monopolization cases are more stringent on the matter of market share than are those in attempt cases. A detailed discussion of the law concerning attempts is beyond our scope. However, it is interesting to note that a circuit court of appeals once held that market share was so inconsequential in cases of attempt that the "relevant market" was irrelevant.[7] The same court held that proof of an attempt requires proof of *specific* intent, which is much more difficult to prove than ordinary, everyday, general intent.

---

[5] *U. S. v. Aluminum Company of America*, 148 F. 2d 416 (1945), 424.

[6] Critics of United States policy claim that many unregulated monopolists are neglected for *political* reasons. See Mark J. Green, *The Closed Enterprise System* (New York: Grossman Publishers, 1972). Keep in mind that the Justice Department or FTC must file suit before the courts can hear a case.

[7] *Lessig v. Tidewater Oil Co.*, 327 F. 2d 459 (9th Circuit, 1964) certiorari denied, 377 U. S. 993 (1964). This is a private case, and one of the reasons we shall pass over "attempt" law is that most such cases are private. For a good summary of "attempt" law see Corwin Edwards, *Studies of Foreign Competition Policy and Practice Vol. 1, the United States* (Canadian Department of Consumer and Corporate Affairs, 1976) pp. 260–69.

Intent

Use of the word "monopolize" in the Sherman Act (rather than "monopoly") implies that simple possession of a large market share is not itself frowned upon, at least not enough to earn a conviction. An illegality requires more: some positive drive, some purposeful behavior, some "intent" to seize and exert power in the market. Only a moment's reflection reveals the wisdom of this policy. What of the innovator whose creativity establishes a whole new industry, occupied at first by just his firm? What of the last surviving firm in a dying industry? What of the superefficient firm that underprices everyone else through genuine economies of scale or some natural advantages of location? What of a large market share gained purely by competitive skill? To pounce on these monopolies would have to be regarded as cruel (since they are actually "innocent"), stupid (since it would be punishing good performance), and irrational (since no efficient structural remedy, such as dissolution, could ensue). Thus a finding of intent to monopolize is essential, even though it may not be easy.

In Section 2 cases a monopolist's intent is not determined by subjecting its owners and officers to lie detector tests or psychoanalysis. Intent is manifested by the firm's particular acts or by its general course of action. With this statement we come to the point at which a crucial distinction must be made between interpretation of Section 2 before the *Alcoa* case of 1945 and after. Before *Alcoa*, the Supreme Court usually held that an offensive degree of intent could be established only with evidence of abusive, predatory, or criminal acts. The types of conduct that qualified included the following: (1) predatory pricing, that is, cutting prices below costs on certain products or in certain regions and subsidizing the resulting losses with profits made elsewhere; (2) predatory promotional spending or predatory pricing on "fighting brands" or "bogus independent" firms or upon new facilities or new products; (3) physical violence to competitors, their customers, or their products; (4) exaction of special advantages from suppliers, such as "railroad rebates"; (5) acquisitions of competitors or their suppliers or customers, or of facilities to be closed down; (6) exaction of excessively long-term "covenants not to compete" from those selling out to the monopolist; (7) "engrossing" supplies of essential raw materials, that is, buying in excess of one's needs; (8) misuse of patents, copyrights, or trademarks; and (9) preclusion of competitive opportunities by refusals to sell, exclusive dealing arrangements, or anticompetitive tie-in sales.

For the most part, this list of "predatory tactics" is derived from the major early cases listed in Table 9-1. The first five cases mentioned there ended in convictions. The last five mentioned ended in acquittals. Notice from the center column that the market shares of the convicted monopolizers are not markedly greater than those of the acquitted firms, although in the latter group there are two with only 50% of industry sales. The big difference lies in the next column, where a "Yes" indicates that obviously predatory tactics were used by the defendant and a "No" indicates a fairly clean slate in this regard. With but one

TABLE 9-1 Major Section 2 Cases, 1911 to 1927

	Industry	Percentage of the industry (%)	Predatory Tactics Present?	Date of Final Judgment
I. Unlawful monopolies				
Standard Oil of N. J.	Petroleum	85–90	Yes	1911
American Tobacco Co.	Tobacco products	76–97	Yes	1911
E. I. duPont	Explosives	64–100	Yes	1911
Eastman Kodak Co.	Photo equipment	75–80	Yes	1915
Corn Products Refining Co.	Glucose	53	Yes	1916
II. Cases of acquittal				
United Shoe Machinery Co.	Shoe machinery	90	No	1917
American Can Co.	Packers' cans	50	Yes	1916
Quaker Oats Co.	Rolled oats cereal	75	No	1916
U. S. Steel Corp.	Steel	50	No	1920
International Harvester Co.	Harvesters	64	No	1927

Source: Milton Handler, *Trade Regulation*, 3rd ed. (New York: Foundation Press, 1960), pp. 378–79.

exception, those guilty of dirty tricks were also found guilty of monopolizing. Conversely, the "good" trusts managed to get off. The obvious implication must be qualified by the possibility that changes in court personnel could have made some difference, as suggested perhaps by the dates of the decisions in the last column. Another qualification that lessens the strength of the argument is the exclusion of several railroad cases from consideration. Between 1904 and 1922, the Supreme Court decided against three railroad combinations that did not employ predatory practices to gain substantial market shares.[8] Even so, we can buttress the message of Table 9-1 by consulting the Court's opinions.

In acquitting United States Steel (1920) the Court held that the corporation's 50% market share (at the time of the case) did not amount to excessive power, and, even if it had amounted to excessive power, the corporation had not abused it: "It resorted to none of the brutalities or tyrannies that the cases illustrate of other combinations." The corporation "did not oppress or coerce its competitors ... it did not undersell its competitors in some localities by reducing its prices there below those maintained elsewhere, or require its customers to enter into contracts limiting their purchases or restricting them in resale prices; it did not obtain customers by secret rebates ... there was no evidence that it attempted to crush its competitors or drive them out of the market ..." In short: "The corporation is undoubtedly of impressive size .... But the law does not make mere size an offense, or the existence of unexerted power an offense. It, we repeat, requires overt acts ..."[9] (Recall from Chapter 7 that U. S. Steel was a combination formed by *merger*. But merger was not then considered evidence of intent even though it is obviously an "overt act." Thus, in those days the "rule of reason" came to mean that a monopolist would not be forced to walk the plank unless he had behaved *unreasonably* in the understanding of the times.)

Although this interpretation may not have gutted Section 2 of the Sherman Act, it certainly bloodied it a bit. Section 2 lay incapacitated until 1945, when the *Alcoa* decision brought recuperation. In essence, *Alcoa* lengthened the list of intent indications beyond predatory and abusive tactics. In fact, the list was lengthened so substantially that it is now easier to explain acceptable evidence of intent negatively by what constitutes *lack* of intent. According to *Alcoa*, unlawful intent can almost be assumed unless the defendant is a "passive beneficiary" of monopoly power or has had monopoly power "thrust upon" him. To *any* extent the monopolist reaches out to grasp or strives actively to hold his dominant position, he is denied the right to claim that he has no unlawful intent. Although this easy negative test of intent is most applicable when the market share involved is especially large (shares below, say, 80% would probably require more positive evidence of purpose), *Alcoa* remains a landmark of antitrust law.

---

[8] Northern Securities Co. (1904) Union Pacific (1912) and Southern Pacific (1922).
[9] *U. S. v. United States Steel Corp.*, 251 U. S. 417 (1920).

Alcoa[10]

The Aluminum Company of America provides many interesting economic lessons, as well as legal lessons. For more than half a century it dominated all four stages of the United States aluminum industry: (1) bauxite ore mining, (2) conversion of bauxite into aluminum oxide or alumina, (3) electrolytic reduction of alumina into aluminum ingots, and (4) fabrication of aluminum products, such as cable, foil, pots and pans, sheets, and extrusions. Alcoa's dominance derived mainly from various barriers to entry.

The Barriers to Entry

Patents. In the beginning, back in the late 1800s, patents protected Alcoa. Until 1886, the processes for extracting pure aluminum were so difficult and costly that it was a precious metal like gold or platinum. In that year, just after graduating from Oberlin College, Charles Hall discovered electrolytic reduction of alumina into aluminum. His discovery was later duplicated by C. S. Bradley. Alcoa acquired the rights to both their patents, and thereby excluded potential entrants legally until 1909.

Tariffs. Electrolytic reduction was discovered independently in Europe at about the same time it was discovered in America, enabling the development of aluminum industries in France, Switzerland, and England. Imports into the United States from these sources could have competed with Alcoa, but imports were stifled until 1945 by tariffs. These varied from a high of 15 cents per pound to a low of 2 cents per pound. On average, however, Alcoa was continuously protected by an import duty equalling about 20% of its domestic list price. The inconsistency of government policy is all too obvious here. Patents and tariffs nurtured the monopoly for 50 years before the antitrust authorities finally attacked it.

Resources Controlled. Resource limitations provided a third barrier to entry. Alcoa integrated backwards into bauxite mining and electric power, the two key resources for producing aluminum. Although these resources were too plentiful to be fully preempted by a single firm, Alcoa vigorously acquired, developed, and built the lowest cost sources of each. Its early bauxite holdings dotted the globe from Yugoslavia and Greece to Dutch Guiana and Istria.

---

[10] Primary sources for this section are L. W. Weiss, *Economics and American Industry* (New York: John Wiley & Sons, 1961), Chapter 5; R. F. Lanzillotti, "The Aluminum Industry," in *The Structure of American Industry*, edited by Walter Adams (New York: Macmillan Publishing Co., 1961), pp. 185–231; Merton J. Peck, *Competition in the Aluminum Industry: 1945–1958* (Cambridge, Mass.: Harvard University Press, 1961).

According to Department of Justice estimates, Alcoa at one time controlled 90% of useful bauxite ore deposits in the United States. As for electricity, "Alcoa had not taken all the low-cost hydrosites, of course, but it had started acquiring sites when the electrochemical industry was young, and any new competition in later years might find that Alcoa had an advantage they could not achieve."[11]

Economies of Scale. As if all that were not enough, economies of scale constituted an additional barrier. Of the several stages of the production process, the second stage—conversion of bauxite into alumina—yielded the greatest efficiencies from increased size. Until 1938 there was only *one* alumina plant in the entire United States. The unit costs of a 500,000-ton per year plant embodying 1940 technology were 10–20% below the unit costs of a 100,000-ton plant. And it was not until 1942 that United States consumption of alumina topped 500,000 tons. The dire implications for entry into alumina production during that era should be obvious. Economies were not nearly so pronounced for reduction and fabrication (there being four smelting plants in the United States during the 1930s and a goodly number of fabricators).

Nonetheless the barriers associated with alumina spilled over into these other stages because Alcoa was *vertically integrated.* However efficient a producer of ingot or fabricated products might be, he was ultimately dependent on Alcoa for his raw materials and simultaneously competing with Alcoa as a seller. This put independents in a precarious position. Alcoa could control the independents' costs *and* selling price. Were Alcoa unkind enough to raise its price of ingot and lower its price of foil, say, the foil fabricators would be in a bind. The "price squeeze" would pinch the margin between their costs and selling price. Just such a squeeze was alleged in 1926 and 1927, when Alcoa reduced the margin between ingot and certain types of aluminum sheet from 16 cents a pound to 7 cents a pound and then kept it there until 1932. Two independent rollers of sheet initiated an antitrust suit that was settled out of court.

Despite these many formidable barriers, several attempts to enter ingot production were made before the government began its big antitrust suit in 1937. All attempts failed. The failures could not be blamed on the weakness of those who made the attempts, for none of them were pantywaists: one threat was mounted by an experienced French group in 1912; another was initiated by the owners of Schlitz Brewing, who were looking for something to do with their money during prohibition; the third threat came from James Duke, founder of another monopoly—the American Tobacco Company. (It is noteworthy that all three aspiring entrants planned on using foreign bauxite, as the best United States reserves were tied up by Alcoa. All three eventually sold their ores, power rights, and plants to Alcoa, thereby enhancing its preponderance.)

[11] Weiss, *op. cit.*, p. 172.

206

Government Intervention

The Antitrust Suit. The government lost its antitrust suit at the district court level in 1941 after a 3-year trial. The district judge relied heavily on the *U. S. Steel* case of 1920. He felt that mere size, unaccompanied by dastardly deeds, did not violate Section 2. The Supreme Court could not hear the Justice Department's appeal because four Court Justices disqualified themselves on grounds of prior participation in the case, leaving less than a quorum. However, the New York Circuit Court of Appeals was designated court of last resort for the case. That three-judge panel, acting under the leadership of Judge Learned Hand, decided against Alcoa, thereby reversing the lower court and boldly overturning precedent.[12]

On the question of market power, the Circuit Court determined that Alcoa controlled over 90% of primary aluminum sales in the United States, the other 10% being accounted for by imports. "That percentage," Hand said, "is enough to constitute a monopoly." On the issue of intent, the Court *rejected* the notion that evil acts must be in evidence. Lacking substantial judicial precedent for his position, the Court looked to Congressional intent:

> [Congress] did not condone "good trusts" and condemn "bad" ones; it forbade all. Moreover, in so doing it was not necessarily actuated by economic motives alone. It is possible, because of its indirect social or moral effect, to prefer a system of small producers . . . to one in which the great mass of those engaged must accept the direction of a few.

By this interpretation a monopolist could escape only if its monopoly had been "thrust upon it," only if "superior skill, foresight and industry" were the basis for its success. Was this true of Alcoa? The Court thought not, emphasizing conditions of entry:

> It would completely misconstrue "Alcoa's" position in 1940 to hold that it was the passive beneficiary of a monopoly . . . . This increase and this continued undisturbed control did not fall undesigned into "Alcoa's" lap . . . . There were at least one or two abortive attempts to enter the industry, but "Alcoa" effectively anticipated and forestalled all competition . . . It was not inevitable that it should always anticipate increases in the demand for ingot and be prepared to supply them. Nothing compelled it to keep doubling and redoubling its capacity before others entered the field.

Assistance to Entrants. Today, partly as a result of this decision, Alcoa accounts for less than one third of all United States aluminum ingot capacity. The government did not bring about this confinement by breaking Alcoa into fragments. Instead, it encouraged and subsidized new entry into the industry. Shortly after World War II, the government's war plants were sold at bargain-basement prices to Reynolds and Kaiser (two former fabricators). This move alone reduced Alcoa's market share to 50%. Later, during the Cold and Korean

---

[12] *U. S. v. Aluminum Company of America,* 148 F. 2d 416 (1945).

Wars of the 1950s, the government aided the entry of Anaconda, Harvey (now owned by Martin Marietta), and Ormet. These firms were the beneficiaries of rapid amortization certificates, government-guaranteed construction loans long-term contracts to supply the government's stockpile of aluminum, and cut-rate government electricity. Changing economic conditions also helped The demand for aluminum in the United States has increased almost 3000% since 1940 and 1000% since 1950. Simultaneously, costs as a function of plant size have not altered appreciably. As a consequence, economies of scale have shrunk to the point at which a minimum efficient scale alumina plant would account for only about 8% of total United States capacity, and a minimum efficient scale ingot plant would account for only about 3%. These developments enabled still further entry during the 1960s and 1970s.

United Shoe Machinery[13]

Subsequent Section 2 cases have repeatedly endorsed the Court's reasoning in the *Alcoa* decision. A major example is *U. S. v. United Shoe Machinery Corporation*, which was tried in 1953 and never appealed to the Supreme Court. United was found to supply somewhere between 75 and 85% of the machines used in boot and shoe manufacturing. Moreover, it was the only machinery producer offering a full line of equipment. United had many sources of market power, but the following are especially noteworthy:

1. Like Alcoa, United held patents covering the fundamentals of shoe machinery manufacture at the turn of the century. These basic patents were long expired by the 1950s, and with some effort competitors could "invent around" United's later patents. Still, at the time of the suit, United held 2675 patents, some of which it acquired and some of which impeded entry.
2. The shoe-machinery industry experienced extremely slow growth. The productivity of shoe machinery increased at a rate permitting the nation's rising volume of shoe output to be produced on a fairly constant number of machines. The number of United's operating machines in 1947 was no higher than that in 1917. This meant that a new entrant could succeed only by taking business away from United.
3. A logical strategy for a new entrant would have been to start with one or two machine types and then branch out into a more complete line. Indeed, this was the approach of United's major rival, Compo, which specialized in "cementing" machines. United's answer to the challenge, however, was a discriminatory price policy that fixed a lower rate of

---

[13] This section is based primarily on Carl Kaysen, *United States v. United Shoe Machinery Corporation* (Cambridge, Mass.: Harvard University Press, 1956), and *U. S. v. United Shoe Machinery Corp.*, 110 F. Supp. 295 (1953).

return where competition was of major significance and higher rate of return where competition was weak or nonexistent.

4. There was same weak evidence of economies of scale. Economies were suggested by the fact that United had only one manufacturing plant (in Beverly, Mass.). The evidence is weak, however, because the plant was essentially a large "job shop" with a wide variety of products and small orders. Mass production techniques were not involved.

5. Finally, United never sold its machines; it only leased them. This policy precluded competition from a second-hand market. Furthermore, the terms of the leases restricted entry into new machinery production. Ten years was the standard lease duration. If a lessee wished to return a machine before the end of his 10-year term, he paid a penalty that tapered down from a substantial amount in the early years to a small amount in the later years. If he was returning the machine for replacement, he paid a lower penalty if he took another United machine than if he switched to a rival manufacturer's machine. Moreover, service was tied in. No separate charges were made for repairs and maintenance, with the result that a newly entering firm had to build a service organization as well as manufacturing and marketing capabilities.

On the basis of these facts, the court ruled against United, saying that the "defendant has, and exercises, such overwhelming strength in the shoe machinery market that it controls that market." What is more, "this strength excludes some potential, and limits some actual, competition." Regarding intent, the court conceded that "United's power does not rest on predatory practices." However, United's lease-only system, its restrictive lease clauses, its price discrimination, and its acquisition of patents

are not practices which can be properly described as the inevitable consequences of ability, natural forces, or law. They represent something more . . . . They are contracts, arrangements, and policies which, instead of encouraging competition based on pure merit, further the dominance of a particular firm. In this sense they are *unnatural* barriers . . . [italics my own]

The court ordered United to sell as well as lease its machines, to modify the terms of its leases, and to divest itself of some assets.

United Fruit Corporation[14]

Not all Section 2 cases end in trial or Supreme Court judgment. The Justice Department may negotiate an "out of court" settlement with a defendant.

[14] Primary sources for this section are Stacy May and Galo Plaza, *The United Fruit Company in Latin America* (Washington, D.C.: National Planning Association, 1958); Complaint, *U. S. v. United Fruit Co.* Civil Action #4560 (July 2, 1954); Indictment, *U. S. v. United Fruit Co.* Cr. 32416 (July 16, 1963); and D. F. Greer, "United States Study," *Restrictive Business Practices* (United Nations Conference on Trade and Development, 1973), U. N. Doc. TD/B/390, pp. 47–50.

These pretrial settlements come in two forms, depending on whether the anti-trust action is civil or criminal. If it is a **civil** proceeding (and this is most common in Section 2 cases), the negotiated settlement is a **consent decree**, which usually includes a series of injunctive provisions regulating the conduct of the defendant. Some divestiture or other fragmentation may also be provided. If it is a **criminal** proceeding, the out-of-court settlement is a *nolo contendere* plea (I do not wish to contend). As former Vice-President Spiro Agnew used to remind us, such a plea is not the same as an admission of guilt. Nevertheless, punishment may still be imposed and often is, although in such cases it cannot take the form of divestiture. One interesting point about the United Fruit (UF) Corporation (now United Brands) is that it recently endured *both* forms of pretrial settlement. Perhaps even more interesting is the fact that UF's allegedly criminal conduct involved modern-day predation.

UF was first organized by merger back in the days of massive horizontal combinations, common-place use of predatory tactics, and William McKinley. Thereafter it accounted for 60–80% of all United States and Canadian banana imports until 1954, when civil charges of monopolization were filed against it. While in North America UF cultivated the image of "Chiquita," in Central America it became known as "el pulpo" (the octopus). Among other things, it controlled 81% of the combined banana exports of Colombia, Costa Rica, Guatemala, Honduras, and Panama during the early 1950s. At the same time UF owned or controlled 56% of the mature banana acreage in these countries. All told, it controlled 2.7 million acres. Of the major banana supplying countries, Ecuador was UF's only weak spot. As for UF's competitors, only Standard Fruit and Steamship is worth mentioning. It accounted for 10–15% of the trade.

Against this background the Justice Department's accusation of 1954 seems plausible. The charges covered three broad areas: (1) general monopolization, (2) dominant control of land and transportation facilities, and (3) exclusionary and predatory practices. This last category obviously reflects intent, and if the case had gone to trial this accusation would have been more fully documented or disproved. As it stands, the complaint merely alleges in rather broad terms such tactics as engrossing, refusal to sell, and flooding local markets. These charges must have had some foundation, however, for UF agreed in 1958 to a consent decree that, by usual standards, was rather strict. Besides prohibiting UF from engaging further in exclusionary or predatory practices, the decree required UF to create out of its own assets a new competitor capable of importing into the United States a million banana "stems" per year—the rough equivalent of 35% of UF's imports in 1957. A plan for the divestiture was to be submitted by 1966.

The ink was hardly dry on the 1958 decree when UF apparently reverted to its old ways. As a result, the Justice Department filed a criminal indictment against the company on July 16, 1963. It charged unlawful monopolization by use of exclusionary and predatory tactics in the banana markets of seven western states. As Table 9-2 shows, UF was at the time more dominant in the

TABLE 9-2   Market   Shares   of   United
Fruit in the Western United States 1958–
1960

| | Percentages | | |
Submarket	1960	1959	1958
Washington & Oregon	96	100	100
California			
San Francisco Area	91	98	98
Los Angeles Area	86	88	88
Nevada	100	100	100
Montana	90	79	99
Idaho	89	78	99
Utah	90	97	99

Source: Indictment, *U. S. v. United Fruit Co.* (1963).

vest than in the United States as a whole. The only other bananas available to wholesalers in the western states were those originating in Mexico or transported overland from ports on the Gulf of Mexico (and these were inferior varieties). Table 9-2 also indicates that UF's dominance in the coastal states began to erode in 1960. It was UF's aggressive response to this that attracted the attention of the antitrust authorities. According to the indictment:

United used concentrated action to eliminate and restrain the importation and sale of bananas in the western States by actual or potential competitors:

(A) Beginning in July 1960, after learning that the Standard Fruit and Steamship Company and the Ecuadorian Fruit Import Corporation (EFIC) had entered a joint venture to import bananas into Los Angeles by ship, the defendant took action to defeat this entry: (1) at various times between July and November of 1960 United discharged two banana vessels per week at Los Angeles instead of the usual one; (2) wholesale customers' ripening rooms were maintained at maximum inventory levels so as to foreclose their purchases from Standard–EFIC; (3) United cut its prices beginning 9 July 1960 to deny a profit to Standard–EFIC; (4) the defendant caused the Port of Los Angeles to deny a secondary assignment on Berth # 147 to Standard–EFIC for the discharging of its bananas;

(B) At various times subsequent to the entry of Standard–EFIC the defendant took various actions against some wholesalers to coerce customers into boycotting the competitor;

(C) Starting in December 1960, United restricted bananas supplied to wholesalers who had bought from Standard–EFIC.

A *nolo contendere* plea terminating this suit was accepted by the court on October 23, 1963. Fines were imposed.

Since that day UF has gone further down hill. Beginning in 1964 Castle & Cooke acquired Standard, applied its "Dole" label to Standard's bananas, advertised heavily that "Dole has gone bananas," increased its merchandising force (by 75% in 1 year alone), and gave UF more competition than that company had ever seen before. The Dole brand is now "top banana" with over 40% of total sales, whereas UF has slumped to second place with a 33% share. Moreover, Del Monte entered the industry in the early 1970s as a result of UF's divestiture order. This newcomer has since become a strong third force in the market, accounting for 15–20% of total sales.[15]

For its own part, UF was plagued by an unusually severe case of management ineptitude from 1968 to 1975. The first date marks UF's acquisition by a smaller conglomerate AMK (mostly Morrell meat packing), and its subsequent conversion into United Brands. Taking command was a New Yorker named Eli Black. He guided the company to its all-time heaviest losses in 1974. He allegedly bribed the Honduran chief of state $1,250,000 in return for export tax concessions. And on the morning of February 3, 1975, knowing that news of these embarrassing events was about to be made public, he filled his briefcase with books, used the case to batter out a window of his 44th floor office, and leaped to his death on Park Avenue.[16]

International Business Machines[17]

The latest computers use semiconductor devices that store 16,000 bits of data on chips the size of a few grains of salt. We shall attempt to pull off a similar feat by putting IBM's voluminous story onto just a few pages.

Market Share and Background

IBM's share of the computer market over the 1960s and early 1970s was in the 65–75% range. Estimates vary depending on market definition, year of reference, method of calculation, and so on. Table 9-3 reports an estimate for 1973 that is based not on annual sales but on the value of the computer equipment then in place and working. Measured against all United States corporations, IBM ranks among the top ten. Its competitors are not nearly so colossal. Honeywell and Sperry Rand, the next closest, are only about one seventh the size. The rest are still smaller and less successful. Indeed, Xerox, listed seventh in Table 9-3, has since dropped out of the industry.

---

[15] *Business Week*, June 16, 1973, pp. 54–55, and July 5, 1976, pp. 56–57.

[16] For a brief account see John Kenneth Galbraith, "Bananas," *New York Review of Book* (October 14, 1976), pp. 10–12.

[17] Primary sources for this section are Gerald Brock, *The U. S. Computer Industry: A Study of Market Power* (Cambridge, Mass.: Ballinger Publishing Co., 1975); *The Industrial Reorganization Act Hearings*, Part 7, "The Computer Industry," U. S. Senate, Subcommittee on Antitrust and Monopoly of the Committee on the Judiciary, (1974); David D. Martin, "The Computer Industry," in *The Structure of American Industry*, 5th ed., edited by Walter Adams (New York: Macmillan Publishing Co., 1977) pp. 285–311; and Ronald Wilder, "The Electronic Data Processing Industry Market Structure and Policy Issues," *Antitrust Bulletin* (Spring 1975), pp. 25–47.

TABLE 9-3   Value of Installed Base of General Purpose EDP Equipment: Systems Manufacturers and Plug-Compatible Companies, United States, 1973

	Value ($ millions)	Per Cent of Total
IBM	17,406	63.8
Honeywell	2,578	9.4
Sperry Rand	2,205	8.1
Burroughs	1,421	5.2
Control Data	973	3.6
NCR	737	2.7
Xerox	390	1.4
Digital Equipment	134	.5
Others (plug-compatibles)	1,457	5.3
Total	27,301	100.0

Source: U. S. Senate, Subcommittee on Antitrust and Monopoly, *The Computer Industry* (Hearings on the Industrial Reorganization Act, 1974), p. 5095.

How did IBM come by this power in the first place? From 1924 IBM has supplied a broad line of business machines (including cheese slicers and grocery scales). Its forte was punch card tabulating equipment. In 1935, just a few years before John Atanasoff of Iowa State College began work on the world's first electronic computer, IBM had under lease 85.7% of all tabulating machines, 86.1% of all sorting machines, and 82% of all punch card installations then used in the United States. However, measured against all United States companies, IBM barely made it into the top 200. IBM did not fully appreciate the computer's potential until 1951, when one of IBM's best punch card equipment customers, the U. S. Census Bureau, accepted delivery of the world's first commercial computer from Univac, a division of Remington Rand (now Sperry Rand). At the time, IBM held 90% of the punch card tabulating machine market, and Remington Rand accounted for the remaining 10%. Hence, IBM rightly viewed Univac I as a threat to its very existence.

Shortly after IBM entered the computer field (delivering its first machine in 1953), two other business machine manufacturers joined IBM and Sperry Rand—National Cash Register (NCR) and Burroughs. In 1956, the industry included these four plus RCA, which had not been involved in business machines before. As it turned out, prior business–machine experience was a crucial determinant of success in computers. IBM's big advantage lay in its accumulation of tabulating machine customers who had vast amounts of data already coded on punch cards, plus a natural interest in any means of rapidly processing them. IBM catered to this group by designing its machines to read their cards IBM had more than just good contacts, it had a good reputation; and during 1956, "IBM shipped 85.2 % of the value of new systems, and Remington Rand only 9.7 %—approximately the same relative shares as then existing in th tabulating machine market."[18]

IBM's "lag-behind-then-recover-quickly" pattern of behavior became al most commonplace thereafter. Remington Rand and RCA were the first to introduce transistorized computers. Philco introduced the first large-scal solid state system. Data General was the first with medium-scale integration and complete semiconductor memories. Honeywell and Burroughs were th most innovative with operating systems and compilers. General Electri developed time sharing. And so on. Attempted entry often motivated thes efforts. What is more, these efforts nibbled away much of IBM's early marke share, but IBM always managed a rebound by duplication. (Patents are freel cross-licensed in the industry.) By contrast, many of these innovators are no longer producing computers. RCA, Philco, and General Electric suffered tremendous financial losses before leaving the trade, as did Bendix, Roya Precision, and Xerox. (RCA sold out to Sperry Rand, General Electric to Honeywell, and Bendix to Control Data.)

How did IBM maintain its dominance in spite of the efforts of such substantia firms? Barriers to entry, of course.

Economies of Scale

When considering economies of scale and other possible barriers to entry one must keep in mind that conditions differ across various segments of th industry. As shown in Figure 9-1, a computer system has numerous com ponents, much as a stereo system has, with its central receiver/amplifier an outlying appendages (turntable, speakers, and tape deck). IBM, Sperry Rand and the other big companies are called **systems suppliers**, for they produce an market a full line of "hardware" equipment together with "software" program and services to run the system. A second sector is made up of **plug-compatibl** or **peripherals** manufacturers. They produce printers, tape drives, disc drive and other individual items of peripheral equipment that can be plugged int the central system. Memorex, Digital Equipment, and California Compute Products rank high among these companies. Third, there are a host of servic bureaus, consulting groups, programmers, and leasing firms that deal pr marily in services rather than manufacturing. They are often lumped togethe as **software houses**. Finally, the newest segment of the industry sells **mini computers**. These are small, relatively low-cost computers that do repetitiv specialized jobs, such as running a single machine tool, regulating a productio line, and quality-testing anything from a carburetor to a cigarette. Respon sibility for development of these devices rests not with the huge systems sup

[18] Brock, *op. cit.*, p. 13.

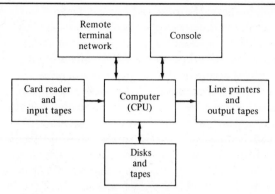

Figure 9-1. Overview of a computer system.

ɔliers but with smaller firms like Data General, Hewlett-Packard, Varian, and Digital Equipment. The following discussion centers on entry into the broadine *systems* segment of the industry, but these three other segments also re-:eive mention.

Gerald Brock finds that size brings moderate advantages in economies of ;cale, but nothing overwhelming. Manufacturing operations one tenth the ;ize of IBM probably incur unit costs of 5–10% higher than IBM, depending ɔn the particular component in question. Such a differential might be extremely ɪmportant in an industry with stable prices and technology. "But in the com-ɔuter industry," Brock says, "with prices rapidly dropping and production :ost only a small fraction of total costs, the manufacturing economies of scale ɪound here are not likely to pose significant barriers to entry."[19]

Mainframe *systems* software also generate moderate economies. Writing, ɪesting, and documenting a systems program incurs large fixed costs. As the ;ales volume of computers using individual programs rises, the fixed costs ɔer unit fall. This spread effect does not hold quite so severely for *applications* ɪoftware because applications software is often tailored to the needs of indivi-ɪual users. The creativity associated with programming also lessens the scale ɪffect, as the existence of several hundred software enterprises attests. Still, ɪmong systems suppliers, a firm with 10% of the market might suffer a 5% ɪnit cost disadvantage overall as compared to a firm with 100% of the market.

Product Differentiation

Two interrelated factors seem to foster fairly intense brand loyalty when it :omes to complete systems—(1) buyer ignorance, and (2) a lack of standardiza-ɪion. In this context buyer ignorance (or irrationality) stems from the extreme :omplexity of the purchase decision. Given the purchaser's particular needs,

[19] *Ibid.*, p. 32.

IBM's system might have the best software; Univac's might be cheapest; NCR's might offer the best input-output equipment; and CDC's system might contain the best central processor and memory. One system of the type required rarely dominates all others in *every* particular. What then? How now? Where to turn? The consequences show up in the confessions of businessmen who must decide:[20] "It is common to get the facts and then ignore or discount them." "Selection has been: any computer as long as it is manufactured by IBM." "We do write specifications and go out for bids, but this is really window-dressing .... Logical computer selection seems almost impossible."

Lack of standardization is a symptom of manufacturers' different specifications for their systems. As a result, the costs to a customer of leaving one mainframe manufacturer for another run high enough to make Hollywood divorces look dirt cheap: personnel must be retrained in procedures, operations, and maintenance; programs have to be rewritten, "debugged," and freshly documented. Switching costs are compounded by any necessary data modifications. Data are housed and organized by certain coding schemes, recording densities, and numbers of tape tracks. A change of systems usually requires a change in one or more of these fundamentals. All this runs into money. The combined costs of personnel, program, and data conversion obviously vary, depending on the particular switch involved. However, Brock estimates that "It probably adds at least 10 percent advantage to the established [computer] companies compared with new firms, and more than that in some cases. The cost to the new firm may be in the form of a lower price [that must be] offered ... or in the form of extra manufacturer costs to insure compatibility and provide conversion aids to the customer."[21]

These dual problems of complexity and transfer are much less pronounced in the industry's other sectors. Plug-compatible manufacturers sell or lease their components separately, not as full systems, thus permitting direct and narrow testing of performance by customers. These components are designed, moreover, to require no retraining or reprogramming or data converting: they are "plug-compatible." The hardest part is bending over to plug them in. Much the same could be said about software and minicomputers. Though less pronounced, product differentiation nevertheless prevails in these sectors too. Recall Table 5-5 in Chapter 5, where we saw IBM keeping more than half of its disk-drive customers, despite rivals' discounts of up to 15%.

Capital Costs

The capital required for entry into the software-service sector is quite small. At a bare minimum, the costs of office space, phone lines, a secretary, and a few programmers are easily met. In the plug-compatible and minicomputer sectors the requirements are stiffer, but not beyond the range of ordinary

---

[20] *Ibid.*, p. 47.
[21] *Ibid.*, p. 51. It is worth noting that IBM has thwarted efforts to attain industrywide standardization because the prevailing system works to IBM's advantage.

TABLE 9-4   Summary of Cost Disadvantages for New Entrants into Three Sectors of the Computer Industry

Item	Integrated Systems	Peripherals Makers	Minicomputers
Economies of scale	20%	10%	5%
Marketing advantages	20–30%	10–20%	5–10%
Capital requirements	Enormous	Moderate	Minor
Total evaluation of entry	No entry possible	20–30% disadvantage	10–15% disadvantage

Source: Gerald Brock, *The U. S. Computer Industry: A Study of Market Power* (Cambridge, Mass.: Ballinger Publishing Co., 1975), p. 65. Reprinted by permission.

financing. For example, the fastest growing minicomputer supplier is Data General, which started out with $50,000 in 1968, raised $20 million more on the stock market during 1969–1971, and, in 1976, enjoyed revenues exceeding $160 million. On a slightly larger scale, Amdahl Corporation, a specialist in central processing units, recently needed $47 million to get off the ground. With respect to integrated systems suppliers, however, the estimates are staggering. When RCA left the computer market in September 1971, it took a $490 million loss write-off. Moreover, RCA reckoned that it would have had to invest $500–700 million *more* over the next 5 years to reach profitability.[22] The evidence suggests that capital requirements are in the neighborhood of $1 *billion* for full-systems entry. In other words, that game is open only to well-healed titans.

Table 9-4 summarizes the industry's manufacturing sectors. The per cent figures indicate the cost disadvantages a new entrant would suffer *relative* to established firms. The figures are only rough estimates, but they indicate three degrees of difficulty. At one extreme, entry into integrated systems seems impossible. At the other extreme, minicomputers display minibarriers. In between, we find manufacture of plug-compatible peripherals.

Antitrust Action

The Department of Justice sued IBM under Section 2 on the last business-day of the Johnson Administration in January 1969.[23] Delays and preparations kept the trial from getting under way for 6 years. At this writing, the trial has been going for 3 years. If the case is not settled out of court, it could continue through appeals for another 10 years. In sum, the case itself is monopolizing the time of scores of people.

[22] *Hearings*, p. 5660 (see footnote 17).
[23] *U. S. v. International Business Machines Corp.*, 69 CIV 200, So. Dist. of N.Y.

IBM's defense strategy hinges on two basic arguments: (1) The "relevant market" for electronic data-processing equipment and services is so large that IBM's market share is closer to 35% than 75%. Indeed, IBM defines the market broadly enough to include $706 million of American Telephone & Telegraph Company's revenues for data communications products and services. (2) IBM's success is due solely to its superior products, services, and technological innovation. In legal terms, this translates into "superior skill, foresight, and industry." IBM is thus arguing that it has neither the power nor the intent to monopolize.

The Justice Department argues the opposite. Its definition of the market is limited to general-purpose computer systems. Accordingly, it alleges that IBM has 75% control and that entry is extremely difficult. As for intent, IBM allegedly tried to maintain control and to inhibit entry deliberately through a wide variety of questionable marketing, financial, and technical maneuvers. These include:

"Bundling," whereby IBM quotes a *single* price for hardware, software, and related support. (IBM unbundled in 1970, after the suit.)

"Fighting machines," whereby IBM introduced selected computers with inordinately low prices in those sectors of the industry where its competitors appeared to be on the verge of success.

"Educational discounts," whereby IBM sold its machines and services to universities and colleges at 20–30% discounts (and in many cases gave them away free), with the effect that computer folks received their training on IBM goods and were therefore ever after more or less brand-loyal to IBM.

"Paper machines," whereby IBM tried to dissuade computer users from acquiring or leasing Control Data's 6600 (an advanced, truly remarkable machine) by announcing that IBM would soon have a comparable and perhaps even superior product, when in fact IBM had no such thing.

How will the courts decide? At present the business press is predicting an IBM victory, and not without good reason. Since 1932 IBM has been sued three times by the federal government and more than a dozen times by private companies for violating the antitrust laws. Technically speaking, IBM has lost only once. That was a tabulating-card monopoly case in 1934. All other cases ended in acquittals or out of court settlements. In one of IBM's biggest settlements, Control Data received roughly $100 million from IBM in return for withdrawal of its 1968 monopolization suit. Much of the government's present case is based on material Control Data gathered for its suit.[24]

[24] Two points of interest here: (1) IBM counter sued CDC, charging CDC with monopolization of the large, scientific computer market (CDC's forte). This means that IBM likes to use narrow market definitions when it suits their purpose. (2) Control Data destroyed its computerized index of 27 *million* IBM documents as a part of the settlement, thereby hampering progress on the government's big case and earning the censure of Federal Judge Edelstein, who is trying the big case in New York.

Proposals to Toughen United States Law

IBM's apparent invincibility illuminates what many see as a basic flaw in current United States policy. The Sherman Act may reach obvious monopolists, but it cannot be used to restructure industries dominated by a few oligopolists, unless those leaders pursue flagrantly unconscionable behavior. An even more probing test of the law than the *IBM* case is another case currently on trial— a Federal Trade Commission suit charging three large breakfast cereal producers with "shared monopoly."[25] Kellogg, General Mills, and General Foods collectively account for 81 % of the ready-to-eat cereal market. But individually, the largest (Kellogg) controls no more than 45 %. The accusations bringing these firms together under one suit are legal novelties:

1. *Brand proliferation*: The companies introduced 150 brands between 1950 and 1970, advertising them heavily and artificially differentiating them, thereby feigning competition and discouraging new entry.
2. *Misrepresentation*: They falsely advertise that consumption of their products will enhance health and reduce body weight.
3. *Control shelf space*: They crowd competitors off grocers' shelves with their countless brands and marketing clout.
4. *Forbearance*: They minimize price competition by tacit mutual agreement not to challenge each other's price increases and by limiting coupons, premiums, and cents-off deals.

The case thus features not only the principle of "shared monopoly" but barriers built by product differentiation. Accordingly, the remedies sought involve more than dissolution. They include the forced licensing to other companies of any new brands developed by Kellogg, General Mills, and General Foods. Still, the prospects for a guilty verdict appear bleak.

A more direct structural attack on large oligopolists would require new legislation. The Industrial Reorganization Act proposed by the late Senator Philip Hart provides an example.[26] Under this scheme, the rule of reason would be abandoned. There would be a *presumption* of monopoly power whenever one or more of the following criteria were met:

1. Four or fewer firms accounted for half or more of an industry's sales in a single year.

---

[25] *In the Matter of Kellogg Co., et. al.*, Docket #8883, Complaint, April 26, 1972.
[26] *The Industrial Reorganization Act, Hearings* before the U. S. Senate Subcommittee on Antitrust and Monopoly of the Committee on the Judiciary, Part 1 (1973).

219

2. There has been no substantial price competition for three consecutive years among two or more firms within the industry.
3. A company's average rate of return (after taxes) exceeds 15 % of its net worth for each of five consecutive years.

However, a company running afoul of one of these criteria would not face automatic fragmentation. A special commission would review the case, at which time the company could defend itself by showing that its power was due "solely to the ownership of valid patents, lawfully acquired and lawfully used," *or* that its divestiture would "result in a loss of substantial economies." Predictably, this proposed legislation touched off a bitter controversy, and nobody is holding his breath while waiting for its passage. It is doubtful whether such a stringent measure can ever pass. Its benefits are too vague to the man on the street, and its business opponents are too powerful in the halls of Congress.

Outside the United States, in Europe and Japan, official policies tend to shy away from any kind of structural approach to monopoly—be it a rule of reason or a presumptive rule. The continued existence of dominant firms is not threatened by restructuring, even when they behave arrogantly. Transgressions lead to direct regulations of behavior or performance rather than restructuring. In the United States the regulatory approach is reserved for "public utilities"; it is the exception, not the rule. The contrast with United States policy can be neatly demonstrated with a *Wall Street Journal* news clip dated December 19, 1975:

> **Brussels**—Common Market antitrust authorities ordered United Brands Co. to lower its wholesale banana prices 15 % in West Germany and 30 % in Belgium, the Netherlands and Luxembourg.
> The order . . . was part of a decision that found the U.S. company had abused a dominant position in the Common Market. The officials also fined United Brands the equivalent of $1.2 million and made it subject to a $1,200 daily fine if it fails to comply with the price-cut order.

Summary

The Sherman Act outlaws monopolization. Establishing a violation requires proof of two elements: (1) substantial market power, and (2) intent. Reason, estimation, and hunch make appraisal of these elements uncertain. Hence we find very big cases in this area. Just about everything is considered except the rainfall in Indianapolis.

When attempting to examine market power, the courts consider barriers to entry of various kinds and profits. The item receiving greatest attention, however, is market share. Broad definitions of the market tend to favor defendants; narrow definitions favor the prosecutors. Which way the court will turn in any particular case is often unpredictable. Once a market definition is established, percentage points become all important. The consensus is that a market share below 60% lies beneath the reach of the law (unless abusive practices are present), whereas shares above 80% make Justice Department attorneys look good in court.

On the question of intent, interpretations are divided by the *Alcoa* decision of 1945. Before *Alcoa*, intent could be demonstrated only by evidence of predatory, exclusionary, or unfair acts. Since *Alcoa*, intent may be demonstrated by evidence that actions are not "honestly industrial," not "passive," or not reflective of "superior skill, foresight, and industry."

The *Alcoa* reading of the Act helped the government to restructure the aluminum, shoe machinery, and banana industries. Limited divestitures were obtained and barriers to entry reduced. Whether the same results can be hoped for in the case of the computer industry remains to be seen. IBM is economically dominant, but it may not be a "monopolist" under current law.

Dissatisfaction with the limited reach of current law has led to efforts for change. Several "shared monopoly" cases have been brought against oligopolists. In addition, "presumptive rules" have also been proposed, whereby defendants would have to prove their innocence if they transgressed some previously specified criteria, such as having more than a 40% market share for 2 years running. These experimental suits and legislative proposals seem destined for defeat, however. Critics who want a stronger policy will continue to think that "trust busting, despite the heroic imagery conjured up by the term, functions as timorous research or a common scold."[27]

---

[27] Robert Engler, *The Brotherhood of Oil* (Chicago: University of Chicago Press, 1977), p. 214.

three

CONDUCT

10

Introduction to Conduct: Profit Maximization (?)

According to legend, economists are supposed never to agree among themselves. If Parliament were to ask six economists for an opinion, seven answers would come back . . .

PAUL SAMUELSON

Passage into Part III signals that our barque of discovery is now well out to sea. Conduct comes next, which means that this chapter must ponder theories of firm motivation in general and profit maximization in particular. Unfortunately, these are deep and choppy waters, but we must sail out on them. Structure alone does not determine conduct. The *combination* of structural conditions and firm motivation determines conduct. According to traditional theory (see Chapters 2 and 3), profit maximization motivates all firms in *all* market settings. It is the diversity of structures that produces diverse conduct from this universal motivation. If a monopolist charges a higher price than a group of purely competitive firms would, it is not because the monopolist is a profit maximizer and the competitive firms are philanthropists. Theoretically, all firms are out to make as much money as they can. The monopolist charges more simply because he faces less competition.

If, contrary to conventional theory, firm motivation varied as much as structure varies, conduct would be less predictable and less readily explainable. Economists would have to step aside in favor of psychologists (or other motivation experts). Unfortunately for economists, variance in structure itself probably promotes some variances in motivation. Owners of purely competitive firms are *compelled* to toe the profit maximizing line lest they go bankrupt. On the other hand, monopolistic and oligopolistic firms may have sufficient market power that their owners and managers need not scratch and scrape for every penny of possible profit. Such firms have the option of enjoying the "easy life," of coasting along with only "satisfactory" or "reasonable" earnings. As an executive of U.S. Steel once claimed, "U.S. Steel has never tried to price to maximum profit ..."[1]

This incalculable relation between structural and motivational variances, as well as related factors, has sparked controversy. Like a ravenous bookworm the controversy has consumed thousands of pages of scholarly journals and dozens of books. Some economists stick to conventional theory. Some advocate alternative possible motivations, such as sales maximization or growth maximization. Some argue that firms are not motivated to maximize anything. They say, without respect for the English language, that firms are merely "satisficers." This brief catalog of positions on firm motivation provides an outline for this chapter. Our own objective is to maximize understanding.

Profit Maximizing— Traditional Theory

The hypothesis of firm profit maximization rests on three essential assumptions concerning the people who own and operate "the firm"; (1) single-minded purpose; (2) rational or forced choice of objective; and (3) the adherence to operational rules of optimality.

Single-Minded Purpose

The first of these assumptions infers that no matter how big and diverse the firm happens to be, all its owners and employees work as one to achieve its objective. Warehousemen may have the hoarding instincts of squirrels. Salesmen may simply want to sell, sell, sell, even at give-away prices. And the typical junior executive may yearn to romance his or her secretary. However, traditional theory holds that while on the job these dedicated souls either set aside their personal obsessions or bend them to benefit the enterprise. All work as a team. No one is ever at cross purposes.

Rationality

What objectives do the efforts of these single-minded individuals further? Since control of a capitalistic firm rests with its owners, and since the owners are rewarded by profits, the traditional assumption of rationality implies a goal of profit maximization. Whether the owner fits the legendary image of the economic entrepreneur or the more common mold of the average upper-crust

---

[1] A. D. H. Kaplan, J. B. Dirlam, and R. F. Lanzillotti, *Pricing in Big Business* (Washington, D.C.: Brookings Institution, 1958), p. 23.

stockholder, he has committed his capital to conditions of uncertainty. The reward for subjecting his capital to some risk of loss is profit. It is only natural, then, for firms to try to maximize profits, just as consumers try to maximize their material well being. Or so it is assumed.

Operational Rules

"Profit maximization" is meaningless unless it can be translated into an operational objective. Left in vague form, the objective does not specifically indicate precisely what businessmen must do in their daily affairs to achieve it. Many operational rules are possible (such as "no one ever went broke underestimating the taste of the American public"). However, as outlined in Chapters 2 and 3, traditional economic theory offers a rather technical rule: *Expand production and promotion as long as added revenues exceed added costs; cut back whenever the resulting reductions in costs exceed the reductions in revenues.* In short, operate where marginal revenue equals marginal cost—or, symbolically, MR = MC.

This rule stems from the standard definition of total profit, which is the difference between total revenue and total cost, that is, TP = TR − TC. We know by now that demand is the crucial determinant of the firm's marginal revenue function. In turn, market structure is a crucial determinant of demand as viewed by the typical firm in the market. Thus, in traditional theory, structure influences conduct through its influence on the marginal revenue portion of the firm's profit maximizing computation.

Criticism of Traditional Theory

If traditional theory is vulnerable to criticism, it must be vulnerable in one or more of these three underlying assumptions. In fact, virtually all criticism may be gathered under three broad labels designating focuses of attack: (1) realism in process, (2) managerialism, and (3) behavioralism. These classifications of criticism are outlined in Table 10-1 according to the degree in which each school of criticism accepts (yes) or rejects (no) the three basic assumptions of traditional theory itemized on the left-hand side.

"Realism in process" thus identifies a form of criticism that generally accepts the assumptions of single-mindedness and rational choice but rejects the notion that MR = MC is an adequate operational objective for businessmen. Conversely, "managerialism" identifies the position of a number of analysts who are not much bothered by the problem of operational feasibility. However, they seriously doubt that the typical firm is run for the single-minded pursuit of the owners' interests. They argue that in most large corporations the owners (stockholders) and managers (president, vice-presidents, and so on) are *not* the same people and they are *not* driven by the same objectives. Since *managers* are allegedly the ones primarily in control, they can pursue objectives in *their*

TABLE 10-1 Outline of Three Main Schools of Criticism According to Their Acceptance (YES) or Rejection (NO) of Traditional Theory's Key Assumptions

Traditional Theory's Assumption	Classification of Criticism		
	Realism in Process	Managerialism	Behavioralism
Single-mindedness	Yes	No	No
Rational profit maximization	Yes	No	No
Operational feasibility	No	Yes	No
Overall acceptance of profit maximization?	No	No	No

self interest rather than the owners'. This split obliterates the assumption of single-mindedness (or redirects it), and opens the door to goals other than profit maximization. Finally, there is a third group of critics called the "behavioralists." They deny that profit maximization is typical of American business for reasons that blend realism in process and managerialism. They stress the complexity of business organizations. They note a diversity of motives among salesmen, production workers, warehousemen, and others in the firm besides those of owners and managers. As for goals, they believe that humans engage in "satisficing" rather than maximizing behavior and that human rules of daily operation reflect this.

The remainder of this chapter is divided into three parts, one for each class of criticism. One important thread of thought to which we shall return repeatedly is this: Pricing policy and cost experience are two largely *separable* issues in this question of profit maximizing. On the whole, a firm is more likely to *price* its wares in conformity with profit maximizing precepts than to manage its *costs* in the miserly, tight-fisted fashion that profit maximization implies. Assume that we (1) drew the name of a *Fortune* 500 firm from a random hat, (2) sent out a team of economists, accountants, and engineers to assess its behavior, and (3) recommended any steps that would move it in the direction of profit maximization. Chances are that our experts would come up with some sound recommendations for cutting costs. You could bet $50 they would. On the other hand, the chances of their coming up with price policy changes are slimmer.

The reason for this asymmetry is simple. The main burden of most price policy adjustments would be carried by persons *outside* the firm—by customers if it is a price increase or by competitors if it is a price decrease. Hence sound price adjustments are likely to have been made *already by the firm*. The main burden of any cost adjustments, on the other hand, would be borne by persons *inside* the firm—by folks who would lose their jobs or would have to work harder. Hence, profitable adjustments in this area are *not* likely to have already been made. It is here we would probably find flab.[2]

Realism in Process

The basic thrust of the realism in process criticism is that the simple rule MR = MC is *non*operational. Businessmen cannot maximize profits by this rule alone, even if they wanted to. Among the many pertinent questions left at least partially unanswered by this rule are the following:

1. *What costs and revenues are supposed to be included in this calculation over what time period?* An accountant's view of "costs" differs from an economist's view, as is illustrated by their differing treatments of "depreciation" and "normal profit." Moreover, the economist's "short run" and "long run" do not correspond to the accountant's "calendar quarter" and "fiscal year." Their decisions on the content of calculations will differ. On top of this divergence, many decisions are nonmarginal from anyone's viewpoint (for example, converting from an open shop to a union shop, acquiring a large subsidiary, or bribing a Senator). The MR = MC rule allegedly collapses under the weight of these big decisions.

   In defense of traditional theory, it ought to be acknowledged that experts in managerial economics have unravelled many of these knotty problems.[3] They have shown that wide application of marginal concepts is by no means impossible. Moreover, as far as the time problem is concerned, profit maximization is now commonly translated into maximization of the discounted present value of the firm. This approach converts future earnings into a present value form that blends the short and long run.

2. *How can risk be properly accounted for?* Even assuming the businessman knows the probabilities associated with the various possible outcomes of his decisions, there is no universally acceptable way of identifying the profit maximizing course of action whenever substantial risk is involved. Scherer explains the situation with the aid of a problem:

   Imagine a decision-maker weighing two alternative policies, one offering a best-guess profit expectation of $1 million with a 10 percent chance of bankrupting the firm (whose net worth is currently $4 million), the other an expected profit of $2 million with a 30 percent chance of disaster. Which is the rational choice?[4]

---

[2] D. C. Hague stresses this point in *Pricing in Business* (London: George Allen & Unwin, 1971), pp. 83–84.

[3] See, e.g., Ralph Turvey, "Marginal Cost," *Economic Journal* (June 1969), pp. 282–98; and E. F. Brigham and J. L. Pappas, *Managerial Economics* (Hinsdale, Ill.: Dryden Press, 1976).

[4] F. M. Scherer, *Industrial Market Structure and Economic Performance* (Chicago: Rand McNally, 1970), p. 28.

Application of sophisticated expected-value criteria cannot yield the "right" answer. The answer requires extensive information on the attitudes of the firm's owners toward increases in wealth versus total loss of their equity, *plus* some technique for properly aggregating these attitudes. Achieving world peace would be easier.

3. *What is the profit maximizing course of action when uncertainty prevails?* In the preceding problem it was assumed that the 10 and 30% probabilities for bankruptcy were *known* to be the true probabilities. Hence, it was purely a case of "risk." As with the toss of a coin, the ultimate outcome was unknown, but the probabilities were certain. When the decision-maker knows *neither* the ultimate outcome *nor* the probabilities of the possible outcomes, he knows about as much as a blind man in a dark room looking for a black cat that may not be there. Economists dryly say he is "uncertain." Accordingly, they have dryly devised a number of techniques to assist rational (cold-blooded) decision making in this situation (including "maximax," "maximin," and "regret hedging"). But none of these really qualifies as profit maximizing.

Defenders of orthodoxy argue that full knowledge is not necessary, that an earnest effort and an "intuitive understanding" are all that are required. Fritz Machlup, for example, uses the analogy of one driver passing another on a two-lane country road, which motorists do all the time without the aid of sophisticated physics and differential calculus. He summarizes his argument by stressing the uses of *subjective* knowledge:

> It should hardly be necessary to mention that all the relevant magnitudes involved —costs, revenue, profit—are subjective—that is, perceived or fancied by the men whose decisions or actions are to be explained rather than "objective" .... Marginal analysis of the firm should not be understood to imply anything but subjective estimates, guesses and hunches.[5]

The critics remain unmoved by this analysis, however. They claim that Machlup's argument rests on a tautology—that "maximization" becomes meaningless if it is allowed that anything businessmen happen to do is considered maximizing. Even if Machlup's theory is interpreted to mean that businessmen merely *try* to—rather than actually do—maximize profits, uncertainty critics would reply that this has little value as a description, prescription, or prediction of business behavior.[6]

(Interestingly enough, Machlup's defense of orthodoxy has received some rather unorthodox support from research concerning executive extrasensory perception. In one test of precognition, a number of business executives were divided into two groups "according to whether they had at least doubled their

---

[5] Fritz Machlup, "Marginal Analysis and Empirical Research," *American Economic Review* (September 1946), pp. 521–22.

[6] Joseph McGuire, *Theories of Business Behavior* (Englewood Cliffs, N. J.: Prentice-Hall, 1964), p. 83.

company's profits over the last five years or not." The profit makers "all scored above chance" in predicting a computer's random numbers. "One executive who had not doubled his companies profits had an average score but all others in his group scored below average [that is, below chance]."[7] Not being one to stick my neck out, I register my reservations by putting this entire paragraph between parentheses.)

Managerialism
(or Realism in Motivation)

There are two parts to this line of criticism:

1. Managers, not owners, are in control of our main corporations.
2. The managers do not want to maximize profits; they hook their wagons to other stars.

Control by Managers

To understand the first point we must look behind the standard pyramid of corporate structure that, as in Figure 10-1, places owners at the top. In *theory*, the stockholders elect a board of directors to represent their views. The board meets only infrequently, and it does not make daily decisions. However, the board hires and fires managing officers according to how well they serve the owners' interests. Hence, power corresponds to placement in the pyramid.

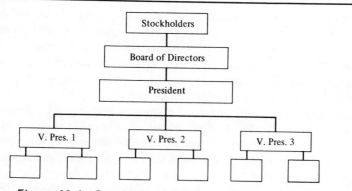

Figure 10-1. Standard corporate organization structure.

[7] *New York Times*, August 31, 1969.

TABLE 10-2 Summary According to Type of Ultimate Control of the 200 Largest Nonfinancial United States Corporations, 1963 and 1929

Type of Control	Number of Corporations		Proportion of Companies	
	1929	1963	1929	1963
Management control	88½	167	44%	83.5%
Minority control	46½	18	23	9.0
Private or majority ownership	22	6	11	3.0
Legal device	43	9	22	4.5
Total	200	200	100%	100%

Sources: R. J. Larner, *Management Control and the Large Corporation* (New York: Dunellen Publishing Co., Inc., 1970), p. 12; A. A. Berle, Jr., and G. C. Means, *The Modern Corporation and Private Property* (New York: Macmillan Publishing Co. 1932), p. 115.

In *practice*, only stockholders or *proxyholders* who attend the annual meeting of owners can cast votes in the election of directors. The emphasis here is on proxyholders because the stockholders of most major corporations are too numerous, too apathetic, too timid, and too far-flung geographically to attend the annual meetings. Hence the usual election procedure is for *management* to nominate a slate of candidates and then ask the stockholders for proxies that is, permission to use the stockholders' votes on behalf of this slate of candidates. Ninety-nine percent of the time a majority of stockholders sign over their proxies to management. In short, the managers select and control the board. Indeed, managers *themselves* hold a majority of seats on the board of many major corporations. "The board of directors becomes, in effect, a rubber-stamping body routinely approving the decisions and recommendations of management rather than an independent watchdog with a vigilant eye to the interests and desires of the corporation's owners."[8]

To illustrate the extent and trend of management control over corporations in the United States, the findings of two prominent studies are summarized in Table 10-2. The first study refers to conditions in 1929, the second, 1963. They both refer to the top 200 United States corporations, and they use similar definitions of "control." It is easy to see that among these firms management control predominates and is on the rise. In 1929, 44% of the top 200 corpora

[8] Robert Larner, *Management Control and the Large Corporation* (New York: Dunellen, 1970) p. 3.

234

ons qualified for the management-control category, more than fell under any ther control group. By 1963 this percentage had risen to 83.5%. The only :maining bastion of stockholder control is so-called "minority control," in -hich no single owner or close-knit group of owners holds more than a majority f outstanding shares, but more than 10% of the voting stock is in the hands f an influential individual, family, corporation, or group of business associates. Of course, owners retain the option of buying and selling stock, no matter ow diverse or detached they may be. Furthermore, such buying and selling nceivably offers a means of rewarding and punishing management. If it does, ockholders are not irredeemably "poor cousins in the corporate family, nored by a management which, if not feathering its own nest with bonuses nd stock options, is yielding to the greater pressure of unions, customers, and overnment."[9] Rather, stockholders are catered to and pampered as a source f capital, even though most capital is raised from other sources. Economists ho hold this view argue that the equity investor is not so unlikely a source of apital as to suffer anyone to treat him highhandedly. Unfortunately, this gument is often exaggerated. Such indirect stock-market control cannot be ringent. At best, share trading is a long leash. After analyzing this form of ntrol in some detail, Oliver Williamson concluded that "individually and llectively, capital market controls experience weaknesses sufficient to warrant uch of the expressed concern over the separation of ownership from control the large corporation."[10]

heories of Managerial Motives

So much for the first introductory proposition. Managers typically *do* sit the driver's seat. What of the second proposition? Do manager's really turn e steering wheel in directions other than that of profit maximization? The nswer is "yes," "no," "maybe," and "sometimes," depending on whom you nsult. Those who say "yes" argue that (1) managers lack the incentive to steer ward profit because their incomes are not directly linked to profit levels, r (2) if there is close linkage, managers are moved by *non*monetary motives. hose who say "no" argue that (1) managerial remuneration *is* atuned to profit erformance, and (2) managers respond accordingly. Those who say "maybe" r "sometimes" stress that it is difficult to generalize. They point out that rporations and managers come in many different sizes, shapes, colors, and ualities. They correctly maintain that no single theory is equally applicable the corner grocer and Alcoa. With these views in mind, let's look into several eories of "managerial enterprise" and then survey the available evidence.

[9] Shorey Peterson, "Corporate Control and Capitalism," *Quarterly Journal of Economics* ebruary 1965), pp. 3, 20–21.
[10] Oliver Williamson, *Corporate Control and Business Behavior* (Englewood Cliffs, N. J.: entice-Hall, 1970), p. 104. Empirical support for this position is provided by B. Hindley, "Separa- n of Ownership and Control in the Modern Corporation," *Journal of Law and Economics* pril 1970), pp. 185–210.

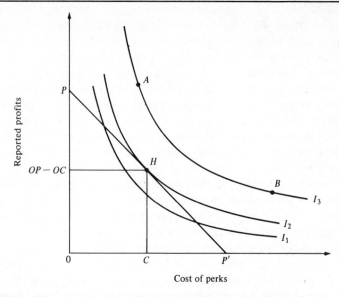

Figure 10-2. *Managerial trade-off between company profits and executive perks.*

Managerial Utility. Oliver Williamson's theories of managerial utility assume that for tax and other reasons managers are interested in executive jets, liberal expense accounts, and other emoluments or perquisites as well as personal income and company profits.[11] Let the horizontal axis of Figure 10-2 indicate the monetary value of "perks" and the vertical axis indicate profits. Each curve I_1, I_2, and I_3, represents a given level of manager satisfaction realized from various combinations of perks and profits. I_1 is the lowest level of satisfaction depicted, and I_3 is the highest. Managers are *indifferent* as between any two points on a given I curve, such as A and B on I_3; that is, all points on I_3 yield the same degree of reward. Accordingly, these are called **indifference curves.**

Managers would obviously like the very generous volumes of perks and profits that lie in the region northeast of I_3, but they are restrained by realities. Point P on the vertical axis represents the *maximum* level of profits the company can earn. Perks at that point are zero, but it defines the extent to which perks are possible. Since $1 worth of increased perks must reduce profits by $1, movement to the right from P reduces profits along the line PP', which has a negative slope of 1. At point H on PP' the value of perks is OC. Hence the corresponding level for profit is OP minus OC, or $OP - OC$, as indicated on the vertical axis. In other words, line PP' is a perks/profits **possibilities curve.** Any point *in*side the triangle POP' is possible. Any point *out*side is not. Managers maximize their

[11] O. E. Williamson, *The Economics of Discretionary Behavior: Managerial Objectives in a Theory of the Firm* (Chicago: Markham Publishing Co., 1967).

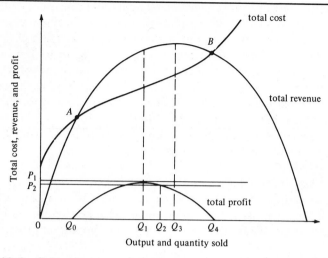

Figure 10-3. *Sale revenue maximization, subject to minimum profit constraint.*

tisfaction by choosing that combination of possible perks and profits landing
em on their highest indifference curve. In this case it is I_2 at point H.

Notice that, according to this model, managers select the *same* price and
tput policies as a simple profit maximizer. If they did not, the PP' line would
closer to the origin, meaning reduced overall managerial satisfaction on an
difference curve such as I_1. However, internal costs will be higher in this model
an in the simple profit maximizing model because perks don't grow on trees.
illiamson has also devised a model wherein perks take the form of additional
aff personnel. The alternative model yields price and output solutions that
ffer, according to the extent variations in staff affect output, from those of
mple profit maximization.

Sales Maximization. Figure 10-3 presents the basic sales revenue maximiza-
n model developed by W. J. Baumol.[12] The horizontal axis measures output
d quantity sold. The vertical axis depicts total dollar cost, revenue, and profit.
ssuming the firm faces a linear negatively sloped demand curve (such as that
cing the monopolist in Figure 3-3 of Chapter 3), total revenue will look like
McDonald's golden arch. Subtracting total cost from total revenue yields
tal profit, which is zero at two quantities (Q_0 and Q_4), corresponding to the
tersection of total cost and total revenue at points A and B. Profit maximizing
tput would be OQ_1, with profit equal to OP_1. Sales revenue maximization
uld require greater output at Q_3. Note that profits are lower at Q_3 than
. Moreover, although it is not shown here, Q_3 implies a lower product price
an the profit maximizing solution Q_1.

[12] W. J. Baumol, *Business Behavior, Value and Growth* (New York: Macmillan Publishing Co.,
9).

If managers were operating under a minimum profit constraint that was abo⟋ the profit level associated with absolute revenue maximization, they would ⟋ forced to raise price, reduce output, and move in the direction of profit max⟋ mization. One such profit floor might be OP_2 in Figure 10-3, in which ca⟋ quantity would be Q_2 instead of Q_3. Why a minimum profit constraint? O⟋ is probably necessary to satisfy the neglected but not totally forgotten sto⟋ holders. Although these are the most often cited conclusions for this model⟋ should be noted that the assumption of monopoly limits its generality. It h⟋ been argued that under oligopoly there is no substantial behavioral differen⟋ between profit and sales maximization.[13]

Maximizing Growth or Present Value of Revenue.[14] We mentioned grow⟋ motivations earlier when discussing mergers. Here we shall focus on simp⟋ theories of "internal" growth maximization, since they follow neatly from t⟋ preceding analysis. We begin by announcing three important principles:

1. Growth of sales requires expansions of capacity and, consequently, adequate capital to finance expansion. Maximum profits can supply the needed funds either directly through retained earnings or indirectly by attracting the capital of additional equity investors and bond buyers. In theory, growth rate maximization often corresponds exactly to profit maximization; in fact, numerous statistical studies demonstrate a close positive association between growth rate and profit.[15]

2. Growth *rate* is only one possible measure of growth. Another is the *present value of the firm's future stream of sales revenues.* This is the sum of each future years' expected sales revenue, discounted by an appropriate percentage rate to account for the fact that each dollar obtained 5 or 10 years from now is worth less than each dollar obtained in the current year. In other words, an added dollar's worth of sales in the current period is actually "worth" more to the firm in terms of present value than is an added dollar's worth of sales in any subsequent period. This principle may be seen in Figure 10-4. Each curve, V_1, V_2, and V_3, indicates a *given present* value of sales revenue, with V_1 being the lowest and V_3 the highest present values explicitly depicted. Any two points on a single curve, such as G and H on V_3, represent the *same* present value. The negative slope of these curves indicates that a given present value can be

[13] W. F. Shepherd, "On Sales Maximizing and Oligopoly Behavior," *Economica* (Novem⟋ 1962), pp. 420–24; B. D. Mabry, "Sales Maximization vs. Profit Maximization: Are they Inc⟋ sistent?" *Western Economic Journal* (March 1968), pp. 154–60.

[14] On growth maximization see Robin Marris, *The Economic Theory of Managerial Capital⟋* (New York: Free Press, 1964); John Williamson, "Profit Growth and Sales Maximizatio⟋ *Economica* (February 1966), pp. 1–16; for a simpler treatment, K. Heidensohn and N. Robins⟋ *Business Behavior* (New York: Wiley & Sons, 1974), Chapter 8.

[15] J. L. Eatwell, "Growth Profitability and Size: The Empirical Evidence," in *The Corpor⟋ Economy*, edited by R. Marris and A. Wood (Cambridge, Mass.: Harvard University Press, 197⟋ pp. 409–18.

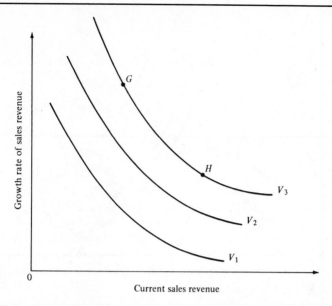

Figure 10-4. *Relationship between the present value of future sales (Vs), growth rate of sales, and current sales.*

achieved *either* by high current sales revenues and low growth (low future revenues), *or* by low current sales revenues and high growth, *or* by some combination in between. To appreciate this, note that the horizontal axis is *current sales* revenue and the vertical axis is the *growth rate* of sales. These V curves may be called **given-present-value lines.**

3. Once again we may take account of the owners' interest by specifying a minimum profit constraint below which profits ought not fall.

These three principles are combined in Figure 10-5, which itself is a modified combination of Figures 10-3 and 10-4. Figure 10-3 has been rotated clockwise degrees and placed underneath Figure 10-4. Thus, all axes move positively. output is measured on the lowest axis; current sales revenue, costs, and profit are measured on the horizontal axis; and the growth rate of sales revenue is measured vertically upward. The first principle may be seen in the close correspondence between the growth rate curve in the upper half of Figure 10-5 and the profit curve in the lower half. When profit is zero, growth rate is zero. When profit is at its maximum level, growth rate too reaches a maximum because profits are needed to finance growth. It should be clear, then, that under present assumptions, the price, quantity, and cost behavior of the growth rate maximizer matches that of the profit maximizer.

237

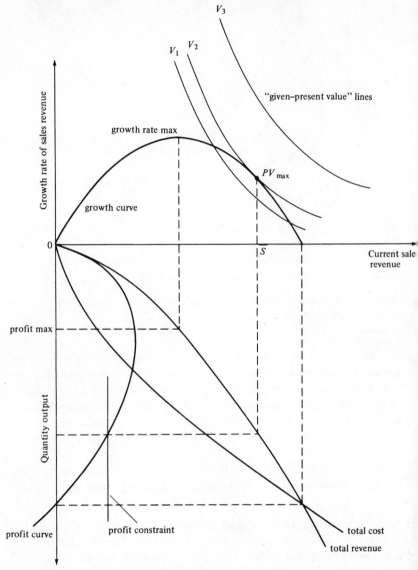

Figure 10-5. *Two views of growth maximization: rate and present value of sale*
Source: Douglas Needham, Economic Analysis and Industrial Structure *(New Yo)*
Holt, Rinehart and Winston, 1969), p. 9.

The second principle is embodied in the given-present-value lines V_1, V_2, id V_3 carried over from Figure 10-4. If "growth" is taken to mean present lue of future sales rather than *rate* of expansion, the higher the V_i the better. owever, the growth rate curve defines those combinations of growth rate id current sales revenue that are within the realm of *possibility*. No point i V_3 is possible. A number of points on V_1 are possible. Maximum present lue is attained at "PV max" on V_2. Because the given-present-value lines ope down from left to right, it follows that PV max will occur at a point to the ght of "growth rate max." Furthermore, this PV max solution implies that present-value maximizer will behave pretty much like a sales maximizer. That to say, the present-value maximizing firm will have a lower price, a lower rate profit, and a higher volume of current period sales than a profit maximizer. the sales maximizer and present-value maximizer were operating under the me profit constraint, that profit constraint would be depicted as in Figure i-5. This of course takes account of principle three.

As in the simple sales maximization model, these theories of growth maxi-ization ignore the problem of oligopolistic interdependence. This is un-ubtedly their greatest weakness because oligopoly is typical of American lustry.

Avoidance of Risk and Uncertainty. Avoidance of risk and uncertainty ould not be regarded as a goal in itself. Nevertheless, recent theoretical and pirical work has established that many firms, especially managerially ntrolled firms, strive to avoid risk and uncertainty.[16] Hence avoidance of k could be considered an important secondary or supplementary objective those already discussed. Introduction of this element increases the complexity the theorizing and alters the conclusions reached by simpler models.

npirical Findings on Manager's Motives

What do you suppose would happen if you went around and asked the ecutives of the 500 largest corporations what their objectives were? Would y give you straight answers? It would be nice if they did, but highly unlikely. though no stigma attaches to profits *generally* (we are after all a capitalist ciety), most folks seem to regard fat profits and giant firms a suspicious, if t loathsome, combination. Mindful of their public image, corporate executives : usually not going to blab about any undying effort they may make to maxi-ze profit. On the contrary, their alertness to public relations would tend to

[16] J. K. Galbraith, *The New Industrial State* (Boston: Houghton Mifflin, 1967), Chapters 3 and 7; E. Caves, "Uncertainty, Market Structure and Performance: Galbraith as Conventional Wisom," *ndustrial Organization and Economic Development*, edited by J. W. Markham and G. F. Papanek ston: Houghton Mifflin Co., 1970); R. Schramm and R. Sherman, "Profit Risk Management i the Theory of the Firm," *Southern Economic Journal* (January 1974), pp. 353–63; and K. J. idreaux, "Managerialism and Risk-Return Performance," *Southern Economic Journal* (Jan-y 1973), pp. 366–72.

239

produce claims of "reasonable profits," "progress," "environmental clean-u and "healthy growth." Existing advertising campaigns trumpeting th purposes predict the answers you would probably hear to your question. I the influences of image-consciousness constitute only one problem stand in the way of fully satisfactory tests of these theories. Others include (1) p data, (2) an enormous number of variables affecting the outcomes in questi (3) limited differences in the conclusions of various theories, (4) the fact t much observed behavior can be explained by more than one theory, and the quirkiness of individual corporate conduct. Nevertheless, a few testa hypotheses emerge from the theories, and economists have attempted test them.

Are managers' incomes more closely associated with profits, sales, or grow Snap judgement might lead you to conclude that most managers steer in direction of sales maximization. Everyone knows that the presidents of II and GM make more money than the president of your local pizza parlor, e when all three firms earn 20% on investment. In this sense raw size does de mine executive remuneration, suggesting perhaps that size guides execu action. Promotion from pizza to computers would call for a hefty raise. E so, an accurate test of the relation between managers' incomes and pr sales, or growth would require an explanation of what happens to the manag income *within* a given firm (or what kind of performance would *cause* manager's interfirm promotion). The best of the appropriate studies h reached the following conclusion: Managers' monetary rewards are m closely and more positively associated with *profit* performance than eit sales volume or growth rate, although these latter factors do have an effec As profits go up, measured in terms of absolute dollars or percentage return capital invested, so do executives' salaries, bonuses, stock options, and price of their ownership shares. These particular studies do not show t managers actually maximize profits. Reaping and sowing are two differ things. Still, the research does tend to bolster traditional theory.

Are managers moved by nonmonetary rewards? Human nature tells us t they are and so does some empirical evidence. Williamson finds that execu compensation is positively associated with "staff" personnel and other em ment expenditures. He has also assembled a number of case studies show "excessive" emoluments.[18] On a less rigorous basis, R. A. Gordon of

[17] Robert Masson, "Executive Motivations, Earnings, and Consequent Equity Performar *Journal of Political Economy* (November 1971), pp. 1278–92; R. J. Larner, *op. cit.*, pp. 33–61; W Lewellen and B. Huntsman, "Managerial Pay and Corporate Performance," *American Econ Review* (September 1970), pp. 710–20; G. K. Yarrow, "Executive Compensation and the O tives of the Firm," in *Market Structure and Corporate Behavior*, edited by K. Cowling (Lon Gray-Mills Publishing Co., 1972), pp. 149–73; Samuel Baker, "Executive Incomes, Profits Revenues: A Comment," *Southern Economic Journal* (April 1969), pp. 379–83; and G. Meeks G. Whittington, "Directors Pay, Growth, and Profitability," *Journal of Industrial Econo (Sept. 1975), pp. 1–14.
[18] O. E. Williamson, *op. cit.* (1967), pp. 85–135.

idence and argument that managers are moved by "the urge for power, the
sire for prestige and the related impulse of emulation, the creative urge, the
opensity to identify oneself with a group and the related feeling of group
yalty, the desire for security, the urge for adventure and for 'playing the
me' for its own sake, and the desire to serve others."[19] These findings are
t necessarily inconsistent with profit maximizing on the price side, but they
suggest cost side conduct that is less than frugal.

Can anything be concluded from direct observation of price and output behavior?
a broad sense we shall be exploring empirical evidence of this sort throughout
st of the remainder of this book. We shall observe many earmarks of extensive
ofit maximization, including price discrimination, positive associations
tween price level and concentration, and positive associations between profits
d market power. However, this evidence does not explicitly refute sales or
owth maximizing because these latter theories include allowance for profit
nstraints. If these profit constraints varied in accordance with market
ucture, the broad empirical findings just mentioned could emerge despite
: adoption of sales or growth maximization objectives. Thus, several
nomists have attempted rather specific tests of these theories, particularly
es revenue maximization. Virtually all of those testing the sales objective
ve concluded that it is not the goal adopted by most firms. Rather, firms
:m to favor some form of profit or growth maximization.[20] For example,
e implication of sales revenue maximization is that firms would attempt to
:rease sales if their actual profits exceeded their minimum profit constraint.

Hall's search for such behavior turned out negative: he found no strong
sitive relationship between sales volume and estimated departures from the
ofit constraint.

Tests of the growth maximization hypothesis are more difficult to devise,
rtly because of the similarity between growth *rate* and profit maximization.
vertheless, Dennis Mueller has argued that a modified version of the growth
pothesis is consistent with the behavior of a substantial number of firms.[21]
: argues, in particular, that managers are probably pushing growth beyond
: rate desired by stockholders, if stockholders want more of the firm's profit
d out in dividends (and less profit retained for internal investment) than the

[19] R. A. Gordon, *Business Leadership in the Large Corporation* (Berkeley: University of Cali-
ıia Press, 1966), pp. 305–16.
[20] M. Hall, "Sales Revenue Maximization: An Empirical Examination," *Journal of Industrial
nomics* (April 1967), pp. 143–56; B. D. Mabry and D. L. Siders, "An Empirical Test of the
es Maximization Hypothesis," *Southern Economic Journal* (January 1967), pp. 367–77; Samuel
:er, "An Empirical Test of the Sales Maximization Hypothesis, ' *Industrial Organization Review*,
. 1, No. 1 (1973), pp. 56–66; J. W. Elliot, "A Comparison of Models of Marketing Investment
he Firm," *Quarterly Review of Economics and Business* (Spring 1971), pp. 53–70. An interesting
eption is C. L. Lackman and J. L. Craycroft, "Sales Maximization and Oligopoly: A Case
dy," *Journal of Industrial Economics* (December 1974), pp. 81–95.
[21] Dennis C. Mueller, "A Life Cycle Theory of the Firm," *Journal of Industrial Economics*
ıy 1972), pp. 199–219.

managers are willing to provide. Interestingly enough, he finds that *matu* firms in relatively slow growth industries, such as those in steel and foods, a the ones that most frequently display excessive profit retention. Rapidly growi young firms in dynamic industries like electronics are, by this standard, *n* the ones guilty of sacrificing profits for growth, despite the fact that they a among the fastest growers in the economy. (Things are not always what the seem.) In addition, Mueller's study underscores the fact that no *one* objecti guides all firms. There is a smattering of evidence for just about every conceivab theory (even sales revenue maximization). Still, variations on the theme profit and growth seem most popular.

When manager controlled firms and owner controlled firms are placed si by side and compared, do any differences appear? The "box scores" for tests this question are presented in Table 10-3, which classifies the names of researche in this area according to their findings. One's immediate impression is that the

TABLE 10-3 **Summary of Tests for Differences in Firm Performance b Type of Control**

| Direction of Managerial Divergence | *Performance Measure* | | | |
	Profit Rate	Growth Rate	Variance in Profit	Retentio Rate
Higher	—	—	Palmer	Williamso
Lower	Monsen, *et al*, Palmer, Radice, Larner, Shelton Boudreaux	Radice	Boudreaux	Kamersch
No difference	Qualls, Hindley, Sorensen, Holl, Kamerschen, Kania	Sorensen, Holl, Kania	Larner, Holl, Kania	Sorensen, Holl, Kani

Sources: Boudreaux, *Southern Economic Journal* (1973), pp. 366–72; Hindley, *Jour of Law and Economics* (1970), pp. 185–221; Holl, *Journal of Industrial Economies* (197 pp. 257–71; Kamerschen, *American Economic Review* (1968), pp. 432–47; Kamersch *Quarterly Journal of Economics* (1970), pp. 668–73; Larner, *Management Control and t Large Corporation* (New York: Dunellen, 1970), pp. 25–32; Monsen, *et al., Quarterly Jour of Economics* (1968), pp. 435–51; Palmer, *Bell Economic Journal* (1973), pp. 293–3C Palmer, *Western Economic Journal* (1973), pp. 228–31 (see also March 1975 issue); Qua *Essays on Industrial Organization* (1976), pp. 89–104; Radice, *Economics Journal* (197 pp. 547–62; Shelton, *American Economics Review* (1967), pp. 1252–58; Sorensen, *Southe Economic Journal* (1974), pp. 145–48; Williamson, *Economics of Discretionary Behavi* (Chicago: Markham Publishing Co., 1967), pp. 135–38; Kania and McKean, *Kyklos* (197 pp. 272–90.

ndings vary widely. Proponents and opponents of "managerialism" have each ad their innings. The results vary because each researcher uses his own blend f sample, time period, and statistical technique, but a few tenative conclusions re possible. First, the "profit rate" column shows that *no* empirical study has ound manager controlled firms earning higher average rates of profit than wner controlled firms, whereas six have found managerial rates to be generally wer (as usually predicted by "managerial" theories), and six have found no gnificant difference. Among those finding "no difference" are several that do nd managerial profits somewhat lower on average than owner controlled rofits, but not "significantly" so. It appears, on balance, that owner controlled rms may have a slight edge in profit performance, but nothing outstanding.

This broad summary conceals two noteworthy refinements. First, one would xpect very little difference in profit rates among firms facing intense com- etition. Profit maximizing for them is a matter of survival, not of type of control. onversely, greater differences are likely among firms with substantial market ower. For them, managerial discretion comes into play. In other words, anagerial discretion ought to depend on the presence of monopoly power. almer explored this possibility and found very little difference in profit rates here monopoly power was "low": 9.98 % for manager control versus 10.59 % r owner control. On the other hand, where monopoly power was "high," e found a significant difference: 11.41 % for manager control versus 14.77 % r owner control. The second refinement concerns the way profits are easured. When profits are measured as a percentage of *sales*, control does not em to have as much effect as when profits are measured as a percentage of ockholders' *equity*. This leads David Qualls to argue that control causes ry little difference in price and output policy, the two key variables in our bsequent discussions of conduct.[22]

Under growth rate, variance in profit (risk), and the rate at which profit rnings are retained (rather than paid-out), Table 10-3 discloses fewer studies d an even greater spread of results, rendering conclusions for these measures l the more tentative. Still, this writer tends to side with those who find *no* gnificant difference between manager and owner controlled firms in these ree categories. Once again, the two types of control seem so similar that we ed not be greatly concerned with the influence "managerialism" may have a motivation.

Are the empirical answers to all the foregoing questions consistent? Broadly eaking, "yes." The fact that managers' compensation is generally tied to ofits leads one to expect that profit performance will not vary markedly by pe of control, which is the case. On the other hand, Williamson's discoveries

[22] If profit as a percent of sales is P/S, and profit as a percent of equity is P/E, then control affect one but not the other if control affects E/S. For more evidence of this point see J. Mingo, Managerial Motives, Market Structures and the Performance of Holding Company Banks," onomic Inquiry (September 1976), pp. 411–24.

concerning perks and emoluments touch a responsive chord in anyone wh can imagine himself in the expensive shoes of a senior executive fairly fr from the reins of influential owners. For this and other reasons, we shou expect some indication that profits of managerially controlled firms are le than those of owner controlled firms, which is also the case, especially whe monopoly power is present. By the same token, there are some indications th monopoly power and management control may permit an attitude towa costs more lackadaisical than otherwise. Finally, these several inferences a consistent with conclusions emerging from direct tests of the sales revenue ma mization hypothesis. These tests reveal that, as a general policy, most firn do not strive after short-term sales, heedless of the consequences for profits.

Behavioralism and "Satisficing"

Although the empirical studies just reviewed typically give primacy to profi (or profitable pricing behavior), they do not prove conclusively that pro maximization is in fact the sole objective of most businesses. General Moto executives might shoot for and attain profits equalling 20% of stockholde equity. This is well above the average for all manufacturers, and the executiv might be generously rewarded for the achievement. However, might they capable of attaining 30% if they *really* tried? No one really knows for su but it is this kind of possibility that leaves room for those holding "behavioralis views. Led by R. M. Cyert and J. G. March,[23] behavioralists attack all thr basic assumptions of the traditional position—single-mindedness, maximizi rationality, and operational rules of thumb.

Against single-mindedness, behavioralists argue that "the firm" cann have goals. Only individuals have goals. And, although a few executives at t top may be rewarded for the firm's profit performance, their benefits may n encourage the tens of thousands of other workers scattered throughout t typical large corporation. Buried in the organization's countless nooks a crannies are specialists in production scheduling, sales, repair service, tra portation, engineering, materials procurement, personnel, safety, insuran tax, finance, accounting, payroll, warehousing, research and developme environmental protection, and so on ad infinitum. To believe that all segme of all echelons can march in lock-step fashion after profits strains credul We are not talking about the cells of a cheetah's body or a bee colony; we talking about imperfect and willful human beings. Assembly line forem may find make-work jobs for surplus workers in order to be "one of the boy Scientists may pursue projects of personal intrinsic interest but of poor pr

---

[23] R. M. Cyert and J. G. March, *A Behavioral Theory of the Firm* (Englewood Cliffs, N. Prentice-Hall, Inc., 1963).

)tential. Environmental engineers may be more dedicated to preserving the liage than to preserving the discounted present value of the firm. Behavioralists •int out that "policy side-payments" are often inescapable to keep some mblance of a "coalition of coalitions." For example, "in order to get the vice-esident of marketing to stay within the organization, it may be necessary commit resources to research on new products."[24] The ramifications involve •litical bargaining, not just economic computing.

In place of maximizing rationality the behavioralists postulate "organiza-)nal slack" and "satisficing." Slack takes many forms they say:

prices are set lower than necessary to maintain adequate income from customers; wages in excess of those required to maintain labor are paid; executives are provided with services and personal luxuries in excess of those required to keep them; subunits are permitted to grow without real concern for the relation between additional pay-ments and additional revenues; public services are provided in excess of those re-quired.[25]

tisficing is a corollary. Whereas a "maximizer" tries to find the course of tion that brings him as close as possible to some objective (often a lofty jective), a "satisficer" does not. He sets *minimum* levels of performance in /eral variables below which he does not want to fall. To explain the matter analogy, suppose the proverbial haystack has more than one needle hidden it. Whereas the maximizer would search until he believed he had found the arpest needle in the haystack, the satisficer would stop when he found one aarp enough" for his immediate purpose.[26] Once such a minimum aspiration el is achieved, the satisficer coasts.

As far as operational rules of thumb are concerned, the behavioralists reject • notion of MR = MC and put a wide variety of rules in its place: (1) standard :centage markups above cost for pricing, (2) smoothing of production aeduling; (3) maintenance of some minimum inventory as a percentage of es; (4) percentage market share goals and salesmens' quotas; (5) minimum)fit measured in an absolute dollar amount or percentage return on invest-:nt. Specific examples of these goals might be a 40% markup for pricing, aarket share of 20%, capacity utilization running at 90%, and a 10% return investment. Whenever one of these minimum aspiration levels is not achieved, aavioralists assume that nonroutine problem solving activities will be tituted to find a "satisfactory" solution. There may be inconsistencies among : objectives, and various efforts at problem solving may proceed in isolation m each other; but complete consistency and coordination are beyond the)ability of human beings (acting individually or as a group).

[24] K. J. Cohen and R. M. Cyert, *Theory of the Firm* (Englewood Cliffs, N. J.: Prentice-Hall, Inc., 5), p. 331.
[25] *Ibid.*, p. 333.
[26] J. C. March and H. A. Simon, *Organizations* (New York: John Wiley & Sons, Inc., 1958), 41.

Behavioralists advance these thoughts largely on the basis of realism. The do not believe that business action can be deduced from theoretical postulate of firm maximization of any variable. They emphasize *observation* of ho businessmen act every day, hoping that perhaps this observation may eventuall through induction, yield some generalizations.

As you should by now expect, traditionalists espousing profit maximizatio and managerialists do not agree with these tenets of behavioralism. Trad tionalists and managerialists criticize behavioralism on several ground three of which may be taken up here.[27]

In the first place, behavioralism is said to suffer from the "fallacy of mi placed concreteness" or "hyperfactualism." A theory is supposed to be like road map of New York State. It is a simplified, condensed, somewhat inaccura view of reality. Nevertheless the map shows the best route from Ithaca t Buffalo without detailing every pothole and traffic light. Thus, the theory (profit maximizing may not be capable of predicting in 1977 the exact price of full-sized 1981 Buick Electra (or even whether Electras will be offered in 1981 but it does suggest an increase in price in the event of a severe fuel consumptio tax. Moreover, one need not know the details of GM's internal clashes an divergence of opinions to make this prediction. Some defenders of the pro maximization assumption go so far as to say that it need not be descriptive realistic *at all*, so long as firms behave "as if" they are maximizing profits. This, however, is an extreme view, which itself is fallacious.

A second line of criticism questions the status of behavioralism as a theor claiming that to a great extent behavioralism is more "framework" tha "theory":

> Frameworks outline the components of a set of phenomena that must be taken into account when efforts to explain the phenomena are undertaken. In themselves, however, they are not explanatory . . . .[29]

Thus, behavioralists may list a number of possible goals, a variety of actor certain bargaining strategies, and several colorful experiences. But witho hypotheses, which are subject to disproof, their list is just a list (like a groce list). Behavioralists might even observe that a 40% markup is the basic pri policy in the lingerie department of a department store, and thereby predi the *exact* retail price of 99% of all garments sold, knowing only the garmen

---

[27] F. Machlup, "Theories of the Firm: Marginalist, Behavioral, Managerial," *Americ Economic Review* (March 1967), pp. 1–33; R. Marris, *op. cit.*, pp. 266–77; W. J. Baumol and Ma Stewart, "On the Behavioral Theory of the Firm," in *The Corporate Economy*, edited by R. Mar and A. Wood (Cambridge, Mass.: Harvard University Press, 1971), pp. 118–43.

[28] M. Friedman, "The Methodology of Positive Economics," in *Essays in Positive Econom* (Chicago: University of Chicago Press, 1953).

[29] N. A. McDonald and J. N. Rasenau, "Political Theory as an Academic Field and Intellectu Activity," in *Political Science: Advance of the Discipline*, edited by M. D. Irish (Englewood Clif N. J.: Prentice Hall, 1968), p. 44.

wholesale cost. Yet this is not the application of a theory. It does not explain *why* the action occurs or *what* might cause the markup to increase or fall substantially. Behavioralism merely predicts that a firm will behave in a certain fashion because past experience of what firms do indicates that a certain course of action is probable. "Such predictions are often *ad hoc* in nature and applicable only to a given situation."[30]

Finally, and perhaps most important, the minimum "aspiration levels" that guide behavioralist managers may actually be "maximizing levels." If the managers of GM state that their profit goal is "no less" than 20% return on invested capital, their phrase "no less" seems to suggest that they are satisficers. On the other hand, 20% might in fact be the best they can do, in which case they would actually be maximizers. How could such a coincidence of "aspiration" and "optimization" come about? One possibility is that initial aspiration levels may be set rather low. Once it becomes apparent that reaching a low aspiration level is as easy as jumping over a 3-foot high bar, the aspiration level may be raised. Subsequent adjustments could follow the familiar sequential pattern of a high-jump bar during a track meet. It is set at ever higher notches until missed. A jumper who is "satisfied" with 7 foot 1 inch might be pretty damn close to his best.

This last problem makes empirical verification of satisficing, as opposed to maximizing, difficult, especially with respect to pricing policy. The difficulty, perhaps even futility, is illustrated by the analysis of an extensive research project headed by D. C. Hague of the University of Manchester in England. It involved four of his colleagues and 6 years of work. The results appear in a book entitled *Pricing in Business*,[31] which upon casual reading seems to provide resounding support for behavioralism. Of the 13 firms studied in depth (by interviews, attendance at meetings, perusal of documents, and so on), only five are said to be profit maximizers; the other eight are judged to be profit satisficers. What is the basis for this division? Hague's primary criterion was each company's *non*operational objective as revealed in the course of interviews with top management. He branded firms as satisficers upon hearing such catchphrase objectives as "to return a satisfactory reward on overall company operations;" "the broad aim is to obtain a given percentage return on investment;" and "to maintain adequate growth while maintaining profitability so far as this is possible."

Reliance on interviews and nonoperational objectives casts doubt on the resulting assessments of motivation. As far as price policy (as opposed to cost policy) is concerned, this information cannot separate the sheep from the goats. Hague himself supplies enough additional information about a number of his satisficers to allow us to substantiate these doubts. Take for example the case

---

[30] J. V. Koch, *Industrial Organization and Prices* (Englewood Cliffs, N. J.: Prentice-Hall, 1974), p. 43.

[31] D. C. Hague, *Pricing in Business* (London: George Allen & Unwin, 1971).

of "Basic Foods" (not the company's real name). On page 71 of *Pricing in Business* we are told that "Pricing decisions were made to meet a combination of marketing (i.e., sales volume and market share) and financial (i.e., sales value and profit) objectives," thereby making Basic Foods a satisficer. Yet, on page 237 we are told that any "final" price change recommendations for Basic Foods were likely to be ones "that gave the best long-run increase in profit, as compared with the no-change case."

Another satisficer that seems misclassified is "Wessex Timber Industries." Its stated objective was a "return on capital of $12\frac{1}{2}$ percent before tax" (page 72). However, this firm operated in an extremely competitive market. "The price at which Wessex Ltd. could sell its products was largely governed by the current market price" (page 316). As a consequence, Wessex had *not* been able to reach its modest profit objective "in two of the three years" prior to the study (page 222), and its salesmen were given flexibility in their use of list prices, being instructed to get the "best price" they could for any sale of lumber (page 73). How could Hague possibly classify this firm as a satisficer? He explains thus: "We suspect, though we cannot prove, that salesmen might have obtained higher prices if greater pressure for profit had been put on them" (page 73). That's all. That is a pretty presumptuous statement (with respect to psychological insight as well as lumber yard expertise).

Several other questionable classifications lead me to believe that maximizers actually outnumber satisficers in Hague's sample. His study thus illustrates our earlier reservations about interview research. It also demonstrates that the biases of social science researchers may affect their conclusions. Hague implicitly admits to bias when he writes that "we were rather surprised by the emphasis that our firms did put on profit."[32] Then a few pages later he tries to argue that "at least four" of the firms he labels maximizers "were satisficers, and not maximizers, at heart." His reasoning? Each of these maximizers was said to be acting like a satisficer whose "aspiration level" had not yet been reached. But of course this is exactly the way a maximizer is supposed to behave. If this sort of reasoning can make satisficers out of maximizers, it can with equal ease make maximizers out of satisficers.

I do not want to press Hague too hard here. There is much truth to behavioralism. And at one point Hague succinctly states much of that truth when he admits that "firms that are satisficers when taking decisions about production, inventories, employment, etc., may become maximizers when they set prices" because they "are forcing those outside the firm to bear the burden of change."[33] What is more, pricing seems to be the province of top drawer executives, many of whom apparently have a monetary stake in policies that improve profits.[34]

---

[32] *Ibid.*, p. 80.

[33] *Ibid.*, p. 83.

[34] Hague presents evidence on this point (pp. 200–43). See also D. Tuson, "Pricing: Whose Responsibility?" in *Creative Pricing*, edited by E. Marting (American Management Association, 1968), pp. 39–48.

Summary

A reasonably correct understanding of firm motivation is essential to a reasonably correct understanding of firm conduct in the market place. According to traditional theory, all firms maximize profits. Conduct differs across firms solely because of differences in the structure of the markets the firms happen to occupy. In monopoly markets, profit maximization often implies a "high" price. In purely competitive markets it implies a "low" price.

The postulate of profit maximization rests on three basic assumptions— single-mindedness, rational maximizing, and operational feasibility. The first of these postulates holds that, despite much diversity, all people associated with "the firm" work together toward a single objective. The second assumption specifies that this objective is profit maximization. Profit is the owners' reward, and, because owners control the traditional firm, profit maximization is both natural and rational. The third assumption rules out any real-world difficulties in following the simple MR = MC recipe.

Attacks on traditional theory have chewed away at the validity of these assumptions. Early on, the critics were most bothered by the *non*operational nature of the MR = MC calculus. Perhaps their most enduring blow in this respect was to point out that rigorous profit maximization is either meaningless or impossible in the face of risk and uncertainty. A second school of criticism, managerialism, has attacked the notion of a single-minded firm and displaced profit as the firm's sole object. Arguing that managers control the largest modern corporations, managerialists have devised such theories as managerial utility, sales maximization subject to minimum profit constraint, growth rate maximization, and maximization of the discounted present value of sales revenues. However, empirical tests of the observable implications of these managerial theories have done no more than tarnish the traditional theory, except on the cost side, and then primarily under conditions of market power. Where competition does not keep costs in check, profit maximization has been rather bruised and battered by the tests.

Finally, the behavioralists attack every one of traditional theory's assumptions. They argue that "the firm" can only be multiminded in light of its complexity and internal diversity. They claim that satisficing makes more sense and is more frequently observed than maximizing. They also deny that profit maximization can be an operational objective. Although common sense and a rudimentary knowledge of the modern bureaucratic corporation tell us that these claims carry much truth, it is difficult to test the extent of this truth empirically. At least one member of the behavioralist school of thought has inadvertently demonstrated that satisficing behavior is very similar to profit maximizing, especially in price policy.

In short, this chapter reads like a ride on an old-time merry-go-round. We repeatedly rode away from the golden ring of profit maximization. Yet somehow we kept coming back to it. After several speedy inspections from different angles, it appears that the ring might be made of brass or tin rather than gold. Nonetheless, those running our major business firms seem to have their eyes on it too. Most of them are also reaching for it with different degrees of effort. As one of the first and foremost critics of traditional theory concedes, "basically profits and profit expectations continue to guide decision-making in the giant as well as the small enterprise."[35]

[35] R. A. Gordon, *op. cit.*, p. 336.

11

Price and Production Behavior in the Short Run: Theory and Cross-Section Evidence

. . true oligopoly is interdependence plus uncertainty.

DONALD DEWEY

Of the several aspects of conduct mentioned previously, none have received greater attention from economists and businessmen than price and production policies. It is only proper, then, that we take these up first and set other forms of conduct aside until later. We begin with *short-run* price and production policies in this chapter and the next. In Chapter 13 we shall deal with their *long-run* aspects.

The principal short-run issues include price rivalry among "existing" sellers, price behavior during slumps in demand, supply control over the business cycle to stabilize price, and price fixing. Considering the long run, our scope will broaden to include not only existing competitors, but also potential and past competitors. That is to say, we shall consider how pricing over the long run influences the birth and death of firms.

Within the short-run context we have already presented simple theories of price determination under perfect competition and monopoly (Chapters 2 and 3). The present chapter will focus on behavior associated with structural conditions that lie between those extremes—namely, oligopoly and monopolistic competition. The first section discusses interdependence, which is a prime determinant of how firms in these settings view their demand curves. The second section introduces complications and uncertainties, particularly those associated with cyclical swings of demand. Next we review several pricing mechanisms used to cope with these complications and uncertainties. The concluding section is devoted to cross-section empirical evidence of short-run price behavior.

Interdependence

When discussing purely competitive and monopoly firms in Chapters 2 and 3, we could have called them lone eagles. The name is most apt for pure monopoly, where price and output are set without regard to rivals because rivals are non-existent. The purely competitive firm also acts independently, taking price as given and setting production level heedless of rival reactions.

The interdependence of oligopolists and monopolistically competitive firms is reflected in the demand curves they confront. Whereas a pure monopolist sees the market-wide demand curve and the purely competitive firm sees a perfectly elastic demand curve, those in between may view *two* demand curves. Two curves are necessary to account for the possible reactions of rivals—followship or nonfollowship—given a change in the firm's price. As explained in Chapter 3, the **followship** demand curve applies if a change in price is aped by rivals. A price reduction under followship conditions will gain added sales for the firm but not at the expense of rivals because they will have lowered prices too. The sales come from added *market-wide* sales, which, if distributed among all rivals according to their pre-existing market shares, would leave each firm's market share unchanged. Conversely, a price increase curtails a firm's sales in proportion to the market's loss of sales, provided all firms act uniformly on the increase. The followship curve could therefore also be called a **constant market share** demand curve.

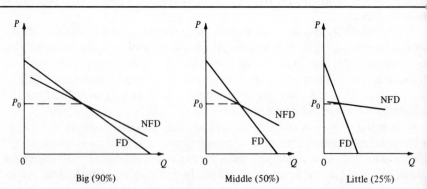

Figure 11-1. Followship (FD) and nonfollowship (NFD) demand curves for various sized firms.

As indicated by the FD curves in Figure 11-1, followship demand varies depending on firm size. Each panel of Figure 11-1 assumes the *same* market-wide demand. But FD for the "Big" firm is drawn on the assumption of a 90% market share; that for "Middle" assumes a 50% market share; and "Little" assumes a 25% market share. The firms could not all be in the same market, but each FD is a reflection of the market-wide demand underlying the illustrations. This may be appreciated by noting that the elasticity of each FD curve at price P_0 is the same, and each such elasticity in turn matches market-wide elasticity. Price P_0 divides each FD curve into upper and lower portions. Elasticity is the same at P_0 because the length of the upper portion *relative* to the lower portion is the same in each case. (A glance back at Figure 2-4 in Chapter 2 may help. Figure 2-4 indicates that the midpoint of *any* linear, negatively sloped demand curve denotes unit elasticity, suggesting a similar consistency across such curves at points one fourth down from the top, one third from the top, and so on.)

Although the followship curves are identical in elasticity, such is not true of the **nonfollowship** demand curves labeled NFD. They do vary in elasticity across firms within a given market because the assumption underlying their construction—that rivals do *not* match price changes—yields substantially different quantity results depending on firm size. Big firm's NFD will have an elasticity very similar to its FD though slightly higher. An unfollowed price cut below P_0 would cause customers to switch to Big. But the most Big could gain from competitors would be an additional 10 percentage points of market share, since at price P_0 Big already enjoys 90%. Comparing 10 to 90 implies a low elasticity for Big's NF curve. At the other extreme, an unfollowed price cut of similar magnitude on the part of Little could easily double Little's sales volume, implying that Little's nonfollowship demand curve at P_0 is highly elastic. Putting two and two together we may conclude that: the smaller the firm relative to its market, the greater the divergence between its followship and nonfollowship demand curves and between their elasticities. Since product differentiation also influences demand, a related conclusion holds that the more differentiated the firm's product is, the less the divergence will be. Or, the more standardized the product the greater the divergence between FD and NFD and their elasticities.

As structure affects a firm's demand elasticities in this fashion, it will also affect the firm's opportunities for earning sales revenues and thereby its price behavior. The linkage between demand elasticity and total revenue is summarized in the two-part diagram of Figure 11-2. The horizontal axis of both parts is quantity. The vertical axis of the upper part is price; that of the lower part is total revenue. Because total revenue is price times quantity, the *area* under the demand curve at any point equals the vertical *distance* under the total revenue curve of the lower part. At point H, for example, total revenue is $OJHK$, and this corresponds to GF using the total dollars vertical scale of the total revenue diagram. It should be clear, then, that a price reduction will increase total revenue if demand is elastic, as it is in the AH range and below to $E = 1$.

253

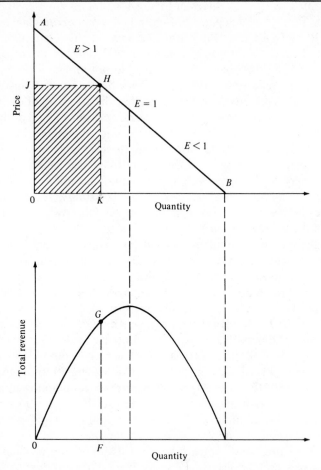

Figure 11-2. *Relationship between demand elasticity and total revenue.*

But a price reduction will decrease total revenue if demand is inelastic, as it is between $E = 1$ and B. Conversely, a price increase will boost the firm's total revenue if demand is inelastic but trim total revenue if demand is elastic. In the event of unit elasticity ($E = 1$), total revenue will be unchanged by a change of price in either direction.

These relationships tell us a great deal about which of the three firms of Figure 11-1 has the most to gain from a trip down its nonfollowship demand curve via price cuts below P_0. Little has the most elastic NFD; hence, it would gain the most, assuming that it could in fact move down its NFD. Conversely, Big has the least to gain from such behavior. Putting two and two together once again, we can surmise that relatively small firms are more likely to cut prices and bestow bargains than big firms. Turning the issue around, we may ask which firm is most likely to gain from a price *increase*. Big is the most likely gainer in this case. We can expect, therefore, to find relatively large firms most frequently cast in the role of upside price leader.

These deductions are fair and proper, but they are nevertheless a bit premature. We have not considered two important factors that may affect their accuracy: (1) Costs are as important as revenues in determining behavior, for costs as well as revenues determine profits. (2) Just as we mortals cannot be in two places at one time (except when reading science fiction), so, too, the firm cannot be on more than one demand curve at any one time (except where the curves intersect). A price cut will take it down either NFD *or* FD, not both. A price increase is an either/or journey in the opposite direction. Because the elasticities of NFD and FD differ, we must discover *which* curve the firm regards as its *actual* demand curve under various circumstances. The firm's view of its terrain determines what steps the firm takes, if it takes any at all. We shall demonstrate the significance of these additional considerations by exploring two classical models of firm conduct—"monopolistic competition" and the "kinky demand curve" of oligopoly.

Monopolistic Competition

Assume, as did the originator of this model, Edward Chamberlin, that *all* firms in the market are small, smaller even than Little of Figure 11-1. Indeed, Chamberlin had in mind firms similar in size to purely competitive firms.[1] Assume further that each firm nevertheless has a negatively sloped though highly elastic nonfollowship demand curve because each has a differentiated product. These assumptions yield a model of short-sighted price cutting. In other words, the interdependence of the firms goes *unrecognized* in this case, with the result that price competition predominates.

Figure 11-3 depicts the situation as viewed by a typical small firm. We begin with all firms charging price P_1. The typical firm is earning excess total profits equal to the difference between P_1 and total unit cost (TUC) directly below point *A times* the quantity produced (assuming that the total unit cost curve includes a normal profit as a cost). Though adequate, the firm's profit could be increased if it cut price to P_2 without being followed by rivals. In that event, it would move down its nonfollowship demand curve NF_1 to a point such as *B*. Notice the very high elasticity of NF_1. Quantity nearly doubles. So this ploy yields a substantial increase in total revenue, while declining unit costs (TUC) keep total costs from rising by as much. However, the profit gains last only as long as rivals fail to follow, because these gains are procured at their expense. Their demand curves will have shifted to the left, leaving them with fewer customers, higher costs, and lower profits. To regain their former market shares, these rivals cut their prices to P_2 as well, an action that shifts the firm of Figure

[1] Edward Chamberlin, *The Theory of Monopolistic Competition*, 8th ed. (Cambridge, Mass.: Harvard University Press, 1962).

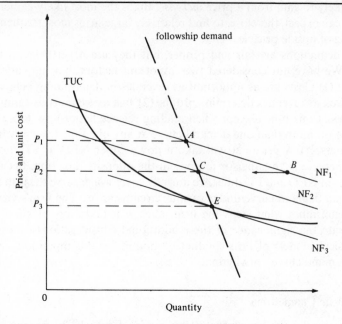

Figure 11-3. *Short-sighted price cutting under monopolistic competition.*

11-3 from point *B* to point *C*. After cut and countercut, the result is a movement down the followship demand curve from *A* to *C* and to a new nonfollowship curve NF₂. As the firm of Figure 11-3 is typical of all firms in the market, this descent carries all other firms with it. If our typical firm is short sighted enough to try the same stunt again, the others will naturally follow and further downward shifts will ensue. Equilibrium is reached at point *E*, at which point any further price cutting takes the firm below total unit cost. Here, theory posits a truce.

Of course the key to this scenario is the inability of the small firm to see beyond its first step down the nonfollowship curve. The firm does not consider the inelastic followship curve relevant. The temptations of NF's high elasticity are too great. The firm feels it is too small to have an impact on others in the market. The consequence is price competition. The pattern may be illustrated with an example taken from grocery retailing, which in certain cities might qualify as monopolistically competitive. In 1975 and 1976 price wars broke out in several cities, despite the fact that industry executives unanimously decried them, saying that "price wars always hurt profits and rarely change market shares among the combatants—the supposed goal." Except for consumers, who obviously benefit, "everybody fights harder and everybody loses."[2] Here is the story of one of the bloodiest battles of this period:

[2] "Supermarket Scrap," *Wall Street Journal*, July 19, 1976.

The Chicago price war, undoubtedly one of the longest and costliest in supermarket history, began abruptly. On a Saturday afternoon in April . . . , the manager of a Jewel Food Store heard from a visitor that a nearby Dominick's store was changing a lot of prices. Unusual for a Saturday, the manager thought. He sent an employee to check.

The employee found Dominick's aisles swarming with stock boys repricing merchandise. *And all the prices were being reduced.* Within minutes, Jewel employees throughout the area were scouting Dominick's stores. Their reports were startling . . . . Dominick's was slashing prices as much as 15% on "hundreds and hundreds" of items.

On Tuesday, Jewel's response was ready. Jewel was cutting prices on 3,327 items from 2% to 30%. On Friday, National Tea announced it was reducing prices . . . . Other competitors jumped in quickly.

Mr. DiMatteo [the manager of Dominick's] says he thought he could batter the competition. So he ordered the price cuts . . . . However, "the competition jumped in a lot faster than I thought they would," he concedes, "I thought we'd be alone for a while." [3]

Although the following demand curve was not wholly invisible to Mr. DiMatteo, it was certainly obscure and broken as depicted in Figure 11-3. As for the ultimate effects on market share, "Progressive Grocer, a trade magazine, found that 95% of the Chicago shoppers it questioned at one point during the price war said they were going to the same store as they had before the battle broke out." [3]

The Kinky Demand Curve of Oligopoly

Fewer firms in the market, with larger market shares, convert conditions to **oligopoly**, and the interdependence becomes *recognized.* [4] A nifty way of demonstrating this conversion is the theory of "kinked demand," a theory designed to explain much of the behavior of middle sized firms. Such firms are big enough to realize that their overt price reductions are almost certain to be followed by rivals, but they are not big enough to qualify as dominant-firm price leaders on the up side. Let P_0 in Figure 11-4 represent the going market price. Q_0 is then the firm's output, and K indicates the firm's position on its demand curves. Given these conditions, what action is best for the firm? Is it likely to slash price, boost it, or leave it unchanged? If the firm thinks its prices below P_0 will be followed, then *below* point K the followship demand curve alone is relevant. The NF demand curve thus disappears below K. Conversely, if the firm is doubtful that its price increases will be followed, then above K only the NF demand curve is applicable, and the F curve does the vanishing act.

Now, a split personality may be okay for anyone with too many friends, but schizophrenic demand curves such as these put the firm in a straightjacket.

[3] *Ibid.*
[4] R. L. Hall and C. J. Hitch, "Price Theory and Business Behavior," *Oxford Economic Papers* (May 1939), pp. 12–45; P. M. Sweezy, "Demand Under Conditions of Oligopoly," *Journal of Political Economy* (August 1939), pp. 568–73.

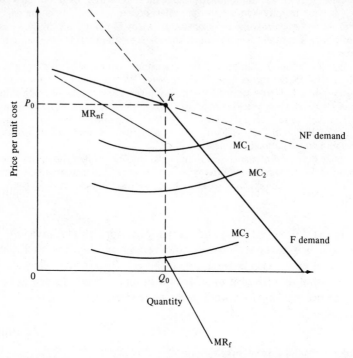

Figure 11-4. *The kinked demand oligopoly model.*

Explanation

Costs aside, it should be clear that a price cut below P_0 would substantially diminish total revenue because the F curve below K is inelastic. Moreover, things are just as bad the other way around. A price increase above P_0 would reduce total revenue substantially because NF above K is highly elastic. With total revenue falling from a step in either direction, the best strategy is to stand pat.

Furthermore, this rigidity of price may not be compromised by cost considerations. If the firm is operating under the $MR = MC$ rule of profit maximization, marginal costs can vary over a spacious range without causing price to flutter from its P_0 perch because the marginal revenue curve is discontinuous. The discontinuity arises because the marginal revenue applicable to price increases is MR_{nf}, which is derived from the *nonfollowship* demand curve above K, whereas the marginal revenue applicable to price reductions is MR_f, which is derived from the *followship* demand curve below point K. Marginal cost is shown to vary from MC_1 to MC_3, but it always remains equal to marginal revenue.

e.g. Perhaps the most striking example of this situation was uncovered by Bjarke Fog in the course of interviewing business people in 139 Danish firms about their pricing policies. He came across a leather tannery that charged

258

a higher price for dyed shoe leather than it did for black shoe leather, even though the costs of making the former were lower than the costs of making the latter. It seems that the price differential originated in 1890, when cost differences did warrant the price differential. When asked why the price differential continued long after costs had changed, the firm's manager replied:

> Perhaps we ought to raise the price of black leather somewhat and lower the price of dyed leather to a corresponding degree, but we dare not do so. The fact is that we shall then run the risk of being unable to sell black leather shoes, whereas our competitors will also reduce their prices for dyed shoes.[5]

In sum, kinked demand theory yields two basic predictions: (1) Oligopolists will refrain from price cutting when their followship demand curves are inelastic; and (2), except in rapid inflation, oligopoly prices will tend to be rigid, despite moderate changes in costs. Although both predictions are consistent with the opinions of businessmen and much of their observed behavior,[6] the model suffers several limitations.[7] In many respects it is a model of rigidity that, as presented above, is itself too rigid.

Consider first the matter of moderate increases in costs. The theory is most applicable when the costs of an *individual* oligopolist rise but those of others in the market remain unchanged. A firm confronted with unique cost increments has no reason to expect that a compensating price increase on its part will be followed by its less troubled rivals. The up-side nonfollowship demand curve may in this case materialize. But what about cost increases that confront *all* rivals simultaneously? A hike in the cost of steel to automakers, for example? A jump in the cost of sugar to soda pop producers? Or a 15% rise in labor costs due to a newly signed collective bargaining contract? The oligopolist who attempts to initiate price increases to cover these costs is not really sticking his neck out very far. Followship is likely. Thus, the business press is riddled with news accounts of oligopolists raising prices after such across-the-board cost increases. Oligopolists have even been accused of predicating price increases on the mere *expectation* of future cost increases.

A second limitation is suggested by the first. Kinked demand theory may partly explain the rigidity of an *existing* price level, but it does not explain how prices reached that level in the first place. In other words, it is an instructive, but *incomplete*, theory of oligopolistic price behavior. Besides uniform cost increases, it ignores the possibility of price leadership and cartelization. It yields no solid predictions as to whether prices will be higher in concentrated

---

[5] B. Fog, *Industrial Pricing Policies* (Amsterdam: North-Holland Publishing Co., 1960), p. 130.

[6] Many references in these footnotes support this assertion.

[7] For a critique see G. J. Stigler, "The Kinky Oligopoly Demand Curve and Rigid Prices," *Journal of Political Economy* (October 1947), pp. 432–49. For critiques of Stigler see C. W. Efroymson, "The Kinked Oligopoly Curve Reconsidered," *Quarterly Journal of Economics* (February 1955), pp. 119–36; R. B. Heflebower, "Full Costs, Cost Changes, and Prices," in *Business Concentration and Price Policy* (Princeton: Princeton University Press, 1955), pp. 361–92; J. M. Clark, *Competition as a Dynamic Process* (Washington, D.C.: Brookings Institution, 1961), pp. 287–89.

markets as compared with unconcentrated ones. And it does not tell us whether profits will be greater where barriers to entry prevail.

These criticisms may be expanded into a third and somewhat different shortcoming of the theory. In its simple form, the theory imparts an impression of interfirm uniformity that is often unrealistic. A cursory reading of the theory conjures up notions of a market in which all firms are exactly the same size and weight (say, 10 firms each with one tenth of the market), all offer identical products, and all charge exactly the same price. Such an image must be rejected, however. Everyone knows that oligopolists often differ in size, products, and prices—even within the same narrow market definition.

Take the auto industry, for example. Do GM, Ford, Chrysler, and AMC all see a kinky demand curve? Probably not. In the main, GM acts as price leader by virtue of its substantial cost efficiency and 45% market share (counting imports too). Leadership implies followship, which means that GM can generally ignore its nonfollowship demand curve altogether—up side and down. Since the nonfollowship demand curve creates the kink on the up side, GM usually sees no kink. We qualify these remarks with "generally" and "usually" because GM might *not* be followed on the up side during times of depressed demand, in which case the kink would materialize. Now consider Ford. Ranking second, it is half GM's size. As a result, it is certainly big enough to be followed on the down side. Given GM's long history of leadership on the up side, however, Ford probably sees *non*followship on the up side and therefore the kink as well.

In turn, Chrysler, with roughly 10% of the market, is less than half the size of Ford. This limitation precludes up-side leadership, and Chrysler would therefore certainly see a kink if it feared followship on the down side. But what about the down side? Is Chrysler small enough to sneak down its nonfollowship demand curve untouched? Generally not. But there is one interesting episode to the contrary that began in January 1961, when Chrysler cut prices on commercial fleet sales. Ford did not follow wholeheartedly until 2 years later. GM held back until 1966, by which time its share of fleet sales had fallen to 41%, down from 61% in 1963, and Chrysler's share had risen to 24%, up from 10% 5 years earlier.[8] Thus Chrysler was allowed a temporary though lengthy trip down its nonfollowship demand curve in this submarket—a kink-free vacation you might say.

The diversity of prices in many real-world markets is illustrated by Table 11-1, which presents data on retail gasoline prices in Washington, D.C., by brand, as of late 1969. The first column reports the number of stations selling each brand, except that independents are lumped in one category at the bottom. The second column converts these numbers of stations into estimates of market share. Thus, Exxon's 144 stations comprise 20.7% of all stations. In addition, the brands are arrayed from largest market share to smallest. Pricing is conveniently

---

[8] L. J. White, *The Automobile Industry Since 1945* (Cambridge, Mass.: Harvard University Press, 1971), pp. 111–35; S. E. Boyle and T. F. Hogarty, "Pricing Behavior in the American Automobile Industry, 1957–71," *Journal of Industrial Economics* (December 1975), pp. 81–95.

TABLE 11-1   Price Levels of Gasoline Stations Located in Washington D. C.—Fall 1969

Brand	Number of Stations Surveyed	Total Stations (Market Share) (%)	Brand's Stations	
			Pricing above Reference (%)	Pricing below Reference (%)
Exxon	144	20.7	36.8	14.6
American	90	12.9	20.0	15.6
Shell	73	10.5	15.1	13.7
Texaco	66	9.5	9.1	36.4
Sunoco	61	8.8	4.9	16.4
Gulf	59	8.5	10.2	23.4
Mobil	50	7.2	4.0	54.0
Sinclair	32	4.6	9.4	53.1
Citgo	28	4.0	7.1	42.9
Atlantic	26	3.7	0	84.6
Scott	15	2.2	0	100.0
Phillips	14	2.0	0	50.0
Hess	9	1.3	0	100.0
Independents	30	4.3	0	100.0
Total	697	100.0		

Source: F. C. Allvine and J. M. Patterson, *Competition, Ltd.: The Marketing of Gasoline* (Bloomington: University of Indiana Press, 1972), p. 13.

summarized by reporting the percentage of each brand's stations pricing above and below the reference price for regular gas in the market. For example, 53 Exxon stations, or 36.8% of Exxon's total, priced above reference. The "reference price" (which at that time was a measly 35.9 cents) is a kind of base or modal price that guides the actions of most gasoline retailers, especially the so-called "major brands." The majors are of course familiar to every driver and television viewer. They stress service, saturation of locations, credit cards, advertising, tires, batteries, accessories, clean restrooms, gasoline additives, steak knives, and other nonprice forms of competition. As Table 11-1 suggests, they also have the lion's share of the business. They may be contrasted with the independents, which generally offer spartan accommodations, abbreviated service, very little advertising, and "competitive" prices. (Quite often they also carry quaint names like Hi-Rev, Rotten Robby's, and Stinker.)

Our earlier discussions of product differentiation led to expectations of the majors charging higher prices than the independents, and Table 11-1 bears out those expectations. The vast majority of major brand stations priced at or above reference. *All* independents priced below reference (by at least 4 cents a gallon, or 11 %). Moreover, theories concerning nonfollowship elasticity and monopolistic competition suggest that firms with small market shares are more likely to charge lower prices than firms with large market shares. This, too, is borne out by these data. As one reads down Table 11-1, the percentage of stations pricing above reference dwindles as the percentage of stations pricing below reference grows. It should also be mentioned that this generalization holds not only for majors within a given market, but also for a *given* major operating in *various* markets. Exxon, for instance, had the largest market share and highest prices in Washington, D.C. Yet at the same time in San Francisco, Exxon ranked ninth with only 3.8 % of the market. There, 87.4 % of its stations were pricing *below* reference. In other words, majors often behave like independents, at least with respect to price, when their market share is like that of independents.

As for kinks, they are somewhat ill-defined and variable across firms and geographic markets, but they are not destroyed by price differentials. A price differential may not cause continual shifting of market share in favor of the low priced brand because of product differentiation. In the gasoline industry it is "customary" for independents to price a few cents below dominant majors. At that point the independents could very well see a kink. Cuts below the customary differential tend to be followed by the majors.

One final limitation of the simple model is that prices may be rigid for reasons other than kinked demand.[9] Consider first the cost of changing prices. It may be high enough to inhibit frequent alterations, especially when price lists are voluminous and complex. What's more, buyers of certain products may prefer a stable price, even though it may on average be higher than a fluctuating price. A molder of plastic houseware products enunciated this point somewhat incoherently when he upbraided his suppliers at a trade convention:

> When you producers were selling polyethylene to us molders at the stable price of 41 cents a pound, my company made much more money than we do now, when price is much lower but bounces up and down with every deal. Why? Simply because I didn't have to spend all my time rushing around to see if I could make as good a deal as the next guy—and never be quite sure.[10]

Finally, the last factor worth mentioning helps to introduce our next section. Many changes of condition that would normally provoke price changes under pure competition do not do so under oligopoly because they are considered *temporary* changes, which, if responded to, might prove unsettling. Swings in the business cycle are the most important of these. Since frequent price revisions can shake up even the coziest nest of oligopolists and jostle them into occasional

---

[9] Stigler, *op. cit.*; T. Scitovsky, *Welfare and Competition* (Chicago: Richard Irwin, 1951), Chapter XII.
[10] E. Marting, *Creative Pricing* (American Management Association, 1968), p. 37.

price wars, oligopolists tend to favor stable prices. As we shall see more clearly, recognized interdependence often leads to tacit collusion, cartelization, and other forms of pricing cooperation. But cooperation can be a delicate thing. And fluctuating prices may camouflage "chiseling" and provoke serious "misunderstandings"—two factors corrosive to cooperation.

Cyclical Complications and Uncertainties

On June 14, 1977, St. Joe Minerals Corporation announced a massive cutback in zinc refinery output from 95% capacity utilization to 65% capacity utilization. Why the cut? To keep price from falling. As the company's spokesman put it, "We're hoping production restraint . . . will be sufficient to prevent further cuts and allow zinc price to move back toward a more healthy level."[11] At about the same time, *Business Week* was explaining to its readers why prices on paper goods had held fairly steady during 1975 despite the worst decline in paper demand in 40 years: "Instead of running their mills flat-out in good times and bad, paper company managers now try generally to cut production instead of prices when demand weakens."[12] These are two examples of a very important and fundamental rule of economics: if prices are to be controlled in either the short or long run, one must control demand or supply, or both. In the case of oligopolists coping with cyclical swings in demand, the only option usually open is supply control. Cyclical swings in demand are either inherent in the product[13] or a result of economy-wide difficulties. Both causes are beyond the control of individual firms.

A Bit of Theory

The principle is illustrated in Figure 11-5.[14] It depicts demand and unit costs for two firms. The underlying conditions are the same for each, except that 11-5(a) assumes a kinked demand whereas 11-5(b) assumes an elastic demand. The horizontal axis in each case is capacity use, which is simply an alternative way of expressing quantity. The vertical axis measures price and costs per unit of output. For simplicity, unit variable costs (UVC) are assumed to be the same for each unit of output up to full capacity. (They are still

[11] *Wall Street Journal*, June 15, 1977.
[12] *Business Week*, May 2, 1977, p. 55.
[13] A curious example of this is textiles. For many decades this industry experienced a mysterious and never fully explained cycle of high demand in odd-numbered years and low demand in even-numbered years. J. W. Markham. *Competition in the Rayon Industry* (Cambridge: Harvard University Press, 1952), pp. 112–15.
[14] For a similar discussion see R. Sherman, *The Economics of Industry* (Boston: Little, Brown and Co., 1974), pp. 148–50; Markham, *op. cit.*; and Robert E. Smith, "A Theory for the Administered Price Phenomenon," (mimeograph release, 1978).

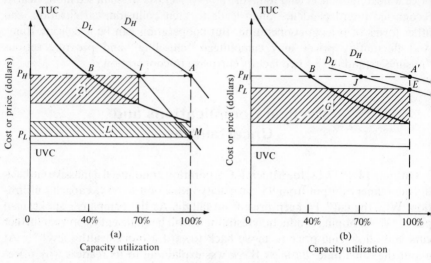

Figure 11-5. Price and quantity responses to fluctuations in demand.

"variable" in the sense that total dollar costs rise with added output.) When fixed costs per unit are added to UVC, the result is total unit costs, TUC (which in this case do not include a normal profit). Thus at price P_H the break-even point for each firm is at point B, which corresponds to 40 % capacity utilization. Demand is shown to fluctuate cyclically between a high level, D_H, and a low level, D_L.

Looking first at Figure 11-5(a), we can compare the implications of adjusting to slack demand by cutting price, as opposed to cutting quantity, when demand is price inelastic (which is typical below the kink in the short run). For demand D_H, the firm is at point A. Capacity utilization is 100%, and profit with price P_H is lucrative. As demand shifts back to D_L, full capacity can be maintained only by cutting price from P_H to P_L, moving the firm from A to M. However, unit costs exceed price at that point, yielding losses indicated by shaded area L. The firm would continue to produce in the short run, despite the loss, because it is covering its variable costs, UVC, and part of its fixed cost. In short, absorbing the slack by a move from A to M is distasteful to the firm (but not to its customers). Had the firm been able to maintain price at P_H by cutting back capacity use to 70%, it would be at point I. Even though this tactic boosts unit costs substantially, they are still less than P_H at I. Hence, total profits are indicated by shaded area Z. From the firm's viewpoint, the superiority of this A to I supply adjustment is quite plain. Profits are not only maintained over phases of the cycle, they are more stable over numerous cycles. Why, then, would any firm want to end up at M, as many often do? Although they do not want to, they may be *forced* to by price competition, which brings us to Figure 11-5(b).

264

Quantity curtailment plus price maintenance are the preferred combination only under the right circumstances—of which inelastic demand is the most important. If on the other hand short-run demand is very responsive to small price shadings, as is assumed in Figure 11-5(b), quantity maintenance, coupled with price cutting, would be the more profitable combination. In 11-5(b) demand shifts by the *same* magnitude as in 11-5(a). A constant price P_H begets 70% capacity use in both cases. Point J in 11-5(b) corresponds to point I in 11-5(a). Thus the profit consequences of maintaining price in 11-5(b) are the same—that is, total profit at J would equal area Z. Area Z may be compared to area G in 11-5(b) to see the greater rewards bestowed by cutting price to P_L and moving from J to E. Area G clearly exceeds area Z. Adjustment A' to E is superior to I' to J.

The only remaining question is *when* does each model apply? As already suggested, the inelasticity of Figure 11-5(a) seems typical of medium and large firms in most oligopolistic industries because their followship curves reflect market-wide demand, which itself is typically inelastic in the short run—especially in producer goods industries such as steel, zinc, aluminum, paper, and chemicals. These oligopolists will try to avoid price cuts in periods of declining demand, recognizing the likelihood of their detection and imitation by competitors, with a resulting loss of profits by all. Figure 11-5(b) on the other hand seems typical of (1) the small firms in these same oligopoly industries, (2) the small firms *wholly populating* monopolistically competitive markets, and (3) the few large oligopolists who just happen to be in markets with highly elastic short-run demands.

To small firms in monopolistically competitive industries, the high elasticity of Figure 11-5(b) is a tempting illusion of nonfollowship. The consequences of their price cutting copy those of Figure 11-3 seen earlier. Their price competition magnetically draws them down the followship curve to points like M in Figure 11-5(a). On the other hand, these elastic curves may *not* be illusory to the small firms that play in the yards of large oligopolists. If the large firms in an oligopolistic industry are intent on maintaining price for reasons defined in Figure 11-5(a), their smaller rivals may correctly see nonfollowship curves of the Figure 11-5(b) variety. At the very least, those who play at the knees of big oligopolists would be strongly tempted to test just how real their nonfollowship curves really were. Several predictions concerning the cyclical variability of prices and quantities naturally follow:

1. Within oligopolies, small "fringe" firms are more likely than large firms to be the sole price cutters or to lead the industry in a general round of price shading when demand flags.
2. Within oligopolies, the large firms are more likely than small firms to cut output in the face of slack demand.
3. Price stability and quantity variability should be associated with concentrated oligopolies—as opposed to unconcentrated oligopolies, monopolistic competition, or pure competition.

Although considerations of demand elasticity have led us to these hypotheses cost considerations would bolster them, especially the first two. For variou reasons the short-run cost curves of smaller firms are often higher and steeper in slope than the cost curves of large firms. The implications of this for price and output policy may be seen by mentally lifting the TUC curve of Figure 11-5(b) a little higher than it is, then giving it a slight clockwise twist. The break-even point shifts to the right. The firm then would want all the more to maintain full capacity utilization.[15]

The Evidence

Evidence for the first two hypotheses comes mainly from *intra*industry experiences. The third hypothesis receives its greatest support from systematic *inter*industry statistical studies. Hence, we postpone our empirical exploration of the third hypothesis, and turn directly to the first two.

For small-firm price cutting during slumps we have space for only a few stories:

- During the 15 months prior to January, 1975, the U.S. sank into its worst recession since the Great Depression; U.S. auto sales plunged 25% from mediocre 1973 levels; and the industry cut back capacity use close to 50%. Price reductions were resisted. Indeed, GM led price increases averaging $1,000 per car. Then that January, Chrysler, the smallest of the big three, broke the ice by cutting price as much as $400 per car under its "Car Clearance Carnival" rebate program. For a while GM and Ford did not join the carnival: "It will be late in January before anybody really knows what's happening," said a Ford executive. Chrysler was sufficiently successful, however, that the Big Two and AMC soon followed.[16]

- The rebates lasted only six weeks. Thereafter, general recovery lifted *big* car sales substantially but *small* car sales only moderately. This created particular problems for "tiny" AMC. Hence, in November, 1976, AMC cut prices on Gremlins and Pacers by $253, or roughly 7%. AMC said it was hoping this would boost its sales 30%, which implies a high non-followership elasticity estimate of 4.3. Unfortunately for AMC, GM followed with a $200 rebate program for three of its small car models that were also in excess supply.[17]

- The president of a small rayon company once summarized price cutting in that industry with these words: "... when demand is not so great and there are large stocks on hand, some of the smaller producers, ourselves

[15] This point is stressed by Markham, *op. cit.*, pp. 150–57.
[16] *Business Week* and *Wall Street Journal*, various issues. Benefits to consumers were in the neighborhood of $100 million.
[17] *Wall Street Journal*, Nov. 5, 1976 and Nov. 17, 1976.

included, must of necessity be a little under the price of Viscose and Dupont ..."[18]

- In 1960–61, capacity use in the steam turbine generator industry dropped to 60%. Allis-Chalmers, the industry's smallest producer, led a "dramatic plunge in price levels."[19]

- Sales volume was pretty good in the synthetic ammonia industry during the 1950's, but "in 1958 prices were cut both in California and in the lower Mississippi Valley under the threat of excess capacity. In both instances, the cuts were announced by a smaller producer and followed, with a lag, by the larger firms."[20]

That should give you the idea. Many similar illustrations of the second hypothesis are available,[21] but one clear case will suffice. Column 1 of Table 11-2

TABLE 11-2   Distribution of Aluminum Capacity and Capacity Utilization, 1975

Company	(1) Per Cent of U.S. Capacity (Dec. 1974)	(2) Per Cent Capacity Utilization Rate (May 1975)
Alcoa	32.0	74
Reynolds	19.8	67
Kaiser	14.7	73
Conalco	7.0	66
Anaconda	6.1	77
Howmet	4.4	85
Martin Marietta	4.2	80
Revere	4.0	62
National-Southwire	3.7	100
Alumax	2.7	99
Noranda	1.4	100

Source: Council on Wage and Price Stability, Staff Report, *Aluminum Prices 1974–75* (Washington, D. C., 1976), p. 122.

[18] Markham, *op. cit.*, p. 75.
[19] R. G. M. Sultan, *Pricing in the Electric Oligopoly, Vol. I* (Cambridge, Mass.: Harvard University Press, 1974), pp. 151, 211.
[20] W. H. Martin, "Public Policy and Increased Competition in the Synthetic Ammonia Industry," *Quarterly Journal of Economics* (August 1959), p. 388.
[21] For examples see Markham, *op. cit.*, p. 136–38; *Business Week*, October 28, 1972, pp. 39–40, and December 14, 1974, p. 27; D. O. Parsons and E. J. Ray, "The United States Steel Consolidation: The Creation of Market Control," *Journal of Law and Economics* (April 1975), pp. 214–15.

presents the rated capacity of United States aluminum ingot producers i December 1974, expressed as a percentage of total industry capacity. Thes percentages would be market shares if all firms were producing at full capacit The industry was not operating at full capacity during the first half of 197; however, because of the severe recession. Thus, the second column of Tabl 11-2 reports each individual firm's percentage rate of capacity utilization i May 1975. It is not difficult to see that size and capacity utilization are *inversel* related. As the source of these data explains:

> The three smallest firms operated at full capacity for the year 1975. These are remarkably high levels . . . considering that the impact of the recession on the aluminum industry was the worst in magnitude since the Great Depression. The explanation for this disparity in capacity utilization across firms of different size appears to be that the smaller firms used small discounts from list price to operate at full capacity levels, while the majors were holding prices at list. The larger firms chose to hold price and cut back production . . . [22]

Although these experiences indicate that concentration helps secure shor run supply control (and thereby price control), concentration is not a conclusiv or even a necessary condition. **Linear cost curves**, such as those used in drawin Figure 11-5 are also helpful. If, for reasons of plant design or inherent technolog unit costs were to rise steeply on either side of 98 % capacity utilization, th utilization rate would be much less flexible.[23]

Durability of product aids as well. Style change, organic decay, whateve shortens product life span: perishables tend to be marked down quickly if the are not moving briskly into the hands of consumers. Durability permits a alternating current of inventory accumulation and discharge that cushion the shock of abrupt swings in demand, thereby smoothing out the rough linkag between consumer's pantry and manufacturer's plant.[24] Indeed, the aluminu ingot industry usually relies more heavily on inventory variation than pro duction variation because ingots are more than durable; they are cheapl storable. A measure of these ingot qualities is that the majors used to maintai 2 pounds of fabrication capacity for every 1 pound of ingot capacity.[25]

For related reasons, **vertical integration** also helps supply control, althoug in its case the linkage secured may run from the consumer all the way back t

[22] Council on Wage and Price Stability, Staff Report, *Aluminum Prices 1974–75* (Washingto D.C., U.S.G.P.O., 1976), p. 121. See also *Business Week*, Nov. 17, 1975, pp. 151–53.

[23] G. Stigler, "Production and Distribution in the Short Run," *Journal of Political Econom* (June 1939), pp. 305–27. For an example of "go" or "no go" facilities, see J. M. Blair, *Econom Concentration* (New York: Harcourt Brace Jovanovich, 1972), p. 282.

[24] F. M. Scherer, *Industrial Market Structure and Economic Performance* (Chicago: Ra McNally, 1970), pp. 149–56.

[25] M. J. Peck, *Competition in the Aluminum Industry 1945-1958* (Cambridge, Mass.: Harva University Press, 1961), Chapter 6.

he mineral pit, as in petroleum and steel.[26] An example of a *lack* of vertical integration contributing to price combat arose recently in the paper linerboard industry. It started in January 1977, when a nonintegrated company, Great Northern Nekoosa, slashed prices from $215 a ton to $195 a ton:

> Most of the other major producers have integrated operations that produce both linerboard and the finished box. But Great Northern sells all its linerboard on the open market. Mr. Bellis said, "It is fine for the integrated producers to say don't cut price when half the time they're taking it out of one pocket and putting it into another." He added: "If we hadn't cut prices our customers would have deserted us."[27]

Finally, and perhaps most important, there are a variety of **pricing mechanisms or rules of thumb**, that, when either imposed or voluntarily adopted, contribute to price stability by providing guidance, uniformity, or centralization to what might otherwise tend to be a rather diffuse, chaotic, even competitive pricing process. These mechanisms or rules of thumb serve purposes other than cyclical price stabilization. Indeed, they are vital to daily decision making and they foster industry discipline in good times as well as bad. Therefore, they warrant special attention.

Pricing Mechanisms and Rules of Thumb

One thing to remember while reviewing these pricing mechanisms and rules of thumb is that their incidence and effectiveness varies according to market structure. Their usage is not randomly distributed; their impact is not always benchant. Incidentally, their names are not exactly catchy either; cost-plus pricing, target-profit pricing, price leadership, cartelization, and government tampering.

Cost-plus and Target-profit Pricing

Cost-plus or "full-cost" pricing usually involves estimating the average variable costs of producing and distributing the product, adding a charge for overhead, and then adding a percentage markup for profits. In retailing, adding a common percentage markup to the wholesale cost of goods sold is quite common. Target-profit pricing is a variant of cost-plus pricing with an important application in manufacturing. It was originally devised by GM executives to achieve a target rate of profit while maintaining price and flexing output. The

---

[26] M. G. de Chazeau and A. E. Kahn, *Integration and Competition in the Petroleum Industry* New Haven, Conn.: Yale University Press, 1959), Chapter 17; W. Adams and J. B. Dirlam, Steel Imports and Vertical Oligopoly Power," *American Economic Review* (September 1964), pp. 26–55.

[27] *Wall Street Journal*, February 4, 1977.

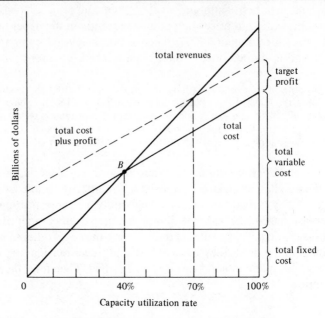

Figure 11-6. *Target profit pricing model.*

technique is illustrated in Figure 11-6, which may be considered a total-dollar version of Figure 11-5(a).

Target profit is defined as a certain percentage of investment, not sales. Hence the technique is not simply a matter of wedging a nice profit percentage int price. Multiplying the target of, say, 40% before taxes times total investmer yields a "hoped-for" dollar target profit. When this target profit is added t total cost, the result is the top broken line of Figure 11-6. Notice that targe profit does not vary with output, but total costs do. Since target-dollar prof does not vary with output, the apparent implication is that the firm will have t *raise* price in recessions and *cut* price in booms. But such actions would driv customers away just when they are most needed and attract them when alread abundant. The trick is to set price in such a way that the firm earns its targe *on average* over the cycle while holding price fairly constant.

The firm achieves this balance by calculating cost and profit per unit on th basis of **standard volume**, or average output, which in Figure 11-6 is 70% c capacity. Thus, for example, if GM's standard volume is 5 million cars and i pretax target profit $5 billion, profit per standard volume car would be set a $1000 ($5 billion/5 million cars). If hypothetical overhead is $10 billion, fixe cost per standard volume car is then $2000 ($10 billion/5 million cars). Wit variable costs of $2500 per car, price comes to $5500 ($1000 + $2000 + $2500 and this price will determine the slope of the total revenue line in Figure 11-

27

Of course, this example abstracts from the realities of many model lines, occasional rebate programs, and escalating costs of production over time. But the idea is clear. In good years, with production above standard volume, realized profit will exceed target profit, as total revenues in Figure 11-6 exceed total cost plus target profit. In slack years, the opposite holds. On average, the target will be grazed if not hit squarely.

Interview surveys and case studies reveal widespread use of these various techniques. R. L. Hall and C. J. Hitch canvassed 38 firms and determined that 30 of them followed some form of cost-plus or target pricing.[28] Fog's study of 38 Danish firms turned up evidence that the most usual method among them could be considered "flexible full-cost pricing."[29] A. Silberston concludes his review of British pricing studies by saying that "full cost can be given a mark of beta query plus."[30] Finally, A. D. H. Kaplan, J. B. Dirlam, and R. F. Lanzillotti interviewed officials in 20 large United States corporations, ten of which were apparently using target-profit techniques. Besides GM, the ten included such renowned companies as U.S. Steel, DuPont, General Electric, Alcoa, International Harvester, and Union Carbide.[31] However, few of these firms had targets as high as GM's 20% after taxes. In fact, one aimed for only 8%.

These several studies touched off a heated debate over whether firms maximized profits. In light of our last chapter, we shall not pursue this question here other than to note that target-profit and cost-plus pricing are not necessarily inconsistent with profit maximization, especially in the long run. As A. E. Kahn has observed, one should not confuse *procedures* with *goals*.[32] Some may use the target procedure to shoot for only 8%, but that may be the best they can do. One thing all successful target pricers share in common is a substantial ability to control supply in the short run.

Price Leadership

Many of the firms not classified as target or cost-plus pricers in the studies cited previously could be considered followers of larger "price leaders" who do employ such techniques. "The development of price leadership in large-scale industry," according to some experts, "has roots in the earlier experience

[28] Hall and Hitch, *op. cit.*

[29] Fog, *op. cit.*, p. 217.

[30] A. Silberston, "Price Behavior of Firms," *Economic Journal* (September 1970), p. 545.

[31] A. D. H. Kaplan, J. B. Dirlam, and R. F. Lanzillotti, *Pricing in Big Business* (Washington, D.C.: Brookings Institution, 1958); and R. F. Lanzillotti, "Pricing Objectives of Large Companies," *American Economic Review* (December 1958), pp. 921–40. An executive of U. S. Steel once explained their policy as follows: "If customers don't buy their steel [in a slump] there isn't too much you can do about it . . . I doubt that you would go out and buy two new cars instead of one if steel prices were cut . . . . Over the long pull, American steel mills have operated at about 75 percent average capacity. If you operate at 90 percent over a stretch, you've then got to figure on a stretch at 60 percent of capacity. Basically you must be able to make adequate profits at the average." G. J. McManus, *The Inside Story of Steel Wages and Prices 1959–1967* (Philadelphia: Chilton Book Co., 1967), p. 63.

[32] A. E. Kahn, "Pricing Objectives of Large Companies: Comment," *American Economic Review* (September 1959), pp. 670–78.

TABLE 11-3 Outline of Three Broad Types of Price Leadership

Characteristic	Dominant Firm Leadership	Collusive Price Leadership	Barometric Price Leadership
Concentration ratio	Very high one-firm ratio	Medium to high four-firm ratio	Low four-firm ratio
Leader's Qualification	Immense relative size and efficiency	Size, age, custom, efficiency	Forecasting ability, sensitivity
Cost across firms	Diverse	Roughly similar	Diverse
Changes in who leads?	Never	Occasionally	Often
Disciplinary problems	Never	Sometimes	Frequently
Followship lags	Never	Temporary	Leader "lags
Examples	Aluminum (until recently), computers	Steel, cigarettes	Gasoline, turbines

of violent price fluctuation and cut-throat competition, which culminated i consolidation of competitors, as in steel, copper, oil production, tin cans, an farm equipment. Such experience has generated a distinct predisposition on th part of managements to avoid price changes except through periodic, wel considered, and well-publicized alterations in recognized *base* prices." Under a diversity of structural conditions, price leadership takes many form but compressing them into three broad types will simplify the situation. The: types are dominant-firm leadership, collusive leadership, and barometr leadership.[34] Table 11-3 summarizes the salient characteristics of each type.

Dominant-Firm Leadership. Dominant-firm price leadership is a giant/pygm situation. One firm controls 50-95% of the market. Awed by its immen: size and efficiency, the smaller firms willingly, if sheepishly, accept its leade

[33] Kaplan, Dirlam, and Lanzillotti, *op. cit.*, p. 271.
[34] J. W. Markham, "The Nature and Significance of Price Leadership," *American Econom Review* (December 1951), pp. 891–905; Scherer, *op. cit.*, pp. 164–73.

ship. Because unit costs of the fringe firms typically exceed those of the dominant firm materially, the small fry refrain from cutting prices below those set by the leader. Moreover, they virtually always follow the leader's up-side price changes without hesitation. This means that the leader's disciplinary problems are few and far between. It also indicates that fringe firms probably prefer a higher level of price than the leader usually sets for the market. As with the other summary descriptions of Table 11-3, the illustration posits generalities that do not fit any particular industry perfectly, but there are a few examples that fit the dominant firm mold fairly well. Not surprisingly, many examples come from the annals of Section 2 Sherman Act prosecutions—United Shoe Machinery, IBM, and Alcoa. In the case of Alcoa, we refer to the period 1946–1965, during which time Alcoa did face some domestic competition but was still quite dominant. In those years Reynolds and Kaiser repeatedly expressed their preferences for prices higher than those Alcoa selected.[35] Of late, Alcoa's dominance has waned, as was implied by our earlier discussion of Table 11-2.

Collusive Price Leadership. This might better describe aluminum nowadays. Typifying this category are medium-to-high four-firm concentration ratios; a leader whose relatively large size (say, 20–30% of the market) and ancient lineage signify qualities befitting an industrial chieftain; a cost structure across firms that is uniform enough to generate fairly harmonious notions about what the industry's price level should be; widespread agreement among the oligopolists over long periods of time as to who their leader should be; few disciplinary problems with "chiselers"; and lags in followship short enough to save the leader from repeated embarrassment.

The cigarette industry provides a classic example from the era when non-filtered regulars were all you could buy.[36] After the Sherman Act dissolution of American Tobacco in 1911, the industry came to be divided primarily between Reynolds, American, and Liggett & Myers. The popularity of "Camels" gave Reynolds a 40% share of the market by 1920, top spot, and rights to leadership. Between 1923 and 1941, American and Liggett & Myers stuck to Reynolds' prices like a Marlboro tattoo. There were eight list price changes during the period. Reynolds led six of them, five up and one down, with the others following usually not more than a day behind. The two Reynolds did *not* lead were price cuts initiated by American in 1933 that were necessitated by remarkable circumstances.

The circumstances were these: As the nation slid into the Great Depression and the prices of leaf tobacco and other cigarette materials were falling along with commodity prices in general, R. J. Reynolds led two bold increases in the wholesale price of cigarettes—7% in October 1929 and another 7% in June

---

[35] M. J. Peck, *op. cit.*, Chapter 4.
[36] William Nicholls, *Price Policies in the Cigarette Industry* (Nashville, Tenn.: Vanderbilt University Press, 1951); R. B. Tennant, *The American Cigarette Industry* (New Haven, Conn.: Yale University Press, 1950).

1931. Consequently, retail prices of popular brands wound up at 15 cents. Now this may not seem like much by today's inflated standards, but it was enough to give the three companies profits that exceeded 30% of net sales less tax. At the time of the last of these 7% increases the so-called "10-cent" brand accounted for less than 1% of the total market. For obvious reasons, however, their sales thereafter skyrocketed to account eventually for more than 20% of the market in the final two months of 1932. Upon feeling this slap, the three large companies retaliated. American led a 12% wholesale price cut on January 3, 1933, then initiated a second cut of 8% one month later, bringing the retail prices of the three companies down to 10 and 11 cents. This knocked the 10-cent brands' market share back to 7% almost immediately. After about a year the three large companies slowly began to raise their prices again. The renewed escalation enabled the 10-cent brands to regain a bit of their lost ground but never to recoup it completely.

From 1901 until 1962 U.S. Steel served as leader in steel, thus providing another example of collusive leadership. Even in 1939, after U.S. Steel's market share had dwindled to less than 40%, the president of one of its larger rivals said that the "pace is set, if that is a good word, by the Steel Corporation."[3] During the first 15 years after World War II, U.S. Steel led the industry in 11 of its 12 price increases. But then in April 1962 U.S. Steel fell from grace. Just 5 days after signing a modest wage settlement with the steelworkers union that could not have increased the industry's unit labor costs, U.S. Steel announced a price increase of $6 a ton that was quickly followed by all but a few other producers.

Only 4 months earlier President Kennedy had introduced his wage-price "guidepost" program, designed to stem inflation. He also had a hand in the union's wage restraint. Thus Kennedy could not ignore big Steel's brassiness. He publically castigated the industry's executives, calling them "irresponsible." (Privately, he called them "S.O.B's" and "bastards."[38]) This helped Inland and Kaiser Steel to decide a few days later that they would not follow U.S. Steel's lead. Whereupon first Bethlehem, then U.S. Steel, and then the others rescinded their increases. The general consensus is that Bethlehem, which is number two in the industry, now serves as price leader.

The reader should not conclude from this discussion that except for this one incident the industry's leader has been followed religiously. As suggested in Table 11-3, price shading is not at all uncommon, especially among the smaller firms when demand turns sour. They maintain their official "list" prices while giving secret, "under-the-table" discounts in hopes of moving down their elastic nonfollowship demand curves. In fact, one of the main reasons U.S. Steel's market share shrank from more than 60% in 1901 to less than 25% today is that its efforts at price maintenance were gently and intermittently exploited by smaller producers.

[37] L. W. Weiss, *Economics and American Industry* (New York: John Wiley & Sons, 1961), p. 293.
[38] A. M. Schlesinger, Jr., *A Thousand Days* (Boston: Houghton Mifflin Co., 1965), p. 531.

Barometric Price Leadership. Under barometric price leadership, conditions are substantially more competitive. Use of the word "leadership" in this case may even be misleading. The leader is often no more than the first firm to announce formal revisions in *list* or *book* prices to reflect prevailing *realized* or *transactions* prices. In other words, the leader's main qualification in this case is his acute sensitivity to market pressures. As George Stigler explains it, the barometric leader "commands adherence of rivals to his price only because, and to the extent that, his price reflects market conditions with tolerable promptness."[39] If the firm actually does lead, it should be a good forecaster of the imminent trend, especially on the up side. International Paper Company illustrates the consequences of up-side error. Its unsuccessful attempt to lead an increase in late 1976 cost it 100,000 tons of production, 1.4 percentage points off its 12.7% market share, and a bundle of profits.[40] Other indices that iron-clad coordination is lacking under barometric leadership include a diversity of cost levels across firms, frequent changes in the identity of the leader, bigger disciplinary problems than are found under dominant firm and collusive leadership, and substantial lags in followship should the leader act more as a forecaster than as an announcer of prevailing reality.

Barometric leaders usually occupy unconcentrated industries as well, but not always. This last fact underscores the lack of precision in these three categories of leadership. For example, during the 1950s the steam turbine electric generator market was highly concentrated. General Electric (GE) (with a 60% share), Westinghouse (with 30%), and Allis-Chalmers (with 10%) accounted for all United States production. Moreover, in book prices, GE was the undisputed leader. GE's price book was the Sears' catalog of the industry, and the others copied it to the letter.[41] Still, in *transactions* prices, GE appears to have been only a barometric leader. This is shown in Figure 11-7, which charts an index of the industry's transactions prices together with GE's transactions prices *relative* to those of its rivals. Notice that GE's transactions prices were slightly *below* its rivals' prices during periods of high demand and rising industry prices. Conversely, GE's transactions prices were slightly *above* its rivals' prices during periods of slack demand and falling industry prices. A partial explanation for this behavior was GE's desire to maintain a 60% market share while serving as leader. During slumps GE's share would diminish as rivals priced beneath it. During booms its share would be restored as rivals eagerly took advantage of the opportunity to advance their prices while GE acted in a more leisurely way.

Cartelization

Another feature to notice in Figure 11-7 is the sharp rise in turbine generator prices after 1954, a rise that is followed by an equally sharp fall after 1959. During

---

[39] Stigler, *op. cit.* (1947), pp. 445–46.
[40] *Business Week*, May 2, 1977, p. 54.
[41] Sultan, *op. cit.*, pp. 213–14.

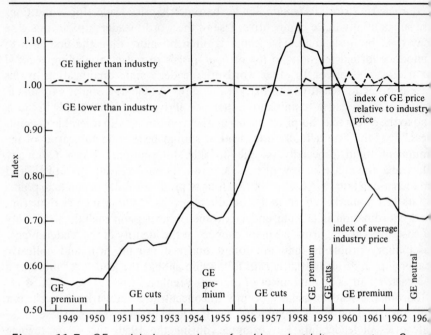

Figure 11-7. *GE and industry prices of turbine electricity generators. Sourc[e] Ralph G. M. Sultan,* Pricing in the Electrical Oligopoly, *Vol. 1 (Boston: Division [of] Research, Graduate School of Business Administration, Harvard University, 1974[)] p. 282.*

the years in between GE, Westinghouse, and Allis-Chalmers conspired to f[ix] prices—that is, they operated a loose-knit cartel. All in all, the price fixir[g] extended to 19 other electrical equipment products, to 26 other firms, and, i[n] these broader respects, to many years before 1955. This is a fascinating bit [of] evidence drawn from a much larger topic than we can treat now. Hence t[he] next chapter is devoted entirely to cartelization. Here we may note in passir[g] that securing a uniformity of behavior among otherwise competitive firm[s] is the essence of cartelization. Cooperation is refined, formalized, and ofte[n] pursued with vigor. When cartelization is applied to pricing, the results ca[n] include less variation across firms, greater stability over time, and, as suggeste[d] in Figure 11-7, higher absolute levels of price. It will be shown in the next chapt[er] that structural conditions affect the ease with which cartel agreements can b[e] privately devised. As you might guess, fewness of firms and high market co[n]centration are conducive to cartel conduct.

Government Intervention

With minor exceptions *private* cartelization is illegal in the United State[s.] Cartelization nevertheless permeates many industries. Sanctioned and supe[r]

sed by various governmental bodies, it has spread under the cover of more
phemistic names such as "parity price supports," "marketing agreements,"
il prorationing," "collective bargaining," and "regulation." The list could
sily be expanded to include various forms of cartelization affecting United
ates foreign trade. In many instances, the government was pushed into these
licies at the insistence of politically powerful commercial groups. These
oups believed that supply control and price stability would be of dramatic
nefit to them. They also perceived the possibility of gaining higher *absolute*
ices, profits, and incomes as well, but they were not in a position to attain
ese several objectives without the government's help. Generally speaking,
eir industries and markets were *too* competitively structured to secure these
ds by price leadership or similar informal cooperation (or even secret, illegal
rtelization). Thus, stripped to its essentials, the government's agricultural
ice support program attempts to curtail production and keep "surplus"
mmodities off the market during periods of slack demand or inadvertently
undant production. When demand expands or nature withholds, land is
owed back into production, excess inventories are disgorged, and so forth.
f course in this industry the business cycle causes only a fraction of the demand
rves' volatility. Foreign demand for our exports dances to the cruel tune of
reign droughts, freezes, floods, blights, and pestilent hordes. Forms of governent cartelization other than those in agriculture will be taken up in later
apters.

Cross-Section Statistical Evidence[42]

We are finally ready for the evidence concerning *inter*industry differences
cyclical price behavior. Figure 11-8 restates the main hypothesis. Its
rizontal axis measures positive and negative percentage changes in quantity,
ereas its vertical axis indicates positive and negative percentage changes in
ice. Instances in which competitive industries have displayed almost perfect
rtical movement along the vertical axis exist. In these cases quantity has
mained fairly constant, while price has absorbed the cyclical swing. Con-
rsely, there are also instances of highly concentrated industries moving
rizontally along the $+\Delta Q - \Delta Q$ axis, displaying very little change in price
r enormous variations in quantity.[43]
Although these are the extreme patterns our earlier theory may have
ggested, the theory was deliberately oversimplified. A more realistic but still

[42] Other surveys of the statistical evidence that have influenced this section are A. E. Kahn,
"Market Power Inflation: A Conceptual Overview," in *The Roots of Inflation* (New York: Burt
anklin & Co., 1975); R. E. Beals, "Concentrated Industries, Administered Prices, and Inflation:
Survey of Recent Empirical Research," Report to the Council on Wage and Price Stability
ocessed June 17, 1975); F. M. Scherer, *op. cit.*, Chapters 12, 13.

[43] F. C. Mills, *Price-Quantity Interactions in Business Cycles* (New York: National Bureau of
onomic Research, 1946), pp. 29, 46–47.

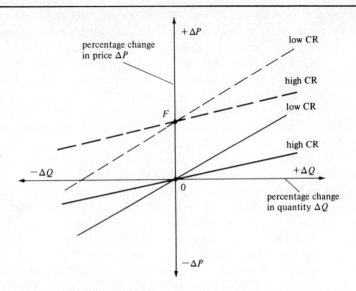

Figure 11-8. *Price movements relative to quantity movements and concentratio*

abstract view of the matter is depicted by the diagonal lines of Figure 11-
The solid lines going through the origin show prices in unconcentrated industri
(low CR) rising more during booms and falling more during slumps than pric
in highly concentrated industries (high CR). So oligopolistic prices might n
be absolutely "rigid"—merely "sticky," or, more precisely, "relatively sticky
as compared to competitive prices. The dashed lines of Fig. 11-8 indicate that th
hypothesis could still hold during broad-based secular inflation. In other word
both diagonals going through the origin have equal parts of plus and min
price change for an overall average of zero net change. Regrettably, we ha
of late experienced *general* inflation, with prices typically going up faster
slower but almost always going up. The dashed diagonals thus indicate t
same degree of stickiness and variability amidst secular inflation as the sol
diagonals do with no net inflation.

The first evidence confirming the presence of relatively inflexible pric
among oligopolistic industries was presented by Gardner C. Means in 1935.
He called them "administered prices," and the name has stuck. Since that tin
Means has presented further positive evidence for subsequent periods. U
fortunately, he has been overselective in his choice of industries and time period
overzealous in propounding his views; and occasionally inconsistent in h
interpretations. As a consequence, he has stirred up a string of formidable criti

[44] *Industrial Prices and their Relative Inflexibility,"* Senate Doc. 13, 74th Congress, First Sessi
1935.

ed by George Stigler and Fred Weston.[45] A blow-by-blow account of their perennial debates is unnecessary. The lessons to be learned may be stated simply: (1) There are many factors, for example, costs, that are much more important than concentration in determining price changes, and (2) prices vary widely across industries for reasons too complex to pin down easily.

This is not to say, however, that concentration has no influence or that its influence is trivial. The weight of accumulated evidence now seems to rest on the side of Means (although it is not as impressive as Means would like to think). Among the more recent studies is one by David Qualls.[46] He computed year-to-year price change variance of 30 four-digit industries for which wholesale price data were available over the period 1957–1970. He then divided his sample into two groups, depending on whether the industry's four-firm concentration ratio was greater or less than 50%. Comparing the two groups, he found that average variance in the unconcentrated industries greatly exceeded average variance in the highly concentrated industries, 39.0% to 6.2%.

Philip Cagan's comprehensive study of pricing during our post World War II recessions also lends support to the pattern of Figure 11-8.[47] He used wholesale price indexes for over 1000 narrowly defined industries that he divided into three concentration categories—high, medium, and low. In all five recessions studied up through 1970, average prices in the high concentration category decreased less than those in the low concentration category. Moreover, Cagan found a shift over time that would correspond to a shift of the solid diagonals of Figure 11-8 up toward the dashed diagonals. Thus, during the 1969–1970 recession, only the low concentration category experienced any decline in average price levels. Prices in the medium and high groups actually increased.

This family of results is perhaps most easily visualized in Figure 11-9, which traces prices over time. Prices in the "oligopoly" sector rise at a fairly steady pace, whereas prices in the "competitive" sector fluctuate widely, falling rather sharply during the shaded recessionary periods. Over the long haul there is no growing divergence between the two series. Oligopolistic prices do not seem to inflate over decades any more rapidly than competitive prices do. (Some have taken this to mean that market power does *not* contribute an inflationary bias to the economy, but we shall see in Chapter 21 that such a conclusion cannot be founded on this kind of evidence alone.)

Instead of examining raw prices, some researchers have explored changes in prices *less* variable costs, otherwise known as **price-cost gross margins**. The

[45] See, e.g., G. J. Stigler, "Industrial Prices as Administered by Dr. Means," *American Economic Review* (September 1973), pp. 717–21; J. F. Weston, S. Lustgarten, and N. Grottke, "The Administered-Price Thesis Denied: Note," *American Economic Review* (March 1974), pp. 232–34.

[46] P. D. Qualls, "Price Stability in Concentrated Industries," *Southern Economic Journal* (October 1975), pp. 294–98.

[47] P. Cagan, "Changes in the Recession Behavior of Wholesale Prices in the 1920's and Post-World War II," *Explorations in Economic Research NBER* (Winter 1975), pp. 54–104. See also S. Eichner, "A Theory of the Determination of the Mark-up Under Oligopoly," *Economic Journal* (December 1973), p. 1187.

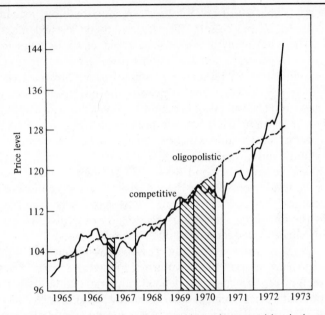

Figure 11-9. *Wholesale prices in oligopolistic and competitive industries, 196!* *1973 (1957–59 = 100). Source: A. S. Eichner, The Megacorp and Oligopo (Cambridge: Cambridge University Press, 1976), p. 269.*

foregoing findings with respect to price fluctuations do not rule out the po sibility that gross margins might behave independently of market powe On the other hand, our earlier theories suggest that margins, like prices, shou be more flexible in competitive industries than in oligopolies. That is, they shou compress more during slumps and expand more during booms, everythir else being equal. Evidence on this point also goes as far back as the Gre Depression. Once again it must be acknowledged that the evidence has bee less than crystal clear and that conflicts of opinion have abounded. Still, t bulk of the best evidence seems to show an inverse relationship between co centration and margin flexibility. During cyclical *up*swings, margins tend rise in competitive industries relative to those in oligopolistic industries; durir *down*swings, the opposite occurs.[48]

[48] A. C. Neal, *Industrial Concentration and Price Inflexibility* (Washington, D.C.: Americ Council on Public Affairs, 1942); L. W. Weiss, "Business Pricing Policies and Inflation Recons ered," *Journal of Political Economy* (April 1966), pp. 177–87; P. Cagan, "Inflation and Mar Structure," *Explorations in Economic Research* (Spring 1975), pp. 203–16; J. A. Dalton, "A ministered Inflation and Business Pricing: Another Look," *Review of Economics and Statist* (November 1973), pp. 516–19; H. N. Ross, "The Determination of Industrial Price Flexibility *Industrial Organization Review* (No. 3, 1975), pp. 115–29; H. J. Sherman, *Profits in the United Sta* (Ithaca, N.Y.: Cornell University Press, 1968), Chapters 6 and 7.

These several findings concerning prices and gross margins in the United States receive independent corroboration from other studies. First, these patterns have been observed abroad in Canada and Japan.[49] They are supported also by United States and United Kingdom studies of a different genre. Tests of the relationship between market power and the temporal variance of profits as a per cent of assets or stockholders equity disclose an inverse association between concentration and profit variance.[50] Then, too, there appears to be a consistent and significant positive relationship between *employment* variability and seller concentration within four-digit industries.[51]

In short, the evidence does not refute the foregoing theories, and your patience with this chapter has not gone for naught. Unfortunately, the behavior observed does wear on the patience of our aggregate economic policy makers. Historically, their main weapon against price inflation has been the occasional curtailment of aggregate demand by means of fiscal and monetary restraint. The idea is that reduced demand reduces prices. But to the extent that market power inhibits price reductions, application of this policy does little more than increase unemployment. Arthur Burns, former chief of United States money supply operations, has often expressed his frustrations. He once said that "Improved policies of managing aggregate demand, important though they may be, will not of themselves suffice to assure prosperity without inflation. Structural reforms are also needed."[52]

Summary

Analysis of short-run price and production policy under oligopoly and monopolistic competition centers on the firm's twofold demand curves. These curves' price elasticities, shapes, visibilities, and shifts tell most of the story. The follow-up curve reflects market-wide demand and is typically rather inelastic.

---

[49] W. Sellekaerts and Richard Lesage, "A Reformulation and Empirical Verification of the Administered Prices Inflation Hypothesis: The Canadian Case," *Southern Economic Journal* (January 1973), pp. 345–60; K. Dennis, "Market Power and the Behavior of Industrial Prices," *Essays on Price Changes in Canada* (Ottawa: Prices and Incomes Commission, 1973), pp. 53-91; R. E. Caves and M. Uekusa, *Industrial Organization in Japan* (Washington, D.C.: Brookings Institution, 1976), p. 97. A study by L. Philips turned up nothing for Europe, but limitations of data and time period were worse than usual in his case.

[50] J. Samuels and D. Smyth, "Profits, Variability of Profits, and Firm Size," *Economica* (May 1968), pp. 127–39; F. R. Edwards and A. A. Heggestad, "Uncertainty, Market Structure, and Performance," *Quarterly Journal of Economics* (August 1973), pp. 456–73. The last one complements F. R. Edwards, "Concentration in Banking and Its Effect on Business Loan Rates," *Review of Economics and Statistics* (August 1964), pp. 294–300, where it is shown that bank concentration and interest rate flexibility are inversely related.

[51] D. S. Smith, "Concentration and Employment Fluctuations," *Western Economic Journal* (September 1971), pp. 267–77; H. Demsetz, "Where is the New Industrial State?" *Economic Inquiry* (March 1974), pp. 1–12. On a related point see D. F. Greer and S. A. Rhoades, "Concentration and Changes in Productivity in the Long and Short Run," *Southern Economic Journal* (October 1976), pp. 1031–44.

[52] Arthur Burns, *Industrial Reorganization Act Hearings*, U. S. Senate Subcommittee on Antitrust and Monopoly, Part 1 (1973), p. 47.

Conversely, the nonfollowship demand curve reflects switches of market share. The smaller the firm and the more standardized the product, therefore, the more price elastic the nonfollowship curve is. Under monopolistic competition all firms face highly elastic nonfollowship demand curves. The phoney promise these curves give price cutters of increased total revenue are too alluring to resist. Abundant small firm populations also keep interdependence unrecognized and followship demand curves invisible. The result is price competition.

Under oligopoly, with its fewer and larger firms, interdependence is recognized. Kinked demand theory explains why price cuts are resisted. To large firms the nonfollowship demand curve is less elastic and therefore less alluring than to small firms. Even more important, only the followship demand curve is visible on the down side. On the up side, only strong dominant price leaders see the followship demand curve. The theory's major implication is rigid prices, or when amended by certain realities such as inflation, *relatively* rigid prices (especially on the down side).

This implication holds even in the face of fluctuating demand. Supply control facilitates the maintenance of prices and profits within a given cycle, plus greater stability across numerous cycles. Comparatively large firms (with relatively inelastic demand curves) appreciate this quality of supply control the most. The elastic nonfollowship demand curves of smaller firms often entice them into secret discounting or thinly veiled price cutting when demand is slack. Intra-industry experiences repeatedly demonstrate the different views large and small firms have of the same market.

Short-run stability, guidance, coordination, and uniformity are furthered by various "mechanisms" or pricing procedures. The most important of these are cost-plus pricing, target-profit pricing, price leadership, and cartelization. These techniques tend to be most highly refined, most consistently adhered to, and most commonly observed in markets displaying stronger as opposed to lesser market power. Those in markets of lesser market power must rely on government intervention, usually in some form of cartelization, to secure the discipline that cyclical supply control requires.

Finally, cross-section evidence is not altogether solid. Still, it seems to show relatively inflexible prices and gross margins in industries bearing ossified structures as compared to those displaying more competitive characteristics. Interindustry studies of profits and employment corroborate this inference.

12

Price and Production
Behavior in the Short Run:
Cartel Practice and Policy

Between 1969 and 1973 I saw the retail price of a loaf of bread in Phoenix go from 5¢ to 69¢. At least 15% of that increase could be traced to our conspiracy. There's no question that price-fixing is a cost factor for the consumer.

Confession of DONALD PHILLIPS, former vice-president of Baird's Bread Co.

In a word, the subject of this chapter is cartelization. Broadly defined, a **cartel** *is an explicit arrangement among, or on behalf of, enterprises in the same line of business that is designed to limit or eliminate competition among them.*[1] The concept includes price-fixing, explicit collusion, and conspiracy. It might involve no more than a sociable discussion of prices over cocktails, or it might be so complex as to involve sales quotas, customer allocations, exclusive sales agencies, weekly meetings, enforcement committees, penalty formulas, and kangaroo courts. There are buyer cartels and seller cartels. They may be open or secret, governmental or private, legal or illegal, local or international.

Cartels fit within the short-run context of the preceding chapter for many reasons. When privately devised, they are often short lived. Their purpose, moreover, is frequently (if not usually) price stabilization rather than flagrant price escalation. Then too, their popularity among businessmen seems to vary inversely with the business cycle. But the fit is very imperfect. Cartels, it must be emphatically acknowledged, are not always "short-run" phenomena. As suggested by this chapter's opening quote, cartels may last for years. The

[1] G. W. Stocking and M. W. Watkins, *Cartels or Competition* (New York: Twentieth Century Fund, 1948), p. 3.

British/Indian ocean liner shipping "conference" celebrated its *centenni* anniversary in 1975. The electrical equipment price fixing conspiracy operate intermittently for over 20 years.

Cartels may also raise prices and profits sharply. Some recent evidence i dicates that a sample of large United States firms involved in illegal pri fixing had *lower* profits than other large firms, thus suggesting a short-ru "preventive" purpose to their activity.[2] But there are also numerous instanc of prices increasing from 30 to 60 %, even hundreds of per cents, under cartels The most famous cartel of all time—the Organization of Petroleum Exportir Countries, or OPEC—gained global notoriety by quadrupling the price crude oil in 1973 and then tacking on moderate price increases at fairly regul intervals thereafter. Further evidence to such effects is found in a once-co fidential 1929 study undertaken by duPont (itself an erstwhile participant various cartels):

> Statistics compiled in Paris and Berlin show the difference between the rise in the price of goods subject to Cartels and those supplied in open markets. In 1927 open-market products oscillated in price between 85.7 and 91.3 on the index figure of 100 in 1925, whereas the price of cartel products was stationary at 97.6. In 1928 the respective figures remained about the same, but in January 1929 open-market products were at 86.9 percent and cartel products had jumped to over 101.[4]

In short, "the typical purpose and effect of cartelization is to set prices high than would prevail under competition, to reduce them as seldom as possibl and to raise them further whenever the opportunity permits."[5] Attainment these ends often requires restrictions extending beyond price and outpu Advertising, product quality, and other variables have felt the grasp of co certed business practices. Unavoidably, then, this chapter is more than ju an elaboration of the preceding chapter's short-run pricing subjects. It i troduces the long-run subjects of the next chapter and other aspects of condu as well.

We begin by surveying United States government policy. A study of structur conditions favorable to cartelization follows. We then review the electric equipment cases and conclude with an extended discussion of the crude petr leum industry and OPEC.

[2] P. Asch and J. J. Seneca, "Is Collusion Profitable?" *Review of Economics and Statist* (February 1976), pp. 1–12.

[3] See, e.g., W. B. Erickson, "Price Fixing Conspiracies: Their Long-term Impact," *Journal Industrial Economics* (March 1976), pp. 189–202; and W. F. Mueller, "Effects of Antitrust Enfor ment in the Retail Food Industry," *Antitrust Law & Economics Review* (Winter 1968–69), pp. 86–

[4] Corwin D. Edwards, *Economic and Political Aspects of International Cartels* (Washingtc D.C.: Subcommittee on War Mobilization of the Committee on Military Affairs, U. S. Sena 1944), p. 13.

[5] *Ibid.*

United States Government Policy

"Every contract, combination ... or conspiracy, in restraint of trade or commerce among the several States, or with foreign nations, is hereby declared to be illegal." So reads Section 1 of the Sherman Act of 1890. It is the backbone of United States antitrust policy. There are numerous exemptions (regulated industries, export cartels, and milk among them), but this is the basic policy applying to most interstate commerce. As enforced, the law is rather empty of economic content, for violation is a *per se* offense. That is to say, explicit (albeit secret) collusion to fix prices, allocate territories, or otherwise rig the market is illegal *regardless* of the reasonableness or unreasonableness of the economic consequences. The only proof required is proof that conspiracy actually occurred. Indeed, mere *attempts* to fix prices are punishable. This dictum contrasts markedly with the "rule of reason" approach to monopolization cases.

Stringent interpretation of the law dates back to 1897, when the Supreme Court decided *U. S. v. Trans-Missouri Freight Association*. The Court's most explicit early expression of the *per se* doctrine is found in its 1927 opinion *U. S. v. Trenton Potteries*. Twenty three corporations producing 82% of the vitreous pottery fixtures (bathroom bowls, tubs, and so on) in the United States were accused of conspiring to fix prices and limit production. The Court rejected their argument that the "reasonableness" of their prices should be considered, saying that

> The aim and result of every price-fixing agreement, if effective, is the elimination of one form of competition. The power to fix prices, whether reasonably exercised or not, involves power to control the market and to fix arbitrary and unreasonable prices. The reasonable price fixed today may through economic and business changes become the unreasonable price of tomorrow. Once established, it may be maintained unchanged because of the absence of competition secured by the agreement for a price reasonable when fixed. Agreements which create such potential power may well be held to be *in themselves* unreasonable or unlawful restraints ...[6]

This rigorous standard of illegality might lead you to think that businessmen strenuously shun complicity in conspiracies for fear of being caught. Alas, life is not so simple. Well over a thousand civil and criminal prosecutions have been brought under Section 1 and many more will surely follow. Of late, the Justice Department has launched an average of 20 criminal cases a year. With bathroom bowls still fresh on our minds, we should mention that since *Trenton Potteries* in 1927, members of the vitreous plumbing fixture industry have twice been caught and found guilty of further price fixing (a most unsanitary record). The latest conspiracy, in the 1960s, came to light when Internal Revenue

---

[6] *United States v. Trenton Potteries*, 273 U. S. 392 (1927), p. 397. (Emphasis added.)

Service agents stumbled onto three tape recordings of price-fixing meeting stashed in the abandoned desk of a man they were investigating for incom tax evasion. The 15 firms involved include American Standard, Borg-Warne and Kohler Company. Estimates of impact indicate that prices were lifte roughly 7% on $1 billion worth of business. "Price fixing rather than com petition has been a way of life in the industry," commented an industry offici who testified as a key government witness.[7] Unfortunately, this example is n unique. Recidivism is quite common in antitrust.

A major contributor to the problem of widespread and repeated offens is the prevalence of kid-glove penalties. Until very recently, criminal violatio were merely misdemeanors; fines could be measured in peanuts ($50,000 most); suspended sentences were fashionable; jailings were extremely ra and brief; and many civil cases were brought. In short, crime paid. Dona Phillips, the confessed price-fixer we quoted at the outset, put it this wa "When you're doing $30 million a year and stand to gain $3 million by fixir prices, a $30,000 fine doesn't mean much. Face it," he said, "most of us wou be willing to spend 30 days in jail to make a few extra million dollars. Mayl if I were facing a year or more, I would think twice."[8]

Some trend toward more deterrent penalties has developed. Of the 54 perso who went to prison for price fixing and other pure antitrust violations betwe the passage of the Sherman Act in 1890 and January 1977, most of them serve time after 1959. In addition, the Act was amended in 1974 to make crimin violation a *felony*, punishable by as much as 3 years in prison, with fines high as $100,000 for individuals and $1 million for corporations. Of course, remains to be seen whether actual penalties will approach these new maximum Under the old law, maximums were largely ignored. Penalties imposed on t plumbing fixture price fixers, for instance, were harsh by normal antiru standards. Yet jailings in that case ranged from 1 to 60 days as compared wi the 1 year maximum. And fines *totaled* only $752,500, with just five of the firms paying the $50,000 maximum then prevailing.

Violators not only face these criminal sanctions, they may be sued by the victimized buyers for *three times* the financial loss suffered from the co spiracy. In the plumbing fixture case, treble damages were reckoned at $2 million, but out-of-court settlements with the victimized plaintiffs broug actual payments down to $28 million. In broader terms, the popularity treble damage suits has burgeoned since 1960. At one time recently they we running at a rate of more than 2000 suits per year, largely because the electric equipment conspiracies had an immense scope. Since 1960, total damag collected by electric-cartel victims (plus the enviable fees collected by th lawyers) probably exceed $500 million.[9]

[7] See *Washington Post*, June 6, 1971; and *Fortune*, December, 1969.

[8] *Business Week*, June 2, 1975, p. 48.

[9] For more on penalties see K. G. Elzinga and W. Breit, *The Antitrust Penalties: A Study in L and Economics* (New Haven, Conn.: Yale University Press, 1976).

Of "Hunting Grounds" and "Dancing Partners"

Given a punitive *per se* rule, the key remaining question is *what* constitutes "price fixing" or "collusive restraint." There are of course several ways to skin a cat; some are obvious, some obscure. The same applies to cartels. Businessmen have demonstrated brilliant surgical skills when it comes to colluding. Among their more obvious efforts are **single sales agencies**, whereby producers refuse to sell directly to their customers. Instead, they sell through a common central agency. Another fairly clear-cut approach is **market allocations** (or carve-ups), whereby each cartel member is assigned exclusive access to certain geographic areas or customers. An example of this is the "Hunting Grounds Agreement"—a recent international cartel in red phosphorus that, broadly speaking, assigned the Western Hemisphere to the United States company; gave the British Commonwealth countries to the United Kingdom company; restricted northern Europe to the German company; placed eastern Europe plus "The French Community" in the hands of the French company; and left an open "hunting ground" in Asia where all four cartel members could compete for business.[10] Notice that under market allocation arrangements colluders need not do anything so obvious as pool their outputs or set prices collectively (except by quoting high in the other guy's territory). The arrangement converts each firm into a monopolist within his assigned area, thereby achieving a fix.

Still more subtle forms of agreement often involve no direct communications concerning price. Nevertheless, Justice Department lawyers have been able to ferret out many such offenses. One of their most celebrated victories was *U. S. v. Socony-Vacuum* (now called Mobil) in 1940. The defendants were major integrated oil companies accounting for 83% of all gasoline sales in the midwestern states. They instituted a "dancing partner" program in the midwest, under which each major agreed to buy the "surplus" gasoline of some particular independent refinery. "Surplus" was gasoline that could not be disposed of except at "distressed" prices. The independents were small and lacked spacious storage facilities. They consequently sold their "surpluses" at whatever discounted price they could get.

The defendant majors were not accused of direct price fixing. Indeed, their surplus purchases from "partners" were at prices determined by the force of competition in the other sales made by all refiners. The essence of the accusation was that removal of excess supply from the market *indirectly* propped up the price. To be sure, the defendants argued that their activities did not constitute price fixing. They were even so bold as to argue before the Court that their innocence was confirmed by their buying most heavily when prices were *falling* and lightly when prices were *rising*. But of course this is exactly the way

---

[10] Canadian Restrictive Trade Practices Commission, *Report on Trade Practices in the Phosphorus Products and Sodium Chlorate Industries* (Ottawa, 1966).

287

an indirect method of price support should work. And the Court was no fooled:

> That price-fixing includes more than the mere establishment of uniform prices is clearly evident from the Trenton Potteries case itself . . . purchases at or under the market are one species of price-fixing. In this [oil] case, the result was to place a floor under the market—a floor which served the function of increasing the stability and firmness of market prices. . . . Under the Sherman Act a combination formed for the purpose and with the effect of raising, depressing, fixing, pegging, or stabilizing the price of a commodity in interstate or foreign commerce is illegal *per se*.[11]

Trade Associations

Notwithstanding the Court's strong language here, not all collective activity is forbidden. Competitors are still free to form, and to take active part in, trade associations. These associations raise problems, however. Because "education" is a prime purpose of trade associations, it is quite common for them to collec and disseminate information on a wide variety of subjects, prices included Moreover, trade association meetings are conducive to talk of prices. As a former assistant manager for a textile firm said recently: "I don't know wha people would do at a trade association meeting if not discuss prices. They aren' going to talk just about labor contracts and new technology."[12] Fortunately for the consumer, trade association cover cannot immunize outright con spiracies from prosecution. In truth, approximately 30% of all cases brough by the government involve trade associations.

Still, the "information" activities of trade associations do pose ticklish problems for drawing the legal line between what does and what does no constitute price fixing. On the one hand, it can be argued that enhanced knowl edge on the part of industry members lessens market imperfections, thereby fostering more effective competition. On the other hand, too much knowledge may inhibit price competition. Recall from the previous chapter that price cutters often attempt to *conceal* their discounts in order to forestall followship They know that their down-side nonfollowship demand curves may disappea when exposed to the full light of day, leaving them only the inelastic, unat tractive, and unprofitable followship demand curve to contend with.

Illegal information activities are illustrated by the *American Column an Lumber* case of 1921.[13] The hardwood flooring trade association involve required each of 365 participants to submit six reports to its secretary: (1) a daily report of all actual sales: (2) a daily shipping report, with exact copies o the invoices; (3) a monthly production report; (4) a monthly stock report (5) current price lists; and (6) inspection reports. In turn, the trade associatio secretary supplied detailed reports to the firms from this information. The exchange was supplemented by monthly meetings where, among other things

[11] *United States v. Socony-Vacuum Oil Co.*, 310 U. S. 150 (1940).
[12] *Business Week*, June 2, 1975, p. 48.
[13] *American Column and Lumber Co. et. al. v. United States*, 257 U. S. 377 (1921).

speakers urged cartel-like cooperation with exhortations such as, "If there is *to increase in production,* particularly in oak, there is going to be good business," and *"No man is safe in increasing production."* The Supreme Court decided this was "not the conduct of competitors." In subsequent cases the Court has frowned upon trade association programs involving elaborate standardization of the conditions surrounding sales, reports of future prices, and requirements that members must adhere to their reported prices. As regards *permissible* trade association activities, Clair Wilcox once summarized the situation by saying that programs appear to be lawful "when they limit price reports to past transactions, preserve the anonymity of individual traders, make data available to buyers as well as sellers, and permit departure from the prices that are filed."[14]

Conscious Parallelism

We saw in the last chapter that cartelization was only one of a number of suppressors of price competition. Recognized interdependence produces cartels, but it also produces kinked demand curves, price leadership, and uniform cost-plus pricing, all of which—*despite the absence of any explicit agreement*—may yield behavior that closely resembles cartel behavior (namely, high and stable prices). Stated differently, "economic theory has suggested that this kind of noncompetitive behavior might well arise in an 'oligopoly' situation ... without overt communication or agreement, but solely through a rational calculation by each seller of what the consequences of his price decision would be, taking into account the probable or virtually certain reactions of his competitors."[15] Such oligopolistic uniformity of behavior has been called **tacit collusion** or **conscious parallelism**.

How have the courts handled this problem? Does mere conscious parallelism fall within the meaning of "contract, combination, ..., or conspiracy," which are specified by the Sherman Act? In short, is it illegal? The simplified answer that we must limit ourselves to here comes in two installments. First, *in and of itself,* conscious parallelism is *not* illegal. It does not provide conclusive circumstantial evidence of conspiracy. The Supreme Court's clearest statement to this effect is found in the *Theatre Enterprises* case of 1954:

> this Court has never held that proof of parallel business behavior conclusively establishes agreement or, phrased differently, that such behavior itself constitutes a Sherman Act offense ... "conscious parallelism" has not yet read conspiracy out of the Sherman Act entirely.[16]

[14] C. Wilcox, *Public Policies Toward Business,* 3rd ed. (Homewood, Ill.: Richard Irwin, 1966), p. 129.
[15] D. F. Turner, "The Definition of Agreement Under the Sherman Act: Conscious Parallelism and Refusals to Deal," *Harvard Law Review* (February 1962), p. 661.
[16] *Theatre Enterprises, Inc. v. Paramount Film Distributing Corp.,* 346 U. S. 537 (1954). See also *United States v. National Malleable & Steel Castings Co.,* 1957 Trade Cases, para. 68,890 (N. D. Ohio, 1957), *affirmed per curiam,* 358 U. S. 38 (1959).

Second, and on the other hand, consciously parallel behavior may well in dicate an unlawful conspiracy or agreement *when viewed in conjunction wit additional facts.* These additional facts may be subdivided into two categories

1. Additional independent evidence of a more formal agreement, as illustrated by the following:[17]
   (a) Identical sealed bidding on nonstandard items (for example, large turbine generators).
   (b) Basing-point pricing systems, whereby all sellers quote identical delivered prices to any given buyer despite substantial transportation costs and widely differing delivery distances.
   (c) Elaborate exchanges of information, such as those encountered in trade association cases.
   (d) Unnatural product standardization or false denials of interfirm quality differences.
   (e) Simultaneous and substantial price increases (coupled with output reductions) unexplained by any increase in cost.
2. Additional independent evidence that the conduct is restrictive or *exclusionary*, such as
   (a) Parallel buying up of scarce raw materials that are not, in fact, used.
   (b) Parallel and predatory price cutting.
   (c) Crosslicensing of patents.

The *American Tobacco* case of 1946 discussed in the preceding chapter i illustrative.[18] Unlawful conspiracy was found in that case, even though ther was no evidence of meetings in smoke-filled rooms or other rendezvou Parallel pricing behavior (based on Reynold's leadership) was placed in th context of additional facts. In particular, (1) prices were raised despite cos reductions and a massive depression; (2) the three largest companies bough up cheap tobacco they did not use but the "10-cent" brands would have used and (3) the three largest companies cut prices only after the "10-cent" brand won a healthy market share. The Court declared that "No formal agreemen is necessary to constitute an unlawful conspiracy." In this case, conspirac was proved "from the evidence of the action taken in concert" and from "othe circumstances."

Basing-point Pricing

Of all the items listed, perhaps the one in greatest need of further explanatio is the item (b) in group 1—basing-point pricing systems. An example of thi

---

[17] Turner, *op. cit.*, and R. A. Posner, *Antitrust Law, An Economic Perspective* (Chicago: Un versity of Chicago Press, 1976), pp. 62–70.
[18] *American Tobacco Co. v. United States*, 328 U. S. 781 (1946).

s the old "Pittsburgh Plus" single basing-point system of the steel industry. Until 1924 all steel producers, regardless of their mill locations, quoted prices as if they were shipping from Pittsburgh. A steel company located in Gary, Indiana, when quoting a price to a buyer located in nearby Chicago, would add to the factory price the railroad freight cost from Pittsburgh to Chicago, rather than the slight freight cost from Gary to Chicago. The excess transportation charge pinned on the buyer was called "phantom freight."

Conversely, if the Gary plant was quoting a price to a buyer in New York, it would add to the factory price the freight cost from Pittsburgh to New York, rather than the larger and truer freight cost from Gary to New York. This undercharging of New York buyers meant that the seller had to "absorb freight." The mills located at the "base," in Pittsburgh, neither charged phantom freight nor absorbed freight on *any* sale. Their transport charges matched their transport costs. But sellers at all other locations dealt shamelessly in fictitious transport figures. When they were located closer to the buyer than the Pittsburgh mills, they quoted phantom freight. When they were located farther from the buyer than the Pittsburgh mills, they absorbed freight.

The system achieved one particularly important result. As a given *buyer* saw it, *all sellers* were quoting *exactly* the same price to him. This did *not* mean that all buyers were quoted the same price. Buyers close to the base saw low identical quotes. Buyers distant from the base saw high identical quotes. Yet each buyer saw only one price that was cited by all sellers. This result still held true after the industry converted to a *multiple* basing-point system by introducing Gary and Birmingham as additional bases. The base closest to the buyer then provided the key to all quotes. Why would the sellers want to quote identical prices to each buyer? To facilitate collusion and effective price leadership. The systems simplify the pricing of colluding firms. They nullify any interfirm cost advantages attributable to geographic location. They enable the leader to lead with ease from the base. They have also been attacked on these grounds as indicative or supportive of restrictive agreements.[19] In the main, they are therefore now illegal in the United States.

To summarize the overall legal situation, we may call upon a panel of experts, the Supreme Court:

[P]rice fixing is contrary to the policy of competition under the Sherman Act . . . its illegality does not depend on a showing of its unreasonableness, since it is conclusively presumed to be unreasonable. It makes no difference whether the motives of the participants are good or evil; whether the price fixing is accomplished by express contract or by some more subtle means; whether the participants possess market control; whether the amount of interstate commerce affected is large or small; or whether the effect of the agreement is to raise or decrease prices.[20]

[19] *Corn Products Refining Company v. Federal Trade Commission*, 324 U. S. 726 (1945); *FTC , Cement Institute*, 333 U. S. 683 (1948).
[20] *United States v. McKesson & Robbins, Inc.*, 351 U.S. 305 (1956), pp. 309–10.

Determinants of Cartels and
Their Potency

A pet theory of anti-antitrusters is that cartels cannot "really" get off the ground. Or if they do, their life is "short and turbulent." Indeed, an economic Nobel laureate of this persuasion embarassed himself when, shortly after OPEC quadrupled the price of oil in 1973, he publicly predicted that OPEC would self-distruct within a few months. (Now it looks as if OPEC may outlive the laureate.) In a related vein, a few other economists of this persuasion believe that collusive behavior is unrelated to such important structural features as concentration and the number of firms in the market.

The aim of the present section is to show that these views are wrong. They stem from preconceived notions and an empirical literature replete with instances of cartel collapse. This literature is useful, but it gets more respect than it deserves. As George Stigler remarks, "This literature is biased: conspiracies that are successful in avoiding an amount of price-cutting which leads to collapse of the agreement are less likely to be reported or detected."[21] Thus, many cartels endure, even as many fall apart. The feasibility, incidence, and endurance of collusion are all largely determined by structural and technological conditions.[22]

Feasibility and Necessity

Before considering specific conditions, we must make a few preliminary observations. Perhaps the most important thing to keep in mind is that the purpose of all collusion is to maximize joint profits, for only if firms act together can they price and produce like a monopolist. Furthermore, common sense tells us that cartelization occurs only when it is both *feasible* and *necessary* to achieving the objective of joint-profit maximization. If cartelization were not feasible, it surely would not occur. If it were not necessary to achieving the objective, it would likewise not occur, especially if it is illegal and heavily penalized.

The trick, then, is to recognize that "feasibility" and "necessity" are determined by structure. In particular, they vary *inversely* with structure. This relationship is most readily seen through two extreme but simple circumstances, both of which would preclude cartelization. First, where there are hundreds of small firms selling a standardized product (for example, wheat), cartelization is absolutely *necessary* to achieving joint maximization but it is *im*possible to

---

[21] G. J. Stigler, "A Theory of Oligopoly," *Journal of Political Economy* (February 1964), p. 46.
[22] *Ibid*; Posner, *op. cit.*, pp. 47–61; P. Asch, "Collusive Olipology," J. M. Kuhlman, "Natur and Significance of Price Fixing Rings," and W. B. Erickson, "Economics of Price Fixing," al in *Antitrust Law & Economic Review* (Spring 1969), pp. 53–122.

ring off privately (without government approval and imposition). Recognized interdependence is too remote. The incentives for price cutting are too great. Private enforcement of an agreement is too costly in manpower and money. And, if collusion is illegal, detection by the antitrust authorities would be too easy. The result is *no* cartel (unless the government wants to use its police power to establish one). Second, moving to the opposite extreme, imagine a market occupied by just two sellers of a simple standardized product (for example, aluminum ingots). In this case, a private cartel is quite *feasible* but wholly unnecessary to achieving the joint-profit maximization objective. Recognized interdependence is unavoidable, The incentives for price cutting are virtually nil. The opportunity for simple price leadership is clearly open. The chances that "conscious parallelism" will yield a monopoly outcome are very good. And, if explicit collusion is illegal, the wisdom of private cartelization in this case is questionable to say the least. Again the result is *no* cartel. Tacit collusion prevails instead.

To repeat, only when cartelization is both *feasible* and *necessary* to achieving the profit objective are we likely to find it, given a hostile legal environment. When structural conditions are highly unfavorable, necessity and impossibility combine to produce competition. When structural conditions are highly favorable, possibility and a lack of necessity combine to produce *tacit* collusion. In between, necessity and feasibility blend, and cartelization is likely to occur. Stated differently, as important structural conditions vary from most favorable to least favorable for the emergence of collusive behavior, and as legal penalties suppress express collusion, it may be assumed, in general, that conduct ranges from tacit collusion to formal cartelization to independent competitive action.

Effect of Number of Firms

With respect to numbers of firms, these considerations of likelihood lead us to expect that cartel occurrence is least common in markets with either a very large or a very small number of firms. Some intermediate range of "fewness" seems most conducive, since it offers a combination of necessity and feasibility. The present author and Art Fraas tested this expectation by (1) compiling a useable sample of 606 illegal price-fixing conspiracies from the records of all Section 1 prosecutions dispatched between 1910 and 1973; (2) counting the number of firms involved in each of these cases; and (3) computing a frequency distribution for these cases based on the number of firms.[23]

[23] Arthur G. Fraas and D. F. Greer, "Market Structure and Price Collusion: An Empirical Analysis," *Journal of Industrial Economics* (September 1977), pp. 21–44. For related studies see G. A. Hay and D. Kelley, "An Empirical Survey of Price Fixing Conspiracies," *Journal of Law and Economics* (April 1974), pp. 13–38; and A. Phillips, "An Econometric Study of Price-Fixing Market Structure and Performance in British Industry in the Early 1950s" in *Market Structure and Corporate Behavior*, edited by K. Cowling (London: Gray-Mills Publishers, 1972), pp. 177–92.

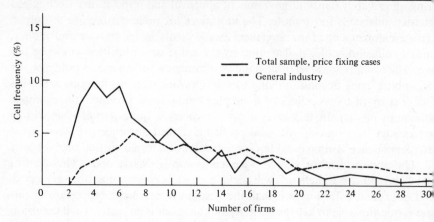

Figure 12-1. *Frequency distribution of numbers of firms involved in price fixing*

The resulting frequency distribution is shown in Figure 12-1 by the solid line The vertical axis there is percentage frequency of each number of firms, a given on the horizontal axis. (Note that no fewer than two firms can conspire For example, in roughly 10% of all the sampled cases of cartelization, fou firms were party to the illegal conspiracy. If by contrast 50% of the sample cases involved four firms and 50% involved five, the distribution would loo like a limbless tree, 50 percentage points tall, rooted at 4 and 5 on the horizonta axis. But this is obviously an improbable vegetable. Rather, the distributio looks more like a camel's back. And, generally speaking, it bears out expecta tion. It has a roughly arched, positive-negative configuration. The positivel sloped portion of the distribution (beginning with two firms and rising) seem to reflect a trade-off between tacit and express collusion, with the incidence explicit collusion rising and the incidence of tacit collusion falling as the numbe of firms in the explicit conspiracies (and in the market)[24] rises. On the othe hand, the negatively sloped portion of the price fixing distribution (beginnin at about six firms) probably reflects a region of trade-off between express collu sion and competitive independence. As the number of firms rises over thi range, express collusion becomes less and less feasible even though the nee for it (in terms of joint-profit maximization) continues to rise.

This plot may be compared to the dotted line distribution of Figure 12-1. I represents all industries generally, not just instances of price fixing. Data fo 1569 narrowly defined manufacturing markets of fairly uniform geographi scope underly the distribution. Moreover, these data are probably neutral t any long-run trend in the number of firms in typical markets because they wer

[24] Hay and Kelley (*op. cit.*) report data on the number of firms in each of 34 conspiracies an the total number of firms in each of the 34 markets involved. The simple correlations between th two is 96.

collected in a year near the midpoint of the period spanned by the sampled price fixing cases—1937. A comparison of the two distributions indicates that a low number of firms is indeed conducive to collusion. The general industry distribution is spread out, whereas the price-fixing distribution is bunched toward the low numbers end. Moreover, the median number of firms for the overall industry distribution is significantly greater than the median for the price fixing sample—18 versus 8.

We now have our first hint as to why many cartels are feeble and fragile while others are strong and durable. If the behavioral trade-off is between tacit collusion and cartelization—that is, if a cartel is set up because tacit collusion is not working well for profit achievement—then the cartel is probably built upon a fairly solid structural foundation. Its prospects appear promising. On the other hand, if the behavioral trade-off is between cartelization and competition—that is, if the cartel amounts to a last gasp effort to pull the industry from the pit of vigorous competition—then the cartel's life expectancy and potential effectiveness naturally seem dim. One implication is that fewness of firms and cartel effectiveness go hand in hand. Unfortunately, no accurate data are available to test this notion systematically. Still, the circumstantial evidence seems favorable to it.[25] One problem with any test of such a proposition is that many factors *other* than firm numbers have an influence. Even as few as two firms might compete wholeheartedly given the right surrounding circumstances.

Other Structural Factors

The theoretical influence of other structural factors is outlined in Table 12-1. The format of the table is illustrated by inclusion of the number of firms in the market as the first condition listed. From left to right across the three columns, the number of firms mentioned rises from "very few" to "many." This pattern accords with the column headings that indicate a declining feasibility but a a rising necessity of cartelization for joint-profit maximization as one reads from left to right.

Concentration. The second condition listed is concentration. The theory behind the table's specifications for this variable should be obvious because concentration is inversely correlated with the number of firms in markets and in conspiracies.[26] High to moderate four-firm concentration would seem to be most conducive to cartelization, as indicated in column (2). Extremely high

---

[25] Fritz Voigt, "German Experience with Cartels and their Control during Pre-War and Post-War Periods," in *Competition, Cartels, and their Regulation*, edited by J. P. Miller (Amsterdam: North-Holland Publishing Co., 1962), p. 171; G. W. Stocking and M. W. Watkins, *Monopoly and Free Enterprise* (New York: Twentieth Century Fund, 1951), p. 112. On the other hand, see R. A. Posner, "A Statistical Study of Antitrust Enforcement," *Journal of Law and Economics* (October 1970), p. 402.

[26] Using Hay and Kelley data again (*op. cit.*), the correlation between concentration and the number of conspirators is −0.69.

TABLE 12-1   Outline of Conditions Affecting the Incidence of Cartelization: Graded on the Basis of Feasibility and Necessity

Market Condition or Characteristic	(1) Feasibility: Excellent Need: Unnecessary (Tacit Collusion)	(2) Feasibility: Good Need: Helpful (Cartel)	(3) Feasibility: Poor Need: Essential (Competition)
Number of firms	Very few (2–5)	Several (5–25)	Many (30+)
Concentration ratio	Very high	High-medium	Low
Type of product	Standardized	Slightly different	Differentiated
Rate of technological change	None	Slow-moderate	Rapid
Frequency (and size) of sales	Frequent (small)	Often (medium)	Lumpy (large)
Opportunity for secret deals	None	Some	Great
Rate of growth	Slow	Medium	Rapid
Elasticity of demand	Low (less 0.5)	Medium	High (2)
Production costs across firms	Identical	Similar	Diverse

concentration would of course foster tacit collusion, and vice-versa for competition. Moreover, George Hay and Dan Kelley found that concentration and cartel stability are positively associated. For their sample of 65 cases "the preponderance of conspiracies lasting ten or more years were in markets with high degrees of concentration."[27]

Firm numbers and concentration are listed first because they seem to be the most important variables mentioned. The other variables can be influential, however, as fewness of firms and high concentration are not sufficient in themselves to assure tacit collusion (although they appear to be essential to such a result). The other variables affect feasibility and necessity for the same basic reasons that numbers and concentration do. They affect the ease of reaching an agreement, the incentive to "cheat" or "double-cross" one's co-conspirators, and the ease of detecting double-crossers.

Type of Product and Technological Change. Type of product and rate of technological change are alike in their influences. Product differentiation or rapid change inject complexities that make it hard to reach an agreement in the first place. These complexities, moreover, make detection of double-crossers more difficult. Price cuts may be shrouded in the folds of product variations.

[27] Hay and Kelley, *op. cit.*, p. 26.

Double-crossing itself can take forms other than price cutting—namely, escalations in advertising or styling or research or some other nonprice variable. In light of these possibilities, it is not surprising that many cartels attempt to standardize their product, restrict advertising, and regulate technological change, for standardization and stagnation are most conducive to cooperation.

Type of Sale and Opportunity for Secret Dealing. If sales move in large lots over intermittent time intervals, then each sales transaction produces a particular and important surge in the seller's revenue stream. The pay-off to any given instance of price shading in this situation can be very lucrative. Temptations to cheat may therefore tug strongly here. This intermittent sales factor, plus healthy doses of rapid technological change and product differentiation, help to explain why the market for commercial airliners is intensely competitive despite its dominance by just two firms—Boeing and McDonnell-Douglas. Infrequent orders of multimillion dollar denominations tend to knock airliner prices into tail spins. As S. L. Carroll observed, "If any collusion, market sharing or market splitting has occurred among the airframe companies, it has been well hidden indeed . . . . The lumpy and discrete nature of orders makes competitive concessions quite tempting."[28] Conversely, an even flow of *frequent* and *small-sized* sales is most accommodating to colluders.

Much the same could be said of opportunities for secret dealing. Where these opportunities are slight, agreements are easy to police and the incentive to double-cross is considerably reduced. Conversely, a prevalence of secrecy enables price discounting under the table, which improves the down-side viability of the seductively elastic nonfollowship demand curve.

Rate of Growth and Elasticity of Demand. A rapid rate of growth in industry demand can upset the best laid plans for several reasons. Perhaps the most important is that the gains to be had from collusion then appear less attractive to potential participants. This may explain why cartels are often called children of depressions. Rapid growth may also confound policing and enforcement efforts. With new customers flocking to the market and old ones expanding their buying, it is difficult to measure market shares and to detect diversions of business that may be caused by double-crossing. Conversely, shares can be pinpointed and diversions due to price shading can be more easily discovered under stable conditions.

Elasticity of demand enters the picture for related reasons. As Hay and Kelley put it, "The more inelastic is industry demand, the greater are the potential rewards to the price fixers. Concomitantly the smaller will be the sacrifice in terms of capacity utilization."[29]

---

[28] Sidney L. Carroll, "The Market for Commercial Airliners," in *Regulating the Product Quality and Variety*, edited by R. Caves and M. Roberts (Cambridge, Mass.: Ballinger, 1975), pp. 150, 163.

[29] Hay and Kelley, *op. cit.*, p. 15.

Production Costs. Finally, it should be obvious why production costs might influence collusion. Widely divergent costs across firms would breed divergent opinions concerning what price should prevail, threatening the success of negotiations. An efficient way of coping with divergent costs is to close down inefficient plants and firms; then devise a profit pooling arrangement whereby the benched third stringers are rewarded for their idleness. But, of course, this also raises difficulties. No one likes being a third stringer, and the compensation fringe firms may therefore request of the first stringers might seem "unreasonably" high. Moreover, such a plan would be more readily detectable by antitrust prosecutors. When discussing costs and cartels F. M. Scherer has also stressed the unsettling impact of uneven cost *changes* across firms: "The more rapidly producers' cost functions are altered through technological innovation, and the more unevenly these changes are diffused throughout the industry, the more likely conflict in pricing action is."[30] He cites an example drawn from an industry now sitting on the edge of your mind: "In the sanitary pottery fixtures industry, conflicts attendant to the introduction of tunnel kilns (replacing more costly beehive oven processes) were in part responsible for the failure of producers to eliminate widespread price-cutting despite repeated attempts to reach collusive agreements."[30]

The Importance of Each Factor. The relative importance of these numerous conditions is difficult to test empirically. Aside from the obvious problems of measuring them and uncovering observations of them (cartelization is after all secretive), their effects in real life are not nearly so neat and straightforward as our simple outline in Table 12-1 implies. The conditions may interact on behavior. Various combinations may be particularly potent or weak. In short, the factors do not willingly submit themselves to systematic analysis. For example, Table 12-1 says that rapid technological change nourishes spirited competition. But, if most other factors favor tacit collusion, rapid technological change may merely force cartelization upon the industry, something which can hardly be considered spirited competition. For another example, Table 12-1 suggests that ten firms are too plentiful to permit effective tacit collusion. But no one would strain himself imagining a ten-firm industry in which nearly all the other conditions point in the direction of tacit collusion—with the result that tacit collusion consequently prevails.

Empirical work is also hampered by the fact the cartels differ in *design.* Two industries might have virtually identical structural conditions. Yet one industry might be successfully cartelized and the other not, despite very serious attempts in the latter case to smother competition. A researcher observing the two industries might well conclude erroneously that some obscure and irrelevant structural difference caused the disparity. However, the true explanation might rest instead on the particular design of the successful cartel. Its penalty system, policing technique, and allocation mechanism might be works of art, with

---

[30] F. M. Scherer, *Industrial Market Structure and Economic Performance* (Chicago: Rand McNally 1970), p. 192.

unique and seemingly unimportant details that make them masterpieces (if that is not too noble a word).

Notwithstanding the difficulties, there are many case studies that provide crude evidenciary support for the assertions of Table 12-1.[31] Further support may be found in a statistical analysis of the 606 cases of illegal price fixing mentioned earlier. Public records on those cases give brief descriptions of the cartels' activities as well as the number of firms involved in each. When applicable, the descriptions mention details such as bid rigging, patent pooling, allocation of territories or customers, production quotas, basing point systems, and trade association involvement.

This information can be used to test the impact of structural conditions and the effectiveness of certain cartel practices if two key assumptions are accepted. First, we assume that specific features of explicit price-fixing arrangements indicate the presence of relevant structural characteristics in the markets involved. To give but two examples, if bid rigging is a part of the cartel's arrangement, it suggests that the flow of product purchases is lumpy rather than smooth. Similarly, if patents occupy a key place in the arrangement, we may suppose that rapid technological change is stirring up competitive "problems" in the market. The second broad assumption is that the official summaries of these cartels are sufficiently accurate about the nature of the arrangments for us to draw inferences from statistical analyses of the data they contain. Unfortunately, this last assumption is a bit shaky because the official summaries are rather sketchy. In fact, they do not contain enough information to allow tests of all the conditions mentioned in Table 12-1. They were written by lawyers, not economists, and they give no inkling of such things as elasticity of demand, opportunities for secrecy, or rate of growth. Complete trial records on these cases would be more revealing, but most price-fixing cases are not tried. The vast majority are settled by *nolo contendere* pleas and consent decrees. Thus the summaries are all we have. Still, they offer enough information to render analysis practicable.

Analysis of Factors Leading to Cartelization

Figure 12-2 illustrates the analytical technique employed. It contains three stylized frequency distributions of numbers of firms, such as those seen earlier in Figure 12-1. In Figure 12-2 each distribution represents a different subsample of price-fixing cases, but all the curves are price-fixing distributions. The solid center curve of distribution represents cases of "simple" price fixing. That is to say, it is assumed that these conspiracies involved nothing more than

---

[31] F. Voight, *op. cit.*; Stocking and Watkins, *op. cit.*; H. C. Passer, *The Electrical Manufacturers: 1875–1900* (Cambridge, Mass.: Harvard University Press, 1953); G. B. Richardson, "The Pricing of Heavy Electrical Equipment: Competition or Agreement?" *Bulletin of the Oxford University Institute of Economics and Statistics* (1966), pp. 73–92; S. M. Loescher, *Imperfect Collusion in the Cement Industry* (Cambridge, Mass.: Harvard University Press, 1959).

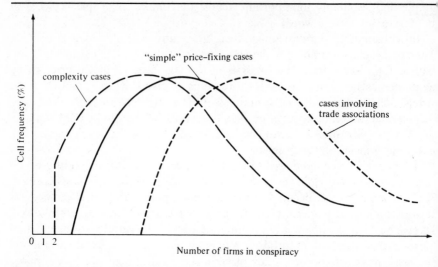

Figure 12-2. The effects of structural complexities and "efficient" cartel devices.

an agreement to charge certain prices. The positive-negative bell shape indicates that the number of firms in the market affects the incidence of cartelization in the same manner as in Figure 12-1. The positive slope suggests a region of trade-off between tacit and explicit collusion. The negative portion implies a region of trade-off between explicit collusion and competition. Aside from the number of firms, however, the solid-line distribution assumes no further structural complications—that is, no bid rigging, no patent pooling, no efforts to standardize a differentiable product.

The introduction of other structural complexities into the market setting would complicate the process of obtaining any collusive agreement, tacit or explicit. Were they present, we should expect them to produce a leftward shift of the observed frequency distribution. The added complexities should cause tacit-explicit *and* the explicit-competitive trade-offs to occur at *fewer* firms than otherwise. Such a leftward shift is shown in Figure 12-2 by the "complexity cases" curve. In contrast, some of the arrangements actually identified in the case summaries were probably devised not so much for purposes of coping with a particular structural complexity as for purposes of improving the efficiency and effectiveness of the price fixing arrangement. As the number of parties to a conspiracy increases, coordination becomes increasingly difficult, but trade associations, single-selling agencies, and coercive or disciplinary practices should serve to bolster coordination. Because these arrangements or activities extend the range of possible price fixing over larger numbers of firms, we should expect to see the frequency distribution of cases with these arrangements to be located to the *right* of the "simple" price fixing distribution. This shift is indicated by the dotted line distribution on the right-hand side of Figure 12-2.

TABLE 12-2   A Statistical Portrait of 606 Cases of Illegal Price Fixing

Subsample Group	(1) Number of Cases	(2) Mean Number of Firms	(3) Median Number of Firms	(4) Relative Location of Dist.
Total cases	606	16.7	8	—
Indications of complexity				
Bid rigging	113	9.7	6 [a]	Left
Patents involved	62	7.8	6 [a]	Left
International scope	62	8.2	5 [a]	Left
Standardization attempted	28	17.1	9	(Center)
Basing point system	14	15.1	9	(Center)
Market allocations	158	13.4	7 [b]	Left
Potency enhancers				
Trade associations	219	30.3	16 [a]	Right
Single sales agent	16	35.8	16 [b]	Right
Coercion-exclusion	70	16.6	10 [c]	Right
Price discrimination	40	30.4	8	(Center)

[a] Median significantly different from all other cases at the 1% level.
[b] Median significantly different from all other cases at the 5% level.
[c] Median significantly different from all other cases at the 10% level.
Source: A. G. Fraas and D. F. Greer, "Market Structure and Price Collusion: An Empirical Analysis," *Journal of Industrial Economics* (September 1977).

Table 12-2 provides a summary portrait of the 606 cases. Aside from the top line, which gives an overall report, the cases are assigned to subsamples according to the characteristics attributed to them in the official records. An attempt has been made, using liberal doses of subjective judgment, to divide the subsamples into two groups. The characteristics listed under "indications of complexity" suggest that the market serving as the scene of the crime suffered structural complications. Conversely, the characteristics listed under "potency enhancers" seem to be devices or elements that improved the reach and effect of the price fixing effort. Perhaps "market allocations," which are included in the first group, should be transferred to this latter group, but it can be argued that allocations might indicate particularly acute cost difficulties.

Looking now to the body of Table 12-2, note that column (1) reports the number of cases displaying each characteristic. Of course any single case could entail more than one characteristic (for example, attempted standardization of product plus basing-point pricing). Hence, the number of cases in this column adds up to more than 606.

Columns (2) and (3) present the mean (average) and median number of firms involved in each case in the total sample and in each subsample. The frequency distribution of the number of firms in each of these subsamples is more or less bell-shaped but skewed to the right (as suggested in Figures 12-1 and 12-2), so the median number of firms falls short of the mean in every instance. Because of this skewness, the mean is exaggerated by extremely high values; therefore the median is the better summary statistic of location among the subsamples When the median of the cases in each subsample is compared to the median of all the cases (or, more precisely, of all the other cases outside each subsample) we obtain a rough index of whether the number of firms in the subsample's cases tends to be relatively high or low. Stated differently, we see whether the subsample's distribution is an instance of "shift left" or "shift right," as suggested in Figure 12-2.

This directional view is summarized in column (5). Thus we find that relatively small numbers of firms appear to be involved in cases concerning bid rigging, patents, international trade, and market allocations—that is, cases evincing structural complexities. Conversely, trade associations, single sales agencies, and coercion-exclusion appear to be typically associated with a relatively large number of colluding firms. Trade association involvement seems especially significant in improving the reach and effectiveness of price-fixing activity. Such associations apparently foster a "social climate" favorable to effective collusion. In addition, trade association gatherings may provide good "neutral" grounds for price-fixing meetings, and their officials may often serve as impartial mediators for the resolution of disputes.

In short, evidence indicates that the structural conditions most favorable to tacit cooperation are a relatively small number of rival firms in a market setting relatively free of complications. Moreover, a variety of regimental or disciplinary devices facilitates tacit or explicit collusion under more adverse structural conditions. To state these results somewhat differently: evidence suggests that, as the number of firms in the market or the complexity of structural conditions increases, conspirators must resort to arrangements of increasingly elaborate design or efficiency to achieve their joint profit-maximizing objectives. Indeed, this finding probably explains why many elaborately formal cartels are eventually undermined by double-crossing, bickering, and dissolution. Elaborate cartels probably arise most often where structural conditions are more favorable to *competition* than to collusion. However, to conclude from this that cartels are nearly always short-lived and feeble would be wrong. In the region of trade-off between tacit and express collusion, at least, cartels probably yield stable and substantial gains for their organizers (as well as losses for their customers).

The Electrical Equipment Cases[32]

The electric equipment cases are to American price fixing what Watergate is to American political corruption. The collusive activity began some time in the

---

[32] This section draws from R. G. M. Sultan, *Pricing in the Electrical Oligopoly, Vol. 1* (Cambridge Mass.: Harvard University Press, 1974); C. C. Walton and F. W. Cleveland, Jr., *Corporations on Trial: The Electrical Cases* (Belmont, Calif.: Wadsworth, 1964); and R. A. Smith, *Corporations in Crisis* (Garden City, N.Y.: Anchor Books, 1966), Chapters 5 and 6.

TABLE 12-3 Extent and Coverage of the Electrical Equipment Price Fixing Conspiracies

Product	Annual (1959) Dollar Sales ($ millions)	Number of Firms Indicted	Share of Market (%)
Turbine generators	$400*	3 (6)*	95 (100)
Industrial control equipment	262*	9*	75*
Power transformers	210	6	100
Power switchgear assemblies	125	5 (8)*	100
Circuit breakers	75	5	100
Power switching equipment	35*	8 (15)*	90–95*
Condensers	32	7	75–85
Distribution transformers	220	8	96
Low-voltage distribution equip.	200*	6 (10)*	95*
Meters	71	3	100
Insulators	28	8	100
Power capacitors	24	6	100
Instrumental transformers	16*	3 (4)*	95*
Network transformers	15	6	90
Low-voltage power circuit breakers	9	3 (5)*	100
Isolated phase bus	7.6	4	100
Navy and marine switchgear	7	3	80
Open-fuse cutouts	6	8	75
Bushings	6	4	100
Lightning arresters	16	7	100

* Includes companies named as co-conspirators but not indicted.

Source: Adapted from *Corporations on Trial: The Electrical Cases* by Clarence C. Walton and Frederick W. Cleveland, Jr., © 1964 by Wadsworth Publishing Company, Inc., Belmont, California 94002. Reprinted by permission of the publisher.

1920s or 1930s (it was so long ago no one seems to know exactly when). At first it was a rather casual adjunct to the industry's trade association activities, involving just a few products. By the 1950s, however, conspiracy had spread to every corner of the trade. Table 12-3 gives some idea of the vast scope of the price fixing and of the structure of the markets involved. Roughly $7 billion of business was involved. The products ranged from $2 insulators to multimillion dollar turbine generators. The average number of firms participating in each market was 6.6. Several of the larger participants—such as General Electric, Westinghouse, Allis Chalmers, McGraw-Edison, and I-T-E Circuit Breaker—operated and conspired in many of the markets. Smaller firms—like Moloney

Electric and Wagner—were more specialized. In all, 29 firms and 44 individual were indicted during 1960 for criminal conspiracies in 20 separate produc lines.

Table 12-3 gives the impression that high concentration and a paucity of firm might have permitted tacit collusion in four or five of these markets. But con ditions not revealed in the table provided substantial competitive pull, thereb abetting explicit collusion. First, many of these products were not standardizec but custom made and differentiable. Various collusive steps were taken to standardize product quality, especially in the early years. Second, many item of equipment were sold in big chunks, which amplified the incentive to cu prices to gain business. Even without given product lines, large orders receivec larger discounts off "book" price than small orders. A third factor was the volatility of the business cycle in the electrical apparatus field. These good are durable capital equipment and experience fluctuations in demand fa beyond those encountered by most other industries. Slack demand seems to hav caused much price cutting, even when the conspiracies were in high gear Finally, technological change was fairly brisk during the decades involved.

Collusive procedures and experiences varied from product to product, fron sealed-bid sales to off-the-shelf transactions, and from higher to lower level of management. One common thread, however, was the atmosphere of skull duggery surrounding all the conspiracies. Code names, pay-phone communica tions, plain envelope mailings, destruction of evidence, clandestine meetings in out-of-the-way places, faked expense account records, and secret market al locations all entered the plot. Perhaps the most sensational technique devisec was the "phase of the moon" system developed for sealed-bid switchgea sales:

> This system was intended to fix automatically the price each conspirator would quote, with a rotation of the low price among competitors to create the illusion of random competition. The contemplated range of bid prices was modest. According to the "moon sheet," which was in effect from December 5, 1958 through April 10, 1959, position would be rotated among the five major competitors every two weeks.[33]

Disclosure of the system inspired some jokester in General Electric to rewrite the words to the then popular song "Moonglow." Sung to the same tune, the first verse went like this: "It must have been Moonglow/ Way up in the blue, It must have been Moonglow/ That brought that bid to you."[34]

Despite all the shenanigans, it is not clear that the conspirators were able to raise or stabilize prices appreciably in all product lines. Double-crossing wa fairly commonplace. A "white sale" drove prices down to 60% of book in 1955 Many participants have made self-serving claims that their efforts failed, anc it can be argued that supply and demand remained prime determinants of price

[33] Sultan, op. cit., p. 39.
[34] The second verse is less entertaining: "I still hear them saying/As they rigged the price/The customer's paying/Too much but its so nice." J. G. Fuller, The Gentlemen Conspirators (New York Grove Press, 1962), p. 66.

evel.[35] On the other hand, a federal trial judge was persuaded by the evidence that prices of turbine generators would have been 21% lower were it not for the conspiracy. In addition, much evidence indicates a substantial price impact in the sealed-bid sector of the trade plus some indirect overall effect via stabilization of market shares.[36] In any event, economic consequences were relevant only to the treble damage suits, which yielded $400 million, or thereabouts. The government's criminal suits were settled under the *per se* rule, with seven executives serving brief stints in the slammer and with fines totaling $1,954,000, the bulk of which was paid by the companies.

The Oil Industry and OPEC[37]

Of the oil industry's several sectors—crude extraction, transportation, refining, and marketing—crude extraction (hereafter called "crude") is the most interesting to us here. Both in the United States and abroad that sector has spawned some rather remarkable cartels or "near" cartels. At the same time competition has not been altogether absent. For most of its history, the crude industry seems to have been caught in the region of trade-off between cartelization and competition. Calouste Gulbenkian, a pioneer of Iraqui oil development, may have said it best when he quipped, "Oilmen are like cats; you can never tell from the sound of them whether they are fighting or making love."

This turbulent blend should lead anyone who has followed the discussion this far to anticipate at least two aspects of the oil story: (1) many oil cartels have been less than love-ins, and (2) the most enduring and significant cartels have been encouraged, supported, and run by government agencies (exempted thereby, or beyond the reach of the Sherman Act). The crude industry's habit of falling under collectivized or centralized control—either private or official— has led many observers to argue that "socially acceptable operation of the

---

[35] Sultan is the industry's best defender, *op. cit.*

[36] Sultan, *op. cit.*, 85, 210, 273; J. D. Ogur, "Competition and Market Share Instability," Staff Report to the Federal Trade Commission (August 1976), pp. 30–47.

[37] Main sources for this section are M. G. de Chazeau and A. E. Kahn, *Integration and Competition in the Petroleum Industry* (New Haven, Conn.: Yale University Press, 1959); M. A. Adelman, *The World Petroleum Market* (Baltimore: Johns Hopkins University Press, 1972); J. M. Blair, *The Control of Oil* (New York: Pantheon Books, 1976); N. H. Jacoby, *Multinational Oil* (New York: Macmillan Publishing Co., 1974); R. Engler, *The Brotherhood of Oil* (Chicago: University of Chicago Press, 1977); Anthony Sampson, *The Seven Sisters* (New York: Viking Press, 1975); U.S. Senate, Subcommittee on Multinational Corporations of the Committee on Foreign Relations, *Report on Multinational Oil Corporations and U. S. Foreign Policy* (U. S. G.P.O., 1975); U. S. Senate, Subcommittee on Antitrust and Monopoly of the Committee on the Judiciary, *Hearings on Government Intervention in the Market Mechanism: Petroleum*, parts 1-5, 91st Congress, First and Second Sessions (1969, 1970); Walter Measday, "The Petroleum Industry" in *The Structure of American Industry*, edited by W. Adams (New York: Macmillan Publishing Co., 1977); E. T. Penrose, *The Large International Firm in Developing Countries* (Cambridge, Mass.: The MIT Press, 1968); S. L. McDonald, *Petroleum Conservation in the United States* (Baltimore: Johns Hopkins Press, 1971). For a theoretical discussion see Richard Gilbert, "Dominant Firm Pricing Policy in a Market for an Exhaustible Resource," *Bell Journal of Economics* (Autumn 1978), pp. 385–95.

industry *necessarily requires* either government regulation of output or th
domination of the industry by firms large enough to excercise a strong contro
over total output and to keep competition, especially price competition
within very narrow limits."[38]

In short, the belief of such observers in a "natural" need for centralization
rests on the assumption that the industry is inherently unstable, so unstable a
to bring forth booms and busts unless somehow "regulated."

The instability is blamed on a combination of four main characteristics
(1) uncertain and violently erratic results of oil exploration that whip the in
dustry's supply curve about like a sapling in changes of the wind, (2) hig
overhead or fixed costs (plus in the United States a "law of capture") tha
impart price inelasticity to the supply curve, (3) very low price elasticity o
demand in the short run, due to the "essential" nature of the product, and (4
cyclical swings in demand. Given the inelasticity conditions, prices must fa
abysmally low to choke off supply or stimulate demand. Conversely, price
must climb sky-high to curb demand or boost output significantly. Althoug
inelasticity alone is no problem, the added presence of shifts and swings mea
that prices are frequently called upon to perform these difficult feats. In othe
words, the industry is said to be less self-adjusting than most: "hectic prosperit
is followed all too swiftly by complete collapse, and redress can be hoped fo
only from the efforts of 'eveners', adjusters, and organizers."

Not all experts hold this view; many refute it. Although we cannot pursu
the debate here, there seems to be enough truth to the instability argument to
give industry leaders and governments an excuse to play the part of "eveners
adjusters, and organizers." (Of course governments have also been spurred to
action by the strategic military and economic importance of oil.) Our discus
sion of these cartelization efforts is split between the domestic United State
and foreign markets.

United States Domestic Crude Oil

Figure 12-3 reveals that prior to 1934 the price of domestic crude oil wa
highly unstable. The solid line shows peaks and valleys in price level of alpin
proportions in those years. Moreover, the high frequency of change—as in
dicated by the dashed line—was equally unsettling. The data traced ther
actually understate the true volatility because they refer to a representativ
posted price, not to actual *transactions* prices, which fluctuated even mor
wildly. For example, discovery of the immense East Texas Field in 1930 anc
the country's simultaneous slide into depression combined to press down th
posted price shown in Figure 12-3 to 61 cents a barrel in 1933, but some transac
tion prices fell to the amazingly low figure of 10 cents a barrel. As just mentioned
this instability may be attributed to the "law of capture" as well as to inelas
ticities and shifts of supply and demand. Under the "law of capture" crude oi

---

[38] Penrose, *op. cit.*, p. 165.

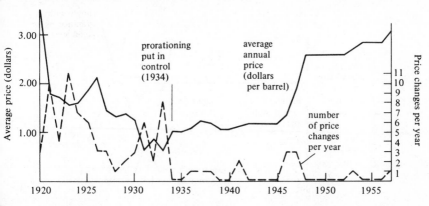

Figure 12-3. Price level and changes for U.S. crude oil, Oklahoma 36° gravity.
Source: M. G. deChazeau and A. E. Kahn, Integration and Competition in the Petroleum Industry, *(New Haven: Yale University Press, 1959), pp. 138, 148-9.*

belongs to whomever gets it out first. Couple this law with (1) fragmented property ownership over a given oil reservoir, (2) the fluid nature of the stuff, plus (3) generous amounts of greed, and you have a mad rush to drain the reservoir. The goal of each owner was simply (and crudely): "get it out while the getting's good." The results were:

- Appalling *physical waste*, because of reckless damage of the reservoir's natural drive pressures, loss of oil by evaporation in makeshift open-air storage vats, loss of oil by ground seepage from pit storage, and so forth.
- Enormous "*economic waste*," because of extraction and consumption of crude oil when its value was low and excessive investment in drilling and rigging.
- Shameful *environmental damage*, both because of the ugliness of oil rig forests and the pollution of streams and soils from oil run-off.
- Added *instability* of prices and producer incomes.

Broad-based private cartelization was impossible, given the thousands of producers. Hence, during the depths of greatest difficulty in the early 1930s, remedial steps were taken by state and federal authorities that eventually led to a table-like structure of price support resting on four legs: (1) demand prorationing, (2) the Connally "Hot" Oil Act, (3) the Interstate Oil Compact, and (4) import quotas.

State Controls. **Demand prorationing** is a system of flexible production control first instituted by state authorities in Oklahoma and Texas, later

307

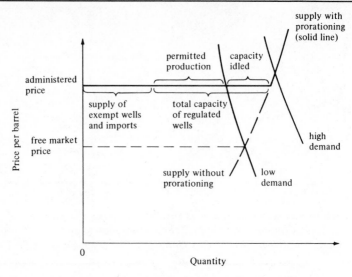

Figure 12-4. *Restriction of supply under demand prorating, lifting prices to "administered level" above free market level.*

emulated in Louisiana, Kansas, and New Mexico (thus including the states most bountifully blessed with oil). Its effects on prices may be seen in Figure 12-3, where after 1934 prices are much less volatile than before. Moreover, those changes that do occur thereafter are almost always increases.

Operation of the system is illustrated in Figure 12-4. In essence, supply is restricted or expanded to whatever level is necessary for price to be at or above the "administered price" level. The supply curve looks like an L lying down. This configuration means that supply is perfectly price elastic up to full capacity use (at the corner of the L). Thereafter, the supply curve that prevails in the absence of prorationing takes over. (Thus if underlying supply capabilities should expand or contract, the long arm of the L lengthens or shortens with rightward or leftward shifts of the unfettered supply.) Not all wells are subject to regulation, the main exemptions being "discovery" wells and inefficient "strippers," the latter being wells physically incapable of producing more than a few barrels a day. Moreover, state authorities have no control over imports into the United States. Hence, exempt and import supplies are subtracted from projected demand before determining the output allowed from the regulated wells. In short, the fraction of allowed capacity utilization is reckoned monthly by the following formula:

$$\text{fraction of capacity utilization for regulated wells} = \frac{\text{demand} - (\text{exempts} + \text{imports})}{\text{total capacity of regulated wells}}$$

Allowable utilization therefore decreases with decreased demand or increased imports, exempt capacity, and total regulated capacity. In Figure 12-4 the fraction for "low demand" is about 0.7, whereas that for "high demand" is 1.0. Competitive drilling is limited indirectly through regulations defining what constitutes "total capacity" for each producer. These definitions embody well pacing formulas, which for many years were faulty in not eliminating law-of-capture competitive drilling completely.

Federal Controls. As for the three other legs of price support, all are federal measures. The Connally "Hot" Oil Act of 1935 prohibits the interstate shipment of crude oil (or products refined from crude oil) produced in excess of the state allowables. Without this law, state officials doing the prorationing were handicapped. Cheating was easy. The year 1935 also saw passage of the Interstate Oil Compact Commission Act, which provides a forum for the prorationing agencies of producing states. There they can collude and coordinate their "conservation" efforts lest they compete with each other at the state level for ever larger shares of national output. Finally, mandatory import quotas came much later, beginning in 1959.

During the early years of prorationing, restrictions on imports were not needed. The United States dominated world oil in those days, being the richest in then-known reserves, the most productive, and the largest exporter. As late as 1949 the United States accounted for 36% of the world's reserves and 55% of its production. Until World War II, moreover, all international shipments of crude were priced according to a "Houston-plus" single basing-point system. Thereafter, United States fortunes began three decades of decline. Development of superabundant and cheap Mideastern supplies threatened the United States industry. A new basing point was established in the Persian Gulf, and United States prices rose relative to those of the new base. As this price differential widened, United States imports multiplied several times over, gushing in at a rate of 18.3% of total United States crude consumption by 1958, the year before mandatory quotas.

The consequences for United States production were enormous. In that year capacity utilization of Texas's regulated wells was only 33%, down from 100% utilization in 1948. Imports were not the sole cause of this, however. Ample exemptions from prorationing in states with prorationing, an absence of prorationing in less nicely endowed and more costly crude-producing states (such as Mississippi, Colorado, Wyoming, and Montana, which in 1958 were producing at 86 to 100% of capacity), some unchecked competitive drilling in several states, and tax incentives that encouraged needless drilling everywhere also contributed to the problem. These several factors raised United States costs, precluding a painless price cut to meet the foreign competition. Indeed, the price of Texan crude was actually *increased* at the behest of producers, once in mid-1953, then again in January 1957.

Bloated by high costs (which pinched consumers $2.15 billion a year) but flush with political clout (owing to campaign contributions and bribes as well

309

as popular votes), the industry escaped threat when the federal government se quotas to limit imports (quotas of sufficient magnitude that they cost cor sumers an additional $7 to $8 billion a year). "National defense" was prc claimed the reason. The regrettable influence of factors other than imports ma be seen by the fact that later, in 1964, after the quota program was in full swin regulated wells in Texas were held to only 28 % of their full capacity. Those i Louisiana and Oklahoma were also working only 32 % and 28 % of the time Finally, the effect of prorationing can be seen by comparing the price develo ments in states with and without prorationing; the latter generally maintaine full capacity utilization. Prices in *non*prorationing states were from one t *nine times* more variable than prices in prorationing states over the perio 1948–1967.[39]

As this is written (1977), prorationing allowables are pegged at 100 %, an they have been since 1972. Import quotas have been discontinued since 197. The Connally "Hot" Oil Act and Interstate Compact Commission Act al still on the books but superfluous. The first sign of change occurred withou popular notice in 1969; ominously, United States productive capacity began continuing decline. At current rates of consumption and growth in consum tion, the United States will virtually run out of crude petroleum within ou life-times—namely, the year 2005, give or take a decade or so. Another sign c exhaustion that may influence policy is a trend toward higher concentratio in reserve ownership and production. The eight largest firms accounted fc 36 % of United States crude production in 1955, but 54 % in 1973. With eve greater centralization of domestic control, something that seems certain, privat collusion of various sorts might be able to take over the government's job c "evening, adjusting, and organizing."

The International Crude Oil Market

Inside the United States the last three decades have seen some decline i government cartelization plus some increase in private centralization, be opposite trends have occurred in the international sphere. Prior to about 195 the foreign sector was rife with the cartel handiwork of the major companie the eldest of the Seven Sisters in particular. Between 1950 and 1970 the powe of the Seven Sisters diminished. And finally, since 1970, OPEC, a cartel con prised of the *governments* of 13 of the world's leading crude exporting countrie (controlling 85 % of all exports), has taken command.

Before 1950. The **Seven Sisters** are Exxon, BP (British Petroleum), Shel Gulf, Texaco, Socal (Standard of California), and Mobil. They came by the

---

[39] McDonald, *op. cit.*, pp. 190–91.

.llective name because, like mortal sisters, they fought and competed with
.ch other while preserving a family affinity.[40] As E. Penrose once wrote:

> The problem of deciding whether the operation of the industry in any period is best
> described in terms of an "international petroleum cartel" or of the rivalries among the
> firms engaged in it, is precisely the problem of deciding how much weight to give to
> the competitive as contrasted to the co-operative elements, and it must be admitted
> that the latter often seemed to be predominant.[41]

.e Seven Sisters stood virtually (but not virtuously) alone in foreign trade
.ior to 1950. They controlled crude prices and output in the producing
.untries through cartel arrangements among themselves and by concession
.reements with foreign producing country governments. Under "concessions"
.ese governments ceded to the oil companies authority to engage in the
.ploration and exploitation of certain territories, which in the early days
.nounted to entire countries. In exchange, the companies paid royalties and
.xes on oil extracted.

We shall skip over the "Red Line" and "As Is" agreements, two cartels of
.e pre-World War II era instigated by Exxon, Shell, and BP. Instead, we shall
.cus on the postwar origins of Aramco, which brought Socal, Texaco, Exxon,
.d Mobil together in what eventually proved to be the richest concession of
.l—Saudi Arabia. Strictly speaking Aramco was a joint-venture, not a cartel,
.t it typifies the cooperative arrangements that replaced the prewar cartels
.d formed the basis for intercompany cooperation during the 1950s and
.60s. Moreover, it neatly illustrates the competitive-cooperative behavior of
.e Sisters.

Here is the story.[42] As of 1947 the Saudi Arabian concession was entirely
.the hands of Socal and Texaco, two newcomers to the international scene of
.e times, who had developed it from scratch, beginning in 1936. They operated
.ramco through a joint-venture called "Caltex." More important, their ex-
.usive ownership of those enormous oil reserves made the industry more
.mpetitive by threatening the market power of the then more well-established
.ternational majors—Exxon, Mobil, and BP:

> By 1947, Caltex had tripled its market share both East and West of Suez. With 33¢ a
> barrel production costs, Caltex could market Arabian crude for as little as 90¢ a barrel
> while the older international majors were selling for $1.30 and up . . . . Exxon and
> Mobil rightly concluded that their longterm market prospects in Europe were un-
> favorable if they failed to get a share of the vast low-cost reserves of [Aramco].

Exxon and Mobil launched a two-part plan: (1) buy into Caltex's Aramco,
.d (2) once in, secure a 50% price increase for Aramco's crude. As Exxon and
.obil saw it, there were only two main obstacles to their scheme. First, if

---

[40] Sampson, *op. cit.*, p. 59.
[41] Penrose, *op. cit.*, p. 150.
[42] Distilled from *Report on Multinational Oil Corps.*, *op. cit.*, Chapters II and IV.

TABLE 12-4 Outline of the Shift of Power from the Seven Sisters to OPEC, 1950–1973

Index of Power	Year			
	1950	1960	1970	1972/3
A. Power of the 7 sisters				
1. Market share abroad (%)	88	72	71	71
2. Strength of collusive agreements	Joint-ventures	Independents arrive	Independents a problem	Disarray
3. U. S. production as per cent of world (%)	54	36	23	21
4. Spare capacity (U. S. imports per cent of consumption) (%)	9	13	23	36
B. Power of OPEC				
1. "Free" world production (%)	(No OPEC)	45	61	63
2. Knowledge	—	Poor	Good	Very good
3. Unity of interest	—	Weak	Moderate	Strong
4. Boldness	—	Meek	Pushy	Brassy
5. Strength of demand (oil as per cent of total world energy) (%)	—	36	44	46

altex discovered their true intentions, the deal would collapse. Part two of the
an was therefore kept secret pending completion of part one. The second
obstacle concerned antitrust. Mobil's chief attorney explained the problem in
confidential memo:

The arrangement would place practical control of crude reserves in the Eastern
Hemisphere in the hands of seven companies . . . . there is, of course, possibility that
the mere existence of the potential control might under the American Tobacco Company decision be construed as an antitrust violation. I cannot believe that a comparatively few companies for any great length of time are going to be permitted to control
world oil resources without some sort of regulation.

As it turned out, he was wrong. The deal went through without any antitrust
position, Exxon buying 30% and Mobil buying 10%, leaving Caltex 60%.
For its part, Caltex agreed to the arrangement because it was short of develop-
ent capital and marketing outlets, both of which Exxon and Mobil had in
abundance. In addition, Caltex deliberately decided that some cooperation
ght be better than competition. When drawing up the papers, Exxon and
Mobil were able to insert technical language, which went unnoticed by Caltex,
facilitate the price increase part of their plan. Hence, "No sooner had the
Aramco merger contracts been signed than a major fight erupted between
altex and Exxon/Mobil over the price of Arabian Oil." The fight was bitter.
Caltex felt cheated. But Exxon and Mobil pressed hard. A Mobil representative
en turned sarcastic. "I hope and trust," he said, "our Texas friends will . . .
rn to Webster's and look up the definition of 'partnership.' I am quite sure it
es not define it as 'a combination of people welshing on their original agree-
ent because it temporarily does not suit their own self-interest.'" In the end
Exxon and Mobil won. Aramco's price jumped 40% to $1.43.

From 1950 to 1973. Table 12-4 outlines the shifting balance of power from
50 to 1973, a period of "recognized interdependence" rather than carteliza-
on. As of 1950, OPEC had not yet been formed. The Seven Sisters lorded over
with 88% of all foreign production and a seamless web of joint-ventures
ch as Aramco) binding them together. However, as the first two lines of
ble 12-4 indicate, their power thereafter declined. Among the many "in-
pendent" companies entering the foreign market during the 1950s and 1960s
re Amerada-Hess, ARCO, Citgo, Getty, Occidental, Phillips, Marathon,
d Sun. A number of government-owned oil companies, such as ENI of Italy,
so began shouldering their way into ever larger roles.

The added competition was one major cause of foreign market price reduc-
ons during the 1950s. A second factor pulling prices down was the United
ates import quota program of the late 1950s. It sealed off the world's most oil-
irsty market and diverted foreign supplies elsewhere. A third cause of price
pression grew with an enormous increase in Russian oil exports, from zero
1950 to 380,000 barrels a day in 1960.

313

These several developments combined to lower transactions prices fir
then posted prices. By 1959, some discounts off the posted price of $2.08 r
as high as 40¢. To the oil companies the "posted" price was essentially fictior
because it applied to *intra*firm sales. The owners of Aramco, for examp
sold to themselves at this price. However, the posted price was by no mea
fictional to oil-producing country governments, for their revenues were key
to that price. Hence, when the majors unilaterally reduced posted prices
1959 and 1960 to better reflect transactions prices, Saudi Arabia, Iran, Ira
Kuwait, and Venezuela threw tantrums. More important, they responded
forming OPEC to make their views felt and protect their interests.

Before discussing OPEC, however, we should mention lines A3 and A4
Table 12-4. Much of the Sisters' strength depended on the relative position
the United States in the world market. And the numbers in those lines indica
a steady decline in United States position as measured by production sha
and dependence on foreign supplies. Decline may also be measured by Americ
inefficiency at the end of 1972. The United States then had 526,000 producing
wells yielding an average output of 18 barrels a day. In the Middle East, wi
different laws of man and Nature, 3000 wells each produced an average
5530 barrels a day. (The numbers may astound you, but they ought not
given our earlier discussion of the United States industry.)

Turning to the bottom half of Table 12-4, we see that at first, in 1960, OPE
was not much to look at. Accounting for less than half of "free" world produ
tion, OPEC lacked full knowledge of the trade, solidarity, and boldness. OPEC
only real achievement in its early years was to prevent further cuts in post
prices. With time, and with the addition of Indonesia, Nigeria, Libya, Alger
Qatar, United Arab Emirates, Gabon, and Ecuador to its membership, OPE
grew powerful in measurable and unmeasurable ways. Its shares of wor
production and exports burgeoned, while the world's dependency on oil reach
addictive dimensions.

In such intangeables as knowledge, solidarity, and boldness, changes occurr
that can only be touched upon here. For example, one of OPEC's first ad
was to commission an independent research study of the profits the Sisters we
earning on their investments in the Middle East and Venezuela. They fou
that "between 1956 and 1960, the rate of return on net assets was 71 per cent
Iran, 62 per cent in Iraq, 14 per cent in Qatar, 61 per cent in Saudi Arabia, a
20 per cent in Venezuela."[43] (Later, in 1970, the U. S. Department of Co
merce released estimates that Mideastern oil industry investments earned
79% return, thus exceeding OPEC's numbers. These amazing profits a
partly explained by the fact that unit costs amount to no more than about 2
a barrel in the Middle East.)

The eagerness of newly entering independents to bid high for concessio
taught other lessens. Libya correctly foresaw that its oil reserves would be mo

[43] Mana Saeed Al-Otaiba, *OPEC and the Petroleum Industry* (New York: Wiley & Sons, 197
p. 109.

oidly developed by granting a number of concessions instead of just one
d by encouraging independent entry. One pay-off from this strategy came
1966 when Armand Hammer of Occidental submitted to Libya a bid of
ceptional financial generosity that included two sweeteners (an agricultural
velopment project and an ammonia plant) and came brilliantly wrapped in
bons of red, green, and black, Libya's national colors.[44] Still other lessons
re learned when reports of the Sister's pre-1950 cartel activities were made
blic. As one Kuwaiti has said; "OPEC couldn't have happened without the
cartel. We just took a leaf from the oil companies' book. The victim had
irned the lesson."[45] Capping these lessons, OPEC members expanded their
perience by gaining increased control of their concessions.

Things came to a head in October 1973. United States demand had far out-
ipped its domestic supplies, forcing abandonment of import quotas and
0% capacity use in prorationing states. Moreover, European consumption
iched an all-time high. In point of fact, for the first time in more than 14 years
e transactions price of oil rose *above* the posted price, which was $3.01 a
rrel. In sum, events could not have put OPEC in a more powerful position.
ien, just as oil company executives and OPEC ministers were boarding planes
d otherwise preparing to meet in Vienna to renegotiate posted prices, war
oke out between Israel and the Arabs. A partial oil embargo followed, lifting
ction prices of crude oil as high as $17 a barrel. And what a lesson that was!
ith a hop and a skip, OPEC abandoned negotiations and moved unilaterally.
pping first to $5.11, then skipping to $11.65 within a few month's time, OPEC
ried everyone else in dust. Since December of 1973, price has continued
ward—5% here, 10% there—always by unilateral decree. OPEC's announced
licy is to base these further increases on world inflation and thus protect
fourfold increase of late 1973 in *real* terms. (The overall upward trend could
sily be graphed, but it makes a gloomy picture.)

OPEC Since 1973. OPEC shuns the name "cartel," preferring "structured
gopoly" instead. Nevertheless, it is a cartel, with a secretariat, a conference
ministers, a board of governors, and an economic commission. Although
e organization has tried repeatedly to devise a plan of systematic production
ntrol, such as demand prorationing, it has not been able to reach any formal
reement in this regard. The basis for opposing a formal agreement on pro-
ction varies from member to member, ranging from poverty to pride. Even so,
PEC could not have achieved the success it has without curtailing production
some degree. Taken as a whole, OPEC countries have at times since 1973
oduced at only 60% of capacity.

The burden is not shared equally, however. Just as Texas for many years
rried the main burden of supply control in the United States, so, too, Saudi
abia serves as the main "evener and adjuster" in OPEC. It's eligibility for

[44] Other examples of exceptionally generous independent bidding include, Getty in Saudi
abia. ENI in Iran, and Japan's national company in several places.
[45] Sampson, *op. cit.*, p. 162.

315

the role is based primarily on its vast reserves and small population (8 millio
Its devotion to the cause is indicated by one stretch of 50% capacity utilizati
And its philosophy is reflected in the comments of its oil minister, Shei
Zaki Yamani: "Usually any cartel will break up, because the stronger memb
will not hold up the market to protect the weaker members. But with OPE
the strong members do not have an interest to lower the price and sell more."

This is not to say that OPEC has been free of internal conflict. Differen
have been sharp. In 1977, for example, Saudi Arabia expanded output su
stantially in order to prevent other OPEC members from achieving th
announced objective of a two-part 15% price increase. At other times, dispu
concerning price structure have outweighed those concerning overall pr
level, the problem arising because of intercountry differences in petrole
gravity, sulfur content, and proximity to markets. In light of our earlier analy
of cartels, these traces of competition seem inevitable, especially when
number of parties involved exceeds eight, which was the median number
our sample of 606 cases of price fixing. Still, our earlier analysis also sugge
that mere *traces* of competition may be all we observe in OPEC for many ye
to come. With respect to other factors influencing collusion, such as prod
standardization, smoothness of sales, and price inelasticity of demand, OPI
seems to be on sturdy ground. Moreover, success breeds success, and
strongest bond among OPEC's members is undoubtedly the hundreds
billions of dollars their cooperation has already paid. Some of this money I
been used by OPEC countries to nationalize the producing assets they conta
thereby ending their concessions. As of early 1975, 57.7% of OPEC producti
was owned by OPEC governments. Now their ownership is closer to 100
The shift may further strengthen the cartel.

Summary

When successful, cartels stifle competition. They restrict and regulate outp
thereby raising and stabilizing price. United States antitrust law genera
forbids such "restraints of trade" on a *per se* basis. Violators face civil
criminal prosecution (or both), regardless of the reasonableness of their
tentions or the success of their efforts. Given a *per se* rule, the key question th
becomes: What consitutes a "contract, combination ... or conspiracy, in
straint of trade," as specified by Section 1 of the Sherman Act? Certain fai
obvious activities clearly come within reach of these words, activities such
market allocations, explicit price fixing, and single sales agencies. In additi
prosecutors have tracked down, and courts have found guilty, some m
devious undertakings, including concerted purchases of "distressed" surplu
and certain trade association information schemes. Plain and simple "c

[46] *Ibid.*, p. 295.

ious parallelism" lies beyond the clutches of the law. But "conscious paral-
ism" has been found in violation when coupled with either (1) additional
cumstantial evidence of conspiracy (for example, basing-point pricing), or
) concerted activities of an exclusionary or predatory nature.

Public records of prosecuted conspiracies and other evidence enable limited
idy of the incidence and endurance of private cartels. Conceptually, the
ound most fertile for cartelization lies between the spacious acreage where
mpetition thrives and the narrow plots where tacit collusion grows. Thus
ivate cartelization requires that the number of firms in the market be few,
it not "too" few. Likewise, concentration must be high but not "too" high.
id so on. Other conditions favorable to private collusion, either tacit or ex-
icit, comprise a standardized product, slow growth, slow technological
ange, smoothly flowing sales, little opportunity for secret deals, low elasticity
demand, and uniform production costs among competitors. Of course
rtels can be established by the government even in market environments
rsh on private cartelization.

Our case studies of electrical equipment and crude oil illustrate these points.
arcity of firms and high concentration in some sectors of the former industry
ight have permitted tacit collusion, were it not for large and "lumpy" sales,
me product differentiation, and fairly rapid technological change. Con-
inted with these impediments to tacit collusion, formal cartelization seemed
e only means of securing stability and better profits. In the case of crude oil,
e domestic and foreign industries present different pictures. Stateside, a
iffuse market structure and an unsteady record of price and output led to a
rm of government cartelization that was particularly important from 1933 to
73. Dwindling domestic supplies and unquenchable demand have since set
e control machinery on "idle." Abroad, the Seven Sisters have alternated
tween cartelization and competition, the former predominating prior to
50, the latter breaking through more and more regularly with the entry of
gorous independents between 1950 and 1973. Since 1973, the Organization
Petroleum Exporting Countries, or OPEC, has established itself as the
eatest and wealthiest cartel of all time. Ever-present undercurrents of com-
tition may eventually sink OPEC, but for now that day seems far off.

13

Price and Production Policy in the Long Run: Theory and Cross-Section Evidence

Count the day lost
  whose descending sun
Sees prices shot to hell
  and business done for fun.

    ... BUSINESSMAN'S LAMENT

Like the anatomy of an insect, our prior discussion of short-run price and output behavior can be reduced to three segments:

1. *Objectives* (stability and avoidance of falling profits)
2. *Conditions* affecting achievement of these objectives (number of firms, concentration, lumpiness of sales, and so on)
3. *Mechanisms* used for or arising from interdependence (cartelization, kinky demand, price leadership, and so on)

The issues in this chapter's long-run analysis may be similarly segmented for purposes of comparison. As for firm *objectives*, long-run profit maximization heads the list. Other objectives—such as long-run supply control or market share maintenance—can be considered derivatives or translations of this main objective. *Conditions* affecting the achievement of long-run profits include many resurrections from our short-run analysis, namely, the number of firms, concentration, product differentiation, and technological change. But two additional conditions distinguish long-run analysis—the condition of entry nd long-run price elasticity of demand. Finally, we may list *mechanisms* in rder of their treatment hereafter, as if pinning moths to a collection board:

1. Entry limit pricing
2. "Open" pricing
3. Price discrimination
4. Predatory pricing
5. Tying arrangements
6. Exclusive dealing

hese items deserve special notice not only because they have a long-run use n exploiting a given degree of market power but because they may affect market ower itself. That is, they may influence the life and death of rivals as well as bserved prices, outputs, and profits. We must therefore begin to acknowledge nat structure-to-conduct is not the only possible direction of causal flow. 'onduct may determine structure as well, providing a feed-back effect. Still nother way of contrasting the present long-run and the more limited short-run ntexts involves the scope of recognized interdependence. In the short run, :cognized interdependence extends only to *existing* rivals. In the long run, :cognized interdependence enlarges to include *potentials*—the potential try of a new rival or the potential demise of an old rival.

We start with a review of some cross-section evidence. We next discuss the six echanisms listed.

Structural Conditions and Some Evidence

Contrary to custom, we shall begin rather than end this chapter with cross-ction empirical evidence. The approach enables us to emphasize at the outset e importance of structural conditions to what follows. Without this emphasis, ructure could easily get buried under all the curve bending yet to come. Moreover, most of the available cross-section evidence relates indirectly, as pposed to directly, to the details of these long-run theoretical models.

An army of theories probes the long-run implications of numbers of firms nd levels of concentration. These theories date from Cournot's work in 1838 to e latest issues of scholarly journals and differ in assumptions, complexity, nd reality. They drift into and out of theoretical fashion. And, although ey do not pinpoint what constitutes a competitive structure, they almost variably indicate the same general tendency:

> *As the number of firms in the market shrinks and as concentration rises, price competition usually lessens to the point of encouraging increased prices and restrainted output in the long run.*

These price and output effects are of course not ends in themselves. They a steps taken by businesses to secure higher profits. Hence a corollary hypothes holds that fewness and concentration favor (but do not assure) excessively hi; long-run profits.

We shall see later (in Chapter 19) that evidence concerning the profit corolla is easy to come by. More than 80 cross-section statistical studies have confirme more or less strongly, a positive association between concentration and profi However, statistical tests of the price-concentration relationship are not easy because prices usually cannot be compared across markets. Profit rat may be standardized as a percentage of assets or stockholders equity, but pric cannot be so standardized. Thus, the profit rates of panty-hose knitters, ste rollers, auto assemblers, and candle dippers may be meaningfully arrayed fi tests of competitive effect. But the prices involved are obviously not of the san species (insect or otherwise). Any array would be awry.

Statistical tests of the price-concentration hypothesis are therefore relative few—numbering only 20 or so. The only such tests possible are intraindustr intermarket, and cross sectional. That is to say, they compare prices of a giv product or service in diverse geographic markets at one point in time. Produc and services so studied include life insurance, bank checking accounts, au loans, business loans, newspaper advertising space, bread, beer, and drug a: grocery retailing.[1] Note that most of these are services because the approa; requires relatively narrow geographic markets. Note also that we have alread

---

[1] J. D. Cummins, H. S. Denenberg, and W. C. Scheel, "Concentration in the U. S. Life Insuran Industry," *Journal of Risk and Insurance* (June 1972), pp. 177–99; John H. Landon, "The Relati: of Market Concentration and Advertising Rates: The Newspaper Industry," *Antitrust Bulle.* (Spring 1971), pp. 53–100; B. M. Owen, "Newspaper and Television Station Joint Ownership *Antitrust Bulletin* (Winter 1973), pp. 787–807; F. R. Edwards, "Concentration in Banking and Effect on Business Loan Rates," *Review of Economics and Statistics* (August 1964), pp. 294–3C P. A. Meyer, "Price Discrimination, Regional Loan Rates, and the Structure of the Banki Industry," *Journal of Finance* (March 1967), pp. 37–48; D. Jacobs, *Business Loan Costs and Ba Market Structure* (New York: Columbia University Press, 1971); F. W. Bell and N. B. Murph "Impact of Market Structure on the Price of a Commercial Bank Service," *Review of Econom, and Statistics* (May 1969), pp. 210–13; George Kaufman, "Bank Structure and Performance: t Evidence from Iowa," *Southern Economic Journal* (April 1966), pp. 429–39; A. A. Heggestad a: J. J. Mingo, "Prices, Nonprices, and Concentration in Commercial Banking," *Journal of Mon. Credit and Banking* (February 1976), pp. 107–17; F. R. Edwards, "The Banking Competition Co troversy," *NationalBanking Review* (September 1965), pp. 1–34; Douglas F. Greer and Robert Shay, *An Econometric Analysis of Consumer Credit Markets in the United States*, Technic Study Vol. IV, National Commission on Consumer Finance (Washington, D.C., 1973), Cha ters 2 and 4; H. W. de Jong, "Industrial Structure and the Price Problem: Experience in t European Economic Community," in *The Roots of Inflation*, edited by G. C. Means *et. al.* (N(York: Burt Franklin & Co., 1975), pp. 199–209; *Prescription Drug Price Disclosures*, Staff Rep(to the Federal Trade Commission (processed, 1975), part III; pp. 41–44; L. P. Bucklin, *Competiti and Evolution in the Distributive Trades* (Englewood Cliffs, N. J.: Prentice-Hall, 1972), pp. 126–3 Almarin Phillips, "Evidence on Concentration in Banking Markets and Interest Rates," *Fede, Reserve Bulletin* (June 1967) pp. 916–26; R. C. Aspinwall, "Market Structure and Commerc Bank Mortgage Interest Rates," *Southern Economic Journal* (April 1970) pp. 376–84; S. A. Rhoad("Does the Market Matter in Banking?" Research Papers in Banking and Financial Econom (Washington, D.C., Federal Reserve Board, 1977); C. C. Slater, *Baking in America: Mark Organization and Competition* (Evanston, Northwestern University Press, 1956), pp. 254–5

reported the research results concerning business loans (in Chapter 8). Those results agree with the others—prices and concentration *are* positively related. The result for commercial bank new auto loans may be seen by comparing the average interest rate on a standardized auto loan in the ten states having the highest and the ten states having the lowest bank concentration as of 1971. The former was 10.71 % annual interest, the latter 9.90 %.[2]

One of the best studies of this type, concerning grocery retailing in 1974, was conducted by a team of University of Wisconsin economists. A major strength of their study is the unusually good data they used. Their data were obtained by force of subpoena through a U.S. Congressional Committee. From these data, the Wisconsin group compiled observations of the weighted average price to consumers of a "grocery basket" comprised of 94 comparable grocery products. Cross-section observations for several retail chains operating in 5 United States cities were included in the analysis.

The statistical upshot is summarized in Table 13-1. Row numerals indicate representative values of "relative firm market share," which is the individual retailer's market share in a single city divided by that city's four-firm concentration ratio, expressed as a percentage. For example, a top-ranked retailer with 15% market share in a market where the next three largest retailers enjoy 5% each would have a "relative" market share of 50%, because 15/(15 + 5 + 5 + 5) = 0.5. If all four leading firms held 15% shares, the result would be 25%, because 15/(15 + 15 + 15 + 15) = 0.25.

The column headings indicate four representative values of four-firm concentration (40, 50, 60, and 70), each with two types of summary results. The dollar figures are estimates of "grocery basket" prices to consumers, holding all variables not mentioned in the table constant. The figures in parentheses show the percentage difference between each price and $90.95, which is the price when concentration is 40 and relative market share is 10 (the first cell in the upper left-hand corner of the table). Thus, for any given level of relative market share, it appears that grocery prices rise as concentration increases from 40 to 70. Price across the first row goes from $90.95 to $95.78, a leap of 5.3%. Across the bottom row, price jumps from $94.18 to $99.01, this last figure being 8.9% greater than the first cell's $90.95. At first glance these findings seem to conflict with our earlier stories of price wars in grocery retailing. However, they do not. City markets *vary* in structure, some being more competitive than others. Table 13-1 spans the range of possibilities.

A scan down the columns of Table 13-1 conveys the impression that a large relative market share also lifts prices. In light of our earlier discussion of gasoline retailing (see Table 11-1), these particular results should not strike you as a bolt from the blue (however financially unsettling they may be). Translating the combined results for concentration and relative firm market share into even more arresting numbers, the Wisconsin team estimated that, nationwide,

---

[2] *Consumer Credit in the United States*, Report of the National Commission on Consumer Finance (December 1972), pp. 118–19.

TABLE 13-1 Estimated Prices of Grocery Baskets for Different Combinations of Relative Market Share and Four-Firm Concentration, October 1974

Relative Firm Market Share	Four-Firm Concentration Ratio							
	40		50		60		70	
	Price ($)	Difference (%)	Price ($)	Difference (%)	Price ($)	Difference (%)	Price ($)	Difference (%)
10	90.95	(0)	91.84	(1.0)	93.64	(3.0)	95.78	(5.3)
25	91.65	(0.8)	92.54	(1.8)	94.34	(3.7)	96.48	(6.1)
40	93.16	(2.4)	94.05	(3.4)	95.85	(5.4)	97.99	(7.7)
55	94.18	(3.6)	95.07	(4.5)	96.87	(6.5)	99.01	(8.9)

Source: B. W. Marion, W. F. Mueller, R. W. Cotteril, F. E. Geithman, and J. R. Schmelzer, *The Profit and Price Performance of Leading Food Chains 1970–74*, A Study for the Joint Economic Committee, U. S. Congress, 95th Congress, First Session (1977), p. 66.

TABLE 13-2 Comparison of Average Prices in Countries with and without Patent Protection for Drug Products, Spring 1959

Product (Producer)	Price in Countries with Product Patents ($)	Price in Countries without Product Patents ($)
Meticorten (Schering)	21.55	15.10
Altown (Carter-American Cyanamid)	3.31	2.52
Diabinese (Pfizer)	4.87	4.82
Penicillin V (Eli Lilly)	13.80	10.97
Chloromycetin (Parke, Davis)	4.08	3.46
Aureomycin (American Cyanamid)	5.53	4.71
Achromycin (American Cyanamid)	5.68	4.68

Source: U. S. Senate, Subcommittee on Antitrust and Monopoly of the Committee on the Judiciary, *Administered Prices Drugs, Report,* 87th Congress, First Session, (1961), p. 109.

"monopoly overcharges" in the industry were in the neighborhood of $662 million during 1974, with great variations across cities.[3]

It almost goes without saying that the group also found a significant positive association between profits and these two measures of market power. However, we shall not pursue the profit issue now except to note that these results for prices and those from similar intraindustry, intermarket, cross-section studies are essential to a proper interpretation of the 80 and more profit studies reviewed later. Without these price studies we could never be certain that the observed positive association between profits and concentration (or profits and market share) was indeed due to "market power." A skeptic could argue with some honest conviction that the cause of the positive profit association was not market power pushing up prices, but rather some *nonprice* profit-enhancing variable like productivity or efficiency, which could be positively but unmeasurably associated with concentration. In other words, profit studies substantially outnumber price studies, but the latter carry as much weight as the former in condemning excessive market power.

As we have seen, high concentration and high barriers to entry typically go hand in hand. We may assume, then, that these concentration-price studies reflect some positive price influence from substantial barriers to entry. But we need not stretch the implications of these studies that far. More direct evidence of the relationship is available in Table 13-2, where patents serve as the entry barrier in question. This table's data come from a study sponsored by the Senate Subcommittee on Antitrust and Monopoly, which explored the effect

[3] B. W. Marion, W. F. Mueller, R. W. Cotterill, F. E. Geithman, and J. R. Schmelzer, *The Profit and Price Performance of Leading Food Chains 1970–74,* A Study for the Joint Economic Committee, U. S. Congress, 95th Congress, First Session (1977), p. 4.

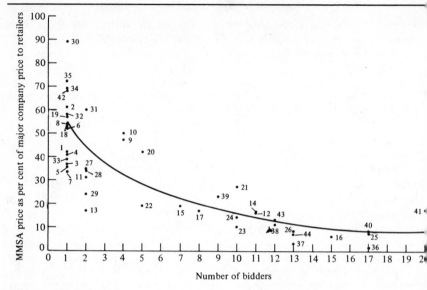

Figure 13-1. *MMSA drug procurement: relationship of number of bidders MMSA price expressed as percent of commercial price, 1959 and early 196 Source: U. S. Senate, Subcommittee on Antitrust and Monopoly of the Committ on the Judiciary,* Administered Prices of Drugs: Report. *87th Congress, 1 Session (1961), p. 95.*

of patent protection on drug prices. A survey was taken of prices in 18 countri —7 with patents for drug products and 11 without. Two columns of man facturers' prices are presented in Table 13-2: those "with" and those "without Both prices in each pair of average prices are derived from a *single* multination company, apply to a *single* brand-name product and refer to *identical* dosag All that changes is country group. As can be seen, prices tend to be higher countries with drug product patents than in those without. The greatest d ferential is 42.7 % for Meticorten. The smallest is 1 % for Diabinese. Thus, hi barriers to entry apparently also boost prices.[4]

Cross-section price studies concerning other structural variables are equal informative. Figure 13-1 presents further findings in the drug market th reflect the combined effects of numbers of firms, product differentiation, ar buyer power. Each of the 44 dots represents a major drug purchase by the U. Military Medical Supply Agency during 1959 and early 1960. Two characte istics of each sale are plotted there: (1) the number of firms bidding on the supp contract, as shown on the horizontal axis, and (2) the lowest price at whic MMSA was able to buy the drug, which is expressed as a percentage of the pri charged to retail druggists for the same product sold under brand name. Tl

[4] For related findings see H. D. Walker, *Market Power and Price Levels in the Ethical Dr Industry* (Bloomington, Ind.: Indiana University Press, 1971), Chapters 6, 7.

atter diagram clearly shows that all sales to the government's MMSA were iced below sales to retail druggists. The discount may be explained partly the larger lot sizes of these sales and partly by the fact that product differentiation is much more prevalent in the general commercial sector than in e government sector. Moreover, the diagram plainly shows an inverse relationip between MMSA prices and the number of bidders.

Finally, it should be observed that power on the *buyer's* side of the market ay influence price level. As if turn-about were truly fair play, conventional eory holds that concentration on the buyer's side may yield sufficient nonopsony" or "oligopsony" power to *reduce* seller's prices. Some of the irgain prices enjoyed by the government in Figure 13-1 probably reflect is buyer power. Government is a *big* buyer. In other areas, cross-section atistical studies of raw materials and labor supplies have shown that, indeed, onopsony or oligopsony power often does depress prices.[5]

Entry Limit Pricing

Barriers to entry are crucial to any discussion of long-run price policy, for thout them excessive prices and profits could not endure. The theory of "limit icing" reflects this nicely: sellers in concentrated markets will set prices high ough to make excess profits but not so high as to attract new entry. Three sumptions underlie the theory:[6]

1. Established sellers and potential entrants seek maximum profits over the long run.
2. Established sellers think potential entrants will expect them to maintain their outputs in the event of new entry, letting price fall with the entrant's added output.
3. Established sellers have no difficulty colluding to determine and set the entry-limiting price.

[5] W. J. Mead, *Competition and Oligopsony in the Douglas Fir Lumber Industry* (Berkeley, lif.: University of California Press, 1966), Chapters 11 and 12; J. H. Landon, "The Effect of oduct-Market Concentration on Wage Levels: An Intra-industry Approach," *Industrial and bor Relations Review* (January 1970), pp. 237–47; J. H. Landon and R. N. Baird, "Monopsony the Market for Public School Teachers," *American Economic Review* (December 1971), pp. 6–71.
[6] D. K. Osborne, "On the Rationality of Limit Pricing," *Journal of Industrial Economics* eptember 1973), pp. 71–80; J. S. Bain, *Barriers to New Competition* (Cambridge, Mass.: Harvard niversity Press, 1956); P. Sylos-Labini, *Oligopoly and Technical Progress* (Cambridge, Mass.: arvard University Press, 1962); D. P. Baron, "Limit Pricing, Potential Entry, and Barriers to itry," *American Economic Review* (September 1973), pp. 666–74; D. Needham, "Entry Barriers id Non-price Aspects of Firms' Behavior," *Journal of Industrial Economics* (September 1976),). 29–43. For purposes of exposition, this section relies heavily on Douglas Needham, *Economic nalysis and Industrial Structure* (New York: Holt, Rinehart and Winston, 1969), Chapter 7, and Modigliani, "New Developments on the Oligopoly Front," *Journal of Political Economy* une 1958), pp. 215–32.

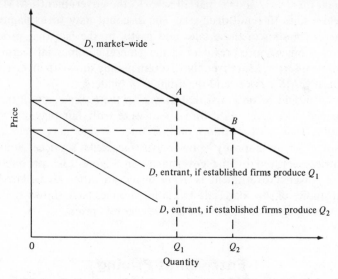

Figure 13-2. *Derivation of postentry demand facing a potential entrant.*

The first postulate explicitly recognizes that anticipated profitability guid both classes of decision makers—entrants and established firms. Potenti entrants calculate prospective profits from expected postentry demand a cost conditions. In turn, the entrant's postentry demand and cost conditio depend on the postentry behavior of established sellers. The dependency is mo readily seen with respect to postentry demand. In essence, the more t established firms produce after the new firm's entry, the lower the entran demand will be at any given price. Figure 13-2 depicts this with a set of thr demand curves. The long, uppermost curve is market-wide demand. The tw shorter and lower curves represent the *entrant's* postentry demand given tw specific levels of postentry output by *established* firms—Q_1 and Q_2. Giv postentry output Q_1, the entrant's demand curve is that segment of the marke demand curve extending southeast of point A. Given Q_2, the entrant's dema curve is that segment of the market's demand curve to the right of point These segments are shifted to the vertical axis to accord with the entran view of them.

These entrant demands are merely illustrative. Others are obviously possib And the theory would now come to a grinding halt without further specificatic as to what the postentry output of established firms will be. This, then, is whe assumption 2 comes in. It is essential to much existing theory and is often call the "Sylos postulate" in honor of an entry theorist, P. Sylos-Labini, wl relied heavily upon it. Given the Sylos postulate, the potential entrant mu contend with a demand curve derived from that segment of the market-wi demand curve extending to the right of the *pre-entry* quantity produced l

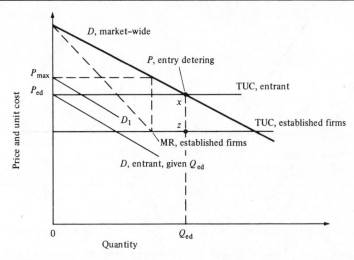

Figure 13-3. Entry limit pricing with absolute cost differences.

existing firms. In other words, established firm output is assumed to be fixed in the event of entry. We shall explore the reality of this assumption shortly. Present acceptance of it permits immediate consideration of the cost side of the potential entrant's profit calculations. For given the Sylos postulate demand curve, the potential entrant need only compare his cost conditions to this demand in order to reach a yes or no decision on entry.

As suggested earlier in Chapter 8, most entry barriers may be categorized as either (1) absolute cost differences between established firms and potential entrants, or (2) economies of scale. Figure 13-3 illustrates the first of these possibilities. It is like Figure 13-2, except that total unit costs (TUC) have been added in simplified form for both the entrant and established firms. As depicted, the potential entrant, compared to established firms, suffers an absolute cost disadvantage at every level of output. Distance xz indicates the extent of disadvantage per unit of output.

Now, if established firms set price at P_{max} in hopes of maximizing their short-run profits, they would be inviting entry. Given the Sylos postulate, the entrant's postentry demand curve would then be D_1, which exceeds the entrant's unit cost (TUC, entrant) over a substantial range. Entry would be profitable for the newcomer. Entry would also cut price and profit of established firms, however, so they may attempt to prevent the entry. The key question is what pre-entry combination of price and quantity will block the newcomer? According to assumption 3, the established firms know the answer and act together to implement the impediment. Price P_{ed} corresponds to output Q_{ed}, and, given the Sylos postulate, the combination will deter the entry. With Q_{ed}, the entrant's postentry demand curve falls below D_1. More important, it falls below the

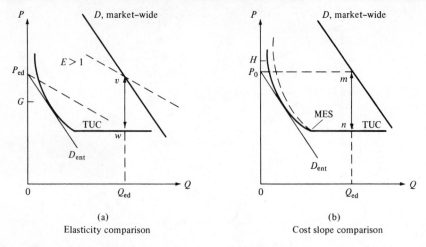

Figure 13-4. *Maximum price-cost premiums with economies of scale.*

entrant's unit costs at every level of output, preventing the entrant from earning any postentry profit. In other words, P_{ed} is the highest price the established firms can charge without attracting entry. If the extent to which industry price can exceed unit cost of the established firms is used to measure the height of entry barriers, then distance xz is the barrier premium in this case.

Barriers attributable to economies of scale add complexities to the theory since the barrier premium will then be a function of (1) the size of the market, (2) the elasticity of market-wide demand at any given price, (3) the scale at which economies of scale are exhausted, and (4) the rate of decline in the unit cost curve when moving from zero output to minimum efficient output. At least two diagrams are called for in this case—Figures 13-4(a) and 13-4(b). Their solid-line total unit cost curves (TUC) display identical economies up to a minimum efficient scale (MES). Furthermore, it is now assumed that existing firms and potential entrants confront the *same* TUC curves. Thus, everyone is equally efficient or inefficient at a given level of output.

Figure 13-4(a), then, illustrates the effect of differing elasticities of demand. When the solid-line market-wide demand applies, P_{ed} and Q_{ed} are the entry deterring price and output. The resulting entrant's demand of D_{ent} is insufficient to cover cost at any output. And vw is the barrier premium associated with this particular solution. Note, however, that demand is inelastic at point v. In contrast, the dashed demand curve of lesser slope is elastic. Were it applicable, P_{ed} and Q_{ed} would no longer deter entry because the entrant's dashed demand curve would then exceed extrant's cost. Given the Sylos postulate, established firms must cut price to G and expand output beyond Q_{ed} to deter entry in this instance. As a result, their barrier premium would shrink to less than one half the value of vw. Conversely, if we imagined a *lower* elasticity than that displayed by the solid line demand at v, entry deterring price would be higher than P_{ed} and the premium would be greater than vw.

Turning to Figure 13-4(b), we see that for a given level of minimum efficient scale, MES, the barrier premium will be greater the more rapidly unit cost rises at less than MES scale. Entry deterring price associated with the solid unit cost curve is P_0, and the resulting barrier premium is mn. A more rapid ascent of unit costs, though, as indicated by the dashed curve, would permit an an even higher pre-entry price at point H plus a correspondingly larger barrier premium. Conversely, a flatter, less sharply rising unit cost curve would force the entry deterring price and barrier premium below P_0 and mn.

The reader should be able to see the similar effects ensuing from a shift right or a shift left of the MES, holding everything else about the unit cost curve constant (that is, its height and shape). The reader should also be able to work out the effects of market size, which may be accounted for by shifts of the market-wide demand curve. Lest your efforts go sour, however, we shall include the implications of such moves in the following summary of limit pricing theory: Entry deterring price and barrier premium will be higher (1) the greater the absolute cost disadvantage of potential entrants, (2) the lower the market-wide elasticity of demand at any price, (3) the sharper the increase in entrant's unit costs below minimum efficient scale output, (4) the larger the level of output at minimum efficient scale, and (5) the smaller the absolute size of the market.

However neat and tidy these conclusions may seem, they can be misleading. The theory underlying them is too tightly bound and gagged by assumptions to give us any more than a very vague prediction of actual behavior. Our brief critique below will center on the Sylos postulate of identical pre- and postentry established-firm output.

Can the pre-entry conduct of established firms be predicted? . . . No. The thinking of potential *entrants* is fairly straightforward. Their behavior depends on their expectations of *postentry* established-firm reaction. But the theory is not based on entrant behavior. It is primarily grounded upon a very delicate balance of established-firm mental reasoning that may or may not be true. Established firms are presumed to *think* that potential entrants *think* not in terms of *postentry* reactions but rather in terms of *pre-entry* policy. To be sure, pre-entry policy may signal something about postentry reaction, but the meaning of such signals is not chiselled in granite on Wall Street. Moreover, the gap between signal senders and receivers is large, and the number of parties involved great enough to foul up communications. Indeed, the signal the theory postulates seems unrealistic. Established firms set price at the blocking point *and keep it there indefinitely.* A more realistic theory might have established firms reducing price when entry is imminent and raising it when the threat has subsided. Take, for example, Shop-Rite's attempted entry into the Washington, D. C., grocery retailing market in 1967:

> This chain came into the Washington market by opening three stores. It has since closed two of them. *Just prior* to this chain's entry into the Washington market, the stores of two leading Washington area chains [Safeway and Giant] located near the

stores of the new entrant cut their prices substantially below those charged in the rest of the metropolitan area. In doing so, these stores operated on abnormally low margins and . . . sustained substantial losses.[7]

Thus, contrary to the theory, established firms are often capable of identifying specific entry threats as they arise, especially where substantial plant and equipment purchases must precede entry. Moreover, established firms might deliberately maintain excess capacity, which capacity could be used to increase output and depress price at the appearance of an entrant on the horizon. This approach is not always optimal, but J. Wenders has shown that, when it is profitable, it invalidates the Sylos postulate.[8]

Can the postentry conduct of established firms be predicted? . . . No. Theorists who rely heavily on the Sylos postulate like to argue that a constant output policy is plausible because it is most unfavorable to entrants. As we have just seen, however, this conclusion is unwarranted. Postentry reactions of established firms can be much more nasty than this. On the other hand, they can also be rather accommodating. Established firms often cut back output to make room for entrants. Established firms are not necessarily moved to this action by the spirit of benevolence; it may be better for their profits to see that price is maintained. Several examples are provided by the large electrical equipment manufacturers, who, during the great price-fixing conspiracies, allocated market shares of certain product lines to smaller rivals that had not produced in those submarkets before. To accommodate the entrants, General Electric and Westinghouse had to give up some of their market shares.[9] In short, the postentry behavior of established firms is largely unpredictable. And where it *is* predictable the Sylos postulate is superfluous. In particular, postentry behavior predictably abides by the Sylos postulate only under structural conditions that are so competitive to begin with that collusive limit pricing is *impossible* and entry is *very easy* anyway—namely, pure competition and monopolistic competition. As Douglas Needham points out:

> Under pure competition or monopolistic competition . . . no individual established seller will take account of entry, any more than it will take account of the behavior of its existing rivals. By definition, in such markets the actions of any individual seller, whether established firm or new entrant, will have no noticeable effect upon the sellers, and will not, therefore, provoke any reaction.[10]

[7] Federal Trade Commission, *Economic Report on Food Chain Selling Practices in the District of Columbia and San Francisco* (Washington, D.C., 1969), pp. 4, 23. For a related example see J. B. Dirlam and A. E. Kahn, *Fair Competition* (Ithaca, N.Y.: Cornell University Press, 1954), pp. 213–14.

[8] J. T. Wenders, "Excess Capacity as a Barrier to Entry," *Journal of Industrial Economics* (November 1971), pp. 14–19.

[9] C. C. Walton and F. W. Cleveland, Jr., *Corporations on Trial: The Electric Cases* (Belmont, Calif.: Wadsworth, 1964), p. 52.

[10] D. Needham, *op. cit.* (1969), pp. 104–105.

Can potential entrant conduct be predicted? . . . No. Entry will not necessarily occur even if price is maintained well above the so-called "entry deterring" level. Potential entrants know that it is postentry price that counts, and nightmares of bloody postentry price wars may keep them out. Conversely, entry may very well occur despite the diligent efforts of established firms to keep pre-entry price below the probable unit costs of potential entrants. Inexperienced entrants may be overly optimistic about their cost prospects or about the mood of existing sellers. (After all, a pessimist is just an experienced optimist.) In sum, the theory provides predictions about the behavior of potential entrants that seem no more solid than those concerning established firms.

Does limit pricing theory explain maximum long-run price level? . . . No. Despite appearances, it can be argued that the theory does not really explain maximum long-run price level.[11] The theory predicts a price level low enough to ward off entry, and presents this prediction as the more plausible of two possible options—(1) an especially high price that invites entry and (2) a lower entry-deterring price. Because the lower of the two options is chosen, it appears that this conduct establishes *maximum* long-run price. But there really is no such price option in the *long run*. Under either option, price will end up at the *same* level. If price is initially set high enough to attract entry, then a multiplication of competitors will drive price down until it equals the entry-deterring price (at which point entry stops). If price is initially set at entry-deterring level, it obviously ends at the entry-deterring level. The only long-run difference in these two options is the number of firms eventually in the market and the likely level of concentration, with the first distinction obviously yielding the more competitive structure of the two. Since the high initial price option yields a more competitive structure, a further unwinding of the theory might produce predictions concerning different long-run price levels, but only indirectly. That is to say, the more competitive of the two structures might foster a relatively lower price level in the long run, a level *below* entry-deterring price. Aside from this possibility, however, the theory of limit pricing conduct is more important from the standpoint of *concentration* than of price.

Notice: we are *not* saying that barriers to entry themselves are unimportant to price level. We are saying that, in theory, barriers to entry *alone* explain *maximum possible* long-run price (and the higher the barriers, the higher this maximum long-run price will be relative to the purely competitive price). Simple price setting does not determine that maximum. We are also saying that pricing conduct can, and does, affect *actual* long-run price level, but only through two channels: (1) As already suggested, conduct together with concentration will determine *where* observed price actually lies between maximum long-run (entry-deterring) price and purely competitive price. (2) Conduct other than simple price setting may affect the height of barriers to entry, thereby *indirectly* affecting maximum long-run price.

[11] D. K. Osborne, "The Role of Entry in Oligopoly Theory," *Journal of Political Economy* (August 1964), pp. 396–402.

Open Pricing

Disenchantment with limit pricing theory has led many theorists to devise models of "open pricing." Early theories of open pricing stressed the notion that established firms might actually earn higher profits by pricing high and inducing entry than by holding prices down. By open pricing, established firms deliberately give up part of the market to newcomers; however, they earn hefty profits in the short run before entries divide demand. Of course established firm profits will fall as entry proceeds; their market share will shrink and market price will fall. This profit trend is shown by the declining curve in Figure 13-5. Lucrative early profits turn into skimpy profits with time. By contrast, the profit stream associated with a limit pricing strategy is fairly steady over time and may actually rise slightly if the market is growing. This too is shown in Figure 13-5.

Although the limit pricing profit stream is below the open pricing profit stream at the start, it eventually intersects and supercedes the latter. This raises a pertinent question: Is open pricing therefore a model of *short-run* profit maximizing and limit pricing a model of *long-run* profit maximizing? Despite your eyeball's affirmative answer, your mind should be telling you

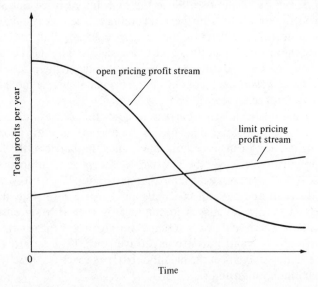

Figure 13-5. *Profit streams of established firms under two price strategies.*

"No, both models are similar in that both assume *long-run* profit maximization as the goal of established firms." Both models can be put on the same footing for long-run comparison by (1) properly *discounting* each profit stream to reduce the value of distant and therefore less useful dollar revenues, (2) adding up the discounted values in each resulting series, and (3) thereby converting the profit streams to *present values*. Given a common objective of long-run profit maximization, the strategy yielding the highest present discounted value will be chosen.

Advocates of the open pricing model tend to think that "the present value of a series of declining profits . . . may exceed the present value of a perpetual profit rate . . . ."[12] Not surprisingly, advocates of the limit price model think the opposite. Actually, recent theorists have refined and elaborated this basic issue until it is now inaccurate to regard it as a stark either-or matter. Their models do not speak in terms of open pricing's flood of entry versus a drought induced by limit pricing. Theorists who continue to assume that established firms control the entry spigot try to determine what *intermediate and varying rate* of entry will maximize the present value of established firm profits under diverse assumptions.[13] Unfortunately, these assumptions suffer many of the problems that plague the Sylos postulate.

Empirical tests of these various hypotheses are extremely difficult. Attempts tend to crack up on many of the same rocks endangering empirical explorations of whether firms try to maximize profits. Business intentions hide beneath brain folds, and observable outcomes may not correspond with intentions. Nevertheless, a few pieces of empirical evidence are available, and they indicate a mixed pattern. Open pricing, limit pricing, and intermediate pricing all appear.

Prominent examples that appear to fit the open pricing mold include the steel, corn-product, and copper markets. U. S. Steel's early high price policy and continued loss of market share received earlier mention. But one does not have to look far for equally valid examples of what appear to be limit pricing. During the first half of this century Alcoa and United Shoe Machinery reported no more than moderate profits despite their considerable power. Similarly, General Foods Corporation is said to price its specialty products at low to moderate levels in "full realization that a high price will restrict the volume and . . . speed up the process of developing competition."[14] Another example from the food industry is Campbell Soup, which "has steadfastly refused to raise prices far enough above costs to reap a short-term deluge of profits, thereby discouraging any real competition."[15]

---

[12] G. J. Stigler, *The Theory of Price* (New York: Macmillan Publishing Co., 1952), p. 234.

[13] P. B. Pashigian, "Limit Pricing and the Market Share of the Leading Firm," *Journal of Industrial Economics* (July 1968), pp. 165–77; D. W. Gaskins, "Dynamic Limit Pricing: Optimal Pricing Under Threat of Entry," *Journal of Economic Theory* (September 1971), pp. 306–22.

[14] A. D. H. Kaplan, J. B. Dirlam, and R. F. Lanzillotti, *Pricing in Big Business* (Washington, D.C.: Brookings Institution, 1958), p. 216.

[15] T. Horst, *At Home Abroad* (Cambridge, Mass.: Ballinger Co., 1974), p. 16.

Finally, there are examples of single firms demonstrating *both* theories at the *same time* in different markets. One is Xerox. It appears to have engaged in limit pricing for its very high-volume market (serving customers making more than 100,000 copies per machine per month); simultaneously it used open pricing in the low-volume market (below 5000 copies per machine per month). In the middle volume range, Xerox followed an "in between" policy. Who threatened entry? Patents prevented any "dry process" entry in the early years of Xerox's success. But electrofax technology was developed at about the same time and was liberally licensed to all comers by RCA. Thus the impact of Xerox's pricing policies may be gauged in terms of electrofax firm entry into these sub-markets up through 1967. Limit pricing held entry down to just three firms. Open pricing brought in twenty-five. In between, ten newcomers entered the middle volume segment of the copy machine market.[16]

A few cross-section studies have sought a more general answer to the question than these individual examples provide, but they too yield mixed results. The basic method they employ to test whether open pricing or limit pricing dominate business practice is simple. First, a sample of concentrated markets is selected. Second, the histories of these markets and their leading firms are traced to discover any general trends in concentration or leading-firm market shares. Falling concentration and declining market shares are said to indicate open pricing; contrary trends are said to indicate limit pricing.

David Kamerschen traced the 1947–63 histories of several dozen highly concentrated oligopolies and found stability or positive concentration trends in about 55 % of them. His was thus a "split decision," but limit pricing won by a slight edge.[17] In another study, W. G. Shepherd worked over a sample of 245 large United States industrial firms, tracing their histories for the period 1960–1969 and incorporating consideration of their profits as well as their market shares.[18] He too found a split, but his results came out somewhat more favorable to some kind of limit-pricing model than Kamerschen's did. Shepherd concluded that "in the normal case, managers attempt to maintain or increase market share." Where declines do occur, they "usually occur involuntarily and under stress." However, after moving from intentions to realizations, he found that

> High market shares *are* usually eroded over time. The average decay process is strong enough to abate monopoly positions in the course of 20 to 30 years. Yet this rate is exceedingly moderate. And there are major exceptions, in which dominant firms maintain high market shares and profit rates for many decades.[19]

---

[16] E. A. Blackstone, "Limit Pricing and Entry in the Copying Machine Industry," *Quarterly Review of Economics & Business* (Winter 1972), pp. 57–65.

[17] D. R. Kamerschen, "An Empirical Test of Oligopoly Theories," *Journal of Political Economy* (July 1968), pp. 615–34.

[18] W. G. Shepherd, *The Treatment of Market Power* (New York: Columbia University Press 1975), pp. 113–29.

[19] *Ibid.*, pp. 124–25.

Rather than end this section on such an ambiguous note, we ought to mention a heart-warming generality that is only rarely refuted by experience. Fresh entry of material significance is usually followed by price reductions.[20]

Price Discrimination

Like a pesky housefly, price discrimination unavoidably invaded the foregoing discussion. Safeway and Giant Foods used it to repulse Shop-Rite's entry into Washington, D.C. The large multinational drug companies used it with results shown in Table 13-2. Most every enterprise and market provides examples. For *price discrimination occurs whenever a seller sells the same commodity or service at more than one price*, for example, Meticorten at $21.55 and $15.10. Moreover, even if the sale items are not exactly the same, price discrimination is said to occur if the seller sells very similar products at different price/cost ratios. IBM, for instance, used to rent two disk-drive systems that differed only slightly in cost and model number (the 2314 and 2319) but immensely in price ($1455 a month versus $1000). The broad definition includes cases in which costs differ and identical prices are charged, and cases involving high prices on low-cost sales coupled with low prices on high-cost sales (as frequently occurred under the single basing point system discussed in Chapter 12).

Essential Conditions

Three conditions are essential for price discrimination: (1) The seller must have some *market power*. A purely competitive firm does not have sufficient control over price to engage in discrimination. (2) The seller must confront buyers who have *differing price elasticities of demand*. These elasticity differences among classes of buyers may be due to differences in income level, differences in "needs," differences in the availability of substitutes, differences in use of the product, and so on. Without different elasticities, buyers would not willingly pay different prices. To practice price discrimination, of course, the seller must be able to identify these different demands. (3) These various buyer elements must be kept *separate*. Without separation, low-price customers could resell their purchases to the high-price customers, subverting the seller's ability to identify and segregate the different demands. A grisly example of the importance of market separation was furnished during the early 1940s by Röhm & Haas, in connection with its sale of methyl methacrylate plastic.

---

[20] Cases are too numerous to list, but a few interesting instances should be cited: W. H. Martin, "Public Policy and Increased Competition in the Synthetic Ammonia Industry," *Quarterly Journal of Economics* (August 1959), pp. 373–92; Elizabeth Marting (ed.), *Creative Pricing* (American Management Association, 1968), p. 30; "A Painful Headache for Bristol-Myers?" *Business Week*, October 6, 1975, pp. 78, 80; M. N. Harris "Entry and Long-Term Trends in Industry Performance," *Antitrust Bulletin* (Summer 1976), pp. 295–314.

General industrial users were charged 85 cents a pound, whereas dental laboratories and dentists who used the stuff for making dentures were charged 45 *dollars* a pound. After many dental buyers discovered the difference, "bootlegging" or, more technically, arbitrage became a problem. To stifle bootlegging the company considered poisoning the industrial plastic. The Food and Drug Administration would have then unwittingly enforced separation of the markets for Röhm & Haas. To quote from Company correspondence:

> A millionth of one percent of arsenic or lead might cause them [the FDA] to confiscate every bootleg unit in the country. There ought to be a trace of something that would make them rear up.[21]

Röhm & Haas eventually rejected the idea, but it did start rumors that the industrial material had been adulterated.

Analysis of Price Discrimination

Theoretically, price discrimination is usually analyzed in three categories—first degree, second degree, and third degree.

First Degree Discrimination. This is perfect discrimination. Each and every unit sold goes for the very highest price above cost it can fetch. Each and every buyer pays as much as he is willing to pay for the quantity he wants. Figure 13-6 compares first degree price discrimination with single, uniform pricing. With a single price of OB, OQ units would be purchased, yielding total revenues equal to $OBCQ$, which is price times quantity. Given constant total unit costs of OB, including a normal profit, the seller earns no more than a normal profit. Buyers willingly pay $OBCQ$. Indeed, by definition of the demand curve, they would actually be willing to pay $OBCQ$ *plus* the shaded area ABC, or $OACQ$. The difference between what they actually pay and what they are willing to pay is called "consumers' surplus," which in this case is $OACQ - OBCQ$, or ABC. Under first degree price discrimination, sellers are able to extract this consumers' surplus as well as the $OBCQ$ revenue obtained from the single price. Seller's total revenue then equals the entire area under the demand curve between A and C, and profits bulge.

For obvious reasons, such perfect discrimination is extremely difficult in the real world and is never achieved in practice. However, E. Blackstone argues that Xerox may have come pretty close to perfection, at least during the 1960s.[22] The company did not at first sell its 914 copy machines. It *leased* them and *metered* the intensity of their use, charging $25 per month plus 3.5 cents per copy.

[21] Corwin D. Edwards, *Economic and Political Aspects of International Cartels*, U. S. Senate, Subcommittee on War Mobilization of the Committee on Military Affairs, 78th Congress, Second Session (1944), p. 19.
[22] E. A. Blackstone, "The Copying-Machine Industry: Innovations, Patents, and Pricing," *Antitrust Law and Economics Review* (Fall 1972), pp. 105–22.

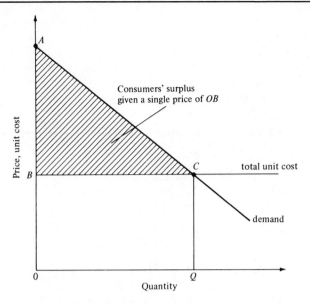

Figure 13-6. First degree price discrimination.

Low intensity users paid little; high intensity users paid a lot. In this way price was tailored to each individual customer's willingness to pay and elasticity of demand. Was this profitable? You bet!

> The estimated cost of producing the original 914 copier was approximately $2500. Some users, because of the large number of copies thay make on their leased Xerox machines, have paid Xerox an *annual rental* of more than $20,000 per machine or—assuming at least a five-year machine life—a total "purchase price" of more than $100,000 for each such machine.[23]

The key to the system was the meter. Most sellers cannot practice first degree discrimination because they cannot measure the depth of each buyer's desire and ability to pay. In addition, leasing kept buyers separate from each other. Had Xerox *sold* its machines at widely differing prices, bootleggers would not have gone begging.

Second Degree Discrimination. Second degree price discrimination is illustrated in Figure 13-7. Demand is partitioned into three blocks. Quantity OQ_1, is sold at price OG. Quantity $Q_2 - Q_1$ is sold at price OK. And finally, quantity $Q_3 - Q_2$ is sold at price OJ. Total revenues obtained are $OJHQ_3$ plus the shaded area. In other words, this system is like first degree discrimination only less refined. Much less consumers' surplus is extracted. Standard examples include "quantity

[23] *Ibid.,* p. 112.

337

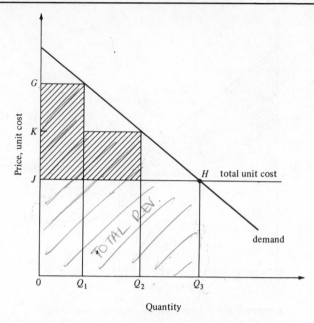

Figure 13-7. *Second degree price discrimination.*

discounts" and "block rate" pricing of electricity and gas. Xerox used such a scheme during the late 1960s for its copier-duplicators (not it 914s). Its charges were 4¢ each for the first three copies from the same original, 2¢ each for the fourth through the tenth copies, and 1¢ each for every copy above 10. (This too was profitable. Overall, Xerox earned 21–30% after-tax return on net worth during the period 1962–1970.)

Third Degree Discrimination. This is depicted in Figure 13-8. The negatively sloped demand curves indicate monopoly power. Differences in their angles of descent and intercepts indicate differing elasticities of demand at each possible price, with the result that buyers in market X have the relatively more elastic demand. Total unit cost (TUC) is the same in both markets because the product is basically the same. Moreover, TUC is again assumed to be constant. This means that TUC and marginal cost (MC) are identical. Following the conventional profit maximizing formula of MR = MC, we find that P_x and Q_x are the optimal combination in market X, whereas P_y and Q_y are the optimal combination in market Y. Shading again indicates excess profits. Notice that price in the relatively elastic market, P_x, is substantially below price in the relatively inelastic market, P_y. Indeed, nothing would be sold in market X at price P_y. Notice also that if these markets could not be kept separate, their demands, their elasticities, and of course their buyers, too, would blend, leaving only one market for the seller instead of two.

338

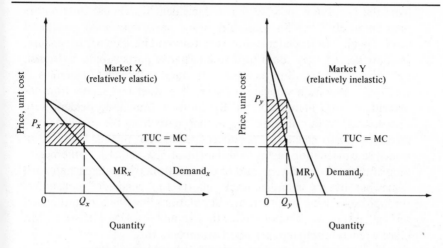

Figure 13-8. *Third degree price discrimination.*

Third degree discrimination is considerably more widespread than second degree and much more so than first degree. Examples abound. The auto industry alone provides many interesting illustrations:

1. Fleet buyers have frequently been able to buy new cars at unit prices considerably below those paid by individual consumers.
2. Manufacturers' markups apparently vary across model lines, with luxury line cars carrying the greatest spread between wholesale price and direct manufacturing cost. For reasons of secrecy, specific data are rare, but an anonymous Ford employee divulged some numbers to Ralph Nader, who in turn revealed the following 1966 markups as a per cent of manufacturer's price: Ford "Custom" two-door sedan, 6.7%; "Galaxie 500" sedan, 13.4%; and "LTD" two-door hardtop 21.1%.[24]
3. Manufacturers charge a much higher profit markup on repair parts than on parts in the form of fully assembled new vehicles. Two key factors help to explain the difference: (a) parts generally have a very low price elasticity of demand, and (b) assemblers may try to use parts sales to "meter" each consumer's intensity of auto use.[25]
4. When selling repair parts, the Big Three vehicle manufacturers have apparently discriminated against their own dealers. Rough estimates

[24] U. S. Senate, Select Committee on Small Business, *Hearings on Planning, Regulation, and Competition: Automobile Industry—1968*, 90th Congress, Second Session (1968), pp. 273–321.

[25] R. W. Crandall, "Vertical Integration and the Market for Repair Parts in the U. S. Auto Industry," *Journal of Industrial Economics* (June 1968), pp. 212–34.

from the late 1960s indicate that independent warehouse distributors paid about 30% less for assembler brand parts than what franchised dealers paid.[26] Independent wholesalers enjoyed bargain prices because, to some degree, they could turn to alternative parts suppliers. In fact, only about 40% of all parts moving through independent channels at that time came from vehicle producers; the other 60% came from independent parts manufacturers. By contrast, franchised dealers were "persuaded" to buy at least 75% of their parts from the vehicle manufacturers. Instruments of producer persuasion included threat of franchise cancellation, delayed shipment of new vehicles at the beginning of the new model year, and so on. The dealers' burden is lightened somewhat by the manufacturers' efforts to "persuade" consumers through advertising and warrantee stipulations that "factory authorized service" is the only kind of service they should get. GM's massive "Mr. Goodwrench" campaign is a good example of this.

5. Finally, discrimination occurs in dealers' showrooms, as cars are one of the few (legal) commodities still available to consumers at negotiated and therefore variable prices. No more than about 40% of all buyers pay full "sticker" price. Those not paying sticker, dicker. And some dicker better than others.

Other common examples of third degree price discrimination relate to firms selling in several product lines, with differing degrees of market power across those product lines. In accord with the empirical findings reviewed earlier, intrafirm price/cost ratios tend to be positively associated with the firm's market power across products.[27]

Social Effects

Actually, the catch-as-catch-can price discrimination of auto showrooms fits none of the theoretical models just outlined. Other real-life forms also fail to fit, such as discrimination associated with basing-point pricing, or with secret "off-list" discounting during recessions, or with predatory pricing. Even so, the social desirability of all forms of price discrimination may be judged by three criteria—income distribution effects, efficiency effects, and competitive effects. The first two of these criteria will be fully explored in Part IV when we come to performance. However, it should be recognized now that blanket labels of "good" or "bad" are inappropriate.

[26] R. W. Crandall, "The Decline of the Franchised Dealer in the Automobile Repair Market," *Journal of Business* (January 1970), pp. 22–23.

[27] For examples see Kaplan, Dirlam, and Lanzillotti, *op. cit.*, pp. 72–74; and C. Kaysen, *United States v. United Shoe Machinery Corporation* (Cambridge, Mass.: Harvard University Press, 1956), pp. 74–77, 125–34; M. J. Peck, *Competition in the Aluminum Industry 1945–1958* (Cambridge, Mass.: Harvard University Press, 1961), Chapter V.

With respect to income distribution, for instance, price discrimination quite clearly adds to profits at the expense of consumers. Since this may contribute added inequality to society's unequal distribution of income, many would say that is bad. On the other hand, profit-enhancing price discrimination may occasionally make the difference between profit and loss, in which case the very existence of the enterprise in question depends on its ability to discriminate. Suppose, for example, that some small town could not attract the services of a physician unless it allowed him to charge the well off higher prices than the poor, there not being much income from that particular practice under a flat fee system. The profit-enhancing properties of discrimination in this instance would be good. Good and bad competitive effects can also be found. It is these competitive consequences that we shall develop more fully now and in the next chapter, beginning with predatory pricing.

Predatory Pricing

There are two elements common to all phenomena called "predatory pricing." *First*, predatory pricing involves temporary price cuts, not for purposes of enlarging demand but rather for purposes of eventually restricting supply. Once the predator is in a position to restrict supply (either by himself or with the cooperation of others), price is then increased. Since "predation" usually requires price to be cut at least below total unit cost, and since the eventual increase carries price well above total unit cost, the stream of profits generated by this ploy is the opposite of that generated by open pricing, as depicted in Figure 13-5. That is to say, losses lead profits. Predatory pricing would make no sense if the losses incurred during the predatory campaign were not rewarded by profits after the campaign is over.

The *second* element of predatory pricing is the predator's "staying power" or "deep pocket," which must be greater or deeper than that of the rivals who are to be preyed upon. As with Nature's great predator *Felis leo*, large absolute size is an advantage. "If such a concern finds itself matching expenditures or losses, dollar for dollar, with a substantially smaller firm, the length of its purse assures it of victory."[28] As with Nature's other ferocious predator, *Homo sapiens*, versatility and guile also help. The business counterparts of these advantages are diversification and price discrimination. Thus, business predation typically involves selling at a loss in one geographic area or in one product line while selling at a profit, perhaps even a substantial profit, elsewhere.

In short, these two elements of predatory pricing relegate the beast to the family tree of "limit pricing" and "price discrimination." Let us now consider the three specific forms it takes: (1) driving competitors from the field, (2)

---

[28] Corwin D. Edwards, "Conglomerate Bigness as a Source of Power," in *Business Concentration and Price Policy* (Princeton, N. J.: Princeton University Press, 1955), p. 334.

disciplining uncooperative competitors, and (3) hindering entry. These are simply three roads to the broad objective of eventually restricting supply.[29]

Driving Competitors Out

Use of predatory pricing to drive competitors out is obviously what gives the practice its name:

> The most extreme form of predatory pricing takes place when a seller holds price below the level of its rivals' costs (and perhaps also its own) for protracted periods, until the rivals either close down operations altogether or sell out on favorable terms. The predator's motivation is to secure a monopoly position once rivals have been driven from the arena, enjoying long-run profits higher than they would be if the rivals were permitted to survive.[30]

Of the two forms of victim liquidation, *bankruptcy* and *merger*, the one more favorable to the profit positions of both predator and prey is merger. Unless the victimized rival is very weak to begin with, or unless the predator applies nonprice harassments such as sabotage or patent infringement suits, a price war to the finish can be very expensive for both combatants. As Lester Telser puts it, "Since both firms can benefit by agreeing on a merger price, and both stand to lose by sales below cost, one would think that rational men would prefer merger."[31]

Indeed, the attractions of merger may be great enough to make price cutting of any kind seem superfluous. But merger is often illegal, and selective and controlled price cutting can serve several purposes even when merger is legal and the ultimate goal. The price the predator must pay to acquire rivals will be lower according to the vigor of the warfare or the *threat* of warfare. If mere threat can cause victims to sell out cheaply, so much the better. But a threat is hollow unless occasionally carried out. Another purpose served by combining predatory pricing and merger, as opposed to simply buying up rivals, is that such a policy discourages entry. A predation-free policy of merger at attractive prices to those selling out would stimulate the entry of new firms, thereby

---

[29] What follows is a distillation of a rather lengthy debate between those who argue that predatory pricing of any kind is essentially irrational and nonexistent versus those who take a less skeptical view. Among the former group are J. S. McGee, "Predatory Price Cutting: The Standard Oil (N.J.) Case," *Journal of Law & Economics* (October 1958), pp. 137–69; L. G. Telser, "Cutthroat Competition and the Long Purse," *Journal of Law & Economics* (October 1966), pp. 259–77; R. O. Zerbe, "The American Sugar Refinery Company 1887–1914: The Story of a Monopoly," *Journal of Law & Economics* (October 1969), pp. 339–75; and R. H. Koller II, "On the Definition of Predatory Pricing," *Antitrust Bulletin* (Summer 1975), pp. 329–37. On the other side are R. C. Brooks Jr., "Injury to Competition Under the Robinson-Patman Act," *University of Pennsylvania Law Review* (April 1961), pp. 777–832; F. M. Scherer, *Industrial Market Structure and Economic Performance* (Chicago: Rand McNally, 1970), pp. 273–78; and B. S. Yamey, "Predatory Price Cutting: Notes and Comments," *Journal of Law & Economics* (April 1972), pp. 129–42.

[30] Scherer, *op. cit.*, p. 273.

[31] Telser, *op. cit.*, p. 265.

piling plans for eventual monopolization. Case histories of firms that have used predatory pricing to gain monopoly power seem to bear out this reasoning. As mentioned in Chapter 9, most of the interesting examples occurred around the turn of the century, and antitrust has made even uninteresting examples now rather rare. Tobacco, sugar, oil, and business machines are among the industries with interesting skeletons in their closets.[32]

Disciplining Uncooperative Competitors

In October 1953, after a costly union wage settlement had substantially increased the labor costs of brewing beer, Anheuser–Busch (AB) attempted to lead a general price increase everywhere except Wisconsin and Missouri. However, several local and regional brewers failed to follow. According to AB's president, August A. Busch, Jr., that was the first time he could remember when, after the large brewers increased their prices, all locals and regionals did not increase their prices also. In an apparent attempt to punish selected mavericks, AB cut its price in the St. Louis market from $2.93 a case to $2.35 a case, thereby eliminating the price "premium" AB maintained between itself and "inferior" regional brands such as Falstaff. Although failure to follow had not actually occurred inside St. Louis (because there had been no attempt by AB to raise prices there), the maverick St. Louis brewers, Falstaff among them, sold beer *outside* St. Louis where price increases *were* attempted and ignored. Perhaps AB feared that its punative motive would have been obvious to anti-trust authorities had it cut prices in, say, Illinois, where an up-and-down sequence would have stuck out like a sore thumb. In any event, motive may be inferred from President Busch's later testimony that AB might not have "done anything" if these regional rivals had also raised their prices in October 1953. AB's price cut in St. Louis lasted 13 months, during the course of which its market share there jumped from 12.5% to 39.3%, a *tripling* at the expense of the mavericks. Then, in February 1955, AB announced a 20% price increase. Not wanting to make the same mistake twice, the battered regionals followed.[33]

In sum, this is an example of predatory pricing for disciplinary purposes. It has both the main elements of predation—deep, temporary price cuts plus an imbalance of power. But the objective is not one of driving rivals from the

---

[32] Besides the preceding references see U. S. Bureau of Corporations, *Report of the Commissioner of Corporations on the Tobacco Industry* (Washington, D.C., 1909, 1915), Parts I, II, and III; A. S. Eichner, *The Emergence of Oligopoly* (Baltimore: Johns Hopkins Press, 1969); William Rodgers, *Think: A Biography of the Watsons and IBM* (New York: Stein and Day, 1969), Chapters 3, 4.

[33] R. C. Brooks, Jr., offers a good brief account of these events, U. S. Congress, House of Representatives *Hearings on Small Business and the Robinson-Patman Act*, Vol. 2, 91st Congress, (1970), pp. 721–38. It should be admitted that this interpretation is not universally accepted among economists. For example, Koller claims there was no predation in the AB case ["The Myth of Predatory Pricing: An Empirical Study," *Antitrust Law and Economics Review* (Summer 1971), p. 105–23].

market. Other examples could be drawn from gasoline retailing, grocery retailing, cement, building materials, and sugar.[34]

Predatory Pricing to Deter Entry

We have now come full circle, for our earlier Shop-Rite example would certainly fit under predatory pricing to deter entry. IBM has also supplied an engrossing if controversial instance. In 1969 and 1970 IBM began to suffer substantial competition from "plug compatible" manufacturers, or PCMs. By May 1971 the PCMs had 14.5% of IBM's disk-drive market and 13.7% of its tape-drive market. Moreover, these shares would have been about 20% by 1976 had IBM not done something. But IBM did do something. On May 27, 1971, it introduced long-term leases coupled with price reductions of 20–35% on equipment vulnerable to such competition.

Within 48 hours PCM company stock-prices began a nose dive (Telex down 14%, Memorex down 15%, Marshall Laboratories down 18%), and within the year following, PCM equipment orders were off 44% from the previous year, despite deep defensive price cuts by the PCM companies. They lost money for the next 2 years. For its part, IBM made up its lost revenues by increasing prices in other product lines—central processing units, card equipment, and maintenance services—just two months after the May reductions. These increases varied from 4 to 8% on equipment, and some maintenance charges rose 25%.

IBM apparently considered this program successful, for little more than a year later the corporation extended it to provide protection against significant PCM entry into memory components. On August 2, 1972, IBM announced what it fittingly called project "SMASH"—a memory price cut of 57% coupled with central processing unit price increases of 36–54%. As the editor of *Datamation* observed soon after the SMASH announcement: "This kind of pricing can't do very much for IBM revenues, but it may drive independent memory suppliers up the wall (or out of business)."[35]

To summarize, predatory pricing may affect market structure as much as limit pricing and open pricing, especially in its starker forms. When used to

---

[34] Federal Trade Commission, *Economic Report On the Structure and Competitive Behavior of Food Retailing* (January 1966), pp. 121–42; *Federal Trade Commission v. Cement Institute, et. al* 333 U. S. 683 (1948); C. D. Edwards, *Maintaining Competition* (New York: McGraw-Hill Book Co., 1964), pp. 169–70; A. S. Eichner, *op. cit.*, pp. 243–46; F. C. Allvine and J. M. Patterson *Competition, Ltd.: The Marketing of Gasoline* (Bloomington, Ind.: Indiana University Press, 1972) Chapters 5–7.

[35] For this quote and details on the rest see G. W. Brock, *The U. S. Computer Industry: A Study of Market Power* (Cambridge, Mass.: Ballinger, 1975), pp. 109–34; and U. S. Senate, Subcommittee on Antitrust and Monopoly, *Hearings on the Industrial Reorganization Act* Part 7, "The Computer Industry," 93rd Congress Second Session (1974), pp. 5637–794. For a summary of recent predatory pricing in gypsum see *Recent Efforts to Amend or Repeal The Robinson-Patman Act*, Hearings before the Ad Hoc Subcommittee on Antitrust . . . and Related Matters of the Committee on Small Business, U. S. Congress, House, 94th Congress Second Session (1975–76), Part 1, pp. 514–20; Part 2, pp. 36–57. The gypsum case illustrates "discipline" as well as entry "deterence."

discipline mavericks, its structural effects are slight but its price-level effects can be substantial. Because predatory pricing inflicts injury on the predator as well as the prey, it is much less common than merger or cartelization, two techniques that often substitute for predatory pricing.

Tying and Exclusive Dealing

Earlier we said that conduct other than simple price setting may affect the height of barriers to entry. Terms and conditions of sale such as tying and exclusive dealing occasionally have this influence. Under **tying arrangements** the seller allows the buyer to buy one line of the seller's goods *only* if the buyer also buys other goods as well. For instance, if Xerox required users of its machines to buy copy paper from Xerox, that would be tying. **Exclusive dealing** is closely related. A seller, usually a manufacturer, gives the buyer, who is usually a wholesaler or retailer, access to the seller's line of goods only if the buyer agrees to handle no goods from any of the seller's rivals. In other words, exclusive dealing binds a buyer to make *all* his purchases from a particular seller. It differs from tying in that (1) it may cover a considerable range of goods, and (2) it limits buyers to a single source of supply. For a hypothetical example, General Electric might require its appliance wholesalers to carry only General Electric appliances, thereby excluding Westinghouse, Whirlpool, and others from the wholesaler.

Tying and exclusive dealing are treated extensively in the next chapter for they are the focus of much antitrust policy. We mention them here because they may be used to further price discrimination or hamper entry.

Summary

The principal objective assumed for this chapter's analysis is long-run profit maximization. Given favorable structural conditions concerning the number of firms, concentration, condition of entry, product differentiation, and long-run elasticity of demand, pursuit of this objective may lead to higher prices and lower output than would prevail under pure competition. These effects are most readily seen in intraindustry, intermarket, cross-section statistical studies that reveal a positive association between prices and high concentration, fewness of sellers, product differentiation, and high barriers to entry. For buyers, "monopsony" power appears to reduce prices paid.

Mechanisms provide some crucial linkage here. Objectives and structural conditions alone do not produce these price and output effects directly. Given the profit objective, conditions may permit limit pricing, open pricing, price discrimination, predatory pricing, tying, and exclusive dealing. Substantial barriers and high concentration, for instance, are prerequisites to limit pricing. In turn, these mechanisms may be used either to exploit or expand market power, or both. When used to enhance market power—that is, to increase concentration or hamper entry—we have a case of reverse causal flow. Whereas the conventional model posits structure causing conduct, here we find instances of conduct altering structure. Later chapters will see even greater attention paid to this possibility.

14

Price and Production Policy in the Long Run: Public Policy

That the Robinson-Patman Act . . . is the most controversial of our antitrust laws may be the understatement of the century.

FREDERICK ROWE

There are many things in life that can be either good or bad or both simultaneously, depending on the circumstances—wealth, wine, and, of course, marriage, to name just a few. The same applies to price discrimination, tying, and exclusive dealing. Under some circumstances, these practices increase competition. At times they lessen competition. It is this good/bad dichotomy that makes public policy in this area a delicate exercise. Indeed, public policy itself can be procompetitive or anticompetitive. And when public policy attempts to govern such dichotomous practices it may do more harm than good. Policy cannot easily extract pure essence of good when treating acts of uncertain and variable virtue.

The purpose of this chapter is to review and assess public policy governing price discrimination, tying, and exclusive dealing (there being no policies concerning "limit" or "open" pricing). The statute law in these areas began in 1914 with Sections 2 and 3 of the Clayton Act. Section 2, concerning price discrimination, was greatly altered by the Robinson–Patman Amendment of 1936. Now, more than a thousand enforcement actions later, we confront a large body of case law that requires summary consideration. Controversy sparked by price discrimination policy also receives attention. A discussion of Section 3 of the Clayton Act, concerning tying and exclusive dealing, concludes the chapter.

Price Discrimination

The Clayton Act's original Section 2 outlawed only flagrantly predatory price discrimination. Its limited scope, plus several loopholes, yielded few prosecutions. As mentioned in the previous chapter, predatory pricing is rare, especially when illegal. While this law lay idle, chain stores revolutionized grocery, drug, and department store merchandising. Small, single-shop, "mom-and-pop" stores suffered and, during the Great Depression, began dropping like blighted apples. The outcries their owners caused the Federal Trade Commission (hereafter called FTC) to study and report. Although the FTC's report found much virtue in chain stores, it also found that "a most substantial part of the chains' ability to undersell independents" could be attributed to the chains' ability to buy goods from manufacturers more cheaply than independents could. The chains' **oligopsony** buying power "forced" manufacturers to discriminate in favor of chains. Moreover, their large size enabled chains to buy directly from manufacturers, thereby sidestepping independent brokers, wholesalers, jobbers, and other middlemen as well as underselling independent retailers. So Congress went to bat for small business. In the words of Congressman Patman, mid-1935:

> The day of the independent merchant is gone unless something is done and done quickly. He cannot possibly survive under that system. So we have reached the cross road; we must either turn the food . . . business of this country . . . over to a few corporate chains, or we have got to pass laws that will give the people, who built this country in time of peace and who saved it in time of war, an opportunity to exist . . . .[1]

In short, the purpose of the Robinson–Patman Act of 1936 went well beyond the traditional antitrust purpose of maintaining competition. It injected two new objectives: *protection* of small business and maintenance of "fair" or "equitable" price relationships between buyers who compete with each other as sellers.

Subsection 2(a) of Robinson-Patman

The aims of protection and equity lurk beneath the tortured language of al six main subsections in the Act, especially 2(a). Subsection 2(a) prohibits a seller from charging different prices to different purchasers of "goods of like grade and quality" where the effect "may be substantially"

1. "to lessen competition or tend to create a monopoly in any line of commerce," or

[1] Hearings Before the House Committee on the Judiciary on *Bills to Amend the Clayton Act*, 74t Congress First Session (1935), pp. 5–6.

2. "to injure, destroy, or prevent competition with any person" (or company)
   (a) "who either grants or"
   (b) "knowingly receives" the benefit of the discrimination, or
   (c) "with customers of either of them."

Thus, there are two definitions of **illegal competitive effect**: (1) a *broad* definition, that refers to substantial lessening of competition in the *market as a whole*, and (2) a *narrow* definition that refers to injury to *particular competitors*. The broad definition reflects the traditional antitrust aim of maintaining competition, and its language matches that applying to mergers. In contrast, it is the narrow definition that reflects the aims of protection, equity, and fairness. Either of these two forms of competitive damage may occur in

(a) the seller's market, which is called **primary level injury**
(b) the buyers' market, which is called **secondary level injury**
(c) the market containing customers of the buyers, which is called **tertiary level injury**.

If, for example, a manufacturer cuts price to one wholesaler but not to others, it might damage competition among manufacturers (primary level), or among wholesalers (secondary level), or among retailers who buy from the wholesalers (tertiary level). If it were a matter of direct sales to retailers, then retailers would be the buyers of the discriminating seller, and they would then be considered "secondary" level. If this sounds confusing, take heart. You are not alone, as indicated by itemization of the first common criticism of the Act.

> *Common Criticism 1 : The Act is "a roughly hewn, unfinished block of legislative phraseology," a "masterpiece of obscurity," a source of "crystal clear confusion."* [2]

Compounding the confusion, several types of price discrimination have been found injurious to competition. Some of these were merely alluded to in the previous chapter. They are (1) volume or quantity discounts, (2) territorial price discrimination, (3) functional discounts, and (4) catch-as-catch-can price discrimination. These are outlined in Table 14-1, together with indications of the level at which they are said to damage competition and the specified breadths of injury typically used in the past by the FTC and appellate courts when enforcing the statute. The dashes in the table identify combinations of level and type that are rarely if every attacked under the law. These blank combinations are eligible for illegality, but the authorities tend to ignore them. The bottom row of Table 14-1 shows the defenses discriminators of each type occasionally

[2] "Eine Kleine Juristische Schlummergeschichte," *Harvard Law Review*, (March 1966), p. 922.

TABLE 14-1   Summary Outline of Injury Definition Applied, Given the Basic Types Discrimination Found to be Illegal and Market Level of Reference

| | Type of Price Discrimination | | | |
| | | | | |
Level of Injury	Volume or Quantity Discounts	Territorial Price Discrimination	Functional Discounts	Catch-as-Catch-Can Pricing
Primary level	Broad or narrow	Broad or narrow	—	Narrow
Secondary level	Narrow	Narrow	Narrow	Narrow
Tertiary level	—	—	Narrow	—
Main line of possible defense	Cost	Good faith	Cost or good faith	Good faith

use to fend off FTC attorneys. These defenses—"cost" and "good faith"—are explicitly recognized by the Robinson–Patman Act:

- *Cost defense*: "nothing herein . . . shall prevent differentials which make only due allowance for differences in the cost of manufacture, sale, or delivery resulting from [differing methods of sale or delivery]."
- *Good faith defense*, Subsection 2(b): "nothing herein . . . shall prevent a seller rebutting the prima-facie case . . . by showing that his lower price . . . was made in good faith to meet an equally low price of a competitor . . ."

Unfortunately, these defenses do not offer much protection in practice. The cost defense has fallen into disuse because the FTC and appellate courts have been very stingy in allowing its application. They require elaborate proofs and reject justifications based on reallocations of overhead costs. The meeting competition in good faith defense is disallowed if the price reduction is excessively aggressive (gaining business rather than merely keeping it); if it continues after lower prices of competitors are known to have been raised; or if there is a lack of precise knowledge concerning competitors' prices. Moreover, the firm may not meet competition if it has reason to believe that the price being met is itself unlawful. In light of their rare use, these defenses do not deserve detailed treatment here.

Common Criticism 2: By amendment or reinterpretation, the defenses open to discriminators ought to be liberalized.

Before delving into the case law concerning the Act, we may note in· its language two major anomalies. First, despite its origins, the statute's fire is focused not on the power or conduct of oligopsonistic *buyers* but rather on the conduct of *sellers*. As Corwin Edwards observes:

> The avowed purpose of the Congress was to use the law of price discrimination to curb the buying power of chain stores and other large buyers. However, the means to be employed consisted primarily in forbidding sellers, the presumed victims of that buying power, from granting the concessions that were exacted from them . . . . If the statute was an effort to protect competition from the pressure of powerful buyers on weak sellers, it was anomalous to provide that protection primarily by action against weak sellers who succumbed to the pressure. Such a process bears some resemblance to an effort to stamp out mugging by making it an offense to permit oneself to be mugged.[3]

Our roster of antitrust defendants has so far been dominated by giants like IBM and Alcoa. The roster of Robinson–Patman defendants, however, introduces a population largely composed of midgets such as Samuel H. Moss, Inc., and Fruitvale Canning Company. The possibility that this oblique approach on sellers might backfire is illustrated by the *Jens Risom* case of 1967, in the office furniture field. Furniture manufacturers such as Risom sold to retailers at a discount off list price amounting to as much as 50%, whereas their sales to interior decorators, who competed with the retailers, were at no more than 40% discount. As a result of the FTC's order ending the discrimination, Risom and some other manufacturers eliminated interior decorators as direct buying customers. These decorators thereafter had to buy furniture for their clients through retailers. Thus, although the intent of the FTC's order was to place decorators on an equal competitive footing with retailers, decorators ended up at the mercy of the retailers with whom they competed. Subsequent to the order, several decorators reported that their clients' costs had increased— one giving estimates of increases ranging from 10 to 20%, depending on which retailer supplied the decorator's clients with furniture.[4]

A second notable quirk concerns the statute's definition of price discrimination. Price differences unjustified by cost differences are "discriminatory," but cost differences unaccompanied by price differences are not. In other words, the economic definition of discrimination—differing price/cost ratios, even if prices are identical—is rejected by the statute in favor of a definition that hinges almost entirely on price differences alone. The consequences of this approach are illustrated by the *Binney & Smith* case. Binney & Smith, Co., was found by the FTC to have sold school supplies at a uniform price to both jobbers, who are middlemen, and large retail chains. This price uniformity, though obviously injurious to jobbers, was not questioned by the FTC.[5]

---

[3] Corwin D. Edwards, *The Price Discrimination Law* (Washington, D.C.: Brookings Institution, 1959), p. 63.

[4] *Recent Efforts to Amend or Repeal the Robinson-Patman Act*, Part 1, Hearings before the Ad Hoc Subcommittee on Antitrust . . . and Related Matters of the Committee on Small Business, U.S. Congress, House, 94th Congress, First Session (1975), pp. 282–312.

[5] Edwards, *op. cit.*, p. 311.

Common Criticism 3: Even accepting the Act's purposes as proper, the statute is ill-conceived. Indeed, many proponents of protection and fairness are disappointed with it.

Before discussing the types of discrimination listed in Table 14-1, we should first specify the kinds of evidence that indicate "broad" or "narrow" injury, the two designations comprising the body of Table 14-1. **Broad** (or **market-wide**) **injury** to competition is indicated by substantial reductions in the number of competitors in the market, elevated barriers to entry, a lack of competitive behavior in pricing, or foreclosure of substantial parts of the market to existing competitors. **Narrow** (or **competitor**) **injury** is indicated by simple price differences among customers, or a price difference coupled with diversion of business from the disadvantaged buyer toward the favored buyer, or diversions away from a nondiscriminating seller toward a discriminating seller. Injuries embraced by this narrow definition are clearly more personal than those embraced by the broad definition. That is, the discrimination appears to cripple a *single* firm or particular *class* of firms. Obviously, the broad definition coincides more nearly with a purely economic definition of competition, while the narrow definition coincides with some notions of fairness.

To search out the extent to which the FTC relies on these two options, R. Brooks studied the records of 73 subsection 2(a) cases that were actually tried (rather than settled by consent degree) between 1936 and mid-1969. He found evidence of broad injury in only one third of the cases (with some trend away from strictly narrow injury during the 1960s).[6] A quick glance at Table 14-1 also reveals that narrow evidence of injury is more commonly used by the FTC, especially when judging injury at secondary and tertiary levels. At primary level, broad injury has been found only in cases concerning volume or quantity discounts and territorial price discrimination.

Volume and Quantity Discounts. These are first cousins to second degree price discrimination. Quantity discounts are based on the amount purchased in a *single* transaction, with large quantities lowering price. Volume discounts are based on *cumulative* purchases, involving numerous transactions, during some stated period of time, such as 1 year. Of the two, volume discounts are least likely to be cost-justifiable and more anticompetitive in the broad sense. For these reasons the FTC has attacked volume discounts much more vigorously than it has quantity discounts. At primary level, volume discounts can heighten barriers to entry or foreclose small sellers from substantial segments of the market.[7]

---

[6] R. C. Brooks, Jr., Testimony, *Small Business and the Robinson-Patman Act*, Hearings before the Special Subcommittee on Small Business and the Robinson-Patman Act of the Select Committee on Small Business, U. S. Congress, House, 91st Congress, Second Session (1970), Vol. 2, p. 657.

[7] R. C. Brooks, Jr. "Volume Discounts as Barriers to Entry and Access," *Journal of Political Economy* (February 1961), p. 65.

Although such discounts may have genuine anticompetitive effects at primary (sellers') level, very few cases have actually been argued on these grounds. The rarity may be due to a dearth of situations causing broad injury at primary level. Then again, it may also be a consequence of the fact that, under the Act, volume and quantity discounts are more easily prosecuted on grounds of narrow injury at the secondary or buyer level. Recall that a major purpose of the Act was to make such prosecutions as these easier.

The classic case here is *Morton Salt*, decided by the Supreme Court in 1948. Morton sold its table salt at $1.60 a case in less-than-carload lots, at $1.50 a case for carload lots, and at still lower prices of $1.40 and $1.35 for annual volumes exceeding 5000 and 50,000 cases, respectively. In defense of these prices, Morton claimed that they were equally available to all, that salt was just one tiny item in grocers' inventories, and that therefore competitive injury could not arise. Rejecting these arguments the Court concluded as follows:

> The legislative history of the Robinson-Patman Act makes it abundantly clear that Congress considered it to be an evil that a large buyer could secure a competitive advantage over a small buyer solely because of the large buyer's quantity purchasing ability . . . . Here the Commission found what would appear to be obvious, that the competitive opportunities of certain merchants were injured when they had to pay [Morton] substantially more for their goods than their competitors had to pay . . . . That [Morton's] quantity discounts did result in price differentials between competing purchasers sufficient to influence their resale price of salt was shown by the evidence . . . . Congress intended to protect a merchant from competitive injury attributable to discriminatory prices on any or all goods sold in interstate commerce, whether the particular goods constituted a major or minor portion of his stock . . . . [In] enacting the Robinson-Patman Act Congress was especially concerned with protecting small business . . . .[8]

This narrow, numerical interpretation of injury was later carried to such extremes that during the 1950s the FTC inferred injury despite evidence that "the beneficiaries of the discrimination were small and weak," and despite "unanimous statements by the disfavored customers that they were not injured."[9] Since then, this hard line has softened somewhat, but a fairly stringent interpretation of secondary line injury still prevails.

Critics of this policy argue that although individual *competitors* may suffer, *competition* may not. Such discrimination in favor of large buyers is said to "introduce flexibility into the distributive system, helping to compress traditional markups, and prevent or disrupt a rigid stratification of functions."[10] Moreover, a large buyer "which does indeed make possible cost savings on the part of its suppliers may yet, in facing impure markets, have to coerce suppliers into giving it the concessions which its greater efficiency justifies."[10] In short,

---

[8] *Federal Trade Commission v. Morton Salt Co.*, 334 U. S. 37 (1948).

[9] Edwards, *op. cit.*, p. 533, referring to Standard Motor Products (Docket No. 5721), and Moog Industries (Docket No. 5723).

[10] J. B. Dirlam and A. E. Kahn, *Fair Competition* (Ithaca, N.Y.: Cornell University Press, 1954), pp. 204–05.

price discrimination may increase price flexibility and rivalry at primary and secondary levels; it may also contribute to efficiency. Even so, enhanced competition is not automatic. Price concessions are not always passed on to consumers or spread throughout the market. Moreover, loss of even a few competitors diminishes competition where there are only a few to begin with. The ultimate effect depends heavily on the circumstances. Hence controversy will continue.[11]

Territorial Price Discrimination. This type of discrimination takes two forms: (1) selective geographic price cutting and (2) fictional freight charges imposed under basing-point pricing systems. Both received earlier mention. The former has produced many illegal primary line injuries, whereas the later has been charged with injuring competition at secondary level. As indicated in Table 14-1, neither can be defended by cost justifications. Because geographic price cutting includes "predatory pricing," several primary line cases of this sort cast a good light on the Robinson–Patman Act. In fact, they give the FTC its finest hours of enforcement.[12] These cases contain poignant examples of genuine broad injury to competition; they also contain striking evidence of predatory intent. Some excerpts from business correspondence follow:

"So by continuing our efforts and putting a crimp into him wherever possible, we may ultimately curb this competition if we should not succeed in eliminating it entirely."

"Don't try to follow me. If you do, we will put you out of business."

The latter message was no idle threat; ensuing below-cost prices ultimately throttled the smaller competitor.[13]

Still, geographic price discrimination may also be procompetitive. It may be used for promotional purposes; for entering new geographic markets; or for further penetrating established markets to spread overhead costs. When used for these laudable purposes, it is usually less systematic than the "sharp-shooting" associated with predation. Nevertheless, procompetitive territorial pricing has occasionally been attacked by the FTC. In the *Page Dairy* case, for instance, the FTC myopically went after a firm whose unsystematic price discrimination was actually undermining its competitors' efforts at cartelization:

---

[11] For a good discussion of the circumstances see *ibid*, Chapters 7 and 8. See also L. S. Keyes, "Price Discrimination in Law and Economics," *Southern Economic Journal* (April 1961), pp. 320–28.

[12] *E. B. Muller & Co. v. FTC*, 142 F. 2d 511 (6th Cir. 1944); *Maryland Baking Co. v. FTC*, 243 F. 2d 716 (4th Cir. 1957); *Forster Mfg. Co. v. FTC*, 335 F. 2d 47 (1st Cir. 1964). Among private cases see *Volasco Prods. Co. v. Lloyd A. Fry Roofing Co.*, 346 F. 2d 661 (6th Cir. 1965); *Moore v. Mead's Fine Bread Co.*, 348 U. S. 115 (1954); and *Continental Baking Co. v. Old Homestead Bread Co.*, 476 F. 2d 97 (10th Cir. 1973).

[13] *Forster Manufacturing Co.*, *op. cit.*

From the trial record it appears that before the complaint against Page Dairy, other dairies had made an unsuccessful effort to draw it into agreement to fix prices .... It is a reasonable inference that the competitors of the company brought its prices to the Commission's attention, not because the local discrimination was unusual, but because Page Dairy was a price-cutter and would not co-operate with other dairies.

The Commission's order in 1953 required Page Dairy to cease selling to any buyer at a lower price than to any other buyer where it was in competition with any other seller. The immediate effect of the order was a price increase by Page Dairy, as a result of which various dairies that had been troubled by price competition of the company felt that their problems had been met.[14]

The line between geographic price cutting that is predatory or destructive of competition and that which promotes or expands competition is obviously difficult to draw. "But," according to the critics, "one thing is certain: it cannot be drawn merely at the point where a price reduction diverts trade from a competitor."[15]

Common Criticism 4: As interpreted, the law stifles genuine price competition, thereby raising and stiffening price levels.

Returning to the bright side of the coin, the FTC put the Robinson–Patman Act to good use in attacking collusive basing-point price systems in the *Corn Products Refining* case of 1945 and others.[16] As we have seen, basing-point systems are price-fixing mechanisms, but the FTC's initial assault was based on narrow secondary line injury under Subsection 2(a). (Later, in *Cement Institute*,[17] a restraint of trade approach was applied.) The defendant in *Corn Products* produced glucose in Chicago and Kansas City plants, but maintained Chicago as a single basing point. Thus, both plants sold only at delivered prices computed as if all shipments originated in Chicago. Kansas City candy manufacturers who bought glucose from the Kansas City plant were charged phantom freight, as if the sweetening had come all the way from Chicago. After hearing the case on appeal, the Supreme Court accepted the FTC's finding that the candy manufacturers located in Kansas City competed with those in Chicago. The Court also bought the idea that, though small, the price differentials on glucose would affect the candy makers' costs and final prices. The cost differences were said to be "enough to divert business from one manufacturer to another." Consequently, narrow competitive injury was adjudged at the secondary or buyer level (between candy manufacturers), and the price system was banned.

---

[14] Edwards, *op. cit.*, pp. 443–44. For a related example see William K. Jones, Testimony, *Small Business and the Robinson-Patman Act*, Hearings before Special Subcommittee on Small Business of the Select Committee on Small Business, House, 91st Congress, First Session (1969), Vol. 1, p. 109.

[15] Philip Elman, "The Robinson-Patman Act and Antitrust Policy: A Time for Reappraisal," *Washington Law Review*, Vol. 42 (1966), p. 13.

[16] *Corn Products Refining Company v. FTC*, 324 U. S. 726 (1945).

[17] *FTC v. Cement Institute*, 333 U. S. 683 (1948).

Functional Discounts. As indicated by Table 14-1, primary level injury is not usually associated with functional discounts, but findings of narrow injury at secondary and tertiary levels have been frequent. By definition, functional discounts are determined not by amounts purchased or buyer location but rather by the functional characteristics of buyers. Functions in the "traditional" distribution network are well known: Producers sell to wholesalers, who sell at a higher price to jobbers, who in turn sell at a higher price to retailers, who finally sell at a still higher price to consumers. Other functional differences may be based on other buyer classifications, such as government versus private.

The problem of illegal price discrimination arises when folks of different functions compete. Most commonly, "traditional" channels get jumbled, as when resale competition crops up between resellers in different classifications, or when a producer sells at various levels in the distribution network to someone's disadvantage. In other words, discrimination between buyers who are *not* in competition with each other is *not* a violation. The FTC has never ruled against a functional discount *per se*; somebody down the line must be disadvantaged relative to his competitors.

For example, if a producer charges a lower price to its direct-buying retailers than to its independent wholesalers, competition may be injured at the *retail* level between its direct buyers and the *customers* of the independent wholesalers. In *Tri-Valley Packing Association v. FTC*, a processor of canned fruits and vegetables sold its canned goods at lower prices to certain retail chains with buying agencies in San Francisco than it charged retailers and wholesalers who did not have buying agencies in San Francisco. The FTC and appellate court found violation of Subsection 2(a) because the direct buying retailers had an advantage over their competitors who had to buy from the higher paying wholesalers.[18]

A different problem arises when a buyer performs a dual role, say wholesaling *and* retailing, in which case he may get a large wholesaler's discount that gives him a competitive advantage when reselling as a retailer but not when reselling as a wholesaler.[19] Critics point out that compliance with the Robinson–Patman Act in these instances often raises a serious inconsistency. Compliance implies that the producer must control the prices at which his independent middlemen resell. But such control involves the producer in "resale price maintenance," or vertical price fixing, which is generally illegal under Section 1 of the Sherman Act.[20]

Common Criticism 5: Compliance with the price discrimination law in this and other respects is inconsistent with other antitrust policies.

[18] *Tri-Valley Packing Ass'n v. FTC*, 329 F. 2d 694 (9th Cir. 1964).
[19] *FTC v. Standard Oil Co.*, 355 U. S. 396 (1958) and 340 U. S. 231 (1951); *Mueller Company v. FTC*, 323 F. 2d 44 (7th Cir., 1963).
[20] Edwards, *op. cit.*, p. 312.

One of the most intriguing and controversial cases of functional discounting is *FTC v. Borden Company*. The issues involved were

1. Definition of "like grade and quality."
2. Cost justification.
3. Primary level injury in a functional discount case.
4. Secondary level injury in the face of equal availability.

What triggered issue (1) was Borden's sale of "Borden" label evaporated milk at a uniform price of $6.27 a case, while selling *exactly the same* canned milk without "Borden" labels at an average price of $5.17 a case to merchants who affixed their own "private" labels before reselling it to consumers. An expansion of Borden's private label operations in the late 1950s caused seven midwestern private label producers to lose 7% of their business to Borden. This minor diversion of business prodded the FTC into charging Borden with unlawful discrimination between "Borden"-label and private-label milk sales (even though the diversion was solely a private-label affair). Borden's first line of defense was to argue that, although the two products were physically and chemically identical in every respect, they were *not* goods of "like grade and quality" for purposes of the Robinson–Patman Act. Borden felt that product differentiation established by advertising distinguished the two products for commercial if not for nutritional purposes. The FTC rejected this defense, but the Court of Appeals accepted it.[21] Finally, the Supreme Court sided with the FTC against Borden, saying

[Our] view is that labels do not differentiate products for the purpose of determining grade or quality, even though one label may have more customer appeal and command a higher price in the marketplace from a substantial segment of the public . . .[22]

Borden also lost on issue (2) when it was decided that Borden's cost justification relied too heavily on "broad averaging." At this point things looked bleak for Borden. A cry of protest arose from those who feared that this turn of events would set precedents that would eventually cripple if not kill low-priced, high-quality, privately-branded consumer products. However, Borden prevailed on issues (3) and (4), thereby preventing such a dire outcome. These issues were decided on remand from the Supreme Court at the Circuit Court level.[23]

With respect to *primary level* injury, the Circuit Court noted that "Borden's share of the market increased only from 9.9 percent in 1955 to 10.7 percent in

---

[21] *Borden Company v. FTC*, 339 F. 2d 133, (5th Cir. 1964).

[22] *FTC v. Borden Company*, 383 U. S. 637 (1966); several commentators have pointed out that this view is inconsistent with other policies [E. M. Singer, *Antitrust Economics* (Englewood Cliffs, N. J.: Prentice-Hall, 1968), pp. 237–38], but, as already noted, consistency is not the hallmark of policy in this area.

[23] *Borden Company v. FTC*, 381 F. 2d 175 (5th Cir. 1967).

1957," a change that could hardly be considered "substantial." Moreover, the Court found no causal relationship between these shifts of business among private-label producers and Borden's brand-versus-nonbrand price policy: "none of the evidence adduced by the testifying competitors relates to the price difference between the milks marketed by Borden; instead it relates to the price difference between their own private-label milk and Borden's private-label milk." Hence, no primary level injury.

The Court found two reasons for favoring Borden on the question of secondary level injury. First, no buyers could be injured except by *self-inflicted* wounds because there was "no evidence in the record that Borden refused to sell private-label milk to any customer who specifically requested it." It was, in other words, *equally available* to all merchants, immense or minute. Second, and more important for permitting brand-name manufacturers to make private-label sales, the Court held the following:

> We are of the firm view that where a price differential between premium and non-premium brand reflects no more than a consumer preference for the premium brand, the price difference creates no competitive advantage to a recipient of the cheaper private brand product on which injury could be predicted. Rather, it represents merely a rough equivalent of the benefit by way of the seller's national advertising and promotion, which the purchaser of the more expensive brand enjoys.

In sum, to the extent consumers are fooled into paying more for brand image, a price differential is all right because the merchants who pay the producer's higher price will eventually recoup from those so fooled.

Catch-as-Catch-Can-Discrimination. This is a miscellaneous category, best explained by illustration. In four cases, brought during the 1940s, the FTC found that competition among manufacturers of rubber stamps (that's right, *rubber stamps*) had been injured by price discrimination. This was a highly competitive market, with 70 manufacturers in New York City alone. The companies chastised were very small, 10–20 employees being typical. Moreover, they charged whatever prices were necessary "to get the business." That is, concessions varied from one customer to another in catch-as-catch-can fashion: "Moss's price for a one-line stamp, two inches long, varied from 4 cents to 15 cents, and for a one-line stamp three inches long, from 4 cents to 30 cents . . . [and so on]."[24] The FTC found primary line injury on grounds that this diverted trade *to* the discriminator *from* his competitors. Since price concessions typically have the effect of diverting business, "the principle adopted in these cases means that *any* discrimination large enough to serve as an effective inducement to buy is unlawful in the absence of one of the statutory justifications [cost or good faith]."[25]

---

[24] Edwards, *op. cit.*, p. 479.
[25] *Ibid.*, p. 482 (emphasis added).

Need we say this policy was injurious to competition? The effects of this brand of policy emerged from an extensive study conducted by Corwin Edwards on the effects of decisions in 83 pre-1957 cases of all kinds (so far as these effects could be ascertained by interviews with the businessmen involved): "There is a consensus of opinion among both buyers and sellers that the result has been to diminish the flexibility of prices."[26] Edwards found no clear tendency for prices to rise or fall as a result of early Robinson–Patman enforcement. Adjustments in all directions were observed. However, the interviews "strongly" indicated stickier and less flexible prices. (Neither of which qualities suits a rubber stamp.) Fortunately, the FTC seems to have responded to this criticism, for it has not prosecuted any cases like those in rubber stamps since the mid-1960s.

Another form of miscellaneous price discrimination that may be procompetitive is "under-the-table" discounting by oligopolists who want to probe their nonfollowship demand curves:

> Oligopolists may be unwilling to chance price reduction unless . . . they can make them secretly and selectively; they may similarly be unwilling to attempt promotional pricing except in a selective fashion. To require open, nondiscriminatory pricing may therefore deprive oligopoly markets of their only sources of price flexibility and rivalry.[27]

Although critics of the law have accused the FTC of discouraging such under-the-table discrimination, the charge cannot be verified by specific cases of the past 20 years. This paucity of cases may stem from FTC constraint coupled with the probability that, given the experience reviewed in Chapter 11, such cases would have to originate with a big firm's complaint against a smaller price-cutting rival. The unseemliness of such a situation is self-evident.

An Overview. Critical analyses of the Robinson–Patman Act suggest that procompetitive discriminations may be distinguished from anticompetitive discriminations by whether they are unsystematic or systematic and whether they are perpetrated by firms with small or large market shares. Systematic, large-firm discriminations tend to be anticompetitive, whereas unsystematic, small-firm discriminations tend to be competitive. But there are exceptions.

The criticism may give the added impression that enforcement zealous enough to crush many small-firm discriminations must have also stamped out large-firm discriminations altogether. But this inference would be fallacious. Discrimination can take many forms not reached by the law. A powerful seller may favor particular buyers by making uniform price reductions upon that part of his product line most important to those particular buyers. Moreover, a powerful seller can sometimes refuse to sell to those he disfavors. Similarly,

---

[26] *Ibid.*, p. 630.
[27] Dirlam and Kahn, *op. cit.*, p. 204.

a powerful buyer, deprived of discriminatory price concessions, can nevertheless obtain substantial advantages in acquiring goods:

It can (a) take a seller's entire output at a low price; (b) obtain low prices from sellers who are meeting some other seller's lawful competition; (c) buy goods cheaply abroad; (d) obtain low prices upon goods so differentiated from what bears higher prices that the prohibition of the law is inapplicable; (e) obtain goods of premium quality without paying a premium price; (f) buy large amounts under long-term contract when prices are unusually low; or (g) produce goods for itself.[28]

For these many reasons, chain stores have thrived despite the law. The shrewd reader may think up other avenues of evasion. Brokerage payments and preferential promotional services or allowances cannot be among them, however. Discrimination via these routes is foreclosed by Subsections 2(c), (d), and (e) of the Robinson–Patman Act, each of which warrants a few words.

Subsections 2(c), (d), and (e)

As may be seen from Table 14-2, these portions of the Robinson–Patman Act are *not* simple extensions of Subsection 2(a) governing seller's price differences. Whereas some kind of probable competitive injury must be shown under 2(a), such is not the case for (c), (d), and (e). Furthermore, whereas 2(a) discriminators may defend themselves by cost justifications or demonstrations of meeting competition in good faith, those running afoul of Subsections 2(c), (d),and (e) may not, except for (d) and (e) with respect to good faith. In other words, these

TABLE 14-2 Comparative Outline of Subsections 2(a), (c), (d), (e), and (f), of the Robinson-Patman Act

Subsection	(1) Competitive Injury Required?	(2) Cost Defense Available?	(3) Good Faith Defense Available?	(4) Violator is Buyer or Seller?
2(a) General	1. Yes	2. Yes	3. Yes	4. Seller
2(c) Brokerage	1. No	2. No	3. No	4. Both
2(d) Promotional pay	1. No	2. No	3. Yes	4. Seller
2(e) Services	1. No	2. No	3. Yes	4. Seller
2(f) Buyer inducement	Buyer liability for knowingly inducing violation of one of the above			

[28] Corwin D. Edwards, "Control of the Single Firm: Its Place in Antitrust Policy," *Law & Contemporary Problems* (Summer 1965), p. 477.

additional provisions of the Act specify what could be considered *per se* violations.

Subsection 2(c), the **brokerage provision**, outlaws payment or receipt of brokerage fees that cross the sales transaction from seller to buyer. It also prohibits any compensation *in lieu* of brokerage. Brokers (whose job it is to match up buyers and sellers without ever taking title to the goods) are quite active in the grocery game plus a few other distributive trades. Subsection 2(c) was aimed primarily at a practice in the food industry by which chain stores large enough to buy direct, without benefit of brokers, got price reductions equivalent to the brokerage fees that sellers would have otherwise paid. In practice, however, this provision outlawed *all* brokerage commissions, large or small, except those paid to a truly independent broker. At times, 2(c)'s vigorous application has harpooned marketing arrangements that helped small concerns. In the *Biddle* case, for instance, Biddle sold market-information services to 2400 grocery buyers—placing their orders with sellers, collecting brokerage from sellers, and then passing some brokerage on to the buyers in the form of reduced information fees.[29] This practice was declared illegal, however, as were others equally beneficial to small independents.[30] The courts held that "The seller may not pay the buyer brokerage on the latter's purchases for his own account" (period). The Supreme Court's *Broch* opinion of 1960[31] has since introduced a modicum of flexibility into brokerage cases, but a modicum is not a magnum.

Subsection 2(d) makes it unlawful for a seller to make any **payment to a buyer** in consideration of the buyer's promotion of the seller's goods, unless similar payments are made available on "proportionately equal terms" to *all* competing buyers. Subsection 2(e) makes it unlawful for the seller himself to **provide promotional services** to or through a buyer unless he provides opportunity for such services on "proportionally equal terms" to *all* other competing buyers.

For example, if Revlon were to provide Macy's, Bullock's, and Sears, with in-store demonstrators of Revlon cosmetics, or if they *paid* these large retailers to conduct these demonstrations, then Revlon would have to make equal-proportionate opportunities of some kind open to all retailers who compete with Macy's, Bullock's, and Sears in cosmetics. You may ask proportionate to what? And in what way? Does that mean that Revlon must circulate a midget giving one-shot, 15-minute demonstrations amongst independent corner drug stores for every fully developed model it sets up in Macy's for a week-end visit?

The FTC and the courts have chopped through a thick jungle of questions such as these during the past 40 years. And, in order to guide the ordinary, time-pressed businessman through the treacherous path so cleared, the FTC has

---

[29] *Biddle Purchasing Co., v. FTC,* 96 F. 2d 687 (1938).
[30] See, e.g., *Quality Bakers v. FTC,* 114 F. 2d 393 (1940); and *Southgate Brokerage Co. v. FTC* 150 F. 2d 607 (1945).
[31] *FTC v. Henry Broch & Co.,* 363 U. S. 166 (1960).

kindly drawn-up a long "Guide for Advertising Allowances and other Merchandising Payments and Services" that attempts to clarify the case law for laymen. Among other things, it states that a seller's burden under the law is heavier than mere selection of the appropriate allowances or services. He must (1) know which customers compete with each other, (2) notify each competing buyer that these aids are available, and (3) police the destination of any payments to make sure they are properly spent.[32] Although the general economic effect of these regulations is unclear, a multitude of small merchants seems to support them on grounds of fairness and equity. Interviews with apparel merchants, after intensive FTC activity concerning 2(d), turned up the following typical response: "It cleaned up the problem of individually negotiated advertising allowances which was inherently unfair to the small guy."[33] Although most economists do not ridicule such sentiments, they tend to be skeptical, even cynical.

> *Common Criticism 6: Subsections 2(c), (d) and (e) should not pose per se violations. Discriminations of any kind should be subjected to tests of competitive injury and be allowed liberal cost and good faith defenses.*

Subsection 2(f), Buyer Inducement

Subsection 2(f) makes it unlawful for any buyer "knowingly to induce or receive a discrimination in price which is prohibited by this Section." Here Congress finally addressed the problem it was really most worked up about — the big buyer who pressures his suppliers for discriminatory concessions. However, this subsection has been used more sparingly than a spare tire because the Supreme Court has made it difficult for the FTC to apply. The FTC's attorneys have the burden of proving (1) that an illegally injurious discrimination occurred, (2) that it was not cost justified, and (3) that the buyer *knew* it was not cost justified.

Ordinary 2(a) cases require no more of the FTC's attorneys than item (1). In 2(a) cases the burden of proof regarding costs naturally rests with the discriminator who wants to defend himself, and buyer knowledge is irrelevant. This absence of items (2) and (3) makes "kid stuff" of typical 2(a) prosecutions. But according to the Supreme Court's view of 2(f), a buyer cannot be expected to know the details of his supplier's cost, and a buyer may therefore be unaware that the bargain prices he pays are illegal.[34] Off hand, this ruling might make any such prosecutions seem impossible, since wiley buyers might evade offenses by maintaining a state of carefully contrived ignorance. But prosecution is merely difficult. The Court has said that buyer knowledge of unjustified dis-

---

[32] P. Areeda, *Antitrust Analysis* (Boston: Little, Brown and Co., 1974), p. 951–60.
[33] *Recent Efforts . . .* , *op. cit.*, p. 346.
[34] *Automatic Canteen Co., v. FTC*, 346 U. S. 61.

counts may be inferred "where his experience in the trade should make it clear that a difference in price exceeds a difference in cost."[35]

Declining Robinson-Patman Enforcement

On the one side we have seen corrective action appropriate to antitrust policy. On the other side we have seen official applications of dubious merit— attacks on harmless trade practices, protective interventions where injury was slight, and even anticompetitive proceedings. The controversy between those seeing Dr. Jekyll and those seeing Mr. Hyde reached a particularly high pitch during the late 1960s and early 1970s. Two task forces on antitrust policy appointed by two successive presidents (Johnson and Nixon), plus a blue-ribbon committee appointed by the American Bar Association, severely criticized the Act and the FTC's enforcement of it. Later, President Ford's people in the Justice Department proposed radical modifications in the statute. Central to this and similar proposals is abolition of the narrow-injury test, but some critics have urged *complete abolition* of the Robinson–Patman Act. In response to these developments, Congress held three sets of hearings,[36] but no new legislation came of them, primarily because small-business trade associations mobilized to thwart reform. Small business merchants seem to revere the current law with religious fervor, despite the fact that it has often been used to their disadvantage. "Please don't let the Robinson–Patman Act die," they plead. "All small businesses need it to survive."[37] Admittedly, the Act's principal achievements lie in the realms of protection and fairness (though not necessarily fairness to consumers).

For its part, the FTC seems to have responded to the criticism by drastically altering its enforcement policies. In 1963 the FTC issued 219 complaints and 150 orders under the Act; in 1969 it issued just 8 complaints plus 9 orders; and, for the year ending June 30, 1975, the FTC issued only 2 complaints and 2 orders. As one Commissioner recently put it, "Robinson–Patman is being slowly anesthetized."[38] Although the FTC's formal proceedings have diminished to token proportions, its informal efforts have apparently not flagged as much. The FTC's nonlitigative procedures include Industry Guides and Trade Regulation Rules, each of which gives the FTC a "guiding presence" of varying compulsion in targeted industries. Even more informally, the Commission's attorneys may issue "warnings" to possible violators and may accept assurances of voluntary compliance." Aside from official enforcement, private

---

[35] C. Wilcox and W. G. Shepherd, *Public Policies Toward Business* (Homewood, Ill.: R. D. Irwing, 1975), pp. 183–84.

[36] *Recent Efforts to Amend or Repeal . . . , op. cit.*, Parts 1, 2, and 3; *Small Business and the Robinson-Patman Act, op. cit.*, 3 volumes; *Price Discrimination Legislation—1969*, Hearings before the Subcommittee on Antitrust and Monopoly of the Committee on the Judiciary, U. S. Senate, 91st Congress First Session (1969).

[37] *Recent Efforts to Amend or Repeal . . . , op. cit.*, Part 3, p. 207.

[38] "Robinson-Patman is not Dead—Merely Dormant," address by Paul Rand Dixon, May 21, 1975 (mimeo).

suits are also possible and quite common. In truth, a private treble damage suit, *Utah Pie Co. v. Continental Baking Co.*,[39] was the fuse that ignited much of the recent debate. The Utah Pie Company, a small Salt Lake City purveyor of frozen pies, sued three formidable pie opponents—Continental, Carnation, and Pet—for injuriously cutting prices below cost in Salt Lake City while maintaining prices elsewhere. In 1967, the Supreme Court held that the three national firms had violated Subsection 2(a) despite the fact that Utah Pie had enjoyed the largest share of the local market and had maintained profits throughout the price war. According to one critic, the Supreme Court used subsection 2(a) "to strike directly at price competition itself."[40]

Tying

Season tickets, book club memberships, and the razors that come packaged with blades all have one thing in common: they are tie-in sales, where the sale of one item is tied to the sale of another. These particular ties are innocuous, since one has the option of making separate purchases at reasonable prices. But policy problems arise when the customer is *required* to buy a second product in order to get the one he wants. Under Section 3 of the Clayton Act, such required tie-in sales are prohibited where the effect "may be to substantially lessen competition or tend to create a monopoly." Tying is also occasionally attacked under Section 1 of the Sherman Act as a restraint of trade. These prohibitions suggest that tying may bolster barriers to entry or enable a monopolist controlling the tying (or principal) good to extend his monopoly power into the market for the tied (or second) good. Both are real possibilities. Although policy is complicated by the fact that tying serves other purposes that may not be anticompetitive, these other purposes are not necessarily *pro*-competitive. Hence, this area is not plagued by bitter controversy. Four purposes of tying deserve mention.

Economies or Conveniences

Shirts sold with buttons, autos with tires, and pencils with erasers illustrate combinations more efficiently manufactured and distributed than constituent parts. These ties are so close that we think of each as being one product, the parts of which come in fixed proportions, such as seven buttons to a shirt. Since consumers would probably have to pay more for the privilege of buying separate parts, these ties are economically "natural."

---

[39] *Utah Pie Co. v. Continental Baking Co.*, 386 U. S. 685 (1967).
[40] W. S. Bowman, "Restraint of Trade by the Supreme Court: The Utah Pie Case," *Yale Law Journal* (November 1967), p. 70.

Goodwill

A manufacturer of a delicate machine that consumes, dispenses, or processes materials may tie machine and materials together, thereby denying machine users the option of purchasing materials from independent sources. IBM, for example, used to require that IBM punch cards be used in its key punch, card sorting, and other processing equipment. Defending itself against anti-rust prosecution, IBM claimed that the tie-in was necessary to protect its reputation, that use of just anybody's cards would clog its machines and tarnish its industrial honor. The Supreme Court rejected IBM's goodwill defense because there was ample evidence that other manufacturers' cards met high standards of quality.[41] However, in other cases, some not involving machines and materials, this justification might be valid.

Price Discrimination[42]

In the previous chapter we saw how Xerox practiced price discrimination by leasing and metering the use of its copy machines. A machine's "consumption" of materials, such as paper, ink, staples, or film, may also, like a meter, measure intensity of use. Thus, when meters are impractical, easily tampered with, or prohibitively expensive, manufacturers of machines may try to sell or lease their machines at a low rate and tie-in the sale of materials priced well above cost. In this way, customers with intense demands would pay more than marginal users. Moreover, profits would be greater than those obtained without such price discrimination, especially if the producer has monopoly power in the machine's market. Notice that this tie-in may merely *exploit* more fully some already existing monopoly power. It does not necessarily entail an *extension* of market power into the tied good's market. For example, even in the absence of antitrust policy, Xerox could not monopolize the paper industry by tying copy paper to its machines because very little paper is used for that specific purpose.

Leverage

Under certain conditions, however, a firm with monopoly control over the tying product may be able to extend its power by tying. One key condition is that the tying and tied goods be complements used in varying proportions, such as bread and butter. William Baldwin and David McFarland explain it thus:

Assume that a seller with a complete monopoly on bread ties sales of his brand of butter to the bread, where butter was formerly sold in a perfectly competitive market. If there is no use for butter except to spread on bread, the tie-in will lead to a complete

[41] *International Business Machines v. U. S.*, 298 U. S. 131 (1936).
[42] M. L. Burstein, "A Theory of Full-Line Forcing," *Northwestern University Law Review* March-April, 1960), pp. 62–95.

monopoly in the butter market. In any event, the bread monopolist will achieve some degree of monopoly power in the butter market. But as he raises the price of his butter, the amount of bread he can sell at what used to be the best monopoly price will fall. The amount of leverage he can exert depends upon the elasticity of the demand curve for butter and the magnitude of the shifts in the demand curve for bread caused by increases in the price of butter.[43]

The lower the elasticity and the smaller the shifts, the greater the leverage.

When enforcing the law, the Department of Justice, the FTC, and the federal courts give little weight to any but this last motive. In the Supreme Court's view, "Tying agreements serve hardly any purpose beyond the suppression of competition."[44] Accordingly, violations tend to fit a three-step formula:[45]

1. Economic power in the market for the tying goods, *plus*
2. Substantial commerce in the tied goods, *equals*
3. A violation of the antitrust laws.

Of these steps, the first is most crucial since "substantial commerce" seems to mean anything over a million dollars worth of business. To determine power in the tying good market, however, the Supreme Court has relied on a loose variety of indices: (1) large market share or "market dominance" for the tying good, (2) patents or copyrights for the tying good, (3) high barriers to entry in the tying good market, and (4) uniqueness or "special desirability" of the tying good.

For example, a landmark case in patents is *International Salt* of 1947.[46] International had a "limited" patent monopoly over salt dispensing machines used in food processing. Users of the machines had to buy their salt from International or find other machines. International argued that preservation of goodwill required the tie-in, that only its own salt was of sufficient purity to provide top-quality dispensing. The Supreme Court rejected this assertion, observing that no evidence had been presented to show "that the machine is allergic to salt of equal quality produced by anyone except International." Moreover, the presence of the patents caused the Court to dispense some salty *per se* references, such as, "it is unreasonable, *per se*, to foreclose competitors from any substantial market."

Requisite power based on copyrights and uniqueness is illustrated by *U.S. v. Loew's, Inc.* (1962), which involved "block-booking." When selling motion pictures to television stations, Loew's had "conditioned the license or sale of one or more feature films upon the acceptance by the station of a package or block containing one or more unwanted or inferior films." Put bluntly, the

[43] W. L. Baldwin and David McFarland, "Tying Arrangements in Law and Economics," *Antitrust Bulletin* (September–October 1963), p. 769.
[44] *Standard Oil of California et. al., v. U. S.*, 337 U. S. 293 (1949).
[45] E. M. Singer, *Antitrust Economics* (Englewood Cliffs, N. J.: Prentice-Hall, 1968), p. 196. Much of this discussion is based on Singer.
[46] *International Salt Co. v. U. S.*, 332 U. S. 392 (1947).

ractice could tie *Gone With the Wind* and *Getting Gertie's Garter*. On the uestion of economic power, the Supreme Court decided that each film "was a itself a unique product"; that feature films "were not fungible"; that "since ach defendant by reason of its copyright had a 'monopolistic' position as to ach tying product, 'sufficient economic power' to impose an appreciable estraint on free competition in the tied product was present."[47]

Despite the appearance of hard-line enforcement, it should be stressed that ying is not *per se* illegal. In particular, goodwill defenses have been used success- lly on several occasions.[48]

Exclusive Dealing

Under an exclusive dealing agreement, the buyer obtains the seller's product n condition that he will not deal in the products of the seller's rivals. The buyer, ay an appliance wholesaler, agrees to secure his total requirements of a par- cular product, kitchen appliances, from one supplier, say General Electric. uch an arrangement may carry anticompetitive effects, especially when used y a seller or a group of sellers with a large market share:

> Once a large or dominant supplier in a market obtains for his exclusive use a cor- respondingly large share of available outlets on a lower level of distribution, he has probably imposed prohibitive cost disadvantages on existing or potential rivals, since they are likely to have to create new outlets in order to participate in the market. The same is true where a group of suppliers collectively (if not collusively) obtain exclusive obligations from dealers—and thus produce an aggregate foreclosure.[49]

uch arrangements advance the supplier's interests not only because they have possible exclusionary effect but because they also assure that distributors ill devote their undivided energy to the supplier's products, something articularly important where personal sales, repair service, and promotion re required. Moreover, the arrangement offers the possibility of more pre- ictable sales.

From the buyer's or distributor's point of view, there are a number of reasons or accepting exclusive dealing:

- Supplies may be more certain and steady, especially in times of shortage.
- Specialization entails lower inventories than would be required with several brands of the same product.

[47] *U. S. v. Loew's, Inc.*, 371 U. S. 38 (1962).

[48] *U. S. v. Jerrold Electronics Corp.*, 365 U. S. 567 (1961), and *Dehydrating Process Co., v. A. O. 'mith Corp.*, 292 F. 2d 653 (1st Cir.) *cert. denied*, 368 U. S. 931 (1961).

[49] D. N. Thompson, *Franchise Operations and Antitrust* (Lexington, Mass.: Heath Lexington ooks, 1971), p. 59.

- If exclusive dealing is rejected, the buyer may no longer be a buyer (that is, the seller "forces" acceptance).
- Acceptance may be conceded in exchange for a commitment from the seller that protects the buyer-dealer from competition of other buyer-dealers handling the same brand (for example, territorial assignments or limits on the number of dealerships).

According to Section 3 of the Clayton Act and the Supreme Court's interpretation of it, exclusive dealing is not now *per se* illegal. Hence, the Court considers economic conditions and purposes when determining illegalities. Two main factors are the seller's market share and the prevalence of the practice among all sellers. Beyond this, uncertainty is rife, as illustrated by the Supreme Court's decisions in *Standard Stations* (1948) and *Tampa Electric* (1961). At issue in the former case were contracts obligating 5937 Standard service stations to take their full gasoline requirements and in some instances tires, batteries, and accessories as well, from Standard Oil Company of California. In addition, all other major suppliers used similar contracts. The Supreme Court *refused* to consider economic justification for the contracts and chose a test centering on the "quantitative substantiality" of the restraint. Stressing the fact that Standard's contracts covered 6.7% of the market and the fact that sales of $58 million were involved, the Court found a violation of Section 3 because the contracts "foreclosed competition in a substantial share of the line of commerce affected."[50] District and circuit courts thereafter applied the quantitative substantiality test until 1961.

In the *Tampa Electric* opinion of 1961, the Supreme Court said it *would* consider economic justifications for exclusive dealing. However, it is still uncertain just how important economic justifications will eventually become because the contract at issue in *Tampa* involved only 1% of the market, and according to the Court, it would probably have gotten by the substantiality test anyway:

> There is here neither a seller with a dominant position in the market . . . nor myriad outlets with substantial sales volume, coupled with an industry-wide practice of relying upon exclusive contracts . . . nor a plainly restrictive tying arrangement . . . . On the contrary, we seem to have only that type of contract which may well be of economic advantage to buyers as well as to sellers.[51]

At this point the reader may be wondering why, if all but the most measly of such contracts are banned, any kid on Main Street can observe extensive exclusive dealing in the retailing of gasoline, autos, tires, fast-foods, and other products. The answer comes in two parts. First, vertical ownership and integration lie behind some of those observations, in which case the absence of a truly independent dealer precludes the possibility of exclusive dealing. Second, much

[50] *Standard Oil of California and Standard Stations, Inc. v. U. S.*, 337 U. S. 293 (1949).
[51] *Tampa Electric Co. v. Nashville Coal Co., et. al.*, 365 U. S. 320 (1961).

tacit exclusive dealing occurs.[52] This latter phenomenon is on all fours with tacit price fixing. Tacit "understandings" are not illegal; only explicit ones are. And a powerful manufacturer may be able to impose tacit exclusive dealing by refusing to sell to those who cannot or do not take the manufacturer's hint that this is what he wants. *Collective* refusals to sell are essentially *per se* illegal.[53] So are refusals whose *clear* purpose it is to secure cooperation in an illegal scheme.[54] But, beyond these narrow boundaries, the right of refusal to sell poses an ever-present punitive threat.

Much the same could be said, in terms of both law and business practice, about another form of exclusive dealing—namely, assignment of exclusive territories. The buyer or distributor in this case receives the exclusive right to handle the seller's product in a given geographic market. Such agreements obviously curtail *intra*brand competition among distributors. But they may also bolster *inter*brand competition under certain limited circumstances.[55]

Summary

The Robinson–Patman Act has been called the "Magna Carta" of small business. Others have named it "Typhoid Mary." Ever since it amended section 2 of the Clayton Act in 1936, it has stirred controversy. Perhaps *any* law governing price discrimination would be controversial. Price discrimination always entails a high price somewhere and a low price somewhere else. Those who see evil in price discrimination tend to see the high price more readily than the low price. Those who see goodness in price discrimination seem to have reverse viewing capabilities. In addition to viewer attitudes, circumstances make a difference.

In any event, the Robinson–Patman Act outlaws price differences where the effect may be broad or narrow competitive injury at any one of three levels—primary, secondary, or tertiary—unless the difference can be defended on grounds of "cost justification" or "good faith" price mimicry. Four major classes of price discrimination have been found to violate these standards at least occasionally: (1) volume or quantity discounts, (2) territorial discrimination, (3) functional discounts, and (4) catch-as-catch-can pricing. The first two are particularly prone to true anticompetitive effects, and a number of these cases cast the FTC in good light. On the other hand, attacks against all four have produced instances of ill-advised enforcement.

[52] Thompson, *op. cit.*, Chapter 4. See also A. R. Oxenfelt, *Marketing Practices in the TV Set Industry* (New York: Columbia University Press, 1964), p. 123; and L. P. Bucklin, *Competition and Evolution in the Distributive Trades* (Englewood Cliffs, N. J.: Prentice-Hall, 1972), pp. 272–75.

[53] *Klor's, Inc. v. Broadway-Hale Stores, Inc.*, 359 U. S. 207 (1959).

[54] C. H. Fulda, "Individual Refusals to Deal: When does Single-Firm Conduct Become Vertical Restraint?" *Law and Contemporary Problems* (Summer 1965), pp. 590–606.

[55] Thompson, *op. cit.*, Chapter 7.

Subsections 2(c), (d), and (e) prohibit any discrimination that takes the form of brokerage payments, discounts in lieu of brokerage, payments for promotion or other services, and direct provision of promotion or other service. These are generally *per se* prohibitions because potential competitive injury need not be shown and, for the most part, these practices cannot be defended on grounds of cost or good faith. Finally, Subsection 2(f) addresses the problem that Congress was most concerned about, for it bans knowing inducement or receipt of an unlawfully discriminatory price. Despite the efforts of Congress and the FTC, the Act has apparently not stemmed the advance of chain stores. Chains have found ways around the law. In addition, the FTC has recently eased up on the Act's enforcement, at least in terms of formal proceedings and orders.

Section 3 of the Clayton Act outlaws tying and exclusive dealing where the effect "may be to substantially lessen competition or tend to create a monopoly." The key legal test of tying is whether the firm has monopoly power in the tying-good market, and, if so, whether a substantial volume of business is accounted for by the tied good. Even where power and substantiality indicate a violation, the tie-in may escape illegality, at least temporarily, on grounds that it protects goodwill. The illegality of exclusive dealing hinges mainly on the market power of the seller and the prevalence of the practice in the relevant market. The extent to which competitively innocuous economic justifications can save otherwise illegal exclusive dealing is uncertain. Be that as it may, it appears that many anticompetitive exclusive dealing arrangements escape the law's embrace because they are tacit rather than explicit.

15

Product Differentiation Conduct: Theory and Evidence

...ll Miller to come right along, but tell them to bring lots of money . . .

AUGUST A. BUSCH III, chief executive,
Anheuser-Busch Inc., (in response to
Miller's threatened dethronement of the
"King of Beers," late 1970s)

What is the relationship between concentration and advertising? To what extent does product differentiation contribute to market power? How do business rivals wield advertising as a weapon of competition? These are some of the grand mysteries of industrial organization economics, and over the past two decades research has rapidly piled up clues to their solution. The job of this chapter is to sift through these clues and reach some tentative conclusions.

The scene is set by Figure 15-1. The double-shafted arrows indicate causal connections we have already explored. Of those connections, the most important for our present purposes is that between product differentiability and advertising, style, and other forms of product differentiation. It was shown in chapter 4 that advertising intensity corresponds positively to product differentiability. In particular, advertising as a percentage of sales tends to be higher for consumer goods as compared with producer goods; for "experience" goods as opposed to "search" goods; for nondurable "convenience" goods as compared with durable "shopping" goods; for goods susceptible to promotion by strong emotional appeal; and so forth. Much the same was said of other

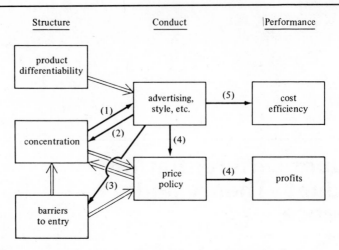

Figure 15-1. *Product differentiation issues in the context of structure, conduct and performance.*

forms of product differentiation, though less rigidly. Variations in packaging flavor, style, and the like are not uniformly profitable across all products.

Nothing said in this chapter will alter those conclusions. They provide a base upon which we now build. For the time being, we shall stuff produce goods into the nearest closet and consider only consumer goods. We shall also assume a condition of *ceteris paribus* or "other things being equal" throughout most of this chapter's analysis. That is to say, we shall take differentiability as "given" or "already accounted for" when postulating various swellings and contractions of differentiation effort.

The numbered, single shafted arrows of Figure 15-1 indicate causal connections discussed in this chapter. Their numbers specify sequence of treatment. After a few preliminary remarks about profit maximizing theory, we consider

1. Concentration as a cause of advertising intensity.
2. Advertising as a cause of concentration.
3. Advertising as a barrier to entry.
4. Advertising's influence on prices and profits.
5. The cost efficiency implications of advertising activity.

Advertising is emphasized throughout because data for other forms of differentiation effort are deficient. Still, these other forms will not be completely ignored. The sketchy evidence concerning them is intriguing.

Profit Maximization and Overview

imple Theory

Advertising can be profitable because it can enlarge sales volume or permit rice increases. But advertising costs money, and its potency as a generator of :venues during a single year is limited. Hence, each firm confronts the question f how much should be spent on advertising to maximize profits. A simplified heoretical answer assumes (1) a short-run time horizon with no lagged effects) advertising, (2) constant advertising outlays on the part of all rival firms, 3) constant product quality, and (4) full knowledge of certain elasticities. Jnder these conditions the firm's profit maximizing advertising-to-sales ratio ould be[1]

$$\frac{A}{S} = \frac{\dfrac{\% \, \Delta \text{ in } Q}{\% \, \Delta \text{ in } A}}{\dfrac{\% \, \Delta \text{ in } Q}{\% \, \Delta \text{ in } P}}$$

'here A/S is advertising outlay relative to sales revenue, Q is quantity of product ›ld, P is price, Δ is change, $(\% \, \Delta \text{ in } Q)/(\% \, \Delta \text{ in } A)$ is advertising elasticity of :mand, and $(\% \, \Delta \text{ in } Q)/(\% \, \Delta \text{ in } P)$ is price elasticity of demand. Lurking eneath this maximization equation is the familiar rule of $MR = MC$, but you ust realize that this equation gives a simplified view of the impact of market ructure on advertising intensity.

Consider first the upper term on the right-hand side, namely, advertising asticity of demand, $(\% \, \Delta \text{ in } Q)/(\% \, \Delta \text{ in } A)$. This is a measure of sales response › advertising, and it is largely determined by product differentiability. The reater the advertising elasticity, the greater the sales responsiveness. Hence 1e greater the advertising elasticity, the greater the firm's A/S, everything .se being equal.

So much, of course, is not really new. What is new concerns the lower term n the right-hand side, that is, *price* elasticity of demand $(\% \, \Delta \text{ in } Q)/(\% \, \Delta \text{ in } P)$. his term's placement indicates an inverse relationship between the firm's dvertising intensity, A/S, and the firm's price elasticity of demand (holding dvertising elasticity constant). The greater the price elasticity, the lower the rm's ad outlay relative to sales. Conversely, the lower the price elasticity, the reater the ad effort. Because a firm's price elasticity of demand is a function of s market share, this discovery leads to a simple theory connecting concentra- on to ad intensity at market-wide levels. As a firm's market share rises, its :mand curve becomes more and more like market-wide demand and thereby

---

[1] Robert Dorfman and Peter Steiner, "Optimal Advertising and Optimal Quality," *American conomic Review* (December 1954), pp. 826–36.

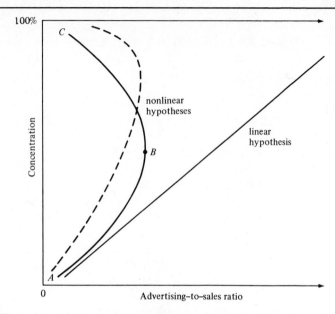

Figure 15-2. *Hypothetical relations between advertising intensity and concentr* tion.

becomes less and less elastic. Hence, rising market share might be associate with rising A/S for the market as a whole. And rising market concentratic might likewise be associated with rising A/S.

The gist of the theory is most clearly seen in the extreme case of purely con petitive firms selling a perfectly standardized product in a market of very lo concentration. With $(\% \Delta$ in $Q)/(\% \Delta$ in $P)$ being infinitely high for each firr A/S will be zero. Or, in terms of real world inquiry: Do wheat farmers advertise (Do hermits fraternize?).

This reasoning, unqualified, yields a "linear hypothesis," with advertisir intensity and market concentration positively related throughout their rang as depicted in Figure 15-2. A few economists believe this to be the true relatioi ship between advertising and concentration.[2] They bolster their belief wit causality theories reaching well beyond matters of elasticity. Some of the theories will be taken up later. We do not pursue them now, however, becau the linear hypothesis is plagued by various problems. Although there is son evidence supporting the positive linear hypothesis,[3] there is also much eviden

[2] E.g., H. M. Mann, J. A. Henning, and J. W. Meehan, Jr., "Advertising and Concentratic An Empirical Investigation," *Journal of Industrial Economics* (November 1967), pp. 34–45.

[3] *Ibid.*, S. I. Ornstein, "The Advertising-Concentration Controversy," *Southern Economic Jourr* (July 1976), pp. 892–902; S. I. Ornstein, J. F. Weston, M. D. Intriligator, and R. E. Shriev "Determinants of Market Structure," *Southern Economic Journal* (April 1973), pp. 612–2 Steven Cox, "A New Look at the Concentration-Advertising Relationship" (mimeograph, 1977

to the contrary.[4] Differing samples and differing perspectives have produced these differing results, thereby igniting controversy. All in all, this author is convinced that the linear hypothesis sits on thin ice.

Problems and Complexities[5]

The main problem with the linear hypothesis as presented is that its underlying assumptions are unrealistic. For one thing, advertising *has* lagged effects, so the assumption of a short-term time horizon is myopic. For another, the theory assumes that business executives have accurate estimates of the effect of advertising and price variation on sales volume. To credit most executives with such insight would be fanciful. Estimates are clouded by a vast array of other variables affecting sales volume, such as general economic trends, tastes, and competitive activity.

Mention of competitive activity raises a third and more significant shortcoming in the simple theory, namely, the theory's unrealistic assumption of constant rival firm advertising. What one firm does will often affect the behavior of others, in advertising as well as price policy. This reciprocal dependency is illustrated by the estimate that, on average, a 1% increase in advertising by one cigarette company provokes a 1.12% increase in the advertising of its competitors.[6] Similarly, a statistical study of 60 firms showed that the most important determinant of each firm's advertising outlay was the A/S ratio of the industry it occupied.[7]

There are other problems as well, and, on the whole, a "nonlinear" hypothesis is theoretically and empirically more tenable, at least in this author's eyes. Two versions of the nonlinear hypothesis are depicted in Figure 15-2— the line labeled *ABC* and the dashed line. In contrast to the linear hypothesis, it is assumed that concentration and advertising intensity are positively related only up to a point, after which point, in the region of high concentration, the relationship becomes negative. The implication is that advertising as a percentage of sales will *not* be highest where concentration is highest but rather where concentration is moderately high, such as at point *B*. Cross-section statistical tests of the nonlinear hypothesis using four-digit industries suggest

---

[4] Leading papers are L. G. Telser, "Advertising and Competition," *Journal of Political Economy* (December 1964), pp. 537–62; and R. B. Ekelund, Jr., and W. P. Gramm, "Advertising and Concentration: Some New Evidence," *Antitrust Bulletin* (Summer 1970), pp. 243–49. For reviews of these and other papers see James M. Ferguson, *Advertising and Competition: Theory, Measurement, Fact* (Cambridge, Mass.: Ballinger, 1974), Chapter 5; and Richard A. Miller, "Advertising and Competition: Some Neglected Aspects," *Antitrust Bulletin* (Summer 1972), pp. 467–78.

[5] For details see K. Cowling, J. Cable, M. Kelly, and Tony McGuinness, *Advertising and Economic Behavior* (London: Macmillan, 1975).

[6] H. G. Grabowski and D. C. Mueller, "Imitative Advertising in the Cigarette Industry," *Antitrust Bulletin* (Summer 1971), pp. 257–92.

[7] D. C. Mueller, "The Firm's Decision Process: An Econometric Investigation," *Quarterly Journal of Economics* (February 1967), pp. 58–87.

that A/S reaches a maximum where four-firm concentration is from 36 to 72% Other estimates peg the maximum at still higher levels of concentration, a suggested by the dashed line in Figure 15-2.[9] What is more, this depiction behavior raises the possibility that *two* directions of causality prevail, not one advertising-to-concentration as well as concentration-to-advertising. Thus, th next several sections cover theories and evidence surrounding the nonline hypothesis.[10] The material is too bulky to be swallowed whole, so it is slice into the following pieces:

1. Concentration as a cause of advertising
    (a) Positive range
    (b) Negative range
2. Advertising as a cause of concentration
    (a) Positive range
    (b) Negative range

Concentration as a Cause of Advertising

Positive Range (Concentration as a Cause)

What was said previously about elasticities and advertising could obvious be reapplied here as one explanation for a positive relation between co centration and advertising where concentration is low to moderate. That rising concentration reduces individual firm price elasticity of demand, there boosting A/S at firm and industry levels.

---

[8] Allyn D. Strickland and Leonard W. Weiss, "Advertising, Concentration, and Price-C Margins," *Journal of Political Economy* (October 1976), pp. 1109–21.

[9] Cowling, Cable, Kelly, McGuinness, *op. cit.*

[10] Principal sources are *ibid*; Strickland and Weiss, *op. cit.*; D. F. Greer, "Advertising a Market Concentration," *Southern Economic Journal* (July 1971), pp. 19–32; D. F. Greer, "So Case History Evidence on the Advertising-Concentration Relationship," *Antitrust Bulletin* (Su mer 1973), pp. 307–32; John Cable, "Market Structure, Advertising Policy and Interma Differences in Advertising Intensity," in *Market Structure and Corporate Behavior*, edited by Cowling (London: Gray-Mills, 1972), pp. 105–24; C. J. Sutton, "Advertising, Concentration, a Competition," *Economic Journal* (March 1974), pp. 56–69; and N. Kaldor and R. Silverman, *Statistical Analysis of Advertising Expenditure and of the Revenue of the Press* (Cambridge, U. F Cambridge University Press, 1948), pp. 34–35. For similar nonlinearity in nonprice variables ot than advertising see F. F. Esposito and Louis Esposito, "Excess Capacity and Market Structure *Review of Economics and Statistics* (May 1974), pp. 188–94; F. T. Knickerbocker, *Oligopolis Reaction and Multinational Enterprise* (Cambridge, Mass.: Harvard University Press, 197 Chapters 3 and 4; and John T. Scott, "Nonprice Competition in Banking Markets," *South Economic Journal* (January 1978), pp. 594–605. See also Chapter 23 in this book.

In addition, there may be a trade-off between price and nonprice competition as concentration rises. At low levels of concentration, price competition seems preeminent. Firm survival and expansion depend mainly upon efficiency and price shading. However, at moderate levels of concentration firms begin to appreciate the financial dangers and futility of price rivalry. In this range of concentration firms may therefore shift their emphasis from price to *non*price competition. Indeed, if tacit or explicit collusion in price is easier to achieve than collusion in nonprice factors, price combat may well lapse while advertising warfare rages. Collusion over price policy is likely to be easier than collusion over nonprice policy because price double-crossing is often more readily detectable and more quickly countered than *non*price double-crossing. Whereas price policy is often clearly definable and highly visible, nonprice policy usually entails a myriad of subtle dimensions, lags, and complexities. Thus, even though equal advertising outlays might be mutually agreed upon, media mix, message content, timing, and other important factors remain variable and potentially corrosive to collusion.

Unrestrained nonprice rivalry may be more rousingly described in game-theory terms, using an example developed by Willard Manning and Bruce Owen to analyze nonprice competition in television networking.[11] It seems that ABC, NBC, and CBS do not compete with each other in the prices they charge advertisers or the rates they pay to their affiliated local stations (who receive a percentage cut of the networks' ad revenues as reward and inducement for airing the networks' programs). On the other hand, the networks do compete rather strenuously in "programming" because (1) popular programming attracts viewers, (2) advertisers "buy" viewers from the networks on the basis of viewer ratings, and (3) each rating point represents about $40 million in additional network revenues over the course of a season. A game-theory model is particularly appropriate to this case because the networks vie with each other in the context of what they assume is a *given* overall viewing audience. That is to say, the networks think total audience size is determined by factors beyond their control, such as age composition of the population and the number of women working outside the home (which affects daytime audience size). The networks are, in effect, dogs fighting over the same bone (the collective viewer's head).

Assume for simplicity two networks, two levels of programming input, and a total audience worth 100 units of advertising revenue. The situation is then captured in Table 15-1, which is a four-cornered "pay-off" matrix. Each corner has six numbers labeled A, C, and π: where A is audience measured in advertising revenues, C is cost of programming, and π is A minus C, or dollar profit from networking. The three numbers to the left in each group belong to Network 1. Those on the right, in italics, belong to Network 2. Note that each pair of A's always adds up to 100, in accord with our assumption that total audience

[11] Willard G. Manning and Bruce M. Owen, "Television Rivalry and Network Power," *Public Policy* (Winter 1976), pp. 33–57.

TABLE 15-1   Network Payoff Matrix

Network 2 (in italics)

		Low Input Level			*High Input Level*	
Low Input Level	A	50	*50*	A	0	*100*
	C	25	*25*	C	25	*50*
	π	⟨25⟩	*25*	π	⟨−25⟩	*50*
Network 1		*compare*			*compare*	
High Input Level	A	100	*0*	A	50	*50*
	C	50	*25*	C	50	*50*
	π	⟨50⟩	*−25*	π	⟨0⟩	*0*

A = Audience in dollars of advertising revenues
C = Cost of programming effort in dollars
π = A − C = profit in dollars

size is exogenously fixed. The distribution of the 100 between the two network
however, is determined by the relative intensity of their programming effor
When *both* are "low" or *both* are "high," there is a 50:50 split. When one
"low" and the other is "high," the latter garners all the bones. In turn, "low
and "high" levels of expense are assumed to be 25 and 50, respectively. Th
crucial question is, then, what level of programming will the networks pursue
The answer is found in the profit figures and network strategies.

Let's look first at Network 1. If Network 1 assumes that Network 2 wi
adopt a "low" effort for next season, then the profits Network 1 compares ar
those circled on the left-hand side—that is, 25 if it opts for a "low" effort vers
50 if it opts for a "high" effort. Network 1 would obviously choose "high
effort under this assumption. However, what if Network 1 assumes a "high
level of effort on the part of its arch rival? The answer is the same. In this cas
Network 1 compares −25, which its "low" effort would bring, and 0, whic
its "high" effort would bring. Although the 0 profit is unsavory, it is better tha
a loss of −25. Hence once again a "high" effort is chosen.

Now, what about Network 2? Which option will it pursue? Its profits (an
losses) are in italics, and, since the pay-off matrix is symmetrical, it too choose
the "high" level option. If it assumes a "low" for Network 1, it compares 2
and *50*. If it assumes a "high" for Network 1, it compares −25 and *0*. The latte
pay-offs are preferable in each case. So Network 2 likewise pursues the "high
option. With both 1 and 2 pursuing a "high", they "overdose". Outlays fc
programming are excessive, and profits are miserably zero. Only collusiv
agreement to follow a "low" policy can cheer them, yielding profits of 25 an
25. However, it would be dangerous for one rival to initiate a de-escalation, an
tacit collusive agreement may be difficult.

This type of rivalry game is called the "prisoner's dilemma." Such game theories have been devised for price policy, but most real world applications relate to nonprice competition.[12] Rivalry in real world TV networking has typically not been intense enough to produce losses. Restraint and positive profit have been achieved by various "rules of thumb" applied at various times, such as, for a series, 26 weeks of new episodes and 26 weeks of reruns.[13] Even so, restraint has been less than perfect, and network profits could benefit by more explicit and extensive collusion (if, that is, the antitrust laws were scrapped). A similar, pertinent example of excessive advertising in oligopolistic manufacturing is drawn from cigarettes. Julian Simon calculates that a $2.2 million reduction in cigarette advertising in 1961 would have led to only a $1.25 million decline in total sales revenue.[14]

Negative Range (Concentration as a Cause)

When concentration reaches really lofty heights, a negative relation (such as in the BC range of Figure 15-2) may be expected for at least two reasons. The higher industry price levels implied by ever higher concentration raise the industry's price elasticity of demand. And, according to the profit maximizing formula outlined earlier, rising price elasticity should shrink the industry's advertising to sales ratio. More obviously, ever higher concentration makes tacit or explicit collusion in nonprice activities more and more feasible.

An especially interesting example of the collusive aspect of concentration concerns advertising in the British soap industry.[15] At the turn of the century a loose oligopoly prevailed with the largest firm, Lever Brothers, holding a 60% market share. Advertising competition throbbed painfully. So in 1906 William Lever openly tried to organize a cartel, arguing that some "measures must be adopted by the leading soap-makers in conference to allay the fierce competition which has arisen amongst them, to terminate the frenzied competitive advertising which was daily becoming more intolerable ..." But the newspapers would have none of this. After receiving their first advertising contract cancellations, they editorially attacked the "Soap Trust" with such fervor that it soon had to be disbanded. Lever slowly alleviated his frustration, however, by acquiring one competitor after another until in 1920 he could claim control of 71% of the industry. Advertising appropriations declined concurrently. Other examples of express collusion cover a wide variety of products

[12] John McDonald, *The Game of Business* (Garden City, N.Y.: Doubleday, 1975).
[13] Rerun rules are easy to police and profitable. Reruns cost 20% of the original, yet they deliver 60% of the original's audience levels and ad revenues. During the late 1970s ABC shook things up a bit, however, by abandoning old rerun formulas and adopting a "living schedule." The resulting outbreak of competition led to frenzied programming rivalry and jittery financial forecasts. *Wall Street Journal*, October 4, 1977, p. 40; and November 30, 1977, p. 1.
[14] Julian Simon, "The Effect of the Competitive Structure Upon Expenditures for Advertising," *Quarterly Journal of Economics* (November 1967), p. 621.
[15] See Greer, *op. cit.* (1973), pp. 318–19.

and a diversity of nonprice activities, including trading stamps, coupon offer, product quality, and product style, as well as advertising.[16]

Just as rising concentration should eventually reduce nonprice competition so, too, falling concentration in this region should increase it. Falling concentration reduces the ability of oligopolists to hold differentiation outlay down to joint profit maximizing levels. Deteriorating collusion is important in this respect, but there are other factors as well. Examples of such inverse relations abound in both time-series and cross-section forms:

- In 1911, when tobacco was chewed as often as smoked, an antitrust decree fractured the monopolistic American Tobacco Company into several successor companies. Comparing A/S during the 2 years preceding the decree with A/S during the 2 years following, we find that A/S rose 32% for navy plug tobacco, 15% for flat plug, 148% for plug-cut smoking, 41% for long-cut smoking, 81% for granulated smoking, and 93% for domestic blend cigarettes.[17]

- Cross-section evidence on advertising in the drug industry is shown in Figure 15-3. The observations are supplied by John Vernon, who found an inverse relationship between concentration and advertising intensity. The beginnings of a nonlinear form are evident as well.[18]

- For a sample of 40 highly concentrated city banking markets, Lawrence White found a very robust inverse relationship between commercial bank concentration and the intensity of *branching activity*. He estimated there were 47.5% more banking offices in the least, as compared with the most, concentrated market in his sample (everything else being equal).[19]

- In another cross-section study of local banking markets, which are generally highly concentrated, Arnold Heggestad and John Mingo found inverse relationships for a wide assortment of nonprice variables, including

[16] *Government Intervention in the Market Mechanism, The Petroleum Industry, Part 1*, Hearing before the Subcommittee on Antitrust and Monopoly, U.S. Senate, 91st Congress, First Session (1969), pp. 569–70; L. P. Bucklin, *Competition and Evolution in the Distributive Trades* (Englewood Cliffs, N. J.: Prentice-Hall, 1972), p. 131; T. A. Murphy and Y. K. Ng, "Oligopolistic Interdependence and the Revenue Maximization Hypothesis," *Journal of Industrial Economics* (March 1974) pp. 229–30; Corwin D. Edwards, *Cartelization in Western Europe* (Washington, D.C.: Bureau Intelligence and Research, U. S. Department of State, 1964), pp. 10, 14; and C. L. Pass, "Coupon Trading—An Aspect of Non-price Competition in the U. K. Cigarette Industry," *Yorkshire Bulletin of Economic and Social Research* (November 1967), pp. 124–36.

[17] Greer, *op. cit.* (1973), p. 327.

[18] John M. Vernon, "Concentration, Promotion, and Market Share Stability in the Pharmaceutical Industry," *Journal of Industrial Economics* (July 1971), pp. 246–66. See also J. J. Lambin, *Advertising, Competition and Market Conduct in Oligopoly Over Time* (Amsterdam: North Holland Publishing Co., 1976), p. 135, Table 6.23, lines 4 and 6.

[19] Lawrence J. White, "Price Regulation and Quality Rivalry In a Profit-maximizing Model," *Journal of Money, Credit and Banking* (February 1976), pp. 97–106. The most and least concentrated markets in his sample had Herfindahl indexes of 0.48 and 0.15, respectively. In terms of number-equivalence this is two and seven firms.

extraordinary banking hours and the availability of trust services and overdraft privileges.[20]

To summarize, concentration of intermediate orders seems most conducive to igorous nonprice competition. Concentration of either high or low extremities ems least conducive.

Advertising as a Cause of Concentration

Positive Range (Advertising as a Cause)

There are three ways in which advertising may foster high degrees of concentration. First is the existence of economies of scale to advertising. As stated arlier in Chapter 8 the incidence of such economies varies across industries. Where such economies do prevail, they contribute to concentration, but only p to the point of their exhaustion.

Second, and aside from scalar effects, one or several of the largest firms in n industry might consistently maintain greater advertising outlays relative to ales than smaller firms maintain. The big spenders could possess larger financial esources, greater foresight, or predatory designs. A striking instance of predatory advertising occurred in the tobacco industry around the turn of the century, efore the antitrust action of 1911.[21] The story centers on James Duke, whose ower-play started in cigarettes, then spread to other branches of the trade. By 885 Duke has secured 11–18% of total cigarette sales for his company through n arduous promotional effort. He then escalated ad outlays to nearly 20% of ales, thereby forcing a five-firm merger in 1889 and acquiring 80% control f all cigarette sales. His American Tobacco Company grew still further until e held 93% of the market in 1899. Coincident with this final gathering of power, igarette ad expense as a per cent of sales fell to 11% in 1894, then to 0.5% in 899. And cigarette profits swelled to 56% of sales in 1899.

With these stupendous profits Duke was able to launch massive predatory ampaigns to capture other tobacco markets. One measure of this effort is the American Tobacco Company's annual advertising and selling cost as a percentage of sales at crest levels in the target markets—28.9% for plug and twist, 4.4% for smoking tobacco, 31.7% for fine-cut chewing, and 49.9% for cigars. Duke even went so far as to introduce deliberately unprofitable "fighting

---

[20] A. A. Heggestad and J. J. Mingo, "Prices, Nonprices, and Concentration in Selected Banking Markets," *Bank Structure and Competition* (Chicago: Federal Reserve Bank of Chicago, 1974), p. 69–95.

[21] Greer, *op. cit.* (1973), pp. 311–15.

brands," one of which was appropriately called "Battle Ax." Losses ensued; mergers followed; and after the entire industry (except for cigars) was under American's thumb, advertising receded substantially to such relatively peaceful neighborhoods as 4 and 10% of sales. Thus the episode traces a full nonlinear course (ABC in Figure 15-2), illustrating more than mere predation.

A third positive force of advertising on concentration is similar to predation in that it produces an escalation of outlays; it is different in that no single firm plays the role of "heavy." How might innocent escalation come about? There are any number of possibilities. Some firms, large or small, might have outstanding success in their advertising campaigns or might establish initially favorable A/S ratios, thereby inadvertently or advertently enjoying unusually rapid growth at the expense of rivals. But, after suffering losses in market share, most of the rivals attempt to emulate these successful companies through increased advertising outlays. Then everyone is off to the races. Competitive rounds of escalation could continue, resulting in cost-price squeezes, losses, bankruptcies, mergers, and ever higher concentration. Prisoners' dilemma game theory is obviously applicable here.

Fantastic as this scenario may seem, the beer industry played it just recently.[22] The traces are sketched in Figure 15-3 in terms of five-firm concentration ratio and advertising as a percentage of sales. (The concentration ratio is based on national sales, thereby understating the "true" level of concentration, which would be based on regional, not national, markets. You may compensate, however, by mentally shifting the Figure 15-3 curve up a bit.) Beginning in 1947 concentration was low to moderate, and advertising was just slightly above 3% of sales revenue. Promotion expense rose rapidly thereafter, as one firm then another leap-frogged ad outlays relative to sales. The process was apparently aggravated by the advent of TV advertising, a decline in tavern sales, the rise of package sales, the geographic expansion of many brewers, and a massive labor strike that closed down Schlitz, Pabst, and Miller for over 2 months in 1953. By the early 1960s, advertising relative to sales was hovering near the 7% level. (And expenditures for packaging differentiation had also burgeoned.[23]) As a result, profits wilted. Profits after taxes as a per cent of equity fell from 19% in 1947 to 6% in 1960 and 1961. All firms, big and small alike, were pulled down financially, as if by quicksand. Most of those effectually engulfed were small, however, suggesting that economies of scale may have been at work as well.[24] In 1947 there were 404 brewing companies, in 197 only 58. Many disappeared by merger (distress sales). Others simply folded. As concentration continued to climb, advertising activity eventually subsided and profits recovered.

[22] D. F. Greer, "Product Differentiation and Concentration in the Brewing Industry," *Journal of Industrial Economics* (July 1971), pp. 201–19.

[23] Kenneth Fraundorf, "The Social Costs of Packaging Competition in the Beer and Soft Drink Industries," *Antitrust Bulletin* (Winter 1975), pp. 803–31.

[24] On the other hand, the fact that profits of *all* firms suffered indicates that economies of scale were not the sole cause.

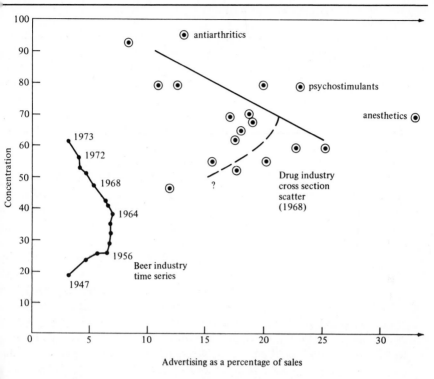

Figure 15-3. Concentration and advertising intensity. Source: D. F. Greer and J. M. Vernon in Journal of Industrial Economics, July 1971, updated.

The sources underlying Figure 15-3 show this subsidence of advertising during the early 1970s. But they are not sufficiently current to show the advertising scuffle touched off by Miller in the late 1970s. Miller has had remarkable success in gaining market share by spending on advertising three times as much per barrel as the other brewers (its parent company, Philip Morris, subsidizes any losses), and by "segmenting" the market with different buyer images for each of its labels—"Miller High Life," "Lite," and "Löwenbräu." Between 1972 and 1976, Miller tripled its market share from 4% to 12%. And in 1978 it punched its way into the number 2 spot. At this writing, Anheuser-Busch, Schlitz, and the others are cranking up to retaliate (whence cometh this chapter's opening quote). The outburst will alter the neat nonlinear pattern of Figure 15-3, but probably only temporarily.[25] Advertising wars are like price wars: they can erupt and subside almost any time.

[25] *Business Week*, November 8, 1976, pp. 58–67; *Advertising Age*, September 26, 1977, p. 112.

Negative Range (Advertising as Cause)

In the range of inverse relationship, advertising may push up concentration as long as advertising outlays exceed the industry (or monopoly) optimum level. The heavy cost burden, particularly in the region of most intensive non-price competition, may provoke mergers and failures, as just illustrated in the case of beer.

A still more interesting possibility entails rising advertising as a cause of *decreasing* concentration, where concentration is initially very high. Most obviously, advertising may assist new entry. In fact, entry can sometimes be accomplished through little or nothing more than an ingenious or lavishly financed advertising campaign. It can also be achieved through product differentiation generally, in which advertising plays only a part. Even if technological innovation or price discounting rather than advertising or differentiation are the means of a newcomer's entry into a highly concentrated market, his eventual success could be endangered if he did not vigorously promote his sales. In any event, it is not likely that entry will dent concentration appreciably or durably unless the entrant spends considerably more on advertising relative to sales than established firms spend. This expenditure in turn hoists the market-wide A/S ratio. Thus, in a study of 34 new brands of grocery and drug products that were successful enough to gain 2–39% market shares within 2 years after introduction, James Peckham found the entrants had advertised much more intensively than established firms. On average, the entrants' share of total industry advertising exceeded their share of total sales by 70%.[26] And these were not just "me too" products.

Pepsi-Cola provides a good example, even though it was not included in Peckham's analysis. During the 1930s Coca Cola enjoyed 60% of all soft drink sales and Pepsi-Cola was languishing in receivership. Pepsi was successfully revived after some modification of its flavor and an exuberant ad campaign financed at a cost per case nearly three times greater than Coke's cost per case. By 1940 Pepsi had 10% of the market to Coke's 53%. Pepsi's market share continued to grow and Coke's continued to wither as long as Pepsi held a substantial edge in ad cost per case. By the early 1960s, Pepsi held about 19% to Coke's 38%. At that point their shares began to stabilize. Coke had by then escalated its ad outlays per case to match those of Pepsi more closely, and it has since yielded little further ground. The result is less power for Coke and the Pepsi generation of a threefold increase in industry ad cost per case.[27] (And you thought "the Pepsi generation" was an age group.) Notice that this example illustrates more than the entrant's contribution to a rising industry A/S ratio. Coke's reaction to Pepsi's entry illustrates a *second* source of rising A/S. Established firms are not likely to stand idly by and watch their market

---

[26] James O. Peckham, "Can We Relate Advertising Dollars to Market Share Objectives?" in *How Much to Spend for Advertising?* edited by M. A. McNiven (National Association of Advertisers, 1969), pp. 23–30.

[27] Greer, *op. cit.* (1973), pp. 330–32.

shares evaporate. They retaliate, counter punch, throw "empties," whatever. This observation brings us once again to entry barriers.

To recap briefly before continuing, an escalation in advertising may cause concentration to rise or fall; which alternative results usually depends on the initial level of concentration.

Advertising as Entry Barrier

Earlier, in Chapter 8, we considered the possibility that product differentiation could pose a barrier to entry. That discussion, however, was mainly confined to *static* barriers, such as the barrier implied by large economies of scale. Here we acknowledge a *dynamic* advertising barrier. When Coke suffered insults at the hands of Pepsi, its response was slow and moderate. But such is not always the case. Established firms may lash out at newcomers, uncoiling massive barrages of advertising, promotion, and other nonprice artillery. Here are a few examples:

- Between 1900 and 1902 a tremendous jump in the popularity of Turkish tobacco cigarettes trimmed 16 percentage points off the American Tobacco Comapny's 93% market share. The Company rushed its own Turkish brands to market and jacked up its cigarette ad outlay from 0.5 to 20.3% of sales.[28]
- In 1961 a new firm entered the Australian soap market, which was then essentially split between two dominant firms. The two old-timers inflated their ad outlays 45 and 100% within a year.[29]
- During the late 1950s Purex was attempting to enter or expand its share in a number of local United States markets, particularly in the east. But Clorox retaliated at every turn, as explained by Clorox's ad agent: "you generally don't wait in most instances to let him [Purex] get much of an inroad ... we ... move to counter with one of this pool of things. We have used as different devices, price off labels, the coupon on the bottle, the newspaper coupon, and so on, and in some territories, we did not meet it with a promotion, but tried to meet it with whatever increase there was in an advertising schedule."[30]

In short, product differentiation may pose a barrier to entry for reasons other than those mentioned in Chapter 8—lagged carry-over, economies of

---

[28] *Ibid.*, p. 326.

[29] M. A. Alemson and H. T. Burley, "Demand and Entry into an Oligopoly Market: A Case Study," *Journal of Industrial Economics* (December 1974), pp. 109–24.

[30] *Federal Trade Commission v. Procter & Gamble Co.*, 63 F.T.C. 1465, at p. 1518. For further examples see Greer, *op. cit.* (1973); Alan Bevan, "The U. K. Potato Crisp Industry, 1960–72: A Study of New Competition," *Journal of Industrial Economics* (June 1974), pp. 281–97, and R. W. Shaw and C. J. Sutton, *Industry and Competition* (London: Macmillan, 1976), p. 42.

scale, and static capital costs. Moreover, these examples help to explain the emphasis businessmen give to product differentiation when voicing their opinions on barriers.

Advertising, Prices, and Profits

Given the flip-flop nature of our preceding remarks, you might suspect that advertising can either increase or decrease prices and profits. You would be right.

Advertising and Prices

In 1977 Seagram Distillers proclaimed a dramatic doubling of its ad budget to boost sales of "7 Crown," "Seagram VO," and its other brands of booze. To cover the $40 million annual cost of this "most aggressive marketing program" in industry history, the company also announced a sequence of price increases—5–10% per case.[31] Businessmen are rarely this willing to admit that advertising increases prices, but this effect is anything but rare. It was alluded to earlier when we mentioned that product differentiation can give firms power over price. Now we elaborate.

Perhaps the best evidence of this relation of advertising to price is shown in price differences between "distributor" (or private label) brands and "advertised manufacturer" brands, a distinction made earlier when discussing the Borden price discrimination case. Table 15-2 shows the retail prices and market shares of these two types of brands for seven food products, as estimated by the National Commission on Food Marketing. In every instance, price of the advertised brand exceeds average price of the distributors' brands, by a low of 5% for canned peaches to a high of 32% for frozen orange juice. On average, these advertised brands are 21% more costly to consumers than the distributors' brands. In a similar study of British markets, David Morris found price differences of 18%, 16%, and 29% for instant coffee, margarine, and toothpaste.[32] To conduct your own research, make a quick visit to the nearest Safeway, A & P, or other large chain. (For really whopping price differences, check out the drug and detergent shelves.)

At this point the defenders of advertising cry, "Foul, foul!! These are unfair comparisons! As any fool can plainly see, heavily advertised, higher priced brands are of higher quality than those cheap, good-for-nothing house brands." Indeed, some defenders claim that folks get *more* for their money by buying advertised brands, inflated prices notwithstanding. Well, what about this

---

[31] *Business Week*, August 22, 1977, p. 68. It should be noted that the market was stagnant at the time.

[32] David Morris, "Some Aspects of Large-Scale Advertising," *Journal of Industrial Economics* (December 1975), pp. 119–30.

TABLE 15-2   Relative Prices and Sales of Distributors' and Manufacturers' Brands, 1966

Product	Average Retail Price per Case		Percentage of Sales Accounted for by	
	Distributors' Brands ($)	Advertised Brands* ($)	Distributors' Brands (%)	Advertised Brands (%)
Frozen orange juice	8.74	11.57	79	20
Frozen green beans	4.94	6.42	77	21
Canned green peas	4.76	5.54	29	60
Canned peaches	6.24	6.54	47	53
Catsup	4.46	5.51	28	70
Tuna fish	12.72	15.46	31	63
Evaporated milk	6.52	7.49	45	54

* These data are for a typical advertised brand. All others are averages.
Source: National Commission on Food Marketing, *Special Studies in Food Marketing*, Technical Study 10 (Washington, D. C., 1966), pp. 66, 70–71.

quality claim? Is it the "real thing"? As you might guess, rigorous research into this question is very difficult to conduct. Nevertheless, a few bits of reliable evidence are available, and they yield a tentative, two-part answer: (1) On the whole, advertising intensity is apparently *not* positively associated with product quality, but (2) there is sufficient variance across products to include many instances where a correspondence between advertising intensity and quality is indeed the case. (Whether the occasional quality premium *fully* justifies the associated price premium is, however, another issue.) Consider the following:

1. One of the most notorious instances of price difference concerns prescription drugs, where unadvertised "generic" products are dirt-cheap compared to advertised brand names—for example, for reserpine $1.10 versus $39.50, for meprobamate $4.90 versus $68.21, tetracycline $8.75 versus $52.02, and penicillin G $1.75 versus $10.04. Yet drug quality is very closely regulated by the U. S. Food and Drug Administration, and no notable quality differences between "generic" and "brand" named drugs has been found despite extensive testing.[33]
2. H. J. Rotfeld and K. B. Rotzoll studied 12 product classes, including drain cleaner, laundry detergent, cooking oil, peanut butter (smooth and chunky), cat food, and toothpaste. They correlated quality rank

[33] Milton Silverman and Philip R. Lee, *Pills, Profits and Politics* (Berkeley, Calif.: University of California Press, 1974), pp. 138–89, 334.

(as determined by *Consumer Reports* and *Consumers Bulletin*) with brand advertising intensity (as measured by absolute dollars spent on national media) for each product. They concluded that quality and advertising intensity were *not* positively related when comparing only nationally advertised brands. *But,* when comparing nationally advertised brands with "local," nonnationally advertised brands, they found the quality of the former generally surpassing that of the latter. Results were thus "mixed."[34]

3. As for distributor versus manufacturer brands, many come off the *same* assembly line to the *same* technical specifications. They differ only in label and perhaps "trim." Thus, more than half of all tires sold in the United States under distributor labels are produced by Goodyear, Firestone, Goodrich, Uniroyal, and General. And according to the editor of *Modern Tire Dealer Magazine,* "there is no noticeable quality difference among nationally advertised tires, the associate brands made by the smaller companies, and private-label brands made by both."[35]

It appears, then, that the quality argument has many weak spots. However defenders of advertising have two further arguments debunking the notion that advertising inordinately raises prices. The first, and shakiest, is the "subjectivist" argument. This holds that advertising adds a "value" not in the product for which the consumer may rightfully wish to pay extra. The housewife pays more for the Borden brand, thinking that she thereby gets more for her money. Since she *thinks* she is getting more, she *must* be getting more, or so it is argued. Perhaps the "security" of the advertised brand warms her heart. Perhaps she feels that her family will love her more for using a familiar brand. In other words, advertising sells hope, confidence, elation, and faith with each unit of canned milk, detergent, soda pop, aspirin, and drain cleaner. The problem with this argument is that it is tautological.[36] *By definition,* the consumer is *always* right and rational, even if he or she continues to pay extra after being informed that to do so is foolish. *By definition,* higher prices are *always* justified by higher "quality." But arguments by definition are dead-end streets.

The second line of defensive argument denies that advertising does in fact raise prices. All evidence of positive association is pooh-poohed. And evidence of a *negative* association, indicating that advertising *reduces* prices is pointed to as proving the opposite effect. In fact, this contrary evidence, which always relates to retailers' advertising, is quite impressive. Lee Benham, for instance, examined retail prices of eyeglasses in states that legally restricted merchant

---

[34] H. J. Rotfeld and K. B. Rotzoll, "Advertising and Product Quality: Are Heavily Advertised Products Better?" *Journal of Consumer Affairs* (Summer 1976), pp. 33–47.

[35] *Washington Post,* April 20, 1975, pp. M1, M3. On TV sets see *Washington Post,* June 8, 1975, pp. F1, F8. Principal TV suppliers for Sears, Wards, and J. C. Penney have been General Electric, Sanyo, Panasonic, RCA, and Admiral. For both tires and TVs, private label prices apparently average 8–10% less than manufacturer label prices.

[36] William Breit and K. G. Elzinga, "Product Differentiation and Institutionalism: New Shadows on an Old Terrain," *Journal of Economic Issues* (December 1974), pp. 813–26.

advertising and retail prices in states that had few or no restrictions on advertising. Comparing the most and least restrictive states, he discovered a $20 difference in average prices in 1963. Where advertising was prohibited, the price of eyeglasses averaged $37.48. Conversely, where advertising was wholly unrestricted, prices averaged $17.98.[37] Moreover, Benham surveyed several large "commercial" retailers, such as Sears, asking which states they felt were the most and least difficult to enter with respect to eyeglass merchandising. According to Benham, "The states ranked as most difficult were classified as 'restrictive,' those ranked least difficult were classified as 'nonrestrictive,' and the remaining states were classified as 'other.'"[38]

Similarly, John Cady analyzed prescription drug retail prices for the effects of state restrictions on retail drug *price* advertising. Comparing the retail prices of 10 representative prescription drugs across states, he found that restrictions on price advertising *raised* prices an average of 4.3%, with the highest differential being 9.1% for one sampled product.[39]

Well, now we really have a mystery. How can these seemingly contradictory results be reconciled? Prescription drugs epitomize the puzzle. How can manufacturers' prices be *positively* associated with manufacturers' advertising while retail prices are *negatively* related to retailers' advertising? Profit studies seem to hold the answer.

Advertising and Profits

The dichotomy carries over into research concerning profits. Positive, negative, and nonexistent associations have been found by comparing profit levels and advertising intensity. Early cross-section studies of the profit issue, commencing in the late 1960s, showed very high *positive* correlations between advertising intensity and profit rates in consumers'-goods industries. This was true regardless of the unit of observation (firm or industry), the time period in question (1950s or 1960s), or the source of advertising data (tax records or trade publications).[40] Moreover, the estimated magnitude of the effect was large.

[37] Lee Benham, "The Effect of Advertising on the Price of Eyeglasses," *Journal of Law & Economics* (October 1972), pp. 337–52.

[38] L. Benham and A. Benham, "Regulating Through the Professions: A Perspective on Information Control," *Journal of Law & Economics* (October 1975), pp. 426–27.

[39] John F. Cady, "An Estimate of the Price Effects of Restrictions on Drug Price Advertising," *Economic Inquiry* (December 1976), pp. 493–510. See also W. Luksetich and H. Lofgreen, "Price Advertising and Liquor Prices," *Industrial Organization Review*, Vol. 4, No. 1 (1976), pp. 13–25.

[40] W. S. Comanor and T. S. Wilson, "Advertising, Market Structure and Performance," *Review of Economics and Statistics* (November 1967), pp. 423–40; Richard A. Miller, "Market Structure and Industrial Performance: Relation of Profit Rates to Concentration, Advertising Intensity, and Diversity," *Journal of Industrial Economics* (April 1969), pp. 104–18; William H. Kelly, *Economic Report on the Influence of Market Structure on the Profit Performance of Food Manufacturing Companies* (Washington, D.C.: Federal Trade Commission, 1969); Blake Imel, Michael R. Behr, and Peter G. Helmberger, *Market Structure and Performance* (Lexington, Mass.: Lexington Books, 1972); J. M. Vernon and Robert Nourse, "Profit Rates and Market Structure of Advertising Intensive Firms," *Journal of Industrial Economics* (September 1973), pp. 1–20.

Results for food manufacturing in the 1950s show an advertising to sales ratio of 1 % is associated with profits of 10.3 % relative to equity, whereas an ad ratio of 5 % is associated with higher profits of 14.7 %.

This raft of positive findings demonstrated two things. First, higher ad intensity may raise prices to produce *higher profits* as well as to pay for higher ad costs. Indeed, the phenomenon observed for beer of rising ad costs and falling profits may be considered a transitory, short-run development. In the long run the more general tendency may be one of positive contribution. The second point explains the form of that contribution, namely, persistent intensive advertising *may indeed constitute a barrier to entry*, since persistent excess profit signal the presence of barriers.

However, more recent cross-section studies have not been nearly so unanimous in finding a positive effect. Some have found *no* relationship, some a *negative* relationship. So once again the question arises: Why the flip-flop Why the coincidence of contrary results?

The answer, in my opinion, is outlined in Table 15-3, which draws heavily upon three profit studies—Phillip Nelson's, Michael Porter's, and Kenneth Boyer's—as well as upon the price findings discussed previously and the material in Chapter 4 (see especially Tables 4-3 and 4-5). Nelson divided consumer goods into three groups, then ran advertising-profit correlations for each using data on *manufacturers*, not retailers. He found[41]

1. A significant *positive* correlation of 0.78 for *nondurable experience* goods, which, it will be recalled, are goods like soap, beer, and cigarettes, goods whose "quality" may be judged only by consumption after purchase. For reasons given earlier these are highly susceptible to exhortative (persuasive) advertising.
2. A significant *negative* correlation of −0.65 for *durable experience* goods such as autos, tires, and appliances. Exhortative advertising for these goods is relatively less important.
3. A nonsignificant *negative* correlation of −0.02 for *search* goods, such as clothing, hats, and furniture, whose "quality" may be judged largely before purchase. These are least supportive of exhortative advertising and most conducive to informative advertising.

Porter's analysis yielded similar results for manufacturers. He divided consumer goods into two groups, then made multiple regression estimates. He found[42]

1. A strong *positive* association between advertising intensity and profits for *nondurables* (or what he calls "convenience" goods). His explana-

[41] Phillip Nelson, "The Economic Consequences of Advertising," *Journal of Business* (Apr 1975), p. 237.
[42] Michael E. Porter, "Consumer Behavior, Retailer Power and Market Performance in Consumer Goods Industries," *Review of Economics and Statistics* (November 1974), pp. 419–36.

tion: These goods are "presold" and inexpensive, so retailers have little influence over brand choice and persuasive advertising is especially effective.

2. *No* association (either positive or negative) between advertising intensity and profits for *durables* (or what he calls "shopping" goods). His explanation: Manufacturers' exhortative advertising is of little influence here because of hefty product prices, heavy retailer influence, and emphasis on other forms of differentiation.

Finally, Boyer analyzed two separate subsamples, one of which was retail and service enterprises (such as grocers, drugstores, auto dealers, laundries, and hotels). He compared their behavior with that of consumer goods manufacturers generally. He discovered

1. A strong *positive* correlation for *manufacturers* (as usual, when all consumer goods are included).
2. A weak negative correlation between advertising intensity and profits in *retail and service trades.*

His explanation: Manufacturer advertising tends to be of the exhorative type, which builds brand loyalty and reduces consumer price elasticity of demand. In contrast, retail and service advertising tends to be highly informative, stressing price bargains, availabilities, and such.[43]

All the various strands of evidence thus seem to add up, very roughly, to Table 15-3. Advertising's impact on prices, profits, and entry barriers apparently depends on type of product, type of enterprise, type of advertising, and type of consumer effect. For simplicity, two realms of impact are distinguished in Table 15-3—anticompetitive and procompetitive or neutral realms.

Experience goods, especially nondurable experience goods, lend themselves to exhortative advertising, which instills brand loyalty and tends to reduce consumer price elasticity—two results that can be exploited by manufacturers of those products. Breakfast cereals, drugs, razor blades, and detergents offer prime examples. Within this first realm, prices, profits, and barriers seem to be positively associated with advertising intensity.

Conversely, there is a second realm where exhortative advertising is less potent, and where informative advertising takes center stage. This realm includes the manufacturing of search goods and, to a lesser extent, durables. More important, it includes retail trade, even the retailing of goods in the first realm. The informative advertising typical of these second sectors often encourages brand switching and raises consumer price elasticity. The empirical result here is thus an inverse or independent relationship between advertising

[43] Kenneth D. Boyer, "Information and Goodwill Advertising," *Review of Economics and Statistics* (November 1974), pp. 541–48.

TABLE 15-3 Summary of Dichotomous Effects of Advertising on Prices, Profits, and Barriers to Entry

Nature of Division	Anticompetitive Realm Advertising raises Prices, Profits, and Barriers	Procompetitive or Neutral Realm, Advertising lowers (or has no Effect on) Prices, Profits, and Barriers
1a. Type of *product*	1b. Experience goods, nondurables (e.g., soap, beer, soda pop)	1c. Search goods,* durables* (furniture, appliances)
2a. Type of *enterprise*	2b. Manufacturing of the above goods (plus banking and insurance?)	2c. Manufacturing of the above goods plus retailing and some services
3a. Type of *advertising*	3b. Exhortative	3c. Informative
4a. Type of *consumer effect*	4b. Brand loyalty, reduced price elasticity	4c. Brand switching, increased price elasticity

* Note: Nonprice activities other than advertising (for example, styling) may have anticompetitive effects for these products.

intensity on the one hand, and prices, profits, and barriers to entry on the other. As Benham explains his findings with respect to eyeglass retailing:

> In general, large-volume low-price sellers are dependent upon drawing consumers from a wide area and consequently need to inform their potential customers of the advantages of coming to them. If advertising is prohibited, they may not be able to generate the necessary sales to maintain the low price.[44]

Retailer advertising tends to be informative for the same reason that search good manufacturers' advertising is informative—that is, consumers have powers of prepurchase assessment; and price receives great emphasis. This is particularly true of drug and eyeglass retailing, where the beneficial effects of advertising are most thoroughly documented. Once a doctor prescribes the drugs or glasses needed, the question of where to buy them can be answered by fairly simple search, a search focusing mainly on price. Availabilities and convenient location also carry weight; hence, they too receive roars in retailers' informative advertising.

[44] Benham, *op. cit.*, p. 339.

This is not to say that suppliers of goods and services in the second realm do not vie for customers with nonprice weapons that may build loyalties, grant power over price, and inhibit entry. On the contrary, style changes, services, prize games, long hours, and the like are all heavily traveled avenues in this realm. It is merely the case that advertising has relatively innocent and often even favorable consequences in these markets.

This overall view is misleading in that it implies more agreement among economists than actually exists. This is a synthesis of debated issues, not really a survey. In fact, some staunch friends of advertising refuse to concede that there is *any* meaningful evidence of a positive association between advertising and profits in *any* class of markets. One of the most popular arguments among sophisticated ad sympathizers is that accounting profits of intensive advertisers are exaggerated because accountants and tax collectors treat advertising as a *current expense* even though, given its lagged effects, it is actually an *investment*. They argue that, once relevant adjustments are made, the positive profit effect vanishes.[45] Those arguments will not be discussed here, however, because in my judgment their importance is demonstrably less than overwhelming.[46]

Is Advertising Excessive?

The last item on our agenda alludes to the possibility that advertising may be burning up more scarce productive resources than is socially optimal. Early debate of this issue tended to lump all advertising together and assume an "either-or" answer—either it was excessive or it was not. More recently the debate has entered a new and more refined phase, pushed by the discoveries outlined in the preceding discussion and by the work of William Comanor and Thomas Wilson, whose theories cast fresh light in this old corner.[47]

To appreciate the current view, we must recognize that there are *two* demand curves for advertising messages—one generated by advertisers who seek to make sales and one representing the desires of consumers seeking information. Of course, these demands may vary from one market to another, and the type of

---

[45] Harry Bloch, "Advertising and Profitability: A Reappraisal," *Journal of Political Economy* (March 1974), pp. 267–86; and Robert Ayanian, "Advertising and Rate of Return," *Journal of Law and Economics* (October 1975), pp. 479–506.

[46] In particular, they are overly contrived and they rely on unreasonably high goodwill retention rates to make adjustments. Compare, for instance, Ayanian's 0.949 rate for autos with Peles' estimate of zero, "Rates of Amortization of Advertising Expenditures," *Journal of Political Economy* (September 1971), pp. 1032–58. See also Darral Clarke, "Econometric Measurement of the Duration of Advertising Effects on Sales," *Journal of Marketing Research* (November 1976), pp. 345–57. Reasonable adjustments do not eliminate the positive effect: L. W. Weiss, "Advertising, Profits and Corporate Taxes," *Review of Economics and Statistics* (November 1969), pp. 421–30; W. S. Comanor and T. A. Wilson, *Advertising and Market Power* (Cambridge, Mass.: Harvard University Press, 1974), pp. 169–93. For a profit study that answers other criticisms see Cowling, Cable, Kelly, and McGuinness, *op. cit.*, pp. 114–27.

[47] Comanor and Wilson, *op. cit.*, pp. 16–21.

messages demanded by the sellers may be quite different from the type of messages demanded by consumers. If we grant that social welfare is measured by the extent to which consumers' demands are met, "excessive" advertising may be measured by the extent to which the sellers' demand for messages in any given market exceeds the consumers' demand for messages in that market.

Although real world measurement of this potential divergence is impossible, a few educated guesses are feasible. First, as we have seen, interbrand rivalries may rocket advertising intensity to stratospheric levels, especially in the middle range of market concentration. It seems safe to say that such cross-cancelling "competitive" advertising is excessive from the social point of view. Indeed, it is excessive from the sellers' point of view as well as the consumers' because the sellers' hyperactive demand for messages stems from a "prisoners' dilemma," and escape via collusion would presumably curtail this demand.

A second broad class of excesses probably occurs where intensive advertising permits firms to raise prices, reap supernormal profits, and bar entry. Under such conditions (outlined in Table 15-3), sellers' demand for messages is likely to outdistance that of consumers by a country mile. "It is in such markets," Comanor and Wilson explain, "that one can infer that advertising is clearly excessive from a social standpoint, since those benefits to the firm that are not benefits to consumers accrue precisely because of the anticompetitive effects of the advertising."

Finally, it is not preposterous to suppose that markets thick with exhortative advertising also inflict excesses detrimental to the social interest. Such markets are substantially the same as those just mentioned, but they deserve this slightly different acknowledgement because the message demands of sellers and consumers may differ in *quality* as well as *quantity*. Consumers would probably prefer a maximum of information and a minimum of exhortation in the messages they demand of the media. (Consumers' demand, if known, would indicate their willingness to pay money for the ads.) Conversely, sellers often find it profitable to maximize exhortation and minimize information, even to the point of lying. Thus, wherever persuasion predominates there is again a big gap between the two demands and an indication that society's scarce resources are being squandered.

In markets *other* than those identified, advertising quantity and quality should be more nearly optimal. Although this is not a happy ending, it is at least a mitigating circumstance.

Summary

The foregoing discussion went well beyond what is usually considered "conduct." Profits and cost efficiencies are not yet fully fair game, since they are more comprehensively treated later under "performance." Still, limited consideration of them is appropriate here, and it certainly cannot be claimed that we have ignored conduct.

Having discussed the close connection between product differentiability and nonprice activities earlier, we focus in this chapter on the relationship between concentration and advertising. The causal flow between these latter variables is two-way; just about everyone agrees on that. There is less agreement concerning the nature and form of the relationship. Of the several competing theories, the "nonlinear" hypothesis is preferred here. It holds that peak nonprice activity occurs where concentration is neither extremely high nor especially low but rather somewhere in the middle or upper-middle region. As for causality, the nutshell view of the present author is this:

Concentration as a cause: (1) Firm level price elasticities fall with rising concentration, thereby initially boosting industry A/S. However, as concentration reaches very high levels, price level is likely to rise, which, in turn, increases price elasticity and lowers A/S. (2) At moderate concentration, price competition wanes while nonprice competition rages. With greater market power, however, collusive understandings may hold even nonprice competition in check.

Advertising as a cause: Economies of scale to advertising, predation, and inadvertent ad warfare are three ways by which this causal flow may operate in low to moderate ranges of concentration. Indeed, whenever nonprice costs are significantly excessive from the industry-wide standpoint, there is pressure for coalescence. In the range of negative relationship, advertising may assist entry, and this added A/S may reduce concentration. Of course the prospect of retaliation always poses a barrier to entry, too. So advertising is not unambiguously pro-entry.

This last observation is reflected in the discussion of prices and profits. Persistent advertising of promiscuous intensity is positively associated with prices and profits, but only under certain circumstances. These are outlined in Table 15-3. The table also summarizes the conditions where advertising appears to be neutral or even favorable in these respects.

Finally, there seems to be a number of markets where advertising is unsatisfactory on a scale of social optimality (or cost efficiency). These markets may be grouped in three not necessarily exclusive classes: (1) those in the throes of white-hot nonprice rivalry of the prisoner's dilemma type, (2) those in which advertising makes a major contribution to market power, and (3) those saturated with persuasive, exhortative advertising.

395

16

Product Differentiation Policy: Unfair and Deceptive Practices

If there is a dividing line between liberty and license, it is where freedom of speech is no longer respected as a procedure of truth and becomes the unrestricted right to exploit ignorance and to incite the passions of people.

WALTER LIPPMANN

The next 20 pages are stunning, dazzling, thrilling, blazing, chilling, tremulous with passion, and even haunting. The chapter is, in short, a blockbuster.

These are lies, of course. But can you think of a better way to herald a discussion of deceptive practices? The statute under review here is Section 5 of the Federal Trade Commission Act (as amended by the Wheeler–Lea Act of 1938), which states that "*Unfair methods of competition in commerce, and unfair or deceptive acts or practices in commerce, are declared unlawful.*" Since passage of the FTC Act in 1914, more than 3300 cases of deception have been prosecuted by the FTC.

To place this policy effort in perspective, it may be recalled from Chapter 5 that product differentiation is governed by three forms of "consumerist" policy

1. Forced *disclosure* of information, for example, contents labeling, grade rating, and unit pricing.
2. *Prohibitions* against unfair or deceptive promotion, and the like.
3. Direct regulation of *product features* affecting safety, quality, pollution, and the like.

Broadly speaking, each form aims at a different target—structure, conduct, or performance, respectively. Policies of the first kind were covered in Chapter 5. Those of the second kind are discussed here. And those in group three will be treated in Chapter 26.

Before delving into the details of what is prohibited by Section 5 of the FTC Act, it would be wise to note briefly what is *not* prohibited or controlled. Much to the disappointment of advertising foes, the law does not protect the public from crass, inane, absurd, tasteless, and boringly repetitious advertising. Likewise, United States policy places no limits on levels of dollar outlay, although much advertising is anticompetitive and wasteful as well as odious. Outlay limits have occasionally been imposed in Europe, but not in the United States. Finally, "puffing" is permitted, even though, strictly speaking, much of it is clearly mendacious.[1] Thus, our senses are pelted by such exaggerations as

Budweiser is the King of beers

Zenith Chromacolor is the biggest breakthrough in color TV

Breakfast of Champions (Wheaties)

State Farm is all you need to know about insurance

The Greatest Show on Earth (Barnum and Bailey)

Perhaps no area of marketing is more infected with "puffery" than that concerning proprietary medicines. Milton Silverman and Philip Lee summarize the situation deftly: "For decades, enormous sums have been spent to convince the public that failure to have a daily bowel movement is a medical emergency, perspiration odor and bad breath represent offenses as heinous as treason and child-beating, spooning a laxative into a child can be equated with giving mother-love (and *not* giving such a laxative is tantamount to withholding parental affection), sleeplessness for a few minutes needs treatment for insomnia, tension is both bad and quickly curable, mouthwashes and gargles are effective in the treatment and even prevention of the common cold, home cold remedies actually cure or shorten cold infection, and it is wise to ingest a pain remedy for the relief of 'imperceptible pain'."[2]

Our survey of what is illegal comes in five parts and focuses primarily on advertising: (1) the criteria applied to determine deception; (2) specific examples of advertising that have collided with the criteria; (3) FTC procedures; (4) remedies applied to clean-up; and (5) miscellaneous unfair practices.

---

[1] I. L. Preston, *The Great American Blow-Up* (Madison, Wis.: University of Wisconsin Press, 1975).

[2] M. Silverman and P. R. Lee, *Pills, Profits, and Politics* (Berkeley, Calif.: University of California Press, 1974), p. 216.

What is "Unfair" and "Deceptive"?

Truth, Falsity, and Deception

Innocent and naive souls tend to think in simple terms: truth should be legal, falsity illegal. But this rule would be impractical, the controversies over truth being what they are. A better rule, the one actually applied by law, centers on the *deception* of potential buyers: "that which is not deceptive is legal, and that which is deceptive is illegal." The two rules differ because, as any con artist can tell you, falsity and deception are *not* necessarily the same. Although most false claims are deceptive, a claim may be false but not deceptive. Conversely, although most true claims are not deceptive, some true claims may be deceptive. These divergences arise because of the gap between any message's sender and receiver. Whereas truth and falsity hinge upon the literal content of the message sent, deception depends upon what goes on in the minds of folks receiving the message—that is, the potential buyers.

Take for example Exxon's promise to put a tiger in your tank. The claim is patently false. There is no tiger. Yet you are not deceived and neither is anyone else. So the FTC does not flinch. Another example of nondeceptive falsity is supplied by the Pittsburgh Brewing Company. Each Christmastime the brewery boosts holiday spirits by offering "Olde Frothingslosh" (which is actually its regular Iron City Beer in different dress). Among other things, the label claims that Olde Frothingslosh is the only beer in the world with its foam on the bottom.[3] Preposterous, right? But we would not want a law that outlawed such levity.

Examples of literal truth that actually deceive are equally easy to come by. In 1971 the FTC found deception in nonfalse television ads showing Hot Wheels and Johnny Lightning toy racers speeding over their tracks. To the TV viewer the racers seemed to move like bullets. But this was merely a "special effect," which was achieved by filming the racers at close range from clever angles. The representation was technically accurate but nevertheless misleading. Many further examples relate to "half-true" advertisements that, although literally true, leave an overall impression that is quite incorrect. Thus, in the late 1940s the makers of Old Gold cigarettes boldly proclaimed: "Old Gold found lowest in nicotine, Old Golds found lowest in throat-irritating tars and resins," citing research published in *Reader's Digest*. The claim was true in the sense that Old Golds did happen to be lowest of the brands tested. But the point of the *Reader's Digest* article was contrary to the ad's innuendos. To quote the article, "The differences between brands are, practically speaking,

[3] Preston, *op. cit.*, p. 163.
[4] *Mattel*, 79 FTC 667 (1971); *Topper* 79 FTC 681 (1971).

small, and no single brand is so superior to its competitors as to justify its selection on the ground that it is less harmful." The FTC and appellate court found deception, saying that "To tell less than the whole truth is a well known method of deception; and he who deceives by resorting to such method cannot excuse the deception by relying upon the truthfulness *per se* of the partial truth."[5]

Who is deceived? Given that deception lies in the mind of the observer rather than in the body of the advertisement, the next question is who among observers is to be protected? If one gullible person is misled, does that constitute illegal deception? What about 3%, or 15%, of the population? When reviewing a case in 1927 the Supreme Court held that Section 5 was "made to protect the trusting as well as the suspicious." Accordingly, the FTC and the appellate courts have adopted a fairly stringent standard, one that protects the ignorant, the unthinking, and the trusting as well as the suspicious and hard headed.[6] The authorities have decided, for example, that the word "rejuvenescense" could not be used as a trade name for a facial cream because it might imply to some the actual restoration of youthful complexion, and that a hair coloring could not claim that it colored hair "permanently." The FTC is especially protective of the ignorant, unthinking, and trusting when it comes to claims of safety or health. Were a huckster to intimate falsely that cleaning solvent "X" was nonflammable, he would ignite a blast of official rebuke.

Still, the authorities have not gone so far as the protect the "foolish or feeble minded." They permit obvious spoofs, such as errant beer foam (Olde Frothingslosh), love-starved girls feverishly attacking a defenseless boy (who uses Hai Karate recklessly), and a rampaging bull that is released merely by uncorking a malt liquor (Schlitz). Moreover, as already noted, the authorities permit generous amounts of puffery, not to mention "minor" sleights of hand and tongue. Thus, as this is written, American Home Products Company can spend tens of millions of dollars annually in its effort to pound into our heads the notion that Anacin is an "extra strength" analgesic with "more of the pain reliever doctors recommend most," while neglecting to tell us that Anacin is merely aspirin ($1\frac{2}{3}$ grains more than the typical 5-grain tablet) plus a trace of caffeine, sold to the consumer at a price three to four times higher than the price of private label aspirin, which, if washed down with coffee, gives the same relief. Obviously more folks than just the foolish and feeble minded are taken in by this pitch (assuming less than one third of the population is foolish and feeble minded).

Intent and Capacity

Prior to the FTC Act, misrepresentation and deception could be successfully prosecuted only with great difficulty. The common law was rigged in favor of the

---

[5] *P. Lorillard Co. v. FTC*, 186 F. 2d 52 (4th Cir. 1950).
[6] *Charles of the Ritz Dist. Corp. v. FTC*, 143 F. 2d 676 (2d Cir. 1944). See also Ira M. Millstein, "The Federal Trade Commission and False Advertising," *Columbia Law Review* (March 1964), pp. 457–65.

con artist because conviction could be obtained only if the injured buyer could prove in court that

1. He understood the seller's claim to convey a fact (not a puff).
2. He had relied upon the claim.
3. He was justified (and not just stupid) in relying on the claim.
4. He had suffered financial or other injury by so relying on the claim.
5. Most difficult of all, the seller *knowingly intended* to deceive him (the buyer).

In brief, conviction required a showing of *actual* deception in the mind of the buyer and *deliberate* intent in the mind of the seller. As you would expect, common law cases were consequently rare—blue moon events at best. Perhaps the only justification for this approach was the fact that sellers could suffer harsh penalties if convicted.

The FTC Act changed all this. No component of this maze of proofs now has to be shown to exist by the FTC in order for it to reach a guilty verdict. The Commission's decision hinges solely on whether or not a sales claim possesses the *capacity or tendency to deceive.* Proof of intent is not required. The Commission attacks the ad, not the advertiser. Likewise, proof of actual deception is not required. The Commission may examine an advertisement and determine on the basis of its own expertise whether there is a *potential* for deception. The Commission need not poll consumers, nor hear from complaining witnesses.[7] Even if suspected deceivers defend themselves by providing a parade of witnesses who say they have not been misled, the FTC can still find a violation.[8]

Despite the power of the FTC to rely upon its own expertise, it has nevertheless tended in recent years to supplement its own intuitive understanding with consumers' testimony, public opinion polls, and outside experts. Whereas prior to 1955, 92% of all FTC cases were decided solely on the basis of Commission expertise, between 1955 and 1973 no more than 57% of all cases were so decided. And over the years 1970–1973, only 36% of all cases were so decided.[9] Greater reliance on outside experts' and consumers' views may be due to the Commission's recent attempts to stem more subtle forms of deception and to counter criticisms that its traditional methods were too presumptive, too shoddy, and too arbitrary.

Given the FTC's fairly free hand, what of punishment and remedy? Does a guilty verdict bring fines, damage payments, and jailings, as could happen under pre-FTC common law? ... No. As we shall see more thoroughly later when we discuss remedies, lenient standards of offense are coupled with lenient measures of penalty. Reprimands plus orders of "cease and desist" are, in the main,

---

[7] *Montgomery Ward & Co. v. FTC* 379 F. 2d 666 (7th Cir. 1967).

[8] *Double Eagle Lubricants, Inc. v. FTC,* 360 F. 2d 268 (10 Cir. 1965).

[9] M. T. Brandt and I. L. Preston, "The Federal Trade Commission's Use of Evidence to Determine Deception," *Journal of Marketing* (January 1977), pp. 54–62.

what face the two-faced (except in certain cases where the consumer's physical well being is at stake[10]). As Ivan Preston puts it, the present "strategy is one of prevention rather than punishment and remedy. The goal is to give maximum aid to consumers at the sacrifice of less than maximum punishment to offenders, rather than the opposite."[11]

What of competitive effects? The original FTC Act made no specific mention of deception. It simply said: "Unfair methods of competition in commerce are hereby declared unlawful." As a result, early FTC assaults on deception were grounded on the theory that deceivers gain unfair competitive advantages over their more honest rivals. This approach was only partially successful and severely limited. After 1929, when the FTC moved against the blatantly fake claims of Raladam Company (that its "desiccated thyroid" obesity cure was completely safe and effective), these limits materialized. Reviewing the case in 1931, the Supreme Court ruled in favor of Raladam, saying that the FTC must prove competition "to have been injured, or to be clearly threatened with injury," in order to find a violation.[12] Injury to *consumers*, or potential injury to *consumers*, did not count. To rectify this shortcoming, Congress passed the Wheeler–Lea Amendment in 1938. The Amendment removed the FTC's obligation to demonstrate injury to competition by outlawing "deceptive acts or practices" as well as "unfair methods of competition." It was this legislation, then, that made "capacity and tendency to deceive" the sole criteria. Actually, it is deceptive for me to say that "capacity and tendency" are the *sole* criteria. A misleading claim is not illegal unless it is "material," that is, affects the consumer's decision. Thus we all know Joe Namath is fibbing when, in the midst of plugging Hamilton Beach popcorn poppers, he leeringly tells us that his favorite off-the-field pleasure is making popcorn. But this misrepresentation is "immaterial.")

Examples of Deception

Man's imagination seems to know no bounds when it comes to sales pitches. As a result, there is a rich variety of illegal deceptions. Unfortunately, we have space for only a few broad classes:[13] (1) claims of origin, (2) claims of composition, (3) claims of function or efficacy, (4) endorsements, and (5) mock-ups.

---

[10] In Section 14 of the FTC Act, Congress provided criminal penalties in certain cases of deception involving food, drugs, or cosmetic devices: "Any person . . . who violates any provision of Section 12 (a) shall, if the use of the commodity advertised may be injurious to health . . . , or if such violation is with intent to defraud or mislead, be guilty of a misdemeanor." Criminal prosecutions under this section are not brought by the FTC but may be recommended by the FTC to the Justice Department.

[11] Preston, *op. cit.*, p. 136.

[12] *FTC v. Raladam Co.*, 258 U. S. 643 (1931).

[13] For more complete surveys see E. W. Kintner, *A Primer on the Law of Deceptive Practices* (New York: Macmillan Publishing Co., 1971), and G. J. Alexander, *Honesty and Competition* (Syracuse, N.Y.: Syracuse University Press, 1967).

Claims of Origin

Just as people are said to come from the right or wrong side of the tracks a commodity's origin often connotes good or bad quality. German beer, French perfume, Swiss watches, and Cuban cigars are common instances of favorable connotation. Thus, false claims of favorable origins and attempts to disguise unfavorable origins are controlled by the FTC. For example, where consumers are not indifferent to the fact that a commodity is imported, foreign origin must be disclosed. One of the more clever attempts to evade this rule occurred when a Japanese town changed its name to Usa, so that goods made there could be stamped "Made in USA" (proving once again that literal truth can be deceptive). On the other hand, such disclosure need not be made if no variety of the product is produced in the United States (for example, coffee and bananas), or if foreign origin is clearly immaterial. It might also be noted that problems arise when appellations of location take on secondary meanings, as in the case of "Swiss" cheese and "Danish" pastry. These problems are resolved by reference to custom: whenever such names are commonly used to indicate product type or style, they may be used regardless of the geographic origin of the goods.

Claims of Composition

The Fair Packaging and Labeling Act, and similar acts governing textiles, furs, and woolens, now regulate ingredient claims for many products. Those claims not so covered are subject to a host of FTC precedents under Section 5 Naked lies, such as calling pine wood "walnut," are out. Many more slippery representations are now explicitly defined by the FTC. Here is a sampling:

"Down" indicates feathers of any aquatic bird and therefore excludes chicken feathers.

"Hair" unqualified, means hair content, not burlap or other vegetable fiber.

"Leather" unqualified, means top grain leather.

"Linoleum" designates a product composed of oxidized oil and gums mixed "intimately" with ground cork or wood flour.

"Vanilla" unqualified, describes only that which is obtained from the vanilla bean.

In 1977, General Motors found itself confronting more than 100 private suits for deceptively using Chevrolet engines in its Oldsmobiles. There was nothing wrong with the Chevy engines. Indeed, GM had mixed engines amongst its models for years. The problem arose because GM's advertising for the Olds "Rocket V-8" had been particularly effective. As the *Wall Street Journal* explained it, "GM's advertising for years has stressed the purported merits of individual models, including the superiority of Oldsmobile's Rocket engine."

But now, customers "find there is little difference in the engines involved" and they therefore feel deceived. GM has been forced to compensate upset customers for what it calls a "breakdown in communications." ("It just didn't occur to us," GM's chairman said lamely, that "people were interested in where the engines were built.") More interesting, GM has now changed its advertising pitch. Instead of plugging the supposed merits of any given engine, it is advertising its "great family of engines."[14]

Claims of Function or Efficacy

During the late 1960s, Firestone advertised that its "Super Sports Wide Oval" tires were

built lower, wider. Nearly two inches wider than regular tires. To corner better, run cooler, stop 25% quicker.

When sued by the FTC, Firestone presented evidence that cars with these tires traveling 15 miles per hour *did* stop 25% quicker than those with ordinary width tires. However, the tests were done on very low-friction surfaces, equivalent in slickness to glare ice or waxed linoleum. Thus "Wide Ovals" might enable some poor soul who crashes through the end of his garage to step short of the kitchen refrigerator. But slippery surfaces and slow speeds are obviously not typical of United States highway conditions. Hence the FTC decided that Firestone's ads were deceptive.[15]

More recently the FTC moved against STP, ordering STP to stop claiming that its oil treatment is vastly superior to motor oil alone, that it makes cars start easier in cold weather, or that it protects against engine wear, friction, or mechanical breakdown.[16] Whereas Andy Granattelli used to press these claims upon TV viewers, now some other celebrity vaguely tells them that STP is "available everywhere" or "it works."

Deceptive claims of efficacy or function may even run afoul of the law when they are less explicit than those already mentioned, when, that is, they enter the realm of innuendo and suggestion. Indeed, it could be argued that this is an area where puffery is rather limited. Thus, a drug treatment for delayed menstruation was said to violate the law for advertising with such phrases as "at last—it CAN BE SOLD" and "Don't Risk Disaster," which falsely implied the product induced abortion.[17] Another example concerns "Vivarin," a simple but costly tablet containing caffeine and sugar in amounts roughly equivalent to those in a half-cup of sweetened coffee. The offending ad, which ran in 1971, had a

---

[14] "Bizarre Backfire," *Wall Street Journal*, July 27, 1977, p. 1.

[15] *Firestone Tire and Rubber Co.*, 81 FTC 398 (1972).

[16] *Advertising Age*, Sept. 8, 1975, p. 71. For more on STP and its lack of effectiveness see *Advertising 1972, Hearings*, U. S. Senate, Committee on Commerce, 92nd Congress, Second Session 1972), pp. 71–72.

[17] *Doris Savitch v. FTC*, 218 F. 2d 817 (2d Cir. 1955).

middle-aged woman speaking as if she had just discovered a sure-fir
aphrodisiac:

> One day it dawned on me that I was boring my husband to death. It wasn't that I
> didn't love Jim, but often by the time he came home at night I was feeling dull, tired
> and drowsy. [Then I began taking Vivarin.] All of a sudden Jim was coming home to a
> more exciting woman, me. We talked to each other a lot more . . . . And after dinner I
> was wide-awake enough to do a little more than just look at television. And the other
> day—it wasn't even my birthday—Jim sent me flowers with a note. The note began:
> "To my new wife . . . ."[18]

More mundane but equally misleading in the judgment of the FTC was ·
"Wonder Bread" campaign of the 1960s, which, among other things, include·
compelling TV commercials showing bread-eating children growing fron
infancy to adolescence before the viewer's very eyes while a narrator intone·
that since Wonder Bread was "enriched," it "Helps build strong bodies 1
ways." The FTC charged that the ads deceptively represented Wonder Brea·
as an "extraordinary food for producing dramatic growth in children."[1]
(Though no different and no cheaper than other common breads, Wonde
built a strong market share in this way, ranking number one nationally an·
accounting for as much as 30–40% of bread sales in some states.)

Endorsements

Mention of endorsements brings to mind jocks like Joe Namath, Ton
Seavers, Billy Jean King, Jack Nicklaus, and O. J. Simpson. These are certainl·
very important people in advertising, and the FTC has several rules of thum·
governing star testimonials. Thus, for example, an endorser must be a "bon·
fide" user of the product unless such would be clearly inappropriate (as wa
true of Joe Namath's peddling pantyhose). Moreover, the Commission urge
that ex-users not be represented as current users, although this is obviousl·
difficult to enforce.[20]

But celebrity endorsements are not the only kind, or even the most importan
kind. There are "lay" endorsements, "expert" endorsements, "institutional
endorsements, "cartoon character" endorsements, and more, all of which hav
at one time or another reached the FTC's attention. The flavor of the Commis
sion's thinking in these and related matters may be tasted by quoting Sectio
255.3, Example 5, from the FTC's "Guides Concerning Use of Endorsement
and Testimonials in Advertising":

[18] *Advertising of Proprietary Medicines, Hearings*, U. S. Senate, Subcommittee on Monopol·
of the Select Committee on Small Business, 92nd Congress, First Session (1971), Part 1, pp. 24,22·
[19] *ITT Continental Baking Co.*, 83 FTC 865 (1973).
[20] *Wall Street Journal*, Dec. 2, 1976.

An association of professional athletes states in an advertisement that it has "selected" a particular brand of beverages as its "official breakfast drink." [The] association would be regarded as expert in the field of nutrition for purposes of this section, because consumers would expect it to rely upon the selection of nutritious foods as part of its business needs. Consequently, the association's endorsement must be based upon an expert evaluation of the nutritional value of the endorsed beverage [rather than upon the endorsement fee]. Furthermore, . . . use of the words "selected" and "official" in this endorsement imply that it was given only after direct comparisons had been performed among competing brands. Hence, the advertisement would be deceptive unless the association has in fact performed such comparisons . . . and the results . . . conform to the net impression created by the advertisement.[21]

Mock-ups

When filming TV commercials, technicians often substitute whipped potatoes or ice cream, soap suds for beer foam, and wine for coffee. The "real thing" melts under the hot lights, or fades, or looks murky on TV screens. Such artificial alterations and substitutions for purposes of picture enhancement are called mock-ups. Although these mock-ups are obviously innocuous (indeed, they may often reduce deception rather than produce it), advertisers have not confined their "doctoring" to innocent, nondeceptive, and prudent dimensions:[22]

- When Libby–Owens–Ford Glass Company wanted to demonstrate the superiority of its automobile safety glass, it smeared a competing brand with streaks of vaseline to create distortion, then photographed it at oblique camera angles to enhance the effect. The distortionless marvels of the company's own glass were "shown" by taking photographs with the windows rolled down.
- Carter Products promoted its Rise shaving cream with a mock-up that was equally fair to poor old Brand X. A man was shown shaving with an "ordinary" lather, which dried out quickly after application. He then switched to Rise and demonstrated how it fulfilled its slogan, "Stays Moist and Creamy." Unbeknownst to the TV audience, the substance he used on the first try was not a competing brand nor a shaving cream at all. It was a preparation specially designed to come out of the aerosol can in a big attractive fluff and then disappear almost immediately.
- Micky Spillane took a shower with Dove soap in a Lifebuoy commercial because he couldn't get the Lifebuoy to lather enough.

[21] *Code of Federal Regulations*, Vol. 16, "Commercial Practices," p. 347.
[22] Quoting from Preston, *op. cit.*, pp. 235, 243. The cases referred to are *Libby-Owens-Ford v. FTC*, 352 F. 2d 415 (6th Cir. 1965), and *Carter Products v. FTC*, 323 F. 2d 523 (5th Cir., 1963).

405

In 1965, the Supreme Court voiced its opinion of such shenanigans in *Colgate-Palmolive Co. v. FTC.*[23] The TV commercial in question purported to show that Colgate's Rapid Shave shaving cream was potent enough to allow one to shave sandpaper with an ordinary blade razor. The ad's action and words went together: "apply . . . soak . . . and off in a stroke." But it was a hoax from sand to soak. What appeared to be sandpaper was actually loose grains of sand sprinkled on plexiglas. And the soak was a 2-second pause. Curious consumers who tried real sandpaper informed the FTC that it couldn't be done. So the Commission asked Colgate to come clean. In its defense, Colgate claimed that you *could* shave sandpaper that was fine grade with very small grains, soaked for over an hour. It said the mock-up was necessary because such fine grain sandpaper looked like plain paper on TV, and the true soak could not be captured in a few seconds. Indeed, Colgate felt so adamant about defending its ad that it fought the FTC all the way to the Supreme Court. The key questions addressed by the Court were as follows:[24]

1. Were undisclosed mock-ups of *mere appearance* acceptable? That is, could whipped potatoes stand-in for ice cream? The Court said yes.
2. Were undisclosed mock-ups demonstrating *un*true performance acceptable? That is, could Rapid Shave be "shown" shaving the ribs off a washboard? The Court said no, clearly not.
3. Were undisclosed mock-ups demonstrating *true* performance acceptable? That is, assuming Rapid Shave *could* easily shave any sandpaper, was an undisclosed mock-up of this acceptable? The Court again said no. When the appearance is *central* to the commercial, and the clear implication is that we are seeing something real when, in fact, we are not, then the mock-up is illegal unless disclosed by saying "simulated" or something similar. Of course, if the real performance is possible and a real performance is shown, there is no problem.

Absolute truth is thus not a requisite. Inconsequential mock-ups for appearance's sake are permitted without an admission of fakery to the audience. Simulations are also allowed with disclosure. But mock-ups that materially deceive cannot be defended. Now, given your newly acquired knowledge of the law, let's test it. How would you react if you were an FTC Commissioner and you caught Campbell's Soup Company putting marbles in the bottom of its televised bowls of soup, thereby making the vegetables and other solid parts of the soup appear attractively and abundantly above the surface? Is this mere appearance? Or is it a material deception? (Your test is not a mock-up test. The case actually came up in 1970. For the FTC's answer see footnote.[25])

[23] *Colgate-Palmolive Co., v. FTC*, 380 U. S. 374 (1965).
[24] Preston, *op. cit.*, p. 238.
[25] Consent settlement, *Campbell's Soup*, 77 FTC 664 (1970). The FTC thought this was deceptive

Federal Trade Commission
Procedures[26]

When attacking problems of deception (or other problems within its jurisdiction), the FTC may proceed in one of three ways: (1) complaint plus prosecution, (2) guides, or (3) trade regulation rules.

Complaint Plus Prosecution

This is a case-by-case approach in the sense that a particular ad or ad campaign is assailed. The complete chain of formal process is as follows: The advertiser is issued a "complaint"; his case is tried before an "administrative law judge"; the judge renders an "initial decision"; the initial decision is reviewed by the full FTC; the Commission's decision may then be appealed by the "respondent" to federal courts of appeal on questions of law, perhaps even ending up like the *Colgate–Palmolive* case in the lap of the Supreme Court. This procedure may be cut short at the outset by consent settlement, in which instance a remedy is reached without formal trial. The consent decree binds the advertiser to its provisions. Even less formal early settlements are possible if, after initial investigation, the Commission's attorneys accept the advertiser's vocal or written assurances that he will "voluntarily" clean up his act.

Guides

Whereas such case-by-case proceedings are *ad hoc*, piecemeal, and particular, industry guides and trade regulation rules are broader, more general, and less judicial. Their more sweeping scope often improves the efficiency and efficacy of enforcement. Industry guides are distillations of case law, usually promulgated without formal hearings. They are issued to summarize and clarify case law for the benefit of the individuals regulated. These guides are nonbinding; they do not directly affect case-by-case procedure. Offenders who violate a guide are not prosecuted for violating the guide. But they can be prosecuted for violating the overriding statutory standard that the guide interprets.

In short, industry guides are merely an expression of the FTC's view as to what is and what is not legal. There are guides for advertising fallout shelters, advertising shell homes, advertising fuel economy for new autos, advertising guarantees, and many others—a number of which are not directly related to advertising at all. In all, there were 94 guides as of January 1977. One of the

[26] Much of this and the next section is based upon M. J. Trebilcock, A. Duggan, L. Robinson, . Wilton-Siegel, and C. Massee, *A Study on Consumer Misleading and Unfair Trade Practices*, ol. 1 (Ottawa: Information Canada, 1976), Chapter III; and U. S. Congress, House, *Oversight Hearings into the Federal Trade Commission—Bureau of Consumer Protection, Hearings*, Committee 1 Government Operations, 94th Congress, Second Session (1976).

more recent is *Guides Concerning Use of Endorsements and Testimonials in Advertising*, from which we quoted earlier. As suggested by that quotation, guides consist of a textual commentary written in laymen's language supplemented by specific examples.

Trade Regulation Rules

These are, in contrast to guides, much more serious. Like legislation, they embody the full force of law. Respondents may be prosecuted for violating the rule itself, rather than for violating the vague prohibitions of Section 5. Rules ease the burden of proof borne by the FTC's prosecuting attorney because, once a transgression is detected, the respondent's only defense is to prove that the rule does not apply to his case. Since trade regulation rules carry so much force, the Commission formulates them by following an elaborate set of procedures:

> Rule-making proceedings consist of two parts—a preliminary private study conducted by the Commission and the final formulation of the rule with public participation. At the first stage, the Commission gathers through investigation, studies, and discussion information sufficient to support the rule, and then formulates a tentative version of the rule. Upon completion of these preliminary steps, a hearing is initiated: the procedures provide for notice of the proposed rule-making to be published in the Federal Register and for opportunity to be given to interested parties to participate in the hearing through submission of written data or views or oral argument. After due consideration has been given to all relevant matters of fact, law, policy and discretion . . . a rule or order is adopted by the Commission and published in the Federal Register. Rules can take effect only upon the expiration of at least 30 days after the date of their publication.[27]

Since these rule-making procedures were first established in 1962, more than 20 rules have been enacted. The first few were simple, even trivial, governing such matters as size labeling of sleeping bags and use of the word "leakproof" for dry-cell batteries. More recently, the FTC has grown confident, some would even say aggressive. Rules now govern door-to-door sales, grocery store stocking of sale merchandise, gasoline octane disclosure, mailorder merchandise, and warranty disclosure.[28] At this writing the FTC is considering some particularly ambitious rules designed to curb unfair and deceptive practices in a number of major markets, most notably those for used cars, food products, proprietary medicines, and funerals.

Remedies

The product of these and other procedures is a variety of remedies designed to quash current violations, discourage future violations, and, in rare instances

[27] Trebilcock, et. al., *op. cit.*, pp. 153–54.
[28] Leaf through *Code of Federal Regulations*, Title 16.

erase the ill effects of past violations. The remedies include cease and desist orders, affirmative disclosure, corrective advertising, and advertising substantiation.

Cease and Desist Orders

The traditional, and in most instances of trial settlement the *only*, remedy applied is an order to cease and desist. This simply prohibits the offender from engaging further in practices that have been found unlawful or in closely similar practices. Thus Firestone was ordered to stop advertising that its tires could stop 25% quicker; and Colgate was ordered to cease "shaving" sand off plexiglas amidst ballyhoo about sandpaper. By themselves, such orders are of course little more than slaps on the wrist. No penalties are levied. Penalties may be imposed only if the errant behavior persists *after* the order is issued. (Under the FTC Improvement Act of 1975, the Commission may ask a federal court to impose civil penalties of up to $10,000 per day of violation against those who breach its cease and desist orders.) But since penalties do not apply to original violations, it is often argued that advertisers are not significantly deterred from dealing in deception.

In support of the argument, it has been estimated that *one third* of the members of the Pharmaceutical Manufacturers Association have at one time or another engaged in illegally deceptive advertising.[29] Moreover, recidivism is common. Once one deceptive campaign is stopped, another with different deceptions may be launched. Firestone's 25% quicker claim, for instance, was Firestone's third violation in 15 years. These considerations illuminate a major advantage of relying more on the other remedies mentioned, as they are harsher. Still, cease and desist orders (at the end of any of the three main procedural avenues) will probably remain the mainstay of FTC remedies for quite some time to come.

Affirmative Disclosure

This remedy is especially appropriate for two particular types of deception—misrepresentation by silence and exaggerated claims of brand uniqueness. To check the problem of deceptive silence, an affirmative disclosure order prohibits the advertiser from making certain claims unless he discloses at the same time facts that are considered necessary to negate any deceptive inferences otherwise induced by silence. Perhaps the most familiar example of affirmative disclosure is the FTC's requirement that cigarette advertisers disclose the dangers inherent to smoking: "Warning: The Surgeon General Has Determined That Cigarette Smoking Is Dangerous to Your Health." Another noteworthy

---

[29] R. Burack, "Introduction to the Handbook of Prescription Drugs" in *Consumerism*, edited y Aaker and Day (New York: Free Press, 1974), p. 257. The regulations referred to here are actually hose of the FDA, not the FTC, but they are similar.

example concerns Geritol, which ran into trouble for representing its iron tonic as a cure for tiredness, loss of strength, wan appearance, and associated afflictions According to FTC spokesman Pitofsky: "The Commission found that this advertising was an open invitation to any person with tiredness symptoms to self-diagnose this trouble as a deficiency of iron. In other words, by constantly telling *all* tired people that their trouble may be iron deficiency, the advertising implied that iron deficiency is as common an affliction as a cold or a headache which is simply not true."[30] The Commission's order for affirmative disclosure specified that if Geritol was going to sell its tonic as a cure for tiredness, it then had to disclose the fact that there is really very little connection between tiredness and iron deficiency, and that the vast majority of people who are tired are not tired because of iron deficiency (and, by inference, that for them Geritol wa a gyp).

Notice that this is a conditional disclosure: *If* Geritol uses a certain pitch then the facts also have to be aired. Affirmative disclosures designed to check exaggerated claims of product differentiation are usually unconditional. Thus a trade regulation rule requires disclosure of estimated life and brightness on *all* light bulb wrappers; another requires octane ratings to be posted on all gasoline pumps. These examples indicate that the line between the two main consumerist policies covered thus far—positive disclosure and negative prohibitions—is often a fuzzy one.

Corrective Advertising

Whereas affirmative disclosure may prevent the *continuance* of misleading claims into the future, the purpose of corrective advertising is to wipe out any *lingering ill effects of* deception. What do we mean by lingering ill effects There are several possibilities. From a purely economic point of view, deceptive advertising continues to generate sales even after it has stopped because of the "lagged effect" of advertising. So long as the ill-gotten gains in sales continue the deception will return a profit and the deceiver's more truthful competitor will suffer a disadvantage. Moreover, deceptive claims may be downright dangerous to consumer welfare where issues of health and safety are involved If some folks continue to believe their tires stop 25% quicker, even after this claim is taken out of circulation, there is a problem of lingering ill effec Accordingly, the typical corrective advertising order comes in two parts:

1. Cease and desist making the deceptive claim.
2. Cease and desist *all* advertising of the product in question unless a specified portion of that advertising contains, for a specified time period, a statement of the fact that prior claims were deceptive.

---

[30] R. Pitofsky, Testimony, *Advertising of Proprietary Medicines, op. cit.*, p. 29.

This remedy was first applied in a consent decree involving ITT Continental Baking in 1971.[31] The product in question was Profile, which was masquerading as a "diet bread." It was pretty much like other bread except that is was sliced thinner. Thin slicing meant fewer calories per slice despite an ordinary number of calories per 1-pound loaf. Hence, Profile was promoted as a low-calorie bread. Looking at the whole loaf, the Commission's attorneys disapproved, and their efforts led to a year's airing of the following corrective ad:

> I'm Julia Meade for *Profile* bread. And like all mothers, I'm concerned about nutrition and balanced meals. So, I'd like to clear up any misunderstandings you might have about *Profile* bread from its advertising or even its name. Does *Profile* have fewer calories than other breads? No, *Profile* has about the same per ounce as other breads. To be exact *Profile* has seven fewer calories per slice. That's because it's sliced thinner. But eating *Profile* will not cause you to lose weight. A reduction of seven calories is insignificant. It's total calories and balanced nutrition that counts. And *Profile* can help you achieve a balanced meal. Because it provides protein and B vitamins as well as other nutrients . . . . How does my family feel about *Profile?* My children love *Profile* sandwiches. My husband likes *Profile* toast. And I prefer *Profile* to any other bread. At our house, taste makes *Profile* a family affair.[32]

The correction is buried beneath positive claims and among broken chains of thought. Nevertheless, Profile's sales have substantially thinned since the ad's appearance. They presently amount to one third of their former level, and Profile's advertising has ceased entirely. (In an apparent attempt to recoup its losses, ITT-Continental has recently introduced a new "diet" bread, Fresh Horizons, which *does* have fewer calories per ounce than regular bread because, by weight, it is 53% water and wood pulp. Whether it will brighten ITT's financial horizons remains to be seen.[33])

Until 1977, the legal status of corrective advertising was shaky. Although the remedy was imposed in several post-Profile consent settlements, the FTC did not apply it in a contested case, and the appellate courts did not pass on its legality, until the *Listerine* litigation. Listerine, presently the nation's largest-selling mouthwash (with about 40% of the market), was for decades promoted as a cold preventative as well. From 1938 to late 1972 Listerine labels declared that the stuff "KILLS GERMS BY MILLIONS ON CONTACT . . . For General Oral Hygiene, Bad Breath, Colds and resultant Sore Throats." Moreover, countless TV commercials showed mothers extolling the medicinal virtues of gargling with Listerine twice a day. "I think," they would crow, "we've cut down on colds, and those we do catch, don't seem to last as long."

Although the makers of Listerine deny that their ads ever suggested that Listerine would prevent colds, millions of folks got that message. The company's own polls showed that nearly two out of every three shoppers thought Listerine was a help for colds. Medical experts testifying at the FTC trial thought

---

[31] *ITT Continental Baking Co., Inc.* (Profile Bread), 79 FTC 248 (1971).

[32] Trebilcock, et. al., *op. cit.*, pp. 121–22.

[33] E. Marshall, "ITT Branches Out," *New Republic* (April 2, 1977), pp. 9–11.

otherwise. Except for some temporary relief from sore throat irritation more easily achieved by gargling with warm salt water, Listerine was, in the experts' eyes, worthless. Believing the experts and taking into account the magnitude, duration, and prevalence of this particular deception, a unanimous Commission ordered the company to include the following statement in a portion of its future ads: "Contrary to prior advertising, Listerine will not help prevent colds or sore throats or lessen their severity."

Arguing that this order infringed their rights of free speech and exceeded FTC authority, the makers of Listerine (Warner–Lambert) appealed to high federal court. In its opinion of August 1977, the Court of Appeals generally favored the FTC's side of the case. Unlike the FTC, however, the Court thought a "softer" correction would do. It said the words "contrary to prior advertising" should be dropped from the correction because they would serve only to "humiliate" the company. Warner–Lambert remained disgruntled, appealed to the Supreme Court, and lost. Corrective advertising should thus become a well-established, if seldom used, FTC remedy.[34]

Advertising Substantiation[35]

In 1971 the FTC announced that from time to time it would thereafter drop a net into selected industries in hopes of fishing out schools of deceptions (or at least more than the occasional dirty carp discovered by its traditional detection techniques). The net? . . . a requirement that advertisers in the target industries *substantiate* their current claims by submitting to the FTC, on demand, such tests, studies or other data concerning their advertising promises as they had in their possession *before* their claims were made. Moreover, the Commission makes these submissions available to the public, so consumers or consumer groups who are interested may see for themselves the support, or lack of support, for advertising assertions. The program's goals are threefold:

1. *Education*—to assist consumers in making a rational choice between competing claims and in evaluating those claims.
2. *Deterrence*—to discourage advertisers from rashly making unsupported claims.
3. *Enforcement*—to aid the FTC in detecting and proceeding against unfair and deceptive claims.

Understandably, the program has so far focused on objectively verifiable claims regarding such things as product performance, contents, efficacy

[34] *Wall Street Journal*, August 3, 1977 and December 19, 1975; "Back on the Warpath Against Deceptive Ads," *Business Week* (April 19, 1976), pp. 148, 151.

[35] Besides Trebilcock, et. al., *op. cit.*, this section draws upon *Advertising 1972 (op. cit.)*, pp. 336–483.

safety, and price. Purely emotional and noninformative appeals have been, for obvious reasons, ignored.

The first substantiation orders were lowered on manufacturers of automobiles, air conditioners, electric shavers, and television sets. Subsequent orders have been issued against producers of hearing aids, acne preparations, pet foods, and underarm deodorants among others. The orders *specify* questioned claims, such as General Motors' assertion that the Chevrolet Chevelle had "101 advantages" designed to keep it from "becoming old before its time," Schick's claim that one "cannot get a cleaner shave" than with its "Lite Touch" electric shaver, and Fedders claim of unique air-conditioning potency: "RESERVE Cooling Power—only Fedders has this important feature."

The first wave of submissions covered 282 claims made by 32 different firms. The FTC's analysis of these 282 revealed some good news and some bad news. First, the good news: a majority of the claims were adequately substantiated. Next the bad news: "serious questions" arose with respect to substantiation "in about 30% of the responses." To quote some examples from the FTC Staff Report:[36]

Automobiles: General Motors' advertising announced "101 advantages" designed to keep Chevrolet Chevelle from "becoming old before its time." As documentation for the claim General Motors listed such advantages as "full line of models," "Body by Fisher," and such safety items, already required by law, as "two front head restraints" and "back up lights" . . . .

Electric Shavers: When ordered to substantiate its claim that one cannot get a cleaner shave than with a "Lite Touch" shaver, Schick's response was as follows: "Safety razors, while usually providing a closer shave are known to cause nicks and cuts which detract from a clean appearance. These facts are common knowledge. The Lite Touch shaver comprises a balanced design which gives a close shave without nicks and cuts . . . ."

Air Conditioners: Fedders, ordered to document its claim that its model ACL20E3DA alone had "extra cooling power," admitted that the claim was incorrect and stated that the claim would not be made in future advertising.

Abetted by such discoveries as these, the program has led to a large number of formal complaints of violation. Moreover, the program has contributed to the formulation of guides and rules. The ad substantiation program has thus served to improve the efficiency and efficacy of FTC enforcement. As regards the program's other two objectives—education and deterrence—success is less measurable. But, if the FTC claims anything more than a modest advance on these two fronts, it could be accused of "puffing." Consumers have not exploited the opportunity to probe the substantiation materials, and misrepresentation continues to be a problem.

Having reviewed remedies, you can now more fully appreciate our earlier assertions concerning lenient treatment of offenders. Although even the harshest

---

[36] Reprinted in *Advertising 1972, op. cit.*, pp. 412–42.

of these measures may seem to have a relative weight of less than a feather, it can be argued that none should be heavier as long as the burden of proof borne by prosecutors is rather light.

Miscellaneous Unfair Practices

The FTC's enforcement of Section 5 extends considerably beyond "advertising" and "deception." Misleading claims may be dispersed *tête-à-tête* when the consumer encounters the merchant toe-to-toe, just as easily as over the airwaves or on the printed page. Furthermore, our emphasis on deception should not obscure the fact that many practices are banned for being "unfair," even if not deceptive. Although these points cannot be explored fully here, they can be succinctly illustrated with one particularly instructive example. In August 1975, the FTC's Bureau of Consumer Protection proposed a trade regulation rule for the funeral industry. The practices complained of and documented in the proposal relate primarily to "unfairness" as opposed to "deception," and only a few involve advertising.

The reason for the predominance of unfairness in this instance should be obvious. What could be more unfair than taking financial advantage of a dead person's bereaved survivors? Indeed, problems arise in this industry primarily because its patrons pose such easy marks. The consumer is understandably ill-prepared to shop around casually, compare prices cooly, or evaluate services critically. Once a consumer and corpse enter a funeral home, the odds are against either leaving before a substantial amount of money has been spent. (The average funeral costs well over $1500.) Unfortunately, members of the industry are alleged to have taken advantage of their customers in more ways than can be detailed here.[37] We can do no more than quote a few selected passages from the FTC's proposed rule and supporting memorandum.[38] Whether the Commission will eventually approve these portions of the proposed rule is at this writing uncertain. The quotes nevertheless serve the purpose of illustrating the broad scope of FTC concern under Section 5.

Embalming Without Permission

The Practice. In the words of a basic text on the subject, "Embalming forms the foundation for the entire funeral service structure. It is the basis for the sale of profitable merchandise."

Embalming is vital because the funeral industry makes its money from the sale of ornate caskets with silk linings, satin pillows . . . and a variety of other goods and

---

[37] See U. S. Senate, *Antitrust Aspects of the Funeral Industry, Hearings,* Subcommittee on Antitrust and Monopoly of the Committee on the Judiciary, 88th Congress, Second Session (1964) and Jessica Mitford, *The American Way of Death* (Greenwich, Conn.: Fawcett Crest Books, 1963).

[38] Federal Trade Commission "Funeral Industry Practices Proposed Trade Regulation Rule and Staff Memorandum" (processed, August 1975). For the industry's response, in brief, see *Business Week,* October 6, 1975, pp. 93, 96.

services, all of which depend on open-casket viewing of the remains. Viewing, in turn, depends upon embalming and cosmetology to make the remains appear lifelike and attractive.

Embalming is also important to a funeral director because starting the process locks the consumer into dealing with the particular funeral home. It is difficult enough for a consumer to order the body transported to another place because he is not satisfied with the terms offered by the first funeral home, it is almost impossible if the first home has actually started work on the remains . . . .

Because embalming is such an essential part of lucrative undertaking, funeral directors have labored for decades to establish it as common practice. Today, the overwhelming majority of funeral homes perform embalming as a matter of course, often without even asking the family whether embalming is desired. Even at one of the most prestigious funeral homes in the country the manager admitted that embalming is routinely done without asking permission . . . .

Some people do not want embalming because it may result in an additional expense (of $50 to $200 or more) which is considered unnecessary; others find the nature of the embalming personally offensive; for others, such as orthodox Jews, embalming is prohibited by religious law. Whatever the reasons, such persons have the right to not have their wishes foreclosed by the funeral home . . . .

The Proposed Rule. . . . it is an unfair or deceptive act or practice for any funeral industry member . . . to furnish embalming, other services or merchandise without having first obtained written or oral permission . . . .

Display of Least Expensive Caskets

The Practice. Failure to display the least expensive casket is a widespread practice. The 1973 Washington, D.C., price survey found that 14 of the 36 funeral homes with casket display rooms failed to display their least expensive casket available for use in a standard adult funeral. At an investigational hearing in August 1974, the manager of one of Washington's largest and most prestigious funeral homes admitted that his home did not display the least expensive casket because it was financially advantageous to limit its sale. Dr. Charles Nichols, Director of the National Foundation of Funeral Service, the industry's center for advanced management and merchandising training, indicated . . . that he would remove a less expensive casket from the display room if it sold too well. The principle is also taught in the Foundation's courses. A September 1974 report by a Florida state special committee, which surveyed all funeral directors in the state, noted that 23% of the state's funeral homes do not display the least expensive casket available for use in the "Standard/Traditional Adult Service." In some funeral homes the inexpensive caskets are in a limbo state between display and nondisplay. Kept in a separate room or behind closed curtains their existence may be disclosed only if it becomes evident that the customer is not going to purchase a more expensive casket.

The Proposed Rule. . . . it is an unfair and deceptive act or practice for any funeral service industry member . . . whose establishment contains one or more casket selection rooms, to fail to display therein the three least expensive caskets offered for sale or use . . . in the same general manner as other caskets . . . .

Availability of Other Colored Caskets

The Practice. One of the most prevalent and effective ways to steer the customer to an expensive casket is to display the cheaper ones in colors selected because they are known to be unattractive, even repulsive, to consumers. Questions regarding the color of caskets are not left to haphazard guessing. Several national studies have been conducted to determine that people are attracted to warm, natural colors. Thus, expensive caskets are displayed in warm hues while the inexpensive units are presented only in colors that are cold, pallid, or garish.

The importance of color and its effect upon sales arose during a 1974 investigational hearing, when it was revealed that the least expensive casket on display at a large D.C. funeral home was "silver taupe" (a color somewhere between lavender and pink). It . . . was, in fact, admitted that this color was chosen in the belief that not too many customers would like a "taupe" colored casket . . . .

The Proposed Rule. . . . it is an unfair and deceptive act or practice . . . to fail to inform customers, by means of a prominently displayed written notice, that displayed caskets can be obtained in other colors . . . *provided*, that such caskets in other colors can be obtained from regular commercial suppliers . . . .

Disparagement of Concern for Price

The Practice. Even when the low-priced merchandise is displayed, there are ways to make the purchaser reluctant to choose it. Funeral industry exposés from all parts of the country indicate that disparagement of lower priced caskets and other merchandise is common. Cheaper caskets are referred to as "tin cans" or "boxes," while less costly arrangements may be referred to as "welfare funerals." By subtle appeals to guilt feelings or outright chastisement, funeral directors convey the message to survivors that selection of a funeral at a low price below what the family can afford . . . is a sign of disrespect or lack of affection for the deceased . . . . An industry source reports that it is common to discourage interest in inexpensive caskets by use of a comment such as "Do you really want to put her in that?"

The Proposed Rule. . . . it is an unfair and deceptive act or practice . . . to suggest, directly or by implication to any customer in any manner that the customer's expressed concern about prices . . . is improper, inappropriate or indicative of a lack of respect or affection for the deceased.

In short, the proposed rule was "designed to provide the consumer with substantially more information on prices and choices, eliminate the devices used to obtain unfair leverage over the consumer, abolish the outright frauds and deceptions that have been structured into the industry, and free up the market so that the dealings between funeral director and customer will be more fair."

Summary

In April, 1972, the American Association of Advertising Agencies released the results of a poll of some 9000 students from 177 universities and colleges. The students took a dim view of advertising. Fifty-three percent told the AAAA that they considered advertising believable only "some of the time."[39] You can see now that their skepticism was not completely unfounded.

[39] *Business Week*, June 10, 1972, p. 48.

Section 5 of the Federal Trade Commission Act (as amended by the Wheeler–Lea Act of 1938) bans "Unfair methods of competition in commerce, and unfair or deceptive acts or practices in commerce . . ." The key criterion for determining violation by deception is whether a claim has the capacity and tendency to deceive. Truth and falsity are relevant but not conclusive, for true claims may deceive and false claims may not. As deception lies in the mind of the observer, some standard must be set as to who will be protected from deception. United States authorities supposedly protect the ignorant, the hasty, and the trusting as well as those less easily deceived. Still, the authorities have not gone so far as to protect the pathologically credulous and feeble minded. Likewise they allow abundant amounts of "puffery."

Of the many specific types of deception that have collided with this criterion, five were presented—those concerning (1) claims of origin, (2) claims of composition, (3) claims of function or efficacy, (4) endorsements, and (5) mock-ups. A never ending chain of cases under Section 5 has, over the years, outlined certain standards or rules in each of these areas. With respect to mock-ups, for instance, the Colgate Rapid Shave case is a particularly important link in the law. The Supreme Court reaffirmed what advertisers already believed—that undisclosed mock-ups of mere appearance were acceptable, and that undisclosed mock-ups demonstrating *un*true performance were unacceptable. The Court broke new ground also by ruling that undisclosed mock-ups demonstrating *true* performance were unacceptable insofar as the demonstration was central to the commercial. Ever since, the word "simulated" has appeared frequently on TV.

The FTC relies on three main procedures and four principal remedies to enforce the Act. The procedures are (1) complaint plus prosecution or consent decree, (2) advisory guides, and (3) compulsory trade regulation rules. The first is a case-by-case approach. The latter two are broader in scope, reaching entire industries or complete categories of deceptive acts.

The principal remedies are (1) cease and desist orders, (2) affirmative disclosure, (3) corrective advertising, and (4) advertising substantiation. The first is the traditional mainstay. The other three are recent innovations that may be considered a little more stringent.

Finally, the FTC's proposed trade regulation rule for the funeral industry illustrates the breadth of FTC concern under Section 5. Advertising and deception attract most of the public's and the Commission's attention, but unfairness and face-to-face fraud are also controlled.

417

17

Conglomeracy and Vertical Integration: Conduct

Certainly, the consolidation of various corporations into conglomerates could invite a vastly increased concentration of economic power, which gives us pause on both economic and social grounds.

WALL STREET JOURNAL, Editorial, March 26, 1969

Gillette makes hair conditioners as well as razor blades. Esmark counts Swift hams and Playtex girdles among its many products. Beatrice Foods produces ice cream, peanuts, and toilet seats. Mobil Oil owns Montgomery Ward's. ITT is into practically everything—bread, insurance, books, hotels, radios, telephones, and so on, *ad infinitum*. Much the same could be said of a clutch of other alphabet companies—FMC, TRW, and CPC—whose nebulous names signal amorphous corporate masses of billion-dollar dimensions.

To this point, our analysis of conduct has focused on single markets or industries. However, the typical large corporation is not so confined. Its operations span many markets and industries, extending to everything under the sun. Multimarket spread includes vertical integration (that is, operation at several stages of the production process) and conglomeracy (that is, diversity of all kinds).

As suggested earlier, multimarket operations serve a number of purposes, many of which are socially commendable as well as privately profitable. Vertical integration may be shown to achieve several advantages:

1. It may cut production costs for technological reasons. Integrated production of steel, for instance, enables the metal to remain hot from blast furnace to carbon burn-off to rolling and drawing. Costly reheating at each stage is eliminated.

2. Vertical integration may increase managerial efficiency through better control of the production process. It may also reduce marketing costs.
3. It may improve the productivity of research and development efforts. Since vertical integration puts producers in closer touch with ultimate buyers, innovation may be better tailored to demand. Coordination of R & D among diverse component suppliers is also less of a problem. These factors explain much vertical integration in the electronics industry.
4. It may be the best way to achieve new entry. When a firm expands backward to preceding or forward to succeeding stages, it is entering new markets. If achieved without merger, this can stir competition. Thus, nearly all significant entry into aluminum ingot production since 1940 has been achieved by such fabricators as Reynolds and Kaiser integrating backward.

The benefits claimed for conglomerate diversification, on the other hand, are much less substantial:

1. It supposedly enables the exploitation of "synergy" or managerial economies.
2. It spreads risk and lowers the cost of capital.
3. Conglomerate expansion is a source of new entry, provided it is achieved without merger.

These and other considerations may partially justify the multimarket organization of many enterprises. However, our concern here is neither causes nor laudable effects; it is adverse effects.

We can focus on the bad aspects and set aside the good aspects because, in the main, the good aspects fade and the bad aspects balloon as firm size grows in absolute dollar scale or constituent market shares. Consider the farmer who sells his cherries at a roadside stand, operates a feed store, and also owns a body and fender shop. He is advantageously integrated and conglomerated. Yet his economic power is next to nil. At the opposite extreme, consider the possibility of a firm so big that it closely encounters *dis*economies, *dis*jointedness, and perhaps even *dis*aster. Such seems to have been the fate of Penn Central, which through merger became the sixth largest United States firm in 1968 only to go bankrupt in 1970. Among its other problems, Penn Central's management seems to have been more concerned with conglomerate growth than with railroading, its major activity.[1] As for the anticompetitive possibilities

---

[1] John F. Winslow, *Conglomerates Unlimited* (Bloomington, Ind.: Indiana University Press, 1973), pp. 184–222; *Washington Post*, May 4, 1975, pp. G1–G3; and J. R. Daughen and P. Binzen, *The Wreck of the Penn Central* (New York: Signet, 1971).

of immense conglomeracy, this chapter discusses mutual forbearance, reciprocity, and cross-subsidization. As a bonus, a section concerning political power is included. Some related items, such as vertical foreclosure, were discussed earlier and need no further mention.[2]

Mutual Forbearance

Mutual forbearance is akin to tacit collusion and other forms of recognized interdependence, the difference being that mutual forbearance extends *across* markets. It describes a state of noncompetition, or 'friendly" competition, as results from an attitude of live and let live. It pops up in the present context because multimarket operation and large size may (1) *foster collusive conduct in markets where it might not otherwise arise* or (2) *cause "spheres of influence" to develop.* The first effect is perhaps most closely associated with vertical integration, the second with general conglomeracy. We shall treat each multimarket form separately.

Vertical Integration and Forbearance

Figure 17-1 illustrates four integrated and four independent firms operating three stages of a production process—crude materials, C, manufacturing, M, and retailing, R. The first two stages are linked by vertical integration, whereas manufacturing and retailing are free of ownership connections. Quite clearly, the singular ties of vertical integration suggest order, whereas the many trade ties of independence look like the work of a mad spider.

The implications for competitive conduct should be obvious. The independence of retailers tends to undermine any collusion among the manufacturers because (1) the retailers may compete among themselves, eroding prices at retail level and drawing manufacturers into price rivalry; (2) retailers may maintain final prices, but manufacturers might still have an incentive to offer the retailers secret price concessions to induce them to shift their buying patterns. An absence of vertical integration, moreover, tends to undermine collusion among the retailers themselves, because cartel-like agreements at the retail level are then complicated by the need to cover buying as well as selling practices. In short, thoroughgoing, effective cartelization of the industry as drawn in Figure 17-1 would require agreement among eight firms (1, 2, 3, 4,

---

[2] The "pure theory" of vertical integration is also ignored as being a bit too esoteric and unrealistic. Using assorted assumptions concerning fixed or variable factor proportions, contracting costs, pure competition, and pure monopoly, it may be demonstrated theoretically that vertical integration raises, lowers, or leaves unchanged the price of the "final" product. See G. Hay, "An Economic Analysis of Vertical Integration," *Industrial Organization Review*, Vol. I, No. 3 (1973), pp. 188–98; F. Warren-Boulton, "Vertical Control with Variable Proportions," *Journal of Political Economy* (July 1974), pp. 783–802; and Richard A. Ippolito, "A Clarification of the Competitive Significance of Vertical Integration," *Industrial Organization Review*, Vol. IV, No. 2 (1976), pp. 98–107.

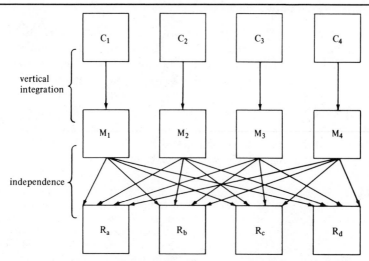

Figure 17-1. Vertical integration versus vertical independence.

a, b, c, d). Complete vertical integration throughout would cut the number of agreeing parties to four. (For the acme of chaos, complete independence everywhere would raise the number of firms to 12.) Since fewness of firms simplifies collusive agreement, vertical integration may do likewise.

Once agreement is reached, vertical integration also eases the problem of enforcement. This is explained by William Adams:

> One reason for such increased adherence to the collusive scheme is the heightened probability that cheating in any one market is more likely to be detected when all participating firms interact in the same economically related markets. As a result, if those colluding in one market find that a colleague has enhanced his market position in other economically related markets they share, they are less likely than otherwise to ascribe the result to chance, and will retaliate accordingly.[3]

Examples of vertical integration's contribution to tacit or explicit collusion include light bulbs,[4] petroleum,[5] steel,[6] textiles,[7] and drugs.[8]

[3] William J. Adams, "Market Structure and Corporate Power: The Horizontal Dominance Hypothesis Reconsidered," *Columbia Law Review* (November 1974), p. 1284.

[4] Lester G. Telser, "Why Should Manufacturers Want Fair Trade," *Journal of Law & Economics* (October 1960), pp. 96–104.

[5] M. A. Adelman, "World Oil and the Theory of Industrial Organization," *Industrial Organization and Economic Development*, edited by J. W. Markham and G. F. Papanek (New York: Houghton Mifflin, 1970), p. 145. See also M. G. de Chazeau and A. E. Kahn, *Integration and Competition in the Petroleum Industry* (New Haven, Conn.: Yale University Press, 1959), pp. 428–49.

[6] W. Adams and J. B. Dirlam, "Steel Imports and Vertical Oligopoly Power," *American Economic Review* (September 1964), pp. 626–55.

[7] Irwin M. Stelzer, "The Cotton Textile Industry," in *The Structure of American Industry*, 3rd ed., edited by W. Adams (New York: Macmillan, 1961), pp. 42–73.

[8] Peter M. Costello, "The Tetracycline Conspiracy," *Antitrust Law & Economics Review* (Summer 1968), pp. 13–44.

Conglomerates and Forbearance

Mutual forbearance among conglomerates has origins similar to those of vertical integration. As the size and diversification of conglomerates expand they meet each other in more and more markets, they become more fully aware of each other's special concerns, and they grow to appreciate their mutual interests.

Although the origins are similar, the incentives motivating conglomerate forbearance may differ. In particular, conglomeracy raises the possibility of massive retaliatory attack in one market as punishment for competitive transgressions in another market. Corwin Edwards outlines the implications:

> A large concern usually must show a regard for the strength of other large concerns by circumspection in its dealings with them, whereas such caution is usually unnecessary in dealing with small enterprises. The interests of great enterprises are likely to touch at many points, and it would be possible for each to mobilize at any one of these points a considerable aggregate of resources. The anticipated gain to such a concern from unmitigated competitive attack upon another large enterprise at one point of contact is likely to be slight as compared with the possible loss from retaliatory action by that enterprise at many other points of contact.[9]

Circumspection finds expression in much business lore. ITT has in the past been so diligent about avoiding the wrath of IBM that a highly paid man was hired by ITT to do nothing more than stop ITT's companies from moving into computers.[10] Less dramatic but no less revealing is the case of National Bank of Commerce of Seattle, which turned down large prospective customers in western Washington on grounds that "our bank did not wish to fish in the Old National's fishing hole . . ."[11]

Perhaps the most interesting example of conglomerate confrontation, threatened retaliation, and eventual accommodation involved Consolidated Food Corporation and National Tea Corporation in 1965. Consolidated was a grocery *retailer* and *manufacturer*, whose credits in this latter capacity include Sarah Lee frozen foods. National Tea was at the time the fourth ranked grocery *retailer* in the United States and, as such, it purchased Sarah Lee cakes plus other items from the manufacturing divisions of Consolidated for resale in its stores. In other words, Consolidated was one of National's manufacturing suppliers and also one of its retail competitors.

The confrontation occurred in Chicago, where Consolidated had seven stores against National's 237. In an attempt to expand its rather measly market share there, Consolidated initiated a "miracle prices" campaign, announcing in double-page ads that it had "smashed" price levels "on over 5000 items."

---

[9] Corwin D. Edwards, "Conglomerate Bigness as a Source of Power," in *Business Concentration and Price Policy* (Princeton, N. J.: Princeton University Press, 1955), p. 335.

[10] Anthony Sampson, *The Sovereign State of ITT* (Greenwich, Conn.: Fawcett, 1974), p. 103.

[11] From company correspondence, government's exhibit, *U. S. v. Marine Bancorporation, Inc.*, 94 S.Ct. 2856 (1974).

The miracle prices menaced National Tea's profits. So, shortly after Consolidated conjured its prices down, National Tea's president warned Consolidated that "there will be fewer of your lines on our shelves." Making good its threat, National apparently ordered no Sarah Lee bakery items for a week and told its store managers to sweep Sarah Lee from their shelves. Consolidated got the message. It made its miracle prices disappear. It eventually went so far as to sell off all its Chicago stores, thereby making *itself* disappear as a retailer in National's biggest market.[12] According to Willard Mueller, the lesson to be learned is obvious:

> Conglomerate interdependence and forbearance eliminated Consolidated as an aggressive rival in food retailing. Because Consolidated was a food manufacturer as well as food retailer, the competitive strategies it followed in one market boomeranged by inviting retaliation in another. Had National not been one of its customers, Consolidated could have behaved independently of National in expanding food retailing operations in Chicago and customers would have benefited from its aggressive price campaign.[13]

Rigorous statistical studies of the importance of mutual forbearance are virtually impossible because the necessary data rarely exist. Nevertheless, some clever work by Arnold Heggestad and Steve Rhoades has demonstrated the significance of such behavior in the one area where statistical testing seems possible—banking.[14] Because commercial banking is primarily a local market activity, and because many banks operate in more than one local market, the following inquiry was pursued: Is competitive intensity within a given local market determined solely by the *internal* structural conditions in that market, such as concentration and barriers to entry, or is it also determined by the frequency with which the firms in that market confront each other on the *outside*, in other local markets? Using a variety of measures for "competitive intensity" —including market share turbulence, price levels, and profit rates—Heggestad and Rhoades found that frequent outside contact *does* make a significant difference in the direction of mutual forbearance. In particular, if the firms in a local market have *no* competitive encounters in other markets, that local market tends to be vigorously competitive (other things equal). Conversely, if the firms in a local market encounter each other extensively and frequently elsewhere, then competition in that local market tends to be muted, puny,

---

[12] Federal Trade Commission, *Economic Report on the Structure and Competitive Behavior of Food Retailing* (1966), pp. 145–46.

[13] Willard F. Mueller, "Conglomerates: A Nonindustry," in *The Structure of American Industry*, edited by W. Adams (New York: Macmillan Publishing Co., 1977), pp. 474–75. For other examples see Federal Trade Commission, *Economic Report on Corporate Mergers* (1969), pp. 458–71; and F. M. Scherer, A. Beckenstein, E. Kaufer, and R. D. Murphy, *The Economics of Multi-Plant Operation* (Cambridge, Mass.: Harvard University Press, 1975), pp. 137, 165, 314.

[14] Arnold A. Heggestad and Stephen A. Rhoades, "Multi-Market Interdependence and Local Market Competition," *Review of Economics and Statistics* (November 1978), pp. 523–32; and "Multi-Market Interdependence in Banking: a Further Analysis," (mimeo, 1978). For a less conclusive test concerning Japanese conglomerates see R. E. Caves and M. Uekusa, *Industrial Organization in Japan* (Washington, D.C.: Brookings Institution, 1976), pp. 83–86.

and lethargic. Hence, Heggestad and Rhoades conclude that "multimarket meetings do adversely affect the degree of competition within markets."

Regardless of whether mutual forbearance springs from vertical or conglomerate multimarket structures, United States policy governing such behavior is the same as that governing price fixing. Explicit agreements are *per se* illegal under Section 1 of the Sherman Act; tacit arrangements escape prosecution.

Reciprocity

Another practice associated with multimarket firms is reciprocal buying. Simply stated, **reciprocal buying** is "the use by a firm of its buying power to promote its sales."[15] "I'll buy from you if you'll buy from me," expresses the philosophy. As old as barter and often as trifling, reciprocity may nevertheless have anticompetitive consequences when used by giant firms.

Reciprocity in Conglomerates

Conglomeracy is an important factor because diversification is often associated with reciprocity. In Figure 17-2, for instance, conglomerate C owns subsidiary U. Firm S is a supplier to C and also a potential buyer of U's product. Thus C can coax S into buying from its subsidiary U by pointing out to S the fact that C and U are essentially the same company and that C is a big buyer of S's goods. Conglomeracy plays its part because C and U would not be linked without it.

Vertical integration may also encourage reciprocal relationships. Suppose, for example, that C owns U, and that S is a potential buyer of U's product, as mentioned. But suppose now that C has no use for S's output and therefore does not buy from S. C would not then be able to induce S to purchase from U because the triangle of Figure 17-2 would be broken where the S to C arrow is squiggled. Notice, however, that C undoubtedly buys from *other* firms, and one or more of those others may buy from S, in which case C could integrate backwards, acquiring those customers of S in order to close the triangle.

To what extent is reciprocity actually practiced? Survey evidence from the early 1960s indicates that, at least in the past, the practice was quite popular. When asked, "Is reciprocity a factor in buyer-seller relations in your company?", 100% of all sampled purchasing agents in chemicals, petroleum, and iron and steel answered "yes." Purchasing agents from services and consumer goods industries reported significantly less reliance on reciprocity, but well over one third of them admitted that it was "a factor" in their trade relations.

---

[15] G. W. Stocking and W. F. Mueller, "Business Reciprocity and the Size of Firms," *Journal of Business* (April 1957), p. 75.

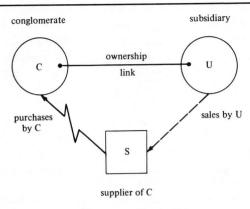

Figure 17-2. *Reciprocity.*

In addition, the same sample survey reveals that large firms practiced reciprocity to a greater extent than small firms; 78 % of the purchasing agents in firms with annual sales exceeding $50 million reported reliance on reciprocity, whereas only 48 % of those in firms with annual sales less than $10 million gave affirmative reports.[16] A separate but less reliable study of the same period suggests that reciprocity was also positively associated with diversification. Firms with their fingers in many pies appear to have relied on it more heavily than did more specialized, less diversified firms.[17] The findings for size and diversification dovetail because firm size and diversification are positively correlated.

Reciprocity may now be on the decline, however. Questionnaire surveys from the 1970s reveal substantially lower reported rates of practice. For example, fewer than 20 % of the large firms responding to a recent Harvard University survey gave any indication of reciprocal dealings.[18] Whether this remarkable drop in affirmative response betokens a genuine and dramatic change in business practice is impossible to say. Nevertheless, between 1963 and 1971 the antitrust authorities criticized reciprocity as being anticompetitive and cracked down with a string of hostile suits that were supported in federal courts by trial or consent settlement. Although reciprocity is not now *per se* illegal, these major events may have produced a genuine reduction in its usage. Then again, events may have merely driven reciprocity underground, with the result that fewer firms are willing to admit that they engage in it, even though business continues

[16] F.T.C., *Merger Report, op. cit.*, pp. 332–36.
[17] Bruce T. Allen, "Industrial Reciprocity: A Statistical Analysis," *Journal of Law & Economics* (October 1975), pp. 507–20.
[18] J. W. Markham, *Conglomerate Enterprise and Public Policy* (Cambridge, Mass.: Harvard University Press, 1973), pp. 77–82.

"as usual." Actually, the downturn in survey statistics probably reflects some unknown blend of both business policy and public pronouncement.[19]

Because reciprocity can be quite innocuous, the picture of its competitive effects is cloudy. Even so, the antitrust authorities' hostility toward the practice is not altogether unwarranted. Any attempt here to sort out the circumstances of harmless and harmful reciprocity would involve tortuous reasoning.[20] We shall therefore simply stress its offensive potentials.

Once again the key to understanding anticompetitive effects is a recognition that competition in one market may not depend solely on conditions inside that market. Conditions outside, in other markets, may have decisive impact. In the case of reciprocity, competition among sellers and potential sellers in one market (that in which U sells in Figure 17-2) is affected by the monopsony buying power of a firm in another market (that in which C buys in Figure 17-2). Note that the monopsony buying power *might* be exploited entirely within the confines of the market where it lodges. The firm with buying power, C, might negotiate preferential price discounts from its supplier S, or might insist that supplier S throw some extra goods into the bargain. If the monopsony power were so confined, there would then be no adverse competitive consequences in any other market. However, there are some good reasons why the monopsonist might prefer to exploit its monopsony power via reciprocity, thereby entangling other markets where (in the form of U) it acts as a *seller* instead of a buyer:

1. Supplier S may not be able or willing to offer special price discounts to the big buyer because to do so might (a) put pressure on the supplier to reduce prices to *all* buyers, (b) violate the Robinson–Patman price discrimination act, or (c) violate some official price regulations.
2. Conglomerate buyer C may not have true monopsony power in the sense of not buying a preponderant portion of all the product sold by supplier S and S's rivals. Rather, the conglomerate may merely be buying a large *dollar volume* of the product, a form of buying power that might be exploited most effectively through reciprocity.
3. Regardless of the strength of the monopsony power, a *shift* of its focus might yield quicker, larger, or more lasting profits. For example, the goods S supplies might be components in a product subject to profit regulation, in which case reduced input prices would yield C no profit gain.
4. Supplier S might *itself* have monopsony power in the market where the conglomerate's subsidiary U operates as seller. In this case reciprocity might not represent the exploitation of S by C. Instead, reciprocity

[19] F. R. Finney, "Reciprocity: Gone But Not Forgotten," *Journal of Marketing* (January 1978), pp. 54–59.

[20] Peter O. Steiner, *Mergers: Motives, Effects, Policies* (Ann Arbor, Mich.: University of Michigan Press, 1975), pp. 218–54.

might be *mutually* advantageous to both conglomerate C and supplier S. Whereas single market monopsony might lead to seller's price concessions, linked monopsony might find expression in reciprocity.

Whatever the reason for shifting buying power across markets into selling power (from the left-hand side to the right-hand side of Figure 17-2), the market of final resting place may suffer competitively. What are these potentially adverse competitive effects? Basically, there are three possibilities: (1) greater concentration, (2) greater price rigidity or higher prices, and (3) augmented barriers to entry. Each deserves illustration and explanation.

Concentration. The classic example here is the *Waugh Equipment* case.[21] In 1924, two high officials of Armour & Company, the giant meat packer, acquired ownership interests in Waugh Equipment Company, a small manufacturer of draft gears, which are components in every railroad freight car. Because these Armour officials were in charge of Armour's shipments traffic, they were able to work out reciprocity arrangements with railroads by promising to give Armour's railroad business to those railroads that agreed to purchase their draft gears from Waugh. As a result, Waugh's share of the draft gear market rose from a tiny 1.5% to a healthy 46% in just 6 years. It should be noted that Armour did not have monopsony power in terms of market share, for it accounted for less than 2% of all railroad shipments in 1929. Still, Armour's railroad purchases were substantial, and Armour was the *only* major shipper enjoying ties with a draft gear supplier.

Multiplications of market share even less dramatic than this carry adverse implications for market concentration. Were such concentration based on superior efficiency or some similar factor, the consequences might be socially tolerable. But this was not the case here.

Price Effects. General Dynamics is an enormous company best known for its manufacture of major weapon systems. It is also a large and diversified purchaser. In 1957, when it took control of Liquid Carbonic Company (LC), General Dynamics had roughly 80,000 industrial suppliers from whom it purchased about $500 million annually. LC was a manufacturer of carbon dioxide and other industrial gases, with a market share equal to about 35% in 1957. Shortly after LC was taken into General Dynamics' corporate family, a "trade relations" program was instituted in hopes of selling LC gases to General Dynamics' many suppliers. As one LC official put it, "Let's not kid ourselves, the ultimate reason for establishing a trade relations department is to increase sales through the proper application of your purchasing power."[22]

---

[21] *Waugh Equipment Co.* 15 F.T.C. 232 (1931).
[22] Erwin A. Blackstone, "Monopsony Power, Reciprocal Buying, and Government Contracts: The General Dynamics Case," *Antitrust Bulletin* (Summer 1972), p. 460.

The program proved successful by almost any measure. Over the peric 1960–1962, "there was a 33 per cent increase in reciprocity sales, wherea general sales of LC increased only 7 per cent. In addition, prior to merger, LC market share had declined by about 2.7 per cent. After merger and the reciproci program, LC's market share regained its earlier position."[23] What is mor these gains were made without price reductions. Quite the contrary. In at lea three instances LC gained reciprocity customers at prices *higher* than tho charged by its rival gas suppliers. Raytheon, for instance, willingly paid L $65 per ton for carbon dioxide, which it could have bought from Thermice i only $60 per ton.

Simply stated, prices are affected in the conglomerate's target market becaus *nonprice* considerations, emanating from other markets, lessen the potency o price as a competitive weapon. For the conglomerate seller pursuing reciprocit buying power elsewhere is the key weapon. As for the conglomerate's smal specialized competitors who lack reciprocal leverage, they can try to fight bac with price cuts. But all the conglomerate needs to do to nullify this effo is stand ready to meet all its rivals' discounts. Price cuts by small specialis would then be futile, since they could never be rewarded with a successful switc of business away from the conglomerate. With price competition rendere needless or unrewarding, prices tend to stabilize or even rise. Ossification the supplants competition. Notice that we have arrived at this conclusion withou even mentioning reciprocity's *indirect* contribution to lessened price competitio through its potentially adverse affects on concentration. All in all, then, re ciprocity may tend to cement trade relations and shrink commercial spaces.

Barriers to Entry. Just as existing firms might be disadvantaged *vis-à-vis* . rival whose sales are based on reciprocity, so too might *potential* entrants b disadvantaged. Large, diversified, potential entrants are usually less handi capped in this respect than small, specialized, potential entrants, because th former can combat the established firms' buying leverage with a bit of thei own buying leverage. Even so, there are instances where reciprocity has im peded the entry of even immense companies.

A case in point is Citgo, which ranks among the top 20 oil companies an among the top 100 industrial corporations with annual revenues well over a billion dollars. In the early 1960s it sought to enter the rubber-oil market which supplies extender and processing oils to tire manufacturers. To asses its prospects, Citgo conducted an extensive survey of major and minor rubbe companies, only to discover that entry would be most difficult because, ac cording to the survey's conclusions:[24]

1. Reciprocity dominates this market to a far greater extent than in our carbon black business.

[23] *Ibid.*, p. 461.
[24] F.T.C., *Merger Report, op. cit.*, p. 383.

2. Each of the large buyers has a favored supplier. In certain cases, this situation is so strong that it precludes entry into the market. The major market supplier line-up follows:

Customer	Supplier
B. F. Goodrich	Gulf
U.S. Rubber	Texaco
Firestone	Shell
Goodyear	Sun & Sinclair

It should also be recognized that reciprocity may impede entry into *both* markets entangled in the give and take. In Figure 17-2, S may gain some protection against interlopers just as the C-U conglomerate gains protection.

A Different Breed of Reciprocity

These same anticompetitive effects can be achieved in the absence of pure conglomeracy if reciprocity is *coupled* with mutual forbearance. In certain industries success may be fostered by a firm's offering a full line of goods, such as a full spectrum of colors in dyestuffs. Where that is the case, existing firms can specialize by producing only one part of the line (thus forbearing to produce the full line) while adopting reciprocal purchasing agreements among themselves to assure that each actually sells a full line to final customers. This practice could stifle rivalry, especially if the reciprocal agreements are closed to entrants. Such reciprocity-plus-forbearance "permits the division of operations into segments, thus helping to insulate each segment from price competition and serving to prevent entry to new firms and smaller firms."[25]

Such was actually the case in dyestuffs during the 1930s. But a much more glamorous example, one involving vertical integration, is provided by the motion picture industry.[26] Prior to the 1950s, when the industry was radically restructured in response to antitrust attack, motion pictures were dominated by the "Big Five"—Paramount, Loew's MGM, Warner Brothers, Twentieth Century-Fox, and R.K.O. As of 1948, each of the Big Five was vertically integrated into movie production, distribution, and exhibition. Together, they were preponderant from top to bottom. In distribution, about 80% of all features were released by the Big Five. At exhibition level, the Big Five operated more than 70% of all the first-run movie theaters in the 92 cities with populations exceeding 100,000. And the 3000 theaters owned or controlled by the Big Five raked in 70% of all United States box office receipts.

[25] H. S. Denenberg and J. D. Cummins, "Insurance and Reciprocity," *Journal of Risk and Insurance* (September 1971), p. 369.

[26] For details see William F. Hellmuth, Jr., "The Motion Picture Industry" in *The Structure of American Industry*, 3rd ed., edited by W. Adams (New York: Macmillan Publishing Co. 1961), pp. 393–429.

The Big Five solidified their power with several applications of reciprocity. At production level, each major studio had its own stable of star performers bound by long-term contracts. Consequently, independent producers could not bid effectively for these key personnel. But the Big Five lent their stars to each other on mutually satisfactory terms. At distribution and exhibition levels the Big Five exchanged motion pictures among themselves to the independents disadvantage. Two facets reflecting forbearance made this exchange possible— and supremely shrewd. First, no member of the Big Five produced enough films annually to be entirely self-sufficient at exhibition level, that is, none could *individually* fill its theaters' screens for the full time available. Second, no member of the Big Five had complete nationwide coverage in theaters. Each tended to be regionally concentrated. Thus, for example, Paramount's theaters were concentrated in the South, Warner's were mainly in the mid-Atlantic states, and Fox's theaters were clustered in the Pacific Coast and Mountain States. Only at the first-run level in a few large cities did the majors meet and compete. Otherwise it was as in Philadelphia, where Warner Brothers alone owned virtually all major theaters and pocketed 75% of the city's box office receipts. William Hellmuth describes the situation bluntly:

> This wide noncompetitive ownership of theaters presented an excellent example of the community of interests between the major companies. Each major wanted to exhibit its own pictures all over the country. No one company had theaters all over the country, but together the majors spanned the area from Maine to California. Each company exhibited its pictures in its own theaters and rented its pictures to the other majors for exhibition in those areas in which they had outlets but the producing company had none. Thus a Fox theater in California showed all the Fox, Paramount, Warner, Loew's, and R.K.O. films in its baliwick, while the Paramount theaters in Vermont and Texas likewise showed the films of all the majors. Only in some major cities were their theaters in competition with each other.[27]

The only production companies having ready access to the Big Five network besides the Big Five were the Little Three—Columbia, United Artists, and Universal (none of which owned theaters but as producer-distributors they together collected 15% of all film rental receipts). Independents were upstaged and snubbed. (It was a caste system with a very small cast.) During the 1930s no less than 95% of all pictures shown in the majors' first-run metropolitan theaters consisted of releases by these eight companies.[28]

The story has a just if not exactly a happy ending. Under antitrust decree the Big Five were forced to divest themselves of their theaters during the 1950s. These divestitures, plus prohibitions on many unfair distribution trade practices, pumped new competitive life into the industry, even though it remained oligopolistic. Independent exhibitors gained more control over their operations. Minor distributors increased their share of the rental market. And, on the

[27] *Ibid.*, p. 405.
[28] Tino Balio, *The American Film Industry* (Madison, Wis.: University of Wisconsin Press, 1976), p. 247.

roduction level, the antitrust action created a boom for independents. In 949 only a small fraction of Hollywood's movies were independently produced. y 1958, 65% were the work of independents.[29] (Still more recently, during the te sixties, the majors were gobbled up by conglomerates—but the effects of iis are not yet clear.)

ummary of Reciprocity

Reciprocity can beget serious anticompetitive effects. When large multi-iarket conglomerates engage in reciprocity, buying power in one market is eployed on the selling side of another. This latter market may consequently xperience greater concentration, less price competition, and impeded entry, ius evincing anticompetitive effects. A second, and less common form of 2ciprocity—one not directly associated with conglomeracy—can yield similar esults. This form entails the division of operations into segments or sub-iarkets, coupled with reciprocal exchanges across the segments on an exclusive asis. Motion pictures, pre-1950, epitomizes this practice.

As for public policy, anticompetitive reciprocity has been attacked directly s a restraint of trade under Section 1 of the Sherman Act. Indirectly, it has been crucial element favoring the prosecution in several conglomerate merger ases.

Cross-Subsidization

A multimarket firm can divert income from one market to another. It can ubsidize losses in one market with profits from another; it can make invest-nents in production, advertising, and research in one market, drawing the iecessary resources from others. This capability gives a multimarket firm 'exceptional leeway in market policy and exceptional possibility of imposing ts will upon its more specialized rivals."[30]

Cross-subsidization includes certain forms of price discrimination and oredation (recall IBM versus the plug-compatible producers). It also includes good deal more. Generally speaking, cross-subsidization is best thought of s a *dynamic* strategy—unlike forbearance and reciprocity, which are rather nore static. Short-run losses, covered by short-term intrafirm transfers, may /ield *future* power and *future* profits, as is evident from examples of both /ertical integration and conglomeracy.

---

[29] *Ibid.*, pp. 316–20; Michael Conant, *Antitrust in the Motion Picture Industry* (Berkeley, 2alif.: University of California Press, 1960), pp. 107–53.

[30] C. D. Edwards, *Economic Concentration*, Part 1, Hearings before the Subcommittee on Antitrust and Monopoly, U. S. Senate, 88th Congress, Second Session (1964), p. 43.

Vertical Cross-Subsidization

The most commonly alleged form of vertical cross-subsidization is the so called "price squeeze." The classic example occurred in aluminum, when Alco had a monopoly on ingots prior to 1940. Alcoa did two things with its ingot Some it rolled and fabricated internally; others it sold to independent rolle and fabricators, such as Reynolds, who at the time had no ingot capacit Survival of these independents obviously depended on prices at two level (1) the price they paid for ingots and (2) the price at which they sold their shee and fabrications.

Alcoa clearly controlled the price of ingots. Alcoa was also big enough i downstream markets to influence the price of sheets and fabrications. Henc Alcoa could, and allegedly did, raise the price of ingots and use the proceed to lower the price of sheets and fabrications. This pinched the independent With their ingot costs rising and their final fabrication prices falling, thei profits were disappearing. Alcoa, for its part, presumably suffered losses a fabrication stage, but these could be covered by its ingot profits.[31]

Conglomerate Cross-Subsidization

Conglomerates may cross-subsidize in a variety of ways for a variety c reasons. Long ago, American Tobacco cross-subsidized advertising fo predatory purposes. More recently, Philip Morris Corp. has subsidized massive advertising campaign for its Miller Brewing Company.[32] Yet Mille apparently wants only the number 1 spot, not a full-fledged monopoly. Indeec most modern cross-subsidization might best be thought of as a "power in vestment" rather than a predatory strategy. Short-run losses may be ultimatel profitable because, as William Adams argues, "The power presently enjoye by a firm depends heavily on the firm's conduct in the past. The greater wa yesterday's advertising, the greater is today's product differentiation. The greate was yesterday's research and development activity, the greater is today' patent control. And so on."[33]

Adams goes on to point out that large diversified firms have a significan advantage over small specialized firms because internal funds are the prim source of capital for "power investments," and giants possess the deepest pool of internal funds. Outside capital from banks and other lenders is relativel scarce for these purposes because power investments are especially high i lender's risk. "Since such investments involve little physical asset creation there may be nothing for the creditors to appropriate if a power bid fails. Th

[31] *U. S. v. Aluminum Company of America*, 148 F. 2nd 416 (2nd Cir., 1945) and 91 F. Supp 333 (S.D.N.Y., 1950). More recently see *Greyhound Computer v. International Business Machines* 559 F. 2d 488 (1977), pp. 498–505.

[32] *Business Week*, November 8, 1976, pp. 58–67.

[33] Adams, *op. cit.*, p. 1287.

rospect of an Edsel trademark as sole surviving asset from a power bid will not ttract lending institutions."[34]

Obviously, the main headwaters of internal pools of funds are likely to be 1ose markets where the conglomerate's monopolistic power is well established. ou will not be startled to learn that as of the late 1970s, blades and razors ccounted for only 30% of Gillette's total *sales* revenue, but blades and razors arned 73% of Gillette's overall *profit*.[35] Nor is it remarkable that in 1958 Jational Tea, the large retail grocery chain referred to earlier, earned only .2% profit "contribution" in cities where its market share was less than 5% ut earned close to 7.0% profit "contribution" in cities where its market hare exceeded 35%.[36]

Such cross-market disparities do not inevitably indicate power grabs. Indeed, hey occasionally reflect an effort at new entry. Gillette used its blade and razor rofits to finance ill-fated entries into pocket calculators and digital watches. till, this seems to be only occasionally true.

Competitive consequences aside, it can also be argued that conglomerate ubsidies, intentional or inadvertent, reduce the effectiveness of markets in llocating resources. As Corwin Edwards observes:

Markets are expected to serve as automatic correctives of misapplied effort—to discourage the production of goods that are not worth their cost and to stimulate the production of profitable goods . . . . So far as conglomerate business structures make the relative costs of different products more uncertain or increase the amount of subsidized production, they make the functioning of markets less adequate.[37]

Conglomerates compound this problem by failing to report their performance openly on a product-by-product basis. Numbers like those cited for Gillette are rarely available. Liberal use of consolidated financial statements masks conditions in individual markets, thereby blinding potential entrants and beuddling investors. Without adequate profit information, the economy's capital markets are not capable of properly allocating resources among various ndustries.[38] Asking investors to operate in this uncertainty is somewhat like asking surgeons to operate in the dark.

---

[34] *Ibid.*, p. 1289.

[35] *Business Week*, February 28, 1977, p. 60.

[36] FTC, *Report on Food Retailing, op. cit.*, p. 89. There are several time-series studies of cross-subsidization, comparing, for example, advertising outlay before and after conglomerate merger and counting instances in which outlay has increased or decreased. The results are usually 50 : 50. But this does not disprove cross-subsidy. Conglomeracy is merely a necessary condition, not a sufficient one. It gives the *option*, not the achievement. Moreover, subsidy *implies* decrease in one place so as to secure increase in another. Thus 50 : 50 is not inconsistent with cross-subsidization.

[37] Edwards, Testimony, *op. cit.*, p. 44.

[38] S. E. Boyle and P. W. Jaynes, *Conglomerate Merger Performance: An Empirical Analysis of Nine Corporations* (Washington, D.C.: Federal Trade Commission, 1972), pp. 87–125.

433

Political Aspects

Corporations do not simply pursue their own self-interest within the existing institutional framework. They also pursue their self-interest in *attempting to determine the nature of that institutional framework*. They are political as well as economic creatures because public policy affects them. As multimarket spread contributes substantially to firm size, and as gigantic size may facilitate political pursuits, the all-important issue of political conduct must be addressed. Even Joseph Schumpeter, who was in his day an eloquent defender of large corporations, betrayed some uneasiness on this point when he wrote that, "Even if the giant concerns were all managed so perfectly as to call forth applause from the angels in heaven, the political consequences of concentration would still be what they are."[39]

This fiercely complex topic has been hotly debated for decades. Quick treatment of it is therefore risky. Let's nevertheless take the risk after first setting some cautious limits. For present purposes it will be assumed that business enterprises *do* have political influence. On that point everyone is agreed.[40] The real dispute concerns the question of whether *giant corporations have more than their fair share of political influence*. Does a $10 billion conglomerate have more political influence than ten $1 billion firms? In turn, does a $1 billion conglomerate carry more political clout than a thousand, $1 million firms? Do the 100,000 stockholders of XYZ conglomerate get their way in Washington, D.C., more often than 100,000 labor unionists, or 100,000 consumers? In short, does economic size award its possessors more than proportionate weight in the political arena?

Of course *any* answers to these questions are heavily spiced with speculation. They may vary greatly with the specific issue at stake (pollution, taxation, antitrust), with the timing of the issue's consideration (1912, 1933, today), with the concurrent seriousness of other issues (such as war and crime), and with a host of other factors. Given all the necessary caveats and qualifications, can anything at all worthwhile be said about the matter? Perhaps.

A Bit of Theory

First, on a theoretical level, there is good reason to believe that political power may indeed grow *more* than proportionately with firm size. Political activity seems predicated on two ingredients—incentive and capability. **Incentive** refers to expected gain relative to probable cost, whereas **capability**

---

[39] Joseph R. Schumpeter, *Capitalism, Socialism and Democracy* (New York: Harper Torchbook, 1962), p. 140.

[40] In case of doubt read Edwin M. Epstein, *The Corporation in American Politics* (Englewood Cliffs, N. J.: Prentice-Hall, 1969).

fers to the resources one can muster to realize the incentive. It has been gued, then, that the strength of *both* elements varies directly with the financial ze of the political actors.

Incentives. With respect to incentives, Lester Salamon and John Siegfried immarize the argument:

> Since each individual consumer-taxpayer typically bears only a small portion of the costs and enjoys only a small share of the benefits from public programs, he rarely has the incentive to spend the energy, time, and resources needed to influence policy. For other political actors, like large corporations, however, the potential benefits and costs of government action are sizeable enough to make political involvement a rational investment. The consequence is a gross disparity in the incentives for political involvement that works to induce the citizen-taxpayer toward passivity while stimulating the large corporation toward political activism.[41]

Capability. As regards capability, there can be little doubt that small units ave the potential for organizing their marchers and pooling their resources. 'et the many bothersome problems they have to confront severely limit their uccess—problems with "free riders," with dissension in the ranks, and so forth. because large corporations are by nature well organized and well funded, ney may steal the march more often than not on this score also. Quoting again om Salamon and Siegfried:

> Large-scale corporate enterprises have important political advantages by virtue of their control over sizeable quantities of several crucial political resources: money, expertise, and access to government officials.[42]

Visibility. Size entails one *dis*advantage: it produces not only disproportionate incentives and capabilities but disproportionate visibility, something that can vork against corporate titans. By philosophy, by education, and by experience, he average believer in democracy tends to be suspicious of size. This innocent istrust of the overdog may curb the political participation of the Goliaths.

The Empirical Evidence

So much is theory. But one cannot assert from theory that disproportionate possession of incentives and capabilities leads inevitably to a disproportionate xercise of political power. Everything depends on whether these advantages are *ctually applied* and whether, if applied, they *actually yield results*. These links n the analytical chain can be verified only by empirical evidence. Such little ard evidence as there is may be viewed under two separate classifications: lectoral politics and governmental politics. Each gives testimony to size's onferral of considerable, though not unlimited, power.

---

[41] Lester M. Salamon and John J. Siegfried, "The Relationship Between Economic Structures nd Political Power: The Energy Industry," in *Competition in the U. S. Energy Industry*, edited by '. D. Duchesneau (Cambridge, Mass.: Ballinger, 1975), p. 349.

[42] *Ibid.*, p. 350.

435

Electoral Politics. When it comes to electing candidates to office, giant co
porations are probably at their weakest. Elections constitute the one slice
politics where people at large are quite active and, by virtue of their votes, mo
influential. This is also the one area in which giant corporations are mo
hampered by their "visibility" problem. Were ITT, LTV, and GM foolis
enough openly and fervently to befriend a presidential candidate, it could ve
well be the candidate's kiss of political death (and an invitation to postelectio
dissolution of the companies).

Even so, corporate giants have more subtle ways of influencing electora
outcomes. According to Senator Russell Long, a Capitol Hill commande
"about 95 percent of campaign funds at the congressional level are derived fro
businessmen. At least 80 percent of this comes from men who could sign a n
worth statement exceeding a quarter of a million dollars."[43] Long goes on t
explain that this money comes from businessmen rather than corporate entitie
because corporations themselves are prohibited by law from making campaig
contributions. Most of the money could nevertheless be considered "corporate
for the simple reason that most of it is either donated by major stockholders c
"solicited" by top corporate executives from their promotion-minded unde
lings in management.[44] For example, the oil industry alone contribute
$4,981,480 to President Nixon's 1972 reelection effort, the money coming fro
413 directors, senior officials, and stockholders in 178 different oil companies.
(And in case you didn't know, Nixon was one of big oil's staunchest supporters
Democrats, too, have generous corporate benefactors.

More to the point, Russell Pittman's detailed statistical analysis of the source
of Nixon's 1972 campaign funds reveals a marked difference in the behavio
of concentrated as compared to unconcentrated industries. Business peop
in highly concentrated industries were much more active campaign contributor
and the volume of their contributions was positively associated with the intensit
of government involvement in those industries as measured by governmen
purchases, regulation, and antitrust investigations.[46]

As if corporate money gained from wealthy stockholders and managemer
employees were not enough, the Watergate scandals and subsequent investiga
tions unearthed corporate "slush" funds and illegal contributions of prodigiou
magnitudes. A parade of huge companies has now confessed to multimillio
dollar wrongdoing—Gulf, Alcoa, Firestone, Reynolds, Phillips, Tenneco, an
Armo Steel among them. Many more companies have confessed to makin
political payments abroad, payments variously described as "illicit,
"improper," "irregular," and "questionable." In part, the money was aime

---

[43] Quoted in Morton Mintz and Jerry S. Cohen, *America, Inc.* (New York: Dial Press, 1971
p. 184.

[44] For details see *ibid* or Morton Mintz and Jerry S. Cohen, *Power, Inc.*, (New York: Vikin
Press, 1976).

[45] *A Time to Choose*, Final Report, Energy Policy Project of the Ford Foundation (Cambridg
Mass.: Ballinger, 1974), p. 241.

[46] Russell Pittman, "Market Structure and Campaign Contributions," *Public Choice* (Fall 1977
pp. 37–52.

t influencing foreign elections. (Incredibly, Exxon even contributed $86,000) the Italian Communist party.) But most of it was apparently spent to buy ιvorable treatment from government officials already in office. By one reliable stimate, over *400 companies* have now admitted that they made a total of more ιan $700 *million in payoffs*, mostly between 1970 and 1976, to foreign heads f state, cabinet ministers, legislators, judges, mayors, generals, and such :sser officials as tax assessors and regulatory agents.[47] Prominent among these ιmpanies are ITT, LTV, Lockheed, Goodyear, Sperry-Rand, and Pepsi.

Mention of these foreign practices carries us well beyond electoral politics nd introduces governmental politics. Before making the full transition, how-ver, it should be noted that corporate campaign contributions apparently ιing the intended results in the voting booth. Rigorous analysis discloses that, ther things equal, campaign expenditures (for mass advertising, travel, and ther promotions) are potently influential in determining who wins and who ιses.[48]

Governmental Politics. There is of course more to politics than electioneering. 'oters do *not* decide the specifics of stockpile procurements, subsidy outlays, ιx exemptions, antitrust prosecutions, tariff revisions, price controls, regulatory nforcement, and countless other policies affecting business. Federal govern-ιent decisions emerge from a disjointed maze of bureaus, committees, com-ιissions, courts, boards, departments, and agencies, as well as from the 'resident's office and Congress's assembly halls. The same is true at state and ιcal levels. Indeed electoral politics seem superficial by comparison. For policy-ιaking power is *primarily* based on access to and influence within these under-ιound chambers, these elaborately structured subsystems.

Such access and influence depend on a combination of legal expertise, :chnical competence, political savvy, personal contacts, public prestige, daily ealings, and abundant financial resources. Virtually all of these qualities can e bought or hired. It is here, then, that firm size confers its greatest political dvantages, probably to a disproportionate degree. Not only are corporate iants blessed with these attributes, they also have very few "visibility" problems ι governmental politics because decision making there is largely hidden from ublic view. Even where it is not hidden, the decisions are so numerous and so ιomplex that the public cannot keep continually abreast of them. Only when he dirt under the rug really begins to stink do people take notice, and even hen not much notice.

ITT activity in 1972–1973 may provide an unfolding case in point. Despite enials, document shreddings, and other attempted cover-ups, the evidence ; now pretty convincing that ITT "bought" governmental approval for its

---

[47] Thomas N. Gladwin and Ingo Walter, "The Shadowy Underside of International Trade," ιaturday Review (July 9, 1977), p. 16.

[48] Kristian S. Palda, "The Effect of Expenditure on Political Success," *Journal of Law & Econ-ιics* (December 1975), pp. 745–71.

acquisition of Hartford Insurance, the fifth largest property and casualt insurance company in the country at the time. ITT apparently "bought the approval of the Connecticut State Insurance Commissioner with promise to build a new ITT-Sheraton hotel and to fund a new civic center, both in th city of Hartford. Furthermore, ITT apparently "bought" favorable settlemer of a federal antitrust suit against the acquisition by bankrolling the 197 Republican Presidential Convention to the tune of $400,000. (Nixon's rol in this and other ITT capers is conveyed by a brief quote: "Listen, you son of bitch," he bellowed at his Attorney General, "don't you understand the Englis language? Don't appeal that goddam case ..."[49])

But bribery is not the only way, or even the most important way, for bi business to influence government. Pressure is more often applied throug "lobbying," "consulting," or "importuning." That the intensity of such activitie is disproportionately associated with firm size is indicated by the followin evidence:

- A 1968 survey by the National Industrial Conference Board shows that a greater proportion of large corporations, as opposed to small corporations, have Washington, D.C., branch offices, keep more federal legislation under continuous review, and communicate more frequently with state and federal officials.[50]
- R. Bauer, I. Poole, and L. Dexter discovered that firm size positively affected political activity of company executives, since only the executives of large firms could afford the extravagance of hiring political staffs and spending time to keep abreast of political issues.[51]
- A now dated House of Representatives' study reports that 173 corporations spent $32.1 million to influence congressional legislation, while farm organizations spent about $1 million and labor unions about $500,000.[52]
- *Business Week* recently reported that the influence of the Business Roundtable has grown to exceed even that of the U. S. Chamber of Commerce and the National Association of Manufacturers. The Roundtable's power is attributed to its very select membership (only 168 of the largest corporations), to its elite participants (only chief executive officers), to its "direct access to the highest levels of the federal govern-

---

[49] For details see Sampson, *op. cit.*; Ovid Demaris, *Dirty Business* (New York: Avon Books 1974), pp. 58–79; Willard F. Mueller, "The ITT Settlements: A Deal with Justice," *Industria Organization Review*, Vol. 1, No. 1 (1973), pp. 67–86. For more wide-ranging revelations of politica "deals" in antitrust cases see Mark J. Green, *The Closed Enterprise System* (New York: Grossman 1972), especially Chapters 2 and 3.

[50] National Industrial Conference Board, *The Role of Business in Public Affairs*, Studies i Public Affairs, No. 2 (New York, 1968), pp. 6–13.

[51] Raymond Bauer, Ithiel de Sola Poole, and Lewis A. Dexter, *American Business and Publi Policy* (New York: Atherton Press, 1963), pp. 197–229.

[52] Cited by Charles E. Lindblom, *Politics and Markets* (New York, Basic Books, 1977), p. 195.

ment," and to its high quality, pragmatic, and nonideological presentation of business views.[53]

In addition, corporate giants often bolster their behind-the-scenes efforts with multimillion dollar grass-roots "public relations" programs. One of the rgest campaigns of this type was launched by the major oil companies in the te 1970s. Their objective was to smother legislative proposals that, if passed, ould have partially dissolved the companies' vertically integrated structures nuch as was achieved by antitrust action in the motion-picture industry). Thus il's behemoths paid university academicians to come up with "objective" udies defending their vertical integration.[54] More important, they spent tens f millions of dollars to advertise their cause, telling TV viewers and magazine aders how crucial to the country it was that the oil companies remain un-uched, how intensely competitive the oil industry already was, how very plain nd ordinary oil company stockholders were, and how little profit they made. erhaps the cleverest advertising pitch of the lot was a magazine ad by Texaco, hich warned readers in bold type, "IF THEY BREAK UP THE OIL OMPANIES, YOU'LL PAY THROUGH THE HOSE" (gasoline hose, at is).[55] Lest you think that such image advertising has no effect on public pinion, it should be mentioned that ITT and Du Pont have studied the impact ' their "public relations" campaigns and found that public opinion has been vayed significantly to their corporate point of view.[56]

At this point a corporate apologist would probably attempt to rebut by saying omething like the following: "Ahh, so it can perhaps be shown, both in theory nd in fact, that corporate giants are disproportionately active in terms of oney spent, time taken, experts hired, and so forth. But it *cannot* be shown at these giants actually enjoy disproportionately favorable *results*, that they tually *win* more than their fair share of the battles. Ergo, they are politically rmless."

Admittedly, there is some truth to this line of defense. It *is* extremely difficult demonstrate rigorously any disproportionate political results. The reason simple: It is impossible to know "what might have been." Say a piece of hard-tting antitrust legislation fails passage amidst intense lobbying by corporate ants. Is this evidence of disproportionate results? It's hard to know since e legislation might have met the same fate without any corporate lobbying.

---

[53] "Business' Most Powerful Lobby in Washington," *Business Week*, December 20, 1976,). 60–63. The Roundtable's credits range from "killing the proposed Consumer Protection gency and a bill requiring audits of the Federal Reserve Board to watering down the new federal titrust and toxic substance control bills."

[54] "Oil Industry Group Plans Big Campaign," *Wall Street Journal*, November 11, 1975.

[55] *Newsweek*, April 5, 1976, p. 73.

[56] R. C. Grass, D. W. Bartges, and J. L. Piech, "Measuring Corporate Image Ad Effects," urnal of Advertising Research (December 1972), pp. 15–22; Erik Barnouw, *The Sponsor* (New ork: Oxford University Press, 1978), pp. 85–86. See also Lindblom, *op. cit.*, p. 206, and *Sourcebook Corporate Image and Corporate Advocacy Advertising*, Subcommittee on Administrative Practice d Procedure of the Committee on the Judiciary, U.S. Senate, 95th Congress, 2nd Session (1978).

Or, to take the opposite tack, suppose that strong safety regulations are passe despite the strenuous objections of GM and Ford. Does this indicate that thes companies are politically impotent? Not necessarily. Had they not fought th battle, the regulations might have been even more stringent than they turne out to be. Maybe the auto magnates were able to get big loopholes writte into the law, severely crippling its enforcement. It is impossible to know wha might have been.

Where does this leave us then? Difficulties notwithstanding, several observa tions seem plausible. First, at a minimum, the "no proof of results" argumen does not establish that large corporations *lack* disproportionate powe. Empirical difficulties work both ways. If one cannot demonstrate dispr portionate results, then one likewise cannot demonstrate their absence.

Second, we may ask why, if the political results are not disproportionate favorable to the large corporations, do these giants spend a substantially dis proportionate amount of time, money, and effort in pursuit of political results Do they squander these valuable resources? Are their leaders stupid? Il advised? Profligate? If they are not, then perhaps the giants are getting politic value for their money. Perhaps they do, indeed, gain disproportionately.

Third, ample circumstantial evidence indicates that, at least on certain issue large corporations do reap disproportionate results. One of these issues governmental protection from bankruptcy. Some corporations have become s large that their failure might seem to endanger the financial stability of the enti country. And this ominous prospect is something that weakens the knees just about everyone in government, fervent foes of big-business include Bailouts take the form of loans, tariffs, import quotas, and antitrust immunit Perhaps the most famous rescue operation to date is that involving Lockhee Aircraft, which lost control of its costs and teetered on the brink of bankrupt until Congress saved it with a $250 million loan guarantee. The overall proble and its consequences are set forth in a 1975 *Business Week* editorial by Joh Cobbs:

> Caught in an explosive inflation and wracked by two painful recessions, an increasing number of giant corporations can no longer claim either flexibility or efficiency. They have lost control of their costs, lost their access to capital, misjudged their markets, and diversified into lines of business they do not understand. In desperation they turn to Washington for help, and if they are big enough and shaky enough, they get it. Neither the Administration nor Congress dares allow a major employer to go down the drain . . . .
>
> [The] willingness of the government to shelter a big corporation from the pain of retrenchment takes the flexibility out of the system. A game in which there are no losers puts no premium on good management or good economic policy . . . . When a big company brings out a bad product, or when it yields to a powerful union and writes an inflationary wage contract, its management should not end up just as well off as good management. If it does, the economy will have no built-in discipline, no way of confirming good decisions and revising bad ones.[57]

[57] John Cobbs, "When Companies Get too Big to Fail," *Business Week*, January 27, 1975, p. 1

Fourth, there is "hard" statistical evidence of disproportionate results oncerning taxes. Using multiple regression analysis, Salamon and Siegfried ave shown that the effective corporate income tax rate falls directly with reater corporate size. The larger the firm, the smaller the tax bite. They found is to be true of industry generally and within the petroleum industry pecifically.[58]

Fifth and finally, the potency of a firm's political activity often depends n the *opposing* activity of other firms. If one firm opposes another, the net al impact may be nil. Since small, single-market firms are much less likely to peak with one voice than are large conglomerates, the political activities f small firms are, pound for pound, probably less potent than those of big rms. Indeed, the diversity of opinions that small and medium firms usually rovide is to be *welcomed* as a desirable contribution to democratic "pluralism." he same cannot be said of immense conglomerates, however, as is indicated y the following observation concerning energy conglomerates:

> The economic effect of the spread of the petroleum companies into coal, uranium, and so forth, may not be significant . . . but the *political effect, by reducing conflicts within the industry, promises to be greater.* The clashes over policy between the coal industry and atomic energy, between natural gas and electricity, and the like are now muted . . . . The opportunity is there for the energy industry to exercise considerable pressure on the political process.[59]

In short, it can be argued that corporate giants are more than just disroportionate *active*. They also seem to be disproportionately *rewarded*. Vhen they lean their great weight on the government's dinner table, it typically lts in their direction.

At this point a paradox ought to be acknowledged. Heretofore it has been nplicitly assumed that when big business *wins* disproportionately the result is ad, or, if not exactly bad, at least unfair to the less powerful. You might thereore tend to think that when big business *loses*, the result is good. Paradoxically, owever, this is not necessarily so. The typical "loss" results in greater governent control and more rigorous regulation. And this result is not *necessarily* ood. Big government may be just as bad as big business. Both suffer common istempers endemic to size. Thus, big business often has an *inadvertent* political fluence of disproportionate dimensions *even when it fails* to get its desired sults. Much regulation *unfavorable* to business would not exist were it not r the existence of big business. Big business, or the fear of big business, often roduces big government that might not otherwise be necessary. The implicaons of this will be explored more fully in later chapters devoted to regulation. or the moment we merely note that conclusive evidence of disproportionate ig business political losses would not wash away the political problem of

[58] Salamon and Siegfried, *op. cit.*
[59] *A Time To Choose, op. cit.*, p. 240 (emphasis added).

big business. Their losses cannot always be equated with social gains. Given choice of worlds—(1) small business plus small government, or (2) big busine checked by big government—many folks would probably prefer the former.

Summary

"Every man for himself, said the elephant as he danced among the chickens Such is the attitude and conduct of ITT according to Representative Emanu Celler. The description might also fit this chapter's other principal character Multimarket firm structure supports massive size and opens new avenues conduct—mutual forbearance, reciprocity, and cross-subsidization. Each m be undesirable.

Mutual forbearance describes a state of noncompetition, or friendly cor petition, arising from an attitude of live and let live. In the context of vertic integration, forbearance emerges because integration (1) reduces the numb of firms in the industry, where "industry" is defined broadly, (2) reduces t complexity of transaction ties, and (3) simplifies enforcement of collusi agreements. In the context of conglomeracy, forbearance typically refers separate "spheres of influence." ITT's studious avoidance of IBM is an examp

Reciprocity, or reciprocal buying, may be perfectly innocent or incons quential. On the other hand it may increase concentration, weaken pri competition, or raise barriers to entry. Conglomeracy facilitates reciproc buying because diversity raises the likelihood of buyer-seller ties. In the absen of extensive conglomeracy, reciprocity may be coupled with forbearance. The each firm can *produce* less than a full line but nevertheless *market* a full line product. The motion picture industry exploited this possibility.

Cross-subsidization entails intermarket transfers within the firm for variety of purposes. When it is used to aid fresh entry or to remain a margin competitor, the result may be procompetitive; when it is used for predato purposes or for "power investments," sour consequences can ensue.

Finally, multimarket structures can pack a political wallop. This issue divided into two main parts: (1) Are giant corporations disproportionate active in the political arena? (2) If so, do they get disproportionately favorab results? The theoretical and empirical answer to the first of these questio seems to be yes. The answer to the second is less certain, but we hazard the gue that, yes, at least in some major areas like taxation and financial protectio (and most likely in others), they get considerably more than table scraps.

four

PERFORMANCE

18

Introduction to Performance

Winning isn't everything. It's the only thing.

VINCE LOMBARDI

Just as the last lap of a long race tests the runner's early strategy, so a study of market performance will prove our survey of industrial organization. To be sure, structure and conduct are momentous and memorable in their own right. They are the economic equivalent of anatomy and action, of form and flight. As stated at the outset in Chapter 1, structure and conduct reflect the setting and process by which we obtain answers to the fundamental economic questions of what, how, who, and what's new. And, as we have seen, structure and conduct are sufficiently important to be the focus of many policies—policies whose main objectives are competitive, decentralized structure and fair, unrestrictive conduct.

Given that structure and conduct reflect *how* the game is played, performance reflects *how well* it is played. Performance consists of the achievements, outcomes, and answers provided by the market.

A few economists look upon performance as Vince Lombardi looked upon winning. They see it as the *only* source of thrill.[1] Most industrial organization economists, the present author included, do not share this view.[2] Nevertheless,

---

[1] John S. McGee, *In Defense of Industrial Concentration* (New York: Praeger Publishers, 1971).

[2] For elaboration see H. H. Liebhafsky, *American Government and Business* (New York: Wiley & Sons, 1971), Chapter 13; Charles E. Lindblom, *Politics and Markets* (New York: Basic Books, 1977), especially Chapter 19; Corwin Edwards, *Maintaining Competition* (New York: McGraw-Hill Book Co., 1949); and F. M. Scherer, "The Posnerian Harvest: Separating Wheat from Chaff," *Yale Law Journal* (April 1977), pp. 974–1002.

performance is important, so the remaining eight chapters give performanc its due. The main topics covered are, in order of their appearance:

1. Allocation efficiency
2. Income distribution
3. Technical efficiency
4. Inflation and full employment
5. Technological progress
6. Product safety and quality
7. Environmental preservation

The first two items are often measured in profit performance, excessively hig profits indicating poor allocation and distorted income distribution. The r maining concepts are largely self-explanatory.

The odd numbered chapters that follow—Chapters 19, 21, 23, and 25—trea these topics theoretically and empirically. Their collective message is simpl *structure and conduct vitally influence performance.* What is more, there is fc the most part substantial correlation between good structure, good conduc and good performance, where "good" means conformity with the value jud ments specified in Chapter 1. This is an important message. It means tha structures displaying low concentration, easy entry, and well-informed buyei are desirable not only because they in and of themselves further such goals a freedom, decentralized decision making, and equal bargaining power bu because such structures also foster fair and vigorous competitive conduct. I addition, these structures and modes of conduct usually foster appropria allocation of resources, low-cost methods of production, brisk technologic advancement, fairly equitable distributions of income, and minimum wag and price inflation.

Were these blanket statements *always* true, everything would be coming u roses, and the odd numbered chapters would be all that were needed. Howeve these statements are qualified with words like "usually" and "for the mo: part," words that warn of exceptions. Unfortunately, for some industrie workably competitive structures do *not* always provide good performance. classic exception is the so-called "natural monopoly," where economies c scale are so significant that a healthy number of competing rivals could exi only in conjunction with horrendous inefficiencies. Low-cost performance i such cases requires monopoly structure. Other structural quirks, such as cer tralized interconnection (for example, telephone service), enormously hig capital costs relative to total production costs (for example, sewage disposal and physical singularities (for example, seaports), also nourish "natura monopolies." Zealous pursuit of competitive structures in these cases woul be futile (because their attainment is impossible) or stupid (because, if attaine they yield poor performance). Hence, government typically approaches thes unruly beasts by condoning and to some extent even encouraging monopolisti structures. In hopes of serving the public interest, government either (1) *take*

44

over ownership and operation or (2) *regulates* performance directly if private ownership is permitted. In short, if monopoly is inevitable, it is preferable that such monopoly be publicly owned or publicly supervised. The latter option, which is the subject of Chapter 20, is called "public utility" regulation.

Regrettably, the exceptions are not limited to a few specific industries whose "good" performance requires "bad" structures. Disharmonies between structure and performance arise under other conditions as well. Three broad classes of exceptions concerning specific aspects of performance warrant discussion.

First, governmental awards of *temporary, unregulated monopoly* may be deemed the best way of rewarding and encouraging good performance. Patents provide the main example of this. A patent gives its owner 17 years of monopoly control over an invention. Because unregulated monopoly often yields handsome profits, patents in theory reward deserving inventors, thereby spurring technological progress that would not otherwise occur. This policy is explored in Chapter 24.

Second, certain aspects of good performance may be furthered by competitive structure and conduct, but procompetitive policies may still not be applied. Such policies may be considered *inexpedient*; their vigorous enforcement may be considered *socially and politically impractical or disruptive*. Assume for sake of illustration that labor unions contribute to aggregate inflation or unemployment because they impose anticompetitive restraints on labor markets. We would then have anticompetitive structures (unions) producing bad performance (inflation or unemployment). Assume further that unions bestow no notable economic benefits on society at large (such as increased productivity) that might broadly justify their existence or outweigh their bad aspects. The solution to the performance problem then seems obvious. Break up or totally dissolve unions, right? Right. But for obvious reasons this may be politically impossible (or if not impossible, politically suicidal). Similar assumptions could be made about oligopolistic industries not sufficiently concentrated to draw attack as monopolies but not sufficiently competitive to be free of inflationary biases. How much labor market and product market power actually contribute to inflation will be taken up later (Chapter 21). The point made here is that structures that are *economically* "bad" may nevertheless be considered *politically* "good," or if not exactly "good," then politically impregnable. Under the problem of inflation, this dilemma has led to "wage-price guide posts," "incomes policies," "freezes," "wage-price jaw-boning," and the like, all of which, as will be seen in Chapter 22, can be considered performance policies. Indeed, they are akin to "public utility" regulation but broader in industrial scope and narrower in purpose.

Third and finally, several important aspects of performance are apparently *unaffected* by structure or conduct. Examples include product safety, pollution, and, to a lesser extent, product quality. In such instances policy need not pursue competitive structures or condone monopoly power to get the desired results. Policy in these instances usually operates *independently* of such considerations, focusing instead directly on performance and applying performance standards

447

to industries of all shapes, sizes, and species. Thus the U. S. Food and Drug Administration regulates the purety, safety, and efficacy of thousands of foods, drugs, cosmetics, and medical devices. Similarly, the grasp of the Consumer Product Safety Commission extends to 10,000 products. And the Environmental Protection Agency governs the pollution performance of all producers—from farms to oil refineries to electric power plants. These performance policies may occasionally cause structure to change. Some evidence suggests, in fact, that these policies sometimes lead to greater market concentration. Still, to the extent such changes occur, they are merely by-products. They are neither intended by, nor integral to, the objectives of these regulatory agencies. For these and other reasons, regulations concerning quality, safety, and pollution are treated in Chapter 26 as a separate category of performance regulation.

In sum, our passage into performance analysis does not put policy behind us. For a variety of reasons, government does not rest content with whatever desirable aspects of performance may be derived indirectly from its extensive (though often less than diligent) attention to structure and conduct. Government often dabbles and deals in performance directly. Whereas most policies governing structure and conduct may be called "antitrust" or "affirmative disclosure" policies, most of those governing performance typically entail "regulation" or "subsidization." Labels aside, you will find one even-numbered chapter on performance policy for each odd-numbered chapter on performance economics.

19

Profits, Wages,
Technological Efficiency,
and Jobs: Theory and
Cross-Section Evidence

The creation of a monopoly involves a principle which can be generally applied . . . when in need of money.

ARISTOTLE

Observations on the social ill-effects of market power date back to Aristotle. He tells of a Sicilian who monopolized the iron trade, thereby profiting 100 %.[1] More recently, over the past 25 years, there have been more than eighty empirical studies of the profitability of market power. These modern studies are more sophisticated, more scientific, and more thorough than Aristotle's. But nearly all of them reach the same conclusion—market power boosts profits. The first purpose of this chapter is to review this mountain of empiricism and explain its implications for two measures of economic performance, namely, allocation efficiency and wealth distribution.

The second purpose of this chapter is to show that market power can affect worker wage rates as well as profits. For this purpose we shall explore power in labor markets (as measured by unionization) as well as power in product markets.

As a third consideration, a growing body of empirical literature indicates that market power spawns technical inefficiency or X-inefficiency. X-inefficiency may economically be more costly to society than either excess profits or exorbitant wages.

---

[1] Ernest Barker (ed.), *The Politics of Aristotle* (New York: Oxford University Press, 1962), p. 31.

Finally, this chapter closes with a brief discussion of two aspects of perfor mance that have only recently caught the eyes of economists—job discrimina tion and job satisfaction. As in the case of X-inefficiency, powerful firms appea to have stained records on both scores. If your value judgements are such tha Aristotle's ancient tale of an iron monger's monopoly profit made you sigh save your breath. Still more stirring revelations are yet to come.

Profits and Market Power

Theory

Figure 19-1 depicts the simple theory of excess profits and resource mis allocation under monopoly. With pure competition, industry price would be OP_c, which equals marginal cost. Marginal cost includes a normal profit, one just big enough that investors are content to leave their capital committed to this industry. Competitive quantity Q_c will then be supplied in the long run Moreover, with price equal to marginal cost, resources are optimally allocated to the production of this commodity. Price indicates resource value "here," whereas marginal cost indicates resource value "elsewhere." Since value here just equals value elsewhere at the margin, any shift of resources will reduce consumer welfare. Consumers' welfare is measured by consumers' surplus which is the greatest sum consumers are willing to pay for consuming quantity

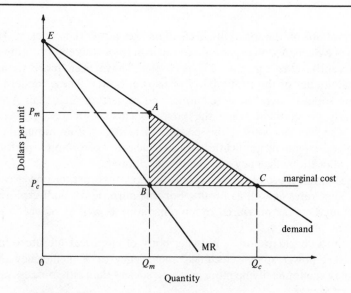

Figure 19-1. Social welfare loss due to monopoly.

OQ_c less the amount they actually pay. In Figure 19-1, assuming pure competition, $OECQ_c$ is the sum they are willing to pay, whereas OP_cCQ_c is the sum they actually pay. Hence triangle ECP_c is the consumers' surplus associated with pure competition.

Monopolization of the industry has at least two effects. First, the monopolist maximizes profit by producing Q_m, where marginal revenue (MR) matches marginal cost. Price jumps to P_m, and the monopolist takes part of what would be consumers' surplus under pure competition. This area, rectangle P_cP_mAB, is the monopolist's excess profit. How markedly the excess profit contributes to an unequal distribution of income and wealth depends on the relative financial condition of (1) those who pay the higher price and thereby lose the surplus and (2) those who earn the excess profit and thereby gain the surplus. If those who pay are generally poorer than those who receive (in the United States only about 2% of all households control over 50% of all business ownership claims), then income distribution is made more unequal than otherwise (Robin Hood in reverse, that is). Regardless of the distribution effect, area P_cP_mAB should be considered a *transfer* from one group to another. It is not a direct measure of allocation inefficiency.

The second effect of monopoly seen here is welfare loss caused by misallocation of resources. When price rises above marginal cost to P_m, a portion of what used to be consumers' surplus disappears completely. This is triangular area ABC, which is neither retained by consumers nor transferred to the owners. In simple terms, misallocation occurs because monopolization underallocates resources to here, as production is cut back; production cut-backs also force overallocations elsewhere. The fact that price P_m exceeds marginal cost indicates that value here exceeds value elsewhere. And society would therefore be better off if resources were moved from elsewhere into here. But monopolization, with entry barred, prevents the necessary reshuffling. Welfare is lost just as welfare would be lost if seismic violence suddenly obliterated our coal resources. From Figure 19-1 it may be seen that welfare loss will be greater, the greater the divergence between P_m and P_c and between Q_m and Q_c. It is also true that welfare loss is a positive function of profit as a percentage of sales and price elasticity of demand.

In short, if market power does indeed generate excess profit, two adverse economic effects could arise—allocation inefficiency and maldistribution of wealth or income. Notice the "if" and the "could." Nothing is certain about these theoretical effects or the extent of actual harm. Research has tried to dispel some of the uncertainty by focusing on three questions raised by Figure 19-1:

1. Is there a positive association between market power and profitability?
2. Given a yes answer to question 1, what is the total welfare loss due to monopolistic misallocation?
3. Given a yes answer to question 1, what is market power's contribution to the above average wealth of the wealthy?

451

We shall take up each question in turn. It should be kept in mind throughou that pure monopoly and pure competition are extreme cases. Research actually centers on the varying degrees of market power that lie between these extremes

Does Market Power Increase Profit?

The relationship between market power and profit performance is the most thoroughly studied of all structure-performance relationships. New evidence appears almost monthly. One reason for the intense attention paid to this issue is the immense policy implications it carries. Another is the wide diversity of possible research approaches. "Profit", for example, can be measured in a number of ways, each of which has a variety of data sources.[2]

An ideal measure of "profit" would be comparable across industries and free from biases that varied systematically but irrelevantly with market power For purposes of comparability, all measures are actually **profit rates**, computed by dividing dollar profit (either pretax or post-tax) by some base figure. There are two broad classes of bases commonly used: (1) balance sheet data and (2 sales revenues. Accordingly, all measures can be divided into two groups.

The first group uses **stockholders' equity or assets** as the base. Indeed, the most widely used measure of profit is the **rate of return on stockholders' equity after tax**. Symbolically, this is $(P - T)/E$, where P is total dollar profit, T is tax on profit, and E is stockholders' equity. This measure has the desirable property of corresponding closely with the profit that stockholders seek to maximize. Moreover, this measure would be the same in the long run for all industries if pure competition prevailed throughout the economy. When assets instead of equity are used as the base, an adjustment must be made because debt capital as well as equity capital stands behind total assets, and debt capital is paid interest rather than profit, which is paid to equity capital owners. Accordingly, the formula for the **rate of return on assets after tax** is $(P - T + I)/A$, where P is dollar profit, T is tax, I is total dollar interest paid, and A is asset value. As compared with return on equity, this measure is probably less affected by irrelevant interindustry variances in debt/equity ratios, but most experts nevertheless consider it to be inferior to $(P - T)/E$. Data for both measures are available from corporation reports or, on a more aggregated level, from Internal Revenue Service documents.

A major problem with this first class of measures is that they may bias all firms toward equal profit rates because the numerator and denominator tend to move together directly rather than independently. Leonard Weiss explains:

> assets are apt to be written up or down according to their profitability. For instance, plant and equipment that have changed hands since they were installed are apt to be valued at their purchase prices rather than at their original costs, and those purchase

[2] For a good review see Leonard W. Weiss, "The Concentration-Profits Relationship," in *Industrial Concentration: the New Learning*, edited by H. Goldschmid, M. Mann, and F. Weston (Boston: Little, Brown, 1974), pp. 196–201.

prices will reflect their income earning prospects. Even when assets do not change hands, investments that turn out badly are sometimes written down to reflect their income potential more realistically. The result of such revaluations is [also] to increase the equity of highly profitable firms and reduce it in unprofitable firms, thus biasing all firms toward equal profit rates.[3]

Another shortcoming of these measures is that available data for them are *firm* specific, not *market* specific. Because many firms are highly diversified, their reported profits are a mix of profits from a number of markets. By contrast, most measures of market power are market specific. The disparity often prevents a precise match-up of observations on market structure and observations on profit.

The most obvious of the second group of measures, which use sales, is **profit after tax relative to sales**, or $(P - T)/S$, where S is total sales revenue. This is not the form of profit that stockholders seek to maximize, but it has the advantage of measuring allocation inefficiency more directly than does profit relative to equity or assets. Moreover, it is not biased by asset revaluations. $(P - T)/S$ is not trouble free, however. It varies across industries for reasons wholly unrelated to market power. In particular, $(P - T)/S$ is largely determined by the capital intensity of the production process. Greater capital intensity implies a greater capital investment per unit of sales, and this in turn requires a greater profit per dollar of sales in order to reward investors with a given level of return on their investments. Letting E/S indicate investment per unit of sales, this may be seen in the following identity:

$$\frac{P - T}{S} = \frac{E}{S} \times \frac{P - T}{E}$$

For a given level of $(P - T)/E$, say 9%, $(P - T)/S$ will be a direct function of E/S. Thus when using $(P - T)/S$, researchers must allow for capital intensity.

This allowance is even more urgent in a similar measure derived from Census data, namely, $(S - CM - PR)/S$, where CM is cost of materials, PR is payroll, and S is sales as before. The numerator of this **price-cost margin** includes much more than profit. It includes depreciation, taxes, advertising, research and development expense, and some managerial overhead. Although this jumble of elements is a defect, the Census price-cost margin is favored by some researchers because it avoids the diversification problem and certain accounting problems. Moreover, it can be argued that oligopoly theory really predicts high prices, prices that may or may not include high profits.

To summarize, there is a variety of profit measures and a variety of data sources, but imperfections affect each of them. If these imperfections spuriously generated positive associations between market power and profit, they would seriously reduce the validity of the measurements. Doubt would be cast on the meaning of such positive findings. However, just about all known errors work

---

[3] *Ibid.*, p. 196.

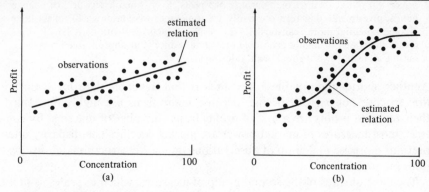

Figure 19-2. *Positive relationships between profit and concentration.*

in the opposite direction. They either lessen the strength of any positive correlation between profits and power or bias it toward zero. Given this direction of error, "we can be pretty sure that if any positive relation does appear there is something there and it is understated. On the other hand, if no relationship is detected, one may still exist."[4]

Concentration and Profits. Earlier chapters theorized that concentration fostered market power. They also reviewed evidence of a positive association between concentration and price level. It will not come as a jolt, then, to learn that all but a few of the many statistical studies correlating profit and concentration find a *similar positive and significant relationship.* Figures 19-2(a) and 2(b) depict examples of these results. Such positive effects have been found for all measures of profit, for many different measures of concentration (four-firm and eight-firm ratios plus the Herfindahl index), and for vastly different time periods (from 1936 to the present). Moreover, the positive relationship holds for broad interindustry samples (including all manufacturing industries), narrow interindustry samples (limited to producer goods or food products, for instance), and intraindustry samples across diverse geographic markets (such as those in banking, grocery retailing, and bread).[5] As if this were not

---

[4] *Ibid.*, p. 201. For statistical demonstration of this conclusion see J. A. Dalton and D. W. Penn, *The Quality of Data As a Factor in Analyses of Structure—Performance Relationships* (Federal Trade Commission Economic Report, 1971).

[5] For surveys see Weiss, *op. cit.*, and Stephen A. Rhoades, "Structure-Performance Studies in Banking: A Summary and Evaluation," *Staff Economic Studies*, No. 92 (Board of Governors of the Federal Reserve System, 1977). Among the many studies not mentioned in these surveys are David Qualls, "Concentration, Barriers to Entry, and Long Run Economic Profit Margins," *Journal of Industrial Economics* (April 1972), pp. 146–58; S. A. Rhoades and Joe M. Cleaver, "The Nature of the Concentration—Price/Cost Margin Relationship for 352 Manufacturing Industries: 1967," *Southern Economic Journal* (July 1973), pp. 90–102; James A. Verbrugge and R. A. Shick, "Market Structure and Savings and Loan Profitability," *Quarterly Review of Economics and Business* (Summer 1976), pp. 79–90; and John E. Kwoka, Jr., *Market Shares, Concentration, and Competition in Manufacturing Industries* (Washington, D.C.: Federal Trade Commission, 1978).

enough, the positive relationship emerges from data gathered from every corner of the world—England, Canada, Japan, Pakistan, India, Mexico, Brazil, Kenya, and France, as well as the United States.[6] Given this wide variety of tests, the general consistency of a positive concentration-profit relationship is impressive.

Two brief numerical examples based on United States data convey the message. Robert Kilpatrick computed the correlation between concentration and three different measures of pretax profit for 91 industries using 1963 Internal Revenue Service data. The correlation coefficients are 0.388, 0.442, and 0.506 for profits as a percentage of equity, assets, and sales, respectively.[7] All are statistically significant at the 95% level or better. All indicate a relationship like Figure 19-2(a).

In another study, one limited to 97 firms producing food products, William Kelly used regression analysis to explain interfirm variance in profit rates as a per cent of stockholders equity. A summary of his results is presented in Table 19-1. Reading the table horizontally discloses the estimated impact of advertising on profit. As advertising intensity increases, profit likewise increases, a result explained earlier in Chapter 15. The estimated impact of concentration is seen by scanning down the columns. For example, when advertising is held constant at 1% of sales, a profit rate of 6.3% is associated with concentration of 40, and a profit rate of 11.5% is associated with concentration of 70. Notice that most of the increase in profit occurs in the range of concentration between 40 and 60. Added concentration above 60 adds very little to profit (regardless of advertising intensity). The table does not present results for concentration ratios less than 40 because the sample did not include observations for low levels of concentration. Still, on the basis of other evidence, it can be assumed that profit would not vary greatly over the low range of concentration, in which case these results would trace the pattern depicted in Figure 19-2(b).

---

[6] J. Khalilzadeh-Shiraz, "Market Structure and Price-Cost Margins: A Comparative Analysis of U. K. and U. S. Manufacturing Industries," *Economic Inquiry* (March 1976), pp. 116–28; J. C. H. Jones, L. Laudadio and M. Percy, "Profitability and Market Structure: A Cross-Section Comparison of Canadian and American Manufacturing Industry," *Journal of Industrial Economics* (March 1977), pp. 195–211; Richard E. Caves and Masu Uekusa, *Industrial Organization in Japan* (Washington, D.C.: Brookings Institution, 1976), pp. 92–96; Lawrence J. White, *Industrial Concentration and Economic Power in Pakistan* (Princeton: Princeton University Press, 1974); P. K. Sawhney and B. L. Sawhney, "Capacity-Utilization, Concentration, and Price-Cost Margins: Results on Indian Industries," *Journal of Industrial Economics* (April 1973), pp. 145–53; John M. Conner and Willard F. Mueller, *Market Power and Profitability of Multinational Corporations in Brazil and Mexico*, Report to the Subcommittee on Foreign Economic Policy of the Committee on Foreign Relations, U. S. Senate (1977); William J. House, "Market Structure and Industry Performance: The Case of Kenya," *Oxford Economic Papers* (November 1973), pp. 405–19; F. Jenny and A. P. Weber, "Profit Rates and Structural Variables in the French Manufacturing Sector," *European Economic Review*, (January 1976); and Stephen Nickell and David Metcalf, "Monopolistic Industries and Monopoly Profits or, Are Kellogg's Cornflakes Overpriced?" *Economic Journal* (June 1978), pp. 254–68.

[7] Robert W. Kilpatrick, "The Validity of the Average Concentration Ratio as a Measure of Industrial Structure," *Southern Economic Journal* (April 1976), pp. 711–15.

TABLE 19-1 Profit Rates of Food Manufacturing Firms Associated with Levels of Industry Concentration and Advertising to Sales Ratios

Four-Firm Concentration	Advertising to Sales Ratio (%)				
	1.0	2.0	3.0	4.0	5.0
40	6.3	7.4	8.5	9.6	10.7
45	8.0	9.1	10.2	11.3	12.4
50	9.3	10.4	11.5	12.6	13.7
55	10.3	11.4	12.5	13.6	14.7
60	11.0	12.1	13.2	14.3	15.4
65	11.4	12.5	13.6	14.7	15.8
70	11.5	12.6	13.7	14.8	15.9

Source: William H. Kelly, *On the Influence of Market Structure on the Profit Performance of Food Manufacturing Companies* (Federal Trade Commission, 1969), p. 7.

The exact *form* of the concentration-profits relationship is a much debated issue.[8] Some evidence reveals a linear relation like Figure 19-2(a). Other evidence indicates a nonlinear or discontinuous form, one example of which is Figure 19-2(b). The present author is open minded on the subject of form, but he suspects that, *if* a nonlinear form does hold under some circumstances, theory would suggest a form like Figure 19-2(b). Evidence of structure's impact on price fixing would suggest the same (see Chapter 12). That is to say, it is in the *middle* range of concentration that the greatest transformation from competitive to collusive conduct is likely to occur. If so, it is in the middle range that concentration and profit are most likely to move positively and significantly together, as shown in Figure 19-2(b).

What about the several statistical studies that show *no* significant positive relationship between concentration and profit? Are they not relevant? To be sure, they cannot be ignored. But almost without exception reasonable explanations can be found for their contrary results. It has been found, for example, that the relationship is weak or nonexistent during rapid spurts of economic expansion or price inflation.[9] Studies drawing data from such periods are

---

[8] Examples include Rhoades and Cleaver, *op. cit.*; Robert Kilpatrick, "The Choice Among Alternative Measures of Industrial Concentration," *Review of Economics and Statistics* (May 1967), pp. 258–70; Norman R. Collins and Lee E. Preston, *Concentration and Price-Cost Margins in Manufacturing Industries* (Berkeley, Calif.: University of California Press, 1968); and A. A. Heggestad and J. J. Mingo, "The Competitive Condition of U. S. Banking Markets and the Impact of Structural Reform," *Journal of Finance* (June 1977), pp. 649–61.

[9] G. Gambeles. "Structural Determinants of Profit Performance in the United States Manufacturing Industries, 1947–1967," Ph.D. dissertation, University of Maryland, 1969.

likely, therefore, to produce contrary results. Another problem is multicollinearity. When a number of variables other than concentration are included in statistical regressions, the effect of concentration is occasionally wiped out. This occurs when concentration and these other variables, such as barriers to entry, are highly correlated. However, this disappearance of concentration does not mean that concentration has no effect. It merely means that computerized statistical procedures cannot sort out the independent contributions that the correlated variables make to profit.[10] Still another group of explicable contrary results arises from the use of limited samples of industries or markets, samples so limited that they do not include observations over a wide range of concentration. As we have just seen, if observations on concentration are limited to either high or low values, positive significant associations are less likely to be detected.[11] The contrary results of studies such as these need not be given great weight.

The fact that contrary results can be explained as aberrations does not silence all skeptics, however. Indeed, there is a small but vocal group of economists who acknowledge the existence of a positive correlation between concentration and profit but who claim that it is entirely spurious, that it is due to some fundamental flaw in the data or to factors unrelated to market power that just happen to be positively correlated with both concentration and profit.[12] This is not the proper place to review the entire debate. Still, we should mention some points made by the skeptics and indicate how each has thus far been answered:

1. Skeptics argue that accounting procedures may differ across firms, making the positive association meaningless. It has been shown, however, that accounting practices do not differ systematically between firms in concentrated and unconcentrated industries.[13]

---

[10] The added variable most commonly at fault is economies of scale computed from data entering the concentration ratio. When an independent measure of scalar economies is used, the problem disappears and concentration attains significance. See R. E. Caves, J. Khalilzadeh-Shirazi, and M. E. Porter, "Scale Economies in Statistical Analyses of Market Power," *Review of Economics and Statistics* (May 1975), pp. 133–40.

[11] In the highs see D. R. Fraser and P. S. Rose, "Banking Structure and Performance in Isolated Markets: The Implications for Public Policy," *Antitrust Bulletin* (Fall 1972), pp. 927–47. For examples of lows see Collins and Preston's results for textiles and apparel (*op. cit.*, pp. 94–97).

[12] John McGee, *In Defense of Industrial Concentration* (New York: Praeger Publishers, 1971), pp. 93–95; Yale Brozen, "The Antitrust Task Force Deconcentration Recommendation," *Journal of Law and Economics* (October 1970), pp. 279–92; Richard B. Mancke, "Causes of Interfirm Profitability Differences: A New Interpretation of the Evidence," *Quarterly Journal of Economics* (May 1974), pp. 181–93; Harold Demsetz, "Two Systems of Belief About Monopoly," in *Industrial Concentration: the New Learning*, edited by H. Goldschmid, M. Mann, and F. Weston (Boston: Little, Brown, 1974), pp. 164–84; Almarin Phillips, "A Critique of Empirical Studies of Relations Between Market Structure and Profitability," *Journal of Industrial Economics* (June 1976), pp. 241–49; George J. Stigler, *Capital and Rates of Return in Manufacturing Industries* (Princeton, N. J.: Princeton University Press, 1963).

[13] Robert L. Hagerman and Lemma W. Senbet, "A Test of Accounting Bias and Market Structure," *Journal of Business* (October 1976), pp. 509–14.

2. Skeptics argue that the positive association is due merely to short-run disequilibrium conditions, that over the long run it disappears under the pressure of dynamic competition brought by new entry, product innovation, and the like. On the other hand, it has been demonstrated repeatedly that the relationship holds across decades of time, not merely months or years.[14] Moreover, study of the market value of firms indicates that investors behave as if firms with market power will keep that power into the distant future. "No indication has appeared that anticipations of entry will erode future excess profits."[15]

3. Skeptics claim that once risk is accounted for the positive relationship will disappear, partly because risk is a major (and positive) determinant of both profit and concentration. Yet a number of studies have shown that even after profits are adjusted for risk-reward, the positive relationship remains.[16]

4. Skeptics claim that small firms' profits are understated because their owner-officers take profit in the form of salaries. In turn, this allegedly understates the profits of unconcentrated industries. However, proper adjustment for this effect leaves the positive relation unscathed.[17]

5. Skeptics argue that the positive relationship arises not because concentration raises prices but because concentration fosters cost reducing efficiencies. This argument is undercut, however, by abundant evidence of positive associations between concentration and price level (see Chapter 13).

6. Skeptics say that the positive relationship is stronger for broadly defined industries than for narrowly defined industries, an anomaly that raises doubts. But careful study of this issue indicates just the opposite—namely, the narrower the definition the better.[18]

7. Skeptics argue that the relationship can be explained by nothing more than luck, luck being the source of both high concentration and high profit. Yet this, too, has been answered by both counter argument and evidence.[19]

[14] David Qualls, "Stability and Persistence of Economic Profit Margins in Highly Concentrated Industries," *Southern Economic Journal* (April 1974), pp. 604–12; R. H. Litzenberger and O. M. Joy, "Inter-Industry Profitability Under Uncertainty," *Western Economic Journal* (September 1973), pp. 338–49; and Dennis Mueller, "The Persistence of Profits Above the Norm," *Economica* (November 1977), pp. 369–80.

[15] Stavros B. Thomadakis, "A Value-Based Test of Profitability and Market Structure," *Review of Economics and Statistics* (May 1977), pp. 179–85.

[16] William G. Shepherd, *The Treatment of Market Power* (New York: Columbia University Press, 1974), pp. 109–10; James L. Bothwell and Theodore E. Keeler, "Profits, Market Structure and Portfolio Risk," in *Essays on Industrial Organization*, edited by R. T. Masson and P. D. Qualls (Cambridge, Mass.: Ballinger, 1976), pp. 71–88.

[17] Robert W. Kilpatrick, "Stigler on the Relationship Between Industrial Profit Rates and Market Concentration," *Journal of Political Economy* (May/June 1968), pp. 479–88.

[18] Frances F. Esposito and Louis Esposito, "Aggregation and the Concentration-Profitability Relationship," *Southern Economic Journal* (October 1977), pp. 323–32.

[19] R. E. Caves, B. T. Gale, and M. E. Porter, "Interfirm Profitability Differences: Comment," *Quarterly Journal of Economics* (November 1977), pp. 667–75.

8. Skeptics claim that high profits are not due to high concentration but rather to high *market shares* based on economies of scale, superior products, and good management. However, it has been demonstrated that once market share is taken into account the positive effect of concentration remains.[20]

9. Finally, skeptics claim that interindustry or intermarket comparisons of profits are irrelevant because they indicate nothing about what would happen to profits if concentration *within* an industry or market *changed*. Policy, they say, brings changes, not comparisons. In reply, it appears that cross-section results are not deceiving. Direct estimates of the effects of change support the positive relationship.[21]

In short, the positive concentration-profit relationship stands up well under close scrutiny (so Aristotle can rest in peace). This is not to say that high concentration *always* produces high profits. High concentration is merely a necessary, not a sufficient, condition.

The Effect of Other Elements of Market Power on Profit. It has already been shown that, besides concentration, advertising intensity is positively associated with profits. What about other elements of market power? They too have been tested. They too make big contributions.

BARRIERS TO ENTRY. If entry were perfectly free and easy, excess profits would quickly evaporate regardless of concentration level. Thus, in theory, high barriers should boost profits (everything else being equal).

This expectation has been borne out repeatedly by the data. An early study by Michael Mann, for instance, found that, among 21 highly concentrated industries, those with "very high barriers" averaged 16.4% profit on equity, whereas those with "moderate-to-low" barriers averaged only 11.9% profit on equity.[22] More recent studies have used more refined measures of entry barriers. All in all, they also indicate that high barriers hoist profitability.[23]

One of the most fascinating recent studies is by Robert Stonebraker.[24] He hypothesizes that the risk faced by the small firms occupying market fringes

---

[20] Weiss, *op. cit.*, pp. 225–30; Dalton and Penn, *op. cit.*; Blake Imel, Michael R. Behr, and Peter G. Helmberger, *Market Structure and Performance* (Lexington, Mass.: Lexington Books, 1972). See also J. A. Dalton and Stanford L. Levin, "Market Power: Concentration and Market Share," *Industrial Organization Review*, Vol. 5, No. 1 (1977), pp. 27–35.

[21] Keith Cowling and Michael Waterson, "Price-Cost Margins and Market Structure," *Economica* (August 1976), pp. 267–74; Maury N. Harris, "Entry and Long-Term Trends in Industry Performance," *Antitrust Bulletin* (Summer 1976), pp. 295–314.

[22] H. Michael Mann, "Seller Concentration, Barriers to Entry, and Rates of Return in Thirty Industries, 1950–1960," *Review of Economics and Statistics* (August 1966), pp. 296–307.

[23] Harris, *op. cit.*; Caves, Khalilzadeh-Shirazi, and Porter, *op. cit.*; William S. Comanor and Thomas A. Wilson, "Advertising, Market Structure, and Performance," *Review of Economics and Statistics* (November 1967), pp. 423–40; Dale Orr, "An Index of Entry Barriers and its Application to the Structure Performance Relationship," *Journal of Industrial Economics* (September 1974), pp. 39–49.

[24] Robert J. Stonebraker, "Corporate Profits and the Risk of Entry," *Review of Economics and Statistics* (February 1976), pp. 33–39.

"can be thought of as the vehicle through which entry barriers work." He reasons that "Most entry occurs on a small scale and entrepreneurs are likely to estimate the risk of entering an industry on the basis of the performance of existing small firms." To test this hypothesis Stonebraker devised two measures of risk for the small firms in each of 33 industries: (1) the *per cent* of observed small firm profit rates falling below normal competitive profit, multiplied by the average *distance* these returns fall below the competitive profit rate, and (2) an index of failure frequency. As it turns out, these measures of small firm risk plus industry growth "explain" more than 60% of the inter-industry differences in large, established firm profits. Simply stated, the *worse* the profit experience of small firms, the *better* the profit experience of their rival large firms. In other words, small firm risk apparently protects large firm profit from entry erosion by serving as a warning beacon to would-be entrants. (Stonebraker also probed the causes of small firm risk. Interestingly enough, advertising intensity was the single most important factor—higher advertising causing greater risk.)

Finally, entry barriers may do more than influence profitability in their own right. They may also *condition* the effect of concentration. In particular, profits ought to rise more rapidly with concentration, the higher the barriers to entry are. Where barriers are low, concentration should have little impact. Where barriers are high, concentration should pack a wallop. Leonard Weiss found this to be so.[25]

IMPORTS. As anyone who has "priced" Japanese television sets or purchased a foreign car knows, imports provide competition for domestic producers. Indeed, they are a form of entry. To see whether such competition affects profit performance, researchers have included import volume in statistical analyses of profits. The results? In general, heavy inbound ocean traffic does seem to mean greater competition because domestic industry profits are inversely related to import volume.[26] (The converse is also true; exports are often positively associated with profit performance.)

BUYER POWER. If the buyers' side of the market is dominated by only a few powerful buyers—as is true for tire cord and primary copper—profits of sellers might be *lower* than otherwise. Theory holds that the monop*sony* power of buyers could negate the monop*oly* power of sellers. Big buyers could play one seller off against another during bargaining or threaten self-supply. Recent tests by Steven Lustgarten and Douglas Brooks bear out the theory. Seller profit margins are inversely related to buyer concentration. Moreover,

[25] Leonard W. Weiss, "Quantitative Studies of Industrial Organization," in *Frontiers of Quantitative Economics*, edited by M. D. Intriligator (Amsterdam: North-Holland Publishing Co., 1971), pp. 375–76.

[26] L. Esposito and F. F. Esposito, "Foreign Competition and Domestic Industry Profitability," *Review of Economics and Statistics* (November 1971), pp. 343–53; Gambeles, *op. cit.*; and J. Khalil-zadeh-Shirazi, "Marketing Structure and Price-Cost Margins in United Kingdom Manufacturing Industries," *Review of Economics and Statistics* (February 1974), pp. 67–76.

the negative impact of buyer concentration is greatest where seller concentration is greatest, as one would intuitively expect.[27]

MARKET SHARE AND DIVERSIFICATION. Firms within a given market are not like peas in a pod. Their profit performance often differs markedly. Hence, when the units of observation under analysis are individual firms, *firm* characteristics must be taken into account, as must the characteristics of the markets in which the firms operate. Two of the most commonly researched firm variables in profit studies are market share and diversification (or conglomeracy).

It is now fairly well established that market share carries a positive impact on profits. By one estimate, pretax return on investment rises about 5 percentage points, for every 10 percentage points increase in market share.[28] Exactly why this occurs remains somewhat mysterious, but a number of hypotheses have been advanced:

Large market share may be expected to yield high profitability (1) by giving the firm a share-based product differentiation advantage, (2) by allowing the firm to participate in an oligopolistic group tight enough to effect some joint restriction of output, (3) by increasing the firms' bargaining power in this oligopoly situation and (4) by allowing the firm to take advantage of economies of scale.[29]

The evidence diversification presents is a mixed bag.[30] Some researchers find a positive association between profit and diversification, suggesting that diversification bolsters market power. Others find a negative relationship. Still others find nothing. Further research is needed to sort things out.

Summary. It appears that the answer to our first question is "yes." There is a positive association between market power (variously measured) and profitability. This does *not* mean you should rush to telephone your stockbroker. Your purchase of ownership shares in GM, IBM, or some other behemoth will not guarantee you fantastic returns. More than likely your rate of return will

---

[27] Steven H. Lustgarten, "The Impact of Buyer Concentration in Manufacturing Industries," *Review of Economics and Statistics* (May 1975), pp. 125–32; Douglas G. Brooks, "Buyer Concentration: A Forgotten Element in Market Structure Models," *Industrial Organization Review*, Vol. 1, No. 3 (1973), pp. 151–63.

[28] R. D. Buzzell, B. T. Gale, and R. G. M. Sultan, "Market Share—A Key to Profitability," *Harvard Business Review* (January/February 1975), pp. 97–106. See also Table 13-1 in Chapter 13.

[29] Bradley T. Gale, "Market Share and Rate of Return," *Review of Economics and Statistics* (November 1972), p. 413.

[30] Kelly, *op. cit.*, R. A. Miller, "Market Structure and Industrial Performance: Relation of Profit Rates to Concentration, Advertising Intensity and Diversity," *Journal of Industrial Economics* (April 1969), pp. 104–18; R. J. Arnould, "Conglomerate Growth and Profitability," in *Economics of Conglomerate Growth*, edited by L. Garoian (Corvallis, Ore.: Oregon State University Press, 1969), pp. 72–80; S. A. Rhoades, "The Effect of Diversification on Industry Profit Performance in 241 Manufacturing Industries: 1963," *Review of Economics and Statistics* (May 1973), pp. 146–55; S. A. Rhoades, "A Further Evaluation of the Effect of Diversification on Industry Profit Performance," *Review of Economics and Statistics* (November 1974), pp. 557–59

be no more than normal because the prices of powerful firms' stocks are in-flated. Expected excess profits are quickly *capitalized* into higher market prices for equity shares.[31] Riches arise mainly in the *process* of this capitalization Hence, only early bird owners (and their heirs) catch the worm of wealth. How ever, this *does* mean that the questions still pending concerning allocation efficiency and wealth distribution deserve careful attention.

What is the Welfare Loss Due to Monopolistic Misallocation?

When the shaded triangle of Figure 19-1 is calculated for individual in dustries then tallied across the economy, what is the result? Arnold Harberger over 25 years ago, was the first to attempt an estimate. Using 1920s data for manufacturing industries and a series of bold assumptions, he concluded tha welfare loss amounted to a piddling 0.06% of that portion of gross national product coming from manufacturing. For the economy as a whole, his estimate was a mere 0.1% of GNP.[32] These calculations led many to dismiss the mono poly problem as trifling. As one commentator quipped, this welfare loss woul only be "enough to treat every family in the land to a steak dinner at a goo (monopolistically competitive) restaurant."[33]

Subsequent researchers have criticized Harberger's procedures and assump tions as being biased downwards. Among other things it has been argued tha Harberger's assumed price elasticities of demand were too low, that his assumed normal profit rate of return was too high, that he ignored the transmission o monopoly distortions through the many vertical stages of most production distribution processes, and that his study was limited to partial equilibrium conditions. Subsequent researchers have attempted to correct these short comings in various ways, and virtually all subsequent estimates of welfare loss are substantially greater than Harberger's. Most are 10 to 20 times greater Yet, Harberger's estimates were so tiny that these multiples likewise yield relatively low numbers. Check the following estimates expressed as a per cen of GNP—Scherer's, 0.5 to 2%; Shepherd's, 2 to 3%; Worcester's, 0.4 to 0.7% Carson's, 3.2%, at most; and Bergson's, 2 to 4% (as interpreted by Worcester).[3]

[31] Timothy G. Sullivan, "A Note on Market Power and Returns to Stockholders," *Review of Economics and Statistics* (February 1977), pp. 108–13.

[32] Arnold C. Harberger, "Monopoly and Resource Allocation," *American Economic Review* (May 1954), pp. 77–87.

[33] F. M. Scherer, *Industrial Market Structure and Economic Performance* (Chicago: Rand McNally, 1970), p. 402.

[34] *Ibid.*, p. 404; William G. Shepherd, *Market Power and Economic Welfare* (New York Random House, 1970), p. 198; Dean A. Worcester, Jr., "New Estimates of the Welfare Loss to Monopoly, United States: 1956–1969," *Southern Economic Journal* (October 1973), pp. 234–45 R. Carson, D. A. Worcester Jr., and Abram Bergson, "On Monopoly Welfare Losses: Comments and Reply," *American Economic Review* (December 1975), pp. 1008–31.

TABLE 19-2   Computation of Welfare Loss in a Hypothetical Industry

	Pure Competition	Oligopoly
Price	P_c = $1.00	P_m = $1.25
Quantity	Q_c = 1,000,000	Q_m = 800,000
Total Revenue	$P_c \times Q_c$ = $1,000,000	$P_m \times Q_m$ = $1,000,000
Excess profit	zero	$0.25 \times Q_m$ = $200,000
Dollar welfare loss	zero	$\frac{1}{2} \times 0.25(Q_c - Q_m)$ = $25,000
Loss as per cent of revenue	zero	2.5%

These more recent estimates are still small, but they should be qualified by two observations. First, *by its very nature* the percentage computation yields small estimates. Only a *portion* of industry suffers any loss at all. Furthermore, within the noncompetitive portion, the percentage loss is computed by comparing a fairly small triangle to a typically large total revenue. Table 19-2 presents a numerical example assuming unit elasticity, a price increase of 25% due to oligopoly, and constant costs equal to the purely competitive price of $1.00. Under oligopoly, price is $1.25; quantity is 800,000 units; total industry revenue is $1 million; and excess profit is the price differential, $0.25, times 800,000. The welfare loss triangle is one half of the price differential (1/2 × 0.25) times the quantity differential (1,000,000 − 800,000 = 200,000), or $25,000. Dividing this by the oligopoly's total revenue of $1,000,000 to reckon loss in percentage terms yield 2.5%. If this hypothetical oligopoly amounted to as much as half of the total economy, then loss as a per cent of GNP would be only half of that, or 1.25%. Thus the percentage loss is *inherently* small. But our second observation is that a small percentage loss can be quite large when translated into absolute dollars; 1% of a $2 trillion GNP would be $20 billion per year (enough to keep college students, or even their colleges, out of rags).

What is Market Power's Contribution to the Above Average Wealth of the Wealthy?

William Comanor and Robert Smiley have done more than anyone "to estimate the impact of past and current enterprise monopoly profits on the distribution of household wealth in the United States."[35] The task is not an easy one. The distributive consequences of excess profit depend on a number of complex factors—on, among other things, (1) how much profit is excessive,

[35] William S. Comanor and Robert H. Smiley, "Monopoly and the Distribution of Wealth," *Quarterly Journal of Economics* (May 1975), pp. 177–194.

(2) who pays the excess profit, (3) who receives the excess profit, and (4) dura
tion of monopoly. Accordingly, Comanor and Smiley draw heavily upon
certain estimates of others and several simplifying assumptions. Example
follow:

1. They borrow Scherer's estimate that excess profit (not welfare loss)
   amounts to 3% of GNP and assume this to have held since 1890, the
   first year of their cummulative computation. As an alternative they also
   use 2%.
2. They make two alternative assumptions concerning who pays: (a) payments are proportional to the distribution of consumption expenditure,
   or (b) the rich spend relatively *more* of their budget on monopolistic
   goods.
3. As regards who receives, they assume that monopoly gains are distributed in proportion to the distribution of business ownership claims.
   This means that wealthy owners are no more or less likely to be monopoly owners than poor owners, a conservative assumption.
4. They assume that the gains are quickly capitalized and are perpetuated
   to some degree by inheritance.

The results are striking. The wealthiest 2.4% of all households *actually*
accounts for slightly more than 40% of total wealth. Under the 3% excess
profit assumption, an *absence* of monopoly power would reduce this share to
"somewhere between 16.6% and 27.5%, which would represent *a decline of
nearly* 50 *percent* in their share of total household wealth."[36] Under the 2%
excess profit assumption, an *absence* of monopoly power would reduce that
40% share to something near 32%, *a decline of roughly* 20%. In addition, an
absence of monopoly would elevate the wealth of the poorest families by
significant multiples. Comanor and Smiley conclude therefore that "past and
current monopoly has had a major impact on the current degree of inequality
in this distribution [of wealth]." Beneath the statistics and technical jargon
is a latter-day Domesday Book headed by names like Rockefeller, Ford,
Mellon, du Pont, and Duke. Of course your reaction to these findings depends
on your value judgements (and your station).

Market Power and Labor Earnings

General Introduction

Excess profits are not the only source of higher prices and lost consumers'
surplus. Other price-increasing excesses are associated with market power.
Table 19-3 illustrates the point with data from grocery retailing. Column (1)

[36] *Ibid.*, p. 191, emphasis added.

TABLE 19-3 Estimated Index of Grocery Prices and Pretax Profit to Sales Ratios Associated with Various Levels of Concentration*

(1) Four-Firm Concentration Ratio	(2) Index of Grocery Prices	(3) Profits as Per Cent of Sales
40	100.0	0.37
50	101.0	0.99
60	103.0	1.22
70	105.3	1.28

* This assumes "relative firm market share" of 10.
Source: B. W. Marion, W. F. Mueller, R. W. Cotterill, F. E. Geithman, and J. R. Schmelzer, *The Profit and Price Performance of Leading Food Chains, 1970–74*, A Study for the Joint Economic Committee, U. S. Congress, 95th Congress, First Session (1977), p. 77.

s four-firm concentration in local markets. Columns (2) and (3) give a price index and profit as a per cent of sales. These last two columns are not perfectly comparable because the data underlying them differ. Nevertheless, to the extent those columns are comparable, they are instructive. Prices clearly rise with concentration. But they rise *much more* than profit. If the price increase of 5.3% associated with an increase in concentration from 40 to 70 were due entirely to profit, then profit would have gone from 0.37 to 5.4% of sales. But this is *not* the case. The observed jump in profit is from 0.37 to 1.28% of sales. Quite clearly, *costs* are rising with concentration as well as *profit*.

The separate cost and profit effects may be illustrated theoretically in Figure 19-3. Let OP_m and OC_m be a monopolist's price and cost per unit, respectively. Then profit per unit is the difference between P_m and C_m. With monopoly output equal OQ_m, total excess profit is area $P_m ABC_m$. The deadweight welfare loss associated with this excess profit is shaded triangle ABH. Thus, in terms of lost consumers' surplus, the combined **profit effect** is represented by trapezoid $P_m AHC_m$, part of which is transfer and part of which disappears. The preceding sections discussed these profit effects. Were there nothing more in monopoly power, the establishment of competition would merely reduce price to C_m and expand output to Q_n, adding $P_m AHC_m$ to consumers' surplus.

The **cost effect** is seen by first drawing a distinction between monopoly cost C_m and competitive cost C_c. If monopoly power raises costs as well as profits, then establishment of competition will reduce price from P_m to C_c, since competitive price will match competitive cost C_c. This is obviously a much greater price reduction than from P_m to C_m. The social gains from competition are correspondingly greater. Elimination of the excess cost adds to consumers' surplus an area represented by trapezoid $C_m HEC_c$.

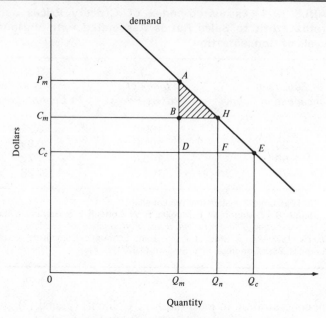

Figure 19-3. Cost implications of market power.

In sum, introduction of competition adds $P_m AHC_m$ from the profit effect plus $C_m HEC_c$ from the cost effect. Together these represent a total gain in consumers' surplus amounting to area $P_m AEC_c$. Stated in terms of loss rather than gain, this area represents the total loss in consumers' surplus due to monopoly, when both cost and profit effects are present. As before, this total welfare loss can be divided into different kinds of losses depending on the *destination* of the loss. Generally speaking, there are four possibilities, two of which should by now be familiar:

1. *Deadweight loss:* First and most obvious is a deadweight loss represented by triangle ADE in Figure 19-3. This is much greater than the deadweight loss associated with excess profit alone (which is ABH), because there is an additional deadweight loss due to higher cost (represented by trapezoid $BHED$). Estimates of this loss are therefore *under*estimates if based on profit alone. As explained earlier, this deadweight loss arises from *allocation inefficiency.* Quantity Q_m is less than the optimal quantity Q_c.
2. *Profit transfer:* A portion of the lost consumers' surplus again goes to excess profit. This is represented by $P_m ABC_m$. Our earlier discussion and estimates of this effect could be reapplied here. Though a loss to consumers, this represents a gain to owners with *distributive consequences.*

3. *Cost that is transfer*: The added total cost of producing OQ_m, represented by $C_m BDC_c$, can take two possible forms. One is excess factor remuneration. Management or labor (or some other factor) may be overpaid at the expense of owners or consumers or both. The overpayments, or "rents," are analogous to excess profit. They are higher than what is necessary to keep the favored factor committed to the industry. Thus, managers may take advantage of the imperfect control stockholders have over the typical large firm to raise managerial salaries or pad expense accounts. On labor's side, it has been argued that unionized workers extract higher pay from concentrated than from unconcentrated industries. As in the case of excess profit, these several excesses may have significant *distributive consequences* depending on the financial strengths of the beneficiaries and the financial weaknesses of owners or consumers who ultimately pay the higher costs.

4. *Cost that is waste*: A second cost element and the final possible destination of lost consumers' surplus is *technical inefficiency* or *X-inefficiency*— that is, the use of more labor, more materials, and more resources than are necessary to produce a given output. This X-inefficiency also shows up in space $C_m BDC_c$. Monopoly could easily give rise to such waste because, in a word, market power permits "slack." Moreover, it has been argued that monopoly power fosters waste because those who seek such power must expend resources to get it and keep it. Thus resources are burned up when established oligopolists escalate their advertising outlays to fight off new entrants. And labor time spent running cartels is a real cost.

Of these four destinations for lost consumers' surplus, the first two have already been traced. Most of the remainder of this chapter is about the last two, which share area $C_m BDC_c$ in Figure 19-3. Excess wages are taken up first, then X-inefficiency. We shall not explore managerial salaries further, so we should at least mention here that high concentration and high barriers to entry apparently do boost top executives' compensation.[37]

Unions, Concentration, and Wages

To some degree labor markets are much like product markets. They have demands and supplies; they have power problems, and so on. What, then, causes the wage rate of a steel worker to exceed the combined hourly earnings of a Greek philosopher and a McDonald's counter attendant? Researchers have uncovered a vast array of variables affecting relative wage earnings. These include skill level, productivity, geographic location, plant size, value of product produced, education, scholastic achievement, work conditions, race,

[37] Oliver E. Williamson, *The Economics of Discretionary Behavior: Managerial Objectives in a Theory of the Firm* (Chicago: Markham Publishing Co., 1967), pp. 129–34.

sex, risk to life and limb, and legal regulations. To determine the influence o unionism on the labor supply side or concentration on the labor demand side these and other factors must first be accounted for. As with price and profi research, there are many ways to skin this cat. Most of them are variants o multiple regression analysis, which allows researchers to control for "other factors.

The market power hypotheses that have been so tested may be divided int three classes: (1) the wage impact of unionism, (2) the wage impact of produc market concentration, and (3) the *interactive* effect of unions *and* produc market concentration.

Impact of Unions on Wages. The hypotheses concerning unionism alone ar most obvious. Workers unionize, that is, join together, to speak with one voice threaten to walk out as one group, and restrict labor supply to one source s that they can demand and obtain higher wages than would otherwise be paid To the extent unions succeed in raising members' wages they may be simul taneously *reducing* nonunion wages. To gain higher wages, unions restrict th number of people who can compete for available jobs in unionized trades This restriction forces workers who are excluded to seek work elsewhere. Con sequently, the reduced union supply may raise union wages but the increase supply of nonunion workers tends to depress nonunion wages. The usua measure of union impact is therefore *relative* wage, the union wage compare to nonunion wage (everything else held constant).

The most widely cited estimate of union impact is that of H. G. Lewis, wh reckoned that for the period 1957–1958 unions enjoyed a relative wage ad vantage somewhere in the neighborhood of 10–15%.[38] Subsequent studie using better data have estimated still larger union-nonunion wage differen tials.[39] Leonard Weiss, for example, used Census data and estimated averag differentials for "craftsmen" and "operatives" of about 30%.[40] More recentl Sherwin Rosen estimated union/nonunion wage differentials ranging betwee 16 and 25%.[41] Of course not all unions are equally powerful, and these estimate must be qualified by the observation that weak unions, such as the Unite Farm Workers, tend to gain very little, whereas particularly strong unions such as the United Steelworkers, may achieve relative wages even above th 25–30% range.

[38] H. G. Lewis, *Unionism and Relative Wages in the United States* (Chicago: University o Chicago Press, 1963).

[39] Frank Stafford, "Concentration and Labor Earnings: Comment," *American Economi Review* (March 1968), pp. 174–80; Victor Fuchs, *The Service Economy* (New York: Nationa Bureau of Economic Research, 1968), Chapter 6; and Adrian Throop, "The Union-Nonunion Wage Differential and Cost Push Inflation," *American Economic Review* (March 1968), pp. 79–99

[40] Leonard W. Weiss, "Concentration and Labor Earnings," *American Economic Review* (Marc 1966), pp. 96–117.

[41] Sherwin Rosen, "On the Interindustry Wage and Hours Structure," *Journal of Politica Economy* (March 1969), pp. 249–73; "Trade Union Power, Threat Effects and the Extent o Organization," *Review of Economic Studies* (April 1969), pp. 185–96.

The Wage Impact of Product Market Concentration. The impact of concentration is more complicated. Theories concerning the impact of product market concentration yield ambiguous indications. On the one hand, high concentration might foster high wages for reasons of "ability to pay." These reasons are 1) the ability of concentrated industries to pass excess wage costs on to customers, and (2) the ability to pay excess wages out of excess profits. Some confirmation of a positive concentration-wage relation is provided by a number of studies.[42] Charles Haworth and Carol Reuther, for instance, find roughly % higher wages where four-firm concentration is 80 as compared to 40 during 1958). Furthermore, Haworth and Reuther show that, like profits, this positive relation weakens markedly during spurts of expansion or inflation (something to which we shall return in Chapter 21).

On the other hand, "ability to pay" does not necessarily dictate actuality. Many oligopolists may be able but *unwilling* to pay extra. In particular, concentration in the product market often means there is concentration on the employers' side of the labor market as well—that is, there are few purchasers of that type of labor. And much conventional theory predicts that such monopsony (or oligopsony) power will *depress* wage rates rather than lift them. Empirically, John Landon has produced a series of studies showing that monopsony power has a negative wage impact at least in some instances.[43] Similarly, Weiss found a negative (but statistically insignificant) relation between concentration and earnings in about half the occupational classes he studied.[44]

Interactive Impact. A moment's reflection reveals why the preceding discussion of unionism and product market concentration is incomplete. It treats unionism and concentration as wholly independent variables. In fact, they are not independent. They are interactive. The influence of one often depends on the strength of the other. Consider unionization first. The positive wage impact of unions is likely to be meager where concentration is low but great where concentration is high. There are two main reasons for this.

1. *Competitive industries seem harder to unionize than noncompetitive industries* (just as competitive industries are harder to cartelize). Competitive industries are typified by a large number of relatively small establishments, each distant from public scrutiny, each tending to have different work conditions, each with

[42] Leonard Rapping, "Monopoly Rents, Wage Rates, and Union Wage Effectiveness," *Quarterly Review of Economics and Business* (Spring 1967), pp. 31–47; Ira Horowitz, "An International Comparison of the Intranational Effects of Concentration on Industry Wages, Investment, and Sales," *Journal of Industrial Economics* (April 1971), pp. 166–78; Charles T. Haworth and Carol Reuther, "Industry Concentration and Interindustry Wage Determination," *Review of Economics and Statistics* (February 1978), pp. 85–95; and J. A. Dalton and E. J. Ford, Jr., "Concentration and Labor Earnings in Manufacturing and Utilities," *Industrial Labor Relations Review* (October 1977), pp. 45–60.

[43] John H. Landon, "The Effect of Product-Market Concentration on Wage Levels: An Intra-industry Approach," *Industrial and Labor Relations Review* (January 1970), pp. 237–47; J. H. Landon and R. N. Baird, "Monopsony in the Market for Public School Teachers," *American Economic Review* (December 1971), pp. 966–71.

[44] Weiss, *op. cit.* (1966).

a potential for "personalized" employer-employee relationships, and a vulnerable to the entry of nonunion competitors. The opposite, in each featur may be said of concentrated studies.

2. *Competitive firms tend to lack both the ability and the inclination to pa excess wage rates.* Unless unionization of the industry is complete, the unionize firm in a competitive industry will go out of business if it pays generous unio wages while its rivals do not. Even if all existing firms in a competitive industr are unionized, the threat of fairly easy nonunion entry may check the union power. Then too, the lack of excess profits may pose a further constraint. Henc unions are likely to have greater positive wage impact in oligopoly industrie where employers act more nearly in unison, have the financial means to me union demands, and enjoy substantial protection from interlopers. Such situa tions do not give unions a completely free hand. There are constraints. Give a negatively sloped labor demand, the ghost of unemployment haunts hig wage settlements even in oligopoly. The ghost is merely less fearsome there.

Turning things around, the impact of product market concentration probab depends on the presence or absence of a strong union on the labor side. A suming the incidence of monopsony power is positively associated with produc market concentration, high concentration is more likely to depress wages i the absence of a union than in the presence of a union. Substantial buyer powe when unchecked by countervailing seller power, could have this effect. Introduc tion of a union, however, places power on *both* sides of the labor market. In th extreme, this creates "bilateral monopoly." And, in theory, the resulting wag is logically indeterminant. The union wants a high wage. The monopsonisti employers want a low wage. The resulting wage could be anywhere in betwee depending on relative bargaining power. This suggests that the impact of con centration may be largely indeterminant, given union presence. On the othe hand, it could be argued that wages will be positively associated with concen tration under unionism. Product market concentration is, after all, a very im perfect proxy for monopsony power. And for reasons given earlier, such a "ability to pay," high concentration plus unionism is more likely to yield highe wages than is low concentration plus unionism.

Empirical exploration of these complex interactive effects is very difficul Perhaps the best study to date is that of Wallace Hendricks.[45] He used di aggregated plant-level data on wage rates paid by 450 United States manu facturing firms in 47 different industries during 1970–1971. The wage rates use were wages per hour (including any cost-of-living allowance) for specifi occupations (for example, electrician, machinist, and painter). The results wer broadly similar for all nine occupations studied, but Hendricks gives janitor special attention because the impact of market power was better isolated fo them than for any other group. These results are summarized in Table 19-

[45] Wallace Hendricks, "Labor Market Structure and Union Wage Levels," *Economic Inquir* (September 1975), pp. 401–416. For European corroboration see A. P. Jacquemin and H. W. deJon; *European Industrial Organization* (New York: Wiley & Sons, 1977), p. 145.

TABLE 19-4   Impact of Product Market
Concentration and Unionism on Hourly
Wage Rates: Per Cent Comparisons

Concentration	Unionism		
	Low	Moderate	High
Low	0 (base)	0.9	9.3
Moderate	7.0	14.1	13.6
High	−8.0	10.6	19.5

Source: Calculated from Wallace Hendricks, "Labor Market Structure and Union Wage Levels,"
Economic Inquiry (September 1975), pp. 401–16.

Concentration and unionism are each divided into three groups—low, moderate, and high. The numbers in the body of the table are *per cent* comparisons, where the low concentration and low unionism category is used as the basis for comparison. Thus, where unionism and concentration are both high, wages are 9.5% higher, on average, than those under low-low conditions. The interactive effects may be seen by comparing the effects of unionism under alternative concentration conditions, then comparing concentration effects under alternative unionization conditions. Thus, unionism generally has a *positive* impact, but the *magnitude* of impact is much smaller where concentration is low than where it is high. High unionism raises wages 9.3 percentage points where concentration is low. But where concentration is high, the difference between high and low unionism is 27.5 percentage points (moving from −8 to +19.5).

As for concentration, it carries a positive then ultimately *negative* impact on wages where unionism is low, suggesting that monopsony power dominates where concentration is really high and unionism is low. On the other hand, concentration has an unambiguously *positive influence* on wages where unionism is high. In this latter case, wages are about 10 percentage points greater for high over low concentration (19.5 versus 9.3).

It appears from these data, then, that interactive effects do prevail. Although this makes generalizations hazardous, it can be concluded that *union power usually raises wages*. As regards concentration, it can go either way. But because concentration seems to foster unionism (the positive correlation in manufacturing runs in the 0.4–0.7 range), and because more often than not concentration's direct impact is positive, it may also be concluded that, on balance, *high concentration produces relatively high wages*. How severely these effects distort income or wealth distribution toward inequality is uncertain. However, these labor gains do not seem to come at the expense of profits, at least that is the general concensus. The gains seem to come largely at the expense of powerless nonunionized workers and consumers.

471

X-Inefficiency Losses Due to
Market Power

X-inefficiency is a form of deadweight loss. Value is not merely transferred from one party to another; it is lost to all. This deadweight loss is, in a word, *waste*. According to Harvey Leibenstein, who coined the term, **X-inefficiency** means "the extent to which a given set of inputs do not get to be combined in such a way so as to lead to maximum output."[46] When inputs are not producing the maximum output possible, there is error, inertia, spoilage, slovenliness, disorder, delay, red tape, ineptitude, or something similar. As a result, costs are higher than otherwise.

It should be stressed that the X-inefficiency concept is not necessarily, or even usually, applied to cost problems that could be cured by massive alterations of plant scale, by adoption of new technology, or by invention of new technology. Think of it rather as a problem of weak motivation and resource misallocation *internal* to the firm. Liebenstein points to the vast efficiency gains that plants and firms have achieved by "simple reorganizations of the production process such as plant-layout reorganization, materials handling, waste controls, work methods, and payments by results."[47] Viewed more broadly, X-inefficiency could reasonably include all forms of pure resource waste: excessive advertising, superfluous packaging, redundant plant capacity, and so on.

How does this dimension of performance relate to competition? We have already answered the question as it pertains to advertising and nonprice competition generally. As regards other forms of waste, theory postulates on at least two grounds that costs are *lower* whenever firms face intense competition:

> In the first place, the process of competition tends to eliminate high-cost producers, while the existence of substantial market power often allows such firms to remain in business .... Second, the process of competition, by mounting pressures on firm profits, tends to discipline managements *and employees* to utilize their inputs, and put forth more energetically and more effectively than is the case where this pressure is absent.[48]

In other words, the "carrot" of greater profits may dangle before all firms seeking to minimize cost, but only the "stick" swung by competition *forces* firms to pursue that objective.

---

[46] Harvey Leibenstein, "Competition and X-Efficiency," *Journal of Political Economy* (May 1973), p. 766.

[47] Harvey Leibenstein, *Beyond Economic Man* (Cambridge, Mass.: Harvard University Press, 1976), p. 37.

[48] W. S. Comanor and H. Leibenstein, "Allocative Efficiency, X-Efficiency and the Measurement of Welfare Losses," *Economica* (August 1969), p. 304.

Tales of business woe constitute some of the most engrossing evidence to this effect. Large, powerful firms often coast merrily along until new entry, lagging demand, or some similar contingency leads to the discovery that costs can be cut drastically without cutting output by so much as one unit. You could build a bulky file of such evidence merely by reading *Business Week*, from which the following examples are taken:

- Suffering from the slap of new entry and slipping profits, Xerox launched a cost cutting drive for the *first time* in its history in 1975. Its Chairman admitted that Xerox was suffering from "sloppy" internal practices and corporate "fat" that had developed during the easy days. Among other things the company fired 8000 employees; deferred construction of a lush new headquarters; sharpened its inventory control; and scrapped plans for a new plant; all while sales grew.[49]
- When Don Burnham took over as chief executive of Westinghouse in 1963, "the company was languishing on a five-year plateau of $2-billion in sales and earning only 5% on equity. By breaking organizational bottlenecks at the top, introducing more productive manufacturing processes, and slashing overhead, including more than 3000 people, Burnham doubled Westinghouse's return on equity within two years to 10%."[50]
- Shell Oil Company sustained some profit setbacks on worldwide operations during the 1960s, whereupon it discovered it could eliminate job duplication by consolidating its British and Dutch head offices and reduce its workforce from 214,000 to 170,000 while increasing output. The result: labor cost savings of 32% per barrel.[51]

Further examples of competitive impact come from cartel case studies. In a study of price fixing in the gymnasium seating, rock salt, and structural steel industries, Bruce Erickson found cost increases of 10–23% due to competition's strangulation.[52] After a massive study of cartel records, Corwin Edwards concluded that available evidence "indicates that the characteristic purposes of cartels point away from efficiency and that their activities tend to diminish

---

[49] *Business Week*, April 5, 1976, pp. 60–66.

[50] *Business Week*, July 20, 1974, p. 56.

[51] *Business Week*, March 8, 1969, pp. 56–57. For further examples involving other major companies see *Business Week* April 13, 1974, pp. 55–58; August 11, 1975, p. 38; August 18, 1975, pp. 80–82; November 3, 1975, pp. 92–93; November 10, 1975, p. 129; December 1, 1975, p. 38; May 10, 1976, p. 66; November 1, 1976, p. 65; and June 19, 1978, pp. 116–18; *Washington Post*, February 11, 1973, p. E5; Carl Kaysen, *United States v. United Shoe Machinery Corporation* (Cambridge, Mass.: Harvard University Press, 1956), p. 128; G. Brock, *The U. S. Computer Industry 1954-1973* (Cambridge, Mass.: Ballinger Publishing Co., 1975), pp. 217–18; L. J. White, *The Automobile Industry Since 1945* (Cambridge, Mass.: Harvard University Press, 1971), p. 12; F. M. Scherer, A. Beckenstein, E. Kaufer, R. D. Murphy, *The Economics of Multi-Plant Operation* (Cambridge, Mass.: Harvard University Press, 1975), p. 299.

[52] W. Bruce Erickson, "Price Fixing Conspiracies: Their Long-term Impact," *Journal of Industrial Economics* (March 1976), pp. 189–202.

efficiency."[53] A research team headed by F. M. Scherer recently uncovere
numerous examples of excessive costs due to cartelization in Europe. Citin
cases from cigarettes, steel, paint, glass bottles, and cement, Scherer's grou
concluded, "Our interviews provided *considerable* qualitative evidence tha
pure X-inefficiency was a *significant* cause of productivity differentials."[54]

Intermarket statistical assessments of X-inefficiency are difficult to devis
Although data on market structure are commonplace, data isolating efficienc
are not. Data on costs offer a substitute for data on efficiency, but only a ver
imperfect substitute because costs are influenced by factors other than eff
ciency—factors such as wage rates, materials prices, and plant location. Neve
theless, a few statistical studies have conquered these problems. So far they a
indicate that *X-inefficiency is positively associated with market power*. Th
data shown earlier in Table 19-3 provide one example. Costs of grocery re
tailing rise with local market concentration, as indicated by the discrepanc
between price and profit behavior. And the authors of the study from whic
those data were taken could find no explanation other than X-inefficienc
for the rise in costs.[55] Further examples follow:

- Walter Primeaux carefully compared costs of electricity production in
  two separate sets of cities—those with electric utility *monopolies* and those
  with direct competition between *two firms* (of which there were 49 cities).
  He found "that average cost is reduced, at the mean, by 10.75 percent
  because of competition. This reflects a quantitative value of the presence
  of X-efficiency gained through competition."[56]
- Franklin Edwards discovered that managers of commercial banks
  tended to hire substantial "excess staff" where bank concentration was
  high compared to where it was low.[57]
- Measuring X-inefficiency as the extent to which firms make more than
  justifiable use of capital-intensive means of production, and drawing upon
  data for Pakistani industries, Lawrence White found that "firms with
  market power do seem to be 'indulging' in more capital-intensive methods
  than are firms facing more competition."[58]

[53] Corwin D. Edwards, *Economic and Political Aspects of International Cartels*, U. S. Senat
Subcommittee on War Mobilization of the Committee on Military Affairs, 78th Congress, Secon
Session (1944), p. 40.

[54] Scherer, Beckenstein, Kaufer, and Murphy, *op. cit.*, pp. 74–75, 168–69, 314–15 (emphas
added). For further evidence concerning European cartels see D. Swann, D. P. O'Brien, W. P.
Maunder, and W. S. Howe, *Competition in British Industry* (London: Allen & Unwin, 1974).

[55] Besides the source of Table 19–3 see *Prices and Profits of Leading Retail Food Chains, 1970-7*
Hearings, Joint Economic Committee, 95th Congress, First Session (1977), especially pp. 88–89.

[56] Walter J. Primeaux, "An Assessment of X-Efficiency Gained Through Competition,
Review of Economics and Statistics (February 1977), pp. 105–08.

[57] Franklin R. Edwards, "Managerial Objectives in Regulated Industries: Expense-Prefe
ence Behavior in Banking," *Journal of Political Economy* (February 1977), pp. 147–62.

[58] Lawrence J. White, "Appropriate Technology, X-Inefficiency, and A Competitive Enviror
ment: Some Evidence from Pakistan," *Quarterly Journal of Economics* (November 1976), pp. 575–8

Economy-wide estimates of monopoly-induced X-inefficiency can only be very rough approximations. It does not seem unreasonable to assume, however, that such waste may amount to as much as 10% of costs where concentration is very high and 5% of costs where concentration is moderate. Compared with our earlier estimates of deadweight loss due to profit-provoked misallocation, these figures are obviously quite large. Conversion to competition would probably reduce X-inefficiency and thereby improve consumer welfare. An overall jump in GNP of 3 or 4% would not appear to be out of the question.

Job Discrimination and Job Satisfaction

To this point it has been assumed that social welfare is measurable solely in terms of *consumer* welfare. We have been concerned with the size of the consumers' pie (as determined by allocation and technical efficiency) and the sharing of its slices (wealth or income distribution). Although consumer welfare is obviously of critical importance, the experiences people face as *workers* may be equally momentous; many if not most people are preoccupied with their occupation. Just as consumer welfare can be broken down into issues of abundance and equity, so too the issue of work experience can be broken down into issues of job satisfaction (or worker "fulfillment") and job equity (or "equal opportunity").

Unfortunately, economists have tended to neglect welfare on the working side of life. We are not completely in the dark, however. Some sociologists and a few economists have devoted a portion of their work to these issues. They find that market structure reaches well beyond consumer welfare, that it reaches the worker as well as his lunch box.

Concentration and Job Discrimination

Discrimination in employment occurs whenever otherwise extraneous characteristics such as race, sex, or religion influence job placement, promotion, or pay scale. Conventional theory holds that discrimination would *not* arise under perfect competition, at least no more than in surrounding society:

> For firms operating under the constraints of perfect competition any significant indulgence of such preferences would impose extra costs and therefore ultimately be incompatible with the survival of the enterprise. Hiring by firms so constrained would be "neutral;" indeed, if Negro wage rates were relatively low because of discrimination elsewhere, Negroes would tend to be substituted at the margin for white employees with equal qualifications.[59]

[59] William G. Shepherd, *Market Power & Economic Welfare* (New York: Random House, 1970), pp. 213–14.

475

As we have seen, market power removes these competitive constraints. More over, insofar as oligopolists pay unusually high wages to their workers generally, oligopolists may attract considerably more job applicants of acceptable quality than they can possibly hire. For these reasons the managers of *powerful firms* *have substantial discretionary power.* Consideration of extraneous character istics may even be unavoidable. Thus, pretty secretaries are likely to win out over the ugly; well-groomed congenial people over the unkempt and uncouth and brothers-in-law over the unknown. Whether or not this discretionary power takes socially harmful forms is largely indeterminate, since discretion can be used to *favor or disfavor* disadvantaged minorities. To quote from William Shepherd:

> With economic constraints eased, and assuming interracial preferences to be negative and significant for at least some managers, then one may expect that . . . employment patterns will embody discrimination . . . . Yet, against this may be set the possibility that managers may exercise their discretion deliberately and "affirmatively" in the social interest, toward open hiring or even "positive" discrimination. The possible social motivation of the modern corporation might prevail in small monopolists as well as in very large oligopolists, and as the rule rather than as the exception . . . . In may cases, the conflicting tendencies within a firm with market power may, at least, yield a standoff between these alternative directions of hiring policy.[60]

Which way, in fact, does the evidence indicate? Studies by Shepherd, Gary Becker, and William Comanor suggest that during the 1960s and earlier blacks experienced better chances of being hired in *competitive* industries than *non*competitive industries, other things equal.[61] Moreover, the discrepancies in hiring practices were particularly severe regarding higher skilled occupation categories, such as professionals, managers, and craftsmen (as compared with lower skilled groups such as laborers and sales workers). Thus, Becker's data for the South in 1940 indicate that competitive industries hired *skilled* blacks at a rate *4 to 8 times* higher than monopolistic industries, whereas competitive industries generally hired *un*skilled blacks at a rate roughly *two times* higher than monopolistic industries. Some of Shepherd's findings for 1966 are shown in Figure 19-4. There it may be seen that as concentration rises, the per cent of total official, managerial, and professional employment accounted for by blacks falls.[62]

Since the 1960s, the plight of nonwhites seems to have improved in virtually all markets, especially noncompetitive markets. Prodded by massive changes in public policy and public opinion, it appears that the discretionary power of

[60] *Ibid.*, pp. 214–15.

[61] Gary S. Becker, *The Economics of Discrimination* (Chicago: University of Chicago Press, 1957), pp. 31–46; W. S. Comanor, "Racial Discrimination in American Industry," *Economica* (November 1973), pp. 363–78.

[62] W. G. Shepherd, "Market Power and Racial Discrimination in White-Collar Employment," *Antitrust Bulletin* (Spring 1969), pp. 141–61.

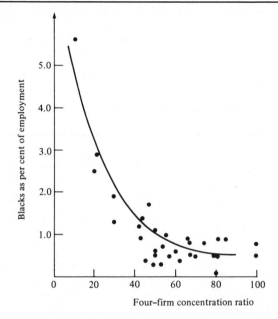

Figure 19-4. *Industry concentration and black employment as officials, managers, and professionals in nine major cities in 1966. Source: William G. Shepherd,* Market Power and Economic Welfare *(New York: Random House, 1970), p. 221.*

noncompetitive firms has pivoted toward improvement.[63] The change shows up in employment rates. Moreover, although the available data on wage rates paid to whites and nonwhites are not sufficiently distributed over time to indicate change in wage earnings, a recent study of wages for 1972 discloses no differential in wage discrimination between competitive and noncompetitive industries.[64]

The empirical evidence concerning women is much more limited than that concerning blacks. Some differential job discrimination against females has been discovered for top level occupational classes, but only as regards *firm size* during 1966–1970, and perhaps earlier. Female participation rates in 231 of the largest 250 United States industrial firms were only about one sixth to one fourth of the national average for officials, managers, professionals, and technicians. On the other hand, a comparison of variances among these 231

[63] See W. G. Shepherd and Sharon G. Levin, "Managerial Discrimination in Large Firms," *Review of Economics and Statistics* (November 1973), pp. 412–22. This paper also shows that on a firm-by-firm basis the effect of concentration is murky. But notice the limited range of size in their sample.

[64] William R. Johnson, "Racial Wage Discrimination and Industrial Structure," *Bell Journal of Economics* (Spring 1978), pp. 70–81.

largest firms revealed no further clear-cut pattern of female employment con
nected to size or concentration.[65]

In short, market power apparently tended to increase discrimination unti
recently. Dissolution of the original pattern can probably be credited to th
solvent of public pressure.

Size and Job Satisfaction

Are job satisfaction and industrial structure in any way linked? The tentativ
answer is "yes," but only in a rather limited way.

The first thing to note is that the question has been thoroughly probed onl
regarding the *absolute size* of production organizations, where "organization
is variously defined as plant, department, or firm. No solid evidence is availabl
concerning corporate diversity, unionism, or concentration (but size and con
centration are correlated). Second, "job satisfaction" has many facets, pro
viding many yardsticks of measurement. Virtually all measures may be divided
into two groups: (1) "subjective" measures, derived by asking workers how
well they like their work surroundings, their foreman, their advancement op
portunities, and so on; and (2) "objective" measures, such as quit rates, job
turnover, and absenteeism.

Despite a diversity of approaches in these various respects, there is sub
stantial agreement on at least one point among the more than 20 studies tacklin
the issue: the larger the organization, the less satisfying the job.[66] The mai
reason for this inverse relationship seems to be that large-scale operation
inevitably entail bureaucratic bulk, impersonal procedures, and rigid rules
Thus in the course of comparing small, single-plant firms with large plant
of large firms G. K. Ingham found that workers in the former settings ex
perienced (1) a greater variety of task assignments, (2) greater interraction wit
their fellow workers, (3) closer contact with their foremen and managers, (4
more frequent nonwork conversation with their foremen, and (5) more "in
teresting" work.[67] It is apparently for these reasons that a number of studie
have found comparatively lower rates of absenteeism among small organiza
tions than among large ones.

If working in a large organization is so much worse than in a small organiza
tion, what, then, keeps workers attached to the larger organizations? Larg
plants have no apparent trouble manning their machines. Indeed, some evidenc
indicates that, although absenteeism runs higher in large plants, there is n
such differential in quit rates or worker turnover. What can explain this anom
oly? The answer is simple—money. Large firms and plants generally pay highe

---

[65] Shepherd and Levin, *op. cit.*

[66] For a survey see F. M. Scherer, "Industrial Structure, Scale Economies, and Worker Aliena
tion," in *Essays on Industrial Organization,* edited by R. Masson and P. D. Qualls (Cambridge, Mass.
Ballinger Publishing Co., 1976), pp. 105–21.

[67] Geoffrey K. Ingham, *Size of Industrial Organization and Worker Behavior* (Cambridge, U. K.
Cambridge University Press, 1970), pp. 72–103.

wage rates and offer better fringe benefits than small firms and plants.[68] In wood products manufacturing, for instance, 1967 average hourly wages in plants of less than 50 workers were about $2.30, whereas they were $3.85 in plants of more than 2500 workers. There is thus a trade-off. Although work in large plants is typically *less* satisfying in nonmonetary terms, it is at the same time *more* remunerative. Accordingly,

> we can conclude that, on the one hand, the workers in the large plants are attached to their organizations almost exclusively by the high earnings they receive. On the other hand, the employees in the small firms are attached not only by the low—but acceptable—earnings, but also by the high level of non-economic rewards they receive. Therefore . . . the similarity of the 'quit rates' and the uniformly high 'stability rates' are the result of different, but *equally effective*, modes of attachment in the large and small organizations.[69]

Intriguing follow-up questions intrude: Does the greater money *fully* compensate for the skimpier psychic rewards of large organizations? Is *overall* job satisfaction, counting *both* monetary and nonmonetary aspects, about equal across sizes? Or does the added money fall short of making up for the difference in psychic reward?

Before considering the answers researchers have arrived at, let us first acknowledge that *no* ironclad answers are possible because folks who work in large organizations are different from those working in small organizations. Given this difference it is very difficult to compare states of happiness. Who can say Jones is truely happier than Smith because Jones says he is "very happy" whereas Smith says he is only "moderately happy." How can we compare the employment pleasures of a Greek philosopher and a Gypsy tinsmith? In fact, survey data show that those who work in large plants hold very different views of what is good and bad from those who work in small plants. Large-plant workers place a great deal of weight on monetary reward and pooh-pooh the nonmonetary aspects of work. Conversely, small-plant workers tend to prize the nonmonetary aspects of work, saying things like "This may sound silly, but I would rather enjoy my work than go for the money." Obviously, comparisons of happiness are hard to make.

Nevertheless, survey studies show that *overall* job satisfaction *diminishes directly with larger establishment size*. This result emerges from questions concerning "overall" satisfaction. It is also suggested indirectly by interpretation of other evidence. For example, the finding that quit rate is *not* a function of size but absenteeism *is* a function of size suggests that those in large plants are generally less satisfied with their work than those in small plants, even though they are not sufficiently dissatisfied to switch jobs. Were the two conditions

---

[68] Scherer, *op. cit.*: Hendricks, *op. cit.*; Fuchs, *op. cit.*; and Haworth and Reuther, *op. cit.*
[69] Ingham, *op. cit.*, pp. 111–12.

truly equal in satisfaction there would probably be *no* effect of size on either variable.[70]

This overall result is somewhat shocking. One would think that any disparity in overall satisfaction level would eventually be erased by workers switching from larger to smaller plants or by employers paying greater-than existing wage differentials to cheer large-plant workers and discourage disloyalty, or by some combination of the two. Of course the amounts large establishments can pay are limited by the degree of productivity advantage they have over the small plants. But still, to an economist, the continued existence of such a disparity is rather mysterious. He is likely to say it is not real. Or he is likely to look for constraints on workers' freedom of choice. We cannot look into either of these dark rooms now. But F. M. Scherer has pried open the door to the latter far enough to conclude that something is going on and further research would be desirable. "One can see wisps of smoke." he says "but we are going to have to break down some doors before we can tell whether a fire is raging."[71]

Summary

This chapter is somewhat like the punchline of a cruel joke. Previous chapters left open the question of market power's impact on *how well* markets work. Now its impact regarding several major measures of performance has been disclosed.

In consumer welfare, market power leads to lost consumer surplus. Surplus is lost because higher prices and lower output prevail under concentration than under competition. The higher prices are due to excess profits, excess wages, excess managerial salaries, and X-inefficiency. The destination of the lost consumers' surplus depends largely on the relative effect of each cause. Excess profits go to those controlling ownership shares. Since roughly 2.4% of the populace controls 50% of all business ownership shares, this transfer from consumers to owners tends to warp the distribution of income and wealth. Excess wages and salaries go to workers and managers in unionized-concentrated industries. These transfers may likewise contribute to maldistribution, but to an unknown extent. Exorbitant costs due to X-inefficiency go to no purpose whatever. They are a form of deadweight loss because they represent resources needlessly consumed.

Yet another form of deadweight loss (and of lost consumers' surplus) is attributable to misallocation of resources. Triangles *ABC* and *AED* in Figures

---

[70] Ingham provides further indirect evidence by showing that (1) there is *no* difference across plants regarding monetary satisfaction (since those in small plants have lower money expectations to go with their lower wage rate) but (2) with respect to nonmonetary aspects, small-plant folks feel *positively rewarded* and large-plant folks feel "indifferent."

[71] Scherer, *op. cit.*, p. 120.

19-1 and 19-3 signify these losses. Unlike the other losses, these are not directly measurable in dollars, but they are no less real.

If one were to hazard a guess as to how much all these losses of consumers' surplus amounted to, something in the neighborhood of 7–10 % of GNP might be reasonable. Individual contributions might be as follows: excess profits, 1–3 %; excess wages and salaries, 2–3 %; X-inefficiency 3–4 %; and misallocation 0.5–1 %.

Finally, market power appears to affect worker equity and welfare as well. In the not too distant past, minorities suffered disproportionate discrimination at the hands of oligopolists and monopolists. Studies of job satisfaction have not been able to test the effect of concentration directly. Still, they have tested the impact of organization size, which may serve as a weak substitute measure for power. In this respect they find that size and satisfaction are inversely related. Relatively high earnings compensate those who are less satisfied. Whether they are "fully" compensated is uncertain.

20

Profits and Policy: Public Utility Regulation

The Supreme Power who conceived gravity, supply and demand, and the double helix must have been absorbed elsewhere when public utility regulation was invented.

F. M. SCHERER

Public utility regulation is an industrial halfway house. Its residents are sheltered from the cruelties of unconstrained competition, yet they do not suffer the restrictions of total government control. Ownership and operation remain private while performance is officially policed in hopes of serving the public interest. Profit level and price structure are the main concerns of utility regulation. Utility regulation also covers such additional matters as accounting procedures, entry, exit, and quality of service.[1] But these we must neglect.

If there is any overall theme to what follows it is this: *profit and price regulation do not guaranty good industrial performance, but in some instances they may curb particularly bad performance.* This mixed verdict is reflected in expert opinion. Most regulatory scholars can be divided into two camps: (1) those who think regulation is good in theory but generally bad in practice and (2) those who believe it is bad in both theory and practice. Very few consider it good in both theory and practice. Still fewer endorse its practice while doubting its theory. Expressions of exasperation thus pepper the field: "Regulation is

---

[1] For an excellent complete treatment see Alfred E. Kahn, *The Economics of Regulation*, Vols. I and II (New York: Wiley & Sons, 1970, 1971). At a less advanced level look into Charles F. Phillips, Jr., *The Economics of Regulation* (Homewood, Ill.: R. Irwin, 1969).

like growing old: we would rather not do it, but consider the alternative."[2]
"Regulation is not an impossible job, but almost."[3]

Our aim is to survey both theory and practice. We begin by seeing what industries are regulated. We then explore why they are regulated and who does the regulating. The heart of the chapter discusses how profits and prices are regulated. Finally, broad problems are surveyed.

What Industries are Regulated?

Table 20-1 lists the main industries subjected to public utility regulation and shows their share of national income in 1976. Together they account for 7.6% of national income. Portions of some of the industries are exempt from regulation. And in some of the industries, government ownership accounts for a considerable part.

Characteristics of Regulated Industries

Several characteristics of these industries set them apart from most others. First, they are usually considered **vital** industries. To be sure, food and clothing (and books) are equally vital yet unregulated, but transportation, communications, and energy are necessities not to be sneezed at.

Second, nearly all regulated industries sell **services** rather than commodities. The movement of goods from here to there is a service, as is a phone call or a kilowatt-hour of electricity. Unlike commodities, services cannot be stored. Their production and consumption coincide inseparably, like a coin's two sides. Most regulated industries must therefore maintain excess capacity to meet peak periods of consumption. In many cases they must also maintain direct connections by wire or pipe with their customers.

Third, most regulated industries are **capital intensive**. The guts of their operations are cables, turbine generators, switches, steel rails, and road beds rather than mill hands, raw materials, or merchandise. This capital intensity can be measured by the value of assets relative to annual sales revenue. It is not at all unusual for assets to be 300 or 400% of annual sales revenue in regulated industries. Three or four years of sales are then necessary to match asset value. In contrast, most asset values in manufacturing are much lower, averaging about 80% of annual sales receipts. Wholesale and retail trade figures are still less, at roughly 35%. Food stores have asset/sales ratios of merely 20%, so for

---

[2] William G. Shepherd, "Regulation, Entry and Public Enterprise," in *Regulation in Further Perspective*, edited by Shepherd and Gies (Cambridge, Mass.: Ballinger Publishing Co., 1974), p. 22.
[3] Charles R. Ross, Testimony, *Controls or Competition*, Hearings before Subcommittee on Antitrust and Monopoly, U. S. Senate, 92nd Congress, Second Session (1972), p. 257.

TABLE 20-1   Principal Regulated Industries in the United States, 1976

Industry	National Income Accruing (in Billions $)	Percentage of 1976 National Income
Transportation		
Railroads	10.2	0.7
Trucking	21.0	1.5
Air	8.5	0.6
Other transport*	9.7	0.7
Communications		
Telephone and telegraph	27.2	2.0
Radio and TV broadcasting	3.2	0.2
Electric, gas, and sanitary		
services	25.8	1.9
Total	105.6	7.6

* Includes local and interurban passenger transit, water transit, and pipelines.
Source: Department of Commerce, *Survey of Current Business* (July 1977), pp. 43–44.

them a single year's sales receipts cover assets five times over.[4] The massive capital intensity of public utilities helps to explain the whys and wherefors of regulation.

Why Regulate?

The selection of industries to regulate rests with government legislatures. State authority is based on "police power." Federal authority is based on the Constitution's commerce clause, which gives Congress the right "to regulate commerce . . . among the several states." Court interpretations of these powers are now quite liberal. Legislatures may impose regulation for just about any reason that strikes their fancy, subject only to the loose constraint that the industries selected must be "clothed with a public interest." Given such flexibility, the regulatory net is woven from diverse strands of reasoning, a net that has grown over time. Despite the rational diversity, the most commonly cited reasons for regulation can be collected under four categories: (1) natural monopoly, (2) conservation of a publicly owned natural resource, (3) destructive competition, and (4) sharp public indignation against "unfairness."

[4] U. S. Internal Revenue Service, *Statistics of Income: Corporation Income Tax Returns*, various issues.

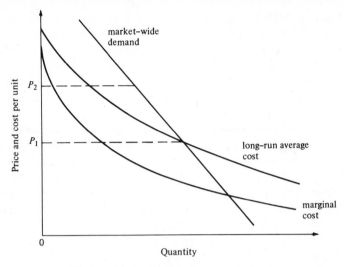

Figure 20-1. *Decreasing cost industry.*

Natural Monopoly

In some situations, economic or technical conditions permit only one efficient supplier, leading to "natural monopoly." The most obvious cause of natural monopoly is substantial economies of scale relative to demand. That is, cost per unit of output declines continuously as scale of operations increases. This is shown in Figure 20-1, where, throughout the range of quantity demanded, long-run average and marginal costs fall for a single firm. Two firms could supply the market's requirements at high price P_2, but only at lofty unit costs. A competitive dual between two such firms could be won handily by the largest rival because greater size brings lower cost, enabling the larger firm to price below its competitor's cost. At price P_1 in Figure 20-1, a sole survivor could meet *all* market demand at a point where the unit cost curve is still falling as a function of output. There is, then, room for only one efficient enterprise.

Among regulated industries, costs decline as scale increases for local water, electric power, gas, telephone, and cable TV. The technology of transmission and the physical fact of direct connection are the main causes of this cost effect. Cables, pipelines, and other conduits have transmission capacities that grow *more* than proportionately to size or material make-up. As a consequence, the least expensive way to transmit electricity, gas, water, or telephone communications is through large lines. Furthermore, local distribution of these services requires direct connection to customers. Competition would therefore entail redundant line duplications, something obviously inefficient and wasteful—not to say damned inconvenient, ugly, and disruptive, given the excessive ditch digging, pipe laying, and wire hanging in which competition would entangle us.

485

An additional factor contributes to natural monopoly in local telephone service. For one caller to reach another, both must be connected to the same central switch. Almost by definition a central switch must be "central"—that is, monopolistic. With two competing phone companies, there would be *two* central switches. Folks having only one phone could then call only patrons of the same phone company. Comprehensive interconnection would require either two phones and two lines for everyone or cooperative switching between the central switches of the rival companies.

Although natural monopoly certainly explains much regulation, many natural monopolies are *not* regulated and, conversely, many regulated industries are *not* natural monopolies. Among the former, imagine an isolated small town so sparsely populated that demand can support no more than one movie theater. This might qualify as a natural monopoly. But such movie theaters escape regulation apparently because they offer something less than a "vital" service (there being other, perhaps even more enjoyable, things to do on a Saturday night than watching movies, even in Hatband, Idaho). Among the latter, transportation services have a long history of regulation, but they cannot qualify as natural monopolies. Major air routes can be served efficiently by a flock of airlines. Trucking can be carried on at low cost by very small-scale operators. And, given the competitive potentials of air, truck, and bus transport, railroads cannot be considered natural monopolies either (even though, six decades ago, they generally did fit that description).

Similarly, certain *segments* of natural monopoly industries are not naturally monopolistic. Although local electricity distribution is best dealt with by a single distributor, there are genuine opportunities for oligopolistic competition in the generation and sale of "bulk" electricity, at least in major metropolitan areas. New York, Chicago, Los Angeles, and Philadelphia, for example, each have more than five nearby firms with megawatt capacities above the 100 mark.[5] Telephone service also has certain segments where competition is possible, even desirable. Monopoly is unnatural and unneeded when it comes to manufacturing telephone equipment, now a $10 billion business. The gadgetry ranges from Mickey Mouse phones to complicated PBX terminals, all within the low-cost capabilities of dozens of electronics firms besides Ma Bell. Long-distance telephone service (which, among other things, connects the central switches of separate cities) is another area ripe for competition, especially since the advent of modern microwave and satellite transmission systems. Unfortunately, regulation has often stifled competition's full flower in such instances.

Resource Conservation

Regulation of radio and television broadcasting is grounded on a different rationale. Economic efficiency requires no more than small-scale local broad-

---

[5] L. W. Weiss, "Antitrust in the Electric Power Industry," in *Promoting Competition in Regulated Markets*, edited by A. Phillips (Washington, D.C.: Brookings Institution, 1975), p. 137.

casting. However, the radio spectrum used by broadcasters is a limited resource, with a limited number of band widths or channels. If broadcasters were granted free and unrestricted entry, they could very well flood the air waves, interfering with each other and garbling the reception of listeners and viewers. Accordingly, access to the spectrum is limited by licensing. Broadcasters, however, are not subject to price or profit control, only to entry restrictions. The arbitrary selection of licensees now in force is supposed to favor those broadcasters who best serve the "public interest," but it is not clear that it actually does. An alternative method of channel allocation recommended by many economists is the periodic "sale" of band widths to competitive bidders, with the monetary proceeds going into public coffers. Whatever the selection process employed, some entry restriction seems necessary. Moving farther afield, conservation has also served, rightly or wrongly, to justify regulation in other areas, such as natural gas, oil, and water.

Destructive Competition

Certain characteristics of many regulated industries—their ponderous capital intensity and susceptibility to excess capacity in particular—expose them to dangers of destructive competition. At least that is what some defenders of regulation contend. Excess capacity is said to induce reckless price cutting. And heavy capital intensity translates into high fixed costs as a proportion of total cost. So once prices start to fall they can plummet deeply before bottoming at average variable cost. The argument concludes, therefore, that such industries will be plagued by periodic price wars financially destructive to producers and disruptive for consumers.

Notice that this argument cannot rationalize regulation in natural monopoly markets, because natural monopolies, once established, face no competition. Notice, too, that the argument is designed to justify *minimum* price regulation, not *maximum* price regulation (as in the case of natural monopolies). Hence, it is an argument that is vociferously applied to justify minimum price regulation in transportation. Yet, as many economists have pointed out, it is precisely in transportation that this line of argument is least valid. Take trucking for instance:

Capital costs are relatively small compared to variable costs, so that unregulated truckers would not be likely to operate at prices much below cost. Also, the labor and capital resources employed in trucking can easily be shifted to alternative uses. In other industries with low fixed costs, such as retailing, prices seldom fall much below cost, and adjustments for changing market conditions are made quickly and with little disruption. In fact, this has been the case in trucking's unregulated sector, which ships agricultural products and has been quite free of "ruinous competition."[6]

In short, the argument has limited application.

[6] L. W. Weiss and A. D. Strickland, *Regulation: A Case Approach* (New York: McGraw-Hill Book Co., 1976), p. 6.

Unfairness

Perhaps the only area where sharp price rivalry can create real problems is railroading. But the main problem is not necessarily bankruptcy. The story begins over a hundred years ago, before trucks and planes, when railroads lorded over freight transportation. On some routes natural monopolies prevailed (because between any pair of cities railroads experience declining costs up to a point). On these natural monopoly routes demand was insufficient to support more than one low-cost company. On other routes, such as those between New York, Detroit, and Chicago, traffic volume was big enough to attract and nurture competition. Given railroads' steep fixed costs, conditions on these latter routes were right for rambunctious, if not completely ruinous, price rivalry. During the 1870s, for instance, a price war broke out on eastbound grain shipments between Chicago and New York, causing rates to fall from $0.56 to $0.15 per hundred-weight and even lower.[7]

In short, railroading in that era fitted two contrasting models depending on route circumstances—the natural monopoly model or the ruinous competition model. The result was a grossly discriminatory railroad rate structure. Towns without rail competition were charged higher rates than those blessed with two or more railroads. Indeed, in many instances rates on noncompetitive short hauls exceeded those on competitive long hauls, despite one's common sense expectation that rates should rise with distance since costs rise with distance. Moreover, large shippers were able to extract more favorable rates than small shippers. Folks on the unfavorable side of the tracks found these several discrepancies "monstrous," "evil," and "unfair." Their clamor caused Congress to pass the Interstate Commerce Act in 1887, which established the Interstate Commerce Commission and directed that rates approved by the Commission be "just and reasonable." That is, the Act outlawed personal discrimination and prohibited short-haul rates in excess of long-haul rates "under substantially similar circumstances." The importance of "fairness" in motivating this historic first step toward federal regulation may be seen in the fact that Congress made no explicit provision for the ICC to fix maximum overall rate levels until 20 years later with passage of the Hepburn Act of 1906.

In truth, "fairness," or some variant of it, has probably had a hand in motivating most subsequent regulation as well. A principal proponent of this view is Donald Dewey, who contends that citizens' expectations of regulation go well beyond protection from economic exploitation or resource conservation:

> [First] we expect group therapy—a release of tension and frustrations . . . . Fortunately, plenty of angry people in this world would rather testify at a public hearing—preferably before a TV camera—than blow up buildings or beat their kids.
>
> Second, we expect regulation to protect us from the kind of sharp commercial practice that is generally impossible in competitive industries . . . The Penn Central

---

[7] Paul W. MacAvoy, *The Economic Effects of Regulation: The Trunkline Railroad Cartels and the Interstate Commerce Commission Before 1900*, (Cambridge, Mass.: MIT Press, 1965).

Railroad will never refund a nickel for a breakdown in service unless it is compelled to do so by a Utility Commission.

Third, we expect regulation to mitigate some of the consequences of the bureaucratization that comes with great size. To say the obvious, in any organization mistakes are made, and the larger the organization, the more difficult it is to pinpoint the responsibility for error. A complaint to a regulatory body is one way that the consumer has of striking back . . . .

Finally, and perhaps the most important, we expect that regulation will introduce a little more predictability into our lives. Nine times out of ten when a railroad petitions to abandon service on a branch line, the service should be cut, according to almost any test of economic welfare. Still . . . the welfare loss can be reduced by drawing out the closing process through hearing and review . . .

In short, it may well be that "as citizens we wish the regulatory agency to serve as a forum for group therapy, a better business bureau, a check on bureaucracy, and a brake on economic and social change."[8]

Who Regulates?

The vast bulk of regulatory power rests with independent regulatory commissions. They are neither legislative, judicial, nor administrative. Rather, the duties of these commissions run the gamut of governmental classifications. They make rules and thereby legislate; they hold hearings or adversary proceedings and thereafter adjudicate; they enforce regulatory laws and thereby administer.

Although commission duties are thus typically broad, their scope of jurisdiction is often narrow. One major division of jurisdiction concerns geography. State regulatory commissions govern *intra*state commerce, whereas federal agencies oversee *inter*state commerce. Product or service determines a second division. Many commissions regulate only one type of utility, or a limited class of utilities. As shown in Table 20-2, which outlines major federal commissions, the Interstate Commerce Commission regulates interstate land transportation (and some waterway carriers); the Federal Energy Regulatory Commission (until 1977 the Federal Power Commission) regulates interstate transmission and wholesale price of electricity, rates and routes of natural gas pipelines, and the wellhead price of gas destined for interstate shipment (although this last authority is being phased out); the Federal Communications Commission licenses broadcasters and regulates interstate (long-distance) telephone and telegraph rates and levels of service; and the Civil Aeronautics Board has jurisdiction over all interstate air passenger service.

State commissions are often less narrowly specialized. With varying scope their main concerns are *local* gas, electric, telephone, water, and transit utilities.

---

[8] Donald J. Dewey, "Regulatory Reform?" in *Regulation in Further Perspective*, edited by Shepherd and Gies (Cambridge, Mass.: Ballinger Publishing Co., 1974), pp. 35–37.

TABLE 20-2 Major Federal Regulators as of 1978

Agency	Vital Statistics	Major Functions
Interstate Commerce Commission (11 members)	Created in 1887, it has 2100 employees, 79 field offices, and a $57 million budget	Regulates rates and routes of railroads, common-carrier truckers, and some waterway carriers
Federal Energy Regulatory Commission (5 members)	Established in 1930 as the Federal Power Commission, it has 1450 employees and maintains five field offices on a budget of $42 million	Regulates interstate transmission and wholesale price of electric power, rates and routes of natural gas pipelines, and the wellhead price of gas for interstate shipment
Federal Communications Commission (7 members)	Created in 1934, it has 2100 employees, 24 field offices, and a budget of $60 million	Regulates broadcasting and other communications through licensing and frequency allocation, and interstate telephone and telegraph rates and levels of service
Civil Aeronautics Board (5 members)	Created in 1938, it has 800 employees, eight field offices, and a $22 million budget. It also administers $80 million in subsidies to airlines	Regulates airline fares and routes. Of late it has spearheaded an effort toward deregulation of airlines.

State or federal, the U. S. Supreme Court summarized the commission concept when it said that these agencies were "created with the avowed purpose of lodging functions in a body specifically competent to deal with them by reason of information, experience and careful study of the business and economic conditions of the industry affected."[9]

Commission panels usually consist of five to eleven members appointed to fixed terms by either the President (for federal posts) or the Governor (for state posts, although several states *elect* commissioners). With but few exceptions, the commissioners so selected do not fit the ideal image of objective experts. They tend to be lawyers and businessmen whose sympathies often lie with the industry they regulate, or obscure politicians (still wet behind the ears and climbing, or washed up and on the way out). Some appointments are even humorous. A nominee for the Federal Communications Commission was asked during his Senate confirmation hearing about his qualifications in communications. "Senator," he replied, "I don't know anything about communications. I came to Washington expecting to be appointed to the Federal Power Commission."[10]

Commissioners are aided by staffs of civil servants comprising mainly accountants, engineers, lawyers, and economists. Many critics of regulation contend that commissions cannot do an adequate job because both staffers and commissioners are underpaid and overworked. The utilities they regulate can afford super personnel in plenitude. Hence, control of corporate giants with this feeble machinery has been called herding elephants with flyswatters.[11] Leonard Weiss and Allyn Strickland explain the machinery further:

> Cases may be initiated by the staff and/or affected firms. The full commission may hear a case, but more commonly it is heard by a trial examiner . . . . The trial examiner is a lawyer appointed by the commission to hear evidence presented by the staff, the affected firms, and any intervenors admitted to the proceeding . . .
>
> The hearing is similar to a court proceeding with prepared testimony, cross-examination of witnesses, and the usual rules of procedure. The participants complete the case by submitting briefs, which summarize their arguments, the relevant evidence, and appropriate precedents. The trial examiner then prepares a proposed decision, which he turns over to the commission. The commission reviews the case record and reaches its own decision, which may or may not be the same as the trial examiner's. Commission decisions are reached by majority vote [and] may be appealed on questions of law or procedure to the courts . . .[12]

This list of procedures may create the illusion that commissions are truly "independent," but that is only an illusion. Many commentators argue that commissions tend to be more responsive to corporate than to consumer interests. Commission appointment and funding are controlled by politicians in

---

[9] *Federal Trade Commission v. R. F. Keppel and Bros. Inc.*, 291 U. S. 304, 314 (1934).

[10] Louis M. Kohlmeier, Jr., *The Regulators* (New York: Harper & Row, 1969), p. 48.

[11] B. C. Moore, Jr., "AT & T: The Phony Monopoly," in *Monopoly Makers*, edited by M. J. Green (New York: Grossman, 1973), p. 82.

[12] Weiss and Strickland, *op. cit.*, pp. 8–9.

491

the legislative and executive branches of government. In turn, these politicians are frequently beholden to the regulated firms, their trade associations, and their unions for political support of various kinds (including campaign contributions, of course). In addition, "commissioners are commonly courted on an informal basis by representatives of the regulated industries. The big broadcasting and airline companies maintain high-paid lobbyists in Washington who regularly socialize with commissioners. Occasionally the press or congressional committees uncover stories of commissioners enjoying golfing weekends in Bermuda as guests of the airlines or travelling to Florida in private railroad cars provided by the railroads. After serving on the commissions, many commissioners and staff members are subsequently employed by regulated firms."[13]

It is probably a sympton of the importance attached to independence that commissions occasionally recruit from academia on the assumption that professors are, on the whole, genuine experts and persons of integrity. Many such appointments have been particularly successful, notably those of Professors Alfred Kahn and Nicholas Johnson, two of regulation's brightest stars. Thus, some commissioners serve outstandingly.

Moreover, personnel and procedures do not deserve all the blame for regulation's shortcomings. Many legislative mandates under which commissions work are vague or misguided. What is more, the task of regulation is *inherently* difficult. There is no regulatory cookbook with recipes for every occasion, no utility child-care guide. There are a few principles, plus plenty of questions lacking pat answers. It is to these that we now turn. The discussion is divided into two topics: (1) rate level, and (2) rate structure. **Rate level** refers to *overall* revenues, costs, and returns. **Rate structure** refers to the *specific prices charged* to specific customers for specific services at specific times.

Rate Level Regulation

Objectives

There are any number of objectives that *could* guide rate level regulation. Among the more obvious possibilities are speedy growth in service, conservation of energy, and optimal allocation of resources in the strict economic sense. For one reason or another, however, *none* of these is the main objective applied in practice. The main objective is to allow the utility sufficient revenues to pay its "full" costs plus a "fair" return on the "fair" value of its capital. Stated differently, *the main objective is to strike a reasonable balance between the interests of consumers* (who should not be gouged by monopoly exploitation)

---

[13] *Ibid.*, p. 10. For elaboration on the causes of proindustry bias see Roger G. Noll, *Reforming Regulation* (Washington, D.C.: Brookings Institution, 1971), pp. 15–46.

and the interests of the utility investors and operators (who should not be ripped off by overzealous commissions, or who, in more legalistic language, should not be deprived of their property without "due process of law").

The effort to balance is captured in a simple equation:

$$\text{Total revenue} = \text{operating expenses} + \text{current depreciation}$$

$$+ \;(\text{capital value} \times \text{rate of return}) \qquad (20\text{-}1)$$

Note that, on the right hand side, operating expenses and current depreciation are both *annual dollar flows*. Capital value is not a dollar flow. It is the asset value of the utility firm at a *given point in time*, also called the **rate base**. However, once this capital value is multiplied by the allowed rate of return (such as 0.10, for 10% per year), the result *is* an annual dollar flow. Thus, the basic problem of rate level regulation is to see to it that the annual flow of total revenue covers the annual flow of "full cost," including depreciation, plus a "fair" or "reasonable" return on capital value, no more and no less. Generally speaking the owners or operators would like to see "more", which means that their interests lie with *high* estimates of the elements on the right hand side. Consumers, on the other hand, would like to see "less" because their interests are generally served by *low* figures for these elements. It is the job of the commission to balance these conflicting interests—to determine that operating expenses, current depreciation, capital value, and rate of return may be neither too high nor too low, and then to permit a rate level that generates the necessary total revenue. Note that if rates are pressed *too* low, service could suffer and the firm could go bankrupt, injuring everyone involved.

The situation may be seen in Figure 20-2 (which is a total dollar view, not a per unit dollar view as in Figure 20-1). The total payments (or total cost) curve has three components corresponding to the right-hand side of the equation (20-1). Thus, utility payments include a fair or normal profit (which is embodied in rate base × per cent return). An *un*regulated, profit maximizing monopolist would charge an overall price level to yield an output of Q_u, placing the firm at point A on the total revenue curve. Excess profit there would be vertical distance AB. The objective of regulation is to lower price level below the monopolist's profit maximizing price, thereby moving the firm from A to C. At point C, total revenue and total payments, including no more than a fair return, just match. Output is greater at Q_r, and consumers are not exploited. At price levels still lower, output would be still greater but total revenue would fall to unreasonably low levels, hurting the utility's investors. The process does not exactly simulate competitive results, but it may be helpful to think of it in that way.

Now, to appreciate fully the problems encountered in the regulatory process, each item of rate level decision making needs to be discussed. We begin with operating expenses.

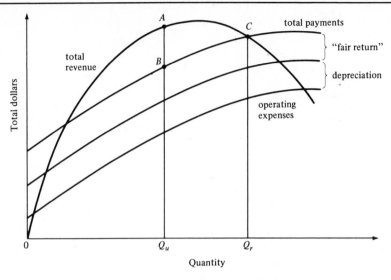

Figure 20-2. Rate level regulation.

Operating Expenses

Operating expenses are to some degree the easiest of all items for a com
mission to determine. They include such things as fuel costs (for coal, oil, and
gas), workers' wages, managers' salaries, materials expense, advertising, and
taxes. Together these expenses typically absorb 70–80% of a utility's total
operating revenue. They are relatively easy to determine because few such
expenses can be padded or fudged. Taxes, for example, are beyond the utility'
control and therefore unquestioned. Similarly, the costs of fuel are shaped in
open markets, and workers' wages are settled by collective bargaining. These
too, are rarely questioned by commissions.

One does not have to go very far down the list of expenses, however, before
one encounters snarls. How much should be allowed for advertising? Does a
monopolist need to advertise at all? What about public relations advertising
which tells us that little 6-year old Suzy is a "typical" AT & T stock holder
that Giant Electric is doing everything possible to clean up the environmen
but smoke-stack scrubbers ought to be scrubbed, that America rolls on rail
road rails, and that *public* ownership of utilities is sinful? Does the tab for these
ads belong to consumers or investors? How much should be allowed for execu
tive salaries, executive secretaries, executive expense accounts, executive liquor
executive jets, and executive travel? Should the gasoline expenses of corporate
Cadillacs be approved when economical Pintos would do? Should all worke:
wage rates be approved? Is it not possible that telephone repairmen could be
overpaid? And what about the costs of company lawyers and accountants who

represent the utility before the commission? Should consumers pay the company's costs of coping with regulation when these costs support efforts contrary to the consumers' interest? Or should these costs be deducted from earnings of the owners, who stand to benefit most from representations that rates ought to be raised to fatten profits? What about donations to charities? Does not "good corporate citizenship" require that community causes be supported? But if it does, what worthy causes should be blessed, in what dollar amounts, and what share of this burden should be borne by consumers?

Answers to these and a stream of similar questions are sticky. Some of these expenses are partly "legitimate," but where does one draw the line? Commissions' answers vary widely, as you might well guess.

Current Depreciation

Current depreciation is an important item of cost because most utilities have a high capital intensity. For all utilities current depreciation amounts to almost 10% of total sales revenue as against only about 3% for all manufacturing.[14]

No one disputes the necessity of including depreciation as a cost. In one sense, depreciation accounts for the "using up" of capital assets through wear and tear or obsolescence. In another sense, depreciation may be thought of as a payment to capital investors, much as wages, salaries, and materials expenses are payments to other factor suppliers. This means that, of the elements in the summary equation, *both* current depreciation *and* capital value times rate of return go to the investors. As Alfred Kahn explains, "The return to capital . . . has two parts: the return *of* the money capital invested over the estimated economic life of the investment and the return (interest and profit) *on* the portion of the investment that remains outstanding."[15]

Although no one disputes depreciation's inclusion as a cost, its computation is even more controversial than the computation of operating expenses. First, the allowance for depreciation is quite different from operating expenses. Whereas operating expenses entail *actual money outlays*, depreciation does not. It is an *imputed cost*, "introduced to take account of the fact that the economic life of capital assets is limited; to distribute the decline in their value—which is a genuine cost of production—over their economic life, in order to assure its recoupment from customers. So the portion of total revenues it permits the company to earn does not, as is the case with normal operating expenses, go out in payments to outside parties—suppliers of raw materials, workers and so on."[16] It goes instead to investors.

Second, since current depreciation is an imputation, there are no hard rules for its reckoning. The actual figure arrived at for any asset in any one year

---

[14] Internal Revenue Service, *Statistics of Income, Corporation Income Tax Returns 1975* (preliminary) pp. 14–16.
[15] Kahn, *op. cit.*, Vol. I, p. 32.
[16] *Ibid.*

depends on three things: (1) the depreciation base, (2) the asset's estimated life span, and (3) the method of write-off during its life. Each element is judgmental; each is therefore open to dispute.

The depreciation base is the original cost of the asset less any salvage value at life's end. Although original cost is straightforward, salvage value is a matter of estimate. Life-span, too, is a matter of estimate. A short life with no assumed salvage value would tend to favor investors over consumers because it would lead to large, early write-offs. Conversely, a long life with high salvage value favors consumers because it leads to small annual write-offs.

As for possible write-off methods, they are too numerous and too complex to summarize here. The most common are called straight line, sinking fund and retirement reserve. The major source of difference among them rests with whether the depreciation base is spread *evenly* or *un*evenly over the estimated life span.

It would be nice if there was an Eleventh Commandment to guide commissioners in all these reckonings, but there isn't. Which way, then, should the estimates lean? How should any biases be checked? It is up to the commissions and whatever conventions they choose to follow.

Capital Value or Rate Base

Far and away the most controversial part of regulation concerns capital value times rate of return (or rate base × per cent return) because this is the computation that determines profit. The Supreme Court's legal guide to commissions is about as solid as natural gas. Specific estimates or formulas are not so important, says the Court. It's the *end result* that counts. The end result must be "just and reasonable." What is "just and reasonable"? Earnings "which enable the company to operate successfully, to maintain its financial integrity to attract capital, and to compensate its investors for the risks assumed ... even though they [the earnings] might produce only a meager return."[17]

This nebulous guide gives commissions great leeway in determining both capital value and rate of return. As regards capital value, there is a wide range of choice concerning (1) accounting devices, and (2) what is counted as real investment. Choice offers opportunities for exaggeration, overstatement, and the exercise of value judgment.

Accounting Devices. At least four methods for computing the rate base have been adopted or proposed:

1. *Original cost* values assets at their "actual" or "book" cost.
2. *Reproduction cost* is the estimated cost of buying, building, and installing the same equipment at today's prices.

---

[17] *Federal Power Commission v. Hope Natural Gas Co.*, 320 U. S. 591 (1944).

3. *Replacement cost* is the estimated cost of replacing the present plant and equipment, much of which may be outdated, with the most efficient and reliable technology available, in amounts sufficient to supply the same service.
4. *Mixed method*, or "fair value," which is some combination, or rough averaging, of the items 1 through 3.

Subtractions for *accumulated* depreciation must be made under any of the options, which expands the horizon for judgment still further.

At present, most federal and state commissions apply the original cost approach, followed in popularity by mixed method and reproduction cost in that order. (Replacement cost is shunned by all.) Still, future changes are possible, and the pros and cons of these techniques are endlessly debated. Among the major points at issue are (1) ease of estimation, (2) inflation, and (3) economic efficiency.

It should be obvious that original cost is the easiest of all methods to estimate (a fact that partly explains its great popularity). The replacement cost approach is undoubtedly the most difficult, because it amounts to little more than a playground for opinion. Reproduction cost lies somewhere in between.

Although original cost is most convenient, it is least competent in accounting for changes over time, especially plant and equipment price changes. During periods of inflation, consumers prefer and investors oppose original cost because it yields a *lower* rate base than the other techniques. On the other hand, during periods of deflation (now about as dated as dinosaurs), producers prefer original cost because it yields a *higher* rate base than the other techniques. What is correct? There is no secure answer, but it can be argued that reproduction cost, which does take inflation into account, might be better economically. Why? Because under the "ideal" of pure competition, industry price will move in the long run to a level that just covers costs plus a normal return on a *new* plant. Moreover, during periods of astounding inflation, original cost valuation might sink the rate base so low as to threaten the firm's viability.

Actually, on grounds of allocation efficiency, the replacement cost approach seems most attractive because the *new* plant alluded to should be one *incorporating the latest in new technology*. Although certainly favorable to replacement cost, this argument is undercut by the fact that the main purpose of regulation is *not* allocation efficiency. Commissions make no attempt to see that utility prices always match marginal cost. They only seek a "fair" balance between opposing parties.

Asset Inclusion. Regardless of accounting technique, there remains the question of what is to be included in the rate base. Buildings, cables, trucks, dams, generators, switches and the like obviously qualify. But what about the $1 billion nuclear power plant completed only a year ago but now shut down because geologists have just discovered an earthquake fault within $\frac{1}{2}$ mile of it? Who ought to pay for it? If the dead plant is included in the rate base, consumers

497

will howl. If excluded, it would surely thrash investors. How would you decide as a commissioner? What, further, about *intangible* assets? Would you permit the cost of patents, franchise papers, licenses, and purchase options to enter the rate base? Some commissions do permit them—to some extent.

Percent Return

Utility investors own utility bonds, preferred stock, and common stock. Each instrument's rate of return differs because each differs in "priority" of pay-out, with bonds enjoying top priority and earning the lowest return. Thus the per cent rate of return referred to in the regulatory equation is actually a *weighted average* rate. Reducing the return to its components, most commissions allow the interest actually paid on bonds, the dividends actually paid on preferred stock, and then they add a "fair" return for stockholders' equity.

Equity Returns. On the whole, equity returns average about 11–12%, which is pretty close to the all-manufacturing average. However, the average masks considerable variety. Examples of 1973 equity returns earned by electric power companies illustrate the diversity: Arizona, 15.6%; California, 11.9%; Montana, 7.4%; New York, 12.1%; Vermont, 13.8%; and Wyoming, 10.9%.[18] These rates underscore the fact that there is no single scientifically correct rate of return. At best, there is (as with Miss America's measurements) a "zone of reasonableness," within which judgment (and imagination) may roam. What are the limits of this zone? The *bottom* limit would be a rate just high enough to attract continuing investor commitments of capital. The *upper* limit would be considerably more generous but not lavish. Obviously, the zone itself is rather elastic.

Perhaps the best way to appreciate this problem is to imagine yourself as the typical investor whose capital the utility is trying to attract. What rate of return would the company have to pay (and the commission have to approve) to get you to bite? If you are shrewd, that rate would depend on the following:

1. The rate you could earn if you put your money elsewhere.
2. The risk of losing your investment (here and elsewhere).
3. The extent to which the company's earnings fluctuate, which in turn may depend on its debt/equity ratio, dividend pay-out policy, general economic condition, and so on.
4. The recent trend in the company's stock price.
5. Your expectations of political changes that may alter regulation.

These would be churning in your head, but the commission cannot read your mind. It therefore has no way of knowing precisely what minimum rate

[18] Clair Wilcox and W. G. Shepherd, *Public Policies Toward Business* (Homewood, Ill.: Irwin 1975), pp. 372–73.

would attract your capital, or that of others. For this reason, commissions must exercise a good bit of judgment, taking these various factors into account because you take them into account.

Rate Structure Regulation

The duty of commissions does not stop once overall revenue is set. The question of what *specific* prices or rates to charge remains. According to judicial and legislative instructions, commissions may permit rates that jump around with time, place, type of buyer, and size of transaction. However, the jumps cannot be "unduly discriminatory"; the differences in rates charged various customers or classes of service must be "just and reasonable." In carrying out this vague mandate, commissions have permitted rates to vary with *cost-of-service* and *value-of-service*. Each is worth illustrating.

Costs and Peak-Load Pricing[19]

For years now we have had to pay more to call long distance during weekday daylight hours than to call during nights and weekends. Likewise, many large buyers of natural gas are charged low prices for "interruptible" service, meaning that they can be cut off if the demand of noninterruptible buyers burgeons. Traditionally, electric power companies have not charged such time based rates, but now there is a definite trend toward them. In 1977, for instance, Wisconsin Power & Light Company began charging business customers 2.03 cents per kilowatt-hour between 8 A.M. and 10 P.M., and just 1.013 cents per kilowatt-hour at other times. Rates may also vary with the seasons. All these are examples of **peak load pricing**, because rates are higher to peak users.

The main justification for higher prices during peak periods is that the costs of providing peak service are greater than those of providing off-peak service. One such cost is plant and equipment. Because a utility must have on hand capacity to satisfy total peak demand, capacity costs can be blamed mainly on those who tap into the utility during peak hours. As for off-peak customers, *the plant and equipment are already there for the peak*, so capacity costs of serving them do not apply, although off-peak users do create costs for fuel and other variable inputs. Indeed, even fuel costs per unit tend to vary with time of demand because utilities usually fire up their least efficient, high-cost plants only during peak periods. The differences between plants can be substantial. In 1973, for instance, a major eastern electric company experienced fuel costs of 3.3 mills/kWh in its most efficient plant and 9.51 mills/kWh in its least efficient plant.[20]

---

[19] This section is based primarily on Weiss and Strickland, *op. cit.*, pp. 18–21.
[20] E. Berlin, C. J. Cicchetti, and W. J. Gillen, *Perspective on Power* (Cambridge, Mass.: Ballinger Publishing Co., 1975), p. 35.

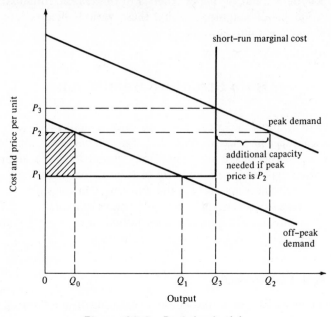

Figure 20-3. *Peak-load pricing.*

(Note that these cost experiences do not contradict the economies of scale mentioned earlier. These are *short-run* cost comparisons, not long-run scale comparisons.)

Figure 20-3 shows peak and off-peak demands set against the short-run marginal cost curve of a hypothetical utility. If a uniform price of P_2 were charged to both peak and off-peak demands, capacity would have to equal OQ_2, which is peak quantity demanded at P_2. Off-peak demand would be OQ_0 given price P_2. Since OQ_2 greatly exceeds OQ_0, it is easy to see that peak demand would be responsible for the plant necessary to produce OQ_2 (even if off-peak demand were nonexistent). Moreover, a uniform price of P_2 would cause inefficient plant usage, because there would be tremendous excess capacity during off-peak periods. In short, such a uniform price is *too low* for peak demand (producing a state of overbuilding) and *too high* for off-peak demand (causing off-peak underutilization). Indeed, off-peak demand is to some extent subsidizing peak demand, since the shaded area in Figure 20-3 indicates the amount by which off-peak revenues exceed off-peak costs.

With a more sensible rate structure, peak customers would be charged P_3 and offpeak customers would be charged P_1. At P_3, peak demand would be curtailed to OQ_3, eliminating the need for capacity over the $Q_3 - Q_2$ range. (It has been estimated that $13 *billion* of electric utility capital spending would be avoided over the years 1977–1985 if all United States electric companies ere using such peak-load pricing.[21]) Conversely, off-peak demand would xpand to OQ_1 under a reduced price of P_1. Off-peak excess capacity would be ut appreciably, thereby achieving more efficient plant usage. Price for off-peak emand could not fall below P_1, however, without falling below marginal cost. nd it is only "fair" and economically "proper" that off-peak users pay those arginal costs.

One consequence of this scheme is that, over time, peak customers may djust their consumption patterns and become off-peak purchasers. The result ould be a leftward shift of the peak demand curve and a rightward shift of the ff-peak demand curve. But these shifts raise no horrendous problems. As ff-peak demand grows to the point of full capacity utilization, off-peak price nould be raised to reflect *some* capacity costs. The distribution of capacity osts among users would then depend on the relative intensities of these de- nands.

As already suggested, a rate structure that fully reflected costs would entail nore than charges sufficient to cover whatever capacity various classes of ustomers were responsible for. Rates would also have to include: (1) A charge er unit of service (for example, per kilowatt-hour, or per phone call) to meet ne costs that vary with output (fuel especially). (2) A fixed charge for connection. 3) A fixed charge per month to cover the costs of metering, billing, and the ke, costs which do not vary with consumption level or timing.

alue-of-Service Pricing

In the main, utility prices are not based strictly on cost of service. Price iscrimination of second and third degrees (as defined and explained in Chapter 3) runs rampant. A common feature of such price discrimination is that those ustomers or classes of service having *in*elastic demands are typically charged nore than those having elastic demands. In 1975, for instance, average electric ites to residential customers were about 3.5 cents per kWh, whereas those harged to industrial customers were only 2.1 cents per kWh.[22] To be sure, upplying a big factory often costs less per unit than supplying a home because any industrial buyers provide their own transformers and other equipment. till, the main explanation for the higher household rate is found in price lasticity of demand. Industrial elasticity appears to be about 1.9, whereas esidential elasticity is closer to 1.2.[23] The difference is due to the greater energy ptions open to industrial buyers. Indeed, many of them economically generate neir own electricity.

[21] *Wall Street Journal*, August 12, 1977, p. 1.

[22] *Business Week*, November 29, 1976, p. 55.

[23] John W. Wilson, "Residential Demand for Electricity," *Quarterly Review of Economics and usiness* (Spring, 1971), pp. 7–22; L. D. Chapman, *et. al.*, "Elasticity Demand in the United States: n Econometric Analysis," Oak Ridge National Laboratory (ORNL–NSF–47), June 1973; L. D. aylor, "The Demand for Electricity: A Survey," *Bell Journal of Economics* (Spring, 1975), pp. 1–110.

Another form of discrimination in electricity is the so-called block rate that, until recently, confronted virtually every residential consumer in the United States. Under a block-rate schedule, price falls as additional "blocks" of electricity are consumed during the month. The idea is that a high rate could be charged for basic uses like lighting, which lacks energy substitutes, whereas a lower rate could apply to electricity used for cooking and heating, where natural gas might be used instead. Of late, many commissions have abandoned block rates in hopes of encouraging energy conservation.

Telephones further illustrate value-of-service pricing. Business users have traditionally been charged *more* than residential users on the theory that phone service is indispensable to businesses but more or less optional in the home. Within the home, it appears that for years Ma Bell imposed equipment rental charges that greatly exceeded the costs of supplying equipment. Conversely, basic phone service was apparently under-priced, drawing a subsidy from equipment. Once folks were permitted to *buy* their own phones, beginning in the late 1970s, Ma Bell said rates on basic phone service would have to go up because she could no longer count on lucrative equipment rentals.

Perhaps an even more striking example of AT & T's price discrimination concerns interstate services of various kinds. AT & T's "Seven-Way Cost Study" in the mid-1960s disclosed a pattern of discrimination generated by competition. Profits as a per cent of investment were 9.7% and 13.4% on message toll telephone and WATS services, where Ma Bell faced no competition to speak of. In contrast, profits were a piddling 0.3% and 1.4% on TELPAK and private line telegraph services, where rivals posed a threat.[24] Clearly Ma Bell's elasticity of demand was higher with competition than without.

Presentation of these examples is not meant to imply that utility price discrimination is always "bad" or "unfair." It may seem unfair because some pay high and some pay low, relative to costs. But there are instances of beneficial price discrimination, "beneficial" in that it can lead to a *lower overall average price* for the company and even allow a *reduction in the high price paid* by those with relatively inelastic demand.

This is best seen by referring to a specific example. Railroad rates are lower for bulky "low value" freight, such as coal, than for "high value" freight, such as watches and auto parts. Indeed, it has been estimated that, in 1960, 65% of railroad freight tonnage moved at rates *below* fully distributed average total costs. This appears unfair to the "high value" freight. However, if the railroad converted to a flat uniform rate per ton equalling average total cost, they would *not* thereby be able to reduce price to those "high value" shippers. The "low value" shippers would stop shipping at the average total cost rate because they could not afford to pay what, for them, would be a rate hike. Traffic volume would consequently decline. And then *all* the railroads' fixed costs would have

[24] Harry M. Trebing and William H. Melody, "An Evaluation of Domestic Communications Pricing Practices and Policies," Staff Paper No. 5, *The Domestic Telecommunications Carrier Industry*, President's Task Force on Communications (1968), p. 217.

כ be borne by the "high value" shippers, which would mean a higher rate than ver for them. In other words, although about 65% of the tonnage moves at a rice below uniform *average total cost*, that tonnage *is* charged a rate above *ariable cost*, and much of that tonnage thereby makes tremendous *aggregate* ontributions to covering overhead fixed costs.[25]

For discrimination to be beneficial, however, certain conditions must hold:

First, there must be a heavy investment entailing high fixed costs *and a substantial amount of capacity standing in idleness*, so that costs per unit can be reduced by spreading the fixed costs over a larger volume of output. Second, the lower rates must be needed to get business that would not otherwise exist. Third, they must be high enough to cover variable costs and contribute something to overhead. And fourth, the whole scale of rates must be regulated to keep earnings reasonable and to keep discrimination within bounds.[26]

In short, rate structure regulation is complex. Cost-of-service pricing is not 1e only option. Value-of-service pricing may sometimes be socially valuable.

Problems and Distortions

As if we have not hung enough problems around regulators' necks, a few 1ore must be mentioned. First, it would be nice if commissions could reward tilities that operate efficiently and progressively and penalize those putting ut poorly. But no tidy incentive techniques have yet been devised. Measure-1ent of efficiency and progressiveness is imprecise at best. And deviations from /hatever measures are adopted may be as much the fault of regulators as 1anagers. Assume, for example, that low profit earnings are taken to signal .oor performance. Such a predicament might, in fact, be the result of some ommission decision. Even if it were not, it is hard to see how a penalty of *still*)wer earnings would allow the utility to improve its efficiency and maintain its inancial soundness. Perhaps the only present source of proper incentive is egulatory "lag." Earnings that rise inordinately from efficiency remain with he firm until regulators act to reduce rate levels, but they act only after a long ag. Conversely, earnings that fall with inefficiency must be borne by the firm intil requests for rate increases are answered, which procedure likewise entails ome lag. Thus the lag imperfectly and temporarily rewards "goodness" and .unishes "badness."

Second, some regulatory theorists—Harvey Averch, Leland Johnson, and tanislaw Wellisz, in particular—argue that profit regulation contains some

[25] Kahn, *op. cit.*, p. 156.
[26] Wilcox and Shepherd, *op. cit.*, p. 381.

particularly unfavorable incentives. Because profit is keyed to the rate base *there is an incentive to expand the rate base* (to substitute capital for labor beyond the point that would be optimal in the absence of regulation.[27] Just how serious this so-called "Averch-Johnson effect" actually is no one can say. Empirical tests of the hypothesis have been mixed, half confirming and half refuting it.[28] Even if the effect does exist, it may not be as bad as it might seem. Although in *static* terms the bias favoring capital over other inputs may lift costs undesirably, the *dynamic* result may be *lower* costs through *improved technological progress*, given that most technological change tends to favor capital intensity.[29]

A third problem is what James McKie aptly calls the "tar-baby" effect.[30] Each swipe regulators take at some supposed utility sin seems to ensnare regulators in ever deeper difficulties. The innocent and well meaning souls who first devised regulation imagined it to be a rather simple matter. What could be easier, they must have asked, than restricting a natural monopolist's profit to some "just" percentage? Yet, as we have already seen, it is not so easy. Taking a punch at profit may mean a bulge in costs; striking at excess cost may hurt quality; close control of quality entails sticky details demanding nearly one bureaucrat for every hard-hat; and so on. Pretty soon regulators are attempting to cover everything from plant purchases to billing frequencies, and in the process they get covered with tar.

Finally, consequently, and most important, the main problem with regulation is that, once it gets rolling, it does not stop with appropriate control of natural monopoly or grossly unfair price discrimination. It keeps right on rolling, crushing many fine opportunities for competition. As Walter Adams once remarked, "Regulation breeds regulation. Competition, even at the margin, is a source of disturbance, annoyance, and embarrassment to the bureaucracy.... From the regulator's point of view, therefore, competition must be suppressed wherever it arises."[31]

This is, to say the least, unfortunate. If you have learned nothing else to this point, you should have learned that regulation is but a very poor substitute for competition (even though it may be a lesser of two evils substitute for unre

---

[27] Harvey Averch and Leland L. Johnson, "Behavior of the Firm under Regulatory Constraint," *American Economic Review* (December 1962), pp. 1052–69; Stanislaw H. Wellisz, "Regulation of Natural Gas Pipeline Companies: An Economic Analysis," *Journal of Political Economy* (February 1963), pp. 30–43.

[28] See L. L. Johnson's survey, "The Averch-Johnson Hypothesis after Ten Years," in *Regulation in Further Perspective*, edited by Shepherd and Gies (Cambridge, Mass.: Ballinger Publishing Co., 1974), pp.. 67–78; plus Charles W. Smithson, "The Degree of Regulation and the Monopoly Firm," *Southern Economic Journal* (January 1978), pp. 568–80; and Robert W. Spann, "Rate of Return Regulation," *Bell Journal of Economics* (Spring, 1974), pp. 38–52.

[29] Kahn, *op. cit.*, Vol. II, pp. 106–07.

[30] James W. McKie, "Regulation and the Free Market: The Problem of Boundaries," *Bell Journal of Economics* (Spring, 1970), pp. 6–26.

[31] Walter Adams, "Business Exemptions from the Antitrust Laws: Their Extent and Rationale," in *Perspectives on Antitrust Policy*, edited by A. Phillips (Princeton, N. J.: Princeton University Press, 1965), p. 283.

ulated natural monopoly). No one has expressed this sentiment better than Clair Wilcox:

> Regulation, at best, is a pallid substitute for competition. It cannot prescribe quality, force efficiency, or require innovation, because such action would invade the sphere of management. But when it leaves these matters to the discretion of industry, it denies consumers the protection that competition would afford. Regulation cannot set prices below an industry's costs however excessive they may be. Competition does so, and the high-cost company is compelled to discover means whereby its costs can be reduced. Regulation does not enlarge consumption by setting prices at the lowest level consistent with a fair return. Competition has this effect. Regulation fails to encourage performance in the public interest by offering rewards and penalties. Competition offers both.[32]

The proper and improper application of regulation may be seen in the starkly contrasting results of regulation's impact on prices that empiricists have uncovered. For electric power and telephone service, regulation seems to have pressed prices *lower* than they would otherwise be, perhaps by as much as -10%.[33] But notice, these markets fit the natural monopoly model fairly well. In contrast, empirical studies show exactly opposite results in transportation, where natural monopoly does *not* prevail and where competition has suffered the greatest official suppression through entry restriction and minimum price control. Regulation there has *raised* prices. Thomas Moore estimates that, as of the mid 1960s, ICC regulation of railroads, trucks, and water carriers cost the American public an astounding $4–$9 *billion* a year in higher rates. Shipping the ICC off to oblivion stamped "Do Not Return" would apparently reduce ground transportation rates by as much as *one third*.[34] Similar conclusions have been reached regarding airline regulation, based on the empirical work of Theodore Keeler and others. Over the period 1969–1974, CAB regulation is estimated to have inflated airfares by an average of 22–52%. In annual dollars, that amounted to between $1.4 and $1.8 *billion*.[35] The major causes of these exorbitant rates are various forms of X-inefficiency.

Lest the reader think that these rather shocking estimates are fabricated from thin air, or unnatural gas, he or she should recognize that some sectors of transportation have always escaped tight regulation, and the experience of these fairly competitive sectors guided the estimates. On the ground, agricultural trucking and private trucking are beyond the ICC's reach. In the air, travel within California and Texas cannot be controlled by the CAB. A comparison of *intra*state air fares and *inter*state regulated air fares in 1975 is shown

[32] Clair Wilcox, *Public Policies Toward Business* (Homewood, Ill.: Irwin 1966), pp. 476.
[33] William S. Comanor, "Should Natural Monopolies Be Regulated?" *Stanford Law Review* (February 1970), pp. 510–18; Kahn, *op. cit.*, Vol. II, pp. 108–11.
[34] Thomas G. Moore, "Deregulating Surface Freight Transportation," in *Promoting Competition in Regulated Markets*, edited by A. Phillips (Washington, D.C.: Brookings Institution, 1975), pp. 55–98.
[35] Theodore E. Keeler, "Airline Regulation and Market Performance," *Bell Journal of Economics* (Autumn, 1972), pp. 399–424; see also GAO Report CED–77–34, "Lower Airline Costs Per Passenger Are Possible In the United States Could Result in Lower Fares" (February 18, 1977).

TABLE 20-3 Comparison Between Inter-state and Intrastate Air Fares, 1975

City-Pair	Miles	Fare ($)
Los Angeles–San Francisco	338	18.75
Chicago–Minneapolis	339	38.89
New York–Pittsburgh	335	37.96
Los Angeles–San Diego	109	10.10
Portland–Seattle	129	22.22
Dallas–Houston	239	13.89*
Las Vegas–Los Angeles	236	28.70
Chicago–St. Louis	258	29.63

* This is the night and weekend rate. Day-time week-day rate was $23.15.

Source: *Civil Aeronautics Board Practices and Procedures,* Report of the Subcommittee on Administrative Practice and Procedure, U. S. Senate (1975), p. 41.

in Table 20-3. It does not take a pilot's eyes to see that, for routes of similar length and paired-city size, the *intra*state fares are substantially lower.

Fortunately, as this is written, there is a movement afoot (or a wing) to deregulate the airlines, led by unconventional CAB Chairman Alfred Kahn and Senator Ted Kennedy. Airlines have been given greater freedom to cut prices and select their routes. Early results indicate lower fares, but no drastic financial danger to the airlines because the lower fares have touched-off an explosion of air travel. Nevertheless, many airlines are squirming under the competitive pressure and squealing for continued regulatory protection. A blunt answer to the airlines' resistance is contained in a letter written by Kahn replying to protestations of doom put out by Continental Airlines. Kahn expressed doubts that Continental would suffer, but added, "if every other carrier ... will feast on Continental, does the public interest demand that we protect you?"[36] Other regulated industries that seem destined for future deregulation are trucking and field production of natural gas.[37]

Summary

Regulation governs major segments of energy, transportation, and communications, which account for about 7% of GNP. These industries tend to

[36] *Wall Street Journal,* May 9, 1978.
[37] There is no question concerning the competitive potential of trucking. However, the case of natural gas is controversial. See, e.g., the contrasting views of John W. Wilson and Norman B. Tur in *The Natural Gas Industry,* Part I, Hearings before the Subcommittee on Antitrust and Monopoly U. S. Senate (June 1973), pp. 353–393, 469–504.

e more capital intensive than others, some experiencing asset/sales ratios of
to 1. Moreover, they provide "vital" services, often reaching consumers
irectly through pipes, wires, and conduits.

Regulation is grounded on several rationales. Natural monopoly justifies
gulation of local electricity, water, gas, and telephone service, where economies
f scale seem to stretch the full range of demand. Resource conservation vindi-
tes some entry regulation of the air waves. These and other areas of regulation
ay also be based on fairness. Another rationale—destructive competition—
ovides a very weak peg on which to hang regulation, especially in transporta-
on, where it is most frequently invoked.

State and federal commissions with broad powers actually do the regulating.
heir procedures are legalistic and their personnel bureaucratic. Among the
any criticisms of commissions, the most commonly voiced are incompetence,
adequacy, and pro-utility bias. Although there may be some validity to these
arges, it should be acknowledged that the task of regulation is *inherently*
fficult.

Profit, or rate level, regulation focuses on the following equation: total
venue = operating expense + current depreciation + (capital value × rate
f return). Each element on the right hand side must be determined to reckon
e total revenue needed. The appraisal entails quantities of pure judgment
ecause there are no scientifically established "rights" and "wrongs." There
e certain principles, such as the need for a rate of return sufficient to attract
pital, but nothing definite. As for objectives, commissions pursue a "balancing
t," forever making compromises between the interests of investors and custo-
ers. Much the same could be said of rate structure regulation.

Probably the biggest problem with regulation is its potentially anticompetitive
fect. To repeat an earlier quote: "Regulation is like growing old: we would
ther not do it, but consider the alternative." Where *un*regulated natural
onopoly (or government ownership) is the alternative, this may be correct.
outhful death and unfettered monopoly are both undesirable. But where
mpetition is the alternative, it ought to be tried.

507

21

Inflation and Macroeconomic Stability: Theory and Evidence

What this country needs is a good five-cent nickel.

FRANKLIN P. ADAMS

Rapid inflation is bad. High unemployment is bad. These two bads rarely hit us at the same time (with a one-two punch). But when they do, as they did during the mid-1970s, the economy goes from bad to worse. The contribution market power makes to inflation and unemployment, whether they occur separately or together, is a subject of controversy. Some believe oligopolists and labor unions are innocent as new born lambs; others claim the two are venal as polecats. This entire chapter could be devoted to a blow-by-blow account of the controversy, but the approach would be confusing. Instead, a brief *synthesis* of views is offered, one that may give a false impression of the degree of agreement among economists, but one that should yield a good understanding of the issues.

Previous chapters have discussed the likelihood that market power will lead to higher and relatively more stable market prices than would be the case under competition.[1] The focus was on individual markets at the *micro*economic level. Thus we must begin this chapter by distinguishing between the issue of aggregate or *macro*-level inflation and unemployment on the one hand, and the issue of high and stable prices in *micro*-markets on the other. Next, we explore

---

[1] See Chapters 11, 12, and 13.

heoretically the inflation-unemployment relationship in terms of three major possible causes of inflation—demand-pull, market-power push, and exogenous hock. Finally, we review some empirical evidence on the roles these possible auses have played in recent economic events in the United States and, with ess emphasis, in other countries as well.

Deliniation of the Problem

Up to this point our analysis has focused on the structure, conduct, and erformance of *individual* markets for products and services. The questions ddressed have been of the following type: Why are cosmetics heavily advertised? Why is the auto industry highly concentrated? It was shown that roduct market power (as measured by concentration or barriers to entry) positively associated with relatively high and relatively stable prices. In abor markets, unionization is the means by which market power is attained, nd union wage rates tend to be both higher and cyclically more stable than onunion wage rates.[2]

Although it may seem that these micro-level findings have some direct and asy application to the question of macro-level inflation, they do not. The micro-evel findings relate to *relative* price and wage levels at a given point in time and elative price and wage changes over the business cycle—for example, the price f autos (under oligopoly) relative to the price of lumber (under atomistic ompetition), and the cyclical stability (up and down) of steel prices relative the cyclical stability of textile prices. In contrast, **inflation** is a macro issue; refers to increases in the *average* level of *all* prices and wages in the economy ver time, and for our purposes it may be defined as being a substantial increase a the consumer price index (CPI) or the wholesale price index (WPI) or overall age index. **Deflation** is the opposite—a decrease in the average level of prices nd wages.

To be sure, the overall average price level is derived from prices in individual aarkets. But to understand the possible contribution market power makes inflation, we must begin thinking in macroeconomic terms instead of micro-conomic ones. Our earlier analysis showed that, if an industry's structure hanges from pure competition to oligopoly or monopoly, the price of this

---

[2] For evidence relating to United States experience see H. G. Lewis, *Unionism and Relative Vages in the United States* (Chicago: University of Chicago Press, 1963); Daniel Hamermesh, Market Power and Wage Inflation," *Southern Economic Journal* (October 1972); and O. C. shenfelter, G. E. Johnson, and J. H. Pencavel, "Trade Unions and the Rate of Change of Money Vages in the United States Manufacturing Industry," *Review of Economic Studies* (January 1972). or evidence relating to British experience see J. H. Pencavel, "Relative Wages and Trade Unions the United Kingdom," *Economica* (May 1974); and R. L. Thomas, "Wage Inflation in the U. K. Multi-Market Approach," in *Inflation in Labor Markets*, edited by P. Laidler and D. Purdy Manchester, U.K.: Manchester University Press, 1974).

509

industry's product is likely to rise. Thus substantial *changes* in market structu toward greater concentration could be a source of inflationary changes prices.[3] But this is a purely microeconomic view of the possible contributic of market power. Its implications are quite limited. The static theory ar empirical evidence of earlier chapters gave no indication that prices wou rise *continually* under monopoly or oligopoly. That analysis applied sole to *relative* prices, and a monopolist's price should *not* rise continually relati to costs or relative to prices of other goods solely by virtue of the monopolis having market power. Moreover, if increased seller's control raises price in o market—that for autos, say—the overall *average* level of prices need not chan; because this increase may be offset by price reductions in other market particularly in those markets becoming more competitive. Indeed, over the pa three decades, there has been no clear cut trend toward greater concentratic in most individual product markets, so *changes* in market power cannot expla the substantial inflation we have experienced since World War II. Inste; of looking at the inflationary impact of changes in structure, we shall be co cerned here with the *mere existence* of market power in both product and lab markets.

The same limitations apply to the evidence cited earlier, that high mark concentration and unionism are associated with greater cyclical stability prices and wages. Contrary to appearances, these findings do not necessar imply that market power is irrelevant to inflation or that market power ten to reduce inflation. The extent to which a product's price moves up and dov with cyclical increases and decreases of demand gives no indication of tl *average* or *net* change in the product's price over the entire span of the busine cycle or over the span of numerous business cycles. The same is true of wa; rates.

Figure 21-1 illustrates this point as it applies to product prices. The horizont axis measures excess demand and supply, with quantity demand exceedi quantity supply to the right of the origin and supply exceeding demand to tl left. The vertical axis measures the *rate of change* in market price (positive negative change over 1 year's time), with the rate of change being a positi function of the extent to which demand exceeds supply. If line *CC* represer price behavior throughout the cycle under competitive conditions, and if li *MM* represents price behavior under oligopolistic conditions, prices will more flexible in the former case than in the latter—ranging between plus a minus 10% compared to plus and minus 4%, respectively. Still, the avera extent of change in both instances would be zero, indicating no net inflatio The only way inflation could occur under such circumstances would be f demand to exceed supply rather persistently in most industries, confining us average to the right of the origin. This describes **demand pull inflation**.

---

[3] For evidence to this effect with respect to wages and the spread of unionism see A. G. Hin "Trade Unions and Wage Inflation in the United Kingdom 1893–1961," *Review of Econor Studies* (October 1964).

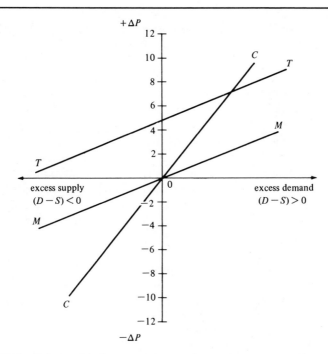

Figure 21-1. Relationship between excess demand, excess supply, and the rate of change in market prices.

Notice next that line TT has the same slope as MM, so that both TT and MM represent the same degree of price flexibility (or inflexibility). The intercept of TT is much greater than that of MM, however, indicating a positive rate of change in price *even in the absence of excess demand.* Thus if TT represented oligopolistic price behavior and CC represented competitive price behavior, market power would contribute substantially to inflation even though the oligopolist's prices were cyclically less flexible than those of competitive firms. This could be called **market power inflation**.

Testing for this type of inflation may look easy. Data on price changes and excess demand in oligopoly industries could be compared with similar data for competitive industries to see if the former industries displayed a TT pattern and the latter displayed a CC pattern. Unfortunately, the task is not so easy for several reasons. First, no wholly reliable measure of excess demand is available for product markets. Second, this test would not be a fair test of the market power hypothesis because a TT pattern versus a CC pattern would imply that, on average, prices in oligopoly and monopoly industries always and continuously rise *relative* to prices in competitive industries, even without structural change. However, as already noted, such a perpetually growing divergence in relative prices is highly unlikely and theoretically unjustifiable.

The only way market power can cause perpetual changes in *relative* price is to have perpetual *changes* in market power. Intermarket equilibrating force of supply and demand tend to erase any changes in relative prices (or changes i their rates of change) based solely on the (long standing) existence of marke power. Thus a fairer test would allow for the possibility that market powe contributes to inflation in such a way that no substantial divergence over tim is observed. If market power were to produce a *TT* pattern for oligopoly, and i these intermarket equilibrating forces were to shift the competitive *CC* lin upward to share the same average and the same intercept as the *TT* line, the market power would contribute to inflation without divergence over time Unfortunately, an empirical test for this form of contribution would be eve more difficult than the test considered earlier comparing *TT* and *CC* as the stand because factors *other* than market power may also cause prices in a industries to rise, on average and over time, even without excess aggregat demand.

Before we take up detailed consideration of these other inflationary force and their relation to market power inflation, we should first gain some familiarit with the **Phillips curve**, which depicts the relationship between inflation an unemployment.[4] Familiarity with the Phillips curve (named after its inventor will allow us to center attention on labor markets as opposed to produc markets, a focus that has the following advantages:

1. A good measure of excess demand in labor markets is both readily available and easily understandable—namely, the unemployment rate.
2. It can be argued that market power inflation is more likely to originate with wage inflation as opposed to product price inflation because labor's wage demands are governed by motives quite different from the profit maximizing motive of firms, which tends to limit discretionary increases in relative prices.
3. If market power inflation does indeed originate with wage changes, it should be more readily observable because, unlike most product prices, union wage rates change only intermittently at well-defined, contractually determined times.
4. There is high positive correlation between the extent of labor unionism within industries and the degree of product market concentration. Thus, evidence reflecting the wage impact of one of these measures of market power will not likely be contradicted by evidence concerning the other measure. Indeed it can be argued that a *combination* of product and labor market power confers the greatest degree of discretion over wage rates and is thereby most inflationary.

[4] A. W. Phillips, "The Relationship between Unemployment and the Rate of Change of Mone Wage Rates in the United Kingdom, 1861–1957," *Economica* (November 1958).

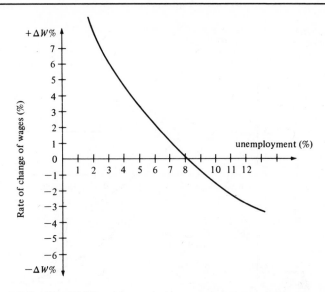

Figure 21-2. The Phillips curve relating unemployment and wage change.

In sum, the labor market is worthy of our attention, for it is there that market power inflation is most likely to arise and, if it does, most readily observable.

Assuming the aggregate rate of unemployment is a good overall index of excess demand or "labor shortage" in the labor market (it is impossible to depict all the individual markets simultaneously), the Phillips curve states that annual percentage rates of change in money wages are a negative, nonlinear function of unemployment. As shown in Figure 21-2, low levels of unemployment (indicating excess aggregate demand) are associated with high rates of wage inflation. The curve does not cross the vertical axis because the unemployment rate cannot be less than zero. Moreover, even with very high aggregate demand and rapidly rising wages, some workers will quit work and accept temporary unemployment while they seek better jobs. Conversely, at high levels of unemployment there is much involuntary unemployment and wages tend to be stable or declining slightly.

This wage-unemployment relationship is important to the issue of product *price* inflation because it can easily be converted into a similar relationship between prices and unemployment. In general, (1) price per unit of product increases in response to an increase in labor cost per unit; and (2) labor cost per unit is a function of the number of units that are produced by 1 man-hour (labor productivity) as well as the wage cost of 1 hour of work.

Specifically, the rate of change of prices, $\Delta P\%$, can be depicted as the difference between the rate of change of money wages, $\Delta W\%$, and the constant

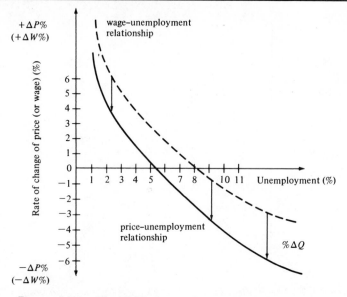

Figure 21-3. The Phillips curve for product price inflation.

trend rate of increase of man-hour productivity, $\Delta Q\%$, such that $\Delta P\% = \Delta W\% - \Delta Q\%$.

A simple example may help: If the hourly-wage of tee-shirt painters doubled from \$3.00 to \$6.00, the cost (and price) of painted tee-shirts need not also rise if a new application of stencils doubled the hourly output of each painter from 2 to 4 shirts per hour. Labor cost per tee-shirt both before and after is \$1.50 (\$3/2 and \$6/4). Thus, a Phillips curve for price change is obtained merely by relabeling the vertical axis of Figure 21-2 to indicate annual percentage rate of change of prices instead of wages, and by shifting the curve of Figure 21-2 downward a few percentage points to account for productivity growth.

These adjustments are made in Figure 21-3, where annual productivity growth is assumed to be 3%, an amount slightly above United States experience over the past 25 years. In this illustration wages can increase at an annual rate of 3% without causing any increase in the overall level of product prices. At rates of wage increase greater than 3% per year, wages tend to "push up" prices. Whether such inflationary rates of wage increase can be attributed to excess demand in labor and product markets (demand-pull), or to the mere exercise of market power on the part of firms and labor unions (market-power push) is an issue that will be explored later. At this point it is important to recognize the two-way causal relationship between price inflation and wage inflation. (1) Wage increases, via their effect on suppliers' cost of production, can cause prices to increase. (2) Product price increases, via their effect on consumers' (workers') cost of living, can cause wages to increase.

One final preliminary step is necessary before discussing causality further. We need to distinguish three different forms of wage-price increase:

1. A once-and-for-all or "one-shot" aggregate increase.
2. Secular inflation, a roughly constant rate of increase over time.
3. Accelerating inflation, with prices and wages increasing at an ever increasing rate.

Each of these is conceptually distinct. Moreover, each is functionally independent: one-shot inflation does not inevitably produce secular inflation, and secular inflation does not inevitably produce accelerating inflation. Under certain circumstances, however, progression up the scale of severity is possible.

The Principal Causes of Inflation

For our purposes, three possible causes of inflation may be considered important: (A) demand-pull or money supply, (B) market-power push or cost-push, and (C) exogenous shock. These are deep, abstract theories, so to avoid drowning we had better begin with a simple wading-pool example. Suppose it is hot. A child's pleasure from a wading pool will depend on three things—the size of the pool, the level of the water in it, and the behavior of the other children in it. If water overflow is thought of as inflation, and low water is equated with unemployment, then: (A) Running water into the pool continually will prevent low water (unemployment) but cause overflow (inflation)—unless the pool expands over time or the water evaporates or something else happens to accommodate the influx. This is analogous to the demand-pull or money supply model if money is thought of as water and pool size is thought of as real income. (B) Next, imagine that a gang of quarrelsome "big kids" occupies the pool instead of a few docile toddlers. As these louts fight over space and splash about, water will overflow (inflation) unless the hose is withdrawn, allowing the water level to fall (unemployment). The situation is analogous to the market-power cost-push model, if the demands of the "big kids" are likened to the money-wage demands of unionized labor or the money-profit demands of powerful oligopolists. (C) Overflow (inflation) would also occur if the pool suddenly shrank or the lip of one edge were bent down or some similar catastrophe hit. These possibilities are analogous to exogenous shock inflation if the size and strength of the pool are thought of as "real" income. Notice for later application that an enlarged pool permits more water and more splashing without overflow.) Now that our toes are wet, we are ready for technical discussions of causes A, B, and C.

515

Cause A: A Growth in the Money Supply
that Exceeds Growth in Real Income

In short, this is the "monetarist" view of inflation,[5] and there is much validit to it. This view can be captured in a single equation:

$$M \cdot V = P \cdot Y \qquad (21-1$$

where M = money supply (a dollar stock value comprised of currency, demanc deposits in banks, and savings deposits)

V = average income velocity (the number of times money suppl: circulates per year)

P = average price level

Y = real output or income (the aggregate annual quantity flow o goods and services)

Since $\Delta(P \cdot Y)$ is approximated by $Y \cdot \Delta P + P \cdot \Delta Y$, which becomes $\Delta P/P + \Delta Y/Y$ if divided by $P \cdot Y$, equation (21-1) can easily be transformed into annua percentage rates of change:

$$\Delta M \% + \Delta V \% = \Delta P \% + \Delta Y \% \qquad (21-2$$

To simplify matters we assume, not too unrealistically, that $\Delta V \%$ is zero in th long run and that growth in real income $\Delta Y \%$ is determined by long-ru growth of productivity and labor force size (or population). It follows, then that, if $\Delta M \%$ is set by the monetary authorities to equal $\Delta Y \%$, average pric change $\Delta P \%$ would be zero. On the other hand, if the growth rate of nomina money stock accelerates in excess of the growth rate of real income, acceleratin inflation ensues. Correspondingly, if the growth rate of money persistentl: exceeds the growth rate of real income by some constant amount, secula inflation ensues. With $\Delta M \% = 9 \%$ and $\Delta Y \% = 4 \%$, for example, $\Delta P \%$ would be 5%, which is $9 \% - 4 \%$. Finally, this theory predicts that a one-sho inflation would result from an appropriate combination of short-run monetar: overflow and underflow relative to $\Delta Y \%$.

According to the monetarists, secular and accelerating inflation cannot b illustrated by the single Phillips curves of Figures 21-2 and 21-3 because eac! such negatively sloped curve depicts only a single *short-run* relationship betweer inflation and unemployment. To develop the monetarists' *long-run* view o the Phillips relation three new concepts are necessary:

1. First, we must distinguish between **money wages**, which are simply dollar and cents wages, and **real wages**, which are money wages translated into

[5] See for instance Milton Friedman, "The Role of Monetary Policy," *American Economi Review* (March 1968); and John T. Boorman and Thomas M. Havrilesky, *Money Supply, Mone: Demand, and Macroeconomic Models* (Boston: Allyn and Bacon, 1972), Chapter 5.

the real goods and services that they can buy—that is, money wages relative to consumer goods prices. Monetarists hold that workers think and act in terms of their real wages, not their money wages. In other words, if overnight all prices and all incomes double in nominal money terms, and all other money values double, people will *not* feel better or worse off than before. They do not suffer "money illusion."

2. Second, people's **expectations** must be taken into account. If prices have been going up 5 % every year for the past 10 years, they will logically expect them to go up 5 % next year as well. And in light of point 1, they will adjust their money wage demands upward accordingly.

3. Third, there is a **natural rate** of unemployment that coincides with a condition of aggregate economic equilibrium, implying an absence of either excess demand or excess supply at the aggregate level. This natural rate is determined by such "real" factors as worker mobility, labor market information, and institutional conditions.

If we assume a condition of pure competition all round, application of these three concepts yields numerous short-run Phillips curves stacked vertically above the natural rate of unemployment, each one of which is associated with a different rate of *expected* price inflation. Put differently, the short-run Phillips curve shifts up or down with price expectations. This family of curves is depicted in Figure 21-4.

Assume initially that the economy is at point A, with unemployment at the natural rate and no actual or expected inflation. The monetary authorities could increase money supply ($\uparrow \Delta M \%$) and consequently cause price inflation ($\uparrow \Delta P \%$), but, because in the *short run* money wages would be set under expectations of zero price change, real wages would fall. As real wages fall, businesses would hire more workers because they are cheaper, reducing unemployment to point B in Figure 21-4 and boosting real output ($\uparrow \Delta Y \%$), both of which are beneficial. However, money supply is now growing more rapidly than before, and this increase in the *rate* of increase ($\uparrow \Delta M \%$) cannot keep unemployment below the natural rate of unemployment over the *long run* because the 3 % inflation experienced at point B will eventually modify expectations, causing a shift to point C, which coincides with a new Phillips curve that embodies expectations of 3 % price *and* wage inflation. With real wages returned to normal, the natural rate of unemployment prevails, and real income returns to its exogenously determined long-run growth rate ($\downarrow \Delta Y \%$).

One major conclusion to be derived here is that inflation at point C is sustained by expectations, even in the absence of excess aggregate demand: workers and firms continue to raise their own wages and prices without injuring their competitiveness because their competitors are raising their wages and prices too. This situation corresponds to an important earlier observation concerning Figure 21-1—namely, lines MM and CC in that diagram can both shift upward in response to forces other than a market-power push led by MM. A second major conclusion is that continued unemployment below the

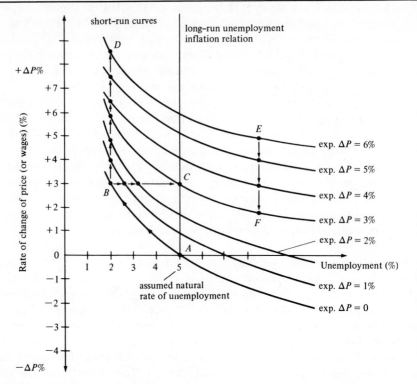

Figure 21-4. *Short-run Phillips curves relative to the long-run natural rate curve*

"natural" level cannot be gained by engineering a given, steady state (secular rate of inflation. It can only be gained by accelerating inflation. Point B in Figure 21-4 was attained only by having actual inflation (3%) exceed expected inflation (0%). As expectations rise to 1%, 2%, 3%, and so on, the actual rate of inflation must accelerate ahead at 4%, 5%, 6%, and so on, if unemployment is to be held at B level. This moves the economy toward point D.

The reverse holds true on the down side. Deflation ($\downarrow\Delta P\%$) will follow a substantial drop in the growth of money supply ($\downarrow\Delta M\%$), as indicated by a movement from point D to point E in Figure 21-4, but only at the expense of greater unemployment, which, if sustained, will lead to still further deflation as illustrated by movement from E to F. Eventually, we could return to point A by bringing actual inflation down to zero and holding the rate there until expectations caught up.

Finally, the most important conclusion to be drawn here is that "full employment" (that is, zero excess aggregate demand) may be defined in terms of this Cause A and the "natural rate." At **full-employment**, the *rate of change* of price is constant, though perhaps positive (that is, 5% year-in and year-out).

Full-employment is that level of employment yielding neither acceleration nor deceleration of prices in *direct* response to variations in the money supply. The qualifying word "direct" indicates an assumed "neutrality" or "passivity" in the other possible causes of inflation, a state that can be fully understood only after we have discussed these other causes.

Cause B: The Exercise of Labor and Product Market Power

In major segments of the economy both labor and management possess enough market power to exercise discretionary control over wages and prices, at least in the short run. This ability to control was shown in previous chapters. Whether or not this market power results in inflation depends on how it is exercised and the nature of the monetary policy accompanying its exercise. It does not necessarily depend on changes in market power.

This feature of market power may be seen by modifying equation (21-1).[6] Broken down into components of national income, price is

$$P = k \cdot W \cdot E \tag{21-3}$$

where P = average price

W = average wage and salary per man-year

E = man-year input per unit of output, that is, the inverse of labor productivity

k = mark-up of prices over unit labor costs $(W \cdot E)$ to cover profits, rents, and interest, for example $k = 1.20$.

Substituting this expression for P into equation (21-1) yields

$$M \cdot V = k \cdot W \cdot E \cdot Y \tag{21-4}$$

which in terms of annual percentage change is

$$\Delta M\% + \Delta V\% = \Delta k \cdot W\% + \Delta E\% + \Delta Y\% \tag{21-5}$$

If we assume $\Delta V\%$ is zero and k is constant (in the absence of structural change) this further reduces to

$$\Delta M\% = \Delta W\% + \Delta E\% + \Delta Y\% \tag{21-6}$$

Note that $\Delta E\%$ will normally be negative because labor requirements per unit of output fall as productivity rises over time. Thus wages can increase $(+\Delta W\%)$

---

[6] This formulation is derived from Sidney Weintraub, "Incomes Policy: Completing the Stabilization Triangle," *Journal of Economic Issues* (December 1972).

at a rate matching that of productivity growth $(-\Delta E\%)$ without increasing prices $(\Delta P\% = 0)$, and full employment (as embodied in $\Delta Y\%$) may be maintained by equating $\Delta M\%$ and $\Delta Y\%$ as before. If however $+\Delta W\%$ *exceeds* $-\Delta E\%$, then $\Delta Y\%$ and employment can be maintained only if $\Delta M\%$ exceeds $\Delta Y\%$ by a similar amount, implying inflation.

One-Shot Inflation. A one-shot market-power inflation would result from the following sequence of events. First, monetary policy is aimed at maintaining full-employment as defined previously. Second, unionized labor attempts to gain a once-and-for-all increase in its long-run share of real income by accelerating its wage level to a growth rate that exceeds average productivity growth. The attempt, however, is eventually thwarted by a commensurate rise in the rate of change of all other prices and wages (a change attributable to **spill-overs** or the long-run intermarket equilibrating forces that restore all preexisting *relative* wages and prices, or their rates of change, in the absence of any significant changes in market power). And third, the unionized sector then abandons its attempt by *decelerating* its wage claims to a rate of increase again matching average productivity growth, whereupon this reverse movement in the rate of increase is followed commensurately in all other sectors.

A numerical example of this one-shot market power inflation is presented in Table 21-1, in which it is assumed for simplicity that the unionized or monopolized sector accounts for 50% of all wages and prices $(0.5 \cdot k \cdot W \cdot E)$; that the competitive sector's prices and wages are set over the course of each time period according to events during the preceding period; and that productivity growth is zero throughout. In period 1, wages in the unionized sector jump to a 10% rate of increase, causing aggregate inflation of 5%. In subsequent periods the competitive sector adjusts under the influence of two factors: (1) the drive to regain real wages lost by aggregate price increases (as in the monetarist model), and (2) spill-over, the forces that tend to return *relative* wages and prices to initial levels. By assumption, the 10% spill-over effect is made up entirely in period 2, but the influence of the aggregate price level is spread over numerous periods due to lagged adjustment. By period 10, all prices and wages are rising at a 10% rate. Thereafter, the sequence of percentage increases is reversed. By period 20, this reversal yields no change in relative prices or wages or real income shares, but this process has resulted in a one-shot increase in all money values of 157.3% (see the index numbers), which remains even after the process has ended.

Secular Inflation. It should be clear from the foregoing that secular rather than one-shot inflation would result if the same "passive" monetary policy were followed (keyed to maintenance of full-employment) and a similarly frustrated attempt were made by the union sector to raise its long-run share of real income, *but no voluntary discretionary deceleration occurred after the attempt was abandoned.* The secular inflation process would leave the *rate of change* of money wages and prices at a new and higher level. In Table 21-1, this movement

TABLE 21-1   Illustration of an Attempt to Enhance Share of Real Income that is Unsuccessful in the Long-Run but Inflationary

Time Period	Union Sector Wage		All Other Wages and Prices		Overall Price Level	
	Change (%)	Index	Change (%)	Index	Change (%)	Index
0	0	100	0	100	0	100
1	10	110	0	100	5	105
2	10	121	10 + 5	115	12.5	118
3	10	132.1	12.5	129.4	11.2	130.7
4	10	145.3	11.2	143.9	10.6	144.6
5	10	159.8	10.6	159.2	10.3	159.5
⋮	⋮	⋮	⋮	⋮	⋮	⋮
⋮	⋮	⋮	⋮	⋮	⋮	⋮
10	10	257.3	10.0	257.3	10.0	257.3
11	0	257.3	10.0	283.1	5.0	270.2
12	0	257.3	−10 + 5	268.9	−2.5	263.1
13	0	257.3	−2.5	262.2	−1.2	259.8
14	0	257.3	−1.2	258.9	−0.6	258.1
⋮	⋮	⋮	⋮	⋮	⋮	⋮
⋮	⋮	⋮	⋮	⋮	⋮	⋮
20	0	257.3	0	257.3	0	257.3

is illustrated by events between periods 0 and 10, but the period 10 situation would then be *perpetuated*, with all money values rising at 10% per period.

Thus, the secular inflation process results in (1) *a short-run* transfer of real income from the competitive sector to the monopolistic sector (for example, the index *levels* of period 2 are 121 versus 115), (2) an increase in the rate of change of all money values, (3) no *long-run* change in relative prices, wages, or income shares, (4) no change in employment, and (5) no further progression to accelerating inflation. Notice that all the basic components of the monetarists' model are retained here. The only concepts that have been added are short-run discretionary power, the long-run constancy of relative wages and prices in the absence of structural change, and spill-overs of rates of change from the monopolistic to the competitive sectors—a consequence of this tendency toward constant relative wages and prices.

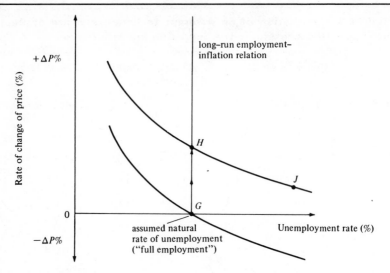

Figure 21-5. *Market-power inflation with monetary policy geared to maintenance of "full employment."*

In Phillips curves, this kind of secular inflation is illustrated by a single upward shift of the short-run Phillips relation at the natural rate of unemployment, as shown by a movement from point *G* to point *H* in Figure 21-5 (corresponding to a combined upward shift of *MM* and *CC* in Figure 21-1, led by *MM*). Progression to accelerating inflation (continuing above point *H*) would result from *persistently* repeated attempts by the monopolistic decision makers to raise their real income share while monetary policy was pegged to the maintenance of full-employment and intermarket equilibrating forces prevented the radical changes in relative prices and wages necessary to reward these efforts.

Labor's Motives. It should be stressed that these Cause B inflations are not due to a growth in market power over time. The mere existence of substantial market power *enables* (and rational behavior encourages) a short-run reach for greater real-income share even in the absence of the structural alterations that would in fact permit the long-run realization of this goal. Among the many *motives* that might translate this ability into action, the following are probably most important in labor's behavior:

1. In contrast to the once-and-for-all attainment of a "monopoly wage" that might be suggested by static theory, unions may strive to maximize their *annual* rate of wage *increase*.[7]

[7] Gottfried Haberler, *Incomes Policies and Inflation* (Washington, D.C.: American Enterprice Institute, 1971), p. 14.

2. They may also strive to enhance interindustry wage inequality.
3. In industries experiencing above average productivity growth, unions will press for money wage increases that also exceed average productivity growth rather than press for product price reductions because the higher wages are of immediate, tangible, and measurable benefit to their members and provide the basis for union-leader reelection.[8]

Empirical research has shown that this type of inflation proceeds without a perpetually growing disparity of money wage rates and income shares between union and nonunion sectors—without, that is, any substantial structural alterations over time.[9] Some evidence even suggests that the general wage level rises faster in countries where wages in different sectors move more closely together and where there is relatively little interindustry dispersal of wage growth rates.[10]

Role of Product Market Power. The role of product market power in this wage-push inflation could be substantial because union motives are likely to be most effectively expressed in highly concentrated industries with barriers to new (nonunion) firm entry.[11] The higher profits of such industries provide a "target" for unions to "shoot at." Moreover, firms in these industries may be less resistant than competitive firms to union demands because (1) they can more easily raise prices, (2) they may want to maintain labor queues in anticipation of fluctuations in production, and (3) they may gain some prestige from paying premium wages. Under these circumstances, product market power would have an indirect inflationary effect through wages. It is also conceivable that some "profit inflation" may occasionally occur among oligopolists with consequences similar to those outlined above for union wage inflation. In equations (21-4) and (21-5), profit inflation would involve an increase in business mark-up over labor cost, k, that is eventually eliminated in the long run by the equilibrating effect of spill-overs.

Role of Money Adjustments. It must also be stressed that these Cause B inflations need validation by passive, full-employment monetary adjustments.

[8] Alfred Kuhn, "Market Structures and Wage-Push Inflation," *Industrial and Labor Relations Review* (January 1959). See also Thomas Wilson, *Inflation* (Cambridge, Mass.: Harvard University Press, 1961), Chapter XV.

[9] Douglas Greer, "Market Power and Wage Inflation," *Southern Economic Journal* (January 1975).

[10] H. A. Turner and D. A. S. Jackson, "On the Determination of the General Wage Level—A World Analysis; or 'Unlimited Labor Forever,'" *Economic Journal* (December 1970).

[11] James R. Schlesinger, "Market Structure, Union Power and Inflation," *Southern Economic Journal* (January 1958); Martin Segal, "The Relation Between Union Wage Impact and Market Structure," *Quarterly Journal of Economics* (February 1964); Harold M. Levinson, *Determining Forces in Collective Bargaining* (New York: John Wiley & Sons, 1966), Chapter 6; George de Menil, *Bargaining: Monopoly Power versus Union Power* (Cambridge, Mass.: MIT Press, 1971).

Strict monetary restraint could probably nullify these inflations, but only by generating sufficient unemployment to negate the inflationary bias at the aggregate level, as indicated by a movement from point H to point J in Figure 21-5. To stem secular and accelerating inflations attributable to Cause B, monetary restraint could mean higher unemployment in the long run. For, only if there was a voluntary discretionary deceleration by the monopolistic sectors, with a short-run transfer of real income share from the monopolistic sector to the competitive sector (like that occurring over time periods 10 through 20 in Table 21-1), would monetary stringency alone be able to curtail these inflations with only a temporary loss of employment and output.

At this point we can explain the phrase **neutrality** or **passivity** in the other possible causes of inflation that was used to qualify our Cause A monetarist discussion. Just as we here had to assume passivity on the part of official money supply managers in order to describe the process by which market power caused inflation, so too we had to assume passivity on the part of monopolistic powers in order to develop the purely "monetarist" model of inflation and deflation, although this assumption was not explicitly discussed for the monetary theory. It should now be clear that passivity of private market power means either an absence of such power or a willingness on the part of those possessing such power to behave as if they do not have it. Those possessing power over wages and prices use it passively if they vary prices and wages only and precisely to achieve a full, "natural-competitive" level of unemployment. This behavior would emulate purely competitive behavior. The extent to which passivity is actually practiced by those with market power or the official monetary authority (in the United States this is the Board of Governors of the Federal Reserve System) is an *empirical* issue, and it will be discussed at length later. Still, a few preliminary comments are appropriate here.

Given the elementary background knowledge provided so far, we can hypothesize *asymmetry* in applications of the passivity assumption. Monopolistic sectors will probably be passive to money supply *inflation* but not pliably passive to money supply *deflation* since in the latter case the monopolistic sector would suffer a temporary but perhaps sizable loss of real income to the competitive sector. Failure of the monopolistic sector to "permit" or "endorse" this deflation passively would increase unemployment. Contrarywise, monetary officials will probably be passive to monopolistic *deflation* (which deflation is unlikely in practice but possible in principle), though not pliably passive to monopolistic *inflation*, particularly an accelerating inflation. Failure of the monetary authority to "permit" or "endorse" this inflation passively would increase unemployment.

The monetary authority, therefore, does *not* have simultaneous control over both the wage-price level *and* employment, and neither does the monopolistic sector.[12] Either power center can play the passive role by bending all its efforts

---

[12] See M. W. Reder, "The Theoretical Problems of a National Wage Price Policy," *Canadian Journal of Economics and Political Science* (February 1948).

to the task of maintaining the "natural rate" of employment, but in so doing it relinquishes control over the wage-price level to the other power center. Since both centers seek to exercise at least some power over prices-wages, even though this can only be partial power, each intentionally abandons the full-employment objective whenever it wants to assert itself actively. In light of this fact, and in light of the asymmetry just mentioned, simultaneous passivity is rather unlikely. Simultaneous activity in opposite directions (Cause B inflation, Cause A deflation) can and apparently does occur, resulting in high "unnatural" unemployment coupled occasionally with inflation. But more often an active-passive seesaw prevails, one that generates unstable, negatively sloped *short-run* Phillips curves that overlap an L-shaped *long-run* Phillips curve (which is vertical at a low "natural rate" of unemployment and horizontal, at least at zero inflation, over a moderately high range of unemployment above that).[13] Finally, because deflationary activity by monopolists is a remote possibility in the event of active money supply inflation, monetarist inflations can easily become "runaway" inflations, and historically almost all "runaway" inflations are attributable to "runaway" monetary growth.

Cause C: Exogenous Shocks

Exogenous shocks (that is, changes in $\Delta Y \%$ outside the control of domestic decision makers, official or otherwise) can cause one-shot, secular, or accelerating inflation, depending on whether they are temporary, permanent and stable, or of increasing intensity. Assuming passivity among other possible causes, we can illustrate this point with a timely example.[14]

Suppose that wages are rising at the same rate as average productivity advance and there is full-employment. Next, suppose this pleasant situation is disrupted when a powerful foreign oil cartel (like the Organization of Petroleum Exporting Countries) raises the price of crude oil from $3 to $12 per barrel. An aggregate increase in the domestic transactions demand for nominal money and a loss of real domestic income ensue. Both results may be either temporary or permanent. It is a temporary loss of real income if, first, oil prices shortly thereafter fall back to $3 while all other prices and wages remain unchanged, or, second, if the price of oil remains at $12 and all other prices and wages also rise fourfold to restore all former levels of *relativity*. The first temporary case amounts to an inflation-deflation attributable to Cause C, with only a temporary increment in money demand, and it suggests a definition of "passivity" in the context of Cause C. **Passivity** in this case requires an absence of such exogenous shocks (that is, constant productivity growth), compensatory positive-negative shocks, or, with respect to an "open" economy, variations in rates of currency

---

[13] Otto Eckstein and R. Brinner, *The Inflationary Process in the United States*, U. S. Congress, Joint Economic Committee Study, Washington, D.C., 1972.

[14] For detailed discussion of this example see J. L. Pierce and J. J. Enzler, "The Effects of External Inflationary Shocks," *Brookings Papers on Economic Activity*, No. 1 (1974).

exchange designed to assure a balance of international accounts—that is, floating exchange rates.[15]

In the second temporary case, where all other prices and wages rise fourfold, we have one-shot inflation with a permanent increment in money demand. But this situation can arise only if passivity does *not* hold in at least one of the other two causes. With Cause A (money) passive but B (monopoly power) not, the microsectors possessing discretionary power will cast aside considerations of full-employment and strive to regain their lost real income by raising wages-prices while the monetary authority strives to maintain full-employment by expanding the money supply. Conversely, with B passive but A not, the roles are reversed and the short-run adjustment process has unemployment falling below rather than rising above the "natural" rate of full-employment, but the result is the same. Thus Causes A or B can convert a "neutral" exogenous shock into one-shot inflation.

If the shock is not temporary and the loss of real income is permanent, Cause C exogenous shock then produces one-shot inflation even when passivity prevails elsewhere. For example, the monetary authority could try to suppress this inflation by curtailing the money supply, but this action would violate passivity because it would raise unemployment in the course of restoring the old aggregate price level, and it would not regain the lost real income. More important for present purposes is the likely action of those possessing market power. In violation of their passivity, domestic monopolistic elements may attempt to restore their real income by boosting their prices and wages (to cover the higher costs of oil), but this too would not regain the lost real income. Assuming passive money supply, this effort would only cause progression to secular inflation and, if the monopolistic parties involved have widespread power and act quickly, it could even cause progression to accelerating inflation.

Because the shock is assumed to be *permanent*, the oil cartel will maintain its receipts in real terms; hence, once the new relative price ratios are established in its favor, the ratios will be maintained by a rate of *further* oil price inflation matching the discretionary "recoupment" inflation of the domestic price-wage setters. We are then on an escalating merry-go-round. Only a fairly long lag pattern would prevent the secular inflation from progressing to accelerating inflation under these conditions. Efforts on the part of the monetary authority to stifle these inflations would most likely result in perpetual and "unnatural" unemployment because passivity does not hold for either Cause B or Cause C in this instance. Both Causes B and C are working to increase prices and wages rather than maintain full-employment.

In brief, the problem of exogenous shock is analogous to the problem of flooded farm land or technological stagnation. If it is temporary and passivity holds for the other causes, the lost real income is temporary and the shock is

---

[15] For a good explanation of this last point, see T. J. Courchene, "Stabilization Policy: A Monetarist Interpretation," in *Issues in Canadian Economics*, edited by L. H. Officer and L. B. Smith (Toronto: McGraw-Hill Ryerson, 1974).

"neutral." If it is permanent to the extent, say, of half our farm land sliding into the sea, or half our productivity growth suddenly disappearing, then the lost real income is a *permanent* loss, and inflations of varying degrees of severity are likely to ensue as people fight for greater shares of a smaller national real income.

Other Possible Causes and a Qualification

Numerous other causes of inflation could be identified, but for present purposes they can either be subsumed under one of the preceding causes or merely acknowledged as potential qualifications to certain aspects of the analysis. Deficit spending at the federal level, for example, is often mentioned as a cause of inflation, but it is not fully distinct from Cause A.[16] Variations in the velocity of money ($\Delta V\%$) can also be considered a cause of inflation, but these too can be subsumed under Cause A. Empirically, velocity inflations seem to be rare and unimportant.[17]

In reality, the operations of Causes A through C are neither as simple nor as direct as our outline suggests because numerous factors may increase or abate their influence. Most of the necessary qualifications are beyond our scope, but one qualification is particularly worthy of mention. A major assumption of our Cause B (monopolistic) discussion is that prices of goods, services, productive factors, and assets outside the monopolistic sectors are all flexible enough over the long run to move in step with prices inside the monopolistic sectors (provided structural change is absent). However, such flexibility does not prevail universally. Many prices and rates of remuneration are inflexibly fixed by long-term contract, regulation, or legislation. To the extent inflexibility applies (and historically its importance seems to be lessening), variations in aggregate inflation and unemployment will be attenuated.

The Evidence Concerning Causes

In theory, the three causes of inflation appear to be quite different. In practice, however, we encounter numerous difficulties when we try to attribute any specific real-world inflation to one of these three causes. The trick is to determine the *unique earmarks* of each cause, and then look for them in instances of inflation. Earmarks that may be associated with more than one cause don't help much, yet most earmarks isolated so far seem to have this failing. For

---

[16] Abba Lerner, *Flation* (Baltimore: Penguin Books, 1972), p. 33.

[17] Phillip Cagen, "The Monetary Dynamics of Hyperinflation," in *Studies in the Quantity Theory of Money*, edited by Milton Friedman (Chicago: University of Chicago Press, 1956); Tibor Scitovsky and Anne Scitovsky, "Inflation versus Unemployment: An Examination of their Effects," in *Inflation Growth and Employment*, Commission on Money and Credit (Englewood Cliffs, N. J.: Prentice-Hall, 1964).

527

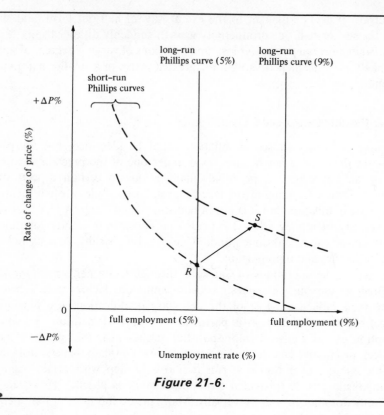

Figure 21-6.

example, if wages were rising more rapidly than productivity during some inflation, one might be tempted to conclude that "market-power push" by unions in concentrated industries was the cause. However, this pattern is also symptomatic of money-supply and exogenous shock inflations; money wages almost always rise with inflated prices.

Another example is illustrated in Figure 21-6. Believers in market-power inflation often claim that rising rates of price increase coupled with rising unemployment, as indicated by the movement from *R* to *S* in that diagram, can only be attributed to market-power push (Cause B). But the validity of this attribution depends on what constitutes full-employment. A monetarist could claim that the *R* to *S* movement is compatible with Cause A, given a true full-employment level of 9% instead of 5% (see Figure 21-6). Indeed, even if 5% were the true full-employment level (ruling out Cause A), this *R* to *S* movement might be due to Cause C (exogenous shock) rather than Cause B.

None of the evidence presented in the following subsections is completely free of this identification problem, and in some instances the doubts will be acknowledged explicitly. Unfortunately, space limitations prevent "full disclosure" in each and every instance.

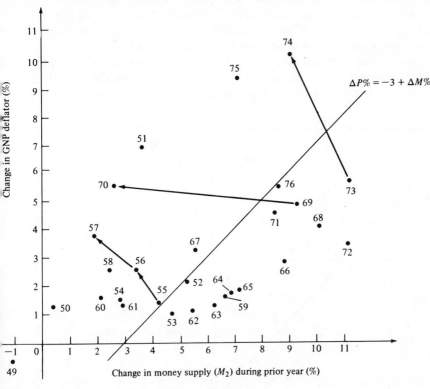

Figure 21-7. U.S. price changes and money supply changes, 1949–1976.
Source: Economic Report of the President, *1977.*

Cause A Inflation: What to Look for?
What's Been Found?

The most obvious way to test the monetarist theory, that is, the effect of money supply, is to check the relationship between changes in money supply and changes in aggregate price level. This has been done repeatedly and variously by numerous investigators using data from many diverse time periods and many different countries. And the answer is almost always the same— prices and money supply do indeed move closely together, especially in the long run.[18] United States experience in this respect between 1949 and 1976 is plotted in Figure 21-7, where the vertical axis measures percentage price change

[18] To list but a few examples, see Anna Schwartz, "Secular Price Change in Historical Perspective," *Journal of Money Credit and Banking* (February 1973), Part II; P. Cagan, *Determinants and Effects of Change in the Stock of Money, 1875–1960* (New York: National Bureau of Economic Research, 1965); R. C. Vogel "The Dynamics of Inflation in Latin America," *American Economic Review* (March 1974).

for each year and the horizontal axis measures percentage change in money supply during the preceding year. A positive line depicting the relation $\Delta P\% = -3 + \Delta M\%$ is included, highlighting the positive association between these variables. (The negative lines are discussed later.)

Since excess demand also plays a key role in monetarist theory, changes of money supply should be negatively associated with unemployment. Recent United States experience in this respect is plotted in Figure 21-8. A rough

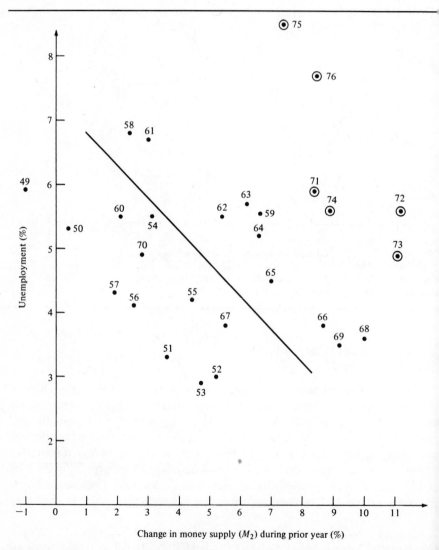

Figure 21-8. *U.S. unemployment and money supply changes, 1946–1976.* Source: Economic Report of the President, *1977.*

negative relationship emerges there, especially if the circled observations of the early 1970s are ignored.

Although these findings support monetarist theory, they do *not* provide ironclad evidence that *all* inflations *originate* from Cause A. Many inflations can be directly attributed to excessive monetary expansion, but other inflations appear to be initiated by Causes B or C, only later to be "permitted" or "endorsed" by passive monetary action designed to maintain full-employment (or prevent excessive unemployment). A further and more rigorous test of whether all inflations are directly attributable to monetary expansions of Cause A, one that acknowledges this lead-lag problem, rests on the observed value of a_3 in the following simplified depiction of the Phillips relation for aggregate wage change:

$$\Delta W\%_{ot} = a_1 + a_2 1/U_t + a_3 \Delta P\%_{ot-1} \qquad (21\text{-}7)$$

Where $\Delta W\%_{ot}$ = percentage change in wage level during year t
$1/U_t$ = the inverse of the unemployment rate during year t
$\Delta P\%_{ot-1}$ = percentage change in price level during the *prior* year

This is merely an algebraic expression for a family of Phillips curves, such as shown earlier in Figure 21-4, that illustrate monetarist theory. If the coefficient a_3 has a value of 1, the short-run negatively sloped Phillips curve shifts up or down to the full extent (one-for-one) that overall prices change up or down. Thus a value of 1 for a_3 tends to indicate Cause A at work. On the other hand, a value of a_3 substantially less than 1, say 0.5, would be observed if wages in monopolistic sectors rose (they almost never fall) *before* the rise in overall price level, a timing implying Cause B.[19]

In fact, statistical estimates of a_3 vary greatly across countries and within countries over different time periods. As regards foreign countries, for example, estimates of a_3 (or its equivalent) are close to or slightly greater than 1 for Austria, Belgium, France, and Italy based on inflation data from the 1950s and early 1960s.[20] Working independently of these estimates and using other criteria, an international team of experts studying European events during this period concluded that these four countries had experienced excess-demand monetary inflation (Cause A).[21] In contrast, estimates of a_3 for England,

---

[19] Despite appearances, a value of a_3 less than 1 for aggregate data does not necessarily imply the presence of money illusion. Still, money illusion could have such an effect, so this test is not airtight.

[20] R. G. Bodkin, *et. al.*, *Price Stability and High Employment: The Options for Canadian Economic Policy*, Economic Council of Canada (Ottawa: Queens Printer, 1967); R. J. Flanagan, "The U. S. Phillips Curve and International Unemployment Rate Differentials," *American Economic Review* (March 1973); Economic Commission for Europe, *Incomes in Postwar Europe: A Study of Policies Growth and Distribution*, United Nations, 1967 (Sales No. 66 II.E.14); L. Ulman and R. Flanagan, *Wage Restraint: A Study of Income Policies in Western Europe* (Berkeley, Calif.: University of California Press, 1971).

[21] W. Fellner, M. Gilbert, B. Hansen, R. Kahn, F. Lutz, and P. de Wolf, *The Problem of Rising Prices*, Organization for European Economic Co-operation, 1961, p. 46.

Ireland, Norway, Sweden, and Denmark during the same period are substantially less than 1, and the experts think "wage-push" (Cause B) played the major inflationary role in these instances. The experts' verdict on West Germany for these years is mixed. During the 1950s West Germany seems to have experienced very mild wage-push inflation, but significant demand-pull pressures developed during the early 1960s. As an apparent consequence, its a_3 coefficient rose from substantially less than 1 to approximately 1.[22]

United States experience since the Korean War is somewhat similar to that of West Germany. Estimates of a_3 based on United States data for the 1950s and early 1960s are substantially less than 1,[23] suggesting a poor fit for the monetarist model during that period. Aggregate statistics for these years also suggest a poor fit for the monetarist model—average annual growth in money supply ($\Delta M\%$) and real GNP ($\Delta Y\%$) were very close at 4.5 and 4.3%, respectively whereas average unemployment was held moderately high at 4.8%. Even so the consumer price index rose by 2% per year. Things changed dramatically however, with the eruption of hostilities in Vietnam. Between 1965 and 1969 $\Delta M\%$ rose from 7 to 10%, unemployment fell from 4.5 to 3.5%, and $\Delta P\%$ as measured by the CPI rose from 2 to 6% per year. Coincidentally, estimates of the a_3 coefficient for these years jumped toward 1.[24] Taken together, these facts point to a clear-cut case of excess-demand Cause A inflation during the war years.

The record for Cause A thus indicates that virtually all inflations are *accompanied* by money supply expansion but not all inflations are *caused* by it. Mere accompaniment involves no more than a "passive," full-employment monetary policy when confronted with *non*monetary inflationary forces. Direct causation involves active stimulation of excess employment and demand.

Cause B Inflation: What to Look for?
What's Been Found?

There are several earmarks of market-power inflation besides the low a_3 coefficient mentioned previously. These include (1) differing discretionary behaviors varying with the strength of market power, (2) spill-over effects, (3

---

[22] Ulman and Flanagan, *op. cit.*, pp. 180–181. It should be noted that these international estimates of a_3 are not positively related to the rate at which prices rose during the period the data apply. For example, recent estimates for the United States, Canada, Germany, United Kingdom, France and Japan based on the 1959–1969 period reveal that the first three had the lowest average annual rate of price increase (2.4 compared to 4.2), yet, on average, their a_3s were higher than those of the last three countries (0.63 versus 0.54). Organization for Economic Co-operation and Development, *Inflation: The Present Problem*, December 1970.

[23] For examples, see G. L. Perry, *Unemployment, Money Wage Rates and Inflation* (Cambridge Mass.: MIT Press, 1966); and the papers by A. Hirsch and S. Hymans in *The Econometrics of Price Determination* (Washington, D.C.: Board of Governors of the Federal Reserve System, 1972).

[24] Eckstein and Brinner, *op. cit.*, C. L. Schultze, "Has the Phillips Curve Shifted? Some Additional Evidence," *Brookings Papers of Economic Activity* No. 2 (1971). For a different interpretation concerning this shift see G. L. Perry, "Changing Labor Markets and Inflation," *Brookings Paper of Economic Activity*, No. 3 (1970).

perverse movements in aggregate variables, and (4) severe political and social disputes over income distribution.

Discretionary Behavior. With respect to differences in discretionary behavior, a number of studies have shown wages increasing more rapidly over fairly long periods in highly unionized, highly concentrated industries than in other industries.[25] These results are impressive, but they run counter to other evidence and to theory, both of which suggest no *long-run*, decades of divergence in wages based solely on the existence of market power. Thus, this author attributes these results either to *changes* in structure (inadvertently reflected in the power variables these studies used), or to a dominance of cyclical effects during the time periods tested in these studies. Once long-run divergence is precluded and spill-overs are accepted, detection of a genuine long-run inflationary bias is much more difficult, for then it must be shown that market power (and not money supply) is responsible for an *overall* inflationary wage pattern, even without excess demand—that is, responsible for an upward shift of the Phillips curve as in Figures 21-5 and 21-6. For this overall pattern, several types of evidence are available.

First, an analysis of 118 wage contracts entered into by 14 major firms during 1954–1970 discloses a significant ratchet effect in wage increases granted by firms in highly concentrated, highly unionized industries, despite the fact that, on average, wages paid by these firms rose no more rapidly over the long run than those paid by firms in competitive labor and product markets.[26] It was estimated that a rise *and* fall of unemployment by 1 percentage point would cause *competitive* wages to rise and fall with *no* net change, that is, no ratchet. On the other hand, with four-firm concentration equal 100%, the same rise and fall of unemployment yields a positive net change of 0.77 in the percentage rate of wage inflation.

A second type of evidence concerns discretionary deflation rather than inflation, but carries similar implications. The deflation occurred under the Kennedy Administration's wage-price "guidepost" program. As will be explained in the following chapter on policy, this was a *voluntary* program exhorting both business and labor to abide by certain noninflationary guideposts when setting prices and wages. Any interindustry differentials in deflation under the program could therefore be attributed to discretionary power. And

---

[25] These include J. Garbarino, "A Theory of Interindustry Wage Structure Variation," *Quarterly Journal of Economics* (May 1950); W. G. Bowen, *Wage Behavior in the Postwar Period* (Princeton, N. J.: Industrial Relations Section Princeton University, 1960); M. Segal, "Unionism and Wage Movements," *Southern Economic Journal* (October 1961); and B. Allen, "Market Concentration and Wage Increases: U. S. Manufacturing 1947–1964," *Industrial and Labor Relations Review* (April 1968).

[26] D. Greer, "Market Power and Wage Inflation: A Further Analysis," *Southern Economic Journal* (January 1975). It is also shown in this paper that there is good reason to believe that wage increases of monopolistic firms *led* the aggregate price increases of the 1950s and 1960s, contributing to a low aggregate a_3 coefficient and fostering market-power inflation.

several studies show that, indeed, the guide posts had greater impact on the wages of highly concentrated, highly unionized industries than on other wages.[27] Graphically, these results would be depicted by a downward shift of the short-run Phillips curve led by those possessing substantial market power. Periods 10 through 20 of Table 21-1 illustrate such an experience.

Spill-overs. Spill-overs, a second identifying feature of market-power push, are wage increases (or decreases) obtained by one powerful group of workers that spill-over into other less powerful sectors of the labor market because other workers attempt to maintain their relative position in the wage structure. In particular, highly concentrated, highly unionized industries that happen to be blessed with above average productivity growth have the option of (1) passing their cost savings on to customers in the form of lower product prices, (2) keeping prices stable and raising wages at a rate that exceeds overall average productivity growth, or (3) raising prices *and* wages. To the extent one of the latter two options prevails, and to the extent the excessive wage increases spill-over into other sectors, wages overall tend to exceed average productivity growth, thereby contributing to inflation.

Otto Eckstein and T. A. Wilson were among the first to demonstrate the presence of spill-overs in the United States, and their "pace-setting" wage leaders were highly concentrated, highly unionized industries such as autos, steel, rubber, and electrical machinery.[28] In a still broader study, J. Eatwell, J. Llewellyn, and R. Tarling analyzed wage and productivity trends in the manufacturing industries of 15 countries for 1958-1967.[29] They found that earnings across industries, within each country, rose more uniformly than productivity across industries. Moreover, the *average* rate of earnings inflation in each country did not equal average productivity growth among all industries in each country. Instead, average earnings rose at approximately the same rate as productivity in the *three* industries with *greatest* productivity growth in each country, suggesting spill-overs from these three industries down to others.

How spill-overs occur is a separate issue. Within unionized sectors there is no doubt but that the wage aspirations of weaker unions are stimulated by inflationary gains of powerful unions. It has been shown that strike activity tends to increase in an industry that deviates substantially from its traditional

[27] Greer, *ibid*; S. Wallack, "Wage-Price Guidelines and the Rate of Wage Changes in U. S. Manufacturing, 1951-66," *Southern Economic Journal* (July 1971); G. L. Perry, "Wages and the Guideposts," *American Economic Review* (September 1967); G. Pierson, "The Effect of Union Strength on the U. S. Phillips Curve," *American Economic Review* (June 1968).

[28] O. Eckstein and T. A. Wilson, "The Determination of Money Wages in American Industry," *Quarterly Journal of Economics* (August 1962). Two related studies are A. G. Hines, "Wage Inflation in the United Kingdom 1948-62: A Disaggregated Study," *Economic Journal* (March 1969); and M. Wachter, "Relative Wage Equations for U. S. Manufacturing Industries 1947-1967," *Review of Economics and Statistics* (November 1970).

[29] J. Eatwell, J. Llewellyn, and R. Tarling "Money Wage Inflation in Industrial Countries," *Review of Economic Studies* (October 1974).

place in the interindustry wage structure.[30] As for other workers toward the bottom end of the spill-over, it can be argued that these workers need not be organized in unions to express their dissatisfaction if their wages fail to keep up with the general pattern.[31] Much spill-over is even governmentally imposed, as when for example the legal minimum wage rate is periodically raised in response to wage-price inflation, or when wages paid by government and its contractors are by law keyed to "comparable" earnings in the private sphere. Spill-overs thus tend to draw competitive wages up, rather than bring non-competitive wages down, erecting a general inflationary bias grounded on what amounts to short-run discretionary power.

Aggregate Variables. Aggregate economic events that cannot logically be accounted for by Cause A theory may also indicate Cause B (monopoly power) at work. Three time periods characterized by such anomalies are identified by the three negatively sloped lines of Figure 21-7, which show price inflation *rising* despite substantial *drops* in money supply growth. The 1973–1974 episode is best explained by exogenous shock, so it will be discussed in the following section. Cause B monopoly power best explains the two remaining anomalies, one of which, 1955–1957, will be discussed at length in the next chapter. Here we focus on the 1969–1970 episode.

Shortly after taking office in 1969, President Nixon announced that he would not rely on "guideposts" or "controls" to bring price and wage inflation down from their lofty Vietnam War levels. Instead, he said he would achieve stability by deliberately reducing aggregate demand through balanced budgets and curtailed monetary growth. Money supply was cut back from an annual growth rate of 10% in 1968 to a 2% annual growth rate during the first half of 1970. And, as shown in Table 21-2, the unemployment rate advanced from 3.3 to 4.8% over the same period, advancing thereafter to 6.0%. Nevertheless, union wages not only *continued* to increase, their *rate of increase increased*, as also indicated in Table 21-2. Nonunion wages continued to increase, too, but they did not accelerate like union wages. Graphically, the situation is illustrated by the R to S movement in Figure 21-6 with a 5% "natural rate" of unemployment.

Confronted with these facts, those who see no inflationary harm whatever in market power might argue that Cause A "expectations" of inflation fed the continuing and accelerating inflation. In other words, they could argue that the "natural rate" of unemployment must have shifted from its prior estimated level of 4 or 5% to 7 or 8%, which would then allow the facts to fit a purely competitive Cause A theory of these events. This argument contains several

---

[30] J. Shorey, "An Analysis of Strike Activity in Britain," unpublished Ph.D. thesis, University of London, 1974, cited by D. Metcalf, "Inflation: The Labor Market," Working Paper No. 61 Industrial Relations Section, Princeton University 1975).

[31] C. L. Schultze, *Recent Inflation in the United States*, Study for the Joint Economic Committee, J. S. Congress, 1959, p. 68; "The Soaring Cost of Employee Compensation" *Business Week*, September 7, 1974, pp. 42–44; "A Boom in White-Collar Salaries," *Business Week*, September 11, 1978, pp. 50–51.

TABLE 21-2 Unemployment and Rates of Change of Union and Non-union Money Wages: 1969–1971

Year and Quarter	Unemployment (%) (Seasonally Adjusted)	Wage Changes Annual Rate %	
		Union	Nonunion
1969 I	3.3	6.7	5.5
1969 II	3.5	7.6	5.8
1969 III	3.7	7.9	6.2
1969 IV	3.6	7.5	7.2
1970 I	4.2	7.6	5.4
1970 II	4.8	8.2	5.2
1970 III	5.2	8.3	6.1
1970 IV	5.8	6.9	5.9
1971 I	6.0	8.0	5.5
1971 II	6.0	8.6	5.6
1971 III	6.0	12.9	5.6

Sources: *Economic Report of the President,* various issues; Marten Estey, "Union and Non-union Wage Changes, 1959–1972" in *Price and Wage Control: An Evaluation of Current Policies* Part 2, Joint Economic Committee, U. S. Congress, 1972, p. 328.

flaws, however. Consider first the inconsistency implied by postulating a long run "natural rate" of unemployment that shifts abruptly about in the short run. Second, a purely competitive seller's expectation that he can actually sell his labor or product at ever higher prices needs to be confirmed by continued brisk sales or full-time employment to warrant the proper Cause A price "expectations." If not confirmed, the seller will begin to expect the loss of his business or job and consequently act more in accord with these distressing expectations than with his price "expectations." Thus, expectations alone cannot explain *accelerating* wages when unemployment climbs to unusual heights. In any event, the Nixon administration foresook its purely monetarist approach by instituting a 90 day wage-price freeze on August 15, 1971. This and subsequent Nixon policies will be explored in Chapter 22.

Political and Social Disputes. Put bluntly, Cause B inflation amounts to no more than a struggle over income shares, a struggle that may occasionally provoke serious social and political conflict. To illustrate this as briefly as possible we borrow liberally from D. Jackson, H. Turner, and F. Wilkinson who analyze "strato-inflation" after World War II in Chile thus:

a wage fixing process developed by which government decreed annually an increase in minimum wages (and salaries) equivalent to the previous year's rise in living costs. On this base, the more powerful unions would proceed to bargain for *additional* increases to cover increased productivity, *plus* some part of the anticipated future rise in prices. Farm prices were guaranteed so as to protect farmers' real income against the consequent rise in industrial prices, and industrial prices were fixed (often by legal controls) to cover the anticipated increases in wages and raw materials charges and to protect profits in real terms. The system inherently involved—granted an initial instability and the large monetary increases that were required to protect the position of individual groups—a cumulative inflation.[32]

The upshot: money claims to national income exceeded 100% of real income. Notice in particular the three part *money* wage demands of unions: (1) an increment for past price inflation (to preserve existing real income), (2) a further increment for productivity growth, plus (3) something extra for *antici-pated* price increases. If achieved in *real* terms, union members would have obviously gained appreciable income share at the expense of others. The resulting strato-inflation ranging between 20 and 50% prevented such a realiza-tion but became intolerable, so the Chilean government made "periodic attempts at 'stabilization,' by severe deflations, credit squeezes, wage freezes and the like." However, the Cause B monopolistic powers were not forced into passivity. These measures

induced violent social conflict—there was a general strike in 1954. And every such attempt at stabilization was finally defeated because the reaction of particular groups to the measures of control or deflation involved was so violent that the government abandoned the effort.[33]

Thus money supply growth does not tell the whole story, even about certain "strato-inflations."

Market-Power Profit Inflation. In this section we have concentrated on market-power *wage* inflation to the neglect of market-power *profit* inflation simply because the available cross-section evidence concerning the latter is sketchy.[34] Disaggregate behavior of profits is similar to that of wages, but the complete step of showing conclusively that beneath this behavior lie long-run inflationary forces has not, in my judgment, been taken. More than half this step has apparently been made because the observed behavior is consistent with

---

[32] D. Jackson, H. A. Turner, and F. Wilkinson, *Do Trade Unions Cause Inflation?* (Cambridge, J. K.: Cambridge University Press, 1972), p. 34.

[33] *Ibid.* Later on the authors note that "the incidence of *recorded* strikes in Chile in the 1960s was ten times higher than that in Britain—for an approximately ten times faster rate of general price increases." For a report on the latest attempt to apply a monetarist deflation in Chile see "A Draconian Cure for Chile's Economic Ills," *Business Week*, January 12, 1976, pp. 70–72.

[34] F. M. Scherer, *Industrial Market Structure and Economic Performance* (Chicago: Rand McNally, 1970), pp. 284–303; R. E. Beals, "Concentrated Industries, Administered Prices, and Inflation: A Survey of Recent Empirical Research," Report to the Council on Wage and Price Stability (processed, June 17, 1975); S. Lustgarten, *Industrial Concentration and Inflation* (Washington, D.C.: American Enterprise Institute, 1975).

537

several plausible theories of such inflationary elements.[35] Some interesting case history evidence is also available, part of which will be reviewed in the nex chapter. In any event, we need not stretch this present knowledge into a whole step to establish the existence of market-power inflation. The available evidence on profits supports all that needs to be said given the labor market evidence just reviewed: discretionary power in product markets is sufficient to enable capitalists to protect their income share from wage inflation and, as already mentioned, such power apparently fosters wage inflation.

Cause C Inflation: What to Look for?
What's Been Found?

As already noted, the unusual episode of 1973–1974 (see Figure 21-7) can largely be attributed to exogenous shock, the principal identifying characteristi in this case being abrupt and violent changes in the prices of a few crucial com modities evincing shortages of supply and low price elasticities of demand. Be tween November 1972 and August 1973, an estimated 64 % of the increase in th wholesale price index was accounted for by increases in agricultural prices alone Another 14 % arose from imported commodities, largely because of devaluation Then, from the fall of 1973 to the end of 1974, domestic prices of all fuels and related products shot up 70 %, thereby replacing food as the major inflationar factor. Since our earlier discussion of shocks (particularly OPEC's shocking price behavior) dealt with these events, only a few points need emphasis here.

First, these shocks noticeably reduced the *real* income and wealth of peopl who had come to take rising real incomes for granted and who were, therefore unprepared for such contingencies. Sufficient discretionary power was spread among corporate and labor groups to enable them to try to regain that lost rea income through escalated wage, salary, and profit demands. These demands in turn raised the costs and prices of most other commodities, converting wha might otherwise have been a simple one-shot, exogenous shock inflation into a continuing market-power push inflation.

Second, these inflationary recoupment efforts may have caused some domesti redistribution of the remaining real income in favor of those having the greates market power. Over the long run, spill-overs into the competitive sectors could restore initial distributive shares. On the other hand, if efforts of powerfu groups to gain a greater share continue as they have until now (1978), it will merely prolong the inflation.

Finally, in their effort to keep the inflation of 1973–1974 below "double-digit" levels, United States monetary authorities had to abandon whatever "passive full-employment objectives they may have held. Their resulting meager ex pansion of the money supply forced unemployment up to heights not seen since the Great Depression—a fact suggestive of the situation's severity.

[35] C. L. Schultze, *op. cit.*; A. S. Eichner, *The Megacorp and Oligopoly* (Cambridge, U. K.: Cam bridge University Press, 1976).

Summary

There seem to be three basic causes of inflation: (A) monetary-fiscal stimulation, which operates on the principle of aggregate excess demand; (B) discretionary power in labor and product markets, which involves wage and profit claims that add up to more than 100 % of real income; and (C) exogenous shocks, which are either capricious or attributable to premeditated acts in the international sphere (unlike the other causes, these shocks are the primary determinants of radical changes in aggregate real income).

These causes are interdependent in that the pure operation of each is dependent on the passivity or neutrality of the others. Cause A passivity is monetary-fiscal policy maintaining the natural-competitive rate of full-employment. Cause B passivity is purely competitive structure or behavior in all markets, something that assures that the natural rate of employment is the *only* equilibrium rate. Cause C passivity is an absence of exogenous shock (or temporary cross-cancelling shocks) plus floating exchange rates. If passivity holds in all these respects, there can be no accelerating inflation and the other types of inflation can be avoided. If passivity holds with respect to any two causes, the remaining cause can generate inflation of any type by becoming an active inflationary force.

Whether one cause can act in a deflationary manner to counter an inflation initiated by another cause depends solely on whether the inflationary cause can be *converted* to passivity (to be a cause it had to be an active cause at some point). If the inflationary cause cannot be so converted, then deflation can be achieved only through greater unemployment. This is as true for Cause A countering a Cause B inflation as it is for the less realistic cases of Causes B or C countering a Cause A inflation. Thus full-employment depends entirely on passivity, and the price level depends on whether the deflationary or the inflationary force is pacified first.

Empirically, there is evidence of all three causes. Indeed, recent United States economic history provides examples of each. From 1954 to about 1967, a period of only mild inflation, Cause B seems to have prevailed. Between 1967 and 1970, the Vietnam War occasioned a serious Cause A inflation. Reversal by means of Cause A (monetary deflation) was prevented in 1970 and 1971 by Cause B developments. More recently, Cause C touched off an even more serious inflation, and once again Cause A deflationary efforts have been hampered by Cause B inflationary forces, which this time spring from a quest to recoup lost real income.

22

Inflation and "Stagflation" Policy

. . . we have learned a lot about wage and price controls but not how to control wages and prices.

SIDNEY L. JONES

Panic, chaos, and disillusion—all are possible if inflation gets out of hand Rapid inflation drastically reshuffles people's real incomes, as some keep u and others, especially those on fixed incomes, fall behind. It creates speculator who dabble in otherwise worthless games of buy and sell. It ambushes savings disrupts corporate finance, undermines long-term projects, and distorts inter national economic relationships. It menaces democracy and invites de magoguery. It now ranks as our number one economic problem.

Policy treatment of the problem is complicated by inflation's diverse causes— monetary demand-pull, market-power push, and exogenous shock. Th difficulties of diversity are compounded by interactions among the causes a period of inflation touched off by one cause can be perpetuated by anothe Annoying as these complications are, they do not totally cripple policy effort: They merely make policy formulation intellectually more challenging than i otherwise would be.

The really big stumbling block to effective anti-inflation policy is the massiv and uneven burden that different sectors of society must bear in the course c any crack-down. Just as the costs of inflation are massive and unevenly spread so too the costs of deflation are massive and uneven. Because those hurt b any crack-down can exercise their democratic right to scream "bloody murder while attempting to "throw the rascals out," anti-inflation policy is complicate if not incapacitated by *political* considerations. Thus one does not solve inflatio is one solves a crossword puzzle. The difficulties are more like those of putting a corset on an elephant—a task requiring brains, cunning, strength, and courage, plus sundry instruments of pain and pleasure (whips and peanuts perhaps).

Introduction—Policy Options

Of inflation's several causes none is more ominously colored by political considerations than the one of greatest interest to us here—market-power push. All the known cures for inflations originated or perpetuated by this cause can be gathered into three categories: (1) curtailment of aggregate demand, most particularly by restricting growth in the supply of money; (2) direct governmental control or influence of wages and prices through "incomes" policies or "guideposts"; and (3) structural reform to gain greater competition in product and labor markets.

Prominent proponents of each approach argue earnestly for accepting or rejecting programs of one bent or another. Among those in the first camp are Milton Friedman, Samuel Brittan, Michael Parkin, and David Laidler. Most folks of this persuasion are **monetarists**, a name we shall use. The pro-controls group includes John Kenneth Galbraith, Sidney Weintraub, Daniel Quinn Mills, and Jerry Pohlman. Those who favor a forced march in the competitive direction number among their membership such luminaries as Gottfried Haberler, Hendrik Houthakker, James E. Meade, Arthur F. Burns, Murray Weidenbaum, and Willard Mueller.

The debate between opposing camps, especially the first two, is often bitter, giving outside observers the impression that scoring is sometimes based on who can deliver the better insult rather than on who can demonstrate the better scholarship. Thus monetarists lambaste pro-controls arguments as being absurd," "fatally flawed," and reliant on "stupid" assumptions. To them, policies of direct control are "the oldest and crudest [of measures] best likened to medieval medicine based on ignorance and misunderstanding of the fundamental processes at work and more likely to kill the patient than to cure him." [1] The pro-controls people reply that the monetarists are full of "wistful rhetoric," that they propound nothing more than "self-sealing ideology," [2] that deflation by simple monetary restraint is little better than a "rain dance." [3] The pro-controls people also take potshots at the pro-competition people. According to Galbraith, for instance, pro-competition policy is "now widely, if not yet universally, identified as the last wavering gasp of the bankrupt mind." [4] In turn,

---

[1] Michael Parkin, "Wage and Price Controls: The Lessons from Britain," in *The Illusion of Wage and Price Control*, edited by M. Walker (Vancouver, B. C.: The Fraser Institute, 1976), p. 101.
[2] Sidney Weintraub, *Capitalism's Inflation and Unemployment Crisis* (Reading, Mass.: Addison-Wesley, 1978), pp. 1–3.
[3] Jerry E. Pohlman, *Inflation Under Control?* (Reston, Va.: Reston Publishing Co., 1976), p. 96.
[4] John Kenneth Galbraith, "The Trouble with Economists," *New Republic* (January 14, 1978), p. 20.

defenders of the pro-competitive faith reply (rather mildly it would seem) that Galbraith "exaggerates," that he is "mistaken," that he has "neglected his homework."[5] As these quotes suggest, the frustrations of past policy failures have taken their toll; the high stakes at issue have raised tension.

We obviously cannot find right or wrong by sloshing further through slanderous prose. So what is the answer? Which of the three policy options is best? Which ought to command the public's greatest allegiance? In this writer's opinion, the policy debate can only find resolution in political and economic *realities*, not in theoretical niceties or rhetorical hostilities. Unfortunately for the truth, the essence of each school's argument, as summarized in the following subsections, is that it alone is more realistic than the others.

Curtailment of Aggregate Demand

The monetarists claim that monetary restraint is both necessary and sufficient to achieve price and wage stability because money supply, relative to produc quantities and labor services, has proved to be the "ultimate" determinant of price and wage level. No inflation flowers without monetary watering. So if things get annoyingly weedy, regardless of the source of the offending seeds, simply turn off the money supply spigot. If those possessing market power do not adapt, be they corporate or union entities, they will be wilted into submission by the penalties of low profits and high unemployment.

This approach takes guts and some temporary time in recession, but it i the only "realistic" way. Acute temporary pain is necessary for long-run stability. Wage-price controls have been tried repeatedly throughout history, and they have failed just as repeatedly. Nay, they are worse than useless; they ar oppressive, wasteful, and economically deadly. Controls admittedly *do* contain inflation in the Soviet Union and other communist countries, but only at the cost of shortages, shoddy quality, suffocating tyranny, and other condition that would never be tolerated in a democracy. As for competition policy, it is politically unrealistic if not irrelevant. The power centers are too powerful to be dismembered. We cannot turn back the clock to the days of decentraliza tion.[6]

Direct Government Intervention

The pro-controls people contend that large corporations, unions, and professional associations have so thoroughly escaped the discipline of de pressed markets that monetary restraint does little or nothing to achieve pric and wage stability; instead, it generates intolerable unemployment. The result is stagnation plus inflation, or **stagflation**. "Monetary policy to control inflation

---

[5] Williard F. Mueller, *A Primer on Monopoly and Competition* (New York: Random House, 1970), pp. 160–71.

[6] For a good statement of the monetarist position see Samuel Brittan and Peter Lilley, *The Delusion of Incomes Policy* (New York: Holmes & Meier, 1977).

is not the solution," says Sidney Weintraub, "it is part of the problem, for in its inability to exercise a direct restraint on the price level it is a major force making for stagflation and slumpflation."[7] The unemployment such an approach entails is politically unrealistic because it is neither slight nor brief. It is sufficiently severe and lasting to topple governments at election time; it crudely tests labor's temperament for a *general* strike; and it toys with the treacherous boundary line dividing recession from genuine depression.

As for vigorous competition policy, that too is unrealistic. The "powers-that-be" enjoy political untouchability. They have a head-lock on Washington, D.C., as well as a favorable image amongst the populace. The inevitable conclusion, then, if one wants to be a realist, is direct government intervention in price and incomes decision making. Responsible monetary policy is in this view still necessary, given its ultimate place in the scheme of things, and given the impossibility of containing by direct controls any considerable inflation caused by reckless money supply growth. But monetary restraint alone is *not sufficient* for stability *and full employment*. Restraint *plus controls* forms the only package that fits actuality.[8]

Structural Reform

Proponents of vigorous pro-competition policies agree that monetary restraint is necessary to keep inflation in check. They also agree that market power interferes with the free and effective exercise of monetary restraint by insulating product and labor markets from the discipline of low profits and unemployment, the two avenues by which monetary curtailment must travel to reach the heavenly bliss of stability. The monetary authorities thus are all too often placed in the precarious position of being unable to attain zero inflation without pushing unemployment up to politically unacceptable and economically dangerous levels and durations.

However, controls do not, in this view, offer a realistic way out of the mess. Controls have been tried and found wanting. In fact, many in the pro-competitive camp agree with the monetarists that controls are economically harmful. In the long run their adverse side effects make them politically unrealistic in a democracy. It follows that the only viable policy solution combines monetary restraint and thoroughgoing competition, not "pure" competition but vigorously "workable" competition.

When defending the realism of this position against skeptical barbs from those in the other camps, pro-competition people point out that most of the economy is *already* workably competitive; or at least near that neighborhood. Why then, they ask, is it impossible to bring the deviant and offending minority sectors into conformity with the more competitive majority? It admittedly takes a bit of grit because the minority is a large minority. But unions account

[7] Weintraub, *op. cit.*, p. 77.
[8] For elaboration see *ibid.*, Galbraith, *op. cit.*, and Pohlman, *op. cit.*

for less than 30% of the total work force. And there is nothing economically inevitable about the immense size of General Motors, General Electric, General Dynamics, or the other "Generals." Indeed, if these creatures are too powerful to be touched structurally, they are also too powerful to be controlled properly by simple monetary manipulations or by governmental directives and urgings. Controls in particular are a sign of governmental *weakness*, not strength.[9]

A Review of "Reality"

The foregoing summarizes this chapter, the remainder of which is devoted to detailed discussions of each school of thought. As long as they all appeal in different ways to the same reality, they cannot all be completely correct. Hence, what follows is mainly a review of reality as it pertains to each of these three positions. Be aware that "reality" applies to both politics and economics in various confusing combinations. This is unavoidable. Be aware, too, that the present writer is of the third school, so this account is, also unavoidably, somewhat biased. To give away my conclusion at the outset, I think realities are such that, given present market structures, neither monetary restraint nor direct controls coupled with monetary restraint can cope effectively, lastingly, efficiently, fairly, and democratically with market-power push inflations, *especially* those that are touched off suddenly by massive exogenous shocks, such as was true of the inflation of 1974 through 1978. The situation can be seen by a crude parable:

Imagine yourself as the president of a small distant democratic country suffering at the hands of well-armed marauding bands. Their plundering seems especially acute during periods of drought or blight, at which times the renegades attempt to preserve their standard of living at the expense of others in your land. You have but three options for reducing the indignities inflicted on your peaceful citizens: (1) engage the marauders head-on in intermittent combat, never decisively defeating, dispersing, or disarming them out of fear that the attempt to do so may bring you down, but periodically subduing them at a substantial cost in lives, including the lives of innocent by-standers; (2) play the conciliatory role using mere bluff and bluster to coax them into an uneasy but controlled truce of some kind, yet once again never dispersing or disarming them, thereby merely papering over the conflict and subjecting yourself to the possibility *and actuality* of occasional erruptions of renewed difficulty; or (3) attempt to defeat the marauders decisively, dispersing and disarming

---

[9] Representative statements include Mueller, *op. cit.*, Gardner C. Means *et. al.*, *The Roots of Inflation* (New York: Burt Franklin & Co.; 1975); Gottfried Haberler, *Economic Growth and Stability* (Los Angeles: Nash, 1974), pp. 117–33; Murray L. Weidenbaum, "New Initiatives in National Wage and Price Policy," *Review of Economics and Statistics* (August 1972), pp. 213–17; the testimony of M. Weidenbaum, W. Mueller, and H. Houthakker in *Controls or Competition*, Hearings before Subcommittee on Antitrust and Monopoly, U. S. Senate, 92nd Congress, Second Session (1972); and Arthur F. Burns, "The Real Issues of Inflation and Unemployment," *Challenge* (January/February 1976).

them if you succeed, thereby finding a long-run solution to the problem, but knowingly risking your presidency in the process. [You may rationalize your choice of the third option with the thought that in the long run you are likely to lose your throne even under options (1) and (2) because of the persistent threat the marauders pose and the disaffection they produce among your loyal subjects.]

The parable is admittedly coarse, and it is not meant to reflect harshly on anyone in our society. (I do not think that union leaders and corporate officers are wicked people bent on bringing the country to its knees. They are paid to wield whatever power they have to further their constituents' interests.) Still, these options approximate (1) monetarism, (2) direct controls (which always require the cooperation of big labor and big business to succeed even temporarily in a democracy), and (3) competitive restructuring. The parable does more than put these policy options under a brighter light. It teaches us that, strictly speaking, there are no perfectly "right" and "wrong" answers, but rather only "better" and "worse" answers.

To return to the parable, one might be able to muddle through with option (1) or (2) or some alternating mix of them. On the other hand, so long as the bands retain considerable power and so long as occasional exogenous shocks rile them up, there will be trouble. Option (3) might thus be better. Moreover, if applications of measures (1) and (2) permit the marauders' power to grow over time, *all* options grow less and less viable. Realism could then eventually reduce to chaos or repressive despotism.

Monetarism (Versus Steel)

The realism of monetarism is based on a long history of close connections between price and wage levels and money supply. The record is incomplete, however, because good data on these variables and unemployment do not extend deeply into the distant past. Even if solid data were available, the competitive structures of older agricultural eras might not yield many instances of market-power push inflation. The dominance of concentrated industries, the rise of mighty labor unions, and the imposition of many anticompetitive governmental restrictions (such as those in agriculture and transportation) are relatively recent developments. Hence our experience of the last three decades is particularly relevant.

As summarized earlier in Figure 21-7, recent experience reveals three instances when price inflation persisted and even accelerated despite substantial reductions in money supply. Two of those episodes, 1969–1970 and 1973–1974, have already been dissected. The latter was due to exogenous shocks; the former to a market-power push that dramatically demonstrated the impotency of monetary restraint. The third episode, spanning the late 1950s, offers another example of market-power push inflation that proved resistant to recessionary pressure. As money supply growth fell, unemployment jumped from 4.4% in 1955 to 6.8% in 1958. Yet contrary to orthodox monetarist theory, prices did not fall or even stabilize. They continued to rise at better than a 2% annual clip.

The Steel Industry and Inflation

The microeconomics underlying this incident are epitomized by the steel industry, where employment conditions may be measured by capacity usage. As shown in Figure 22-1, the price of steel mill products rose roughly 23% between 1955 and 1958; at the same time, capacity usage in the industry fell from a respectable 92.1% to an unhealthy 59.1%. The rate of price increase was almost three times faster than that of wholesale prices generally, contributing substantially to a rise in aggregate price indexes.

The history of steel thereafter, also shown in Figure 22-1, provides further illustration of the grave difficulties encountered by monetary and fiscal policies

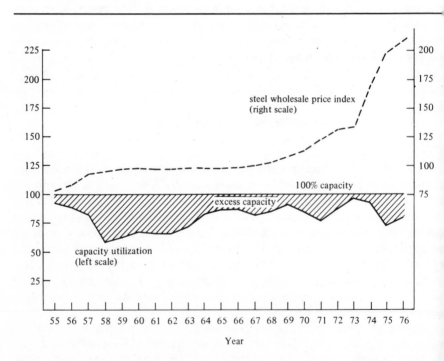

Figure 22-1. Steel mill products price index and capacity utilization. Source: Council on Wage and Price Stability, Prices and Costs in the United States Steel Industry (Oct. 1977), pp. 16, 119.

that attempt to tie prices down by deliberately engineering recessions. After the 1955–1958 increases, steel prices stabilized until about 1966. A substantial amount of excess capacity hanging over the industry for many of those years probably helped to discourage price increases. An additional and equally important restraining influence was the federal government's persistent scolding, probing, and importuning of the industry from 1958 through 1966.

First, the Senate Subcommittee on Antitrust and Monopoly conducted a series of hearings that were sharply critical of the industry's pricing practices. Even President Eisenhower gave a few scowls. According to the industry's trade press these attentions put big steel "on the spot in the battle against inflation."[10] Later, in 1962, U. S. Steel Corporation tried to lead an across-the-board price increase of $6 a ton, only to be shouted down by President Kennedy in a confrontation that for drama must outrank all others in the annals of business-government relations. The price boost would have violated the spirit of Kennedy's wage-price "guideposts," which further restrained steel prices until their lapse in 1966.

When Nixon ascended to the presidency in early 1969, he announced his strong distaste for guideposts or other forms of direct government intervention. ("Free prices and wages are the heart of our economic system," he said.) The steel industry took this to heart and, despite a marked drop in demand, raised prices nearly 23 % during Nixon's first 30 months in office. As shown in Figure 22-1, the price escalation was not deterred by a slump that created more unused capacity in 1971 than the steel industry had seen in nearly a decade. The slump reflects the larger recession that the Nixon administration deliberately induced through tight monetary and fiscal policy in hopes of curbing the inflation stirred up during the Vietnam War. This steel price escalation exemplifies the widespread and persistent inflation that eventually signaled defeat for Nixon's monetarist policy. Steel price hikes then slowed during a period of controls and recovery in 1972 and 1973, but thereafter Figure 22-1 displays a startling spectacle. While capacity usage dipped to levels even lower than those witnessed in the recession of 1971, steel prices skyrocketed over 60 % in just 3 years from December 1973 to December 1976.

Of course the big mystery is what caused this price hike and the other price increases to occur even in the midst of (or especially in the midst of) hard times. Market power was undoubtedly at work. But our inquiry must dig deeper. Was it balooning profit margins or ever-rising steelworker wages? Perhaps productivity fell, driving up unit labor costs? Or was it escalating raw materials prices? After intense study of all the possibilities, two teams of economists working independently, one from the Federal Trade Commission and the other from the Council on Wage and Price Stability, arrived at the conclusion that the main cause of the industry's unruly record was ever-rising steelworker

---

[10] Cited by John M. Blair, *Economic Concentration* (New York: Harcourt, Brace, and Jovanovich, 1972), p. 635.

wage rates and fringe benefits.[11] Among the many numbers notifying us of this fact are the following:

1. Between 1952 and 1977 average hourly employee costs in all of manufacturing climbed 297%. The corresponding inflation rate for steelworkers was 450%.
2. In 1952 steelworkers enjoyed an hourly compensation rate that was 18% above the all-manufacturing average. By 1977 the steelworkers' compensation premium had leaped to 64%.
3. Between 1967 and 1977 the steelworkers outstripped in increases such other strongly unionized industries as autos, railroads, and bituminous coal.
4. If these hourly compensation figures had been offset by fantastic productivity performance, they would have had less serious consequences for unit labor costs and prices. However, although productivity was good as compared to the Japanese or West German steel industries, it was not fantastic. So unit labor costs have climbed inordinately, putting the United States industry at a significant cost disadvantage *vis-à-vis* the Japanese and the Europeans. United States unit labor costs were roughly *twice* those of the Japanese in 1976.

This picture obviously justifies the emphasis given in the last chapter to wage inflation in highly unionized and highly concentrated industries. Steel profit margin increases may also have contributed slightly to short spurts,[12] but no more than slightly if at all. Profits display no clear trend; and for the period covered by Table 22-1, after–tax profits amounted to no more than about 5.3 cents per dollar of sales (or about 8.6 cents per dollar of stockholders' equity). In contrast, total cost per ton of steel would have been 9% lower in 1976 if steelworkers' hourly compensation had grown at a rate equal to that for the rest of manufacturing between 1967 and 1976.

The Inflation of 1973–1978

Casting our net of inquiry farther, we find that general economic events of the 1973–1978 period illustrate the greatest failings of purely monetarist policies. Exogenous shocks in the food and fuel sectors ignited a double-digit inflation during 1973 and 1974, but those forces quickly subsided as agricultural output increased and oil price increases moderated. Subsequent monetary restraint pushed the country into seriously hard times, driving unemployment up to 9% in May of 1975 and putting over 8 million people out of work. Continued

---

[11] Council on Wage and Price Stability, *Prices and Costs in the United States Steel Industry* (October 1977); R. M. Duke, R. L. Johnson, Hans Mueller, P. D. Qualls, C. T. Roush, and D. G. Tarr, *The United States Steel Industry and Its International Rivals: Trends and Factors Determining International Competitiveness* (Federal Trade Commission, November 1977).

[12] John Blair, *op. cit.*, pp. 632–43.

monetary and fiscal restraint kept the unemployment rate in the 7% range and excess capacity in the 20% range over the next 3 *years*, a duration of ill condition not seen since the Great Depression four decades earlier. At this writing the slump has cost the nation an estimated $400 *billion* in lost output.

What did we gain on the inflation front for this vast idleness? The initial jolt of 9% unemployment did pull price inflation below the 10–12% levels of 1974. Yet despite the steady slack thereafter and despite the absence of continued exogenous shocks, price inflation relentlessly persisted at rates between 5% and 8% over the period 1975–1978, a pace of ascent astronomic by historical standards. Contemplating conditions in 1978, economists for the Council on Wage and Price Stability calculated that still more stringent monetary tightness than that prevailing would undoubtedly curb the continuing inflation, but only at horrendous cost: "a one percentage point reduction in the inflation rate would require an annual loss of about $100 billion in output and 2.5 million jobs."[13] Another typical estimate of the time projected that *three* extra percentage points of unemployment would lower the inflation rate by only about *one* percentage point over a year.[14] In other words, inflation could indeed be slashed to zero by turning off the monetary spigot, but only by shoving unemployment well above 10 or 15% for an indefinite but certainly long duration. Would such a plan of attack be politically feasible? Is it realistic to think that big labor and big business (not to mention other folks) would accept the consequences with little more than a whine or two? Monetarists seem to think so. You may judge for yourself. (While judging keep in mind that a week is a long time to a politician.)

What made the situation intractable was simply this: *Under competitive conditions* the exogenous shocks in food and fuel of 1973–1974 would probably have reduced everyone's real income a few percentage points with only temporary price inflation and a mild short-run rise in unemployment, assuming proper monetary tautness. It would have been like events of olden days, when in the face of a partial crop loss our great-great grandparents had no choice but to "lump it" and "wait 'til next year."[15] Nowadays, however, many folks, steelworkers included, enjoy enough market power that they do not have to "lump it" meekly when hit by shrinkage of the real income pie. They can fight to recoup their losses and perhaps gain new ground (even if at the expense of others) by demanding ever higher *money* incomes. The ensuing struggle between power blocks over real income shares generates inflation. Inflationary forces will be greater the greater the original shocks, the mightier the power blocks, and the hotter the battle. The shocks of 1973–1974 were substantial indeed.

In short, monetary restraint appears to be a necessary but not sufficient tool for inflation control. Under present conditions its application severely

---

[13] *Quarterly Report of the Council on Wage and Price Stability with a Special Report on Inflation* (Washington, D.C.; April 1978), p. 9.

[14] *Business Week*, July 31, 1978, p. 94.

[15] The analogy is due to Richard N. Cooper, "Inflation and Recession," *New Republic* (August 24, 1974), pp. 13–15.

aggravates unemployment for prolonged periods, if not permanently. Economic and political realities therefore inhibit the tool's forceful application. Something additional seems needed.

Wage-Price Controls

Monetarists like to point out that wage-price controls have a long and unclean record. They contend that all control efforts have been failures since as early as Roman times, when the Emperor Diocletian fixed the value of 900 goods, 130 grades of labor, and 41 freight rates. The death penalty was prescribed for breaches, of which there were apparently many. According to one historian of the day, Lactantius, much blood was shed "upon very slight and trifling accounts." Even so, failure of the policy lay more in the shortages and disruptions it seems to have caused than in the official savagery. People stopped bringing goods to market "because they could not get a reasonable price for them."[16] History is littered with hundreds of further attempts at direct control that monetarists consider no more than temporary successes (unless one wants to count totalitarian control programs as long-term successes). Of course pro-controls people disagree with this interpretation. They argue in rebuttal that success often needs to be no more than "temporary," as in time of war. They argue further that crude ancient schemes imposed to counter money supply inflations cannot be fairly compared to our more sophisticated modern versions, which are designed to check market-power push inflations.

In fact, there is a spicy variety of "control" policies. Their common element is some form of **direct government supervision** of wages, salaries, prices, and perhaps profits, interest rates, and rents as well. The usual purpose of such controls is to stem inflation, although they have also been aimed at balance of payments improvement and income redistribution. Of present interest are control policies designed to check market-power push inflation. Graphically, the objective is depicted in Figure 22-2. The basic idea is to shift the trade-off between inflation and unemployment, that is, the Phillips curve, especially in the region above the "full" or "natural" rate of unemployment U^*. If achieved, inflation could then be less for any given level of unemployment above U^*. Alternatively, unemployment could be reduced to U^* without adding to inflation. (Monetarists scoff at this theory, saying that the shift would occur anyway if monetary restraint substantially raised unemployment for a sufficient spell. Granting this, a more sophisticated theory of controls would hold that controls achieve a *quicker* shift than monetary policy alone can attain.)

So much for theory. In reality, control policies vary in four major respects: (1) coverage, (2) the nature of wage-price standards, (3) methods of enforcement,

[16] Brittan and Lilley, *op. cit.*, p. 73.

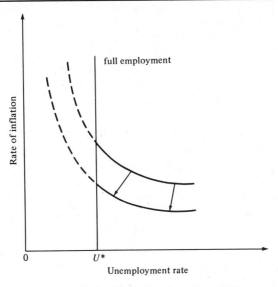

Figure 22-2. *The objective of controls.*

and (4) duration.[17] The scope of **coverage** may be very broad, in which case the program includes virtually all industrial sectors and most income variables—wages, salaries, prices, rents, and so on. Conversely, a program of limited coverage may focus on just a few industries (especially those thought to be sources of inflation) and a few economic figures (wages and prices, say). Between these extremes are countless combinations of industrial breadth and economic depth.

As for **standards**, every control policy must define what behavior is "proper" and "expected." Standards may be simple or complex, vague or specific. An example of a fairly simple and specific standard is a wage-price freeze. Usually, control policies have rather simple and vague *overall* standards, such as "wage restraint" or "increases matching productivity," applying to everyone covered. These standards are then augmented in the course of enforcement by more *specific* standards applying to certain industries or companies.

One extreme of **enforcement** has already received mention—Diocletian's death penalty. At the other extreme are official "urging," "jaw-boning," "exhortation," and "preaching." These latter means of compliance obviously play on peoples' feelings of patriotism or fairness as opposed to their fear of oblivion. They are also the means western democracies rely on most heavily; so voluntary compliance is essential to the success of their control. Even where fines, or worse, serve as penalties, widespread support or acquiescence is

[17] Arnold R. Weber, *In Pursuit of Price Stability* (Washington, D.C.: Brookings Institution, 1973), pp. 10–14.

necessary. (Otherwise the authorities would have difficulty impanelling "pure" juries and quickly run out of jail space.) As you might guess, there are some strong links between compliance method and program coverage. Jaw-boning can only work with limited coverage because it works on the spotlight principle, wherein public opinion is mobilized against offenders. Just as it is impossible for everyone to be famous, it is impossible to splotlight every corner grocer and auto repair shop. Programs of broad coverage consequently require specific legal sanctions.

Regarding **duration**, most control policies have no set life-span. A few, however, do, most notably policies that freeze wages and prices. In such cases the duration is invariably short—60 to 90 days or so. Longer freezes would obviously petrify the economy until brittle.

With this background we are prepared to survey two United States control programs—Kennedy's wage-price "guideposts" and Nixon's Phases I through IV. A brief run-down of European experience then follows.

The Guidepost Program (1962–1966)

Well aware of the wage-price antics in steel and other power-laden industries during the late 1950s, President Kennedy's Council of Economic Advisors introduced an informal "guidepost" program in 1962. As stated in the *Economic Report of the President* the standard for noninflationary wage behavior was that wage increases in each industry should not exceed the rate of *overall* productivity increase.[18] Later, the vagueness of " overall productivity increase" was removed by specifying one number for wage increases, 3.2%, which was an average estimate of the previous 5 year's productivity growth. The theory underlying this standard derives from conditions pictured in Figure 22-3. Regardless of what happens to hourly compensation in dollars and cents, *real* income follows a narrow path cleared by output per worker hour, that is, productivity. Hence the growth of *money* income might as well match the growth of *real* income as determined by productivity improvement. Moreover, if these two figures do match, producers' labor cost per unit will not increase on average because additions to labor cost will be offset by additions to output. With unit labor cost steady, prices need not climb (unless pushed up by raw materials costs).

Prices, that is, need not rise *overall*. The guidepost standard for *individual* industry price changes could not be zero because productivity advance *varies* from industry to industry. Given wage increments of 3.2% for all workers, unit labor costs will *fall* in those industries experiencing above average productivity growth and *rise* in those industries languishing with below average productivity growth. Accordingly, the guidepost standard for prices was that prices fall where productivity improvement was unusually brisk and rise where it was unusually slow. Given uniform wage increases, this price behavior would prevail under competitive conditions. Figure 22-4 conveys the idea because it

[18] *Economic Report of the President, 1962*, p. 189.

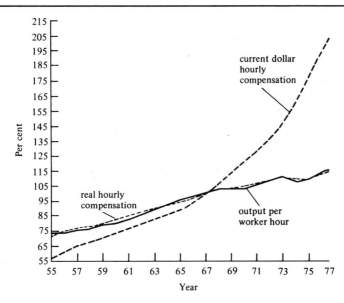

Figure 22-3. *Indexes of output per worker and real and nominal compensation, private nonfarm business, for all persons. 1967 = 100. Source: U.S. Department of Labor, Bureau of Labor Statistics.*

shows price changes plotted against productivity changes in 139 industries over 1958–1968. On average, prices rose, so declines did not offset increases. But the broadly negative relation is plain to see. If price changes had averaged out to zero, the price reductions would clearly have come chiefly from particularly progressive industries.

These general wage and price standards were qualified by certain "exceptions." Wage increases, for example, could be above standard if necessary "to attract sufficient labor." And prices could rise above an industry's standard if necessary "to finance a needed expansion in capacity." Although economically defensible, these exceptions offered loopholes that complicated enforcement.

Jaw-boning, ear-stroking, and related anatomical incantations provided the main fire-power of enforcement, although President Kennedy and later President Johnson were by no means averse to harsher measures. Various threats—ranging from prospective antitrust suits to massive sales from government stockpiles—were occasionally brought in for reinforcements. Still, the program was wholly "voluntary," so the focus of its coverage remained rather narrowly fixed on the biggest, most highly concentrated, and most thoroughly unionized industries. Moreover, no bureaucracy was created to implement the program.

Because most control policies are based on the same economic principles as those guiding the guideposts, the problems arising under this program carry

553

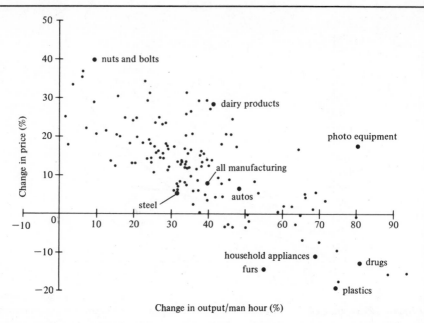

Figure 22-4. Percent of change in output per man-hour and prices, for 139 manufacturing industries, 1958–1968. Source: Bureau of Labor Statistics Bulletin 1710, Productivity and the Economy (1971), p. 29.

special significance.[19] High on the list of difficulties was the necessity of relying on *past* productivity performance to channel *future* wage settlements. In fact, productivity growth exceeded the 3.2% standard while wages generally met the standard. As a consequence, profits balooned, angering organized labor. The Council of Economic Advisors considered raising the wage standard to 3.6%, which union leadership advocated, but stuck with 3.2% in the end. A measure of the delicacy of labor's support is the explosion of tempers caused by this little 0.4 percentage point difference of opinion. Conversely, actual productivity growth under the program could have been worse than standard, in which case the problem would have been one of having a standard that was in fact inflationary. It was this possibility that the Council was trying to avoid when rejecting 3.6%. Unfortunately, it is not possible to solve the problem of finding a correct standard by adopting a short-run estimate based on current experience because productivity is whipped about rather wildly by the short-run business cycle. The problem is thus endemic to all control programs.

A major problem concerning prices lay in getting price reductions in industries experiencing especially favorable productivity growth. Competition

[19] For a thorough discussion see John Sheahan, *Wage-Price Guideposts* (Washington, D.C.: Brookings Institution, 1967).

would normally *force* price reductions in such cases, but of course competition was (and is) lacking in many industries. In particular, the auto industry gained substantial profit increases by refusing to cut prices in the face of above average productivity growth. Auto workers then felt free to press for wage increases that would break the 3.2 ceiling, and their success undermined the program. A similar situation arose in the airline industry, which is curious because the federal government, through the CAB, had the legal power to force air-fare reductions. But the CAB showed a bright yellow streak in the spinal region by not enforcing the guidepost program. Labor unions (not being color-blind) felt wronged. In 1966 they pressed for and received a much publicized ceiling-breaking settlement. This particular breach in the ceiling also damaged the program's foundation, heralding complete collapse shortly thereafter.

The guideposts might have been able to outlast these difficulties. They could not, however, endure the forces of economic boom that began building in 1966 and 1967 with the escalating war in Vietnam. As demand-pull inflation raised prices in competitive sectors outside the guidepost program, the 3.2% wage standard, which was barely acceptable to organized labor even assuming zero inflation, became intolerable. The moral is simple: *strong demand-pull pressure will crush any such voluntary program.* By extension, a substantial exogenous shock inflation would also have destroyed the modicum of social consensus sustaining the program. As we shall see shortly, these contingencies pose hazards for programs of even more refined design and stricter enforcement.

It is of course impossible to "prove" whether or not a given controls policy successfully stems inflation (or reduces unemployment) because one can never be sure what conditions would have been like without the policy. Nevertheless, deviations from pre-policy trends can be estimated statistically. A number of tests by this method show that, despite their several failings, the guideposts were moderately successful, at least temporarily. Overall wage and price inflation were trimmed by 1 or 2 percentage points between 1962 and 1966.[20] Moreover, the bulk of curtailment seems to have been achieved in those sectors receiving greatest policy attention—that is, highly unionized and highly concentrated industries. A positive impact in steel was suggested earlier by Figure 22-1. Particularly noticeable effects have also been found in machinery, chemicals, rubber, and petroleum.[21] These findings indicate more than short-run success for the program; they also suggest that the theory underlying it (that market power fosters inflation) is essentially correct.

---

[20] *Ibid.*, pp. 79–95; Pohlman, *op. cit.*, pp. 182–85; Norman Keiser, *Macroeconomics* (New York: Random House, 1975), pp. 324–33; Otto Eckstein and R. Brinner, *The Inflationary Process in the United States*, U. S. Congress, Joint Economic Committee Study, 1972. On the other hand see S. W. Black and H. H. Kelejian, "A Macro Model of the U. S. Labor Market," *Review of Economics and Statistics* (September 1970), pp. 712–41.

[21] Stanley S. Wallack, "Wage-Price Guidelines and the Rate of Wage Changes in U. S. Manufacturing 1951–66," *Southern Economic Journal* (July 1971), pp. 33–47; D. F. Greer, "Market Power and Wage Inflation: A Further Analysis," *Southern Economic Journal* (January 1975), pp. 466–79; George L. Perry, "Wages and the Guideposts," *American Economic Review* (September 1967), pp. 897–904.

The Wage-Price Freeze of 1971, or Phase I[22]

The guideposts were just a teaser. They were so informal that Council economists learned of price increases through the newspapers. The guideposts likewise had no Congressional authorization, no biting sanctions. It could be said, then, that on August 15, 1971, the United States really lost its virginity in this area of peace-time wage-price controls. On that day President Nixon, acting under stand-by authority granted by Congress in 1970, imposed a 90-day wage-price freeze. The freeze replaced his unsuccessful two and a half year effort to curb inflation by monetary restraint and deliberate recession. Indeed, it should be noted that the steel industry contributed a "last straw" because, just two weeks prior to the freeze, steel producers and the United Steelworkers of America reached a new labor agreement ordaining an immediate increase of 15% in wage and fringe benefits, a sure sign that market-power push was sabotaging Nixon's monetarist policy. Moreover, most folks were by that time growing weary of inflation *plus* unemployment. There was consequently tremendous pressure on Nixon to "do something." Immediately after the freeze began, opinion polls showed 75% approval, including several expressions of near ecstasy from businessmen.[23]

The freeze was supposed to be a short and simple surprise. It was short because it was meant to be no more than a stopgap until a more elaborate Phase II control program could be devised. The element of surprise was necessary because prices and wages in power-laden sectors would have gone up like a gas tank inspected by match illumination had everyone known in advance that controls were in the offing. As for simplicity, a zero rate of change implies a clarity and purity unequalled by any other standard imaginable. Nixon expressly wanted bare-bones bureaucratic requirements.

Yet, the freeze was anything but simple. A listing of its complexities could fill a big book. Such a book would be instructive, however, because its message would be (quite simply) that even the simplest of control programs is a rat's nest. No less than four government agencies got their fingers in the enforcement stew—Internal Revenue Service, Office of Emergency Preparedness, Agricultural Stabilization and Conservation Service, and Cost of Living Council, the last of which was specially created to oversee the controls program. In the short span of 90 days, these agencies had to answer no fewer than 800,000 inquiries at field office level, 2435 special exemption requests, 400 executive-level questions, and 75 key policy issues. Among the latter were the following:

1. What should be covered besides wages and prices? Rents, interest rates, dividends, and profits? What about country club dues, college tuition, social security payments, and the like? Raw agricultural products were exempt from the start, but when are honey and peanuts transformed from

---

[22] This section is based largely on Arnold Weber, *op. cit.*
[23] *Business Week*, August 21, 1971, pp. 21–22.

raw to processed? What about exports and imports? Are their prices to be frozen?

2. The freeze applies in comparison to what? Prices and wages prevailing on August 15, 1971? If so, what about the many items that were "on sale" that day? What about goods whose prices are seasonal—normally rising or falling during the freeze period? Given an exemption for seasonal goods (which was granted), is Halloween candy a seasonal good?

3. There has to be some means of preventing evasion through quality change, but what is a quality change? Are grocery store trading stamps part of quality? And so on, *ad infinitum*.

4. What about price and wage changes that are by contract due to occur during the freeze? Should they be allowed? What about price increases that were posted and paid for *prior* to 8/15/71, but on goods and services not yet delivered? For example, should those who in July bought season tickets to see the Atlanta Falcons play football in the fall be reimbursed for the increase over prior year's prices?

5. Should exemptions go to those businesses whose costs increased substantially just before the freeze but whose prices had not yet been changed to reflect the higher costs? If denied, this could bankrupt some steel fabricators, whose cost of materials rose just before the freeze. What about passing on those costs attributable to government regulations and directives? Should the freeze squeeze?

6. What about enforcement? By the time you catch offenders and push them through court, 90 days will have passed. How heavily do you "lean" on delinquents, then?

The actual answers were stringent enough to decelerate prices and wages ubstantially. Between August and November 1971 the consumer price index ose at an annual rate of 1.6%, well below the 4.0 rate of increase during the 6 months preceding the freeze. Greater reductions were registered in the whole-ale price index and various wage indexes. Whether the freeze had any lasting mpact, however, is debatable. A big "bulge" of increases occurred just after the haw on November 14.

Phase II (November 1971 to January 1973)

The freeze gave way to what turned out to be protracted controls of varying overage and stringency. Table 22-1, which is a terse summary, conveys the ontent and complexity of these regulations.

During Phase II, statutory controls limited price increases on a firm-by-firm basis to a per cent pass-through of cost increases, meaning, for example, that prices could rise 10% if costs rose 10%. Since *increases* rather than *absolute* levels were being controlled, there had to be some base period against which the current costs could be compared, and the period varied. It could be either the ime of the "last" price increase or January 1, 1971, whichever was more

557

Table 22-1 Regulations of the Controls Program, Phases II, III, and IV

Program	Phase II 14 November 1971 to 11 January 1973	Phase III 11 January 1973 to 13 June 1973	Phase IV 12 August 1973 to 30 April 1974
General Standards			
Price increase limitations	Percentage pass-through of allowable cost increases since last price increase, or 1 Jan. 1971, adjusted for productivity and volume offsets. Term limit pricing option available.	Self-administered standards of Phase II.	In most manufacturing and service industries dollar-for-dollar pass-through of allowable cost increase since last fiscal quarter ending prior to 11 Jan. 1973.
Profit margin limitations	Not to exceed margins of the best 2 of 3 fiscal years before 15 August 1971. Not applicable if prices were not increased above base level, or if firms "purified" themselves.	Not to exceed margins of the best 2 fiscal years completed after 15 August 1968. No limitation if average price increase does not exceed 1.5%.	Same years as Phase III, except that a firm that has not charged a price for any item above its base price, or adjusted freeze price, whichever is higher, is not subject to the limitation. Self-administered standards of Phase III. Executive compensation limited.
Wage increase limitations	General standard of 5.5%. Exceptions made to correct gross inequities, and for workers whose pay had increased less than 7% a year for the last 3 years. Workers earning less than $2.75 per hour were exempt. Increases in qualified fringe benefits	General Phase II standard, self-administered. Some special limitations. More flexibility with respect to specific cases. Workers learning less than $3.50 per hour were exempted after 1 May.	

Wages	above $100 million, 30 days before implementation, approval required. For all increases of wages for units of 5000 or more; for all increases above the standard regardless of the number of workers involved.	all firms with sales above $250 million whose price increase has exceeded a weighted average of 1.5%. None.	increases may be implemented in 30 days unless CLC requires otherwise. None.
Reporting			
Prices	Quarterly for firms with sales over $50 million.	Quarterly for firms with sales over $250 million.	Quarterly for firms with sales over $50 million.
Wages	Pay adjustments below standard for units greater than 1000 persons.	Pay adjustments for units greater than 5000 persons.	Same as Phase III.
Special Areas	Health, insurance, rent, construction, public utilities.	Health, food, public utilities, construction, petroleum.	Health, food, petroleum, construction, insurance, executive and variable compensation.
Exemptions	Raw agricultural commodities, import prices, export prices, firms with 60 or fewer employees.	Same as Phase II plus rents.	Same as Phase III plus public utilities, lumber, copper scrap, and long-term coal contracts, initially with sector-by-sector decontrol of prices and wages until 30 April 1974.

Source: Cost of Living Council and *Economic Report of the President, 1974*, p. 91.

recent. But there was a catch. Price increases by this standard could not b
such as to generate "excess" profits, which were defined in historic term
particular to each firm. The *overall* goal was to hold price inflation to 2.5%
per year.

The general standard for wage increases was 5.5% per year. This standard
was based on the theory that, assuming a 3% rate of productivity advance
5.5% wage inflation would attain the 2.5% target level of price inflation. The
ghost of the old guideposts should be obvious here. Unfortunately, organized
labor was disenchanted with this standard (thinking it was too low, of course)
so an additional 0.7 percentage point was added for fringe benefits, resulting
in a total compensation standard of 6.2%. Furthermore, a major exception for
additional increments was granted to workers earning "substandard" wages
Interpretation of "substandard" proved a problem because the Cost of Living
Council, whose administrative responsibility carried over from the freeze
wanted a threshhold figure of $1.90 per hour, whereas organized labor insisted
it be higher. A compromise of $2.75 settled the dispute.

While the Cost of Living Council had overall policy authority, responsibility
for direct supervision of prices and wages was split between a Price Commission
(for prices) and a Pay Board (for wages and salaries), both of which ranked
below the Cost of Living Council. To aid their enforcement efforts, these agencies
developed rules for business notification of intended changes and for reporting
of actual changes. Their basic scheme divided all covered firms into three tiers

1. **Tier I firms** had sales exceeding $100 million or collective-bargaining
   units of 5000 or more employees. These firms had to obtain *prior
   approval* before implementing price and wage increases.
2. **Tier II firms** had sales between $50 million and $100 million or collective-
   bargaining units of 1000 to 5000 employees. These firms did not need
   prior approval for their actions, but they had to *submit regular reports*
   of behavior.
3. **Tier III firms**, with sales and employees below those of tier II firms,
   had no prenotification or reporting requirements.

Beyond these generalities lay hordes of exemptions, special treatments
and individual cases. Major exemptions were raw agricultural commodities
exports, imports, and small firms. One of the main special treatments concerned
public utilities. Rather than duplicate the efforts of public utility commissions
the Price Commission delegated its authority to control prices in those areas
to existing regulatory authorities. A memorable hint of the program's burial
beneath detail arose in this regard when the Price Commission received a
letter from a legal brothel in Nevada that was regulated by health authorities
The letter asked whether the Pay Board considered prostitution a service
industry or regulated utility.[24]

---

[24] Jackson Grayson, "A View from the Outside of the Inside of Upside Down," in *The Illusion
of Wage and Price Control, op. cit.*, p. 169.

In an attempt to avoid any more details than were absolutely necessary, the Pay Board entered into "term limit pricing" agreements with 185 large multi-product firms accounting for about $124 billion in sales. Under such an agreement a firm did not need to seek approval for every change of price for every one of its products. Each firm was free to boost prices substantially without cost justification on some portion of its product line, which portion being left up to each firm's discretion. However, in exchange for this lightened pre-notification burden and greater flexibility, each firm had to agree to raise its overall, weighted average price level by no more than about 2.0%.

Problems with Phase II. Administrators of the Phase I freeze passed a 400 page book of problems on to the officials who took over for Phase II. On top of this, Phase II produced its own brands of perplexity. For one thing, the "term limit pricing" agreements came under heavy fire from critics for being too lenient. Apparently half the firms so bound were unable to raise their weighted-average prices by amounts allowed. In addition, contrary to the intent of controls, the firms could raise prices substantially where they had market power. "By giving the individual firm freedom to decide which prices to increase," stated one critic, "the Price Commission is granting a license to exercise power wherever it is greatest."[25]

A problem now acknowledged even by former price control officials might be called the "great grocery gaffe." During the Phase I freeze grocery stores were required to post prices conspicuously so that shoppers could compare posted prices with actual prices and blow the whistle on any grocer with gross discrepancies. However, the freeze was so short and the signs so difficult to compile that the signs could not be placed in service until a few days before the end of the freeze. Rather than rub grocers the wrong way by scrapping the signs at the start of Phase II, they were kept for reporting "base prices." But the main technique of Phase II was to allow price increases for cost increases, not to freeze prices. So, as grocery prices climbed above posted prices, great confusion ensued. Many consumers thought the posted prices were the only legal prices, but unless the consumer knew specific margins of markup above cost, he could detect no violations by the signs, even if he understood what the signs represented. Hence the signs provoked many groundless complaints, and led many folks to think that Phase II was fake.[26] Indeed, it was probably a mistake to try to regulate retail food prices in the first place because raw agricultural products were exempt and grocery retailing is largely competitive. The Price Commission was so advised at the outset by economists, but for political reasons—namely the notion that "fairness" required control of virtually all sectors, competitive and monopolistic alike—the advice was rejected.

[25] Willard F. Mueller, in *Controls or Competition, op. cit.*, p. 23.
[26] Robert F. Lanzillotti, Mary T. Hamilton, and R. Blaine Roberts, *Phase II in Review* (Washington, D.C.: Brookings Institution, 1975), pp. 54–55

561

The fundamental method of percentage cost pass-through has also been attacked. With few exceptions, price increases were permitted to cover increased costs *plus* a customary profit margin on those added costs. By this method profits could increase with added cost, leading to charges that inefficiency was rewarded. It has been àrgued in defense of the program that the adverse effect was not as bad as it might seem.[27] Still, it can also be argued that a scheme of *partial* cost pass-through might have served better.[28]

Economic distortions provide the most sensational problems of any controls program, including Phase II. The lumber industry, where distortions stemmed from evasion efforts, is perhaps the best example to emerge from Phase II:

> First, since the regulations permitted higher prices when services were added to products, plywood producers performed the "service" of cutting 1/8 inch off plywood sheets and sold the sheets for substantially higher prices. The dimensions of lumber products were also shaved as a device to obtain effective price increases.
>
> Second, since the Price Commission could not control foreign producers and import prices were thus uncontrolled, producers in the Pacific Northwest exported lumber to Canada and reimported it at substantially higher prices.
>
> Third, Price Commission regulations that permitted normal markups at each stage of distribution spawned shipments of lumber from one wholesaler to another; each added a normal markup but did not perform all of the usual wholesaler functions.
>
> Finally, at least for a time, the regulated price on two-by-fours was relatively high as compared with boards; thus, logs were turned into two-by-fours and a shortage of boards developed.[29]

On the *wage* side of Phase II, the biggest problem with the Pay Board was that it leaned toward leniency, especially where strong unions were involved. As compared to the 5.5 % wage standard, the average rate of approved increases in major collective bargain agreements was 7.0 % during 1972. Nonunion wage increases were considerably lower, however, largely as a result of continued slack in aggregate demand during 1972. It was thus these substandard increases in the nonunion sector that permitted overall average hourly earnings to rise at a 5.6 % rate during the year, running just shy of the 5.5 target.

These many sour spots in Phase II would leave less aftertaste today if it could be shown that Phase II allayed wage-price inflation significantly. But econometric studies yield no consensus that it did. Several estimates reveal absolutely no effect for either prices or wages. Several others suggest a down-shift of 0.5 to 2.0 percentage points in price inflation plus some lesser conse-

[27] *Ibid.*, pp. 80–97.
[28] A. Bradley Askin, "Wage-Price Controls in Administrative and Political Perspective," in *Wage and Price Controls: The U. S. Experiment*, edited by John Kraft and Blaine Roberts (New York: Praeger, 1975), pp. 26–27.
[29] William Poole, "Wage-Price Controls: Where Do We Go From Here?" *Brookings Paper. on Economic Activity*, No. 1 (1973), p. 292.

uences for wage inflation. The one thing that seems certain is that *if* there was ny effect at all, prices were restrained more than wages.[30]

Phases III and VI, Plus Another Freeze

President Nixon terminated Phase II on January 11, 1973, replacing it with Phase III. As shown in Table 22-1, Phase III retained the standards of Phase II but removed most prenotification and reporting requirements. The Pay Board and Price Commission were abolished, leaving only the Cost of Living Council. In addition, exemptions were broadened to free rents and free more workers earning "substandard" wages. (Remarkably, the new low-wage exemption was set at $3.50, which was only slightly below average hourly earnings for *all* nonfarm workers.[31]) The stated purpose of the changes was to reduce administrative burdens while continuing controls. Compliance was to be "voluntary." In fact, most people saw Phase III as a *relaxation* of controls rather than a mere *reorganization*.

Price behavior during the next six months seemed to confirm people's impression of an economic dam-break: the wholesale price index leaped to 22.3% annual rate of increase, and the consumer price index rose to an 8.0% annual pace of advance. Actually, conversion to Phase III had little to do with this surge, for it came mainly from sectors uncontrolled from the beginning. In particular, wholesale prices of farm products exploded, elevating at close to a 40% annual rate of increase during the first 6 months of 1973. This jump was due to domestic shortages of agricultural commodities relative to an extremely strong surge of worldwide demand for our exports. Prices for timber and petroleum leaped for similar reasons.[32] On top of these exogenous shocks, the aggregate economy moved into high gear, responding to expansionary monetary and fiscal policies launched with the Phases. Unemployment fell from 6.0% at the start of Phase II in November 1972 to 4.8% in June 1973. In short, the timing of Phase II's demise was a public relations catastrophe.

Amid public pressure to reinstate tough controls, Phase III was abandoned while still in its infancy. A second freeze descended over the land. Like the first freeze, this one hit during the summer, lasting from mid-June to mid-August. *Unlike* the first one, this one hit just when the main inflationary forces at work were chiefly exogenous shock and demand-pull. What is more, this freeze was followed by Phase IV, which, as shown in Table 22-1, was in many respects even more stringent than Phase II. In particular, the new price standards permitted pass-through of cost increases only on a dollar-for-dollar basis, not on a

---

[30] For reviews see Kraft and Roberts, *op. cit.*, pp. 143–49; Pohlman, *op. cit.*, pp. 221–26; Brittan and Lilley, *op. cit.*, pp. 146–50.

[31] Albert Rees, *Wage-Price Policy* (General Learning Press, 1974), p. 16.

[32] Ross E. Azevedo, "Phase III—A Stabilization Program That Could Not Work," *Quarterly Review of Economics and Business* (Spring 1976), pp. 7–21.

percentage basis. (That is, if one's cost rose by 50¢ a widget, price per widget could rise only 50¢, not 50¢ plus some percentage markup.)

The results of Freeze II and Phase IV added up to more than a public relations catastrophe. Their inappropriateness produced some genuine economic catastrophes:

> When prices of more and more commodities were held below market clearing levels in late 1973, symptoms of inefficiency became increasingly widespread and diverse. Curtailment of domestic supply was sometimes threatened by increased exports, reduced production to avoid losses, and failure to expand production through use of marginal production capacity. Lack of availability and wide differences in prices of material inputs complicated production planning and threatened to disrupt production schedules. Distribution and purchasing operations were complicated by multiple prices and instances of bartering in order to reduce costs or obtain scarce materials, and black markets were frequently reported. Shortages were perhaps the most commonly reported symptom of inefficiency . . . [33]

Under these burdens, folks quickly became weary and disenchanted. Phase IV officially died on April 30, 1974. Whereas controls were greeted with rousing cheers in August 1971, no woeful wails over Phase IV's death could be heard the first day of May 1974. The contrast of public emotions seems odd when set against the fact that consumer prices were rising *three times faster toward the end of Phase IV than they were rising before imposition of Phase I.* Of course the explanation is very simple. People began to look upon controls as a sham and a burden. That is, folks learned two lessons: (1) controls cannot suppress a chronic inflationary trend, especially not one "goosed" by exogenous shocks and (2) if controls are given an earnest try, they create distortions, inefficiencies and inequities that may even aggravate the inflation in the long run.[34] Need we add that these feelings cultivated a widespread disrespect for the law?

European Experience

European experience with controls, usually called "incomes policies," is greater than United States experience. Although a few observers look favorably on European policies,[35] most agree that on balance they have failed.[36]

---

[33] Marvin Kosters, *Controls and Inflation* (Washington, D.C.: American Enterprise Institute, 1975) pp. 94–95.

[34] Monetarists are among the quickest to complain of shortages created by government administered price ceilings.

[35] For example, Organization for Economic Co-operation and Development, *Socially Responsible Wage Policies and Inflation* (1975); Ann R. Braun, "The Role of Incomes Policy in Industrial Countries Since World War II," *International Monetary Fund Staff Papers* (March 1975), pp. 1–36

[36] For example, Brittan and Lilley, *op. cit.*; Lloyd Ulman and Robert J. Flanagan, *Wage Restraint: A Study of Incomes Policies in Western Europe* (Berkeley, Calif.: University of California Press, 1971); David C. Smith, *Incomes Policies* (Ottawa: Economic Council of Canada, 1966); Walter Galenson (ed.), *Incomes Policy: What Can We Learn from Europe?* (Ithaca, N.Y.: Cornell University School of Industrial and Labor Relations, 1973); Michael Parkin and Michael T. Sumner (eds.), *Incomes Policy and Inflation* (Toronto: University of Toronto Press, 1972).

Thus, Lloyd Ulman and Robert Flanagan conclude their study of seven European countries by saying that "in none of the variations so far turned up has incomes policy succeeded in its fundamental objective, as stated, of making full employment consistent with a reasonable degree of price stability."[37] Walter Galenson's view is also representative: "Great Britain, Sweden, and Holland have had indifferent success with bouts of formal incomes policy."[38] Even proponents of controls, like Jerry Pohlman, admit that the European record is bleak:

> Certainly, one who attempts to find strong support for the effectiveness of wage and price restraints by looking abroad will be disappointed. Without exception, market controls have broken down at some time or another in all the free economies that have tried them.[39]

It may seem odd, then, that experience has not discouraged advocates of controls. They argue that controls are sound in principle; that failures occur only because of faulty application. They explain away failures as results of (1) inadequate sanctions, (2) lack of public support, (3) failure to constrain money supply in the course of control effort, (4) inappropriate application to money supply inflations, (5) over ambitious coverage and duration, and (6) unsatisfactory supervision of relative income shares.

The Continued Search

Can controls be patched up? Can they be made to succeed? Mention of a few proposed improvements (short of totalitarianism) concludes this review.

Limited coverage is one of the most common corrections called for. The idea is to focus stringent controls solely on big business and big labor, ignoring competitive areas, such as food and lumber, which have been reduced to chaos by past control efforts. There is a problem here, however. Defenders of limited coverage have yet to explain why this narrow lunge at largeness is politically more realistic than a policy of competitive restructuring, or why, if it is equally realistic, controls are superior to competition.

Another modification would be to keep controls temporary, to apply them only occasionally. Although this view has its merits, it seems tantamount to applying a band-aid to cure a malignant tumor. Temporary application of controls may even have the adverse side effect of delaying implementation of more effective long-lasting treatments.

Others see past controls as not being permanent enough. If controls collapse because of disputes over relative income shares, then the solution is to draw up a massive schedule of formulas "fairly" fixing everyone's wage relative to everyone else's wage. Indeed, England has already taken steps in this direction.

---

[37] Ulman and Flanagan, *op. cit.*, p. 216.
[38] Galenson, *op. cit.*, p. xiv.
[39] Pohlman, *op. cit.*, p. 187.

There are two problems with this approach, however. First, if the wage-relative decided upon do not correspond to those that would be cranked out by th market (and there is no reason to think that they would so correspond economic chaos will ensue. Second, the approach is politically unrealistic. A explained by Samuel Brittan and Peter Lilley:

> However resentful they are about it, people will in the last resort accept a relatively low position in the pecking order if it is due to the luck of the market . . . . If, on the other hand, their low position seems to result from a moralistic evaluation of their merits made by their fellow citizens through some political process, they will stop at nothing to get the judgement withdrawn. No one likes being consigned to the rubbish heap by a body of wise men appointed to express the supposed moral evaluations of society.[40]

Finally, a number of economists, most notably Sidney Weintraub and Henr Wallich, advocate a "taxed-based incomes policy," or TIP.[41] The basic ideal i to stiffen the backbone of businessmen against labor's inflationary wage de mands. This would be achieved by heavily taxing those businesses that gran wage increases above some specified standard. An alternative approach woul provide tax breaks for those who voluntarily limit their wage increases to specific amount. In essence, these plans provide streamlined enforcemen mechanisms for a guidelines policy. They have the advantage of relying o market forces more than most incomes policies. Yet they, too, are not withou deficiencies and distortions.

Competition Policy

During the "greenback" period, 1865–1879, the price level in the Unite States was cut in half with very little rise in unemployment. What happene between the late 1870s and the late 1970s to produce prices and wages that ar now unresponsive to recession? It could be that the rise of industrial con centration and union organization explain much of the difference. Indee historical comparisons of this kind moved Milton Friedman, king of th monetarists, to admit that in the course of deflating an economy the existenc of unions may make the problem of unemployment "more difficult" than would otherwise be.[42] But we need not ransack history for evidence of marke power's adverse effects. Recall from our earlier reviews of modern cross-sectio evidence that a given level of slack depresses prices and wages more in con petitive than in noncompetitive contexts.[43]

---

[40] Brittan and Lilley, *op. cit.*, p. 186.

[41] Weintraub, *op. cit.*: and Henry Wallich and Sidney Weintraub, "A Tax-Based Incom Policy," *Journal of Economic Issues* (June 1971), pp. 1–19.

[42] Milton Friedman *et. al.*, *Inflation: Causes, Consequences, Cures* (London: Institute of Eco omic Affairs, 1974), p. 96.

[43] See Chapters 11 and 12 or D. Greer, *op. cit.*, and Phillip Cagan "Changes in the Recessio Behavior of Wholesale Prices in the 1920's and Post-World War II," *NBER Explorations in Eco omic Research* (Winter 1975), pp. 54–104.

Thus we finally come to the last of our options—pro-competition policy. What this means with respect to business has already been suggested in previous chapters. To be explicit but not redundant, proponents of greater competition advocate more vigorous enforcement of present antitrust laws. In addition, many support reform of those laws to achieve extensive restructuring of highly concentrated industries presently not reached by the Sherman Act. An Industrial Reorganization Act," such as that proposed by the late Senator Philip Hart (and discussed near the end of Chapter 9), seems desirable to them. Hart felt that "we must find ways to inject competition into our economy if we are to rid ourselves of government wage and price controls."[44] Competitive restructuring would probably yield economic benefits beyond those concerning inflation. Moreover, without industrial reform, little could be done to lessen the power of labor unions, political realities being what they are.

On the labor side much could be done short of abolishing unions. Restrictions on union membership could be lessened by prohibiting prior apprenticeships and exorbitant initiation fees, thereby lowering barriers to entry. Union-operated hiring halls could be abolished. Compulsory union membership as embodied in the "union-shop" could be outlawed. Labor moderation could also be achieved by staunchly holding unions and their leaders financially responsible for breaches of contracts, illegal strikes, intimidation, and violence.[45]

Mention of some of these items raises an important point. Greater competition can be achieved not only by restructuring markets, but also by *less* anticompetitive government intervention. Many of the privileges and immunities enjoyed by unions are the handiwork of government. Looking beyond unions *per se*, the Walsh–Healy Act and Davis–Bacon Act require that government contractors pay "prevailing" wages, which usually means union wages. These laws artificially prop wages and could be repealed. Moreover, minimum wage laws could be abandoned, as they not only contribute to inflation, they also cause unemployment among the young, inexperienced, and poorly skilled

---

[44] Senator Philip Hart, *Controls or Competition*, Hearings before the Subcommittee on Antitrust and Monopoly, U. S. Senate, 92nd Congress, Second Session (1972), p. 2.

[45] Haberler, *op. cit.*, p. 128. Procontrols people argue against tampering with unions on grounds that they provide "benefits" outweighing their costs. Just what these benefits are, and how much they add up to, is rarely stated. But the argument is not ironclad, as indicated by the following assessment of Albert Rees: "If the union is viewed solely in terms of its effect on the economy, it must in my opinion be considered an obstacle to the optimum performance of our economic system. It alters the wage structure in a way that impedes the growth of employment in sectors of the economy where productivity and income are naturally high and that leaves too much labor in low-income sectors of the economy like southern agriculture and the least skilled service trades. It benefits most those workers who would in any case be relatively well off, and while some of this gain may be at the expense of the owners of capital, most of it must be at the expense of consumers and the lower paid workers. Unions interfere blatantly with the use of the most productive techniques in some industries, and this effect is probably not offset by the stimulus to higher productivity furnished by some other unions." [*The Economics of Trade Unions* (Chicago: University of Chicago Press, 1977 edition) p. 186]. Rees goes on to praise unions for noneconomic benefits, such as political representation and grievance voice, but none of these institutional benefits seems dependent on perpetuation of present union power over workers and wages.

who populate the bottom of the wage ladder. Lowering unemployment com
pensation payments would also loosen labor markets by lessening the luxur
of those out of work. If unemployment is made less of a holiday, workers wi
strike less often and compete more earnestly for jobs, even if it means occasion
ally accepting only modest wages.[46]

In the same vein, all forms of government intervention that officially carteliz
otherwise competitive markets could be annulled. Public utility regulation c
transportation could be abolished or sharply curtailed to great benefit. Agr
cultural price supports, marketing agreements, production quotas, marketin
orders, and the like could be abandoned. Many state sponsored licensing an
regulation boards for opticians, architects, dentists, lawyers, morticians, T
repairmen, barbers, cosmeticians, and other diverse "professionals" effectivel
restrict competition and therefore probably ought to be disbanded or reforme
In the area of banking and finance, removal of regulations would permit great
competition between commercial banks, savings and loans, mutual saving
banks, credit unions, and finance companies. Ceilings on interest rates for bot
deposits and loans could be phased out. Antitrust could also be more vigorousl
applied in financial markets than at present.

Still more competition could be achieved by doing away with shackles o
imports. Tariffs, import quotas, "voluntary" trade restraints, "trigger-pricing
plans, administrative regulations, and related measures have for decad
protected domestic producers from foreign rivalry. Steel, milk, sugar, textile
and TV sets are among the countless products so protected. It is ironic that th
Price Commission of Phase II fame claimed as one of its greatest anti-inflatio
achievements the temporary relaxation of import controls on meat. Th
spectacle of a controls commission fighting to undo controls was somethin
to behold.

The preceding list is limited and unrefined.[47] Even as it stands it may seer
sweeping if not revolutionary (and it is). Monetarists and pro-controls peopl
are undoubtedly more right than wrong when they say that passage of such
program is politically unrealistic, however economically desirable it may b
The connection between the action and the payoff is too complicated fc
most people to understand. And economists do not speak with one voice.

Appreciation of its dim political prospects is furthered by noting that virtuall
all offending government interventions originated in attempts to satisfy th
wishes of "special interest" groups. These groups gained at others' expens
and reform implies that they will lose to others' benefit. These groups ma
therefore be expected to fight like hell to preserve their special interests again:
any attack. Recognizing this, Hendrik Houthakker of Harvard has propose
passage of an omnibus anti-inflation bill, comprehensively including all measur
such as those listed above and others like them. The virtue of this approac

---

[46] See Martin S. Feldstein, "Lowering the Permanent Rate of Unemployment," U. S. Congres
Joint Economic Committee (September 18, 1973).

[47] Moreover, supporting citations would be endless, but many are mentioned elsewhere in th
book.

that losers in one respect would simultaneously gain in other respects. Moreover, the bill could provide for "establishment of an adjustment assistance fund which could make limited grants to firms or workers seriously damaged by provisions of the bill, or guarantee loans to firms for restructuring made necessary by the bill."[48]

Lest the gains and losses, if ever incurred, disturb the reader too greatly, it should be remembered that the market system itself works by gains and losses. Moreover, virtually all these anticompetitive interventions were originally founded on some alleged "unfairness" of the gains and losses doled out by markets. To be sure, privately monopolistic markets may be "unfair." But the "fairness" of competitive markets, such as those advocated by pro-competition people are less open to question.[49]

Summary

There are three broad policy approaches to achieving price stability with full employment—strict monetary restraint, government controls, and greater competition. Advocacy of each is grounded on references to realism. Opposition to each is likewise grounded on references to realism.

Monetarists point to the close connection between money supply and price-wage level for their economic realism. They concede that checking an on-going inflation necessarily creates unemployment, but they argue that, politically, people are willing to pay short-term pains to gain long-term stability. Opponents of the monetarist position concede that monetary restraint is a necessary step toward stability but deny that it is sufficient. They claim that monetary restraint alone cannot contend with the potent inflationary forces caused by concentrations of market power—not without hoisting unemployment to politically unacceptable intensities and durations.

Advocates of controls favor direct but "democratic" supervision of wages and prices, particularly in noncompetitive markets, as a supplement to responsible monetary policy. They concede that controls would be unnecessary in a competitive world, but argue that attainment of competition is politically unrealistic. They also concede that democratic operation of a controls system requires the support or acquiescence of society, especially the big power blocks. However, they see this requirement as no problem. Opponents of controls say that, in reality, controls (1) erode with time, (2) generate distortions, inefficiencies, and shortages, (3) reduce freedom, (4) foster disrespect for the law, (5) detract from more constructive anti-inflation treatments, and (6) achieve no lasting wage-price stability (unless enforced by the iron hand of a dictator).

[48] Hendrik S. Houthakker, "A Positive Way to Fight Inflation," *Wall Street Journal*, July 30, 1974, p. 12.

[49] For a discussion of "fairness" as an inappropriate guide to policies that undermine the market see William Poole, "Carter and the Economics of Fairness," *Wall Street Journal*, May 15, 1978.

Proponents of a pro-competitive transformation of the economy believe that monetary restraint must be supplemented with competition. In particular they contend that exogenous shock inflations ignite market-power push inflations that cannot be suppressed by simple monetary restraint without horrendous and politically unrealistic costs in vast idleness. Neither can these inflations be suppressed by controls because it is just such shocks that have repeatedly ruptured control programs. Opponents of pro-competitive policy have only one basic criticism—it is politically unrealistic. Proponents admit that this is largely true; yet they remain hopeful. After all, they say, political "realities" might change. The economy could very well lurch from crisis to crisis until eventually such a program of reform becomes acceptable. On the other hand they worry that if reform is put off too long, problems may build to the point where all three policy options under discussion lose all touch with reality (leaving only dreadful, unthinkable options that have only been alluded to here).

One last analogy: What would you do about an alcoholic? A monetarist would say lock the liquor cabinet and let the poor guy endure the pain of drying out. A controls person would say that that is futile because the guy has a key to the cabinet, making withdrawal impossible, acutely painful psychologically, or prolonged. Instead, he must be jaw-boned, cajoled, and convinced not to use his key, except for maybe a nip here and there. A pro-competition person would say take away the guy's key then lock the cabinet. Otherwise every one of life's little setbacks will put him on a binge and eventually we might have to lock *him* up.

23

Technological Change: Theory and Cross-Section Evidence

What laws govern the growth of man's mastery over nature?

JACOB SCHMOOKLER

From the first squawky telephone to the latest supersonic transport, techological change has done more than anything else to shape our modern economy and everyday life. Innovation spurs growth, boosts productivity, lifts profits, lengthens lives, generates jobs, and enriches experiences. Nearly half of all this century's gains in real income can be attributed to technological progress. The lion's share of the products we now use and take for granted simply did not exist as little as three generations ago—television, frozen food, zippers, computers, air conditioning, penicillin, nylon, refrigerators, synthetic detergents, Frisbees, and so on. Whereas your investment in a savings account returns 5%, society's investment in research and development (R & D) yields a fantastic return of 30–50%[1].

What is the role of industry in all this? During 1976, a typical year, private companies spent $16.4 billion on R & D. Roughly 60% of this expenditure went for improvement of existing products, 30% for development of new products, and 10% for developing new processes of production. On top of this, private industry conducted more than half of all R & D funded by the federal government, which in 1976 amounted to $23.6 billion. Thus a total of $38.1

---

[1] Edwin Mansfield, "Federal Support of R & D Activities in the Private Sector," *Priorities and Efficiency in Federal Research and Development*, Joint Economic Committee of the U. S. Congress, 4th Congress, Second Session (October 29, 1976), pp. 95–99.

billion was spent on R & D that year, 70% of which flowed through industri. laboratories and research centers.[2]

In this light, questions concerning industry's performance for progress tak on a serious glow. Does high concentration help or hinder technologic advance? What sorts and sizes of firms put forth the greatest R & D effor Are there still active independent inventors cast in the image of Thomas Ediso and the Wright brothers? These queries now occupy our focus. We begin t filling in some background. The remainder of the chapter is then divided int two major portions, one covering the impact of firm size, the other discussir the effect of market structure. It will be seen that bigness comes out lookir better than it has in previous chapters, but only to a limited degree.[3]

Concepts and Conditions

Edison was undoubtedly right when he said that invention is the produ of "one percent inspiration and ninety-nine percent perspiration." But fc present purposes, **invention** is best defined as "*the first confidence that somethin should work, and the first rough test that it will, in fact, work.*"[4] It requires a *initial concept* and *crude proof.* Furthermore, a common caveat is that a invention must possess *utility*, not inanity.

Although invention is surely the seed of technical progress, it is only the see In monetary weight invention accounts for no more than about 5–15% of th total cost of bringing most new products to market or placing new productio processes into service for the first time. By far the greatest amount of time an expense goes into what may be called innovation. **Innovation** *is the first con mercial application of an invention.* It entails refinement of the basic idea, testin prototypes, debugging, development, engineering, initial production, and pe haps initial marketing as well.

In many cases there is no clear boundary between invention and innovatior Conceptually, however, "Invention is the stage at which the scent is fir picked up, development the stage at which the hunt is in full cry."[5] Wherea about 5–15% of a successful new product's cost goes into invention, abou 10–20% goes into engineering and design, 40–60% is spent on toolin and manufacturing set-up, 5–15% into manufacturing start-up, and 10–25 covers initial marketing expenses.[6] A similar pattern is revealed by a breal

---

[2] *Business Week*, June 27, 1977, pp. 62–63.

[3] Excellent surveys guiding this one include F. M. Scherer, *Industrial Market Structure ar Economic Performance*, (Chicago: Rand McNally, 1970), Chapter 15; Morton I. Kamien an Nancy L. Schwartz, "Market Structure and Innovation: A Survey," *Journal of Economic Literatu* (March 1975), pp. 1–37.

[4] John Jewkes, David Sawers, and Richard Stillerman, *The Sources of Invention*, 2nd ed. (Ne York: Norton, 1969), p. 28.

[5] *Ibid.*

[6] U. S. Department of Commerce, *Technological Innovation: Its Environment and Manageme* (Washington, D.C., 1967), p. 9.

own of industrial R & D outlays for 1973, as estimated by the National Science Foundation:

$599 million, or 2.8%, went toward *basic research*, for the advancement of *general scientific knowledge*;

$3,762 million, or 17.9%, went for *applied research*, pursuing what could be called inventions;

$16,561 million, or 79.3%, went into *development*, that is, innovative activities concerned with translating research findings into commercial products or processes.[7]

Innovation also consumes a tremendous amount of time, further separating the first flash of insight from the marketing debut. John Enos estimated the interval between invention and innovation for 44 major discoveries, finding that, on average, the interval was about 13 years. To mention a few examples: radio was 8 years maturing; jet engine, 14 years; catalytic cracking of petroleum, years; ballpoint pen, 6 years; magnetic recording, 5 years; mechanical cotton picker, 53 years; television, 22 years; and dacron, 12 years.[8] In short, innovation is indispensible; an invention without innovation is like an unsung song.

But advance requires still more, a third stage called **diffusion**. The innovation may flop, or it may spread. Clearly, *the extent and speed of any spread can be very important to overall progress*. Like the earlier stages, diffusion usually takes time and money because it, too, is essentially a learning process. Unlike the earlier stages, however, this learning process is not confined to a single research laboratory or a few firms; it can involve multitudes of producers and users. The digital watch provides a timely example of diffusion. Introduced in 1972 at $2000 apiece, it was at first more a curiosity than a chronometer. But then it caught on. With improvements, climbing sales, longer production runs, and cost reductions, prices fell from $2000 to $10 in just 5 years ($10 being the bottom of the line, of course). Forecasts now indicate that in 1980 half of all watches sold will be digital.[9]

It may be concluded that a full assessment of progressive peformance must take into account *invention, innovation,* and *diffusion*. Each is different. Yet each is crucial to progress. And it will be shown that, to some degree, certain firm sizes and certain market structures perform better at one stage than others. These distinctions should therefore be put in warm storage.

One more preliminary comment needs mention. Good performance in these several respects cannot be measured in absolute terms. Given that Eastman Kodak spends $335 million on R & D and Polaroid spends $78 million, as they

[7] National Science Foundation, *Research and Development in Industry 1973* (NSF 75-315), pp. 7, 55.

[8] John L. Enos, "Invention and Innovation in the Petroleum Refining Industry," reprinted in *Economic Concentration Hearings*, Part 3, U. S. Senate 98th Congress, First Session, Subcommittee on Antitrust and Monopoly (1965), pp. 1486–91.

[9] *Business Week*, October 27, 1975, pp. 78–92; January 26, 1976, pp. 27–28; May 2, 1977, pp. 8–80.

573

did in 1976, one cannot conclude therefrom that Kodak is the more progressive of the two. *Relative to sales,* Polaroid spent 8.2% as against Kodak's 6.2%. *Relative to profits* Polaroid spent 97.4% to Kodak's 51.6%. The implication should be obvious. Accordingly, subsequent analysis places heavy reliance on a varied assortment of *relative* measures.

Unfortunately, the problem cuts even deeper than can be controlled by converting all statistics to percentage or per unit values. Let private R & D spending as a percent of sales be 4.4% for instruments and 0.5% for leather and leather products, as shown in Table 23-1 for 1973. One is tempted to deduce from this marked disparity that performance in instruments is "better" than in leather goods. But such a supposition might be wrong. Although relative outlays are plainly higher for instruments, the *opportunity* for technical progress is also much greater for instruments (which includes modern optical, surgical, and photographic gadgetry of all kinds) than for leather goods (which includes such items of ancient craft as belts, gloves, and shoes).

Given a greater opportunity, the profitability of R & D will be greater over a larger range of expenditure. It is only natural to expect, then, that industries

TABLE 23-1 Selected Data for R & D Performing Companies: By Industry 1973

Industry	(1) Total R & D Funds ($ millions)	(2) Total Funds as a Per Cent of Sales (%)	(3) Company Funds as a Per Cent of Sales (%)
Aircraft and missiles	5051	13.5	2.9
Electrical equipment	5333	7.1	3.6
Motor vehicles	2411	3.5	2.9
Machinery	2144	3.8	3.2
Chemicals	2081	3.5	3.1
Instruments	914	5.6	4.4
Petroleum	504	0.7	0.7
Rubber	284	1.8	1.6
Primary metals	272	0.6	0.6
Food products	270	0.4	0.4
Paper	198	0.7	0.7
Textiles and apparel	64	0.4	0.4
Lumber, wood products	55	0.6	0.6
Printing, publishing	32	0.6	0.6
Leather goods	8	0.5	0.5

Source: National Science Foundation, *Research and Development in Industry 1973* (NSF 75–315, 1975).

and firms with richer opportunities will outspend and outinnovate those suffering relatively impoverished prospects. Much of the interindustry variation in outlays observed in Table 23-1 can probably be pinned on just such differences. At the top of the list we find aircraft, missiles, electronics, motor vehicles, chemicals, and machinery (which includes computers). All enjoy dazzling opportunities and spend accordingly. Indeed, these industries alone account for over 80% of all industrial R & D. Toward the bottom of the list are food, textiles, apparel, and wood products as well as leather goods. Centuries of attention paid to their design and production undoubtedly curtails present-day leeway for change. Hence progressiveness ought to be measured *relative to the potential for progress*. Full exploitation of an industry's opportunities would then be good performance. Failure to reach full potential would mean defective performance, even though observed progress may give impressive appearances.

It is of course difficult to know exactly where full potentials of this sort lie. In fact, it was at one time thought that meaningful economic research in this area was impossible, that ignorance of true technological opportunities was fatal to the undertaking.[10] Luckily, this is not so. Ways around the problem have been devised. These ways should therefore be noted.

First, and most obviously, federal contributions to R & D have to be excluded when calculating private industry performance. Otherwise, those few industries benefitting from federal largess—aircraft, electronics, and communications, in particular—would have an unfair edge. This may be seen in Table 23-1 by comparing *total* R & D of column (2) with *company* R & D of column (3), both taken relative to sales. The difference is federally funded.

Second, much can be learned by comparing the progressiveness of individual firms *within a single industry*. All such firms presumably face the *same* opportunities, whatever they may be. Hence we shall review more evidence concerning individual firms here than anywhere else in the book. This evidence is not only intriguing, it is also pertinent; if an industry's small firms out-do their bigger brethren, it might pay to slice the big ones smaller. Then again, the evidence might suggest the opposite conclusion.

Finally, *inter*industry comparisons of progressiveness are possible if potentials are accounted for in some fashion. The techniques tried thus far include use of "dummy" variables in regression analysis and international comparisons. The latter are easiest to explain. French steel and American steel industries presumably face the same opportunities, but one may be more highly concentrated than the other, in which case any differences in progressiveness between them might be due to this structural difference. Still another approach can be used for diffusion. If a single innovation is useable in several industries but adopted at different rates in different industries, one can test whether market structure helps to explain those different rates of adoption. Numerically controlled machine tools is one such innovation.

---

[10] Joe Bain, *Industrial Organization* (New York: Wiley & Sons 1968), p. 460.

Within the confines of these various techniques, it will be assumed that more progressiveness means better performance. This, too, has its problems. Sensitive readers need no prodding to realize that "more" is not necessarily "better." They may object that newness can be unsettling and even dangerous. Faster cars and deadlier pesticides might mark progress in terms of "more," but they might also raise costs of safety and pollution. Other examples abound—synthetic detergents, food additives, nuclear power, and so on. This particular objection to progressiveness certainly has its merits. But we shall have to postpone problems of safety and pollution until Chapters 25 and 26. For the moment, we shall simply assume that "more" R & D, "more" patents, "more" innovations, and "more" rapid diffusion are indeed for the better.

Firm Size and Progressiveness

Theory

Confident that big firms were more progressive than small, J. K. Galbraith wrote some time ago that "a benign Providence . . . has made the modern industry of a few large firms an excellent instrument for inducing technical change."[11] He was not alone in his praise of bigness. Others before and after have expressed the same sentiment. They rest their case on a chain of arguments.

1. *Absolute size*: It is alleged that big firms can better afford R & D outlays. They have bigger bank balances and richer cash flows than smaller firms. Given the immense expense of R & D projects, small firms simply cannot compete.

2. *Economies of scale*: Invention and innovation often require costly specialized equipment—wind tunnels, test tracks, electron microscopes, and so on. Researchers themselves are growing ever more specialized, necessitating teamwork. These R & D inputs can be used more efficiently by large scale enterprises, or so it is argued.

3. *Risk*: Every project is a gamble. Large size enables numerous projects, so the hits can offset the misses. Risk thus diminishes with added size.

4. *Time horizon*: It is contended that a larger firm can wait longer for a payoff than a smaller firm. This argument presumably gives larger firms longer time horizons, and innovation is time consuming.

5. *Diversification*: R & D often yield unexpected outcomes. Search for a synthetic fiber may turn up a new paint. Since bigger firms tend to be more diversified than smaller firms, the giants can better exploit these happenstances.

Though plausible, these arguments are not unassailable. Those who question the view that bigness is better quarrel with these theoretical assertions. It can

[11] John Kenneth Galbraith, *American Capitalism* (Boston: Houghton Mifflin, 1956), p. 86.

be argued that, although many projects are indeed costly and require large absolute size, many are not. Some run into the millions, some into the thousands. The range leaves ample room for smaller firms, and, on average, the cost of a typical project is not gargantuan. By one estimate, "the median project in the combined R & D project portfolio of all sizeable U.S. industrial corporations in 1976 would have a total R & D cost of less than $500,000."[12]

As for economies of scale, a small firm may be able to overcome a handicap by hiring the services of a large independent R & D outfit, whose sole activity is research and whose costs are spread over its many contract customers. The fact that most contracted R & D is done for large firms does not negate this possibility. Moreover, it can be argued that since R & D is a *creative* activity, the bureaucratic tangles that bigness inevitably brings may be stifling rather than liberating, inefficient rather than efficient.

Risk, too, may be questioned as a force favoring bigness. To be sure, the bigger firm may be able to back more projects and thereby assure itself success in some of them, just as "the richer gambler who backs more horses in the race is, other things being equal, more likely to pick the winner."[13] However, it may be doubted whether the returns from this strategy are *more than proportionate* to the outlay. If they are not, then great size gives no particular advantage.

Moreover, it may be questioned whether the risk in funding only a few projects intimidates the smaller firms. Do race tracks draw only the wealthy who can wager on a number of nags each time round? Don't bet on it. There are countless little guys who *really* gamble; there are countless small firms accepting great risks. Conversely, there are many large firms whose bureaucrats seem to shun almost everything short of a sure thing. Approval of projects in big firms typically requires clearance of several managerial layers, something that heightens the chances that uncertain undertakings will be vetoed by "an abominable no-man."[14] IBM repeatedly rejected opportunities to develop and produce the Xerox machine, saying it was too risky. But it was not too risky for Haloid, the half-pint company that actually undertook the task and later changed its name to Xerox. IBM management also ordered IBM researchers to drop development of disk memories, one of the most significant of all computer inventions. Although IBM later claimed credit for these devices, it could do so only because several unruly IBM researchers ignored orders, endangered their jobs, secretly persisted, and eventually succeeded.[15]

Several studies by Edwin Mansfield indicate that the risks of R & D may not be as awesome as commonly supposed. His most recent study summarizes the 1968–1971 experience of 16 firms in the chemical, drug, petroleum, and

---

[12] F. M. Scherer, *The Economic Effects of Compulsory Patent Licensing* (New York: New York University Graduate School of Business Administration, 1977, Monograph 1977-2), p. 15.

[13] Jewkes, Sawers, and Stillerman, *op. cit.*, p. 130.

[14] C. Northcote Parkinson's expression, cited by Scherer *op. cit.*, (1970), p. 354.

[15] *Economic Concentration Hearings*, *op. cit.*, p. 1217.

electronics industries.[16] Mansfield quantifies the probabilities of success at three stages that roughly correspond to invention, innovation, and diffusion but go by different labels. He finds considerable variation, but the average probability of successful "technical completion" was 57%. Of those projects passing "technical completion," 65% were "commercialized." And of those "commercialized," 74% returned a profit. In other words, the probability of prize-winning was better than 50:50 at the purely technical level. These good odds seem "to be due to the fact that the bulk of R & D projects are aimed at fairly modest advances in the state of the art." Eventual profitability is much more precarious, however. Of all projects entering the front end of the R & D pipeline, only about 27% emerge profitably at the rear end (a figure attained by multiplying the several probabilities, $0.57 \times 0.65 \times 0.74 = 0.27$). Still, 27% is not dreadfully risky. The odds do not imply a game of utterly foolish gambles. It may therefore be a game that small firms can play without suffering nightmares.

The remaining arguments favoring large size—time horizon and diversification—are equally vulnerable to counterargument. But the debate will now be dropped. Resolution cannot be reached without recourse to the facts. So let's now turn to the facts as they relate to invention, innovation, and diffusion (keeping in mind that the statistics often blur these stages). Truth on both sides will be revealed.

Firm Size and Invention

The facts concerning invention are best kept in three separate compartments: (1) inputs, (2) outputs, and (3) outputs/inputs, or efficiency. Inputs of R & D money and personnel obviously reflect *effort*, but they may indicate nothing about *results achieved*. The most common and convenient measure of results, or R & D output, is patents. In lieu of patents, which fail to discriminate between marvelous and mundane discoveries, some students of the subject have tried to measure output by selecting only "significant" inventions then tracing their sources. Finally, systematic comparison of outputs and inputs yields a measure of efficiency, such as patents *per dollar* of R & D investment. Such a measure is needed to test the presence of scalar economies.

Inputs: At first glance, statistics reflecting effort overwhelmingly favor the big firms as being most progressive. R & D expenditures are tightly concentrated. In 1958, for which good data are available, "U.S. firms with 5000 or more employees originated 46 percent of all value added in manufacturing. At the same time they accounted for 88 percent of all expenditures on R & D performed by manufacturing companies, including 93 percent of expenditures

[16] Edwin Mansfield, J. Rapoport, A. Romeo, E. Villani, S. Wagner, and F. Husic, *The Production and Application of New Industrial Technology* (New York: Norton, 1977), pp. 21–43.

on federally-supported R & D programs and 83 percent of the privately-financed effort."[17] One of the main reasons R & D effort is so dramatically concentrated is that virtually all large firms undertake some R & D, whereas most small firms have no formal R & D program whatsoever. Over 90% of all firms with more than 5000 employees engage in some R and D, but below this, as firm size drops, the proportion of firms engaging in R & D sinks. The result: about 600 companies account for 90% of all private R & D spending.[18] Thus there is some element of truth to the claim that bigness is better.

These aggregate statistics, however, exaggerate the prominence of the largest enterprises. They take no account of differing technical opportunities across industries, and they make no distinction between what could be considered large middle-sized firms and the genuine giants among those who do have R & D programs. The most pertinent question is this: *Within* a given industry or a cluster of industries of given technological opportunity, is the effort of the largest firms greater, *relative to their size*, than the effort of medium-sized firms? The question is diagrammed in Figure 23-1. The vertical axis is R & D outlay per dollar of sales or some other measure of *relative* effort. The horizontal axis is firm size. The solid line indicates what we already know, namely, the effort of really small firms *is* relatively small. The dashed lines indicate the possibilities among the medium and large sizes. If relative effort always rose with size, pattern *A* would prevail. If medium and large firms put forth the *same* relative effort, pattern *B* would be observed. Finally, pattern *C* would hold if relative effort dwindled beyond the middle range.

There have been at least nine statistical studies of this question.[19] They vary in number of industries and firms included, time periods, and measures of size and effort. Yet there is substantial agreement among them. Patterns *B* and *C* prevail in all but a few industries, chemicals being the most prominent exception. That is to say, inventive and innovative effort tends to increase *more* than proportionately with firm size *only over the small to medium range* ("medium" varying from industry to industry). For still larger firms, intensity of effort is either *constant or decreasing* with size. Hence bigness is better only up to a point; thereafter it is often worse.

---

[17] Scherer *op. cit.* (1970), p. 358.

[18] *Business Week*, June 27, 1977, p. 62.

[19] J. S. Worely, "Industrial Research and the New Competition," *Journal of Political Economy* (April 1961), pp. 181–86; D. Hamberg, "Size of Firm, Oligopoly and Research: The Evidence," *Canadian Journal of Economics and Political Science* (February 1964), pp. 62–75; Edwin Mansfield, *Industrial Research and Technological Innovation* (New York: Norton, 1968), pp. 38–40; William S. Comanor, "Market Structure, Product Differentiation, and Industrial Research," *Quarterly Journal of Economics* (November 1967), pp. 639–57; F. M. Scherer, Testimony, *Economic Concentration Hearings, op. cit.,* pp. 1194–96; H. G. Grabowski, "The Determinants of Industrial Research and Development: A Study of the Chemical, Drug, and Petroleum Industries," *Journal of Political Economy* (March 1968), pp. 292–306; Ronald E. Shrieves, "Firm Size and Innovation: Further Evidence," *Industrial Organization Review*, Vol. 4, No. 1 (1976), pp. 26–33; John E. Tilton, "Firm Size and Innovative Activity in the Semiconductor Industry" (mimeo, April 1972); Douglas W. Webbink, *The Semiconductor Industry* (Washington, D.C., Federal Trade Commission Economic Report, 1977), pp. 103–08; Peter D. Loeb and Vincent Lin, "Research and Development in the Pharmaceutical Industry," *Journal of Industrial Economics* (September 1977), pp. 45–51.

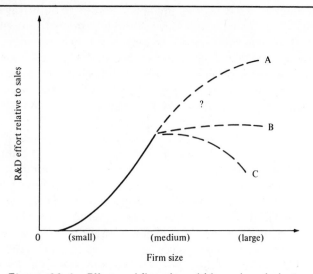

Figure 23-1. *Effort and firm size within a given industry.*

Outputs: Patents and R & D spending are highly correlated, so observations concerning outputs generally conform with those concerning inputs. Still, there are significant differences, and all the differences tend to favor smallness. Take simple patent statistics for instance. Whereas 90% of all private R & D funds can be credited to about 600 firms, they cannot claim the same percentage of patents; 80% of all patents issued nowadays go to corporations, both big and small, while 20% go to *individuals.*[20] Moreover, *within* the corporate sector itself, patents are nowhere near as highly concentrated as R & D dollars. F. M. Scherer made a complete count of patents issued in 1959 to 463 manufacturing firms listed among *Fortune's* 500 largest corporations in 1955. These largest firms "received 56 percent of the U.S. invention patents issued to domestic manufacturing corporations in 1959 and accounted for approximately 57 percent of the 1955 sales of U.S. manufacturing corporations. Thus, the largest firms barely held their own in the receipt of invention patents despite their disproportionate share of both government and private R & D spending."[21]

A defender of large corporations might at this point like to explain the discrepancy in output and input by claiming that the *quality* of large firm inventions is superior to that of small-firm or individual inventions. But the claim would collapse for lack of evidence. One index of quality is commercial utilization, and several studies show that a greater percentage of small-firm patented inventions are used commercially than large-firm patented inventions.[22]

[20] U. S. Department of Commerce, *Statistical Abstract 1977*, p. 557.
[21] Scherer *op. cit.* (1970), p. 358.
[22] Jacob Schmookler, *Invention and Economic Growth* (Cambridge, Mass.: Harvard University Press, 1966), pp. 48–51.

Moreover, as Scherer notes, "Interview studies also reveal that large corporations with an active staff of patent attorneys are less discriminating in their choice of inventions on which patent protection is sought."[23]

As for the inventions of individuals, the evidence is almost astounding. John Jewkes, David Sawers, and Richard Stillerman carefully compiled case histories for seventy momentous twentieth century inventions and found that only 24 of them, or one third, were the work of corporate research laboratories. In contrast, 38, or more than half, "can be ranked as individual invention in the sense that much of the pioneering work was carried through by men who were working on their own behalf without the backing of research institutions and usually with limited resources."[24] Among these individual discoveries are: air conditioning; jet engine; Kodachrome; penicillin; "Polaroid" Land camera; power steering; automatic transmissions; safety razor; cyclotron; xerography; titanium; helicopter; electron microscope; gyro-compass; and Cellophane.

Corroborating these results, Daniel Hamberg found that of 27 major inventions made during the decade 1946–1955, only seven (26%) came from large industrial laboratories. The remainder came from independent inventors, small firms, and universities. Hamberg also found that of 13 major steel inventions he studied, seven were concocted by individual inventors.[25] Moreover, after study of seven major inventions for the refining and cracking of petroleum, John Enos determined that all seven were made by independent inventors.[26] However instructive (and inspirational) these statistics might be, it nevertheless seems to be true that, *over time*, the *relative* importance of individual inventors seems to be shrinking. Whereas today 20% of all patents go to individuals, at the turn of the century individuals garnered 80%.[27]

When the patent output of firms within given industries is analyzed, the results are similar to those obtained for R & D effort. Figure 23-2 shows this, based on a study of 448 corporations conducted by Scherer.[28] The firms are divided into four groups of differing technical opportunity, the most progressive group being group A, electrical equipment and communications. Within each of these groups the firms are arrayed by size classes, and within each class the average number of patents per billion dollars of sales is computed. Small firms, with sales less than $55 million, are excluded. Among included medium and large firms, relative patent performance at first improves with size, then deteriorates. The giants in the sample could not therefore boast of greater inventive output, relative to their size, than their somewhat smaller corporate colleagues.

Output/Input: When the preceding input and output records of the largest firms are compared, it appears that their inventive output is much the weaker.

---

[23] Scherer *op. cit.* (1970), p. 358.
[24] Jewkes, Sawers, and Stillerman, *op. cit.*, p. 73.
[25] Daniel Hamberg, "Invention in the Industrial Research Laboratory," *Journal of Political Economy* (April 1963), p. 96–98.
[26] Enos, *op. cit.*, pp. 1481–86.
[27] Schmookler, *op. cit.*, p. 26.
[28] Scherer, *Economic Concentration Hearings, op. cit.*, p. 1197.

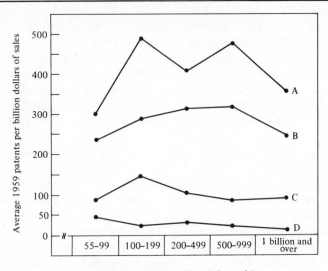

Figure 23-2. *Average 1959 patents per billion dollars of sales by size and technological group. A: electrical equipment and communications; B: basic chemicals and drugs; C: petroleum, rubber, stone–clay–glass, fabricated metal products, machinery, and transportation equipment; D: food, tobacco, textiles, apparel, paper, and primary metals. Source: F. M. Scherer,* Economic Concentration, *Part 3, Subcommittee on Antitrust and Monopoly of the Committee on the Judiciary, U.S. Senate, 89th Congress, 1st Session (1965), p. 1197.*

For this, there are two main explanations. First, the inputs are probably more imperfectly measured than the outputs, and the imperfections shift as a function of firm size. In particular, data on R & D spending tend to understate the inventive effort of small firms and individuals. Such efforts tend to be more casual, less formal, and therefore less fully reported than the efforts of large firms. Conversely, R & D spending data may somewhat overstate the inventive efforts of larger firms because most of the larger firms' money goes into *innovation* rather than invention. And in the area of innovation, many large firms make up for their embarrassing record regarding invention. Thus, for example, virtually all the inventions credited to *individuals* by Jewkes, Sawers, and Stillerman were not innovated by individuals but rather by industrial firms, many of which are immense.[29] Not too much should be made of this qualification, however, because "development" and "innovation" do produce patents, the main measure of invention.

[29] Nelson, *Economic Concentration Hearings, op. cit.,* p. 1145.

TABLE 23-2   Number of Patents Pending per Million Dollars Spent on R & D, 1953

	Size of Firm		
Industry	Under 1000 Employees	1000 to 4999 Employees	5000 or more Employees
Machinery	117.6	70.4	41.3
Chemicals	89.3	50.0	42.4
Electric equipment	63.7	79.4	39.1
Petroleum	100.0	119.0	64.1
Instruments	63.3	69.4	26.7
All other industries	64.9	140.8	35.9
Average all industries	78.1	74.6	39.1

Source: Derived from Jacob Schmookler, *Economic Concentration, Hearings*, Part 3, U. S. Senate Subcommittee on Antitrust and Monopoly, 89th Congress, First Session (1965), p. 1258.

The second explanation for the discrepancy shows bigness in a less praiseworthy light. That is, output/input tends to fall directly with increased size, everything else being equal, because of *diseconomies of scale in invention.* Telling statistics demonstrating these diseconomies were gathered by Jacob Schmookler. They may be seen in Table 23-2, which reports the number of patents pending per million dollars of R & D outlay for firms formally engaged in R & D, broken down by size classes. In short, the data are patent output ÷ million dollars R & D input. Reading across the rows, you will spy a fairly consistent pattern. Patent productivity is always *lowest in the largest size class.* In four of the industry groups it is highest among medium-sized firms. And in two industries—machinery and chemicals—the *smallest* firms display the greatest patent productivity. The smallest firms, in fact, are rarely far below the medium firms, and the smallest are typically twice as efficient as the largest. Using different data drawn from the petroleum, chemical, and steel industries, plus a different analytical technique, Mansfield came up with similar results. He concluded that, "contrary to popular belief, the inventive output per dollar of R & D expenditure in most of these cases seems to be lower in the largest firms than in large and medium-sized firms."[30]

Stated differently, costs per patent rise with size. The obvious next question is why? There is of course no answer universally propounded by all observers,

---

[30] E. Mansfield *op. cit.* (1968), p. 42. See also Tilton, *op. cit.* A major exception is drugs: J. M. Vernon and Peter Gusen, "Technical Change and Firm Size: The Pharmaceutical Industry," *Review of Economics and Statistics* (August 1974), pp. 294–302.

but most seem to agree with the answer derived by Arnold Cooper, whose comparative study of large and small research organizations is widely cited:

> Large firms, he found, seem to become enmeshed in bureaucracy and red tape, resulting in a less hospitable atmosphere for creative contributions by operating personnel. Superior technical personnel tend to be attracted to smaller companies where greater latitude may be afforded them. The larger the firm, the more difficult it may be to recognize the problems needing solution. Finally there is evidence of greater cost consciousness in smaller firms.[31]

This summary has a familiar ring, echoing our earlier discussion of job satisfaction in Chapter 19. But the creative nature of inventive activity adds an interesting twist. Most imaginative inventors seem to abhor procedural manacles and collective research. "Indeed, nothing is more characteristic of the individual inventor than this disposition to fold his tent and quietly steal away to other territory when large-scale organized research comes into his field."[32]

To sum up, inventive inputs, outputs, and output/input ratios all seem to be positively associated with size only among very small and medium-sized firms. Beyond that, no additional gains from size are evident. If anything, losses are thereafter more likely than gains. There is, moreover, still a place for the individual inventor.

Firm Size and Innovation

A rather forceful case can be made that *innovation* is affected by size much as invention is. Observe first that the bulk of R & D money goes to "development," and that many if not most corporate patents are off-spring of "development" instead of "research." So the preceding section's message necessarily overflows to cover much present ground.

Second, there is certainly no shortage of "hare and tortoise" stories, wherein the unlikely little firm outraces the unsuspecting, seemingly swift, all-powerful, large firm, whose brash overconfidence or lackadaisical attitude instills sloth:

- In 1926, Western Electric offered sound equipment to the major movie companies, all of whom rejected it. Warner Brothers, then a minor company, gambled on the sound equipment. The major companies decided to fight the adoption of sound; acceptance would make much of their equipment obsolete; long-term contracts with silent-picture stars might become costly liabilities, techniques would be revolutionized; conversion to sound would require an embarrassing payment of royalties to tiny Warner. Warner won.[33]

---

[31] Kamien and Schwartz, *op. cit.*, p. 10.

[32] Jewkes, Sawers, and Stillerman, *op. cit.*, p. 99.

[33] William F. Hellmuth, Jr., "The Motion Picture Industry," in W. Adams, *The Structure of American Industry*, 3rd ed. (New York: Macmillan Publishing Co., 1961), p. 398.

- It was not the Big Three who innovated small cars in the United States after World War II, but rather Kaiser, Willys, American Motors, and Studebaker. The Big Three resisted, fearing dilution of their large-car sales.[34]
- Much the same could be said of unit-body construction, dual-braking systems, crash panels, auto air conditioning, pollution control equipment, and so on. Some claim that, aside from automatic transmissions, the crowning achievements of GM are tail fins, opera windows, and landau roofs.[35]
- When inventors of the digital watch offered it to the major old-line watch companies for development, they ran into a brick wall. Innovation thus fell to electronics companies like Time Computer, Fairchild, and Texas Instruments.[36]

The foot-dragging behavior of leading firms is so common that theorists have dubbed it "the fast-second strategy." Briefly, the idea is that, for a large firm, *innovation* is often costlier, riskier, and less profitable than *imitation*. A large firm can lie back, let others gamble, then respond quickly with a "fast second" if anything started by their smaller rivals catches fire. Being large to begin with minimizes any eventual market share losses, as explained by William Baldwin and Gerald Childs: "The dominant firm is likely to be favored as an imitator because of such factors as its ability to distribute a new product far more widely and in a shorter period of time than a smaller innovator, its current reputation among a large number of customers, ability to engage in more extensive advertising than its rivals and, conceivably, because its leading position in current markets is attributable to greater efficiency and the general ability to produce better products at lower costs than any of its rivals."[37] In short, "A firm with a dominating position, conscious of its power to pounce if its position should suddenly be put in jeopardy, may be so confident of being able to deal with incipient competition as to become sluggish."[38]

For fairly obvious reasons, the strategy would pay-off best (1) where the innovations in question are easily copied, both technically and legally, and (2) where the leading firm faces an inelastic demand and the innovations in question are "durable" or "economy" models, representing substantial price cuts. (Thus the stainless steel blade was not Gillette's baby.)

On the other hand, there are several good reasons to doubt that the last

---

[34] Lawrence J. White, "The American Automobile Industry and the Small Car, 1945-70," *Journal of Industrial Economics* (April 1972), pp. 179-92.

[35] Blair, *Economic Concentration Hearings, op. cit.*, pp. 1123-24; Lawrence J. White, *The Automobile Industry Since 1945* (Cambridge, Mass.: Harvard University Press, 1971).

[36] *Business Week*, October 27, 1975, pp. 78-92.

[37] William L. Baldwin and Gerald L. Childs, "The Fast Second and Rivalry in Research and Development," *Southern Economic Journal* (July 1969), p. 24.

[38] Jewkes, Sawers, and Stillerman, *op. cit.*, p. 166.

section's conclusions on invention carry over to innovation. The evidence concerning R & D and patented inventions, although instructive, is only loosely applicable to innovation. Given the significant differences between invention and innovation, bigness may well be better for innovation. Moreover, casual empiricism concerning sound-movies and compact cars lacks resolve, even when it is backed up by plausible theories. Counterexamples and counter-arguments are available to defenders of giant enterprises. RCA's color television, Du Pont's nylon, AT & T's transistor, GM's diesel locomotive, and IBM's "Selectric" typewriter are just a few instances of large firm innovation involving vision, risk, and voluminous cost.

What is needed, then, is some *systematic* analysis of the question. To this end, Edwin Mansfield and his associates have conducted detailed studies of innovation in the steel, petroleum, coal, drug, and chemical industries. Their approach was, first, to obtain information on *what* innovations had been made, *which* were the most important, and *who* was most responsible for the pioneering. This information was obtained by canvassing knowledgeable experts on these industries—engineers, scientists, trade associations, and so on. All told, 325 major innovations were included. Next, economic data on each industry were assembled, such as firm size and market concentration. Finally, the innovation information and economic data were compared. Because long time spans were involved, an "early" period and "late" period was selected for each industry within the data's limitations—for example steel was 1919–1938 early, 1939–1958 late; chemicals 1930–1950 early, 1951–1971 late.

The results are reported in Table 23-3. Market shares for the top four firms in each case are given in italics. The top four's percentage share of innovations—weighted and unweighted for estimated importance—is given in regular type. If the largest firms were extraordinarily innovative, their share of innovations would exceed their share of the market. Conversely, if they were relatively slow and staid, their share of innovations would fall short of their market shares. A simple tally tells us that, when innovations are weighted by their importance, the top four's share of innovations exceeded their market share eight times and fell short eight times. Using unweighted raw shares, the top-four performed favorably seven times and unfavorably nine times. These results suggest a toss-up. The largest firms are neither disproportionately innovative nor disproportionately slothful. There is substantial variance across industries, however. The top four petroleum and coal companies performed especially well, whereas the top four steel and chemical companies produced rather embarrassing records.

Though not strictly comparable, available data on the aluminum industry, gathered by Merton Peck and Bruce Smith, paint a picture even worse than steel, thereby tipping the balance of available evidence in favor of lesser sized firms. Over the years 1946–1957, the aluminum industry was dominated by the "Big Three"—Alcoa, Kaiser, and Reynolds—which then accounted for over 90% of ingot sales and 40% of fabrications. Yet at the same time these firms accounted for only 11% of 155 innovations in fabricating, finishing, and

TABLE 23-3 Per Cent Share of Innovations and of Market Accounted For by Largest Four Firms in Steel, Petroleum, Coal, Drugs, and Chemicals

Item	Steel		Petroleum		Coal		Drugs		Chemicals	
	Weighted	*Raw*	*Weighted*	*Raw*	*Weighted*	*Raw*	*Weighted*	*Raw*	*Weighted*	*Raw*
Early period										
Product innovations	20	20	60	71	n.a.	n.a.	45	37	63	61
Process innovations	39	41	34	36	27	18	n.a.	n.a.	56	58
Market share	62	62	33	33	11	11	50	50	67	67
Late Period										
Product innovations	27	27	40	34	n.a.	n.a.	48	27	60	61
Process innovations	58	64	58	57	30	27	n.a.	n.a.	41	43
Market share	63	63	39	39	13	13	33	33	57	57

n.a.: Not available.
Sources: Edwin Mansfield, *Industrial Research and Technological Innovation* (New York: Norton, 1968), p. 91; E. Mansfield, J. Rapoport, J. Schnee, S. Wagner, and M. Hamburger, *Research and Innovation in the Modern Corporation* (New York: Norton, 1971), Chapter 8; E. Mansfield, J. Rapoport, A. Romeo, E. Villani, S. Wagner, and F. Husic, *The Production and Application of New Industrial Technology* (New York: Norton, 1977), Chapter 3.

joining.[39] Over the later period 1958–1968, the Big Three controlled more than 75% of ingot capacity; at the same time they "only accounted for 18 percent of the listed innovations."[40] The only area in which the Big Three might be patted on their backs (one pat each) was alloy innovation. They accounted for 69% of those during 1946–1957, and 35% during 1958–1968.

This presentation of the evidence merely indicates whether, *as a group*, the largest firms could claim a disproportionately large share of innovations. Mansfield and his friends went further, however. They estimated the distribution of performance across *all* innovating firms in each of their studied industries to determine what size of firm was *the* best for innovation. To appreciate this effort refer back to Figure 23-1 and mentally relabel the vertical axis "Innovative performance relative to sales," or "Number of innovations per sales dollar." An OA pattern of performance across all firms would obviously give the top four a disproportionately large share of the innovations. But an OC pattern also could, in which case the biggest four firms would be good but *not* the best. The fifth through eighth firms, say, would then be better than the top four. And perhaps the seventh firm would be best of all. If the seventh were best, the peak in the OC curve would occur at the seventh firm's size level.

Well then, what are the innovation distribution patterns for these industries? Only chemicals had an OA pattern, mainly because the largest firm, DuPont, was also the most intensive innovator of all chemical producers. The other four industries delivered OC patterns, wherein the biggest were not the best. The best (or peak) in coal was ranked fourth; in petroleum, sixth; in drugs, twelfth; and in steel, the peak was always found "among very small firms."

It would thus appear that our previous conclusions concerning invention apply here after all. Innovative vigor typically rises with size only from small to medium-sized firms. Beyond some point, which varies, the zeal fizzles relative to size. The only apparent exception is chemicals.

Firm Size and Diffusion

Diffusion typically traces a path similar to a "logistic" curve, as it is called. Three such S-shaped curves are captured in Figure 23-3, where zero represents the date of innovation. As time passes (on the horizontal axis), the per cent of firms adopting the innovation rises slowly at first, picks up steam over the middle stretch, and then tapers off as the stragglers finally convert. Curves I and II show cases of complete conversion by all members of the industry. Of the two, curve I depicts the more rapid diffusion. Curve III illustrates a case where the innovation is very slow to spread and is never fully adopted by all. Nuclear

[39] Merton J. Peck, *Competition in the Aluminum Industry 1945–1958* (Cambridge, Mass.: Harvard University Press, 1961), pp. 183–97.

[40] Bruce Smith, "Technological Leadership in the Aluminum Industry," in *Technological Development and Economic Growth*, edited by G. W. Wilson (Bloomington, Ind.: Indiana University Press, 1971), pp. 209–29.

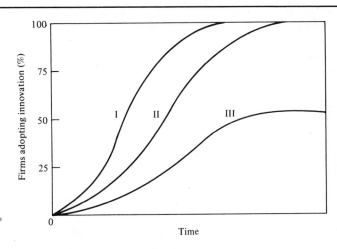

Figure 23-3. Three patterns of diffusion.

power illustrates partial adoption, as it seems highly unlikely that nuclear reactors (as we know them today) will ever be universally accepted.

Whether an innovation spreads quickly or slowly, completely or partially, depends on many factors. Market growth, capital cost magnitude, risk, patent protection, and the technical competency of management are among them. Most important, however, is the potential profitability of the innovation. If it promises remarkable cost savings or skyrocketing sales, converts will not timidly hesitate. Dim profit prospects have the opposite effect. Both ups and downs are illustrated by the textile industry. High speed shuttleless looms were innovated in the 1950s, but United States textile manufacturers delayed extensive adoption until the 1970s when rising labor costs made the new looms significantly more profitable than the older, relatively labor-intensive looms. In 1973, an old-style loom cost $8000 as against $35,000 for a new shuttleless loom. Conversion at that time was nevertheless "the only way to go," according to one textile executive, because the new looms could "get 70% more output with 15% less manpower."[41]

Firm size also has a bearing, and its influence has been measured two ways. The first is merely a matter of positioning. Which firms are the *quickest to begin* using an innovation? Mansfield's studies of diffusion in the coal, brewing, steel, and railroad industries led him to conclude that larger firms were quicker to adopt innovations. He estimated that a 10% increase in firm size would, on the average, reduce delay time 4%.[42] Other results indicating a favorable influence

---

[41] *Business Week*, October 27, 1973, p. 124.
[42] Mansfield *op. cit.* (1968), pp. 155–172.

of firm size have been found for the diffusion of numerically controlled machine tools in a number of industries,[43] and diffusion in the British textile industry.[44]

Although these results seem to conflict with those concerning invention and innovation, they do not. Several qualifications attend them. For one thing, as a matter of sheer statistical probability, one would expect big firms to be quicker, on the average, than small firms. But it does not appear that they are *disproportionately* quicker. Mansfield explains the difference nicely: "To illustrate this, consider an industry with two firms, one large (80 percent of the market), one small (20 percent of the market). If the large firm does its share of the innovating (no more, no less), it will be first in 80 percent of the cases—and it will be quicker on the average than the small firm."[45]

For another thing, one would expect the effect of firm size to emerge only or mainly where the costs of introduction are particularly high or risky because the big firms should be at their best in such instances. In fact, a study of numerous innovations in chemicals turned up just such differential effects. Firm size had a favorable impact only for high-cost innovations.

Finally, there are many cases where firm size appears to have had *no* effect or an *adverse* effect on the speed of adoption, even where high costs are involved. Examples of these innovations and their industries include "special presses" in Canadian paper,[46] nonflammable dry cleaning in British dry cleaning,[47] basic oxygen process in United States steel,[48] and Sulzer shuttleless looms in United States textiles.[49]

There is thus some sketchy evidence favorable to firm size regarding firm-by-firm diffusion. However, the evidence regarding *intra*firm diffusion, the second measure of diffusion, is definitely stacked on the side of small firms. That is to say, small firms may be somewhat slower to take up an innovation once it is introduced, but, once they do pick it up, they adopt it *throughout their operations* more quickly than large firms. Thus, although small firms may be "late starters," they also tend to "catch up" with *internal* rates of diffusion exceeding those of large firms. (Now *that* really is playing tortoise to the big firms' hare.) The phenomenon has been observed in railroading, paper manufacturing, chemicals,

[43] Anthony A. Romeo, "Interindustry and Interfirm Differences in the Rate of Diffusion of an Innovation," *Review of Economics and Statistics* (August 1975), pp. 311–19; Steven Globerman, "Technical Diffusion in the Canadian Tool and Die Industry," *Review of Economics and Statistics* (November 1975), pp. 428–34.

[44] J. S. Metcalfe, "Diffusion of Innovation in the Lancashire Textile Industry," *Manchester School* (June 1970), pp. 145–59.

[45] Mansfield *op. cit.* (1968), pp. 171–72.

[46] Steven Globerman, "New Technology Adoption in the Canadian Paper Industry," *Industrial Organization Review*, Vol. 4, No. 1 (1976), pp. 5–12.

[47] R. W. Shaw and C. J. Sutton, *Industry and Competition* (London: Macmillan Publishing Co., 1976), pp. 108–19.

[48] Joel Dirlam and Walter Adams, "Big Steel, Invention, and Innovation," *Quarterly Journal of Economics* (May 1966), pp. 167–89.

[49] *Business Week*, October 27, 1973, p. 124. See also Jewkes, Sawers, and Stillerman, *op. cit.*, pp. 303–04.

and in ten industries using numerical machine tools.[50] The main explanations for small–firm speed here seem to be (1) that their nonbureaucratic nature enables quicker, more comprehensive decision making, and (2) the later they start, the more certain they are of the innovation's good value, having the benefit of positive experiences among their adopting predecessors.

To summarize, there is some evidence that large firms adopt innovations earlier than small firms, all else being equal. But the big ones may not be disproportionately faster. Indeed, other evidence indicates no differential at all. Moreover, where the small-fry have been slow to pick up a new ball, they run with it faster toward complete internal conversion.

Firm Diversification and Progress

The diversification aspect of the topic has been explored very little. Theoretically, firm diversification is often said to have a favorable impact on invention and innovation. Yet empirical tests have neither confirmed nor refuted this hypothesis. Some studies find a positive effect of diversification on R & D input and output. Others find a negative impact. Still others find nothing. A definite answer thus awaits further study.[51]

Firm Size: An Overview

Overall, medium-sized firms emerge as the most willing and able to spur advance. A little bit of bigness is good; too much often seems bad. Still, a *range* of sizes may be best for an industry, just as they are for a basketball team. Invention, innovation, and diffusion each demand talents and resources. Projects vary widely in size and scope. "All things considered," Scherer aptly concludes, "the most favorable industrial environment for rapid technological progress would appear to be a firm size distribution which includes a preponderance of companies with sales below $200 million, pressed on one side by a horde of small technology-orientated enterprises bubbling over with bright new ideas and on the other by a few larger corporations with the capacity to undertake exceptionally ambitious developments."[52] With inflation, the threshhold size might now be $400 million or so in sales.

Market Structure and Progress

Theory

Theories on the impact of market structure on progress differ from those on firm size by giving greater consideration to *rivalry*, or the lack thereof. Early theorists, like Galbraith, argued that high concentration and high barriers

---

[50] Romeo, *op. cit.*; Globerman *op. cit.* (1976); and Mansfield *op. cit.* (1968), Chapter 9; Mansfield, *et. al. op. cit.* (1977), p. 118 (referring to a study by Peter Simon).
[51] For a survey see Kamien and Schwartz, *op. cit.*, pp. 26–27.
[52] Scherer, *op. cit.* (1970), p. 361–62.

to entry would foster progressiveness. They reasoned that the *lack* of rivalry implied by these conditions would (1) boost profits, thereby supplying abundant monetary wherewithal to engage in risky R & D, and (2) protect inventors and innovators from imitators, poachers, and like-minded creatures who would "steal" the pioneers' ideas, thereby discouraging the initiation of progressive efforts by jeopardizing the chance of just rewards.

Of course these arguments are no more overpowering than those defending large firm size. We have already seen that much, if not most, R & D is neither as risky nor as expensive as one might think. Counterargument concerning blood-sucking imitators and interlopers is even easier. The whole idea behind patents is to protect technical frontiersmen from just such discouraging fates. Patents are an even more efficient protection than indiscriminate approval of monopoly because patents grant *temporary* monopoly control *after* the birth of an invention (when reward for birth may be warrented) rather than *permanent* power *before* (when even pregnancy is less than certain).

More recent and more complicated theories cast added doubt on the notion that progressiveness is necessarily positively associated with monopoly power. Unfortunately, these theories defy compact discussion because they bend and branch with each varying assumption about the ease of imitation, cost contours, technological opportunity, risk, price elasticity of demand, and time horizon.[53] If one were to hazard a crude summary of what appears to be the emerging theoretical consensus, however, it might go something like this:

Two elements are imperative to vigorous progressiveness—ability and incentive. **Ability** includes some modicum of financial treasure that can be sunk into long-term risky projects, and some freedom from the pressures that arise from daily uncertainty about survival. We naturally could not expect a firm whose light of vitality was flickering to take on extra burdens that a firm whose light glowed steadily might assume without strain. Quite obviously, monopolies are usually strong enough to shoulder the added load, for they enjoy both wealth and security. It is indeed these attributes that are emphasized by those who believe that monopolies are ideal for spear-heading technical advance.

On the other hand, **incentive** includes prospects of profit and loss. The larger the prospective profit from some endeavor, the greater the incentive to undertake it. Conversely, the larger the prospective loss from stagnation, the greater the incentive to get moving. For various reasons, competition probably heightens both incentives. The greater the competition, the greater the industry's output and the greater the expansion opportunities for any one firm that gets a jump on the others. Likewise, the greater the profit prospects will be for any technical breakthrough. As for considerations on the loss side, the greater the competition, the greater the chances are that stagnant firms will be outdistanced by their rivals. Competition thus propels movement with fear.

---

[53] Examples include Douglas Needham, "Market Structure and Firms' R & D Behavior," *Journal of Industrial Economics* (June 1975), pp. 241–55; Raymond Jackson, "Market Structure and the Rewards for Patented Inventions," *Antitrust Bulletin* (Fall 1972), pp. 911–26; plus those cited by Kamien and Schwartz, *op. cit.*

All told, it appears that monopolies probably have a great deal of ability but very little incentive, whereas purely competitive firms probably have little ability but ample incentive. Neither structural extreme is therefore particularly conducive to progress. However, the elements blend in intermediate structures, where market power is sufficient to secure ability but not so strong as to eradicate the incentives brought by rivalry. With both ability and incentive present, intermediate ranges of oligopoly may be expected to display the least lassitude.

Elaborations on this theme could generate additional arguments for the same conclusion. For example, more than half of all private R & D effort is aimed at "product improvement," which of course is one form of product differentiation, a form that extends to producer goods as well as consumer goods. The vigor of such product–improvement differentiation could well be most spirited in some middle range of concentration, just as advertising is, and for many of the same reasons. As concentration rises from low to moderate levels, price competition becomes less and less attractive while *nonprice* competition, including competition on the technology front, becomes more and more attractive. However, *further* increases in concentration, above oligopolistic levels, are not likely to continue intensification of R & D aimed in the nonprice direction. Approach toward monopoly tends to subdue rivalry of all forms, especially if under oligopoly that rivalry is excessive from the marketwide, profit maximizing point of view. This restraint at particularly high levels of concentration may obtain despite the fact that collusive agreements restricting R & D could probably never be more than nebulous understandings, given the complexities involved and generous opportunities for double-crossing one's collaborators. Comparing concentration ratios of 60 and 100, then, invention and innovation are likely to be about the same, or the 100 could pump out the inferior record, all else being equal. Pictorially, curves *ABC* and *AC* in Figure 15-2 (of Chapter 15) would depict this hypotheses if the horizontal axis there were relabeled "R & D intensity."[54]

Complicating matters a bit is the possibility that causation may not run just one way, from structure to performance. Particularly rapid technical change, where it is attributable mainly to an independent march of science, could *cause* high concentration. Firms that fail to keep step with the march will fall to the wayside, dying from self-destructive mistakes—such as delays that are never overcome or costly trips down blind alleys. These possibilities appear to be the explanation for rising concentration in aircraft manufacturing,[55] and they could apply to other industries. Patents constitute another mechanism that encourages concentration. Historically, they have contributed to concentration in such fields as electric lamps, aluminum, synthetic fibers, and telephone equipment. On this empirical note we now leave theory behind.

---

[54] More sophisticated theories to roughly the same effect may be found in Scherer, *op. cit.* (1970), pp. 366–370; Kamien and Schwartz, *op. cit.*, pp. 30–31.

[55] Almarin Phillips, *Technology and Market Structure* (Lexington, Mass.: Lexington Books, 1971).

Market Structure and R & D Effort

The evidence of structure's impact is best collected into three classes—one each for R & D effort, innovative output, and diffusion. These classes of evidence present nowhere near as clear a pattern as that traced for firm size. Perhaps interindustry differences in technical opportunity cannot be sufficiently accounted for. Perhaps the available measures of technical vigor are less reliable in the interindustry context. Whatever the reason, the present picture is at best murky. ("Our test tubes are dirty," Richard Miller would say.)

As regards R & D effort, there are at least ten statistical studies exploring the relationship between concentration or barriers to entry and R & D intensity. Most studies measure intensity by R & D expenditure relative to sales, but a few use counts of scientific personnel relative to total employment or patents relative to sales. Unfortunately, the results lack consistency. Several studies find a positive relationship between concentration and R & D intensity.[56] One discloses a negative association.[57] Three detect no significant relationship whatever.[58] Finally, the results of five other studies more-or-less support the nonlinear hypothesis developed earlier. These last tentatively reveal a *positive* relationship between concentration and R & D intensity over a low to medium range of concentration, plus a *negative* relationship over a medium to high range of concentration.[59] I say "tentatively" because in some of these studies the effect of concentration is obscured by the authors' attempts to account for technical opportunity. In one study, for instance, the sample of industries is divided into "low" and "high" technology groups.[60] Concentration and R & D intensity are positively associated in the "low" group and negatively associated in the "high" group. However, average concentration tends to be high in the "high" group and low in the "low" group. So the hypothesized nonlinear relation emerges, but only indirectly and uncertainly.

Still, there are several grounds for accepting the nonlinear results as more than merely tentative. Scherer's study of this issue is among the best, and he

---

[56] D. Hamberg *op. cit.* (1964); F. M. Scherer, "Market Structure and the Employment of Scientists and Engineers," *American Economic Review* (June 1967), pp. 524–31; Blake Imel, Michael R. Behr, and Peter G. Helmberger, *Market Structure and Performance* (Lexington, Mass.: Lexington Books, 1972), pp. 65–75.

[57] Robert W. Wilson, "The Effect of Technological Environment and Product Rivalry on R & D Effort and Licensing of Inventions," *Review of Economics and Statistics* (May 1977), pp. 171–78.

[58] F. M. Scherer, "Firm Size and Patented Inventions," *American Economic Review* (December 1965), pp. 116–21; Richard E. Caves and Masu Uekusa, *Industrial Organization in Japan* (Washington, D.C.: Brookings Institution, 1976), p. 128; Comanor *op. cit.* (1967).

[59] Scherer *op. cit.* (1967); T. M. Kelly, "The Influences of Firm Size and Market Structure on the Research Efforts of Large Multiproduct Firms," Ph.D. dissertation, Oklahoma State University, 1970 (as summarized in Kamien and Schwartz, *op. cit.*); F. T. Knickerbocker, *Oligopolistic Reaction and Multinational Enterprise* (Boston: Graduate School of Business Administration, Harvard University, 1973), pp. 141–42; S. Globerman, "Market Structure and R & D in Canadian Manufacturing Industries," *Quarterly Review of Economics and Business* (Summer 1973), pp. 59–67 (assuming the high technology industries are highly concentrated, as in Scherer); and William J. Adams, "Firm Size and Research Activity: France and the United States," *Quarterly Journal of Economics* (August 1970), pp. 386–409.

[60] Globerman, *op. cit.*

concluded that "technological vigor appears to increase with concentration mainly at relatively low levels of concentration." In the higher ranges, he felt that "additional market power is probably not conducive to more vigorous technological efforts and may be downright stultifying."[61] Furthermore, William Adams' study produces a nonlinear relation, and his is perhaps the best in controlling for technical opportunity. He compared R & D intensity and concentration *industry-by-industry* between the United States and France. For 5 of the 14 industries so studied he found R & D intensity to be higher in the country where concentration was higher. One such industry is textiles: the R & D outlay/sales ratio for textiles was 2.4 in France and 0.5 in the United States, whereas concentration was 30 in France and 19 in the United States. In *all* such cases the concentration comparison was over a low range of concentration. The concentration ratios in these comparisons averaged 19 on the low side of the Atlantic and 31 on the high side. Conversely, seven of the industries compared revealed an opposite tendency, and they were generally more concentrated. That is to say, there were seven instances in which the country with the *higher* concentration had the *lower* R & D intensity, and, for these, top-side concentration averaged 54 as against 42 on the bottom. Combining the averages of these two sets, R & D rose when concentration rose from 19 to 31, but R & D *fell* as concentration rose from 42 to 54. For two industries there were no inter-country differences in R & D or concentration, precluding their comparison.

The notion that R & D intensity is most feverish in the intermediate values of market structure is buttressed by still further tidbits like the following: Analysis of the impact of entry barriers led William Comanor to the conviction that "Where technical barriers either effectively foreclose the entry of new firms or where they are quite low, research spending tends to be limited. Where barriers are moderate, however, and where prospects for some entry exist, research spending is greater."[62]

Market Structure and Innovative Output

Measurement and data problems make interindustry studies of innovative output extremely difficult. About all that can be said with certainty is that, once again, very few if any gains in progressiveness would be obtained by transforming all our industries into near monopolies or tight-knit oligopolies.

This conclusion is suggested, first of all, by reexamining the innovation data compiled by Mansfield and his associates—data reported above in Table 23-3. Those data plotted produce Figure 23-4. The vertical axis is market share of the top four firms, and the horizontal axis is their share of significant innovations. A diagonal line, on which the two shares would be equal, divides the diagram. Thus, all instances of market share exceeding innovation share are plotted in

---

[61] Scherer *op. cit.* (1967).
[62] Comanor, *op. cit* (1967), p. 657.

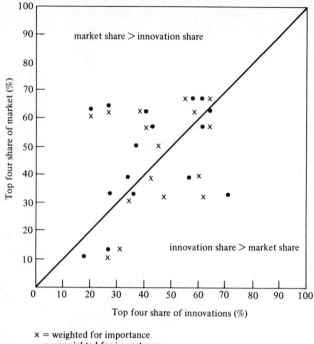

x = weighted for importance
• = unweighted for importance

Figure 23-4. *Concentration and innovation.*

the top left half. On the other hand, all instances of market share falling below innovation share end up in the bottom right half. Put differently, the upper left half is the home for observations that reflect *un*favorably on the performance of the leading firms, whereas the lower right half houses favorable observations.

Now, if concentration had *no* influence on the relative performance of leading firms, the plotted points would present no clear pattern relative to concentration. Notice, however, that above a concentration level of 45%, 15 of the 18 observations appear in the *un*favorable region. Conversely, below a concentration level of 45%, only 2 points appear in the unfavorable region whereas 12 cast reflections of favorable performance. The relative performance of leading firms is therefore markedly better where concentration is lower and competition keener.

Oliver Williamson, who first recognized this pattern, explains it thus,

> in the short run, monopoly advantages may permit the largest firms to neglect the behavior of their rivals, while over the long run the recognized degree of interdependence among the principal rivals may lead to calculated efforts to restrain innovation and thereby preserve stable interfirm relations. Lacking compulsion to innovate in the short run and anxious to moderate competition in the long run, *the relative innovative*

596

performance of the largest firms may decline as monopoly power increases. This is contrasted with circumstances in a competitive industry where differential advantages may be available only to the extent that a firm is a successful innovator. Hence, *the incentives to innovate are held to be particularly keen where competitive conditions prevail.*[63]

The *relatively* poor showing of leading firms in highly concentrated industries suggests that, *in general*, highly concentrated industries perform less laudably than competitive industries when it comes to innovation (other things being equal). By definition the leading firms account for more of the performance where concentration is high than where it is low. So, if their performance is relatively poor, it reflects adversely on the entire industry. Even so, this deduction is not based on hard data. Large-scale interindustry comparisons of industry-wide innovative performance, narrowly defined, have not yet been made.

About the best that has been achieved in this regard are extensive interindustry comparisons of *labor productivity advance*. This measure of innovative performance is perforce limited because (1) it reflects nothing about progress on the *product side*, only the production side; (2) even on the production side, labor productivity is a stunted measure that ignores energy productivity, capital productivity, and other input productivities; (3) an industry's brisk labor productivity advance may be due not so much to the industry's own effort as to the efforts of its capital goods suppliers, in which case there is some misplacement of the performance credits; and (4) any differential push toward labor saving in highly concentrated industries may be motivated by excessively high wages paid in those industries, in which case any "good" performance regarding labor productivity may merely reflect an escape from some self-inflicted "poor" performance regarding wage rates. Nevertheless, for what it is worth, most studies reveal no positive association between concentration and long-run advance in labor productivity. The one fairly trustworthy study indicating a positive relationship produces estimates of only small advances. Thus a substantial increase in concentration would lift labor productivity only slightly at best. Other factors, such as industry growth and R & D activity, are statistically more important and impressive.[64]

Market Structure and Diffusion

Hampered by data difficulties, early tests of structure's impact on diffusion were no more than makeshift. These tests nevertheless suggested that competition was stimulating and monopoly power encumbering. Thus, analysis of diffusion in the coal, steel, brewing, and railroad industries led Mansfield

---

[63] Oliver E. Williamson, "Innovation and Market Structure," *Journal of Political Economy* (February 1965), p. 68 (emphasis added).

[64] Douglas F. Greer and Stephen A. Rhoades "Concentration and Productivity Changes in the Long and Short Run," *Southern Economic Journal* (October 1976), pp. 1031–44.

to a qualified conclusion: "We have too few industries to test accurately the hypothesis often advanced that the rate of imitation is faster in more competitive industries, but the differences seem to be generally in that direction."[65] John Tilton arrived at a similar spot after a book-length study of international diffusion in the semiconductor industry: "The evidence presented in this study about the market structure characteristics conducive to the rapid diffusion of new technology shows that easy entry conditions and new firms were very instrumental in the rapid utilization of new semiconductor techniques and devices in the American market."[66]

More recently, Anthony Romeo has confirmed these suggestions with a convincing test.[67] The power of his test derives from his choice of a single innovation, numerically controlled machine tools, that many industries of varying structure use. These tools are controlled by specially coded cards or tapes, which guide them through their paces. The machines can produce simple or intricate metal parts faster, cheaper, and more flawlessly than old methods. Wide potential usage of the innovation permitted Romeo to gather adoption data from 140 firms in 10 manufacturing industries—aircraft engines, airframes, coal mining machinery, digital computers, farm machinery, industrial instruments, large steam turbines, machine tools, printing presses, and tools and dies. Employing two alternative measures for speed of numerical control diffusion within each of these industries, Romeo discovered that the *less* concentrated among them adopted the innovation significantly *more quickly* than the more highly concentrated. Thus he had good reason to write that "competitive pressures do seem to lead to higher rates of diffusion."

Market Structure: An Overview

All in all, the evidence concerning market structure is in harmony with that on firm size. Whether the measure of performance is R & D effort, innovation, or diffusion does not seem to matter. Towering concentration ratios and obstructive barriers to entry stifle progress. At the same time, there are grounds for arguing that structures of the opposite extreme—atomistic structures with fluid firm turnover—might be less than ideal, especially for R & D effort. Intermediate structures, leaning toward the competitive side of the continuum, seem best.

Summary

Our progress through this discussion took three steps. First, by way of background, it was explained that technological progress itself entails three

---

[65] Mansfield *op. cit.* (1968), p. 154.

[66] John E. Tilton, *International Diffusion of Technology: The Case of Semiconductors* (Washington, D.C.: Brookings Institution, 1971), p. 166.

[67] Romeo *op. cit.* (1975); and A. A. Romeo, "The Rate of Imitation of a Capital-Embodied Process Innovation," *Economica* (February 1977), pp. 63–69.

steps—invention, innovation, and diffusion. Invention is the first realization and crude proof that something will work. Innovation is the first commercial application of the invention. And diffusion is the spread of its adoption. Each step demands somewhat different talents and resources. A surprising amount of invention can still be carried out in basements and garages, although the relative importance of truly independent inventors is waning. Innovation requires refinement, testing, sometimes further invention, and initial production, all of which can be costly. Diffusion involves some risk-acceptance on the part of buyers. Since progress in these three categories is partly determined by technological opportunities, as dictated by divergent growth rates in different branches of science, the impact of market conditions is both limited and difficult to measure. Nevertheless, measurement is not impossible because firms within a given industry face similar opportunities and interindustry comparisons can be devised.

Early theorizing on the relation between progress and *firm size* stressed the virtues of bigness. But two decades of subsequent study have shown that emphasis to be misplaced. In the aggregate, R & D effort is concentrated in the hands of the top 600 firms, but inventive output is not commensurate with the input of these firms. Within specific industries there is no evidence indicating that R & D intensity, relative to firm size, increases beyond medium-sized firms. Indeed, the largest firms are much less spirited than medium-sized firms in many industries. Moreover, within most industries, inventive output does not match measured input, apparently because diseconomies of scale occur beyond moderate size levels.

The record regarding innovation and firm size is much the same. The largest firms cannot claim credit for a disproportionate share of the innovations. Except in chemicals, firms of less than ponderous proportions are the best. The largest firms in some industries lead in diffusion. But their showing in that respect is tarnished by several qualifications, the most important of which is the more rapid *internal* diffusion displayed by small firms.

The influence of market structure is still somewhat uncertain because test results conflict. Nevertheless, several faint outlines seem discernable. First, it is perhaps most plausible to suppose that neither monopoly nor pure competition (nor the nearby neighboring structures of either) are very good for vigorous advance. Incentive and ability blend in the middle ranges of structure, as evidence on R & D effort seems to bear out. Second, the facts concerning innovation indicate that the relative performance of leading firms diminishes as concentration increases. Data on productivity change are mixed, but if concentration does make some positive contribution it is a small one. Finally, several studies of diffusion testify to the benefits of competitive structures. Other things being equal, high concentration and lofty entry barriers hinder the spread of technological breakthroughs.

599

24

Technological Change: Public Policy

The patent system added the fuel of interest to the fire of genius.

ABE LINCOLN

The list of 17 innovations was unimpressive—a stain remover, a construction material, and a sewing thread were highlights. Yet the list produced amazing results when assessed by Edwin Mansfield and his associates. They sought to estimate the private and social rates of return generated by run-of-the-mill innovations. The *private* rate of return is the *innovator's* reward, or profit before tax. The *social* rate of return is the *users'* prize, namely, the cost savings or added consumers' surplus that users of innovations gain.

The difference between private and social reward can best be illustrated with an extreme case not included on Mansfield's list: Dr. Jonas Salk donated his discovery of polio vaccine to the public, declining patent monopoly and, with it, a staggering fortune, thereby minimizing his return. But the public's return was stupendous, amounting to untold millions, perhaps billions, of dollars in reduced medical bills, a more productive populace, and relieved suffering. Although none of the 17 innovations on Mansfield's list could match the polio vaccine, and although none were charitably donated to the public, the median social rate of return for the group was a bountiful 56% as compared to the median private rate of 25%.[1] That is a gap of 2 to 1! For one reason or another —imitators' poaching, "satisficing" rather than profit maximizing prices, and so on—the innovators did not capture all the benefits society received. They shook the tree while others ran off with most of the apples.

[1] E. Mansfield, J. Rapoport, A. Romeo, E. Villani, S. Wagner, and F. Husic, *The Production and Application of New Industrial Technology* (New York: Norton, 1977), pp. 144–66.

Of course we would not want to arrange the world so that every discoverer appropriated the full value of his discovery. Such is not needed to motivate trailblazers, given the alternative inducements of fame and psychic pleasure. Such is not even desirable, given the crazy implications full reward would have for income and wealth distribution. (Imagine the consequences to us and the heirs of Columbus if he could have claimed America as his private property.) Nevertheless, the gap between private and social gain does suggest that reliance on private markets, plain and simple, may lead individuals and enterprises to invest *too little* in research, development, and innovation as compared to a socially optimal investment. Thus, we do not rely on private markets plain and simple. Government intervenes to encourage invention and innovation. Two government policies having this purpose—patents and R & D funding—are the focus of this chapter.

The Patent System: Nature and Scope

Background

A patent is a **monopoly right** to make and sell some product, or use some process, that is governmentally granted for a limited number of years as a reward for invention. The character and duration of this right differs from country to country. United States law grants "for the term of seventeen years [from the patent's date] . . . the right to exclude others from making, using, or selling the invention throughout the United States."[2] The right is a form of private property that can be bought and sold, traded, given away, and leased or licensed for the use of others (who pay a "royalty" for the privilege). The invention covered can even go unused if the owner wishes. Moreover, although only individuals can be awarded patents, corporate employees typically "assign" their patents to their employers, and independent inventors often sell or license their patents to others for commercial application. Regardless of ultimate ownership, roughly half of all patents go unused because the inventions they cover are too far ahead of their time, too costly to develop relative to the potential profit, or too unsettling to the ultimate owner's old way of doing things. Many go unused because close substitutes for the invention are available. Thus, the monopoly granted may be only a measly one.

Leaf through any issue of the *Official Gazette of the United States Patent Office*, which records and summarizes every patent, and you will appreciate how frequently patent monopolies are paper tigers. The December 27, 1977, issue offers these typical examples: No. 4,064,671, a stabilizer strut for a suspended ceiling system; No. 4,064,797, an A-frame bacon cooker; and No.

---

[2] 35 U.S.C. Section 154 (1970).

4,065,099, a tamper-proof, in-post tennis net tightener. As the identifying numbers indicate, more than 4 million patents have been issued since inception of the system. Of late, the annual flow tops 70,000. If these figures are not big enough to suggest to you that many if not most patented inventions are rather pedestrian, consider the following: There is No. 556,248, granted in 1896 for an automatic self-tipping hat. Patent 2,882,858, awarded in 1959, covers a diaper for parakeets. A vibrating toilet seat won patent No. 3,244,168 in 1966.

Lest you think the federal government gets too caught up in comedy, mention of a crucial additional point should not be delayed: enforcement of any patent is left up to the patent holder. Neither the patent office nor the FBI chases infringers. Accused infringers must be hauled into court by patentees. The original Bell telephone patents, for instance, were enforced with more than 600 infringement suits initiated by Bell interests. What is more, the patent office does not have final say as to what constitutes a valid patent. The federal courts have final say. So, once in court, an infringer almost always defends himself against a patentee's attack by claiming the patent is invalid. This defense is by no means futile because court judges generally hold more stringent standards of patentability than the patent office. Approximately 60–70% of all patents coming under court review are declared invalid and unenforceable. In three out of four cases the chief cause for rejection is a lack of "inventiveness."[4] The remaining reasons for invalidation can be understood only after an explanation of what can and cannot be patented under United States law.

Patentability

According to statute law, "Whoever invents or discovers any new and useful process, machine, manufacture, or composition of matter, or any new and useful improvement thereof, may obtain a patent therefor." Embedded in the language are four criteria for patentability: (1) inventiveness, (2) novelty, (3) utility, and (4) subject matter.

To cross the threshhold of **inventiveness** the discovery must be "nonobvious" at the time "to a person having ordinary skill in the art." There must, in other words, be some creativity. But just how much creativity is required and how much creativity went into any claimed invention are often difficult to judge. What is "nonobvious" to one patent examiner may not be to another. The uncertainties in the "nonobvious" standard are, in fact, almost vague and various enough to call for discriminating "creativity" on the part of patent examiners: What is the scope and content of the prior art? What are the differences between the prior art and the claimed invention? If it must be non-obvious to one with "ordinary skill in the art," what constitutes "ordinary skill"? That which is possessed by a Harvard professor, an apprentice chemist, a shop-hand? To restate the problem more concretely, do you think the follow-

---

[3] Stacy V. Jones, *The Patent Office* (New York: Praeger, 1971), pp. 64–69.
[4] *Ibid.*, pp. 43–44.

ng should qualify? Putting a rubber erasure on the end of a pencil? Making doorknobs of clay rather than metal or wood? Devising a motorized golf-bag cart? All three were in fact awarded patents, but when tested in court two were found wanting. Given the nature of the problem, it is hard to disagree with Judge Learned Hand, who once grumbled that the test of invention was little more than a vague and fugitive "phantom."[5]

As for **novelty**, invention must not be previously known or used. Although this standard is fairly straightforward, it takes patent examiners a long time to review past patents and published scientific papers in search of duplication. Of all standards, **utility** is certainly the least demanding. As the extravagant examples given above illustrate, many approved inventions are empty of all but the most fantastic applications.

Because patentable **subject matter** is limited to mechanical or chemical processes and compositions, much is excluded. Discovery of fundamental laws of nature, such as $E = mc^2$, may not be patented, however brilliant or useful their discovery may be. The same holds for mathematical formulas, managerial strategies, teaching methods, and the like. If you were to devise an economic policy that painlessly eliminated inflation while reducing unemployment you might win a Nobel Prize, but you would not be glorified with a patent as well. Admissible inventions must take tangible form. Products of nature are likewise unpatentable, although this rule has exceptions. One patentable exception is new asexually reproducing plants—that is, those cultivated by grafts, or cuttings, or such. These are not to be confused with sexually reproducing plants, which cannot be patented (for reasons other than moral turpitude, of course).

Obtaining a Patent

The rules and regulations of patentability give appearances of an imposing thicket, blocking all but a privileged few. But of the more than 100,000 patent applications filed annually, 70% or so gain patent office approval. Applicants are aided not only by lenient standards of invention and utility but also by an army of clever, well-healed patent attorneys. Indeed, these attorneys are often more crucial to obtaining a patent than an invention is:[6]

Since an application for a patent consists of a series of verbal statements expressing the technological content of what has been invented, much of the patent lawyer's skill is spent in inventing formulas of words that plausibly extend the scope of the claims made in the application. As it reaches the patent office the application combines technological and legal invention, and the latter, if of superior quality, may do much to offset deficiencies in the former. To examine and deflate these highly sophisticated

---

[5] *Harries v. Air King Prods. Co.*, 183 F. 2d 158, 162 (2d Cir. 1950).

[6] Specific evidence is provided by F. M. Scherer, "Firm Size, Market Structure, Opportunity, and the Output of Patented Inventions," *American Economic Review* (December 1965), p. 1111, note 20.

and carefully prepared claims, the patent office has an insufficient staff of relatively inexperienced persons who, because of the press of their work, can give to each application, on the average, only a few hours of attention.[7]

The point is driven home by citing Patent 549,160, which a patent attorney obtained for himself in 1895, and which covered what later proved to be the wonder machine of our modern age—the automobile. According to legend, George Selden stole ideas from genuine auto engineers and successfully bluffed his way far enough along to see his auto patent earn $5.8 million in royalties and gain the approval of a U. S. District Court. The only person willing and able to challenge the validity of Selden's patent was Henry Ford, who eventually won his case in Circuit Court.[8]

Two Case Studies

At its best, the patent system stimulates progress, rewards deserving inventors and innovators, and arouses competition. At its worst, it fosters opposite tendencies. Each extreme may be vividly depicted by a case history.

United States Gypsum and Wallboard[9]

There is nothing especially clever about wallboard, looking at it with today's familiarity. It is plaster sandwiched between two sheets of paper. The ingredients are commonplace and easily produced; the idea is less than ingenious. At the turn of the century, all wallboard was produced with open edges that exposed the plaster filler. Exposure caused the edges to chip and crumble when bumped in transit or when the wallboard was carelessly hammered into place. The obvious remedy for this problem—paper covering for the edges as well as the body of the wallboard—was hit upon in 1912 and won for its discoverer, one Utzman, patent No. 1,034,746. This patent covered the process of closing the edges of wallboard by folding the bottom cover sheet over the edge and then affixing the top cover sheet.

Realizing its great value, United States Gypsum Corporation (called U. S. Gypsum), the leading wallboard producer of the day, acquired the Utzman patent and then used it as a springboard to four decades of industry dominance. On the face of it, the odds against U. S. Gypsum's conquest were rather large, for it was based on a brittle springboard. Aside from the fact that the Utzman

---

[7] Corwin D. Edwards, *Maintaining Competition* (New York: McGraw-Hill Book Co., 1964 edition), p. 218.

[8] Jones, *op. cit.*, pp. 77–79; Irene Till, "The Legal Monopoly," in *The Monopoly Makers*, edited by M. J. Green (New York: Grossman, 1973), pp. 293–94.

[9] This section is based primarily on *United States v. United States Gypsum Co.* 333 U. S. 366 (1947); and Clair Wilcox, *Competition and Monopoly in American Industry*, Monograph No. 21 of the Temporary National Economic Committee, U. S. Congress (1940), pp. 161–63.

patent lasted only 17 years, competitors could easily "invent around" it by closing wallboard edges in other, equally obvious ways. The top cover sheet could fold toward the bottom; the two cover sheets could *both* fold to overlap the edge; the two cover sheets could be imbedded in the center of the plaster edge; a separate sheet could cap the edge, and so on. U. S. Gypsum, however, was able to control the competition these options offered its smaller rivals by tenaciously suing for infringement at every fold. After thus "softening" up its competitors, U. S. Gypsum bought their renegade patents.

In exchange for the cooperation of its rivals, U. S. Gypsum licensed them to use its accumulated patents through agreements that fixed the prices all parties charged for their wallboard. While building these arrangements, U. S. Gypsum seems to have avoided court and favored nontrial settlements as often as possible, perhaps out of fear that its patents would be found invalid if ever truly tested. In other words, competitors were sufficiently strong and U. S. Gypsum's patents were sufficiently weak that the company could not monopolize the trade. At best, it attained a 57% market share. Even so, U. S. Gypsum was resourceful enough to construct a network of license agreements that effectively cartelized the industry. "According to the plans we have," an optimistic executive said at one point, "we figure that there is a possibility of us holding the price steady on wallboard for the next fourteen or fifteen years which means much to the industry."[10] How much it meant is measured by the fact that in 1928, U. S. Gypsum reportedly earned a profit of $11.09 per 1000 square feet of wallboard over the manufacturing cost of $10.50.

But the cartel's edges began to crumble during the late 1920s as a result of several factors. One was the expiration of the crucial Utzman patent in August 1929. Another was the superior "starch process," developed independently of U. S. Gypsum. Despite these adversities the company managed to maintain control (and relieve its edginess) by aquiring applications for patents covering "bubble board," a type of wallboard that was lighter and cheaper than regular wallboard by virtue of its interior bubbles (the blowing of which was achieved merely by adding soap foam to the plaster while wet). During 1929, industry leaders huddled repeatedly, one key meeting occurring on the very same day the Utzman patent expired. The upshot was a series of license agreements grounded on a total of 50 patents and seven patent applications, including the starch patent and the "bubble board" applications. All companies in the industry were a party to the collusion except one small firm. The license contracts gave U. S. Gypsum the right to fix the minimum prices at which licensees would sell. Accordingly, U. S. Gypsum issued a series of bulletins running over a thousand pages combined specifying in minute detail prices and terms of sale for 95% of the industry's wallboard. Success of the rejuvenated price-fixing program permitted its primary sponsor to earn a fat profit even during the Great Depression. By one estimate, U. S. Gypsum's prices were so high that it could break even while operating at only 14% of capacity.

[10] *U. S. v. U. S. Gypsum, op. cit.*, 374.

Although the arrangement would have carried through to 1954, when the "bubble board" patents expired, the cartel's life was cut short by action of the Antitrust Division of the Department of Justice. Attacked for violating the Sherman Act, the cartel was dissolved after the Supreme Court decided in 1947 that "regardless of motive, the Sherman Act bars patent exploitation of the kind that was here attempted."[11]

Chester Carlson and Xerox[12]

Born to the wife of an itinerant barber and raised in poverty, Chester Carlson invented xerography. Various family tragedies compelled Carlson to work unceasingly from age 12 to support his family and his education. His dire boyhood circumstances induced dreams of escape. In his own words:

> At this stage in my life, I was entranced by the accounts I read of the work and successes of independent inventors and of the rewards they were able to secure through the patents on their inventions. I, too, might do this, I thought; and this contemplation gave stimulus and direction to my life.

After working his way through to a physics degree at the California Institute of Technology, Carlson accepted a research position at Bell Telephone Laboratories in 1930, a position made temporary by the Great Depression. Though plagued by financial difficulties during the depression, he found a job in the patent department of another company. His tasks there impressed upon him the need for quick, inexpensive copies of drawings and documents. Thus it was that in 1935 Carlson began a spare-time search for a copy machine. Although he was working full time and attending law school at night (in hopes of becoming a patent attorney!), his research and experimentation were extensive, leading eventually to his key idea of combining electrostatics and photoconductive materials. The first successful demonstration of Carlson's ideas took place in a room behind a beauty parlor in Astoria, Long Island, on October 22, 1938. He used a crude device to copy the message "10-22-38 Astoria."

Four patents awarded to Carlson between 1940 and 1944 covered his basic concepts. During the same years he tried to find a firm that would develop his invention for commercial use, but he encountered a stream of rejections, including those of 20 large firms—IBM, Remington Rand, and Eastman Kodak among them. The project was finally picked up for experimentation by Battelle

---

[11] *Ibid.*, p. 393.

[12] This section is based on J. Jewkes, D. Sawers, and R. Stillerman, *The Sources of Invention* (New York: Norton, 1969), pp. 321–23; D. V. DeSimone, Testimony, *Economic Concentration*, Part 3, U. S. Senate Subcommittee on Antitrust and Monopoly, (1965), pp. 1108–1111; E. A. Blackstone, "The Copying-Machine Industry: Innovations, Patents, and Pricing," *Antitrust Law & Economics Review* (Fall 1972), pp. 105–22; and F. M. Scherer, *The Economic Effects of Compulsory Patent Licensing* (New York: New York University Graduate School of Business Administration, 1977), p. 9.

Memorial Institute, a nonprofit research outfit, which thereby gained partial rights to any future earnings on the patents. Battelle devised a number of major patentable improvements, including use of a selenium plate, which allowed copies to be made on ordinary as opposed to chemically coated paper. But Battelle did not have the resources to manufacture and market the machine.

Quest for a commercial innovator led to another round of rejections from big companies, whereupon, in 1946, the task was undertaken by Haloid Company, a small firm earning an annual net income of only $101,000. Motivated by partial rights to potential earnings and led by a bright, enthusiastic fellow named Joseph Wilson, Haloid pushed the project to fruition. Among the landmarks on the long road that followed were (1) the first marketing of an industrial-use copier in 1950; (2) a change of company name from Haloid to Xerox; (3) first profit earnings in 1953; (4) development by 1957 of a prototype office copier, the cost of which nearly bankrupted the company; and (5) commercial introduction of the famous 914 console copier in 1959, more than 20 years after Carlson began his initial experiments.

All told, over $20 million was spent on the development of xerography before 1959. It is doubtful whether such a large financial commitment would ever have been made by the people who made it without patent protection. Besides Carlson's first four patents, the project generated well over 100 improvement patents for various machine designs, selenium drums, paper feeding devices, copy counters, powder dispensers, and so on. The significance of patents to Xerox is summarized by Joseph Wilson:

> We have become an almost classic case for those who believe the (patent) system was designed to permit small, weak companies to become healthy. During the early years of xerography we were investing almost as much in research as we were realizing in profit. Unless the first faltering efforts had been protected from imitators, the business itself probably would have foundered, thus obliterating opportunities for jobs for thousands throughout the world.[13]

(Carlson, Battelle, and Wilson were each duly and eventually rewarded with eight-digit earnings.)

Why Patents?

The Xerox story implies several justifications for the patent system that now ought to be openly stated. At bottom, support rests on three legs: "natural law" property, "exchange-for-secrets," and "incentives."

Natural Law

The natural law thesis asserts that inventors have a natural property right to their own idea. "It would be a gross immorality in the law," John Stuart Mill

---

[13] DeSimone, *op. cit.*, p. 1111.

argued, "to set everybody free to use a person's work without his consent and without giving him an equivalent."[14] Although this view appeals to our sense of fairness and appears to be self-evident, it is not without its practical problems. For one thing, it implicitly assumes that invention is the work of a single, identifiable mind, or at most a few minds. But today invention is usually the product of a faceless corporate team, and any resulting patent rights rest with the corporation, not with the deserving inventors, individual or otherwise. Of course corporations may fund the research and thereby accept the risks, so the property argument could be extended to corporate research on grounds of "just" compensation.

This extention does not square with the fact that corporations doing research for the U. S. Department of Defense get exclusive patent rights on their defense work without bearing any financial risk. The property rationale is further undermined by the fact that patents protect only a few classes of ideas. If one is seriously concerned about the fair treatment of thinkers, why forsake those who push back the frontiers of knowledge in areas excluded from patent eligibility— such as pure science, mathematics, economics, and business administration? Are these pioneers second-class cogitators? Are their ideas less hard to come by or less worthy? Is the inventor of parakeet-diapers more deserving than the inventor of double-entry bookkeeping?

Exchange-for-Secrets

Patent law requires that inventors disclose their invention to the public. Without patent protection it is a pretty safe bet that inventors would try to rely on secrecy more than they now do to protect their ideas from theft. Thus the exchange-for-secrets rationale "presumes a bargain between inventor and society, the former surrendering the possession of secret knowledge in exchange for the protection of a temporary exclusivity in its industrial use."[15] Widespread public knowledge is assumed to be more beneficial than secret knowledge because openness fertilizes technological advance. One discovery may trigger dozens of others among many inventors. And, although the initial discovery cannot be used freely for 17 years, secrecy might prevent full diffusion of its application for an even longer duration. Just how well society comes out in the bargain is impossible to say. The benefits of openness and the costs of temporary monopoly defy accurate estimation, especially the former. About all that can be said with confidence is that abolition of the patent system would cause the burial of *some* knowledge currently revealed in patent applications.[16]

---

[14] Cited by Floyd L. Vaughan, *The United States Patent System* (Norman, Okla.: University of Oklahoma Press, 1956), p. 27.

[15] Fritz Machlup, *An Economic Review of the Patent System*, Study No. 15, U. S. Senate, Subcommittee on Patents, Trademarks, and Copyrights, 85th Congress, Second Session (1958), p. 21.

[16] C. T. Taylor and Z. A. Silberston, *The Economic Impact of the Patent System* (Cambridge, U.K.: Cambridge University Press, 1973), p. 352.

Still, the *extent* of the graveyard and the *importance* of the knowledge that would be buried cannot be reckoned. The measure is uncertain because (1) many discoveries, especially those relating to products rather than production processes, would be automatically disclosed anyway once placed in use; (2) much of the knowledge that *can* be kept secret *is* kept secret despite the patent system; and (3) much of the knowledge that could be kept secret but is disclosed through patents is outdated or otherwise worthless. The first point needs no explanation (especially not to chemists and engineers who change companies frequently, or to industrial spies). The last point may be illustrated with two simple comments: (a) Delays of inventors, their patent attorneys, and the patent office (which takes $2\frac{1}{2}$ years to clear a typical patent application) render the average scientific information contained in a freshly issued U. S. patent roughly 4 years old.[17] (b) A survey of 22 technologically orientated British companies reveals that they would be willing to pay no more than about $\frac{3}{4}\%$ of their combined R & D budgets to gain access to the information contained in British patents, assuming such information was sold rather than given away, and assuming the information was unavailable otherwise.[18]

The second point—that much knowledge remains secret despite the patent system—has a more complicated root structure. Rough estimates suggest that somewhere between 30,000 and 60,000 patentable inventions are born each year for which no patent application is ever filed.[19] Many of these inventions are not worth the bother and expense patenting entails, even when their use breaks secrecy. Examples include novelty items and toys whose life spans are limited by fashion or consumer caprice. On the other hand, many of these inventions *are* valuable and remain unpatented because their owners feel that long-term secrecy is both possible and more profitable. Undoubtedly one of the oldest and most highly prized trade secrets of all time is the formula for Coca Cola. Though the trade secret approach is risky, it is attempted extensively. The practice weakens support for the patent system because it can then be argued that, for the most part, patents do not cover inventions that would otherwise be secret. As Alfred Kahn put it, "companies presumably keep secret whatever they can and patent what they cannot."[20]

What is more, the disclosure requirement of patent law is not strictly enforced, and some patents are obtained without full disclosure. The problem is not so much one of the patent system in principle as it is of slipshod administrative practice. The patent office has no laboratories to check whether the information given in applications is sufficient to enable replication of the invention by someone skilled in the art. Step-by-step duplication of what is disclosed may or may not produce the claimed effect, and experience has shown that it usually does not—a crucial step is "inadvertently" left out; a temperature is "misprinted," and

---

[17] *Business Week*, December 4, 1971, p. 68.

[18] Taylor and Silberston, *op. cit.*, p. 212.

[19] Jones, *op. cit.*, p. 101.

[20] Alfred E. Kahn, "The Role of Patents," in *Competition, Cartels, and Their Regulation*, edited by J. P. Miller (Amsterdam: North Holland Publishing Co., 1962), p. 317.

TABLE 24-1   Influence of Patent Rights and Prior Commercial Experience on Commercial Use of Inventions

Character of Patent Rights	With Prior Commercial Experience (%)	Without Prior Commercial Experience (%)
Contractor has title	23.8	6.6
Contractor has no title	13.3	2.2

Source: *Background Materials on Government Patent Policies*, Vol. II, U. S. House of Representatives, Subcommittee on Domestic and International Scientific Planning and Analysis, 94th Congress, Second Session (1976), p. 97.

so on."[21] As a result, a word has been coined to describe what is so commonly missing—**know-how**. Indeed, patent licensees have learned that access to another's patents, plain and simple, is normally a worthless proposition without abundant know-how thrown into the bargain.

Incentive

The justification most solidly illustrated by the story of Xerox, and the justification most supportive of the patent system, is that it provides incentive to invent and innovate. This rationale rests on two propositions: first, that more invention and innovation than would occur in the absence of some special inducement are desirable, and second, that giving out patents is the best method of providing such special inducement. In other words, discoveries would surely occur without patents (wheel, pulley, and plow head the nearly endless list), but it is believed that their unearthing will be appreciably hastened, or that more of them will be obtained, if the vast profit potential exclusive patents provide is used to lure inventors and innovators into action.

There can be no doubt but what many inventions and innovations depend on patents for their existence or early arrival. Stories of people like Chester Carlson tell us that garrets and garages shelter thousands of inventors so inspired. As for innovation, Table 24-1 contains convincing evidence that exclusive patent protection encourages commercial use of discoveries. The data in the table derive from an in-depth study of 1720 patented inventions resulting from federally funded R & D. Of those inventions, 1484 could be privately exploited in civilian markets on an exclusive basis because the patent rights fell to the corporate research contractor rather than to the government. Patents on the remaining

[21] Till, *op. cit.*, p. 304.

236 inventions were owned by the federal government, not the research contractor, and their use in civilian markets was open to anyone, nonexclusively.

Table 24-1 shows the percentage of inventions that were used commercially in each of these two classes, holding constant another major determinant of commercialization, namely, the contractor's prior commercial experience in the field of the invention. Among contractors with prior commercial experience, those with patent titles commercialized 23.8 % of their inventions, whereas those without exclusive titles converted only 13.3 %. Among contractors without prior commercial experience in the field of the invention, private patent rights are associated with a frequency of commercial use three times greater than use without title. Hence patents seem to spur innovation as well as invention.

Even so, the incentive thesis needs qualification at two levels. First, social benefits of cost savings and added consumer surplus may be rightly credited to the patent system for fathering "patent-dependent" inventions and innovations, but patent protection of these discoveries also creates social costs. These costs are the usual ones associated with monopoly—that is, higher prices than otherwise, X-inefficiencies, and so on. When these costs are deducted from the social benefits provided by these patent-dependent discoveries, the *net result* is considerably smaller that that suggested by brash talk of the gross benefits. This qualification of the incentive thesis is nevertheless not very serious because theory can demonstrate that the social benefits of these patent-dependent discoveries nearly always exceed those social costs to yield a positive net social benefit.[22]

The second and higher level qualification is critical, however. We may comfortably assume that patent-dependent inventions and innovations are always, on balance, beneficial. But we *cannot* jump from there to conclude that the *patent system itself* is, on balance, always beneficial. Inability to make this leap weakens the incentive thesis. The cause of our shaky knees at this point can only be diagnosed by a more thorough discussion of the patent system's costs and benefits.

Benefits and Costs of Patents

If the net social benefits of patent-dependent discoveries and developments were all that counted, the value of patent systems could not be questioned. However, patents are extended to *all* inventions that meet the legal qualifications, including inventions that are *not* dependent on the patent system for their existence. Whatever social benefits may be claimed for these *non*patent-dependent inventions, they cannot be attributed to the patent system for the simple reason that their existence does not hinge on patent protection. Patent

[22] For a review see Scherer, *op. cit* (1977), pp. 25–34, and William D. Nordhaus, *Invention, Growth, and Welfare* (Cambridge, Mass.: MIT Press, 1969).

protection for these nondependent inventions does create social costs, however, costs of the monopoly kind. So in such cases there will *always be net social costs* from patents. Given that (1) patent dependency always yields net social benefits and (2) *non*patent dependency of patented inventions always yields net social costs, economists have devised the following criterion for judging the value of the patent system. As stated by F. M. Scherer, one "must weigh the *net* benefits associated with inventions which would not have been available without patent protection against the *net* social losses associated with patented inventions that would be introduced even if no patent rights were offered."[23]

Unfortunately, balance scales capable of this weighing have not yet been invented (patentable or otherwise). Some have even said the task is and always will be impossible because there is no sure way of telling whether a given invention is, or is not, patent dependent. Still, the major considerations that would guide educated guesswork on the issue have been sketched, and they include the following.

Tallies of Patent Dependency

Rough approximations have occasionally been made about the number of patent-dependent versus nonpatent-dependent inventions, on the assumption that, if the former number falls considerably short of the latter, the net benefits of the former are also likely to fall short of the net costs of the latter. For example, these two figures have been crudely estimated by classifying discoveries of individual inventors (and perhaps those of small firms too) in the patent-dependent group and relegating those of corporations (or *large* corporations) into the nonpatent-dependent group. Questionnaire surveys of patentees rather consistently reveal that, in general, individual inventors rely heavily on patent protection to sustain their efforts, whereas most corporations claim that patents are neither the chief goal nor principal determinant of their innovative efforts.[24]

By this broad measure it would appear that *non*patent-dependent inventions easily outnumber patent-dependent inventions by a ratio somewhere in the neighborhood of 3 or 4 to 1. However, the very rough nature of this approximation is underscored by substantial differences of patent-dependency across industries. Chemical and pharmaceutical companies claim to lean more heavily on patents than do other corporate classes. A West German study arrived through opinion surveys at the following estimates of patent-dependent inventions as a per cent of all patented inventions in West Germany: chemicals and drugs, 36%; electrical equipment, 21%; instruments and optical, 21%; machinery, 3%; and iron and steel, 0%.[25]

Patent dependency has also been examined by study of situations in which

---

[23] F. M. Scherer, *Industrial Market Structure and Economic Performance* (Chicago: Rand McNally, 1970), p. 384.

[24] For a survey of the surveys see Scherer, *op. cit.* (1977), pp. 50–56.

[25] *Ibid.*, p. 53.

patents have not been available. Neither Switzerland nor the Netherlands had patent systems during the latter half of the nineteenth century and the first decade of this century. According to Eric Schiff, who assessed the evidence provided by these countries, the absence of patents failed to petrify industry in either. On the contrary, industry thrived. As regards inventive activity itself, the evidence for the Netherlands is mixed, meaning that substantial growth was apparently based on technological change borrowed from foreign countries with patent systems. On the other hand, Swiss inventive activity appears to have been totally unaffected by a lack of patents, inasmuch as it was vigorous both during and after the patentless period.[26] Related evidence of present-day vintage is derived from the severely restricted patent coverage of drug products in a number of countries, including Sweden, Japan, Italy, and West Germany. Scherer's cross-national analysis of innovative activity in pharmaceuticals led him to conclude that there were no "clear links between the strength of patent protection and relative innovative vigor."[27]

If, on the whole, patents are no more forceful in stimulating invention and innovation than is indicated by these items of evidence, obviously there must be other sources of incentive, other factors propelling progress. In the first place, to the extent *secrecy* can be maintained, it provides protection in lieu of patent protection. We have already acknowledged the importance of know-how even with patents. Second, many companies engage in progressive activities to remain *competitive* or gain competitive leadership. Introduction of new products or product improvements is a form of product differentiation, much like advertising. Natural lags, including temporary secrecy and retooling requirements, prevent immediate imitation of these efforts, gaining prestige and customer loyalty for the innovators. With all or most firms in an industry competing in this fashion, average industry price level will normally be high enough to cover the industry's R & D costs, just as price level covers advertising costs. Third, even where imitation is not substantially delayed, innovative investments are not always or even usually flushed down the drain by the price competition of imitators. High concentration, stiff barriers to entry, and similar sources of *market power other than patents* furnish a basis for post-imitation price discipline in many industries. Finally, even when R & D does not on average pay its own way, it may nevertheless persist. Like gamblers, inventors and innovators often have distorted visions. They tend to see the Chester Carlsons more clearly than the Feckless Floyd failures. They *overrate their chances* of winning the spectacular treasures, and, as a consequence, they often subsidize their R & D efforts from unrelated earnings.

Note that most of these nonpatent inducements probably apply most strongly to medium-sized or large firms. Secrecy cannot be maintained by a small individual inventor who must go around displaying his ideas in hopes of finding a firm that will commercialize them. A small, newly entering enterprise

---

[26] Eric Schiff, *Industrialization without Patents* (Princeton, N.J.: Princeton University Press, 1971).
[27] Scherer, *op. cit.* (1977), p. 39.

that dares to threaten the established position of existing behemoths cannot count on the restraint of their price discipline should they elect to crush the newcomer. A small company cannot gain much of a jump on its rivals if its brand name is less entrenched and its distribution channels are shallower and thinner than those of its larger rivals. A small company likewise tends to be less diversified than its larger foes, so it may have fewer opportunities to subsidize its R & D during periods of financial drought. Perhaps these considerations explain why individual inventors and small firms profess greater reliance on the patent system, and claim a keener interest in its perpetuation, than big firms. (This does not necessarily mean that the patent system is, on balance, pro-competitive. The story of U. S. Gypsum should dispel hasty conclusions of that kind.)

To summarize, various empirical tallies of patent dependency indicate that the system provides life-support for only a minority of inventions and inno-vations, a minority whose origins are of usually humble size. This minority wins kudos for the system. But since patents are also showered indiscriminately on the nonpatent-dependent majority of inventions, it would appear from tally-type evidence that the net costs of the majority exceed the net benefits of the minority, and the system should therefore be reformed or abolished. However, we must hold off the executioners, at least momentarily.

The Economic Significance of
Patent-Dependent Inventions

Although the weight of numbers suggests the patent system is economically unfit, that measure may be misleading. What if the relatively few inventions that are patent-dependent include the relatively few inventions that are truly revolutionary, whereas, at the same time, the relatively numerous nonpatent-dependent inventions include only simple improvements or inanities? It has been argued that, to some extent, there is a direct relationship between the economic significance of inventions and their patent dependency. F. M. Scherer speaks eloquently for this view:

> It is conceivable that without a patent system some of the most spectacular tech-nical contributions—those which effect a genuine revolution in production or con-sumption patterns—might be lost or (more plausibly) seriously delayed . . . . Such innovations may lie off the beaten paths of industrial technology, where no firm or group of firms has a natural advantage, and the innovator may be forced to develop completely new marketing channels and production facilities to exploit them. They may entail greater technological and market uncertainties, higher development costs, and longer inception-to-commercialization lags than the vast bulk of all industrial innovation. Entrepreneurs may be willing to accept their challenge only under highly favorable circumstances—notably, when it is anticipated that if success is achieved, it can be exploited to the fullest through the exercise of exclusive patent rights.
>
> That such cases exist is virtually certain. Black-and-white television and the devel-opment of Chester Carlson's xerographic concepts are probable examples.[28]

[28] Scherer, *op. cit.* (1970), p. 388.

Undoubtedly it is this possibility, coupled with notions of "natural law" property, that persuades politicians to keep the patent system intact. At a bare minimum, such crude *qualitative* accounting raises serious doubts about the accuracy of negative conclusions derived from simple *quantitative* tallies.

The Social Cost of Nondependent Inventions

But the qualifications cannot end there, not in fairness to those who oppose patents, anyway. Just as the net benefits of dependent cases need qualification, so too the net costs of granting patents in nondependent cases need amplification—an exercise that tips the balance back in the negative direction, especially where revolutionary innovations of this nondependent stripe are concerned. First, granting monopoly rights over knowledge that is not dependent on patents artificially restricts use of that knowledge below what is socially optimal. The marginal cost of using technical knowledge is zero in the sense that knowledge can be used over and over and over again, by one person or many, without even the slightest danger of exhaustion through wear and tear. No one is compelled to get less of it when anyone else gets more.

Ideally, therefore, technology should be *freely* available to all potential users because the "pure" marginal cost of its dissemination and application is zero. But the grant of monopoly leads to exclusions, either directly or by the extraction of a royalty-price that exceeds zero.[29] A second social cost, one stemming from that just mentioned, is a blocking effect. Potential inventors who might like to use a patented invention to further their research in different or related fields may be blocked from doing so, in which case the patent would not be fostering progress but rather inhibiting it. Third, if a patent is extended to a firm with a preexisting monopoly position, then suppression of the patented invention is possible under certain circumstances.[30] Fourth, patents give rise to monopoly powers and restrictive practices that go well beyond those inherent in patents themselves.

It is at this last point that patent policy collides with antitrust policy. Pure and simple patent monopoly escapes antitrust attack for obvious reasons. But, as seen earlier in the story of U. S. Gypsum, patents may be cleverly accumulated and manipulated to construct elaborate fortresses of monopoly power or extensive networks of price-fixing agreements. The line between proper use and malevolent abuse of patent rights is difficult to draw, but the antitrust authorities and federal courts have over time made the attempt. As a result, the following practices, among others, have been declared illegal:

Restrictive licensing: If a number of patent licensees are restricted to charging prices specified by the patent holder, or if a number of licensees

---

[29] Wassily Leontief, "On Assignment of Patent Rights on Inventions Made Under Government Research Contracts," *Harvard Law Review* (January 1964), pp. 492–97.

[30] For a review of suppression cases see, Vaughan, *op. cit.*, pp. 227–60.

collude to allocate markets using patent licenses to formalize their agreement, violation is likely, as in the *Gypsum* case.[31]

Cross-licensing: Two or more patent holders may exchange rights of access to each other's patents, something which is often desirable in light of the fact that several firms may contribute to the technology of a single item, such as a TV set. However, patent "pools" that exclude others, or fix prices, or otherwise restrain trade are illegal.[32]

Acquisition of patents: Monopoly power built on the acquisition of many patents (as opposed to relying on one's own inventiveness) may be attacked under Section 7 of the Clayton Act.[33]

Tying: Tying the sale of an unpatented product (like salt) to a patented product (a salt dispensing machine used in food processing) is virtually *per se* illegal.[34]

In brief, antitrust policy permits patent holders to earn their "legitimate" reward for invention, a reward that may be monopolistically plump. But patent rights cannot be stretched beyond "legitimate" rights. Tight interpretation of legitimacy has held down the social costs of the patent system, but not to the point of quieting cries for reform.

Proposals for Reform

Ideology and evidence lead few folks to advocate complete abolition of the United States patent system. The natural law property thesis rests on strongly held value judgements unrelated to economic benefits and costs. There is also enough incentive provided by the system to produce some social benefits. Whether these benefits exceed the social costs is, as we have seen, uncertain, but the benefits are large enough that abolition of the system might give appearances of throwing the baby out with the bath water. Hence critics of the system usually advocate reform, not abolition.[35]

One of the most obvious improvements that could be made in the system is the elimination of improvident patent grants. The test of inventiveness could obviously be tightened substantially.

Another frequently voiced change is shorter patent life. At present, patent monopolies usually extend to more than 20 years because, in addition to the

---

[31] *U. S. v. United States Gypsum Co.* 333 U. S. 364 (1948); *U. S. v. Masonite Corp.*, 316 U. S. 265 (1942); *Newburgh Moire Co. v. Superiors Moire Co.*, 237 F. 2d 283 (3d Cir. 1956).

[32] *U. S. v. Line Material Co.*, 333 U. S. 287 (1948); *U. S. v. Singer Manufacturing Co.*, 374 U. S. 174 (1963).

[33] *U. S. v. Lever Bros. Co.*, 216 F. Supp. 887 (S.D.N.Y. 1963); *Kobe, Inc. v. Dempsey Pump Co.*, 198 F. 2d 416 (10th Cir. 1952).

[34] *International Salt Co., v. U. S.*, 332 U. S. 392 (1947).

[35] Patent systems in less-developed countries are an entirely different matter, though: D. F. Greer, "The Case Against Patent Systems In Less-Developed Countries," *Journal of International Law and Economics* (December 1973), pp. 223–66.

official 17 years granted from date of patent issue, patent applicants have 1 year of grace after discovery before they have to apply, plus several years of wait while their application stands "pending" neck-deep in the patent office's backlog. Application revisions and amendments may add still more time of useful monopoly. It can be argued that reducing patent life below 17 years to, say, 10 years would not damage incentives appreciably while it would shrink the duration of social costs. A variant of this suggestion is *variable* patent lives, awarding cheaply developed, trivial inventions only three or four summers plus their associated seasons, but giving more significant, more risky, and more difficult-to-develop inventions the benefit of a full 17 years. The main problem with this plan is the administrative difficulty of determining which specific inventions are to be blessed with what patent life span.

Yet another commonly advocated change is compulsory licensing to all who desire licenses at a "reasonable" royalty fee. This cut at exclusiveness would obviously reduce the monopoly power that patents presently bestow. Empirical studies of the proposal indicate that it would also substantially deflate the system's incentives, but by less than abolition would.[36] Assuming the system's incentives are most important to individual inventors and small firms, compulsory licensing could include especially favorable treatment of individuals and small firms so that they would *not* be forced to license their patents to others except under certain limited circumstances.[37]

Federal Funding of R & D

The federal government has seated itself at the dining table of technology, supped gluttonously, and has begun picking up the tab. Back in 1940 federal expenditures on R & D amounted to no more than $74.1 million, which was 0.8% of the total federal budget and barely 0.07% of GNP. A further mark of that prosaic era is the fact that federal spending on *agricultural* R & D exceeded *defense* R & D spending. World War II, the Cold War, the Space Race, and the Vietnam War conspired to change all that. By the mid-1960s federal R & D spending had soared to exceed $14 *billion*, which relative to total federal spending of all kinds topped 12%, and compared to GNP exceeded 2%. Defense R & D spending exploded to 41 times the size of agricultural outlays.[38]

Since the mid-1960s things have slackened off a bit. Total federal R & D funding has continued to climb to ever higher absolute dollar levels, exceeding $24 billion in 1977. Yet price inflation exaggerates these dollars, and, as a proportion of the total federal budget or relative to GNP, federal R & D funding has recently fallen to about three fifths of what it was during the mid-1960s.

[36] Taylor and Silberston, *op. cit.*; Scherer, *op. cit.* (1977).

[37] Scherer, *op. cit.* (1977), p. 86.

[38] National Science Foundation, *Federal Funds for Research, Development, and Other Scientific Activities* (NSF 77–301, 1977), p. 4; Edwin Mansfield, *The Economics of Technical Change* (New York: Norton, 1968), p. 163.

TABLE 24-2   Federal R & D Funding by Function: Fiscal Years 1969 and 1978

Function	Millions of Dollars		Per Cent of Total	
	1969	1978*	1969	1978*
National defense	8354	12,907	53.4	49.0
Space	3732	3,140	23.9	11.9
Energy	328	2,798	2.1	10.6
Health	1127	2,683	7.2	10.2
Environment	315	1,098	2.0	4.2
Science base	513	1,060	3.3	4.0
Transportation and communications	458	805	2.9	3.1
Natural resources	201	610	1.3	2.3
Food, fiber, agriculture	225	488	1.4	1.8
Education	155	269	1.0	1.0
All other (crime, housing, social services, etc.)	233	459	1.5	1.7
Total	15,641	26,317	100	100

* Estimates based on President's 1978 budget to Congress
Source: National Science Foundation, *An Analysis of Federal R & D Funding by Function* (NSF 77–326, 1977), p. 5.

Recent trends in the composition of this expenditure are depicted in Table 24-2. National defense and space head the list of allocations. In 1978 their combined total of $16 billion accounted for about 61% of all federal R & D money. But this proportion was down from 77% in 1969, a drop of 16 percentage points. Quite clearly there has been a substantial revision of priorities, with military and space losing ground to a wide range of civilian R & D programs. Note especially the massive rise in energy R & D funding, from $328 million, or 2.1%, in 1969 to $2798 million, or 10.6% of the total R & D budget, in 1978. By far the biggest chunk of energy money has gone to support the development of nuclear power—projects like the liquid metal fast breeder reactor, uranium enrichment processing, magnetic fusion, and laser fusion. In 1969 these efforts took 93% of the energy outlay. In 1978 these still took a hefty 54%, but other energy sources were then getting much greater attention, including coal gasification, oil shale, and solar power.

Three other areas enjoying rapid relative growth in funding are environment, natural resources, and "science base." The first is self-explanatory. The second entails research in such areas as mineral reserve estimation, watershed management, and forestry protection. "Scientific base" refers chiefly to basic research that has no obvious or immediate application in either commerce or government.

Much of it is "glamorous" science, such as high-energy physics, molecular biology, and oceanography. But it stretches from mathematics to materials–processing to anthropology.

Why has the government opened its purse so widely to these pursuits? Why has the distribution of money moved around so much? What guides Washington in these matters? There are no really solid answers because noneconomic value judgments play a crucial role in the decision making. Which will reduce the threat of death more—a billion dollars spent for a new military weapon or for a cure for cancer? Which will do more to relieve the energy crisis by the year 2000—a billion dollars spent on nuclear or on solar power? No one knows for sure; speculation reigns amidst the inherent uncertainties. Hence, value judgments are inescapable, and these shift like hemlines under the press of political, social, international, and technical developments.

Still, there are a few broad economic foundations for this effort.[39] To begin with, most federal R & D is allocated to areas where the federal government stands as the sole or chief consumer of the ultimate product. National defense and space are the most obvious instances. Because the federal government has prime responsibility for provision of these "public goods" (a responsibility recognized by even the most miserly conservatives), it is strongly felt that the government should also take responsibility for technological advance in these areas.

Other R & D programs are grounded on the belief that private incentives are lacking. That is, the social benefits of advancement greatly exceed the benefits that can be privately captured, or if they can be privately captured, such would be undesirable. Research in basic science, health, environmental protection, and crime prevention probably fit this justification. Still other programs can be defended as offsets to market imperfections of somewhat different sorts. Single R & D projects in such areas as nuclear power and urban mass transportation couple costs of billions of dollars with risks of ominous magnitudes, so much so that even our largest and most courageous private companies are scared to undertake them without government support. The necessity for government R & D funding in agriculture, housing, construction, and coal is often defended because these industries tend to be populated with firms too small and too scattered to shoulder the burdens of even medium-sized R & D projects. As concentration in these industries has increased over time, and as firm size has likewise grown, this justification has lost some of its punch. Still, it remains persuasive to many politicians, and it probably remains valid at least in some areas.

Whatever the reason, federal R & D outlays now exceed those of private industry by a fat margin. Accordingly, our survey of policy would have been woefully lacking had it concealed this contribution.

[39] For details see Mansfield, *op. cit.*, pp. 186–87; *Priorities and Efficiency in Federal Research and Development*, A Compendium of Papers, Subcommittee on Priorities and Economy in Government of the Joint Economic Committee, U. S. Congress, 94th Congress, Second Session (1976); and John E. Tilton, *U. S. Energy R & D Policy* (Washington, D.C.: Resources for the Future, 1974).

Summary

The United States government's promotion of technical progress dates from the days of the Founding Fathers. Patents originate in the Constitution, which authorizes legislation to "promote the progress of science and useful arts, by securing for limited times to authors and inventors the exclusive right to their respective writings and discoveries." Under present law, patent last 17 years and cover discoveries that pass fairly lenient standards of inventiveness, novelty, and utility. Admissible subject matter is limited to mechanical and chemical products or processes, thereby excluding fundamental laws of nature and other worthwhile discoveries.

At its best, the patent system stimulates progress, rewards deserving inventors and innovators, and arouses competition by nourishing small firms. The history of Xerox illustrates these beneficent effects. On the other hand, deserving and getting do not always coincide under the system, with the result that patents protect discoveries that would be available anyway. Moreover, patents often provide hooks on which to hang restrictive practices, and they occasionally even stifle technical progress. Many of these blemishes in the system were underscored by the story of wallboard.

The main justifications for the patent system are "natural law" property, "exchange-for-secrets," and "incentives." Each has appeal; each has problems. As the law presently stands, too much is arbitrarily excluded to make the natural law argument natural, and society gets in on too few of the secrets it bargains for. That patent incentives pull some discoveries from the nether world cannot be doubted, but this effect is easily exaggerated.

Ideally, a benefit-cost analysis would compare the net benefits of patent-dependent inventions with the net costs of extending patents to nonpatent-dependent inventions. Unfortunately, data deficiences permit no more than speculation on this core. What little evidence is available indicates that net benefits have the best chance of exceeding net costs on those patents that are extended to individual inventors and small firms. Chemicals and pharmaceuticals might also enjoy favorable balances. These findings have led reformists to call for greater flexibility in the system—for example, variable patent lives and compulsory licensing rigorously applied to large firms and trivial discoveries.

Federal funding of R & D has grown from little more than a teenager's weekly allowance to amounts in excess of $25 billion. In recent years, defense and space R & D have been deemphasized in favor of civilian R & D. Noneconomic value judgments play a particularly prominent role in this policy area.

25

Quality, Safety, and Pollution: Theory and a Few Scraps of Evidence

... over the past decade, the pendulum has swung strongly toward laws and regulatory agencies geared to meeting social needs that the market system ignores.

BUSINESS WEEK, April 4, 1977

It is often said that markets ignore quality, safety, and pollution. One support for this accusation is that variances in market structure and conduct do not seem to affect these aspects of performance appreciably. In theory, there is no obvious or solid linkage between market structure and these variables.[1] In practice, no empirical studies reveal such linkage as it relates to safety and pollution, and only a few studies link structure to product quality. Those concerning product quality suggest that (1) small firms are typically equal to, and often more than equal to, large firms when it comes to quality, and (2) competition may foster favorable quality performance.[2] Still, these studies are not yet numerous enough to yield ironclad conclusions.

---

[1] The connection between product quality and structure has received the greatest theoretical attention, but these theories are chaotic. Conclusions fluctuate wildly depending on the theorist's assumptions. For recent examples see Dennis Epple and Allan Zelenitz, "Consumer Durables: Product Characteristics and Marketing Policies," *Southern Economic Journal* (October 1977), pp. 277–87 and L. J. White, "Market Structure and Product Varieties," *American Economic Review* (March 1977), pp. 179–82.

[2] K. W. Kepner and D. I. Padberg, "Quality as a Dimension of Competition in the Fluid Milk Industry," *Journal of Farm Economics* (December 1964), pp. 1331–35; Galen Rarick and Barrie Hartman, "The Effects of Competition on One Daily Newspaper's Content," *Journalism Quarterly* (May 1950); L. J. White, "Price Regulation and Quality Rivalry In a Profit-maximizing Model," *Journal of Money Credit and Banking* (February 1976), pp. 97–106; L. J. White, "Quality, Competition and Regulation: Evidence from the Airline Industry," in *Regulating the Product*, edited by R. Caves and M. Roberts (Cambridge, Mass.: Ballinger, 1975), pp. 17–35; Alan Bevan, "The U.K. Potato Crisp Industry, 1960–72: A Study of New Entry Competition," *Journal of Industrial Economics* (June 1974), pp. 281–97.

Markets are also said to ignore quality, safety, and pollution because, when left to themselves, markets of *all* types frequently perform poorly in these respects. Such failings are of course serious. Quality, safety, and pollution often mean more to us than monetary well-being. They may determine the difference between life and death. Hence, we cannot ignore them here.

This chapter covers two questions: (1) Why do markets sometimes fail to perform well in these respects? (2) When is direct government regulation of these aspects of performance appropriate? Because the answers to these questions differ according to which aspect of performance is addressed, the discussion is divided into three main sections, one each for quality, safety, and pollution. The next chapter takes up two further questions: (1) What is the government actually doing to regulate in these realms? (2) How good a job is it doing?

Quality[3]

Why is Market Performance Often Flawed?

As pointed out in earlier chapters, ideal market conditions would yield ideal results. Quality might vary across the brands of any one product in durability, efficacy, consistency, purity, and the like, but no buyer would be ripped-off, no buyer would get more or less than what he paid for. Variations in quality would be fully reflected by variations in price. Shoddy goods would be cheap, premium goods expensive. And, knowing this, consumers would get the most they could out of their limited budgets, buying quality according to their tastes and riches.[4]

Of course, one of the key prerequisites to this paradise is perfect buyer information. Without accurate, complete, and inexpensive information, consumers are, as indicated earlier, susceptible to errors of commission and omission. An error of *commission* occurs when a buyer erroneously *over*-estimates the quality of the good. He commits himself to buying more than he would with full information. Two illustrations of the monetary loss suffered from such errors are given in Figures 25-1(a) and 25-1(b). In each case the incorrect demand curve lies to the right of the correct demand curve because the uninformed buyer wants to buy *more* at every possible price than he would if

---

[3] Much of this section is based on M. R. Darby and E. Karni, "Free Competition and the Optimal Amount of Fraud," *Journal of Law & Economics* (April 1973), pp. 67–88; Sam Peltzman, "An Evaluation of Consumer Protection Legislation: The 1962 Drug Amendments," *Journal of Political Economy* (September 1973), pp. 1049–91; and T. McGuire, R. Nelson, and T. Spavins, "An Evaluation of Consumer Protection: Comment," *Journal of Political Economy* (June 1975), pp. 655–61.

[4] For a complete discussion of this view of quality see E. Scott Maynes, *Decision Making for Consumers* (New York: Macmillan Publishing Co. 1976), especially Chapter 3.

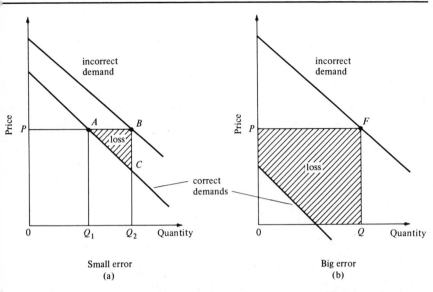

Figure 25-1. Errors of commission due to incorrect overestimation of value.

he were fully informed. Possible prices include the going market price P. The main difference in the two cases depicted is the degree of error. Figure 25-1(a) depicts a *small* error of commission, as the correct demand curve lies only slightly beneath the incorrect demand curve. The buyer's loss in this case is shaded area ABC. You might think that his loss is Q_1ABQ_2, which is the amount he is spending over and above what he ought to be spending ($OPAQ_1$), but it is not. The entire amount of his excess expenditure cannot be considered a loss because he is gaining *some* benefit from that erroneous excess—the benefit being Q_1ACQ_2, which is the area under the demand curve over the range of excess. Hence, loss is the excess expense, Q_1ABQ_2, less the added benefit, Q_1ACQ_2, and the result is ABC.

It can now be seen that Figure 25-1(b) depicts a *big* error of commission. At price P, the buyer should not be buying any of the good, but he is erroneously buying quantity OQ. Once again the benefit derived from these purchases is the area under the "correct demand" curve, whereas the total expenditure is area $OPFQ$. The difference is an enormous loss. In an even more extreme case, where the commodity in question is utterly worthless to the consumer (a vampire protection kit, for instance), the welfare loss would equal the *entire* amount spent, which in terms of 25-1(b) is area $OPFQ$.

Errors of *omission* are the opposite. They occur when the buyer buys *less* than he would with full knowledge. Two illustrations of the monetary loss suffered from such errors are given in Figures 25-2(a) and 25-2(b). In each case the incorrect demand curve lies to the left of the correct demand, and the

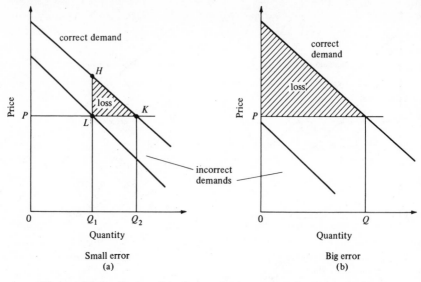

Figure 25-2. Errors of omission due to underestimation of value.

greater the leftward shift the greater the error. Thus Figure 25-2(a) depicts a case of slight error, and the welfare loss is triangle LHK. This is because Q_1 is the amount bought, but Q_2 is the amount that *ought* to have been bought. Correction of the error would cost the consumer an additional amount Q_1LKQ_2, but the added benefit would equal the total area under the demand curve over the Q_1 to Q_2 range, or area Q_1HKQ_2. The difference, which may be regarded as either the net gain from correction or the net loss from error, is area LHK.

A bigger error of omission is depicted by Figure 25-2(b). In that case the consumer is so pessimistic about the commodity he buys none at all at the going price, even though he would buy an amount OQ if fully informed. His loss is the entire amount of consumers' surplus that he would have enjoyed in the absence of error.

In the blissful fantasy land of ideal markets consumers always avoid these errors through low cost acquisition of information. They do this by inspection, experience, and study. In the case of search goods, which we defined earlier as goods whose qualities are visually apparent, inspection is sufficient. In the case of experience goods, whose qualities are hidden to the naked eye, experience and study are the only avenues open to knowledge. Under ideal circumstances neither avenue costs much in time or money.

In the real world, however, there are problems, some of which we discussed earlier. First, and most obvious, experience can be gained only through product purchase and use. Learning, then, is obviously cheap when beer, pizza, and anned corn are under investigation, but not when it comes to expensive, nfrequently purchased products like funerals and automobiles. Second, he private free-market system may not supply information for study in optimal mounts and grades. Thus, although sellers supply abundant information in he form of advertising, it is biased and often misleading. Independent testing ervices, such as Consumers' Union, earn a living by developing and disseminat-ng unbiased information on products. However, they merely survive, not hrive. The independent market for information is stunted by imperfections ind failures such as inappropriability and a lack of buyer knowledge, both of vhich were discussed in Chapter 5.

Finally, and perhaps most important, commodities and services often have qualities other than search and experience qualities—namely, **credence** qualities. Credence qualities are those that, although worthwhile, cannot be evaluated hrough inspection, or normal product use, or even simple study of general nformation. Instead, one's assessment of their value is either impossible or especially costly in relation to any additional information obtained. An example s TV repair. Say your set gets neither picture nor sound because of a burned-out horizontal oscillating tube, the replacement of which actually costs only $15, including the costs of diagnosis and labor as well as parts. But you are no expert. You don't know this. You know nothing other than the fact that repair s needed. So you take the set to what seems like an honest shop, pay the $10 minimum fee, and place yourself and your set at the mercy of the man behind he counter. Two days later he calls to tell you that a new *picture* tube is required, plus two transistors, all for "only" $57. Your response? You take a deep oreath and tell him "O.K.," thereby making an error of commission.

You buy solely on credence, for it would cost you time and money to give up your $10 deposit and take the set to another shop for a second opinion, an opinion that for all you know could well be the same and thereby cost you even more. Besides, it may take another week to obtain the second opinion (causing you to miss "Monday Night Football" two weeks in a row).

Other credence goods of this kind are auto repair, dental repair, and physician services. A common feature of these goods, besides consumer ignorance, is that *information* (that is, diagnosis) and *service* (that is, repair) are provided *iointly* rather than separately. Another class of credence goods is occupied by various drugs, cosmetics, medical devices, vitamin supplements, oil additives, and the like. These goods offer only "iffy" performance. They may or may not work depending on the circumstances, so you can never be sure if they really do work. That is, they may reduce the *chances* of contracting illness, or improve the *chances* of winning a mate, or favorably alter some other *chances*. But they offer no certainty of success. All in all, search qualities are known before purchase, experience qualities become known costlessly after purchase, and credence qualities are expensive or impossible for individual consumers to judge even after purchase. Inevitably, consumers are particularly error prone when it comes to credence qualities.

What Is the Proper Role of Government?

At bottom, government policy in this area is confined to four possibilities:

1. *Do nothing.*
2. *Improve consumer knowledge* by grade rating, subsidizing information, forcing quality disclosures, and labeling regulations.
3. *Prevent distortion* of consumers' knowledge by prohibiting false or misleading claims concerning quality.
4. *Regulate product quality* directly by prohibiting "inferior" quality products or specifying product features and contents.

The first three options were discussed earlier in Chapters 2, 5, and 16. And, as a *general rule*, they are better than the last policy. Why? Because under those three options, the ultimate decision of what to buy is left to the consumer not to the government. Although consumers will make errors of quality judgment, so be it. If someone is dumb enough to buy a vampire protection kit, he deserves to have his financial blood sucked. We value freedom of choice as an end in itself. And to the extent freedom of choice is exercised wisely in a market environment that approaches the ideal, such freedom will further the proper allocation of resources and thereby advance material welfare and happiness. These attributes are summarized in the concept of "consumer sovereignty." Indeed, consumer freedom is so highly prized that some folks argue that even policy options 2 and 3 are bad, that such policies of information improvement and deception prevention "interfere" with free consumer choice, even though they do not totally supplant it. Only a policy of "do nothing" satisfies those of this persuasion.

Moreover, it may be argued that government bureaucrats should not have the power to prohibit or specify the provision of products because bureaucrats can make mistakes just as consumers make mistakes. In particular, product regulation typically implies the application of broad, across-the-board standards protecting the "average" consumer or "most" consumers. Standards usually cannot be tailormade to fit the *particular* needs and tastes of individual consumers. Thus, in simple terms, vampire protection kits might be banned by the bureaucrats as being ineffectual, unnecessary, and vile. This would, however, prevent their purchase as "novelty items," thereby disappointing those folks who derive ghoulish delight from such things.

In more technical terms, our analysis of errors in Figures 25-1 and 25-2 applied only to *individual* consumers, not to *all* consumers as a group. Since individuals differ in tastes, knowledge, and proneness to error, those curves differ across individuals, even for a given product. It follows, then, that when the government makes product decisions for consumers as a group, it could be making errors of commission and omission as regards particular individuals.

The social costs of such regulatory errors may be seen in Figures 25-1 and 25-2, but the reasoning underlying them would be reversed. That is to say, government could ban vampire protection kits in hopes of preventing consumer errors of commission. But this would *impose* an error of *omission* on those who would buy them for novelty purposes if given the opportunity. The loss to those forcibly denied the product would be the shaded consumer's surplus suggested in Figure 25-2(b), which depicts errors of omission.

Conversely, the government could require that all cars come equipped with high quality seat belts, in hopes of preventing consumer errors of omission. But this would *impose* an error of *commission* on all folks who, with full knowledge of the benefits of strong seat belts, would buy cars without them. Those who would otherwise not buy seat belts at any price would suffer a loss equal to the entire amount spent on regulation seat belts, or an area like *OPFQ* in Figure 25-1(b), which depicts errors of commission. Those who would spend less on seat belts than the minimum amount required by law (say $5 for two cheap lap belts with plastic clasps) would lose lesser amounts, as is suggested by the shaded areas of Figures 25-1(a) and 25-1(b).

In sum, policies of direct product regulation tend to be heavy handed, even onerous, whereas policies of information enhancement and deception prevention tend to be more delicate and less oppressive. Accordingly, most people generally oppose direct product quality regulation, and their wishes are largely honored (as indicated by the vast array of junk that is available to American consumers, including shoddy vampire protection kits with pine, instead of more effective oak, stakes for driving into the heart).

Still, direct regulations of quality are by no means unheard of. They seem to be most acceptable in instances where three conditions combine: (1) where credence qualities are abundantly present, (2) where the technology involved is particularly complex, and (3) where consumers' preferences are fairly obvious to outside observers. Where credence qualities are present and technology is complex, consumers are especially susceptible to errors, and information policies are inadequate. Where consumer preferences are fairly obvious to outsiders, expert regulators run less risk of *imposing* errors on consumers. And where *all* these conditions apply, folks more readily tolerate or encourage active government intervention to assure good performance.

Thus, the Food and Drug Administration regulates the efficacy of drugs and medical devices (but not cosmetics), and state governments often regulate the quality of various repair and professional services, such as those of doctors, dentists, veterinarians, lawyers, and TV technicians (but not those of travel agents). Unfortunately, these regulations usually take the form of qualifying examinations and licensing, an approach that evidence suggests is faulty. Qualifying examinations provide no assurance of honesty or *continuing* competence; licensing erects a barrier to entry. Thus informed sources claim that "up to 40 percent of the nation's doctors are 'making a killing' in overcharging patients, performing unnecessary surgery and in other 'gouging' practices."[5] Another indication of physician quality, one which simultaneously reflects drug quality, is this: Before 1962 the Food and Drug Administration did not control the effectiveness of drugs. But in that year the law changed so all the drugs physicians were prescribing at that time have since had to be studied for claimed efficacy. As of January 1, 1976, the FDA's drug effectiveness review had removed from the market a total of 6673 drug products manufactured by 3016 companies. This includes 835 "chemical entities" made by 60 firms and 5838 "me-too" products made by 2515 firms.[6]

Perhaps the most interesting available test of alternative regulatory approaches was conducted by the staff of the Federal Trade Commission (FTC) examining TV repair.[7] Data were collected on TV repair costs and "parts" fraud in Washington, D.C., New Orleans, and San Francisco. At the time of the study in 1973, each of these cities was governed by a different policy:

1. Washington, D.C., had no regulation of repairmen.
2. Under Louisiana law, New Orleans repairmen were subject to competency examination and other entrance regulations plus licensing (all of which were sufficiently exclusionary that between 1960 and 1972 the number of licensed technicians in Louisiana actually decreased by 13%).
3. In contrast, California's technicians faced no entry restrictions, but their behavior was monitored by a state bureau containing two laboratories and a team of experts, who, in response to consumer complaints, tested the honesty and competency of repairmen by running "doctored" TV sets through suspected shops incognito. If fraud or gross negligence was discovered, the evidence was presented to the State Attorney General for disciplinary action.

Well, which system do you suppose gave consumers the best market performance? The FTC's staff had 61 "test" repairs made in the three cities at repair shops randomly selected from the telephone book. All the TV sets used were identical and in perfect operating order except for a burned-out horizontal oscillating tube. As it turned out, 48% of the repair shops in Washington, D.C., and 50% of those in New Orleans committed "parts" fraud by charging for parts and services that were not needed or were not employed. So D.C.'s free market performance must be rated abominable, and Louisiana's performance under licensing regulation rated no better.

In contrast, "only" 20% of the test shops in San Francisco ripped-off the FTC's "consumers," suggesting that California's policy of incognito monitoring

[5] Dr. John Knowles, former director of Massachusetts General Hospital, quoted by Darby and Karni, *op. cit.*, p. 68. See also "Too Much Surgery?" *Newsweek*, April 10, 1978, pp. 65–67.

[6] Food and Drug Administration, *Annual Report 1975*, p. 36. For further examples of questionable competence concerning prescription practices, see *Examination of the Pharmaceutical Industry 1973–74*, Hearings before the Subcommittee on Health of the Committee on Labor and Public Welfare, Part 2, U. S. Senate, 93rd Congress, First and Second Sessions (1974), pp. 597–601.

[7] John J. Phelan, *Regulation of the Television Repair Industry in Louisiana and California: A Case Study*, Report to the FTC (1974).

id have some beneficial effects. As for repair prices, they were lowest in California and highest in Washington, D.C., and New Orleans. The difference was due mainly to the relatively higher incidence of "parts" fraud in the latter two cities, but prices were generally highest in New Orleans, where licensing raised barriers to entry. In short, quality maintenance may be a serious problem for credence goods, but certain forms of its regulation can be costly and ineffectual.[8]

Safety[9]

Why Is Market Performance Often Flawed?

Although product quality, narrowly defined, is not usually regulated, the same cannot be said of product safety. The Food and Drug Administration and Federal Aviation Agency have been active for decades, and since the late 1960s there has been an explosion of new regulations and new federal agencies governing product safety (the Consumer Product Safety Commission and National Highway Traffic Safety Administration, included). From this observation you may conclude that certain aspects of "safety" set it apart from mere "quality." And you would be right. Before we explore these special aspects of safety, however, we should first of all note that, under ideal circumstances, safety is no different from any other product quality. That is to say, if we were blessed with ideal markets, then government regulation of safety would amount to little more than a massive vampire protection kit.

To see how the ideal market would handle safety, one must acknowledge the fact that folks do *not* demand absolute safety, either for themselves or for others. People willingly accept the risk of dreadful injury, disease, and even death, as indicated by all sorts of everyday behavior—smoking, driving without seat belts, hang gliding, whatever. People are especially willing to accept risks when they are fully informed about the potential costs of hazards and they are compensated for them monetarily either by lower prices for hazardous products or higher wages for hazardous employment, as compared with safer alternatives. Thus, under an ideal *caveat emptor* market system, the costs of accidents arising from products would be borne by consumers, but lower prices would

[8] For further discussion of the ill effects of "quality" licensing see E. D. Attanasi and S. R. Johnson, "An Empirical Note on Firm Performance in Government Contract Markets," *Journal of Industrial Economics* (June 1975), pp. 313–20; *Business Week*, November 28, 1977, pp. 127, 130, 132; Keith B. Leffler, "Physician Licensure: Competition and Monopoly in American Medicine" and Lawrence Shepard, "Licensing Restrictions and the Cost of Dental Care," both in *Journal of Law and Economics* (April 1978), pp. 165–201.

[9] Much of this section is based on N. W. Cornell, R. G. Noll, and B. Weingast, "Safety Regulation," in *Setting National Priorities*, edited by H. Owen and C. L. Schultze (Washington, D.C.: Brookings Institution, 1976); V. P. Goldberg, "Consumer Choice, Imperfect Information and Public Policy," (Davis, Calif.: Institute of Government Affairs, University of California, 1973); and R. R. Campbell, *Food Safety Regulation* (Washington, D.C.: American Enterprise Institute, 1974).

exactly cover the costs to consumers assuming the risks. Producers would profit by building safer products only insofar as consumers were willing to defray the producer's costs of adding safety. Consumer sovereignty would prevail, and "optimal" degrees of safety would be provided.

Unfortunately, this happy result can only be found in theory. In reality people have lessened their reliance on markets and increased their reliance on government for at least four reasons—(1) morality, (2) equity, (3) ignorance and (4) adverse third party effects.

Morality. The theory assumes that "optimal allocation of resources" and "consumer sovereignty" are society's supreme values, the ultimate and conclusive criteria by which to judge good and bad. As we have seen repeatedly however, folks often give higher rank to other considerations. This is especially true in matters of life and death, where notions of morality frequently overwhelm economic criteria. Thus, our puritanical heritage seems to be the only possible explanation for many safety regulations that do nothing but protect individuals from themselves. Motorcycle helmet laws, the compulsory wearing of life vests for sailing, and the provision of elaborate barriers to prevent people jumping off bridges are examples.[10]

Equity. The losses produced by hazards do not beset everyone equally. Although many millions of auto travelers run the risk of violent death on the highway, only about 45,000 of them die each year in this way. Similarly, all meat eaters benefit when cattlemen use diethylstilbestrol (DES) to boost the livestock industry's productivity and thereby lower beef prices by 3.5% or so. However, the use of DES also raises the risk of cancer to consumers, a risk that horribly collects its due from only a relatively few families despite the widespread benefits bestowed in the bargain. As with autos, millions gain a little benefit and run a little risk, but only a few are actually forced to pay the dreadful costs of contracting cancer. Many folks might think that these are serious mismatches of getting and deserving, that the imbalances are unfair or inequitable to the few unlucky souls who encounter the Grim Reaper.

Ignorance. The foregoing value judgments might be dismissed as maudlin or irrelevant. However, the problem of ignorance is not so easily dismissed. Even though press, TV, radio, and government agencies pour out massive amounts of information concerning some hazard, the public remains uninformed. Test yourself. As one who is above average in attentiveness and intelligence, how much do you know about diethylstilbestrol, Red Dye No. 2,

---

[10] Tibor Scitovsky, *The Joyless Economy* (New York: Oxford University Press, 1976), Chapter 10. For another angle on this issue contemplate the following: It is conceivable that, given the freedom to decide individually, no motorcyclist would wear a helmet for fear of being looked upon as being a "pansy." But since they all know they "should" be wearing one, they might vote by two thirds majority in *favor* of a compulsory helmet law because the law would relieve them of the pansy problem.

accharin, and zirconium, to name just a few substances given ample recent ress coverage. Could you compute the marginal cost of added risk from using roducts laced with these chemicals? Are you even aware of what products ormerly contained them? Probably not. Although risk poses no problem under onditions of perfect knowledge, risk can be burdensome "(a) when consumers do not know that it exists; or (b) when, though aware of it, consumers re unable to estimate its frequency and severity; or (c) when consumers do not now how to cope with it, and hence are likely to incur harm unnecessarily."[11] t seems safe to say that these areas of ignorance cannot be erased by policies f information enhancement whenever the risk is buried beneath complex echnologies (and technological complexity is growing all the time).

Going beyond risk, there is the additional problem of uncertainty. *Risk* imply refers to a situation in which sufficient statistical evidence exists to llow experts to predict the probability that a particular event will occur. Thus xperts tell us that failure to wear seat belts more than doubles frequency of leath in auto accidents. Similarly, fatal blood clots strike women who use " The Pill" at a rate of about 30/1,000,000, whereas nonusers run a considerably ower risk of 5/1,000,000. As with the flip of a coin, the outcome in any particular nstance of auto wreck or "Pill" popping is unknown, but its *probability* is nown.

In contrast, *uncertainty* is a black abyss. The statistical *probabilities are unnown* as well as the particular outcomes. Thus experts may be able to establish causal link between a hazard and bodily harm, but the linkage may elude numerical expression of risk:

> Giving mice a massive exposure to a chemical and observing that in a short period of time the mice develop cancer establishes that a substance is carcinogenic. It does not establish the extent to which the carcinogenic effect depends on dosage, the type of tissue exposed, the method of exposure, and the other features of the environment in which the dosage was administered. One may conclude that the experimental results make it more likely that the same substance in dosages comparable to human exposure levels causes human cancer, but the extent to which the likelihood has been increased is not even roughly quantifiable.[12]

Uncertainty not only baffles consumers, it also befuddles experts, as indicated by the endless string of health and safety experts who appear before Congress every year with testimony that takes the form of "Well, on the one hand . . . but then, on the other hand . . . ." Senator Muskie expressed everyone's frustration with this when, after listening to a lot of "one hand . . . other hand" testimony, he quipped, "What I need is some one-armed scientists."

N. W. Cornell, R. G. Noll, and B. Weingast argue that uncertainty engenders a political demand for public controls on product safety more stringent than would otherwise be justified. They argue in particular that we should "minimax

---

[11] *Final Report of the National Commission on Products Safety* (Washington, D.C.; U.S.G.P.O., 1970), p. 11.

[12] Cornell, Noll, and Weingast, *op. cit.*, p. 468.

regret" by adopting "strategies that avoid the worst logically possible outcomes, thereby minimizing the maximum possible loss, no matter what the likelihood that the maximum loss will actually occur."[13]

Adverse Third Party Effects. All the foregoing considerations relate to hazards to which individuals expose *themselves* in the course of consumption. Morality, equity, and ignorance may thus persuade some folks that government regulation of product safety is needed to protect people from *voluntary self-inflicted* exposure to hazard. But what if all these arguments are brushed aside in favor of some notion of absolute personal freedom. Is there any "final" flaw in the market system that could justify government regulation? The answer is "yes"—adverse third party effects. Thus, although Hot Rod Charlie may willingly buy and drive a cheap car with faulty brakes and flimsy tires (perhaps even revelling in its risky prospects), the car poses a hazard to *other* people occupying the same roads as Charlie. Stated differently and more technically, people like Charlie have a demand for risk exposure that the market mechanism could satisfy by supplying hazardous autos at reduced prices reflecting the added costs of risk borne by *the buyer.* But the market cannot, and does not supply to people like Charlie the additional items that are necessarily involved in such risky ventures—namely, the arms, legs, and lives of other folks.

Similarly, some people may willingly save a few cents by purchasing pop in bottles that are susceptible to explosion. And the market could fill their needs. However, what about those who want nothing to do with flying glass? They are exposed to risk when searching grocery shelves for safer brands. Hence, once again the market system yields less than satisfactory results.

The problems of morality, equity, ignorance, and adverse third party effects take us considerably beyond the problems concerning "quality." To summarize the differences by analogy, suppose you are sitting in the park playing chess with a formidable opponent named Product Market. You are no expert at chess. You like to win, but you devote most of your time and energy to more important things, such as romance, athletics, music, religion, career, whatever. Market, as a consequence, is giving you some trouble (especially with his rooks). Suppose now that an expert kibitzer steps up, sees your plight, and offers you a few helpful suggestions. Some suggestions you understand and some you don't; some you take and some you don't. So long as it is just a "friendly game" you may like to have the kibitzer's occasional views but no more. You certainly do not want him to play for you. So, too, might you regard government intervention concerning product quality. However, what if more was at stake in the game than a plastic king—your life, for instance, or the lives of others? Your weaknesses as a player would be greatly magnified. Your concerns for morality and equity would loom large. And you might begin to worry about some Hot Rod Charlie running over you with a brakeless auto midway through the game. For all these reasons you might call upon the kibitzer actually to make a few moves

---

[13] *Ibid.*, p. 469.

or you. So, too, might you ask the government to do more than merely disseminate information when it comes to questions of product safety.

What Is the Proper Role of Government?

Any attempt to decide the proper role of government in safety regulation is complicated by the possibility of relying entirely on insurance and rules of legal liability as protectors of consumers. We cannot discuss these complications here more extensively than to note that insurance and liability law are often poor substitutes for active government intervention. Government regulation attempts to *prevent* damages from occurring, whereas insurance and liability law address the problem of compensation *after* damages occur.

For accident prevention, the government relies upon information disclosure and direct product regulation, with a growing emphasis on the latter. Thus, autos are now designed in Washington, D.C., as well as in Detroit; the FDA constitutes an extension of drug company production lines; swimming pool slides must meet government specifications; and there are other instances. In light of the foregoing analysis, this emphasis on product regulation is certainly more appropriate for purposes of safety than of quality. Yet this conviction does not automatically eliminate the problem of governmental errors of commission and omission. Moreover, these errors may partially subvert the intent of safety regulation by yielding some unsafe results.

For example, forcing safety features upon autos may reduce auto fatalities, but they may also increase the price of autos to the point of inducing poor people to ride motorcycles, which, although cheaper, are considerably more dangerous than autos. A more controversial example is provided by saccharin, an artificial sweetener. In 1977, the FDA took steps to ban saccharin as a food additive after Canadian scientists found it caused cancer in laboratory rats. Opponents of the ban argued that without saccharin people would consume more sugar, thereby aggravating such health risks as obesity, heart disease, and arthritis. As this is written, a combination of public outcry and Congressional action has forced the FDA to retreat. For the present, warning labels will take the place of prohibition. (One sarcastic Congressman's proposed label— "Warning: The Canadians have determined saccharin is dangerous to your rat's health.") Related problems of safety regulation will be reviewed in the next chapter.

Pollution

Why Is Market Performance Often Flawed?

Pollution can be measured any number of ways—tons of carbon monoxide, sulfur oxides, and soot in the air; or millions of gallons of oil, raw sewage, and chemicals in the water; or excessive airport noise; or property damage; or human mortality. In whatever way it is measured, the problem of pollution boils down to a misallocation of resources because there is too much of one thing (dirtiness) and not enough of another (cleanliness). As we rely on markets to allocate resources, this misallocation constitutes another instance of market inadequacy.

Under ideal circumstances the market system optimally allocates resources because (1) the *price* of each product reflects *all* of society's benefits from the product at the margin, (2) the *cost* of each product reflects the value of all resources used at the margin, and (3) price equals marginal cost. If the price people are willing to pay does not accurately reflect all marginal benefits (as happens when consumers err), or if the firm's costs of labor, materials, fuel, and other resources do not accurately reflect all marginal social costs, then something has gone haywire. Resources get misallocated. In the case of pollution the problem arises because producers do not themselves pay the costs of disposing of their wastes "cleanly"; rather, they impose these costs on *others* by fouling air, water, and land with their filth. Since these costs are external to the firm, they are called *external costs*. Note that external costs may arise from consumption as well as production, as is true of automobile pollution, or pop bottle litter. Lest you doubt that pollution actually creates costs, stop and reflect. Think of crop damage, houses being painted every 5 years instead of 10, days of labor lost to bronchitis or early death, and medical expenses. Overall, it has been estimated that during the early 1970s pollution cost the American public about $30 billion a year.[14]

Figure 25-3 illustrates the problem in a simplified way. Whereas the problems of quality and safety arise primarily through consumer ignorance, which can be depicted by individual consumer demand curves, the problem of pollution may be depicted by a comparison of two *industry supply* curves. Assuming pure competition, the industry-wide supply curve is the horizontal summation of the marginal costs of firms in the industry. Accordingly, S_1 in Figure 25-3 represents industry supply based on member firms' private costs (for labor, land, and so on). Equilibrium price and quantity are P_1 and Q_1. However, what if the firms in question are beef feed lot operators, and the dung, urine, and other wastes associated with their operations are flushed into rivers and streams? Then for each head of cattle raised, downstream society has to bear added costs —namely, the costs of driving farther to fish or swim, of purifying water to make it drinkable, and so on. Once the external costs per unit of output are added to the firms' private costs of feed, fuel, labor, and such, the result is S_2.

Thus S_2 indicates the supply curve that *ought* to prevail but does not prevail so long as the costs of pollution are registered outside the market place. Optimal allocation would be achieved by a price P_2 and quantity Q_2. Since correction of the error entails a higher price and lower quantity of production, the error was one of *over*allocation of resources to this industry. At P_1 and Q_1, too much

[14] *Environmental Quality*, Sixth Report of the Council on Environmental Quality (Washington, D.C., 1975), Chapter 4.

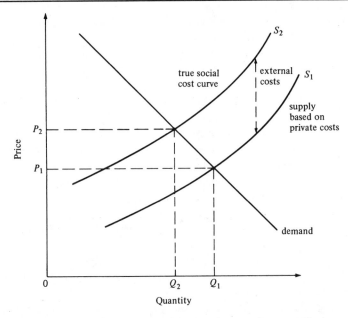

Figure 25-3. *The problem of external costs due to pollution.*

of this good and its by-product pollution are produced. Corrective adjustment implies that buyers of the product will pay higher prices, and that resources will be shifted to other employments (such as producing pollution control equipment). This will obviously hurt the industry's insiders, both buyers and producers, but in the long run it would benefit society as a whole.

To summarize, the central problem of pollution is adverse third party affects, whereas the main problem with quality and safety is one of buyer ignorance.[15]

What Is the Proper Role of Government?

Basically, pollution can be controlled in three ways: (1) regulate the activity that produces it, (2) tax the activity that produces it, or (3) subsidize the polluter to help cover the costs of preventing pollution. These are not mutually exclusive; they can be used in combination.

Regulation. Simply stated, regulation is control by decree. The government enacts laws forbidding DDT, limiting hydrocarbon emissions from autos, requiring the installation of "scrubbers" in smoke stacks, curbing the dumping

[15] For a more thorough discussion of pollution see J. J. Seneca and M. K. Taussig, *Environmental Economics* (Englewood Cliffs, N.J.: Prentice-Hall, 1974); or A. M. Freeman, R. H. Haveman, and A. V. Kneese, *The Economics of Environmental Policy* (New York: John Wiley & Sons, 1973).

of mine tailings, prohibiting the use of lead in gasoline, and so on. The government then enforces its decrees with persuasion, threats, fines, and perhaps even jailings. The main intent of these efforts is to *internalize a previous externality*. That is to say, regulation seeks to impose the costs of clean up on polluters and their patrons, while relieving others (the "pollutees") of the costs of damage and avoidance.

Although the costs of *preventing* pollution are not necessarily the same as the external costs suffered *once pollutants are emitted*, the economic impact of regulation may be depicted by Figure 25-3. If S_1 is assumed to be the industry's cost curve in the absence of regulation, then S_2 could indicate the industry's cost curve after installation of pollution control equipment, after changeover to cleaner burning fuel, and after other preventive measures. The resulting higher costs of production shift the supply curve upward, raising price and reducing output. Just how much price and output alter depend, of course, on the elasticity of demand and the expense of reaching the limits prescribed by law.

Some examples of these effects are shown in Table 25-1, which reports estimated changes due to compliance with the Federal Water Pollution Control Act Amendments of 1972. By 1983 all industries are supposed to be using the "best available technologies" for water pollution control. Column (1) gives estimated price increases and column (2) gives estimated quantity reductions, both in percentages, for compliance in selected industries. A third and corollary effect, plant closure, is estimated in column (3). With less output fewer plants are needed. In addition, some old plants may be just too costly to modernize

TABLE 25-1 Estimated Economic Impact of Meeting 1983 Water Pollution Standards

Industry	(1) Change in Prices (%)	(2) Change in Output (%)	(3) Number of Plant Closures
Iron and steel	1.1	−1.2	n.a.
Metal Finishing	60.0	−8.0	7
Chemicals	3.4	Negligible	13
Canning	0.42	−0.23	128
Beef feed lots	0.1	−0.05	8000+
Dairy products	0.29	−0.13	96
Leather tanning	2.2	−7.0	31
Fertilizer	1.3	Negligible	20

n.a. = not available
Source: *Staff Report to the National Commission on Water Quality* (Washington, D. C., 1976), pp. III–64, 65, 77, 78.

and equip for pollution abatement, in which case they are closed "prematurely." Although the price and quantity effects vary considerably across industries, the estimates for plant closures reveal still more diversity. This is largely explained by differences in underlying plant populations across industries. Whereas metal finishing and chemicals have a relatively few plants, output in the canning and beef feed lot industries (both of which have competitive structures) is scattered among a very large number of plants. Hence plant closings in the latter two industries will be more numerous than those in the former two for any given degree of output reduction.

It should be noted that the objective sought by regulation need not be one of absolute and complete eradication of *all* pollution. The social costs of total prevention undoubtedly exceed the benefits by billions of dollars per year. Nevertheless, there are instances where the pollutant in question is monstrously pernicious, as is true of plutonium and mercury. In such instances absolute prohibitions may well be justified. And one of the major advantages of the regulatory approach is that it can be applied effectively to achieve this end.[16] It is, in other words, the hammerlock of policy options. You may be pleased to learn, then, that United States policy is comprised almost entirely of regulations, the specifics of which we discuss in Chapter 26. Do not get too pleased, however. There are serious problems with the regulatory approach. It can be a weak hammerlock with loopholes, poor execution, and hesitant enforcement.

Taxation. A second way to control pollution is to tax it. Canneries could be charged 25 cents for every cubic meter of raw sewage they dump into rivers or lakes. Electric utilities could be charged a dollar for every ton of coal they burn having more than 1.5% sulfur content. And so on. The *purpose* of such taxes, or effluent charges, is again to *internalize a previous externality*. The *effects* of taxation can be quite similar to the effects of regulation. A tax induces pollution abatement because companies can avoid paying the tax by not polluting. Wherever the costs of clean-up are *less* than the costs of polluting and paying, the firm will clean up. Conversely, where the costs of clean-up *exceed* the costs of polluting and paying, the firm will pollute and pay the tax. It follows, then, that the higher the tax rate, the greater the abatement achieved (because the higher the tax rate, the greater the incentive to avoid it by abatement).

Notice that, regardless of how the firms faced with an effluent tax react, their costs of doing business will have been raised. If they pollute, they pay the tax. If they abate, they pay for new equipment, cleaner fuel, and so on. They pay either way. And the economic consequences of these higher costs are the same as those encountered with government regulation. They lift the industry supply curve, thereby raising price and curtailing quantity, as depicted in Figure 25-3.

Although tax and regulatory approaches thus share much in common, they should not be regarded as the environmental equivalent of such "me-too"

---

[16] David Pearce, "The Limits of Cost-Benefit Analysis as a Guide to Environmental Policy," *Kyklos* (Fasc. 1, 1976), pp. 97–111.

laundry products as Tide and Cheer. Indeed, most economists criticize th regulatory approach and praise the tax approach.[17] Two of the most commonl voiced advantages of the tax approach are *efficiency* and *incentives*. For any give level of pollution prevention short of complete eradication, the tax approac is more *efficient* because it costs less in resources consumed by abatemen It's like saying Tide is half the price of Cheer per unit of cleaning power. Taxe are more efficient because an efficient approach to abatement requires tha *different* firms reduce their pollution by *different* amounts depending on thei *differing* costs of abatement. Those who find abatement cheap should abat *more* than those who find it expensive, for then they can together achieve i given degree of abatement most cheaply. This distribution of abatement i achieved by a tax, because by it abatement behavior is keyed to individual firn comparisons of tax rate and abatement cost, with least-cost abaters abatin the most. This diversity is typically *not* achieved by the regulatory approac because *uniform* pollution cut-backs are usually prescribed by regulators regardless of cost. It is common to decree something like: "O.K., everybody pollute 80% less, or else."

The tax or effluent fee approach offers superior *incentives* for a slightly differ ent reason. As Allen Kneese and Charles Schultze explain:

A firm has no incentive to cut pollution further once it has achieved the effluent limitation specified by regulation. Indeed, it has a positive incentive *not* to do so, since the additional reduction is costly and lowers profits. Because effluent charges must be paid for every unit of pollution firms have not removed, they would have a continuing incentive to devote research and engineering talent to finding less costly ways of achieving still further reductions.[18]

The key words are "incentive to cut pollution further." To see the incentive effect in our laundry detergent analogy, visualize the difference between a policy taxing you 2 cents for every gram of dirt per shirt and a regulatory policy requiring no more than 5 grams of dirt per shirt. Assume also that at current detergent prices you would launder to the 5-gram limit under both policies Now, what would you do if an equally effective new brand of detergent came out costing half as much as the current brands? You would buy the new brand regardless of which policy prevailed because you are always swayed by an *incentive to cut costs*. But only with the tax policy do you have an *incentive to clean further* to reduce your tax burden. Although the tax approach has no caught on in the United States, it is widely used in Europe, especially for water pollution control.[19]

[17] See, for instance, A. V. Kneese and C. L. Schultze, *Pollution, Prices, and Public Policy* (Washington, D.C.: Brookings Institution, 1975).
[18] *Ibid.*, pp. 89–90.
[19] See Organization for Economic Co-operation and Development, *Pollution Charges: An Assessment* (Paris, 1976).

Subsidies. The third approach is to subsidize polluters to curtail polluting. Whereas taxes *goad*, subsidies *entice.* That is to say, the government pays polluters to install abatement equipment and man it, or pays the extra costs of nonpolluting fuels and materials. Because the government pays the costs, this approach does not entail an upward shift of the industry's supply curve. Product price need not rise. Quantity of output need not fall. Thus, one consequence of the subsidy approach is that the total volume of resources committed to pollution abatement might be greater with subsidy than with either tax or regulation.

Because subsidies yield abatement without price increases, the costs of abatement are disguised. Consumers do not confront the true social costs of production, including the costs of cleanliness. As a result, consumers are not encouraged to reduce their purchases of high-polluting products and increase their purchases of low-polluting products. Society's misallocation of resources may therefore persist under the subsidy approach.

A second problem of subsidies is that they may not, in effect, entice much abatement. A subsidy program may pay 75%, say, of the cost of clean-up. But since 25% of the burden still rests with polluters, it is still cheaper for them to pollute than to abate. Thus programs of *partial* subsidy may not accomplish much, unless they are accompanied by some stiff regulations.

For these two reasons sober economists generally oppose the subsidy approach. Although sober economists are often (or even usually) ignored by politicians, it so happens that subsidies have seen little service in the federal government's fight against pollution. Their use is primarily confined to financing municipal sewage treatment facilities. Given the obvious difficulties inherent to "taxing" municipal governments or to "regulating" them under threat of fines and imprisonment, subsidies may be the only real alternative to pollution when it comes to city sewage.

To summarize this discussion of pollution policy, taxes rate "good," regulations rate "fair," and subsidies appeal only if politically expedient. Given the choice between subsidies and choking to death on effluent, subsidies seem irresistible.

Summary

This chapter explores the merits of government regulation in three aspects of performance—quality, safety, and pollution. As direct regulation entails centralized command and control rather than decentralized freedom of choice, and as it is susceptible to errors, inefficiencies, and catastrophies that may exceed those perpetrated by the free-market system, regulation should not be attempted without solid justification. Indeed, a few economists stoutly oppose all regulation. Where problems can be solved by less meddlesome forms of government intervention—such as structural reorganization, information betterment, deception prevention, and curbs on collusive conduct—they are to be favored. As this chapter shows, these more pleasing policies are often insufficient. Simple modifications of market structure and conduct cannot solve problems whose origins are independent of market structure and conduct, problems whose origins derive from inherent market inadequacies.

Although most problems of product quality can be handled by policies of information improvement and deception prevention, some form of regulation is appropriate where (1) credence qualities are important, (2) technology is particularly complex, and (3) consumer preferences are reasonably obvious to outside observers. Credence qualities and complex technology render consumers particularly prone to errors. Consumer preferences that are fairly obvious to outsiders (as in the case of human or mechanical repairs) permit experts to regulate with little risk of imposing errors on consumers. Thus most folks seem to support quality regulation of doctors, dentists, veterinarians, and drugs, among other things. Unfortunately, some forms of quality regulation are themselves of very poor quality.

Four main factors make the free market system inadequate to ensuring *safety* and undermine the adequacy of information policies—namely, (1) morality, (2) equity, (3) ignorance, and (4) adverse third party effects. Perhaps the most interesting of these is ignorance. Although simple information policies can often cure this problem, they are impotent against severe technological complexities and vast uncertainties. Indeed, uncertainties even baffle experts, and, when they do, regulation becomes particularly difficult. However, regulation is still regarded as necessary by many people because lives are at stake.

The key problem of pollution is external costs. Costs are external because they are registered outside the market place. As a result, resources are overallocated to "dirty" doings and underallocated to "clean" ones. Of the three policy options available—regulation, taxation, and subsidization—regulation is the most heavily applied in the United Sates, but taxation offers the most advantages, at least in theory. Regulation is perhaps inescapable when really dangerous substances are involved, but taxation seems superior for efficiency and abatement incentive.

26

Quality, Safety, and Pollution: Product and Process Regulation

There is no shortcut from chemical laboratory to clinic, except one that passes too close to the morgue.

DR. CHAUNCEY D. LEAKE

The quip introducing this chapter is no joke. Sulfanilamide, a potent anti-infective and the first modern "wonder drug," was greeted with worldwide acclaim when introduced in 1936. Hoping to cash in on sulfanilamide's popularity, drug companies rushed to market a vast array of derivative products, one of which was a liquid called Elixir Sulfanilamide. Unfortunately, sulfanilamide does not dissolve easily in water, alcohol, or any other common biological solvent, but it does dissolve in diethylene glycol. After discovering this, the makers of Elixir Sulfanilamide used diethylene glycol as their solvent without even bothering to look up to its toxicity in chemical textbooks. The result was 108 people dead—107 consumers from poisoning and one, the drug company's remorseful chief chemist, from suicide. Another result of this tragedy was the Food, Drug, and Cosmetic Act of 1938.

The story illustrates a crucial point: Current United States policies governing quality, safety, and pollution did not develop in a vacuum. Neither did they derive from theorizing of the type you were exposed to in the preceding chapter nor from socialist dogmas. Almost without exception these policies evolved as pragmatic responses to specific tragedies or general conditions of crisis. Killer smogs, highway death tolls of epidemic proportions, blinding eyelash cosmetics, grotesquely deformed babies, and death-trap cribs propel the history of regulation in these areas. This is not to say that businessmen are evil minded;

641

they merely seek to make money. Likewise, consumers are not always blame-
lessly innocent when it comes to mayhem; they can be grossly negligent. It
merely needs to be understood that these policies have empirical, not theoretical
origins (although the previous chapter's theories help to explain how these
crises arose).

These practical origins must be recognized at the outset because later there
will be little room for horror stories. This chapter's principal purpose is to
explain some major federal regulations governing product quality, safety, and
pollution. A second purpose is to air the views of critics of such regulation. The
critics may be divided into two groups—those who want more regulation and
those who want less. Given that things do not change much in the absence of
disastrous developments, those who want less probably won't get their way
unless our current regulatory agencies make some rather big mistakes, thereby
creating a crisis rather than observing or preventing one. If, for example, a
miraculous cure for cancer was held off the market for reasons the public
thought wrong, deregulation would surely gain support.

The chapter is divided into five main sections. The first reviews the tasks or
duties required of all regulatory efforts of this type. Each of the next four
sections is devoted to a federal agency—the Food and Drug Administration
(FDA), the National Highway Traffic Safety Administration (NHTSA), the
Consumer Product Safety Commission (CPSC), and the Environmental
Protection Agency (EPA).[1] Our discussion of each agency is organized according
to the outline of activities developed in the first section.

Regulatory Activities

Imagine yourself in the shoes of a United States senator 20 years ago. You
perceive a problem of hazardous products or annoying pollution and wonder:
"What the hell can be done about it?" Creating a regulatory agency on which
to dump the problem might seem a good idea, but the key question is what duties
and powers should be invested in the agency to solve the problem? The question
is a treacherous one, because, hypothetically, the bad answers outnumber the
good. And historically we have had our share of bad answers. Weak and halting
efforts at food and drug regulation date back to 1906. Water pollution legislation
goes back to the Refuse Act of 1899, but that law was not enforced until 1970.

Only recently has a distinct pattern of fairly effective regulatory activities
emerged. These are outlined in Table 26-1 together with the purpose of each,
examples of each, and some rough indication of where each activity takes place.
At first glance this looks confusing. The table's cluttered appearance seems to
indicate only "red-tape" and "bureaucratic hassle," but there is method to

[1] For a complete discussion of all these agencies see *Federal Regulation and Regulatory Reform*,
Report by the Subcommittee on Oversight and Investigations of the Committee on Interstate and
Foreign Commerce, House, 94th Congress, Second Session (1976).

the muddiness. Notice first that virtually all major regulatory activities fall into one of three broad categories: (A) standard setting, (B) enforcement, and (C) research. Broadly speaking, **standards** are necessary so that everyone involved— both regulators and regulated—know what they are *supposed to be doing* to attain good performance. In turn, **enforcement** of these standards is necessary to assure that the regulated *actually do* what they are supposed to. Finally, **research** is necessary to *evaluate* the agency's standards and enforcement programs. This last category includes "follow through" to help assure that the regulators are doing what they ought to be doing (and not overlooking something important). Research also embraces the search for new ways of achieving old objectives. Discussion of the specific activities listed under each broad category illuminates these assertions.

Standard Setting

There are typically two types of standards—broad and narrow. **Broad standards** are vague, generalized concepts of what is desirable. Because they are typically set by Congress and because they are found in the legislation establishing regulatory agencies or amending established agency powers, broad standards may be viewed as the goals and limits governing the regulat*ors*, *not* the regulat*ed*. Thus, for example, the Consumer Product Safety Act says vaguely that one goal of the CPSC is "to protect the public against unreasonable risks of injury associated with consumer products." And the Federal Water Pollution Control Act of 1972 calls for "recreation in and on the water . . . by July 1, 1983." The purpose of broad standards is not limited to issuing mandates, it extends to giving time schedules and future goals.

Broad standards may be considered the regulators' standards for another reason. Namely, no private company or citizen can be prosecuted for violating these broad standards because they are *too* vague and *too* ill-defined to guide the actions of those who are regulated. For enforcement and prosecution **narrow standards** are necessary. These are very specific; some so much so that they fill thousands of pages in the *Code of Federal Regulations*. A simple example given in Table 26-1 is the 0.5% lead standard for paint, one purpose of which is to prevent lead poisoning in toddlers who may innocently choose to cut their teeth on the window sill. These narrow standards are usually developed by the regulatory agencies themselves, not Congress, although certain particularly earth-shaking standards may be subject to Congressional approval. Congress delegates this authority for a simple reason: specific, narrow standards tend to be highly technical and complex, involving tens of thousands of products, countless producers, hundreds of different problems, and other large dimensions of perplexity. Moreover, the *procedures* required to develop narrow standards are tangled snarls, involving notifications, hearings, conferences, and so on— in short, many things for which Congress has no capacity.

It should also be noted that narrow standards may be of two types: (1) performance standards or (2) design standards. **Performance standards** merely

TABLE 26-1   Outline of the Major Activities that Regulation Entails

Activity	Purpose	Examples	Locale of activity
Standard setting			
Broad standards	To set goals and limits for regulators	"Safe" products "swimmable" rivers	Set by Congress in legislative mandates
Narrow standards	To set goals and limits for firms and products regulated	Lead level in paint not to exceed 0.5%; dual braking systems in all autos	Usually set by agency after hearings
Enforcement for compliance			
Certification or permit	To approve of regulated firms' intentions and give guidance	Engine design "X" approved; effluent permit granted	Laboratory; agency offices
Sample testing	To monitor regulated firms' activities	Antibiotics batch tested for purity; smoke stack emissions measured	Assembly line; plant floor; sewage outfalls; stacks

Field surveillance	To double check compliance and catch "mistakes"	Annual inspection of autos; investigate consumer complaints	Highway; retail stores; repair shops; homes
Remedies	To bring violators into line	Seize contaminated canned goods; force recall of autos; fine violators	Warehouses; stores; courtrooms; agency offices
Research Technical research	To explore new possibilities	Build experimental "safety" cars; test new monitoring devices	Laboratories
General surveillance	To assess program operation and discover new problems	Collect data on accidents; measure air quality	Hospital emergency rooms; highway patrol offices, weather stations, river banks, etc.

specify some specific level of performance—for example, for auto pollutants, no more than 3.4 grams of carbon monoxide emitted per mile traveled. This approach leaves it up to the regulated firm to devise some means of meeting the performance standard, and many different engine designs or exhaust control devices meet this example of auto regulation. In contrast, a **design standard** specifies the *particular designs* that are acceptable. This alternative approach is much less flexible but equally possible and frequently used.

Enforcement of Compliance

Certification and Permits. Once narrow standards are set, the next step is to get folks to abide by them. Implementation typically requires four distinct activities. The first, as outlined in Table 26-1, is certification or the issuance of permits. The purpose of certification is to approve the regulated firms' intentions, to give guidance *before* massive investments in plant and equipment are made and *before* any harm is done. An example is the FDA's clearance of new drugs. At the time of the Elixir Sulfanilamide tragedy, safety was regulated —but only after the fact. The Elixir was not certified as being in compliance with safety standards prior to its marketing. Now all new drugs have to be certified as being in compliance with standards of safety and efficacy before they can be marketed.

Sometimes certification is undertaken not so much for the benefit of consumers as it is for the benefit of regulated firms. An example of this is EPA's certification of engine designs that meet emission performance standards *prior* to actual production of those engines. Imagine the billions of dollars an auto company could lose if it invested in production facilities for an engine that it thought would meet standards only to find out later that in the view of EPA the engine did not. Where performance standards are involved, certification is particularly important.

Sample Testing or Monitoring. The second major enforcement activity is sample testing. In a word, this is monitoring. Once standards are set and certification (if any) is completed, there remains the question of what is actually going on at the factory. Do the goods coming off the assembly line comply with standards? Is the plant's sewage pure enough to be dumped into the local river? Are gases and particulates escaping in volumes greater than those specified by permit? Are foods and drugs manufactured in surroundings that are clean? The only way these questions can be answered is by extensive on-the-spot sampling, testing, inspecting, scouting, and detecting. Of course an army of enforcement personnel is required for this task, but the army may be smaller than you might think, numbering no more than 20,000 or so snoopers for all the agencies under review here. Budgetary limits hold the number down, so great reliance is placed on "spot" checking and "small" sampling.

Field Surveillance. Field surveillance, the third step outlined in Table 26-1, may be considered a process of double checking or back-up monitoring. When consumer products are under scrutiny (instead of, or in addition to, production processes), sample testing at production sites often is not enough to assure compliance. Because only sample testing is involved, some goods that are not up to snuff will reach retail shelves and showrooms. There may also be a problem of post production tampering, wherein safety devices or pollution control devices are removed by retailers or consumers in order to gain better gas mileage, greater convenience, lower operating costs, or some other advantage. As a result, field surveillance is necessary to (1) detect substandard goods that have slipped through sample testing and (2) assure continued compliance. Field surveillance involves observation and sample purchasing at the retail level. In the case of autos it may include the annual inspection of autos in use. Finally, and perhaps even more important, field surveillance also entails (3) the receipt and investigation of consumer complaints. Swift action may be necessary even where formal standards are absent.

Remedies. Of all enforcement activities, the imposition of remedies is most readily understandable. Some remedies might be considered "light" penalties, such as seizure of the offending goods, closure of production plants, and compulsory product recalls. Yet these are not necessarily "light" at all. They can be expensively onerous in terms of lost inventories, idle plants, and replacement parts. Going one level higher in the echelon of remedies, fines and imprisonment are used under certain circumstances. The purpose served by granting regulators these various armaments should be obvious. They provide incentive. They motivate compliance.

Research

Major research activities may be divided into two groups. Those listed first in Table 26-1 are scientific or technical. Regulatory agencies conduct "in-house" research, or fund private research, to discover new and safer product designs, to devise improved testing equipment, to explore the relationship between poor air quality and human health, and so on. These activities are worthwhile for at least two reasons: (1) without official assumption or funding these areas of research are likely to be slighted, and (2) they enable regulators to keep abreast of technological developments, thereby improving the quality of regulatory effort. Indeed, this research often indicates where standards should be modified, abandoned, or imposed.

A second type of research may be called *general surveillance.* The forms of surveillance discussed earlier under compliance were "over the shoulder" types of surveillance. Their objective is to spot specific violations of specific standards. Although general surveillance may turn up specific violations, that is not the primary function. Rather, its purpose is to "keep the eyes peeled" a cliché connoting a general awareness of what is going on. Perhaps the best

TABLE 26-2 Brief Run-down of Regulatory Agencies Reviewed as of 1977

Agency	Vital Statistics	Major Function	Notes
Food and Drug Administration (FDA)	Founded in 1931, it fields a staff of 7000 with a budget of $240 million	Responsible for the safety and efficacy of drugs and medical devices and the safety and purity of food; it also regulates labeling and oversees about $200 billion worth of industrial output	An entrenched bureaucracy notorious for caution and close identification with the industries it regulates; bold actions can usually be traced to legislative mandates that give the FDA no leeway to stall
National Highway Traffic Safety Administration (NHTSA)	Created in 1966, it has 800 employees, 10 field offices, and a $100 million budget; it also administers $129 million in grants to states	Regulates manufacturers of autos, trucks, buses, motorcycles, trailers and tires in an effort to reduce the number and severity of traffic accidents	An aggressive young regulator, it has promulgated hundreds of regulations on everything from auto bumpers to mandatory seat belt installation.

Agency			
Consumer Product Safety Commission (CPSC)	Established 1972, it employs 890 on a budget of $39 million and maintains 13 field offices	Mission is to reduce product-related injuries to consumers by mandating better design, labeling, and instruction sheets.	Notorious for concentrating on trivia, it has been reorganized to stress rational priorities, but its administrators' effort to reach into too many new areas means poor follow-up
Environmental Protection Agency (EPA)	Founded in 1970, it employs 10,000, maintains 10 regional offices, and operates more than 20 laboratories spending $865 million; in addition, it administers more than $4 billion in sewage treatment construction grants	Develops and enforces standards for clean air and water, controls pollution from pesticides, toxic substances, and noise; approves state pollution abatement plans and rules on environmental impact statements	Preoccupied with developing standards and writing broad rules, it prefers negotiating compliance to twisting arms, but under an active new administrator, it is likely to be a tougher enforcer in the future

Source: *Business Week*, April 4, 1977, pp. 53, 56.

example of this is the National Electronic Injury Surveillance System maintained by the Consumer Product Safety Commission. This system connects the Commission to 119 hospital emergency rooms scattered throughout the country. The hospitals report a daily flow of information concerning product-related injuries and fatalities, thereby enabling the CPSC to maintain an up-to-the-minute vigilance over its area of concern.

Of the several regulatory activities neglected by the preceding review perhaps none is more important than consumer education. As we have seen earlier, information disclosure can often correct the market's faults, and all the agencies of interest here have education programs. We shall not discuss these programs here, however, because information policies were dealt with in Chapters 5 and 16.

Having thus developed our own "standards" and "surveillance techniques" for studying the agencies under review, we are now ready to take up each one in turn—FDA, NHTSA, CPSC, and finally EPA. Equal space cannot be given to each of the activities of Table 26-1 nor to each agency. So we will sometimes resort to sampling. In particular, space limitations compel us to ignore regulatory research altogether. A brief overview of all four agencies is provided by Table 26-2.

The Food and Drug Administration[2]

Standards: Broad and Narrow

The FDA's regulations are like a large, refurbished Victorian house—something old, something new; something lacy, something stark. Their origins date back to 1906. Major modifications occurred in 1938, 1962, and 1976. The FDA's jurisdiction includes food, drugs, cosmetics, and medical devices. Aside from responsibilities concerning information disclosure and deceptive practices, the FDA devises and enforces standards of safety, purity, efficacy, and production cleanliness. However, these broad standards do not apply equally to all products under FDA jurisdiction. The match up between products and broad standards is provided in Table 26-3, which reports the dates the FDA (or its predecessor) was legislatively directed to do its duty in these respects. A listing of more than one date indicates strengthening of the law by amendment.

Thus it may be seen that standards of "safety" and "clean production processes" now apply to all four product groups. Rigorous and complete standards of "purity" apply only to food and drugs. And standards of "efficacy" apply only to drugs and medical devices. Why the differences in standard coverage?

---

[2] This section is based largely on Milton Silverman and Philip R. Lee, *Pills, Profits, and Politics* (Berkeley, Calif.: University of California Press, 1974); *Examination of the Pharmaceutical Industry 1973–74*, Hearings, U. S. Senate Subcommittee on Health, Committee on Labor and Public Welfare, 93rd Congress, First and Second Sessions (1974), Parts 1–7; and a number of FDA publications.

TABLE 26-3   FDA's Broad Standards and Product Jurisdiction, by Date of Congressional Mandate

Broad Standard	Food	Drugs	Cosmetics	Medical Devices
Safety	1906	1906, 1938, 1966	1938	1938, 1976
Purity	1906, 1938	1906	(partially)	(partially)
Production cleanliness	1938	1938, 1966	1938	1938
Efficacy	—	1962	—	1976

A partial answer may be found in the preceding chapter. That is, the inadequacies of the free market system do not strike all products equally, and government regulation of these "qualities" is not equally appropriate to all commodities. (How, for example, could you regulate the efficacy of cosmetics?) A still more complete answer hinges on a more complete understanding of what is meant by "safety," "purity," "production cleanliness," and "efficacy," which brings us to narrow standards.

Safety. In general, the FDA's narrow standards for safety are not absolute but *relative*. A drug that is known to kill 5 out of every 100 patients who ingest it may be approved for sale. At the same time a food additive may be banned if massive doses of it appear to cause bladder cancer in 1 out of every 10,000 laboratory mice. How can these radically different standards be reconciled? They are consistent if relative safety depends upon the *use* to which the substance in question is put. Thus, a drug that is fatal to 5 out of every 100 patients may nevertheless be quite acceptable if it is fairly successful in curing inoperable malignancies for which no other therapy is known. On the other hand, the slightly suspect food additive may be banned justifiably if all it does is provide color, especially if the same color could be obtained with other, safer, and only trivially more expensive substances.

In other words, "safety" cannot be generalized except in terms of trade-off. Seriously hazardous substances are permitted if the benefits they bestow are truly great. There is a catch, however. Such substances are carefully controlled, as in the case of prescription drugs. Prescription drugs can be dispensed only by a licensed physician, dentist, veterinarian, or pharmacist. Nonprescription drugs, or "over the counter" medicines, are generally regarded as safe for the consumer to select and use when he or she follows the required directions and warnings. Indeed, appropriate warnings are required on all drugs, but those on prescription drugs are usually seen only by doctors and druggists.

Safety standards for foods and food additives are similarly strict. The Delaney amendment to the Food, Drug, and Cosmetic Act states that "no additive shall be deemed to be safe . . . if it is found, after tests which are appropriate for the evaluation of the safety of food additives, to induce cancer in man or animal." Under this standard the FDA had no choice but to initiate in 1977 a ban on the use of saccharin in food because it appeared to cause cancer in rats, even though the rats tested were fed such massive doses of the sweetener than an equivalent human intake would amount to a fantastic 140 pounds per year. Only a short time before that the FDA had banned cyclamates on similar grounds. Thus, a ban on saccharin would have left consumers with no artificial sweetener (except one attainable as a drug product). And the public (especially the plump and diabetic public) protested shrilly. Indeed, by the time you read this, the Delaney amendment may itself have been amended because of this incident. A likely substitute standard would be one such as is currently used for cosmetics. A cosmetic is considered "safe" when, *under normal use*, it is not hazardous. Even when normal use is slightly hazardous (as with hair dyes), cosmetics are permitted *if* they carry clear warning of their dangers.

Purity. Purity is not the same thing as safety, although the two often overlap. Pure strychnine is anything but safe. Conversely, watered down milk may be perfectly safe but it is hardly pure. Given the basic difference between purity and safety, it is possible to have *relative* standards of safety while imposing *absolute* standards of purity. And the FDA does have fairly absolute standards of purity for foods and drugs.

The standards concern two main types of purity—composition (or "strength") and contamination. Thus for drug **composition** and **potency** the major official compendia of specific standards are the *United States Pharmacopeia* and the *National Formulary*, which together cover some 2000 drug forms. By these standards, for example, a 5-grain aspirin tablet must contain 5 grains of "aspirin" (and all other drugs so regulated must meet their standards) within a tolerance of plus-or-minus 5%. Similarly, many foods are "identified" as to quality of contents to prevent "watering down." Tomato "paste," for instance, must contain not less than 25% salt-free "tomato solids." Such standards of composition apply only to foods and drugs.

Contamination standards prohibit filthy, putrid, or decomposed products, be they foods, drugs, cosmetics, or medical devices. Thus, for example, the FDA claims that it does not permit any variations from "absolute cleanliness or soundness in foods."

> The Act does not authorize "tolerances" for filth or decomposition in foods. It states that a food is adulterated if it consists *in whole or in part* of a filthy, putrid, or decomposed substrate.[3]

---

[3] Food and Drug Administration, *Requirements of the United States Food, Drug, and Cosmetic Act* (1972), p. 6.

In practice, however, the standards are only "reasonably" absolute, since foreign matter is permitted "below the irreducible minimum after all precautions humanly possible have been taken to prevent contamination." This leniency is illustrated by standards governing tomato canning:

> In judging whether tomato products have been properly prepared to eliminate rot and decay, the Food and Drug Administration uses the Howard mold-count test, and refuses admission to import shipments and takes action against domestic shipments if mold filaments are present in more than 40% of the microscopic fields in the case of puree, paste, more than 30% in the case of catsup, or sauce, or more than 20% in the case of tomato juice.[4]

Lest the percentages that escape bother you, it should be noted that FDA standards for food purity usually go well beyond the point of assured safety.

Production Cleanliness. Standards governing production cleanliness underscore this last statement. In fact, the mere processing of a food under insanitary conditions that may contaminate the food renders such food adulterated under the law:

> The maintenance of sanitary conditions requires extermination and exclusion of rodents, inspection and sorting of raw materials to eliminate the insect-infested and decomposed portions, fumigation, quick handling and proper storage to prevent insect development or contamination, the use of clean equipment, control of possible sources of sewage pollution, and supervision of personnel who prepare foods so that acts of misconduct may not defile the products they handle.[5]

The FDA provides details in *Current Good Manufacturing Practice Regulations*. These cover even such matters as building design, lighting, and ventilation. Similar standards apply to drugs, cosmetics, and medical devices.

(All this may sound comforting. But keep in mind that standards and enforcement are quite different. As with a 55 miles per hour speed limit, compliance is sometimes short of the statute.)

Efficacy. The issue of efficacy is in many ways similar to the issue of deceptive advertising. In both cases the key question is whether the product performs as claimed. However, the FDA's regulation of efficacy differs markedly from ordinary curbs against deception. As we saw in Chapter 16, the FTC's fight against deception sweeps the mass media clean of most false and misleading *claims*, but it leaves even the most worthless *products* so promoted on store shelves. No attempt is made by the FTC to sweep shelves clear of worthless junk. No attempt is made to restrict the use of deceptively promoted products to applications for which they are effective. No attempt is made to stifle misleading "word of mouth" promotion of these products. Whereas regulation

---

[4] *Ibid.*, p. 12.
[5] *Ibid.*, p. 5.

of sheer "deception" entails none of these measures, regulation of "efficacy" entails them all. Drugs are *banned* if "there is a lack of substantial evidence that the drug will have the effect it purports or is represented to have under the conditions of use prescribed, recommended, or suggested . . . . "[6]

The stringency of current regulation is underscored by the fact that before 1962 deceptive advertising of prescription drugs was controlled by the FDA, and by the fact that physicians, who prescribe drugs, are supposed to be knowledgeably immune to hoodwinking. Nevertheless, as of January 1, 1976, with the help of over 200 outside experts, the FDA had found a lack of substantial evidence of effectiveness in 33% of all pre-1962 drugs studied to that point, and 6673 drug products (or brands) had been removed from the market.[7] Shocking? Indeed. Efficacy regulation has been a god-awful blow to the reputation of the entire medical industry:

> Perhaps most disconcerting were the disclosures that much of the drug industry's vaunted research had been shoddy; that much of its publicized scientific evidence consisted only of testimonials; that well over half of its therapeutic claims were unsupportable; that many industry spokesmen and physicians were content to determine drug efficacy by popularity vote; that many medical journals seemed less anxious to inform physicians than to protect advertisers and had been publishing supposedly scientific reports that could not withstand the scrutiny of experts; and that thousands of physicians had often been prescribing drugs without adequate proof of their value.[8]

How had this remarkable situation developed? There are many theories, but two seem to stand out—bandwagon psychology and effective advertising. As one drug promoter explained, "Doctor A used it because we told him Doctor B used it. Doctor B used it because Doctor C used it. And Doctor C used it because Doctor A used it. For further evidence, we could mention that the product was advertised in all the best medical journals. And we could emphasize that it was selling like hotcakes. What doctor is going to question a success record like that?"[9] Or, as two doctors comment, "the whole affair brings to mind Hans Christian Anderson's *The Emperor's New Clothes*. If everyone else seems convinced that the Emperor's new garb is present and beautiful—or that the efficacy of a drug has been scientifically established— it is sometimes difficult to object."[10]

(By the way, drug makers did not hesitate to object strenuously to being called naked. Their objections however, were less than fully efficacious—unlike the advertising. They were contrived, ill-conceived, and, in their ultimate test before the Supreme Court, rejected by a vote of 7 to 0.)

---

[6] Federal Food, Drug, and Cosmetic Act, Section 505 (d).
[7] *FDA Annual Report 1975*, p. 36.
[8] Silverman and Lee, *op. cit.*, p. 132.
[9] *Ibid.*, p. 110.
[10] *Ibid.*, p. 132–33.

654

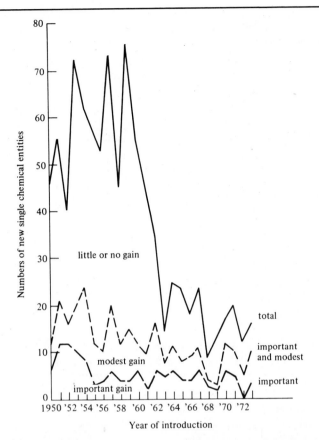

Figure 26-1. FDA classification of annual new drug approvals by degree of therapeutic importance, 1950–1973. *Source:* Examination of the Pharmaceutical Industry 1973–1974, *Part 7, Hearings before the Subcommittee on Health of the Committee on Labor and Public Welfare, U. S. Senate, 93rd Congress, 2nd session (1974), p. 3050.*

FDA Enforcement

Certification. The 1962 Drug Amendments imposed standards of efficacy on new, post-1962 drugs as well as on old, pre-1962 drugs.[11] Enforcement of the standard for new drugs involves FDA premarket clearance or certification based on research materials supplied by the drug companies to FDA. Safety, too, must be demonstrated, but of all aspects of premarket clearance, efficacy has stirred the greatest controversy.

[11] Pre-1938 drugs are exempted from efficacy requirements, but this is an inconsequential exemption because very few drugs currently in use predate 1938.

Since efficacy regulation of "old" drugs led to such a deep drop in "old" market offerings, it will not surprise you to learn that new drug introductions have fallen off substantially since 1962, as shown in Figure 26-1. Between 1950 and 1962 an average of 54 new chemical entities were approved by the FDA each year. Thereafter, from 1963 to 1975 an average of just 16 new chemical entities were cleared each year, a tremendous decline of 70%. This trend incited critics to compile a long list of complaints:[12]

- Drug development costs have soared to more than $10 million per drug.
- The time it takes for research plus FDA approval has more than doubled, averaging 6.6 years in 1973.
- The higher costs of drug R & D have hurt small firms severely and have boosted the four largest firms' share of innovational output from 24% in the late 1950s to 48.7% during the years 1967–1971.
- American drug companies are allegedly being forced to move their operations abroad, costing Americans their jobs.
- Most important, critics claim that American medical care has deteriorated, that the array of new drugs available to American patients has been needlessly and injuriously restricted as compared to new drugs available in foreign countries.

Defenders of FDA regulations concede that the number of new drug introductions has taken a nose dive, but they argue that the post-1962 regulations cannot be blamed for all of the decline. They claim that research *opportunities* have withered as the new mines opened by break-through discoveries during the 1940s and 1950s have petered out. In support of this claim defenders point out that new drug introductions began to decline *before* the 1962 Amendments took hold, and that new drug introductions have declined in Germany, France, England, and other advanced countries as well as in the United States despite no comparable changes in their laws. Moreover, the FDA's defenders deny that United States medical care has suffered under efficacy regulation. They contend that the decline in introductions is mainly accounted for by elimination of drugs representing little or no important therapeutic gain (see Figure 26-1 again). The disproportionately greater loss of trivial drugs is understandable, they say, because rising costs of new drug development would tend to cripple the profit prospects of trivial drugs before crippling the profit prospects of important drugs, given that trivial drugs ordinarily have weaker profit potential to begin with.

As for the problem of extended time lags, there are two issues—(1) prolonged research and (2) bureaucratic delay once research is completed. It can

[12] See, e.g., Sam Peltzman, "An Evaluation of Consumer Protection Legislation: The 1962 Drug Amendments," *Journal of Political Economy* (September 1973), pp. 1049–91; H. G. Grabowski and J. M. Vernon, "Consumer Protection Regulation in Ethical Drugs," *American Economic Review* (February 1977), pp. 359–64; H. G. Grabowsky, *Drug Regulation and Innovation* (Washington, D.C.: American Enterprise Institute, 1976).

be argued that new 1962 regulations concerning *safety in research*, not efficacy, have contributed most to the research slow-down. A weak but ready response is available for the second objection, too:

> There is ample proof to show that FDA can move quickly when necessary. For example, although a new drug application usually requires many months or years for processing, the application for an urgently needed new oral contraceptive product— Searle's Demulen—was cleared in about ten days. The application for *l*-Dopa, urgently needed for the treatment of parkinsonism, went through in a few weeks.[13]

Exactly where the truth lies between the objections and rebuttals is uncertain. In any event, Congress seems to have sided more with the FDA's defenders than its critics. In 1976 Congress gave the FDA power to regulate the efficacy of new and old medical devices as well as drugs. This constitutes a massive extension of FDA authority. There are over 8500 different medical devices, ranging from tongue depressors to heart pacemakers, with annual sales exceeding $4 billion. Once again a sad situation motivated the regulation. Shortly before passage, some 10,000 injuries, of which 731 resulted in death, were attributed to apparently needlessly faulty devises.[14]

Sample Testing and Field Surveillance. During 1975 FDA agents inspected 32,533 establishments, ranging from food warehouses to cosmetic production plants. During the same year FDA technicians analyzed 24,613 samples of food, 8182 samples of human drugs, 2792 samples of animal drugs and feeds, 688 samples of medical devices, and 541 samples of cosmetics. But these are only *domestic* numbers. In addition, the FDA made 78,666 wharf inspections and analyzed 21,769 samples of imported products.[15]

Hidden beneath these numbers are some truly heroic efforts. Consider, for example, the case of Mr. Albert Weber, an FDA chemist with rare talents who was honored with a front-page *Wall Street Journal* article, cleverly written by Jonathan Kwitny. Some excerpts follow:

> Who knows what evil lurks in the hearts of mackerel? Albert Weber's nose knows.
> For, while a nose is a nose is a nose in most cases, Mr. Weber's proboscis stands between this country and one heck of a stomachache. Mr. Weber is the recognized dean of organoleptic analysts—food sniffers. He is one of some two dozen Food and Drug Administration chemists around the country who use their beaks instead of their beakers to check the healthfulness of suspect foods for which there aren't any convenient chemical tests. Mostly, that's rotten fish. Mr. Weber is the only one who does this work full time.
> His sizable snout has been compared to Namath's arm, Heifetz's hands and Einstein's brain. His judgments are accepted almost as law in court cases involving hundreds of thousands of dollars in rejected foodstuffs . . . .

[13] Silverman and Lee, *op. cit.*, p. 251.
[14] *Medical Device Amendments of 1975*, Senate Report No. 94–33 of the Committee on Labor and Public Welfare, 94th Congress, First Session (1975).
[15] *FDA Annual Report 1975*, pp. 144–45.

In the 32 years since [he stared smelling fish], Mr. Weber hasn't grown to like his work any better. "How can you when you have to smell that stink all day?" he asks. But he has made adjustments. He will not allow friends to see him at work. He drives home alone. His wife stays out until after he has had a chance to shower and change. But the FDA needs him, and he says loyalty keeps him on the job . . . .

He smells about 4,000 fish or shrimp in a day and rates them Class I (good commercial), Class II (slightly decomposed) or Class III (advanced decomposed— or, as popularly known, "Phee-Yew!"). Some samples, he says, are "beyond Class III—you have to smell those at arm's length." Often in such cases he says he can tell by looking from across the room that a sample is bad. But visual opinions won't stand up in court if a food dealer challenges the FDA's rejection. Mr. Weber has to smell everything that comes his way.

Usually he breaks the skin of the fish or shrimp with his thumbnails and quickly sticks his nose into the crevice for a sniff. "As a rule, one sniff will do, but on the border line, maybe four. If you can't make up your mind by four sniffs, you shouldn't be doing this work," he says.[16]

By the way, Mr. Weber must rule a shipment acceptable if the portion he samples contains no more than 20% Class II or 5% Class III. Thus, some fish and shrimp of the "Phee-Yew" variety get through. This, and similar standards, some critics claim, is too lenient. Likewise, some critics of the FDA contend that its inspectors do not canvas plants often enough or thoroughly enough. Accordingly, they would like to see *more* FDA regulation, not less. For example, in 1971 the General Accounting Office, a watch-dog agency of Congress, checked up on FDA surveillance by inspecting a representative sample of 97 food plants. The General Accounting Office found that "39, or about 40 percent, were operating under insanitary conditions. Of these, 23, or about 24 percent, were operating under serious insanitary conditions having potential for causing of having already caused, product contamination."[17] The FDA could apparently use more people of Mr. Weber's caliber. With about 90,000 plants, mills, and other establishments needing surveillance, the FDA has enormous enforcement responsibilities.

Remedies. Table 26-4 reveals that constant vigilance is indeed necessary. Serious offenses occur more often than most of us would like to think. The year reported there, 1975, was not unusual. To overcome the drabness of these statistics, one contributory case can be cited:

A Seattle District inspection of a Tacoma, Washington, candy manufacturer revealed evidence of heavy rodent infestation in a raw material storage area. As a result of the inspection, the firm voluntarily destroyed over 37,000 pounds of raw peanuts and almonds, and over 40,000 pounds of finished candy, valued at more than $95,000, made from the rodent-defiled nuts. In addition, the firm recalled from the market a variety of candy produced from the rodent-contaminated nuts.[18]

[16] *Wall Street Journal*, October 7, 1975, p. 1.
[17] *Dimensions of Insanitary Conditions in the Food Manufacturing Industry*, Report of the Comptroller General of the United States, B-164031 (2), April 18, 1972, p. 2.
[18] *FDA Annual Report 1975*, p. 10. Strictly speaking the FDA has no formal authority to force a recall, but it can encourage voluntary recalls under threat of prosecution.

TABLE 26-4   Summary of FDA Remedial Actions During 1975

Program	Recalls	Seizures	Prosecutions	Injunctions
Foods	129	348	43	15
Human drugs	432	46	1	4
Animal drugs				
and feeds	36	26	0	8
Medical devices	266	36	1	3
Cosmetics	26	60	0	1
Totals	889	516	45	31

Source: *FDA Annual Report 1975*, p. 146.

To summarize, the FDA does a great deal. What it does could probably be done better. On that, just about all observers and eaters seem to agree. Whether the FDA should be given greater or lesser jurisdiction is, however, another kettle of fish.

National Highway Traffic Safety Administration

The compelling need for the strong automobile safety legislation . . . lies embodied in these statistics: 1.6 million dead since the coming of the automobile; over 50,000 to die this year. And, unless the accelerating spiral of death is arrested, 100,000 Americans will die as a result of their cars in 1975.[19]

With these words Congress justified its establishment of NHTSA in 1966. Congress could have abolished automobiles or (as in the early days in England) required each moving auto to be preceded by a pedestrian carrying a red flag. But these policies defy practical consideration. So, instead, Congress ordered NHTSA to devise and enforce specific standards in furtherance of "motor vehicle safety." More recently, in 1975, NHTSA was directed to implement a program to improve fuel economy in new automobiles, the ultimate objective being 27.5 miles per gallon, on average, by 1985. Such are the broad standards guiding NHTSA policy.

[19] Senate Report No. 1301, 89th Congress, Second Session (1966), pp. 1–2.

659

Narrow Standards

Upon getting the green light in 1966, NHTSA got quickly into high gear. The agency, which is housed in the Department of Transportation, issued 29 specific equipment standards in its first 4 years. Since that time NHTSA has more or less coasted, issuing fewer and fewer new standards each year while concentrating on enforcing and modifying its old standards. As of 1976, a total of 50 specific standards had been issued.

A simple list of the equipment covered—such as tires, windshields, child restraints, steering columns, brakes, and motorcycle helmets—reveals nothing more systematic than the jumbled contents of an average private garage. Nevertheless, all standards have one prime criterion: they must meet "the need for motor vehicle safety." Moreover, all standards may be classified, analyzed, and organized in three groups.[20]

100 Series, Precrash Standards. These standards improve the capacity of drivers to *avoid* crashes and reduce the capacity of cars to *cause* crashes. Examples include No. 101, which requires that clearly identified, well illuminated essential controls be within easy reach of a driver restrained by safety belts; No. 105, which requires split braking systems, incorporating emergency features capable of stopping the car under certain specified conditions; and No. 109, which requires that tires meet minimum standards of quality, endurance, and high-speed performance.

200 Series, Crash Standards. These are aimed at protecting auto occupants and highway pedestrians *during* a crash. Their implementation softens blows, holds riders snug, and cuts down on flying debris. Examples include No. 202, which requires head restraints hindering "whiplash"; No. 203, which requires padded, collapsible steering systems; No. 205, which requires shatter-proof glass; and No. 206, which requires especially strong and reliable door latches.

300 Series, Postcrash Standards. The purpose of these standards is to keep injuries and losses to a minimum in the period *after* the crash has occurred. As of 1976 only two such standards had been issued—No. 301, which tries to minimize fire hazards by specifying certain features of fuel tanks, fuel tank filler pipes, and fuel tank connections; and No. 302, which requires that flame resistant materials be used in auto interiors.

Intuitively, the equipment costs of complying with all these standards might seem horrendous. But as of 1976 they were only about $250 per car.[21] Given these costs, and given the fact that our own necks are at stake, more than idle curiosity compels us to ask about the benefits these standards bestow. Have they made any difference? Have they saved any lives? a number of studies

---

[20] For a more detailed and more interesting excursion through these standards the reader should look into the *Code of Federal Regulations* Title 49.

[21] *Federal Regulation and Regulatory Reform, op. cit.*, p. 172.

indicate that they have—and significantly. One of the most thorough was undertaken by the General Accounting Office in 1976:

> The GAO analyzed information on more than 2,000,000 cars in crashes in North Carolina and New York, comparing driver death and injury rates and model cars. The GAO found that the 1966–70 standards may have saved 28,230 lives between 1966 and 1974 nationwide. Compared to pre-1966 models, it found from 15% to 25% fewer deaths and serious injuries occurring in 1966 to 1968 model cars and 25% to 30% fewer in 1969 and 1970 models. GAO found little further improvement, however, from standards introduced in 1971–1973 model cars.[22]

The results of a second study are shown in Figure 26-2.[23] It compares occupant fatalities per 100,000 cars in Maryland during 1972–1975 across three classes of cars: (1) unregulated models, (2) belt equipped 1964–1967 models, and (3) post-NHTSA era models from 1968–1975. Comparing the last category with the first reveals an overall 39% reduction in fatality rates. Figure 26-2 also shows the impact of the 55 miles per hour speed limit beginning in 1974. It is estimated that this speed limit saves about 4500 lives per year nationwide.

Although pre-1977 standards invited little opposition, a spectacular clash of opinions occurred during 1977. In that year the so-called "passive restraint" standard was promulgated, requiring very costly "air bags" or comparable restraint systems to be phased in during the 1982–1984 model years. Opponents of this standard have been neither passive nor restrained, and in many respects their arguments are persuasive. Why, for example, should the few who *do* wear their seat belts ("few" meaning 20% of all auto travelers) be forced to pay the heavy costs ($200–$300 for equipment plus $600 in the event of inadvertent set-off) of protecting those who stupidly choose *not* to wear seat belts? The "good guys" would be subsidizing the "bad guys." Indeed, those who do not like to wear seat belts could buy air bags as optional equipment if they so desired. This last observation leads to a second query: Why even force air bags on the "bad guys"? No adverse third party effects are present so long as seat belts are available to all passengers who want to wear them.[24] (The author is, by the way, a regular wearer of seat belts.) Congress could overturn this standard if it wished, but as of this writing it has shown passive restraint. The standard therefore stands.

It should be noted that in addition to the preceding equipment standards, a number of nonequipment standards govern manufacturing and distributing practices. The most important of these concern product identification and record keeping. They enable manufacturers and retailers to track down purchasers of autos, tires, motorcycles, and other equipment long after purchase in the event a recall is necessary.

---

[22] *Ibid.*, p. 169.

[23] *Ibid.*, p. 170. For still further evidence see Leon S. Robertson, "A Critical Analysis of Peltzman's 'The Effects of Automobile Safety Regulation'," *Journal of Economic Issues* (September 1977), pp. 587–600.

[24] See "Public Notice Concerning Motor Vehicle Occupant Crash Protection," Secretary of Transportation (June 9, 1976), for pros, cons, and a brief review of other options.

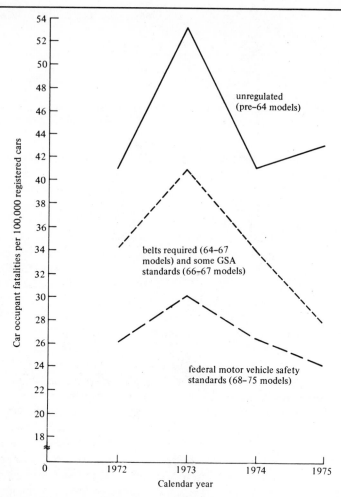

Figure 26-2. Car occupant fatalities per 100,000 registered cars, by type of new-car safety regulations, Maryland, 1972–1975. *Source:* Federal Regulation and Regulatory Reform, *Subcommittee on Oversight and Investigations of the Committee on Interstate and Foreign Commerce, U. S. House of Representatives, 94th Congress, 2nd session (1976), p. 170.*

Enforcement

Certification. To illustrate certification, the air bag system certified as meeting modified Standard No. 208 may be described briefly:

The air cushion restraint system consists of an air cushion and a sensor system which activates it. The sensor detects the impact of a crash by measuring the vehicle's deceleration. Provided the deceleration is sufficiently intense—typically corresponding to an impact into a fixed barrier at 12 mph—the sensor sends a signal to a device which deploys the air cushion by rapidly inflating it. Typical times for deployment and inflation range from 35 to 70 milliseconds.[25]

Pre-market clearance in this case is obviously imperative if multimillion dollar postmarketing errors are to be avoided.

Testing and Surveillance. From January 1968 through September 1976, NHTSA's activities in these spheres can be summarized by the following statistics:[26]

1. 59,000 pieces of equipment or components of equipment were tested for compliance with 13 different standards.
2. 832 vehicles were tested for compliance with 20 different standards, a total of 1574 tests.
3. Tests have averaged a failure rate of 6.0% for all vehicles and equipment.
4. There were 2208 investigations as a result of failures and suspected noncompliance on the part of industry; 85% of these investigations ended without a finding of violation. This includes investigations of safety-related defects not covered by specific standards, as when, for example, Chevy engine mounts began to fail.

Remedies. The NHTSA has a number of remedies at its disposal, including fines (which totalled more than $1.5 million as of 1976). However, recalls are by far the most familiar and most commonly used remedy. The majority of recall campaigns are initiated "voluntarily" by manufacturers (under threat of compulsory recall). Moreover, recalls have resulted in some of the most astounding statistics passing through these pages. Between NHTSA's founding in 1966 and 1976, 122.8 million cars were produced in, or imported into, the United States. Of these, 52.4 million have been recalled—a discomforting 42.7%![27] Moreover, some cars have been recalled more than once. Within 18 months of its first offering, the Vega suffered three recall campaigns. The last of these, involving 95% of the Vegas produced to that point, was to remedy a rear axle that was "a fraction of an inch" too short, so that a wheel might fall off.

The recall record for tires has been cheerier. Substantially less than 1% of all tires produced are ever recalled.

To sum up, we may call upon Chrysler's President, E. A. Cafiero, who in 1977 observed that the auto industry "had very few government restrictions a dozen years ago," but now it "finds almost every action and decision subject to

---

[25] *Ibid.*, pp. 8–9.
[26] *Traffic Safety '76*, Annual Report of NHTSA, p. 27.
[27] *Ibid.*, p. 28.

the control of some government agency."[28] Of these agencies, NHTSA is perhaps the most important.

Consumer Product Safety Commission

Broad Standards

Created on October 27, 1972, the CPSC is the youngest of the four agencies reviewed here. The legislation establishing CPSC states that its primary purpose is "to protect the public against unreasonable risks of injury associated with consumer products." To this end, CPSC administers five laws:

1. The Consumer Product Safety Act
2. The Federal Hazardous Substances Act
3. The Flammable Fabrics Act
4. The Poison Prevention Packaging Act
5. The Refrigerator Safety Act

The last four of these preceded CPSC's creation, and were therefore formerly administered by other agencies, such as FDA and FTC. The overall significance of these regulations may be measured in round numbers thus:

An estimated 20 million consumers are injured each year through the use of consumer products, of which 110,000 are permanently disabled and 30,000 are killed. The Commission also estimates that there are more than 10,000 different consumer products and more than 2.5 million manufacturers, importers, packagers, distributors, and retailers who are subject to Commission regulations.[29]

The only consumer products not included under CPSC's umbrella are those covered by other agencies: foods, drugs, cosmetics, medical devices, firearms, pesticides, motor vehicles, aircraft, and boats.

Given its youth, the CPSC has not yet developed its powers to the full. A sampling of its narrow standards and enforcement activities is nevertheless enlightening.

Narrow Standards

Most mothers do not know it, but 2.375 inches is a very important measure to them. Before 1973 about 150 babies died annually in a rather bizarre fashion.

---

[28] *Business Week*, October 24, 1977, p. 73.

[29] *Better Enforcement of Safety Requirements Needed By the Consumer Product Safety Commission*, Report by the Comptroller General of the United States (GAO), HRD-76-148 (July 26, 1976), p. 1.

When playfully dangling their feet between two slats of their cribs, these babies slipped out—their hips, torso, and other upper body parts following their feet toward the floor. However, their naturally large heads would not clear the slats, causing the babies to strangle or hang to death. The industry's crib slat spacing of 3.5 inches was clearly too great. But what spacing was proper? Formal research into the question led to studies of babies' buttocks, because buttock bulk could protect babies from passing beyond the threshold of danger. Of particular interest was the anterior-posterior measurement of baby buttocks when compressed between two slats by the downward force of a baby's weight. It was concluded that slat spacing of 2.375 inches would protect 95% of all infants from self strangulation. Hence, the Commission's standard for baby cribs reads in part: "the distance between components (such as slats, spindles, crib rods and corner posts) shall not be greater than 6 centimeters ($2\frac{3}{8}$ inches) at any point."[30]

This was one of the first and easiest to formulate of all the Commission's narrow standards. As Steven Kelman comments:

> The CPSC's crib safety standard represents something like an ideal case of product safety regulation, displaying all the potential advantages of such regulation and none of the pitfalls. The decision to intervene in the marketplace with mandatory rules involved a hazard of which most consumers are totally ignorant, and the risks of which are assumed involuntarily by an infant unable to protect itself. The cost of making the product safe was minimal. The safety change did not reduce the utility or attractiveness of the product, and the likelihood that the standard would indeed reduce injury and death was extremely high.[31]

Were all CPSC standards as ideal as this, the Commission would be one big continuous picnic. Unfortunately, that is not the case. Most standards relate to complex problems and may take years to formulate. For this reason CPSC relies mainly upon "voluntary standards" as opposed to "mandatory standards." Whereas mandatory standards are developed by CPSC itself, voluntary standards are developed by industry groups acting under the guidance and prodding of CPSC, which retains rights of final approval. Use of voluntary procedures saves CPSC's resources, broadens CPSC's scope, and improves the chances of self-enforced industry compliance. Still, the voluntary procedure offers no panacea. Proposed ladder standards consumed tens of thousands

---

[30] *Federal Code of Regulations*, Title 16, Chapter II, Section 1508.4, p. 174.

[31] Steven Kelman, "Regulation by the Numbers—A Report on the Consumer Product Safety Commission," *Public Interest* (Summer 1974), p. 86. Kudos may also go to CPSC's poison prevention packaging standards, which are *performance* rather than design standards. They are phrased in terms of how *difficult* it is for a large sample of children between the ages of 12 and 51 months to open containers and how *easy* it is for adults to open these same containers. They require: "(1) Child-resistant effectiveness of not less than 85 percent without demonstration and not less than 80 percent after a demonstration of the proper means of opening . . . (2) Adult-use effectiveness of not less than 90 percent . . . " where the adults are "age 18 to 45 years inclusive, with no overt physical or mental handicaps . . . " *CFR* Title 16, Chapter II, p. 330–31.

of man-hours, reams of paper, and hundreds of thousands of dollars belonging to both industry and government.

Given the difficulties of standard formulation and given the thousands of products subject to CPSC jurisdiction, the Commission has set some vague priorities to guide its endeavors. As of 1977 the three priority criteria were (1) frequency and severity of injuries, (2) causality of injuries, and (3) chronic illness and future injuries. Product data concerning these criteria are obtained through an information gathering network that connects CPSC to 119 hospital emergency rooms. Despite the Commission's earnest effort to be rational and systematic in standards development, it has provoked intense criticism from various quarters. For one thing, its approach has led to charges that CPSC concentrates on trivia and tackles problems over which it is likely to have little or no control. For example, according to some critics,

> the CPSC is hard at work investigating the possibility of safety standards for matches, kitchen knives, and staircases. While many people suffer burns, cut themselves, and fall down stairs, one wonders exactly how effective the Commission can be in significantly reducing the incidence of any of these accidents short of specifying that match flames be cold, knives blunt, and stairways be horizontal.[32]

A second common criticism is that the Commission rejects the use of economic analysis in setting its priorities and standards. At the behest of Congress the agency often shuns benefit-cost analysis as being irrelevant, inappropriate, and inaccurate when applied to product safety. Although there is merit to these CPSC decisions,[33] people who have faith in benefit-cost analysis howl.

In 1977, for instance, the Council on Wage and Price Stability railed against the CPSC's proposed standards for power lawnmowers on grounds that they would cost consumers $240 million to $330 million or more a year and return benefits of only $163 million in accident-cost reduction. Admittedly, the standards would reduce mower-related injuries an estimated 63%. And in 1976 lawn-mower injuries numbered 147,000 and deaths 25. But the monetary value assigned to the reduced bloodshed could not match the monetary costs of required safety equipment, not according to Council economists anyway. Thus the Council contended that "adoption of the standard would make consumers worse off because they would be forced to pay more for a given increase in safety that it is worth to them."[34]

Despite these and other criticisms it appears that CPSC has thus far won more supporters than enemies. Then, too, some folks feel that CPSC has not gone far enough or fast enough, especially in the area of enforcement.

---

[32] N. W. Cornell, R. G. Noll, and B. Weingast, "Safety Regulation," in *Setting National Priorities*, edited by H. Owen and C. L. Schultze (Washington, D.C.: Brookings Institution, 1976), p. 484.

[33] *Federal Regulation and Regulatory Reform, op. cit.*, pp. 173–82, 505–15.

[34] *Wall Street Journal*, August 16, 1977. Of course many CPSC standards would pass tests of benefit-cost. See, e.g., Betty F. Smith and Rachel Dardis, "Cost Benefit Analysis of Consumer Product Safety Standards," *Journal of Consumer Affairs* (Summer 1977), pp. 34–46.

TABLE 26-5 CPSC Testing and Surveillance Activities: Fiscal Year 1975

Activity	Number
Inspections[a]	6372
Investigations[b]	6782
Sample collections	3783
Sample analyses	1211
Import examinations	3941
Monitoring product corrections	1383

[a] "Inspections" are normal visits to manufacturers, distributors, etc., to determine their compliance status.

[b] "Investigations" refer to in-depth injury investigations and the gathering of compliance data at the consumer level.

Source: Consumer Product Safety Commission, *Annual Report* (1975), p. 33.

Enforcement

Testing and Surveillance. Skipping over CPSC's certification activities, we see in Table 26-5 some data concerning testing and surveillance. Although CPSC had written very few standards by the year of reference, 1975, the Commission was charged with enforcing four safety acts that predated its creation. Thus the vast bulk of CPSC enforcement effort measured here relates to those older regulations. Over 40% of all inspection man-hours, for instance, were devoted to the Federal Hazardous Substances Act, and approximately 25% concerned the Flammable Fabrics Act.

These data do not take into account inspections and sample collections funded by CPSC and conducted by state governments. They also ignore the "Volunteer Consumer Deputy Program," which is perhaps the most intriguing of all surveillance programs mentioned in these pages. CPSC deputizes hundreds of plain, ordinary, everyday consumers like you and me, and, after training them briefly, sends them forth to visit retail stores and private homes in search of breaches in CPSC's umbrella of protection. Consumer deputies have engaged in campaigns concerning Christmas tree lights, drug bottles, bicycles, toys, and sleepwear, among other things. Consumers participate in many other CPSC programs as well, to an extent unrivalled in the annals of Washington, D.C., regulatory agencies.

This delegation is probably all to the good. According to critics who would like to see more regulation, or at least more effective regulation, the Commission needs all the help it can get. To take but one example, the General Accounting

667

Office undertook an extensive review of CPSC's operations and concluded that the Commission had failed to[35]

1. Ensure that all manufacturers, packagers and importers of products under CPSC jurisdiction were identified and notified of safety requirements.
2. Verify that companies were complying with Commission safety requirements once hazardous products were found.
3. Evaluate adequately the agency's own compliance actions to determine their effectiveness.

Remedies

According to the same class of critics the Commission has been shy, slow, and inept in applying remedies. When establishing CPSC, Congress blessed the Commission with a wide variety of weapons, including product seizures, injunctions, cease and desist orders, and civil and criminal penalties. To some extent the agency has invoked these, but not to the extent consumer activists would like. Through 1976 the Commission averaged only seven product seizures per year despite abundant opportunities. Recalls, civil penalties, and the other armaments were used just as sparingly. As for slowness, several criminal cases referred to the Justice Department for prosecution were declined because the cases were too old to be handled. Incidentally, one instance of allegedly slow CPSC action concerned a singularly perverse product failure—namely, home smoke alarms that started fires. CPSC's coolness to that problem got its critics thoroughly burned up.

To summarize, CPSC is a crucial but controversial agency. It arouses passions in critics of every stripe. It must move gingerly to gain greater support, doing neither too much nor too little.

Environmental Protection Agency

Broad Standards

It is not the job of EPA to make our air crystal clear or our water diamond pure. EPA's task is nevertheless huge. The agency was created in 1970 to administer 15 environmental programs scattered haphazardly up to that time among five federal departments. Since then EPA's responsibilities have burgeoned still further, inflated by gusty legislative winds. Given our limited space, we can do no more than sketch the agency's activities in one area—auto air pollution.

---

[35] *Better Enforcement, op. cit.*

668

TABLE 26-6   EPA National Ambient Air Standards Relevant to Auto Pollution

Pollutant	Standard in Micrograms Per Cubic Meter of Air	
Carbon monoxide (CO)	Primary:	8-hour = 10,000
		1-hour = 40,000
	Alert:	8-hour = 17,000
Nitrogen dioxide (NO₂)	Primary:	Annual = 100
	Alert:	24-hour = 282
		1-hour = 1,130
Hydrocarbons (HC)	Primary:	3-hour = 160

Source: Council on Environmental Quality, *Environmental Quality— 1975*, pp. 300–03.

EPA gets its primary authority in this area from the Clean Air Act, the main purpose of which is "... to protect and enhance the quality of the Nation's air resources so as to promote the public health and welfare and the productive capacity of its population." This may be considered a broad standard. EPA has also adopted several broad standards for ambient air conditions. Because air quality depends on the density of pollutants per volume of air in a local region, these ambient air standards are stated in saturation thresholds, beyond which danger lurks. The "primary" and "alert" standards most pertinent to auto pollution are shown in Table 26-6.

Narrow Standards

The broad standards guide the formulation of narrow standards applicable to specific sources of air pollution—for example, steel mills, electricity generating plants, and, of present interest, autos. In the case of autos, Congress, not EPA, has set the main specifications. The 1970 Clean Air Act amendments required a 90% reduction below the 1970 model year levels in hydrocarbon and carbon monoxide emissions by the 1975 model year, and a similar reduction in nitrogen oxide emissions below 1971 model year levels by 1976. Interim year standards were also set, so this ultimate objective could be achieved by steps.

To encourage compliance, a dagger was hung over the industry in the form of a $10,000 fine for each and every car produced in violation of standards. As it turned out, however, the industry never met these standards and the dagger never fell. Subsequent legislative actions repeatedly relaxed requirements' in response to industry protests that the standards could not be met without excessive equipment costs and loss of fuel economy. Congress caved in rather than force the industry to shut down, something that surely would follow fines

669

of $10,000 per car. A shutdown would have meant the lay-off of 500,000 workers and a $1\frac{1}{2}\%$ rise in the national unemployment rate, not to mention the loss of hundreds of millions of dollars in wages and profits during each month of idleness. In other words, industry had a sword hanging over Congress, making Congress's dagger look like a fingernail file. It now appears that the standards originally set for 1975 will not be achieved until 1981. Unless there is further backpeddling, 1981 cars will be emitting no more than 0.41 grams of hydrocarbons per mile, 3.4 grams of carbon monoxide per mile, and 1.0 gram of nitrogen oxides per mile.[36]

Enforcement

Certification. Certification of prototype vehicles meeting standards has proceded under Section 206 (a) of the Clean Air Act. No vehicle whose prototype has not been approved may be sold in the United States. This stage of enforcement has thus far carried EPA's greatest compliance burdens because, as we shall see, other areas of enforcement have suffered paralysis.

Testing and Surveillance. EPA's final regulations for assembly-line testing were not issued until July 1976, *six years* after passage of the Clear Air Act of 1970. Once they cleared the bureaucratic tangle, they were attacked by environmentalists as being inadequate. The regulations call for tests of a very small and rather unrepresentative sample of only about 800 vehicles per year (less than 0.01 % of production). Moreover, the regulations provide a lenient threshold of acceptance. A particular class of car is considered acceptable if as few as 60% of the cars sampled in that class meet standard. As originally proposed, the regulations specified a more stringent 90% threshold, but EPA changed its mind, explaining that it did not want the testing program to be "unreasonably burdensome to the auto companies."[37]

Besides assembly-line testing, EPA has explored, and to varying degrees carried out, two additional surveillance programs. The first is the **in-use compliance program**, or IUPC, which seeks to answer the question—Do vehicles in actual use meet standards *when properly maintained by their owners*? Trial runs of IUCP turned up evidence that more than 2 million autos ought to be recalled but, because of various deficiencies in surveillance, no recalls were ordered.

The second surveillance program is **inspection and maintenance**, or I/M, which seeks to answer the question—Do owners properly maintain their vehicles to meet standards? Whereas IUCP looks for violations that are

---

[36] *Wall Street Journal*, August 4, 1977. It should be noted that the 90% reduction from 1970 levels represented an even greater reduction as compared to uncontrolled, pre-1968 autos. Grams per mile emissions of uncontrolled cars were approximately 8.7 for HC, 87.0 for CO, and 3.5 for NO_x.

[37] *Federal Regulation and Regulatory Reform, op. cit.*, p. 125.

the responsibility of the *manufacturers*, the I/M program looks for violations that are the responsibility of vehicle *owners*. This program has failed because of failures in the other programs. That is to say, EPA cannot force vehicle owners to pay the costs of full compliance when the cars they buy do not comply in the first place. If the manufacturers do not hold up their end of the bargain, buyers should not be given the double burden of paying for new but faulty control equipment *and* the repair of that equipment.

As a result of this string of enforcement failures, compliance is lax. EPA tests of consumer-used cars less than 1 year old reveal that, on average, autos typically exceed carbon monoxide and nitrogen oxide standards. The record for hydrocarbons is considerably better, but nothing to shout about.[38] Given the fact that an auto's emissions grow worse as the auto grows older, it is probably safe to say in addition that the vast majority of all cars over 2 years of age violate standard, because by law cars are supposed to be able to meet federal emission standards for their first 50,000 miles (when properly maintained and operated). Such are the consequences of relying on certification as the primary means of enforcement.

Remedies. Do not look for a table of seizures, recalls, and fines in this case. Your search would be in vain. What EPA gives up in shoddy testing and surveillance cannot be recovered in penalties. Although as this is written EPA has not been loath to impose such remedies in other areas of its jurisdiction, such as water pollution and industrial air pollution, it has no record worthy of comment in the area of auto air pollution.

To summarize, some progress is being made as measured by ever cleaner cars and by moderate reductions in overall auto emission tonnages per year. But these achievements have been made amidst postponed standards and stunted enforcement. Certification has carried nearly the entire load. Much the same could be said of EPA's many other pollution control efforts, but rather less caustically.

Summary

The last 20 years have witnessed a revolution in government regulation of industry. Consumer disappointment with free market performance in the areas of quality, safety, and pollution has nurtured the growth of old regulatory agencies and fostered the birth of new ones. This development delights many, but it depresses others. Critics contend that government is more of a problem than a solution, that its centralized control pollutes democracy, endangers freedom, and spreads bureaucratic mediocrity.

---

[38] *Environmental Quality 1976*, Report of the Council on Environmental Quality, pp. 5–8.

Criticism notwithstanding, popular support for these regulations is substantial. For the most part they are grounded on tragedy, crisis, and loathsome conditions. Unless regulation itself produces such regrettables, it is likely to endure.

One factor contributing to regulation's perpetuation is some recent refinement (if not perfection) of certain regulatory techniques. Ignoring information and education programs, virtually all important regulatory activities fall into a triad of categories: (1) standard setting (2) enforcement, and (3) research. As shown in Table 26-1, standards are needed to assure that regulators and regulated know their objectives. Enforcement is necessary to assure that the regulated are actually doing what they are supposed to be doing to achieve the objectives. Finally, research serves a number of purposes, including a check-up on whether the regulators are doing what they are supposed to be doing. In theory, this triad is balanced, effective, self-correcting, and beneficial; in practice it has many kinks. Our discussion of FDA, NHTSA, CPSC, and EPA discloses some of the problems involved. Public vigilance is therefore necessary to see that regulators accentuate the positive and eliminate the negative.

Index of Authors

Index of Major Companies

A & P, 124
Alcoa, 205−208, 267, 271, 273, 333, 432, 586, 588
Allis-Chalmers, 275−276, 303
American Can, 135, 144, 203
American Motors, 191, 260, 266
American Smelting and Refining, 135
American Standard, 286
American Telephone & Telegraph, 502, 586, 602
American Tobacco, 135, 144, 203, 273−274, 290, 381−382, 385
American Viscose, 267
Anaconda, 208, 267
Anheuser-Busch, 343, 382−383
Aramco, 311−312, 314
Armour, 105, 427
Atari, 188−189

Bethlehem Steel, 158−159, 274
Boeing, 297
Borden, 145, 357−358
Borg-Warner, 286
British Petroleum (BP), 310−311
Brown Shoe, 162−164

Campbell Soup, 333, 406
Chrysler, 191, 260, 266
Citgo, 261
Coca Cola, 384
Colgate-Palmolive, 406
Consolidated Foods, 422−423
Continental Can, 159−160
Control Data, 213−214, 218
Corn Products Refining, 203, 355

Diamond Match, 135
Du Pont, 135, 144, 199, 203, 267, 271, 284, 439, 586

Eastman Kodak, 203, 573−574
Exxon (See Standard Oil of N. J.)

Firestone, 403, 409
Ford Motors, 79, 191, 260, 266, 339

General Dynamics, 427−428
General Electric, 79, 149, 152, 271, 275−276, 303−304, 330
General Foods, 79, 145, 219, 333
General Mills, 219
General Motors, 79, 191, 260, 266, 270, 340, 402−403, 413, 586
Gillette, 433, 585
Grinnell, 166, 199−200
Gulf Oil, 310
Gulf & Western Industries, 146, 157

Hazel-Atlas, 159−160, 167
Heublein, 59, 79
Honeywell, 213−214

IBM, 91−92, 197, 212−218, 273, 335, 344, 365, 577, 586
International Harvester, 135, 144, 203, 271
International Paper, 144, 275
IT&T, 146, 156−157, 166, 411, 418, 422, 437−439

Kaiser Aluminum, 207, 267, 273, 419, 586, 588

Index of Industries

Index of Legal Cases

Subject Index